A
PRIMER
OF
POLITICS

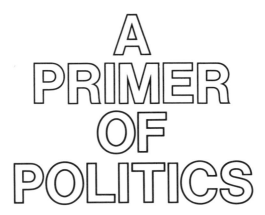

A PRIMER OF POLITICS

James E. Combs
Valparaiso University

Dan Nimmo
University of Tennessee

Macmillan Publishing Company
New York

Collier Macmillan Publishers
London

Macmillan Publishing Company
866 Third Avenue, New York, New York 10022

Collier Macmillan Canada, Inc.

Library of Congress Cataloging in Publication Data

Combs, James E.
  A primer of politics.

  Includes index.
  1. Power (Social sciences) 2. Political science.
3. State, The. I. Nimmo, Dan D. II. Title
JC330.C64   1984   303.3'3   83-9911
ISBN 0-02-324100-4

Printing: 3 4 5 6 7 8   Year: 4 5 6 7 8 9 0 1 2

ISBN   0-02-324100-4

DEDICATION
To the memory of Jackie Combs

Every man should have a little taste of power before he's through.

—Nathan Burdette

PREFACE

One of Aesop's more delightful fables goes like this: Once upon a time, there were some frogs who led a happy life in a marsh, jumping and playing without a care in the world. But some of them, unsatisfied with this easygoing life, declared that they should have a king to rule over them and watch their behavior. So they decided to send a petition to Jupiter—the king of the gods—to give them a king. After some haggling, Jupiter lost his temper and sent them a stork as king, who gobbled up the frogs right and left. After some of this, the survivors sent another message to Jupiter, pleading him to rid them of the stork. "Tell them," said the pitiless Jupiter, "that this is their own doing. They wanted a king. Now they will have to make the best of what they asked for." Moral: Let well enough alone.

Leaving well enough alone is good advice, but it has never been widely practiced. Like the frogs in Aesop's marsh, people have always wanted a ruler, and rulers there have always been. Not all have been as voracious as the stork, but enough of them have caused their subjects enough misery to remind us that politics and government are something consequential and, if done badly, can cause a lot of misery. But it also can be done well. How ruling is done makes a difference, and that is the subject of this book. For if we are to make the best of what we ask for, we have to be able to identify good rulers and what they can do.

To that end, in this text we have returned to one of the classic figures of political science, Niccolo Machiavelli. Machiavelli's work offers a point of departure for a book about political rule and rulers, as this was his major concern. Further, Machiavelli's writings are useful in relating what goes on in politics to the politics of the reader's everyday life.

Each chapter in this book is organized around some great prince. We include here virtually every type of politician—the good and bad, democrats and tyrants, successes and failures, and so on. Our goal is to introduce the reader to politics through the people and subjects we have selected. We plead for no particular cause, ideology, or system, and so the reader will find both admirable characters and sinister ones. But we contend that you can learn from all of them and, through them, choose which ones you would prefer to rule over Aesop's marsh. We include in each chapter a profile of the prince under discussion and conclude with maxims drawn from the chapter.

We believe that a Machiavellian perspective on politics is important and timely. This book takes a frank, nonideological, and honest look at the sometimes unreassuring facts of political life. It is written in the belief that students of politics can handle such painful truths and indeed can even use what they learn from such a book. Both politics and political learning require courage, skill, and work. If you have courage and work, you can learn political skills, the kind of skills useful to you in the conduct of your life. For Machiavelli, this book, and, indeed, all education can teach you much about how to rule yourself. As we shall see, the politics of self is different only in degree and not in kind from the politics of the state, and becoming a Prince in either place is an arduous task. Nevertheless, this book is written in the hope that both individuals and states can learn to rule themselves well. For both, the goal should be the same: to govern with grace.

ACKNOWLEDGEMENTS

The completion of a publishing enterprise such as the one the reader is about to undertake reminds the authors that it was a highly collaborative venture. We can only try to acknowledge the contribution of the main characters in the drama, and gracefully ignore those who hindered the story's completion. The editors and production staff of Macmillan proved to be very professional and punctual. Clark Baxter had the editorial wisdom to see the beauty of the Machiavellian perspective, and Gene Panhorst the editorial tenacity to see the project through to completion; both were a pleasure to work with, proving themselves able to put up with overwrought, harrassed, and stubborn authors, and willing to pick up a check. Joel Brauser and his production staff did an efficient job in transforming the concept into a book. Special thanks are due Carol Lewis, who did an excellent job in turning an indecipherable rough draft into a manuscript. Finally, the authors would like to say thanks to a wide variety of people—who must remain anonymous—who helped in so many ways: Machiavelli scholars, colleagues and friends, bartenders and cocktail waitresses, librarians and student aides, wives and girlfriends, all of whom made their own unique but important contribution to the completion of our long, arduous, but altogether worthwhile task.

TO THE STUDENT

This book is about politics. More specifically, it is a primer of politics. A primer is an introductory book with primary materials for the beginning student of a subject. In this book you will find such primary materials for understanding politics and, indeed, aspects of life in general. The book introduces you to politics through the perspective of Niccolo Machiavelli, a great political thinker. If you learn to think like him, you will learn much about politics and life. We, the authors, invite you to try. For if you choose to learn—to learn *how* to learn and how to *use* what you learn—then this book will help you to understand what is going on in your world and it will help you to get what you want out of your life. Whether you do so choose to learn is up to you. But, as Machiavelli might have said, not everyone will be a good student of politics and not everyone will become a Prince. If you do take the teachings of Machiavelli and this book seriously, you will come away knowing more about what it takes to be a good student of politics and, indeed, what it takes to be a political Prince. These are things worth knowing.

CONTENTS

Part VI

Practicing Power 259

Part VII

Losing Power 385

A PRIMER OF POLITICS

Part

I

Politics Is Not Just for Princes

Chapter

1

The Teachings of Niccolo Machiavelli

In Florence, Italy, there is a monument to Nicholaus Machiavelli, constructed in the eighteenth century, with the Latin inscription *Tanto Nomini Nullum par Elogium*—"No epitaph can match so great a name." Machiavelli lived almost five hundred years ago, during the turbulent and creative period of the Italian Renaissance. He was a native of Florence, the city that came to be called the second Athens because it produced so many great geniuses—Dante, Giotto, Petrarch, Boccaccio, Donatello, Masaccio, Leonardo da Vinci, and Michelangelo. Renaissance Florence was also like Athens in another way: it was politically unstable. Machiavelli's own *History of Florence* is a depressing story of cycles of interminable strife, involvement in both civil and foreign wars, and vacillation between republican and dictatorial rule. He wrote of the Florentines: ". . . though unable to preserve their liberty they cannot endure slavery."

Machiavelli was born into a middle-class family in 1469, and of his early years we know very little. But we do know that he was alert, intense, intelligent, and much interested in books. He appears to have read much on his own and prized a copy of Livy's history of republican Rome (which he read at age seventeen). Machiavelli's wide knowledge of the classics, which appears in his writings, reveals someone who kept reading and pondering history throughout life. He learned much on his own, through private reading and reflection on his own experience.

What experiences he had! Machiavelli was grown by the time of the death of the greatest of the Medici princes, Lorenzo the Magnificent. He witnessed the entry of Charles VIII of France into Florence and the ensuing political struggle that the fall of the Medici brought. He heard the fiery sermons of Savonarola, who damned church corruption and the decadent pope. Savonarola presaged the advent of the Reformation by his martyrdom, which Machiavelli witnessed in 1498. (Savonarola never actually broke with the Church; unbeknownst to Machiavelli but during his lifetime, Martin Luther made the conclusive break in 1517.) After Savonarola was burned at the stake, the government of Florence was purged of officials known to be sympathetic to him. Machiavelli was at this time twenty-nine years old, but still without a profession and an income. But the powers that be had taken notice of him, and he was given an administrative post at the second chancery, handling diplomatic functions. Although he had no administrative experience, it is likely that the republican councils that had to confirm his nomination to office were impressed by his intelligence and learning. For at that time there was a recruitment method by which applicants had to give evidence of their education in the humanities—languages, rhetoric, classic writing style, ancient history, and philosophy. It appears that earlier that year, Machiavelli's professor at his university in Florence had become first chancellor, remembered Machiavelli's talents, and recruited him for an important job.

For the next fourteen years, Machiavelli was a working and traveling diplomat, serving the interests of the Florentine republic. He became familiar with the politics of the various city-states of Italy. It was by any definition a dangerous and changing political scene, complete with wars, assassinations, revolts, palace intrigues, conspiracies and treason, mercenary armies, foreign invasions. Machiavelli must have had strong nerves as well as intelligence, as he was sent on delicate diplomatic missions that involved personal risk. His life was threatened several times, but his reports and dispatches display a cool detachment from and penetrating insight into what was going on. These reports intermingle observation and speculation, revealing his developing political mind. He was the observer of a colorful and dynamic political scene, and he was fascinated with it. He had, after all, met some of the great political figures of his age—the Medicis, Cesare Borgia, Caterina Sforza, Louis XII of France, Pope Julius II. But it was a hard life. It is estimated that in his career Machiavelli traveled over thirty thousand miles on horseback (sometimes thirty-two miles a day). He wrote many long reports, in which he articulated his perspective on politics and his judgment of the political figures he had met.

But involvement in politics, even as a diplomatic legate, had its risks and its price. When Florence tried to maintain its neutrality between 1510 and 1512, a papal alliance forced Florence to capitulate and restored the Medici. Machiavelli was associated with the republic but offered his services to the new government. He was first dismissed, then wrongly accused of being part of a conspiracy, and imprisoned and tortured. He was finally released in an amnesty, tried again to get a government post, but finally withdrew in enforced idleness at his small farm near San Casciano.

Machiavelli chafed at being out of the political action and wrote long letters to an influential friend, asking his help in getting back into politics. He spent his days tending to the farm, visiting his favorite prostitutes, and occasionally slipping into Florence to meet and talk with a group of intellectuals. He disliked the enforced leisure (partly because he was nearly broke), but it gave him time to devise a way of getting back into politics, namely, winning again the favor of the ruling Medicis. This leisure time also gave Machiavelli the opportunity to reflect on his knowledge and experience of politics, and so he began to write about it, usually in the context of his contemporary political and personal situation. But what he penned was to have considerable influence and despite its seeming remoteness, what he said has relevance and uses, even for you.

WHAT MACHIAVELLI SAID

You can learn much from Machiavelli if you are willing. A lot of what he says you will find frank, disturbing, and even shocking. But whether or not you agree with him, it behooves you to understand what he said and the tradition he founded. In this chapter, we shall try to interpret what Machiavelli said. That is not as easy as it may sound: Machiavelli's writings have been interpreted in many different ways. There is even one school that believes that he could not possibly have meant what he said, and thus *The Prince* (Machiavelli's most famous work) must be a satire. However, most people who have read his works—scholars and politicians alike—take him quite seriously and see in his works one of the most important perspectives on human life and politics ever presented. We too shall take him seriously and try to present what he said as fairly and straightforwardly as possible.

THE EXILE OF SAN CASCIANO

In exile, Machiavelli wrote his important political works for both pleasure and profit. He was confined to his little farm in San Casciano, forbidden by the new Medici rulers of Florence from participating in political activity. But he was frustrated at being out of the political action, and so he dedicated *The Prince* to Lorenzo de Medici as a "token of my readiness to serve you." All he had to offer, said Machiavelli, was his "knowledge of the actions of men, acquired through long experience of contemporary affairs and extended reading in those of antiquity." So he had a bound copy of his volume presented to Lorenzo, although there is no evidence that Lorenzo ever read it. Clearly this was a political ploy on Machiavelli's part: he wanted a job with the Medici and thought that maybe a book that revealed his political acumen, as well as flattering those for whom he wanted to work, might impress them enough to hire him. (Machiavelli might have spoiled his case if Lorenzo had read his book: Chapter 23 is entitled "How to Avoid Flatterers" and advises the prince to beware of court flatterers trying to advance their own careers.)

On the other hand, Machiavelli also thought and wrote about politics for the pleasure it brought him. In exile, he had the time to reflect on his political experience and read the works of ancient writers such as the Roman historian Livy. In the evening, he wrote a friend, he would put on his best clothes, attiring himself suitably to "enter the ancient courts of ancient men" with whom he talked, and as they reflected together on life and politics: "I do not feel boredom, I forget every trouble, I do not dread poverty, I am not frightened by death; entirely I give myself over to them." From this conversation across the ages, Machiavelli composed his great works—*The Prince* and *Discourses on Livy*.

Machiavelli would doubtlessly have been surprised that his musings in exile would become the immortal works they have, damned and praised, banned and widely read, and stirring controversy to this day. (Contemporary American evangelical conservatives have revived the image of Machiavelli as a satanic archfiend, one of the villainous secular humanists of history.) His work is close to five hundred years old, but it is still fresh and challenging and probably more influential than ever. One historian noted that all history since Machiavelli has been a "running commentary" on him. A political novelist spoke of the "cold-faced Florentine, who is the founding father of our modern world." A philosopher wrote of the still unresolved "question of Machiavelli," which "has never given men peace since it came to light." And indeed it has not: the literature on Machiavelli now rivals that of Shakespeare, and new works on him appear yearly. Somebody who stirs that much attention must have something to say.

WHAT IS THE WORLD LIKE?

Machiavelli believed that humans were caught in a world of unreasonable change. People live in a world ruled by time. The march of time is an incessant process, both for people and society. "It is a well established fact," Machiavelli observed, "that the life of all mundane things is of finite duration." Elsewhere he mused that if a state could maintain equilibrium, it would enjoy "real tranquillity. But as all human things are kept in a perpetual movement, and can never remain stable, states naturally either rise or decline. . . ." We all would like to be able to govern ourselves and to see the society we live in (and perhaps the whole world) governed so that equilibrium and tranquillity are perpetual. We cannot halt the decay and death of our own bodies any more than we can stop changes in society and politics. We do not stand and watch the world and ourselves change; we take part in that change. We are ourselves passing events, caught in the onrush of time.

For Machiavelli, change is unreasonable in how it affects one's life. Change is often unpredictable and capricious, and time unravels everything, creating problems and obstacles. "Time waits for no man," said Machiavelli, and "men should well consider the state of the times and govern themselves accordingly." The world is temporal, and so you must deal with changing times and circumstances.

There is, then, a joker in the deck of life, which Machiavelli personified as the ancient goddess *Fortuna*. *Fortuna* is the worldly factor of fortune, luck, chance, fate, providence—whatever force makes life uncertain and dependent on outside circumstances over which we have imperfect control. But one can understand and anticipate the changing force of *fortuna*. Machiavelli's vision of the world is dynamic, in which *fortuna* plays havoc with our lives. He compared *fortuna* to a torrential stream that tears up the countryside and before which everybody flees because they are unable to withstand the onslaught.

WHAT CAN PEOPLE DO?

Do the power and whimsy of *fortuna* mean that we are helpless against its power? No, Machiavelli insisted, we are not. After evoking the image of the wild river, he asserted, "this does not mean that men cannot take countermeasures while the weather is still fine, shoring up dikes and dams, so that when the waters rise again, they are either carried off in a channel or confined where they do no harm. So with Fortune, who exerts all her power where there is no strength prepared to oppose her, and turns to smashing things up wherever there are no dikes and restraining dams." Machiavelli refused to believe the pessimistic opinion that human ingenuity cannot sometimes overcome and defeat *fortuna*. He surmised that "Fortune governs half of our actions, but even so she leaves the other half more or less, in our power to control." In other words, at times we can pit whatever intelligence and strength we can muster to oppose Fortune and outwit and master her. (Machiavelli also used the metaphor of Fortune as a woman, exploiting the popular myth that women were unpredictable.)

So what can you do? You can cultivate what Machiavelli called *virtu*. Machiavellian *virtu* has been much discussed, but in general we can think of it as the ability to think and act resolutely and intelligently in order to get what we want. *Virtu* is the power to conquer *fortuna*. Cultivating the qualities of mind and deed that are virtuous in regard to a particular task increases the chance that you will be successful in governing *fortuna,* rather than her governing you. Suppose that you want to be a businessperson. If you want to succeed in business—as, say, a corporate executive—you must cultivate business *virtu*, those traits and actions that will help bring you success. The fortunes of business are such that your moves must be well planned, as anything less will likely fail. There are different types of *virtu* for different jobs—soldier, minister, teacher, or whatever. To improve your chances of overcoming *fortuna* and making your presence felt in the world, you must develop *virtu*. You may have the desire to succeed; you may have the talent to succeed; but *virtu* is that will and that talent put into action as talented will power.

WHAT MUST PEOPLE DO?

What must you do in order to achieve a desired result? Machiavelli believed that you must face up to doing those things that are necessary for human purposes, what he called *necessita*. When we say "necessity dictates," we mean that after assessing the facts of a situation and the realistic choices available, we conclude that the most likely way to achieve a certain effect is to do X rather than Y. In other words, it is necessary to do what it is that we want to do. It is necessary to break eggs to make an omelet; it is necessary to use intelligence and strategy to complete a college curriculum; it is necessary to use force to keep children from tearing up the house. It is necessary to choose what is most likely to achieve the result in mind.

Necessita, then, is gleaned by the use of intelligent *virtu* in the face of *fortuna.* Machiavelli did not think that history was predetermined and governed by inexorable forces over which one had no control. Because we live in a state of constant change, nothing is determined. Our situation is always precarious, the future always seems scary, and what we should do always seems difficult to determine. But the world and our immediate situations are not totally out of control. We have the power to understand and to do what is necessary in order to become masters of our fate. But that requires us to face up to *necessita.* Given whatever purposes or ends you have defined as desirable, what then do you have to do in order to realize them?

It is here that Machiavelli begins to make us uncomfortable. Your determination of what is necessary to do to achieve what you want suggests that you have to use whatever means are necessary for your purpose. And that means that you are going to use power to get what you want. You are powerful to the extent that you correctly define and do what is necessary in situations or, in other words, to use those means that are adequate to gain your end. But remember: the world was not designed for your convenience; other people may not do what you want because you want it, and so to bend the world to your will, you will have to study and use those means necessary for the situation.

Machiavelli recommended practical action. Practical action produces results. Because life, especially politics, is sometimes a rough game, the means sometimes have to be rough too. You cannot always be nice and expect the world to give you what you want just because you are nice. The practical person who plays the games of life—such as politics—cannot always be a lamb; sometimes that person must be a lion or a fox, using force, deception, cunning, manipulation, and indeed the whole range of power relationships that enable mastery of a situation. But Machiavelli did not recommend evil, nor did he say that the end justifies the means. The famous passage from Chapter 18 of *The Prince* explains: "In the actions of all men, and especially of princes who are not subject to a court of appeal, we must always look to the end." It says nothing about justifying actions, but much about what is necessary to achieve results. Machiavelli did not advocate evil; rather, he advised: do what you must. If you cannot get the desired results by being good, then if the end is important enough, you may have to do evil. Sometimes in life you have to turn your mother's picture to the wall. Do what is necessary, and do not lie to yourself about what you are doing and why. If it is accepted that a certain end in politics is good (for example, preventing an invasion of your country), then the question becomes one of envisioning and using the means necessary for your purpose. The use of power at such times may indeed be morally or ethically questionable, but that was not Machiavelli's concern. He was concerned with politics, not ethics, with the difficult questions: in these circumstances, is the use of power in some form politically wise? Are your political means adequate for your political ends? Is it necessary for you to do this now for that end? Are the results worth the price paid? Not easy questions, but ones central to politics and, indeed, ordinary life.

Suppose that you become the head of a struggling company. What do you have to do to make the company succeed? To defeat the *fortuna* of the business world, you must use your executive *virtu* by doing what is necessary to get the job done and maximize profits. Here are some of the things you must do: You "hit the ground running" by firing those tied to the old boss, those not doing a good job, or those who are potential rivals for your job. This immediately gives you a reputation as a tough boss to be respected and feared, and so productivity will increase. Firings open up positions, and you fill them with new people on the make who want to please you and are grateful to you for giving them the job. You reward innovation, demand hustle, fill the place with spirit and energy, and set an example by working long hours. You build a network of informants who tell you what is going on, who is not doing the job, who is bad-mouthing you, and where the bodies are buried. You abandon products or company policies that do not work or sell. You tell the board of directors and stockholders what they want to hear, whether or not it is true. That gives you time to make your upbeat line come true. You use lawyers to bend tax laws to minimize corporate taxes. You keep the son of the board chairman on the payroll and blackmail him into saying good things about you by threatening to tell his father about the girl in the mailroom. You keep down wage demands by lying to the union representatives about corporate profits. You put out company propaganda that makes the corporation look like a version of the Salvation Army, doing all these things out of the goodness of its heart. You give campaign contributions to candidates sympathetic to your problems. You reward your loyal corporate allies with perquisites. You woo new clients by wining and dining them, making inflated promises, and giving tours of your plant with its best face put on for that occasion. And if you use your business *virtu* well, have a little bit of luck, and do what is necessary, you may bring it off, increase profits, and achieve success.

Some of the things you have done may be unethical and illegal. But Machiavelli asked us an uncomfortable question: Could you have succeeded by strictly obeying the rules? If you do and your competitors do not, then where will you be? Can the ruler of any organization—corporation, university, or government—succeed without doing things that are manipulative, mean, and at times immoral? Machiavelli declared what others are reluctant to, that you cannot rule without hurting some people. Your success as a corporate president helped a lot of people—your employees and their families, your staff that shared your success, the board of directors, the stockholders, and even the national economy as a whole. Your end then was good, wasn't it? But in the process, it was necessary for you to hurt a lot of people—the employees you fired, the competitors you squeezed out, the kid you blackmailed, and so on. Was the end worth the means? Were the means necessary to the end? Machiavelli did not flinch from this problem, nor did he solve it. For that matter, no one else has, either. Machiavelli simply recognized that in the rough-and-tumble of real life, what may be necessary is not always nice. Good and bad are mixed up together, and doing what must be done without hurting somebody may be impossible.

WHEN SHOULD PEOPLE ACT?

Machiavelli also discussed what he called *occasione,* variously translated as "historical opportunity," "occasion," or the "right time." What he meant was that *virtu* was best pitted against *fortuna* by the careful planning and execution of actions at the correct time so as to maximize their chances of success. We should try to anticipate what might happen and react to the events that do happen. Fortune, explained Machiavelli, constantly surprises us with the unpredictable, the unlikely, the untimely. A key to *virtu* is the ability to outwit *fortuna* by doing the right thing at the right time. A sense of timing, pacing, and the right occasion are crucial to successful rule. Seize the moment, and act when the historical opportunity is right. Those who hesitate are indeed lost. As the Tammany Hall ward heeler George Washington Plunkitt said, "I seen my opportunities and I took 'em." Knowing what to do must be complemented by knowing when to do it.

If you reflect on this, you can think of many everyday examples of the problem of occasion. You have agreed to marry someone: when do you tell your parents? You want to tell them when the time is right—when they are in a good mood, have met the person and like him or her, after graduation, when you turn twenty-one, and so on. If you are wise, you will wait for the right moment, the moment when what it is that you want to do has the best chance of success.

The corporate president mentioned earlier found it necessary to do certain things to achieve corporate goals. Once defined, his problem then became when to do these things. So upon taking office, he quickly fired the old guard, getting them out of the way fast, establishing his reputation, and putting the fear of God in those not fired. He did it in this way to achieve the maximum effect. If he had fired them one at a time over a long period, the act would not have the effect of sweeping change and a new start. By timing the act in the way that he did, he used the occasion wisely for his ruling purposes.

TO WHAT END?

So far we have dealt with what Machiavelli thought one must do to get things done. You have to recognize and overcome the twists of fortune, use whatever virtue you can teach yourself and apply to problems, face up to and do what is necessary, and learn when to do something. What are you trying to accomplish? You are trying to create what Machiavelli called *ordini,* the "good order" that emerges from your efforts. For yourself, this can simply mean the conduct of a successful life. For those who rule, it may mean the temporary creation of order out of chaos, as *ordini* depends on the *virtu* of a ruler. Princes' task, their "honor," is to bring about *ordini,* a general good that is the aim of politics.

Let us again use the example of the corporate executive. His task is to realize the goals of the corporation, the corporate *ordini.* By using the power of his managerial *virtu,* he creates an "order" in terms of corporate operation and position in the economy, which is good for his organization. Princes have the power, Machiavelli thought, either to create or destroy. Those that create should be honored, and those that destroy should be condemned. The founder of a new state is a hero. But the prince who, through bad ruling, lets a state go to ruin is a villain or a fool. Because order is problematic, the consequences of bad ruling can be devastating, destroying order and creating disorder. For both the corporate president and the political prince, the goal is the same. At their best, princes produce peace and prosperity. But bringing about the worthy goals of good order is not easy. Good order is produced only at a price. The world is not neat or easy, and sometimes the price paid is very high. It may take firings to increase productivity and profits for the corporation. It may take war to bring political peace, and police and prisons to maintain law and order. The question Machiavelli raised was, how much pain is necessary?

THE ECONOMY OF VIOLENCE

At this point we deal with what we might call the *Machiavellian ethic.* Machiavelli did not separate morality and the necessities of ruling. Rather, he pointed to the hard facts of the price that must be paid for the good end of *ordini.* Good ends are not easily obtainable, and good order is not easily achieved or maintained. They are gained by the use of power. Order comes from power. The first sentence of Machiavelli's *Prince* speaks of "power over men," and *Discourses* I:1 says that "security for man is impossible unless it be conjoined with power." The price of good order is that it is produced by the use of power. Order through power is not neat and unmessy, but it is the political way of getting things done, whether in a corporation, university, or government. Machiavelli insisted that ruling did not have to be accomplished badly. Power can be used wisely and prudently and produce good things. But it can also be used unwisely and imprudently and produce bad things. The science of politics is to tell the prince how to use power wisely and prudently.

This Machiavellian principle was termed by Professor Sheldon Wolin as the *economy of violence.* The exercise of power involves telling other people what to do. If they ignore or resist you, then when push comes to shove, you may have to use the threat of force or actual force. In any case, using power means helping some people and hurting others. But Machiavelli insisted that if power is used well, rulers can minimize the amount of hurt and maximize the amount of help. In that way, they can economize violence, reducing rather than increasing the amount of pain in the world through the adroit use of power. Ruling is the controlled use of power, producing *ordini,* with those public benefits that flow from such a happy state.

Let us offer some examples of what Machiavelli meant. Suppose that the newly appointed corporate president does not rule well. He keeps incompetents, intriguers, and disloyalists on the payroll. His employees feel safe in their jobs, even if they goof off. Productivity declines. The president fails to deal with quarrels, problems, conflicting and overlapping work, and sabotage. And on and on. There are a million different things that can go wrong. Always remember Murphy's famous law: If things can go wrong, they will. And so if the prince (corporate president) fails to prevent things from going wrong, he will not be using power well. He will not be creating order. And to the extent that he does not, he is producing disorder—internal strife, trouble, confusion, disillusionment, and hatred; low profits and therefore stagnation of the corporation and low wages; drift and lowered expectations in company plans; loss of reputation and trust among both employees and staff; and lack of support from the board of directors. The violence done to the corporation will be great, and he could have prevented much of it by ruling well. Violence is not simply physical force; it is also things like low wages, staff discord and bitter feelings, tension, strikes and layoffs, wage cuts, alcoholism on the job, family disputes stemming from the corporate situation, and on and on.

Economizing violence is the job of political princes. If you rule a corporation unsuccessfully, there are limits to the harm you can do. But if you rule a country unsuccessfully, you can cause a lot more pain because you are the political power in the land, the ruler of everyone. If you fail to produce *ordini,* the consequences will be greater in terms of the pain you will cause. Machiavelli belonged to that school of thought that saw society as problematic. Peace and prosperity are not a given; people are not always nice and agreeable; and things do not always work out for the best. Rulers who naively believe, with Dickens's Micawber, that "something will turn up" are courting disaster for themselves and their country. There is always the ugly possibility that things will come unglued and that the amount of violence will increase, either in domestic strife or foreign conflict. The task of princes is to solve the problem of ruling and prevent a diseconomy of violence from occurring.

How do princes do that? They do it by skillfully using force and consent. They use the political *virtu* that they should possess in order to mobilize the consent of the governed, which is a source of political power in the form of mass support. If people like and trust princes, they are more likely to be open to compromise and persuasion to achieve peaceful solutions. Consensus helps hold together the political fabric that princes try to keep from being rent. Machiavelli wrote much on the tradition of civic virtue—what the Romans called *civitas*—which economizes violence through social peace. But societies may also become corrupt. If so, the only way to economize violence may be through the direct application of force—police and military—in order to prevent even more bloodshed. And of course princes must concern themselves with the possibility of foreign threat, economizing violence by preventing foreign invasion by means of treaties or military strength. Their inability to obtain consent or use force well means that there will likely be more violence than if they had been able to rule successfully.

It is this theme in Machiavelli that shows that he did not separate politics from morality. To put it another way, he saw in politics a utilitarian ethic. The successful conduct of politics by a prince economizes violence. The utility of the prince is that through his or her rule, the state can be preserved, peace and prosperity can be pursued, and political violence can be minimized. The ethic of the prince is a political ethic, that the social good can be produced by political rule. Politics, of course, is often what increases the amount of pain in the world—war, massacres, suppression, torture, all of people's inhumanity to others. But Machiavelli believed that politics was also the solution, the means by which all these terrible things might be avoided. It all depends on the success of politics, and this explains why the study of ruling correctly is so important. Machiavelli would no doubt agree with Aristotle that political science is the "master science," for the simple reason that until political problems—the problems of ruling—are solved, no other individual or social problem can be safely undertaken.

Machiavelli adhered to the ancient tradition of *civic humanism,* that politics is a noble art, can be studied as an applied science, and can be practiced so skillfully that it sometimes can bring about humane results, the best political results that can be expected under the circumstances. Machiavelli promised no utopia and was not interested in what should be. But he was much interested in discovering what is—what people in fact do—as a preface to discovering what can be—what politics realistically can do. So what Machiavelli wrote is both descriptive and prescriptive. He looked at facts and inferred from them what might be done to produce politically desirable results. He asserted that he wanted to write something "useful to an understanding reader." People in the past "imagined states and princedoms such as nobody ever saw or knew in the real world, for there's such a difference between the way we really live and the way we ought to live that the man who neglects the real to study the ideal will learn how to accomplish his ruin, not his salvation." Machiavelli did not believe in perfectability of people and society but, rather, in political solutions that can economize violence.

Many have asserted that Machiavelli meant that might was right. In this view, power (might) is used to rule people, and right is what the people with power say that it is. And oftentimes that is precisely the case. But that is not what Machiavelli meant; more correctly, he meant that might *made* right. Power may be evil, bringing a diseconomy of violence. But power can also be creative. Whatever you think is right can be realized only in the presence of might. You must understand what has to be done in politics—the use of power—before you can define right.

THE AUTONOMY OF THE PRINCE

This brings us to perhaps Machiavelli's most controversial statement, that the prince must sometimes do bad things in order to realize good things. He asserted:

> Any man who tries to be good all the time is bound to come to ruin among the great number who are not good. Hence a prince who wants to keep his post must learn how not to be good, and use that knowledge, or refrain from using it, as necessity requires.
>
> Thus a prudent prince cannot and should not keep his word when to do so would go against his interest, or when the reasons that made him pledge it no longer apply.
>
> To preserve the state, he often has to do things against his word, against charity, against humanity, against religion . . . he should not depart from the good if he can hold to it, but he should be ready to enter on evil if he has to.

Notice that Machiavelli did not recommend evil in the sense of "go out and do what you want; nothing is wrong." He was not talking about ordinary people; quite the contrary, he believed that the strength—the civil *virtu*—or the state depended on the common morality of the many. But because of the crucial and ultimate nature of ruling the state, princes must be autonomous, not always bound by the very morality that they are committed to defend. They do not seek to do evil, but sometimes politics necessitates that they do so. If they are not willing to do evil, they are bad princes, and their state, people, and moral scruples all may be in jeopardy. A "good" person, in the common moral sense, may very well be a bad prince simply because he or she *is* a good person.

This famous Machiavellian argument has less to do with ethics than with politics. Politics is a dynamic social activity that is autonomous. Politics is not ethics, ideology, religion, or philosophy. Politics is politics. And because it is what it is, politics must be played on its own terms. Thus princes cannot play politics as though it were ethics; they must play it as politics. This means that as political necessity dictates, they must use evil as part of their political virtue, using it as a form of power for the purposes of good order. If in extraordinary circumstances princes are bound by the restraints of ordinary morality and social "niceness," they may endanger their state by not being equal to the requirements of the political situation. Machiavelli did not deny that there was such a thing as political morality, nor that most of the time it was a good thing for princes to be bound by it. He was very much aware that princes operate in the context of political and social morality and should promote morality. If at all possible they should act within the bounds of political ethics and not do things that oppose social morality: "In actual fact, a prince may not have all the admirable qualities ... but it is very necessary that he seem to have them. Indeed, I will venture to say that when you have them and exercise them all the time, they are harmful to you; when you just seem to have them, they are useful. It is good to appear merciful, truthful, humane, sincere, and religious; it is good to be so in reality. But you must keep your mind so disposed that, in case of need, you can turn to the exact contrary." The prince's job is political utility, to rule so that politics produces what can be. That utility requires actions "in case of need" that may not be strictly moral but surely are political.

Let us consider an everyday example of morality: Keep promises. A good rule, but can a political prince always be bound by it *and* accomplish what is good for his or her state? Indeed, in politics can't it have bad results? If you, as a prince, could avoid a destructive war by breaking your words, might it not be worth it? In the crisis in Europe in August 1914, didn't every major nation keep its word and live up to its treaty obligations? The princes were therefore moral because they kept their treaty promises and went to war. The result was World War I. If one prince had been immoral and *not* kept his word, the war might have been avoided. Keeping one's promises is a moral rule, not a political rule. But following a political rule and in the process sometimes breaking a moral rule may have good results. Politics is ruling people, not obeying principles. Sometimes in politics one must rise above principle to get something done. Machiavelli was demonstrating not how to be moral but how to be politic. Being politic and being moral may at times be incompatible, but for princes there is no choice if they are to do what they are supposed to do: be politic.

AN EXAMPLE

Chapter 8 of *The Prince* is entitled "On Those Who Have Become Princes by Crime." This is of interest to the political scientist, since one of the most common ways to gain power is through some form of crime— murder, blackmail, imprisonment without trial, and so on. Such means are crimes in the moral sense, but they are also political methods. Machiavelli closely examined the case of Oliveretto da Fermo, who sought, by means of crime, to become ruler of Fermo. He arranged to have his leading rivals come to a banquet. Afterwards (at least they got a free meal) his soldiers appeared from secret places and killed them all. Oliveretto then terrorized the town council into forming a new government with himself as its head. He then moved quickly to create new laws that strengthened his position, and within a year he was the undisputed master of the region.

Machiavelli admitted that what Oliveretto did was cruel and evil. But that was not what interested him. Politically, how was Oliveretto able to pull this off? Machiavelli offered this: "I believe this depends on whether the cruelty is used well or badly. Cruelty can be described as well used (if it's permissible to say good words about something which is evil in itself) when it is performed all at once, for reasons of self-preservation; and when the acts are not repeated after that, but rather are turned as much as possible to the advantage of the subjects. Cruelty is badly used, when it is infrequent at first, but increases with time instead of diminishing." Machiavelli then generalized even further: ". . . When a prince takes a new state, he should calculate the sum of all the injuries he will have to do, and do them all at once, so as not to have to do new ones every day . . . injuries should be committed all at once, because the less time there is to dwell on them, the less they offend; but benefits should be distributed very gradually, so the taste will last longer." We learn from Oliveretto's crime that the way to secure a new and illegal government is to do away quickly with (although not necessarily kill) those leaders likely to cause significant trouble; and to finish quickly your necessary acts of cruelty (or, as the saying goes, don't cut off a dog's tail by inches) to avoid their threatening your rule; but spread out your benefits over time in order to maximize their positive effects. If Oliveretto was a good ruler, Machiavelli pointed out, the cruelties would be forgotten, save by a few. Oliveretto had economized violence, secured the state, and, for political necessity—to keep himself in power—spread out the public benefits. Therefore, most people were helped by his murders. This is an extreme case, but you should get the point: bad things were done in politics, but good things came of it. We should learn from this that in similar situations we may have to do the same in order to obtain similar results. Like Machiavelli, we can mix description and prescription and imitate the action of the politician when roughly similar circumstances prevail.

Recall our example of the new corporate president. Didn't he figuratively do the same thing that Oliveretto did? Didn't he fire those who were tied to the old boss and who might be disloyal, as well as poor workers and potential rivals? If he were smart, he would do it quickly and then concentrate on the gradual benefits—promotions, higher salaries, pensions and health coverage, and so forth—spreading them out over a long period of time. When a new administration takes power in Washington or Moscow or London, doesn't it immediately let go of most of the people who are associated with the old prince and whose loyalty is in doubt? In the early days of his dictatorship, didn't Adolf Hitler move quickly in 1934 to execute those who were potential rivals for power, in the famous "Night of a Thousand Knives"? Perhaps it is not moral to do these sorts of things, but it certainly is political. But if you are going to be politic, you don't have to fly blind: you can learn from what politicians have done before you and apply the precepts of historical practice to the present.

THE LIMITS OF POWER

Yet despite his belief in the efficacy of political action and the power of wise princes, there also is a sad and pessimistic theme in Machiavelli's works. He accepted the classical idea (from Thucydides and others) that history is a process, and that what he called "the malice of time" eventually would destroy all things—people, families, and governments. For Machiavelli, the world is not an ordered whole. There is no divine order or historical principle that guarantees salvation or progress. History is an endless cycle of rising and falling states: "...I certainly think that if she [a state] could be kept in this equilibrium it would be the best political existence, and would ensure to any state real tranquillity. But as all human things are kept in a perpetual movement, and can never remain stable, states naturally either rise or decline...." Even though we may be able to control our fates and outwit fortune for a while, Machiavelli believed that in the long run, we all would die. So the political *ordini* brought about by princely *virtu* is a temporary truce, a respite in the march of everything to eventual ruin, the tendency of all life and organization ultimately to come apart.

If history were just an endless process of change, then in a sense this would make the efforts of the princes of history—indeed, of all of us— somewhat futile, perhaps a bit absurd. The prince is almost an absurd existential hero, fighting against the *fortuna* of historical entropy. If you reflect on Machiavelli, and on the task and achievements of the political princes that we shall discuss in this book, you should come away from it all with a sense of empathy—understanding, although not necessarily approving, the necessities of politics. Perhaps the political world is insane, history is out of control, and none of it makes any sense. But for Machiavelli, the futility of it all does not stop the imperative of politics and rule. People will try to rule, and someone will succeed, despite the problems and the malice of time. At their best, princes express humanity's temporary control of things, helping us to muddle through as a political order, at least for a moment. Political princes are on the political stage of history, acting out the obligatory drama of human political conflicts. Princes cannot *not* play: they must act and act well, as the play progresses. All human weaknesses and strengths are magnified in them and have consequences for us all. They, more than others, become aware of the anguish of choice, the loneliness of power, and the uncertainty of what might happen. Machiavelli's prince is a man or woman on a tightrope, acting in an episodic political circus, wearing many masks and costumes, and juggling many political balls; he or she performs for many audiences with varying results; sometimes the political magic works, and sometimes it does not. But perhaps more than any other person, the political prince understands the limits of power. Even though princes have more power than ordinary people do, they are aware, as was Machiavelli, that their power to affect events, to magnify their influence on the tides of history, is limited. Even at the height of their moment in the limelight, their power to control the world is circumscribed. *Sic transit gloria mundi,* the Romans warned their returning conquerers at their holiday—"all glory is fleeting."

The Machiavellian prince—many of the best of whom we shall study in this book—is not a monster, but a person whose political aspirations are writ large. Despite the existential limits of what he or she can do, this prince remains one of humanity's most remarkable achievements. The best politicians are models of human excellence, bringing quality and style to politics, making politics into an art. Machiavelli thought that politics—making a state work—was one of humanity's highest artistic achievements. Like the sculptor or the architect, the politicians that Machiavelli admired were creators, not destroyers. They may create with blood and iron and money, but that is because these are the tools of the politician, just as hammer and chisel are the tools of the sculptor.

Machiavelli invited you to learn about this world of politics. It is not a nice, safe, and easy world to enter and understand. But if you fail to understand it, you will be ignorant of one of the most astonishing and consequential parts in your life. The political princes of the world now literally have the power to destroy all human life on this planet, and so if for no other reason, you should know something of why (or why not) you might be blown up. And you also can use what you learn, as we shall again and again point out. In any case, politics is Machiavelli's world, and welcome to it.

POSTSCRIPT

Some of you may think Machiavelli was crazy, or evil, or right on the mark; others will not think at all about what he said, because it is too threatening. In any case, we believe that you should think, and think hard, about Machiavelli. Is what he said the way it is, and more pointedly, the way it *has* to be? Machiavelli posited notions about ourselves, the world, and politics that we still need to consider. That is why we want to use him here to guide you through the maze of political life. In the next chapter, we shall elaborate on what it means to be a Machiavellian.

But wait. What happened, you may wonder, to Machiavelli himself? He did not get the job that he hoped for. He sent a copy of *The Prince* to Lorenzo, but it was never acknowledged. There is an apocryphal story that Lorenzo was more impressed with a pair of hunting dogs that he received on the same day! Machiavelli continued to write in exile—the more elaborate *Discourses on Livy;* poems and essays; *The Art of War;*

The Mandrake Root, a delightful sex farce; and many letters. He was even commissioned by the pope to write a history of Florence. But nothing helped him return to politics. When Rome was sacked in 1527, the republic was restored in Florence, but ironically, because Machiavelli had been commissioned to write the history by a Medici pope, his old job was given to someone else! Broken in spirit and health after so many years of frustration and penury, Machiavelli died the same year.

Even though Machiavelli died, what he wrote did not. "Machiavellism" and "Machiavellian" soon entered the language of politics and life. Is what he wrote a mandate for unscrupulous, immoral, and exploitative actions or a frank and cold-eyed look at what is and what has to be done? *The Prince* was not published until after Machiavelli's death, but handwritten copies were already circulating. By 1529 Thomas Cromwell (a courtier at England's Henry VIII's court) was recommending it to a friend. In England at about that time, Machiavelli came to be associated with Satan, and the latter was popularly called "Old Nick." In 1559, Machiavelli's works were placed on the Roman Catholic index of forbidden books, and in 1572, the Protestants blamed Machiavelli's influence on Catherine de Medici of France for the St. Bartholomew's Day Massacre. There emerged a vast literature in Europe that was either pro-Machiavelli or anti-Machiavelli. The Elizabethan dramatists refer again and again to Machiavelli, and Christopher Marlowe even has a character named "Machiavel" in his prologue to *The Jew of Malta.* Shakespeare's Richard III asserted that he would "send the murderous Machiavel to school." Machiavelli has been admired and condemned by democrats and tyrants, by kings and revolutionaries, and by figures as varied as Napoleon I, Vladimir Lenin, and Adolf Hitler, as well as James Harrington, James Madison, and Alexander Hamilton. Some, such as Frederick the Great, condemned him while practicing what he said. Others, such as Richelieu, openly admired him while practicing what he said. To this day, Machiavelli's work is condemned, denied, and banned but still used. The controversy and the malignant reputation associated with his name remain unabated.

In the next chapter, we shall begin to apply the Machiavellian perspective to life and politics. Then we shall outline some principles of good Machiavellian thinking about life and politics, which should prepare us for our grand tour of Machiavelli's spiritual domain.

"Tacitus writes novels; Gibbon babbles; Machiavelli's book is the only readable one."

—*Napoleon I*

"This collection [*Discourses*] of practical maxims ... seems to have been expressly written to be read on the eve of any great undertaking."

—*Hippolyte Taine*

Politics Is Not Just for Princes

"The authentic interpreter of Machiavelli is the whole of later history."

—*Lord Acton*

"If Machiavelli had had a prince for disciple, the first thing he would have recommended him to do would have been to write a book against Machiavellism."

—*Voltaire*

"Machiavelli is not more the inventor of Machiavellism than Grave's is the inventor of Grave's disease."

—*Mario Praz*

"The maxims of Machiavelli—liberals recite them while kings put them into practice."

—*Allesandro Manzoni*

"Machiavellism is the geometry of politics."

—*Benoist*

"We are much beholden to Machiavelli and other writers of that class, who openly and unfeignedly declare or describe what men do, and not what they ought to do."

—*Francis Bacon*

"Machiavelli's theory was a sword plunged into the flank of the body politic of Western humanity, causing it to shriek and rear up."

—*Friedrich Meinecke*

"[Machiavelli's] achievement is of the first order, if only because the dilemma has never given men peace since it came to light. . . . The sword of which Meinecke spoke has not lost its edge: the wound has not healed."

—*Isaiah Berlin*

"We live today in the shadow of a Florentine, the man who above all others taught the world to think in terms of cold political power."

—*Max Lerner*

"The pocketbook is where it hurts. A man may forget the death of the father, but never the loss of the patrimony, the cold-faced Florentine, who is the founding father of our modern world, said, and he said a mouthful."

—*character in Robert Penn Warren's* All the King's Men

"It is said that No. 1 has Machiavelli's *The Prince* lying permanently by his bedside. So he should: since then, nothing really important has been said about the rules of political ethics."

—*character in Arthur Koestler's* Darkness at Noon

"How could he have been understood?"

—*Maurice Merleau-Ponty*

Chapter

2

What Machiavellians Learn

*Life is, in fact, a battle. . . . Evil is insolent and strong; beauty
enchanting but rare; goodness very apt to be weak; folly very apt to
be defiant; wickedness to carry the day; imbeciles to be in great
places, people of sense in small, and mankind generally, unhappy.
But the world as it stands is no illusion, no phantasm, no evil dream
of a night; we wake up to it again for ever and ever; we can neither
forget it nor deny it nor dispense with it.*
—Henry James, *French Poets and Novelists* (1878)

Machiavelli learned from experience and wrote about it. What he said
about politics and life in general is still of use to you today. *The Prince* is
a book of political advice, and in many respects, so is this one. The
Machiavellian spirit is to use knowledge to decide what we should do to
get what we want, politically and otherwise. Here we shall state the
Machiavellian perspective in brief, as a preface to explaining what you
can do with it. It is our contention that Machiavellism—the tradition
that Machiavelli founded—now constitutes a world view that can be
stated, adopted, and used.

THE WORLD IS CHAOTIC

For Machiavelli, the world made no sense. He saw the world as unstable
and impermanent, with no divine order or moral law governing the
affairs of people. Change is constant, and order an illusion, a temporary
respite in the march to disorder. We cannot control change in the world
any more than we can control our own deaths. There is no inherent,
discoverable meaning in history. This is not to stay that Machiavelli or
Machiavellians are necessarily irreligious; Machiavelli himself appears to have observed the rituals of his faith. He seems to have followed
the tradition of St. Augustine, who considered the transcendent Heav-
enly City of God and Church as being separate from the Earthly City of
human society, economics, and politics. Machiavelli was interested in

Politics Is Not Just for Princes

understanding the Earthly City, human affairs, and what one could do to succeed in it.

Machiavelli was, then, a realist. His eye was on what people actually do, what the world in fact is. Politics is about what is, what is happening, and what people do to, for, and with one another. And because what people do is not always commendable, many of us avoid facing the hard facts of social reality. We want the world to be better than it really is, to look at it through rose-colored glasses, engage in wishful thinking, and rationalize away unpleasant and intruding facts. But Machiavelli insisted that we see things for what they really are, that we face the facts. If you want to understand and master yourself and the world, you first must recognize reality.

This does not mean that you have to become a pessimist or a cynic. Pessimists delude themselves by assuming things will work out for the worst, and cynics prejudge human motives as always being bad. The Machiavellian realist is skeptical about assumptions that things will work out for the best and that people will usually do the right thing. The Machiavellian wants to avoid the fallacy of assumacy: never assume good, stability, reason, progress, or order but also never assume evil, instability, passion, inertia, or disorder. The realist knows that there are alternative outcomes, different possibilities, and no certainties. This violates the fundamental principle of realism, searching for the truth of what is happening and suspending judgment of what may come to pass, as several things may happen. Do not impose your expectations on unfolding reality; expect the unexpected, and remember that the world was not created for your wishes or convenience.

For the Machiavellian, the world is dynamic, a temporal process of change and chance that proceeds without a clear direction and without any discernible purpose or justice. Perhaps the greatest fallacy of assumacy is assuming permanence. History is an onrushing succession of events, over which no one has control and in which nothing is permanent, including yourself. We live life in time, attempting to cope with a problematic and ever-changing world. Life is one damned thing after another, and we do things because they seem to be right to do at the time.

LIFE IS ACTION

As suggested by the quotation from Henry James that opens this chapter, life is a battle, and as much as we might wish it, the world just will not go away. We may delude ourselves into thinking that "life is but a dream," but it is not. The world impinges, the blood we bleed is real, and the pleasure and pain we feel are not illusions. But as Machiavelli declared, we are not helpless. We must learn to cope with the world. Many people do not or will not; not everyone leads a successful life, nor does everyone who tries to cope succeed in doing so. But most of the time, those who try to master themselves and their circumstances have a better chance of doing so than those who do not. The race is not always to the swift, nor the battle always to the strong, but that is where you should place your bets.

The Machiavellian perspective stresses that in order for you to get what you want, you must be willing to learn. Your goal is competence at whatever it is you want to do—be a good student, lawyer, lion tamer, spouse, politician, or whatever. Being competent means that you have taught yourself to do well what it is that you want to do. As you live your life, you will be amazed by the extent of incompetence around you. Many, perhaps most, people simply do not know what they are doing and do not conduct their lives wisely. But you do not have to be one of them. Machiavelli taught that competence is available to those who are willing to pay the price—self-criticism, cultivation of talent and temperament, willingness to learn. The ideal of competence is relevant to any area of life in which you wish to excel, including politics.

Machiavellism, then, is a philosophy of conduct. Machiavelli was interested in what people can do to attain their goals. The Machiavellian perspective is more than a tough-minded, realistic view of the world; rather, it is an injunction to act in a certain way so that one may overcome the problems and obstacles that are certain to arise. The ideal of competence enjoins rational action to solve problems. The Machiavellian studies the most competent way to do things, given the nature of the world. To the extent that you are competent, you will attain a degree of autonomy, a freedom of choice and action that stems from your ability to control situations. You are free to the extent you are autonomous, and competent conduct is the means by which you can become autonomous. Life is action, and the Machiavellian studies the ways in which action can bring about desired results.

BE PRAGMATIC

Machiavelli's approach has been described as "naturalistic activism." Even though the world you confront is a torrential and turbulent river of events, if you use your head you can some of the time, channel and control the flow of the river for your own purposes. To do so, you must cultivate an attitude toward the world that is open, honest, and reflective. Machiavellian competence begins with not only observing and understanding the world but also learning from it for your own purposes. Simply put, competence is achieved by learning from experience. You may learn from your own experience or from the experiences of others. You can learn from successes or failures. But the important thing is that you do learn and incorporate what you have learned in your future actions.

Machiavellians call this attitude pragmatic sagacity. If you are going to cope with the world, you will have to be pragmatic. The world is a practical place, and coping with it is a practical art. You must learn how

Politics Is Not Just for Princes

to compromise and negotiate with the world if you want to do something in it. To do what you want, you will have to take practical actions to succeed. This means that you will have to use knowledge to guide your actions. You can gain that knowledge by studying your own and others' experiences. Such knowledge is worthwhile not in itself but for what it tells you to do.

Pragmatic sagacity is an attitude that uses informal logic to guide action. Pragmatic logic is not an abstract set of rules remote from the real world but, rather, is a "logic in use." This kind of logic is not thinking about thinking but, rather, thinking about doing. The practical sage cultivates logic not as an academic but as a real-life discipline. People use pragmatic logic to solve the problems of life, gathering facts and formulating rules that guide their actions.

Suppose that you are pondering what career to pursue. To make the best decision, you must be brutally frank with yourself: What are my talents? What am I good at? What can I realistically expect from myself? Where are my best chances? Whose advice should I seek in deciding? Once I have decided, then what should I do? What knowledge and skills must I have? How do I get to where I want to go? If I get there, what do I have to do to stay there? Once decided, you must seek competence, plan what to do, and act. Remember, the world will not seek you out, you have to seek it out. With talent, temperament, and luck, you can increase the chances that you will enjoy some worldly success. But there are no guarantees: there may be someone else who is more talented and has a better temperament and is luckier. In all of this, you should use pragmatic logic to decide what to do.

Machiavellian logic, then, teaches us to learn from experience and to apply that learning to our conduct. The logic that we learn to use in everyday life is not strictly inductive or deductive but, rather, is abductive. The world is changeable, difficult to understand, and often recalcitrant. To deal with it, we use facts to formulate rules that we put into practice to get what we want. Our logic is rough and flexible, but from it we develop rules that work for us. We learn from experience not to touch hot stoves, to be nice to our professors, and never to believe that the check is in the mail. We are interested in results, and use maxims—rules of use—for our pragmatic purposes.

USE POWER

The Machiavellian understands that one of the central realities of the world is power. We shall say much in this book about power, that you have to use power in order to get what you want. Everyone uses power in everyday life, but some use it better than others do, probably because they understand its necessity and do not shrink from using it. At the core of learning to be competent is the cultivation and use of power. In a very general sense, power is mastery—mastery of oneself, of nature, of others. Machiavellian logic teaches one to seek knowledge for ruling and formulating rules about rule. As the maxim goes, knowledge is power, but the opposite is true too—power is knowledge. You are exercising power if you use knowledge to guide action, thereby gaining control over something. There is nothing necessarily evil about power. Power is simply the ability to master.

Consider the question of power over self. In your career, your chances of success will be much enhanced by the effective exercise of power over yourself. If you let someone else dominate you, you not only will not be able to rule yourself, but you also will be allowing someone else to dictate what you do. Too, power over yourself means disciplining yourself to do the things necessary for a successful career. Many people drift from day to day, year to year, without that discipline. Power over self means mastery, not drift.

It is also a Machiavellian fact of life that if you are going to go to the top in your chosen career, you will have to exercise power over others. By getting good grades and going to a good law school, you will exercise power. By ruling a hospital or a business or a family, you will exercise power. You exercise power over others anytime you tell other people what to do and they do it. Remember that someone has to rule, someone is going to rule, and there is no reason that it cannot be you. To be effective, you must overcome whatever qualms you may have about dominating others.

In order to gain power and to use it well, you will have to study power. This book is about political power, but the Machiavellian lessons of political power can also be applied to whatever area of life you choose. If you study power and its uses, you can overcome the forbidding feeling you might have about it. Knowledge of power is power too: to the extent that you study power, you will increase your chances to assume power and also the likelihood that you will use it wisely. The study of power does not necessarily teach you to be mean and nasty; rather it teaches you the realities, possibilities, and limits of power for both good and evil. Machiavelli believes that power was necessary for any human purpose and was available to both saints and sinners. But he also believed that nothing, good or bad, could be done without power. If you want to do good things for yourself and others, you will have to use power to do them.

PLAY THE GAME

It is convenient and useful for you to think of life as a game. When you enter the "game of life"—or more accurately, the games of life—you will see that such areas as love, work, war, and politics do indeed have the dimensions and qualities of games. The games of life are complicated, fluid, informal, and less well defined than are formal games (e.g., chess, poker, baseball), but they share features that illustrate the Machiavellian concept of everyday life. Game is a metaphor for often various serious and even deadly human transactions, as when we speak of the "war game" and "theaters of war." The logic of games is helpful in teaching you how to play the games of life and win.

A game, formal or informal, contains rules, players, strategies, plays, chance, and outcomes. A spectacular formal game such as the Super Bowl has all these features. The contest is conducted according to football rules as to what you can and cannot do, although of course these rules are bent, broken, and interpreted. Football players have differing talents and temperaments, and the teams use strategies to win the game ("game plans"). They use different plays as the game develops, changing and altering their strategic perspective by means of tactical maneuvers. Chance is important: the "way the ball bounces" can affect the outcome. And of course, the game does have an outcome: someone wins and someone loses. The contest is Machiavellian: people using conscious game logic and competence to guide their actions and master the situation.

In a less formal sense, your college career as a student is the same. College has certain rules—curricula, majors, course requirements, and so on. You bring your talents and temperament to the academic game. To the extent that you develop a strategy, develop discipline and skills, study the game and the way to master it, you then can play competently and minimize the effect of chance. If you are aware, you can change strategies and tactics and maximize the chances that you will "win" a high grade point average, the accolades of your professors, the admiration of family and peers, and admission to elite advanced programs and to a promising career—another game you can begin to learn how to master. Your brilliant academic career is Machiavellian: an academic contest in which you use conscious academic logic and develop academic competence in order to gain mastery over the college curriculum. You win; most others lose.

It is useful for you to think of other, larger areas of action as games that you might enter and certainly want to understand. Here we shall use the metaphor of the game to understand politics. The Machiavellian understands that politics is a game with loose but understandable rules (constitutional, cultural, ethical, personal); the political game has players who must be studied so that their actions can be understood and predicted. Political players make coalitions and deals with other players to form a team that will affect the outcome. Politicians develop strategies that will help them get what they want and plot new moves and tactics as the game develops. Some players become master politicians, good at playing the game and usually more successful than those who do not play well. Chance intervenes at times, and sometimes politicians become the prisoners of events and political tides, for good or ill—they are assassinated, overthrown, elected at an emotional and irrational time, or victimized for problems they did not create. Political games, such as electoral contests, do have outcomes—someone wins an election, someone else loses.

Politics is a complicated game. Indeed, the politician is not involved in just one game, but many, at the same time and successively. It is useful to think of politics as an ecology of games, both independent and interdependent, in which the politician must play—balancing them off, putting out brush fires, using different skills in different games, anticipating what new games might emerge, and so on. Politics is not an easy game to play, and often it takes the best players many years to develop the talent and temperament it takes to master them. Even then, there is no guarantee that they will win all the games, master all of them, or keep new games from beginning.

STUDY POLITICS

The Machiavellian perspective includes the idea that no matter what you are interested in doing and no matter what games you wind up playing, you should study politics. There is an important sense in which all games, all areas of social action, are political. We may speak of the politics of sex, the politics of the family, the politics of the classroom, the politics of car repair, the politics of divorce, the politics of the career. Everyday life is political for the simple reason that people want things from themselves and for themselves and will try to get other people to help them get these things. People are in constant negotiation with one another over who will get what, when, and how. We all are politicians in our efforts to negotiate what we want with other people who have their own needs. To the extent we get what we want, we are practicing successful politics.

When we say that everyday relationships are political, we are not saying that what you do in mundane life is the same as what the president does or what the prime minister of the Soviet Union does, or what even your own town mayor does. Politics is not reserved for, nor practiced only by, those people generally labeled as politicians. Politics is practiced by all of us.

Politics is not something remote from your life. Your life, after all, is an effort to cope. You try to understand the world in order for you to move through it. You use past experience for present purposes of ruling. You use whatever power—an arsenal of means—you can garner to tell yourself, nature, and others what to do. You use power over yourself to make yourself study. You use strength to move physical objects out of your way. You use powers of communication to get other people to do your bidding. If you write a good term paper in a course, you encourage your professor to give you a good grade. You have gained the professor's compliance. If you get the career and job you want, it is because you have practically used power over the right people for you to gain their compliance and entry into the job you want. In that mundane, personal sense, then, politics is simply the pragmatic rule of experience.

In this conception, politics is understandable to you because you practice the activity daily. When you decide something, for example, you are confronted with choice: Which career should I pursue? Should I marry him or her? Should I study for that exam tomorrow or go to the movies? Your decision may be impulsive and irrational: You may choose a career because that is what your parents want; you may marry the first willing person; you may go to the movies. But you know that is *not* the right way to decide something. An important decision should be considered and rational; that is, it should be logical: what is the best thing for me to do given what it is that I want to be doing? You assess what you want to do in several ways. You have values, principles, and goals to consider. You have desires and weaknesses of the flesh. You have dreams and fantasies about yourself in the future to think of. But at your best you also assess the situation: in fact, what is the situation? Whom do I have to consider and convince in my decision? If I am making a decision that my parents will not like, what strategy can I use to change their mind or at least to get them to acquiesce in what I want to do? When you use such assessment, you are being pragmatic. You want to rule the situation, deal successfully with the people involved, and attain the results you desire. You use pragmatic sagacity: What precepts of practice—rules and maxims—can I draw from my fund of experience? If this were a game, what strategies and tactics would I use to win? How can I best negotiate with the people concerned to gain their compliance? How should I use my own experience? When you go through this process and translate your plan of action into reality, you are being political. You are using power. You are playing a political game. You are practicing political pragmatics. You are ruling. You are being Machiavellian.

We are using what Machiavelli discovered and applied to the area of action that he was interested in: political logic. The logic of pragmatic social action is logic in use to gain a result that we shall term *political*. The difference between the logic you use and the logic used by professional politicians is not a difference in kind but in context of action. We all are politicians, but some of us practice it as a profession. What politicians do to get what they want is something that we can intuitively understand because we do it all the time. One dictionary definition of *logical* is "that which is in accordance with inferences reasonably drawn from events or circumstances." Like all of us, the politician draws inferences from experience and situations about what to do in politics. Those inferences inform and guide political action, those things done in the dynamics of political situations because they seem to be the right thing to do at that place and time. Even the most irrational and impulsive responses are explained in retrospect as the correct response. But Machiavelli understood, as you do, that such responses are stupid. The political logician responds with an attitude of rational calculation: now given this, what should I do to gain what is politically correct and advantageous to do? Like any good logician, the political logician must watch for fallacies of reasoning, emotional responses, ideological blinders, and all other barriers to effective political thinking and doing.

This is no idle enterprise. Nor is it easy. The kind of honest and unblinking calculation that the Machiavellian uses makes many people uncomfortable. But we contend that political logic, wisely used, is necessary for the realization of any purpose, however noble or ignoble. Being well intentioned is not enough; the road to hell is indeed paved with good intentions. What must inform your intentions is the hard analysis of how to use the power of political thinking to shape and guide political action. Machiavelli understood that action has consequences and that action undertaken without proper foresight may be worse than wasted. If purposes are to be realized, then actions equal to the task of realizing them must be found. If you approach your goals, immediate or long range, with an uncaring, lazy, and insensitive attitude, you are less than likely to get what you want.

The cultivation of political logic, then, is a discipline. It requires work. The Machiavellian believes that political intelligence is more effective in action than is political ignorance. We agree with Goethe's warning: "There is nothing more frightful than ignorance in action." The intelligent person develops the habits of thinking that permit the use of knowledge as power. At the core of Machiavellian *virtu* is the disciplined habit of thinking in political-logical ways, using one's fund of political wisdom as political intelligence in action. The basic tool for effective political thinking is political logic. Machiavellians do not depend on luck, fate, or the gods; they use pragmatic sagacity in the hope that pragmatic results can come from the wise use of power. You will have a better chance of getting what you want if you are smart about it. There are no magic formulas that guarantee success, but at least you can develop Machiavellian habits of mind and conduct.

Political logic is both a science and an art. It is a science in that it enjoins political knowledge and rationality, applying standards of thinking and acting to the politician and, by extention, to the rest of us. Through disciplined habit, the political actor can understand the nature of politics, develop the proper attitude toward political situations, apply knowledge and rules to situations, and help draw sound and useful conclusions as to what to do. A Machiavellian political science develops standards for political thinking and political acting, rules for how to think about politics and what to do in politics. Political logic is also an art, the art of logic in use, of applying standards of action to political action. Politics is often called the art of the possible, of what can be done here and now, because politicians translate logic into action, doing what they can to gain the results desired. Politics is a highly practical art, and the proof of good political logic is in what is created. Machiavelli considered a well-ruled state to be a thing of beauty, a creation no less aesthetic than a statue, painting, or building. We admire political intelligence not only for its rationality but also for its creativity. The politician is an artist, and politics is a creative art.

Therefore you should study politics not only to help you understand the nature of politics but also to help you in your personal quest for pragmatic rule of experience, your own politics. There is no real difference between using political logic to govern a state and using political logic to govern your own life. You must study political situations because they will help you conduct your own life. Study the careers of politicians, for they will tell you how to be a prince.

BE A PRINCE

Above all, Machiavelli was committed to quality: at whatever it is you decide to do, be a prince. Machiavellian *virtu* is a quality of mind and deed available to virtually everyone but achieved by very few. A prince is anyone who effectively rules himself or herself and others. In an irrational world, a prince uses pragmatic sagacity—political rationality—in order to understand and control experience. In your everyday life and long-term career, you will constantly have to use your personal qualities (virtues) to combat the unforeseen, the hostile, the uncaring, and the accidental aspects of the world. Your success in life—career, love, friendships, family—are by no means decided beforehand, nor will they come easily. Steering your ship successfully through the tempests and shoals of the oceanic world will not happen if it is left to drift by chance.

What are princely qualities? The Machiavellian ideal has two dimensions: princely characteristics and princely actions. Machiavellian *virtu* includes identifying and cultivating the habits necessary for princely activities—courage, integrity, gallantry, composure, and any quality that contributes to successful pragmatic rule of oneself and others. There is no established list of what you should be. Instead, you should cultivate those personal qualities that work. At the core of *virtu* is the willingness to learn—becoming a prince means that you learn to use those qualities of thought and deed that contribute to pragmatic rule. Virtuous characteristics are inseparable from virtuous actions. Princes recognize that the world is political and think and act accordingly. Princes learn those qualities that permit them to adjust to changing circumstances and direct them toward their desired goals. Princes acquire the qualities that contribute to political competence through their willingness to learn.

It is not difficult to prove just how important is the willingness to learn. Think of the people that you know in school. For several reasons, many of them are not willing or able to learn. But a few are. They seek learning, knowing that it is essential to the realization of their purposes. They understand that knowing is linked to doing and that their chances of doing depend on the quality of their knowing. If you do not see that, you may not belong in school. This is not to say, of course, that you cannot be a prince at something—plumbing, cooking, selling, whatever—that does not depend on academic knowledge. The Machiavellian ideal simply urges that you seek your area and level of competence and avoid what you are not competent to do. Incompetence in any field is ignorance in action.

It is also not difficult to see that competence in any field generally has good consequences and that incompetence has bad consequences. If you have an incompetent teacher, you probably will not learn anything. But if you have good teachers, you may learn something. If you want your plumbing fixed, a good dinner at a restaurant, or your house sold, you want somebody competent at those skills. The ideal of Machiavellian virtue celebrates professionalism at whatever is done. Princes are pros, those who learn well, excel at, and take pride in their profession. A profession is a vocation requiring specialized knowledge and intelligent execution to achieve a beneficial result. The ideal of the professional exalts the practice of *virtu* in almost every area of life. If you are going to be good at what you do, you must become a pro. True professionals study and try to excel at their craft.

At the heart of the Machiavellian perspective on politics is the simple but powerful idea that politics is probably the one area in which competence is crucial. For Machiavellians consider politics the most difficult and consequential areas of social action, the one on which all the others—economy, society, culture—depend. If political rule is not successful, if political problems are not solved, then all other human purposes—running a business, raising a family, watching a movie—are put in jeopardy. Political peace is necessary for any human purpose; we cannot live and get on with our business in a state of perpetual anarchy. And because politics is so consequential, incompetence among political princes has more disastrous results than any other human vocation does.

For this reason, princes should be professionals, people whose vocation is politics. They have trained themselves for their craft, the craft of governing, statecraft. They apply standards of political thinking and political acting to themselves and other politicians. They like politics and are not afraid of or unwilling to use power. They have political experience, a fund of political knowledge from their own careers and from political history and biography. They are political scientists and political artists, understanding that facts and rules can be used in contemporary political situations to create political reality. They bring whatever political virtue they can muster to bear on the chaos of the present, producing whatever political order possible through their mastery of political forces. They are strategic masters of political logic in action. They are princes, distinguishable from the rest of us by their political characteristics and acts. The perfect political prince is, of course, never realized completely but is a reminder of what a prince should be. And as we shall point out in this book, there have been princes who approximate the model.

THE PRINCE'S STUDENT

Very few of you will be princes. Not all of you can be, and certainly not all of you should be. Not every outfielder can be Joe DiMaggio, not every violinist Itzhak Perelman, and not every physicist Albert Einstein. Not everybody is talented, ambitious, and lucky. We all know that in many ways life is unfair and that cream is not the only thing that rises to the top. Fortune smiles on some of us and frowns on others. Imbeciles indeed may be in high places, making life miserable for the rest of us because of their incompetence. Talented folk may fritter their life away or be prevented from gaining power by the fears of the mediocre. Finally, many of you may just have a temperamental distaste for the frustrations and stupidities of politics and prefer to turn your attention elsewhere.

Yet, as we have urged here, you can learn much by becoming a student of princes. You can, if you so choose, learn much about how the world works, not only the world of politics per se, but also those of business, sports, colleges and universities (oh, yes), and so on. You can understand not only the high politics of presidential elections or peace negotiations, but also the more mundane politics of situations you will encounter throughout your life. Suppose that you go to work for a business. You would be wise to learn the politics of the business—who has power, how things are done, whom to see to get something, how promotion works, who is useless, who is efficient, and so forth. This knowledge is essential to you to do your job, whether or not you choose to try to become the prince of the business. You cannot escape politics, and so you might as well try to understand how it works.

If you have princely ambitions, you obviously should study politics to help you in your struggle. But you should also need Machiavelli's warning: it is not easy to be a prince. Before you attempt to rule, remember that rule of any kind—including self-rule—means agonizing costs, risks, and dilemmas. It is easier to be ruled than to rule. The ruler has to make decisions, do the work, deal with not-always-nice people, take the heat, make gambles, weigh choices that may be bad, do nasty things, sweat out crises, try to figure out what is going to happen next, and tell others what to do. Power means responsibility. If you are in charge, you are expected to lead, to know what to do, to win, to keep your followers busy and happy, to ward off threats, to reward and punish, and to express and implement what the group believes: in a word, to rule. Are you willing and able to do that? Could you do it well? This book is an invitation to political education. We want to help show you the ways of politics. We are not interested in "civics"; we are not going to elaborate on the methods of political science; nor are we going to tell you what political values you should hold. Instead, we are going to introduce you to politics by demonstrating the perspective and method of Machiavelli, pointing to the whys and wherefores of political life and illustrating how politics works by using the careers of notable Princes of the past. In the next chapter, we shall show in more detail how to think politically. But first, let us turn to a case that reveals the agonizing burden of being a prince.

THE COVENTRY DECISION

Winston Churchill had to make many difficult decisions in his long political career, but perhaps none was more difficult than the Coventry

WINSTON CHURCHILL: WAR LEADER

If it had not been for World War II, Winston Churchill might have been barely remembered as just another minor Tory politician and, indeed, something of a political failure. Up to 1940, he had led a long and colorful life. His youthful adventures in Afghanistan, the Sudan, and the Boer War had made him a well known and dashing figure in England, because he had written best-selling books about his experiences. But he retired to devote himself to the sport of politics, which, he said, was more dangerous than war, because in war you can be killed only once, but in politics you can be killed many times. And many times he was. He resigned in disgrace from the goverment after the disaster at Gallipoli during World War I. He switched political parties twice, was in and out of the House of Commons, and served in various cabinets. But during the 1930s, his warnings about the rise of "hungry tigers," the new dictators such as Adolf Hitler and Benito Mussolini, went unheeded. In *While England Slept* (1936), Churchill wrote, "[England] decided only to be undecided, resolved to be irresolute, adamant for drift, solid for fluidity, all-powerful to be impotent." The appeasement of Hitler at Munich made war inevitable, he thought, but still England would not face the crisis.

The policy of appeasement and Prime Minister Neville Chamberlain's government collapsed with the Nazi spring offensive of 1940. Faced with the Nazi overrun of Europe, the British formed a coalition government with a compromise candidate (by no means universally liked), the old war-horse Churchill, already in his sixties. The situation was bleak: France was soon to fall, and England stood alone against the German juggernaut. But the out-gunned and outnumbered British did not give in. Much of the reason for this was Churchill. He was the embodiment of the stubborn John Bull, and he mobilized the English language and sent it into battle. His radio speeches to the nation stiffened its will to resist either invasion or bombardment. He offered himself as the leader of that fight: "I have nothing to offer but blood, toil, tears, and sweat. . . . Victory at all costs, victory in spite of all terror, victory however long and hard the road may be; for without victory there is no survival." He reminded the British that the future would see that "this was their finest hour" and the Germans that they would fight them everywhere, and "we shall never surrender." "We have not journeyed all this way," he said defiantly, "across the centuries, across the oceans, across the mountains, across the prairies, because we are made of sugar candy." It is worth noting that Churchill's memorable speeches did not come easily. He learned how to write and speak over long years of training and painstaking preparation. He would often rewrite important speeches twenty-five times, search for memorable phrases, and practice their delivery over and over. He became the "speaker of the century" even though he stuttered and had a congenital lisp and intense stage fright, once collapsing during a speech in the House of Commons.

In any case, Churchill's rhetoric helped the British persevere. Hitler attacked the Soviet Union, and after its defeat at Pearl Harbor, the United States finally entered the war. The tide began to turn, and Churchill kept urging his new allies to pursue the fight to the end. Once challenged in regard to his courtship of Stalin and the Soviets, he replied that if the devil came out against Hitler, he would make a favorable remark in Parliament about Satan himself. In 1945, Hitler was defeated, and Churchill was able to tour the wreckage of the Fuehrerbunker in Berlin and sit in Hitler's chair. But he was then defeated for

　　　　　　　　　　　　　　　　　Politics Is Not Just for Princes

reelection and had to retire again to private life. (He served again briefly as prime minister in the early 1950s but spent most of the rest of his life writing.)

Churchill remains one of the great politicians of the twentieth century and also one of its most remarkable characters. His capacity for hard liquor, for example, is well known: "I have taken more out of alcohol," he once remarked, "than alcohol has taken out of me." (He also lived well into his nineties.) He never lost his interest in politics nor his belief in parliamentary democracy. "Democracy," he once said, "is a very bad form of government, except for all the others that have been tried from time to time." But democracy has its limits, and he warned, "People get the government they deserve."

---

decision. This story is worth telling because it illustrates how a competent prince, following the dictates of political logic, has to make decisions that are not easy but that may be the politically right thing to do at the time. A few historians dispute the following story, but here we rely on the testimony of Churchill's own secret intelligence officers.

In the late 1930s, with war looming, British intelligence managed to obtain a replica of a German cipher machine, used to send scrambled messages to diplomatic and military units. British cryptographers finally broke the machine's code, and by April 1940, with England and Germany at war, the British began to intercept German coded messages.

Churchill and the war cabinet then had to decide how to use the information gained. They knew in advance every major military operation the Germans were going to undertake, but if they used this advance information too obviously, the Germans might become suspicious and change their codes, thus robbing the British of this valuable information. Having the information gave the British a great strategic advantage, but if they misused it, they would lose it. So Churchill had to weigh the costs and benefits and decide on the basis of political logic whether the machine was worth using in a particular case.

In November 1940, German Luftwaffe chief Hermann Goering convinced Hitler to change their bombing strategy in the blitz of England, hitting cities other than London. Some historians believe that on November 12, a British operator intercepted the message that the English city of Coventry would be the target of mass bombing on the night of November 14. Churchill was immediately notified, and the war cabinet was convened.

Coventry was a large city, with a population of over a quarter of a million people filling thirty square miles. It was an ancient city, the site of the famous St. Michael's Cathedral. It was also a major industrial center, with plants and military arsenals. But Goering's main reason for bombing cities with big populations was to kill civilians and demoralize the British.

Thus some believe that Churchill knew of the impending Luftwaffe raid on one of his own country's major cities. It was going to be a big raid, and there would be large loss of life and valuable property. Churchill was a humane man, but he was also a consummate strategist. His larger political and military aim, the political logic that guided him, was to do those things that would win the war. England's survival as a nation was at stake, and every decision had to be taken with that political aim in mind. Churchill's alternatives were few. The damage that could be done to Coventry would not seriously cripple the British military machine. If he evacuated the city, spies and German pilots would realize that the British had had advance warning, and they might discover that the British had broken the German cryptographic code. Evacuation would also create panic and chaos, and if the attack were delayed because of weather or other reasons, the British risked losing their secret information for no gain. All these considerations aside, if indeed this story is true, for Churchill the choice was simple: he could save some lives and prevent some suffering now by warning Coventry, or he could sacrifice them and keep the secret, gambling that it would be worth it by saving a great many lives and even his own country later. So he decided to do nothing. In other words, other than the normal alert procedure whenever a raid was expected, Coventry would be sacrificed to prevent the Germans from finding out that the British knew what they were going to do.

On the brilliant moonlit night of November 14, 1940, with no industrial haze to block the aerial view, the Germans attacked Coventry. Air-raid sirens went off at 7:05 P.M.; five minutes later planes were heard; and only then were police, hospital, fire, and civil defense forces informed. After eleven hours of bombing, the entire central city, including the cathedral, was destroyed. Casualties included 554 civilians killed, 865 seriously wounded, and over 4,000 suffering wounds and burns; 50,749 houses were destroyed or damaged. Germany boasted through propaganda broadcasts that now every English city would be "Coventryized."

Churchill relied on his political experience to guide him. His political aim meant that terrible and agonizing things had to be done. If he did know about the impending attack on Coventry, he used power in order to achieve a long-term political result by not protecting his fellow citizens from foreign attack. He suppressed his humane and moral impulses to stop the horror visited on Coventry. His decision was political and pragmatic. His political logic was simple: his power was his responsibility to the entire nation to win the war, and the power to win the war would come only from advance secret knowledge carefully applied; saving Coventry was not worth the risk, on balance, of losing the use of the code; therefore Coventry had to be sacrificed. Knowledge of the German code later proved invaluable in sinking the German warship *Bismarck,* in battles in North Africa and the D-Day landing, and indeed in the balance of the war. President Franklin D. Roosevelt later commented on the agony of such decisions, that it was "forcing us more and more to play God ... I don't know what I should have done."

Now ask yourself: Could I make such a decision? If you could not decide, or sacrificed the code for Coventry, would you belong in politics?

If you had saved Coventry, and the Germans had changed their code, eventually won the war, and subjugated your country to Nazi rule, then how would you have felt? The point, of course, is that such decisions of life and death are not easy, nor are there simple rules or answers to tell you what to do. Not every decision or action, to be sure, has such consequences or requires such a terrible choice, but the inescapable fact is that a prince has no exit: what you decide to do has consequences that are real and not always good for everybody, and yet you are responsible for them.

"Life is, in fact, a battle. . . ."

—*Henry James*

"There is nothing more frightful than ignorance in action."

—*Goethe*

"[The war] is forcing us more and more to play God . . . I don't know what I should have done."

—*Franklin D. Roosevelt*

"[England] decided only to be undecided, resolved to be irresolute, adamant for drift, solid for fluidity, all-powerful to be impotent."

—*Churchill*

"Without victory there is no survival."

—*Churchill*

"People get the government they deserve."

—*Churchill*

"There is no less likely way of winning a war than to adhere pedantically to the maximum of 'Safety First'."

—*Churchill*

"No leader should ever suppose he can invariably take the safe course, since all choices involve risks. In the nature of things, you can never try to escape one danger without encountering another; but prudence consists in knowing how to recognize the nature of the different dangers and in accepting the least bad as good."

—*Machiavelli*

Chapter

3

Princely Thinking About Politics

People called it the Great War. It was, they thought, "the war to end all wars." It was not. Within two decades after the ink had dried on the peace treaties, a fiercer and far wider conflict began. So the Great War became known as World War I, the prelude to World War II.

In October 1917, one year before World War I eventually ended, a twenty-eight-year-old American working with the War Department left his duties to join a highly secret project. The project had no name, but the young man was Walter Lippmann. Lippmann, a journalist by trade, became a member of a highly select, five-member group known only as the "Inquiry." Of the other four members, one was a philosopher of religion, another a historian, one a lawyer, and the fourth a geographer. Despite its secrecy, word of the group's existence leaked out, and several famous Americans asked to join. A noted jurist, Judge Learned Hand, offered his services. John Dewey, the nation's leading philosopher, volunteered. But the group stuck with its original five members, eventually acting as the directorate of a much larger staff.

The Inquiry came into existence at the behest of the president of the United States, Woodrow Wilson. It was Wilson's desire not only to end the global war that the United States was fighting but also to play a major role in drawing up the peace agreements that would follow. Therefore, he instructed his key aide, Colonel Edward House, to put together a group of experts to assemble materials for the peace conference. The Inquiry was the result. Its task was to formulate a peace plan that would set the boundaries and rules for nations once the war to end all wars was over.

Lippmann was the general secretary of the Inquiry. His job was to coordinate the work of the specialists and to provide overall direction for the project. In short, he was to formulate a plan for a durable peace. The task was not easy. For one thing, the Inquiry had to act quickly. President Wilson had to have soon a peace plan to present to the world, as there was a genuine fear that the victorious Allies might dictate a peace so harsh and selfish as to make another war inevitable. But there was another problem. A durable peace would require that national frontiers be drawn in such a way as to minimize rivalries among nations over coveted territories and ethnic groups. Doing that was not easy. Some national groups—the Czechs, Slovaks, Serbs—wanted new states of their own. Others, such as the Poles, wanted their old kingdoms restored. Still others, most notably the French, wanted Germany punished for the war. To compound all this was another difficulty: there were remarkably few facts from which to form a sensible peace proposal. For example, maps showing the precise economic, ethnic, language, and social characteristics of territories in Europe and other portions of the world either did not exist or were so outdated as to mislead.

Such was the problem facing the Inquiry. Working with the information available in the form of maps, statistics, and historical facts, the group (sometimes sitting on the floor peering at documents before them) compiled charts of where various national groups were concentrated. Lippmann then weighed these documents against the Inquiry's prime goal: to give national groups the opportunity to determine their own destinies without intensifying existing national rivalries. Matching ethnic aspirations with geographic and economic factors, Lippmann organized a political solution to the Inquiry's problem, which he sent to Colonel House in late December 1917, just a little more than two months after joining the Inquiry. House presented Lippmann's proposals to the president; Wilson required clarification of certain points. Finally, on January 8, 1918, Wilson addressed the U.S. Congress. It was a speech that became famous as "Wilson's Fourteen Points." Accepting the Inquiry's basic points and adding six general principles of his own, Wilson outlined his plan for a stable peace. Before 1918 came to a close, the Germans asked for an armistice on the basis of the Fourteen Points. The war was over.

But there are many reasons that this was not the last war. First among them was that the Fourteen Points did not serve as the basis for the final peace treaty, the Treaty of Versailles. The political logic of the peace conference took its toll of Wilson's (and Lippmann's) plans. Logical thinking about a political problem, so successful for Wilson's purposes in early 1918, was sacrificed for other ends a year later. The peace treaty that ultimately derived from postwar negotiations did not please Lippmann. Writing in the *New Republic,* he declared, "It will require at least a generation of force to secure the execution of this treaty."

Even though the Inquiry's efforts did not provide the basis for the treaty ending World War I, the problem faced by Lippmann and his fellow Inquiry members is instructive. Just what did such political thinking require?

THINKING ABOUT PROBLEMS

Everybody thinks. It may not seem so at times, especially when you come across a "thoughtless" person, but people do think. But as philoso-

WALTER LIPPMANN: PRINCELY THINKER

"Gentlemen, the future President of the United States." This is how John Reed in 1908 introduced his fellow classmate Walter Lippmann to a gathering of Harvard undergraduates. (Reed later became a successful journalist and in 1917 wrote an eyewitness account of the Bolshevik Revolution in Russia, entitled *Ten Days That Shook the World.* Movie fans may recall Reed as the leading character, played by actor Warren Beatty, in the popular and highly acclaimed film *Reds.*)

Walter Lippmann (1889–1974) did not become president of the United States, but like Reed he did become a journalist, one of the most respected and influential in the world. So influential was he that those who did reach the office of president of the United States flattered him, courted his favor, and sought his advice. President Theodore Roosevelt thought him the "most brilliant young man of his age in all the United States." (Lippmann was twenty-five at the time.) He wrote eight of President Woodrow Wilson's famous Fourteen Points in World War I, and forty years later, after advising many presidents in the intervening years, Lippmann helped write the inaugural address of President John F. Kennedy, convincing the new president that it was better to describe the Soviet Union as an adversary than as an enemy, thereby suggesting a shift away from the Cold War. Lippmann's experience as a diplomat, however, was not always so indirect. In 1927, when the United States and Mexico were on the verge of military conflict, Lippmann drafted the letters that President Calvin Coolidge sent to the Mexican president *and* the letters that the Mexican president sent to Coolidge! Lippmann also drafted the letters that both presidents sent to a third party, the Mexican archbishop who was mediating the dispute.

But from the time of his very first political job—as secretary to the mayor of Schenectady, New York, in 1912—Lippmann avoided a career as a full-time politician. Hence, although for six decades he was a "behind-the-scenes" adviser to practicing politicians, his life's work was that of a journalist. He began as a cub reporter for the *Boston Common* after graduating from college and wrote for the *New Republic* magazine before World War I. In 1922, he joined the editorial staff of the New York *World* and soon became the director of its editorial page. When the *World* folded in 1931, the New York *Herald Tribune* made Lippmann an offer he could not refuse, to write his own political opinion column. Although a few other journalists had written independent columns, this was the first opinion column, that is, a systematic reflection on politics, political events, and political actions and recommendations of what should be done. Today, such columns are common in newspapers and newsmagazines and have their counterparts in commentaries on television news programs. But latter-day columnists and commentators are only imitators: Walter Lippmann invented the art.

Besides Lippmann's ten books, there are also many compilations and reprints of his articles, lectures, and other writings. Lippmann wrote almost three hundred articles and more than two thousand editorials. But his four thousand newspaper columns were what made him influential, as they were the vehicles of his political thinking. Most of all, Walter Lippmann was a political thinker.

At the height of his career in Washinton, D.C., a legend grew about Walter Lippmann. As reporters made their daily rounds of government officials, trying to clarify a complicated policy or discover what course of action officials might take, they encountered over and over again from those officials the same question, "Have you read Lippmann on that?"

---

pher John Dewey wrote, some ways of thinking are better than others are. In the remainder of this chapter, we shall consider how you might learn to think more constructively about politics, what Dewey called *reflective* thinking.

Reflective thinking has several characteristics. First, it is active. When you are thinking, or reflecting, you are consciously dealing with a problem. You are not daydreaming, nor are you jumping from one thing to another. Second, reflective thinking is persistent. You reflect on a problem until you find a solution or until you consciously give up. Third, reflection is the careful consideration of the information that supports the ideas that constitute thoughts. The Inquiry's efforts in 1917 illustrate these three characteristics. Lippmann and his cohorts actively considered the problem of how to draw new national boundaries for a postwar world. In spite of the difficulties they faced, they persisted in their inquiry, and they made careful use of the maps, charts, facts, and other materials they could assemble. Active, persistent, careful consideration. In short, reflective thinking is inquiry—assembling facts, generating ideas, comparing ideas with supporting facts, and considering the possible consequences of each idea if put into practice.

When you think reflectively, you do so in phases. You begin with a problem. For John Dewey, anything that might challenge or confuse the mind, no matter how commonplace or trivial, could be a problem if it stimulated questions, challenged beliefs, and provoked inquiry. You pass a stranger on the street. The stranger smiles. "I wonder what that meant," you wonder. That problem may be less earth shattering in its implications than the one faced by the Inquiry, but for you it is no less a problem (especially if the stranger is of the opposite sex and the smile beguiling).

The next phase is to search, hunt, seek, or whatever for facts and ideas that will help solve the problem. For example, you are registering for classes at a college or university. You note that there are long lines at each of two tables at which your registration forms must be approved. Which line should you join? One way to deal with the problem is to ignore it, thereby accepting Etorre's Observation (one of many addenda to Murphy's Law that "if anything can go wrong, it will"), namely, that "the other line always moves faster." Instead, recognize that you have what John Dewey called a *forked-road situation*. A forked-road situation is ambiguous, offers a dilemma, and proposes alternatives. Which alternative to take? The reflective thinker looks for facts that will serve a purpose. Assume that your purpose is to get through registration quickly. To gather such facts you could do several things: ask people which line is moving faster, climb on a chair and gauge the relative speed of the two lines, or stroll up front and see which table seems to have the more speedy registrars. In short, you seek signs, clues, helpful hints.

Reflective thinking, thus, is not very complicated. Dewey boiled it down to a couple of points. He wrote that the "demand for the solution of perplexity is the steadying and guiding factor in the entire process of reflection" and that "the nature of the problem fixes the end of thought, and the end controls the process of thinking." Thus Lippmann's Inquiry group had a problem that guided their reflection; the end they sought—an outline for a lasting peace—controlled their thinking.

Reflective thinking is relevant to everyday life and to politics. Machiavelli understood that, and because politics has its own logic, the type of reflection that Machiavelli recommended applying to politics must be distinctive. It must, first, be realistic, that is, not concerned with abstract political ideals, but with practices and policies. Princely thinking about politics must discover what works and does not work, not what we would like but cannot realistically achieve. Second, reflective thinking is active. By considering alternatives, by exploiting forked-road situations, people can actively strive for new ways of living. This leads to the third aspect of Machiavelli's guidelines for political thinking, that it must be applied. A realistic appraisal of what is, an active exploration of alternatives, will lead to a new problem, which is: How can we effect a change?

If these are the characteristics of reflective political thinking, how should you use them? How Machiavelli and Lippmann thought about politics offers you some suggestions. Machiavelli in the fifteenth century and Lippman in the twentieth century believed in learning and thinking about politics by taking part in it. They were what today's social scientists call *participant-observers*. Both princely thinkers were active in politics at various times in their lives. Their activity provided opportunities for studying firsthand what goes on in politics. But because both wanted to learn about politics (the "end" that "controls the process of thinking," to use Dewey's phrase), they were careful. Their emphasis was on observation, description of what they observed, and comparisons of what they observed in order to derive lessons from their participation. Instead of deciding beforehand what should be done in each case, they suspended that judgment until they had accumulated a description of what was happening. Instead of randomly or haphazardly gathering facts, they observed systematically. Each sought concrete facts rather than hasty impressions. Each compared several instances of politics to discover general patterns and, each thought, general principles.

But, you say, how can I be a participant-observer in politics? Doesn't it take time, money, and interest to be involved in politics? That, of course, depends on your definition of politics. If you define politics as what governing officials do—how they obtain their office and what they do with it—then most people are indeed unlikely to take part. Even then, however, there are some options: campaigning, voting, working for a public official, and the like. But suppose that you expand the meaning of the word *politics* to include any relationship between two or more people that involves trying to get one or the other to do something, something the person might not otherwise do. Such relationships are power relationships. Put slightly differently, you are in politics! You are a participant-observer. By the time you have finished reading this text, you will, we trust, have learned how to sharpen your powers of political observation.

Machiavelli and Lippmann did not limit their observation to areas of their immediate political involvement, nor must you. They also studied history, examining what happened in the past, drawing inferences from previous examples, comparing those ideas, and learning what could be applied in the present and future. They were not so foolish as to believe that the past always repeats itself. Machiavelli recognized the danger in too easily assuming that the past is prologue for what is to come. Nonetheless, he wrote in his *Discourses* that "the custom of praising the old and condemning the new does exist, but it is not always wrong. Sometimes such a judgment has to be correct since human affairs are always in motion, either rising or declining." In short, history does not always repeat itself; yet, similar situations and problems recur, requiring similar reflection. The prudent prince accepts this and draws such lessons from the past as may be applied to and tested in the present. Five centuries later, Lippmann echoed Machiavelli's thought: "The changing world that confronts us is both new and old. It is never wholly what it used to be, and therefore the old rules are never wholly reliable. It is never entirely new, and therefore we are fools if we do not look for guidance in the book of experience."

Participant-observation. Historical analysis. These are the sources of princely reflection on politics. How can they be applied well? To assist your reflection on that problem, let us consider the case of the dog that did not bark.

"WATSON, YOU KNOW MY METHODS"

Silver Blaze was a famous racehorse. He had a brilliant record and hence was favored to win the Wessex Cup. Then without warning, he disappeared. And another strange thing happened. Silver Blaze's trainer, John Straker, was found dead a quarter of a mile from the stables. This was the case presented to Mr. Sherlock Holmes, accompanied by his friend and assistant, Dr. John H. Watson. As always, Arthur Conan Doyle's famous but fictional detective solved the case, exercising his superior powers of reason and deduction, though not before this exchange took place between Holmes and the police inspector assigned to the mystery. The inspector speaks first:

"Is there any point to which you would wish to draw my attention?"
"To the curious incident of the dog in the night-time."

"The dog did nothing in the night-time."

"That was the curious incident," remarked Sherlock Holmes.

What made it curious? The dog was in the stables at the time that Silver Blaze was removed. It did not bark. Holmes deduced that the dog did nothing because he knew the intruder who nabbed Silver Blaze. The intruder must have been Straker, intent on removing the horse, taking him away from the stables, and inflicting on the thoroughbred a slight but disabling injury. The horse then would not be able to win the Wessex Cup, and his trainer would profit by betting against him. But when Straker moved to cut Silver Blaze with a small knife the horse kicked the culprit. Straker died from the blow. The murderer, that is, Silver Blaze, then wandered off, to be found later by Holmes, in an ironic and amusing ending to the tale.

What does this have to do with political thinking? Indeed, the fictional Sherlock holmes was not a political thinker at all; he was scarcely even interested in politics. Watson rated Holmes's knowledge of politics as "feeble." Yet, the very methods invented by Arthur Conan Doyle for Holmes's use are precisely those required for sound political thinking. They are very much in the tradition of Niccolo Machiavelli, Walter Lippmann, and John Dewey, and to study them is to learn a great deal about what is required of princely political reflection.

You should start with knowledge. To be a competent detective, you must know, said Holmes, a great deal about a vast variety of things, some seemingly trivial. "Breadth of view is one of the essentials of our profession," said Holmes, for "the interplay of ideas and the oblique uses of knowledge are often of extraordinary interest." Contained in Holmes's "vast store of out-of-the-way knowledge" were detailed and precise distinctions among types of tobacco ashes, shapes of ears, perfume scents, newspaper types, bicycle tires, typewriter ribbons, tattoos, and countless other items. Machiavelli, as well, taught that a prince must know about many things: history, events, people, places, laws, customs, religions, cultures, and so on. "All knowledge comes useful to the detective," lectured Holmes. Machiavelli could have said as much about a prince.

Observation is no less important to detection or reflection than knowledge is. Holmes observed that his thinking was founded "on the observation of trifles," for "the greatest issues may depend upon the smallest things." That, of course, was why the dog's doing nothing in the nighttime was a "curious incident," which led to the solution of the Silver Blaze mystery.

Doyle's Holmes specifies aspects of observation that have general and political importance. First, observation must be based on experience. Holmes was a great believer in traveling to the scene of a crime in order to see for himself what had taken place, to search for clues, and to reconstruct events. "Evidence on the spot has special value," he argued. Political thinking also requires exierence. Political scientists refer to evidence gained through experience and "on the spot" as empirical.

Much of what you will learn about politics in this book, such as why people vote as they do or fail to take part in elections, is based on empirical evidence acquired by surveys of people's attitudes and beliefs. Moreover, you have already seen that political thinkers such as Machiavelli and Lippmann strongly believed in observation through experience. That is the basis of what we described earlier as participant-observation.

A second feature of observation is that it checks misleading and/or false impressions. Holmes warned, "Never trust to general impressions ... but concentrate yourself on details." Political scientists label the technique of checking one's impressions against the facts as *hypothesis testing*. It is vital to sound political thinking. In his book *A Preface to Morals* Walter Lippmann could have been describing Machiavelli's princely ruler when he wrote, "The mature man would take the world as it comes and within himself remain unperturbed. When he acted he would know that he was only testing an hypothesis, and if he failed, he would know that he had made a mistake."

Observation, then, is a means of testing hypotheses, whose aim is to gather pertinent evidence: "Data! Data! Data! I can't make bricks without clay!" cried Holmes in the case of *The Copper Beeches*. But evidence should not be gathered simply for its own sake, but for a specific end. That is what you should have learned from Dewey's admonition that the nature of a problem fixes thought and the end sought controls thinking. Holmes put it this way: "It is of the highest importance in the art of detection to be able to recognize, out of a number of facts, which are incidental, and which are vital." In princely thinking about politics this is the trait of sagacity, the ability of "reasoning backwards" that Holmes described in *The Cardboard Box*. It involves taking a complex idea and breaking it down into parts in order to consider each subdivision separately, to test it, and thereby to obtain a clear picture of the whole.

Analysis, the final phase of princely thinking, is reasoning backwards. It has three overlapping, interdependent features. One is induction. You are engaged in induction when you look at a series of facts without prejudice, without deciding in advance where they will lead you. Suppose that you are a member of a jury at the trial of someone accused of a crime. As you listen to and sift through the evidence presented by the prosecution and the defense, you have no fixed idea of the defendant's guilt or innocence. That is something you must decide once all the evidence is presented, the basis for the saying that "a person is innocent until proven guilty." "It is a capital mistake to theorize before you have all the evidence," remarked Holmes. Walter Lippmann had to practice that inductive rule in his peace settlement prepared for President Wilson. Unswayed by the jealousies and rivalries of national groupings, the Inquiry sought to establish frontiers that would preserve the peace. But the delegates to the peace conference saw it differently, and their theories took precedence over the facts of geography, economics, and ethnic cultures.

Analysis also requires abduction. Any set of facts can be interpreted in differing ways, and different theories can be created to fit a common body of evidence. Abduction is applying different interpretations and determining their relative plausibility. Holmes described the problem as follows: "Circumstantial evidence is a very tricky thing. It may seem to point straight to one thing, but if you shift your own point of view a little, you may find it pointing in an equally uncompromising manner to something entirely different." In Holmes's abductive reflections, according to Watson, the detective would spend "hours of intense concentration during which he weighed every particle of evidence, constructed alternative theories, balanced one against the other, and made up his mind as to which points were essential and which immaterial." If you, as a citizen, are to reflect in princely fashion about politics, you must do the same thing. Think of the circumstantial evidence presented to you by rival candidates in elections. You must seek suporting evidence, listen to claims from various points of view (construct alternative theories), and make up your mind as to what is essential and what is immaterial.

This leads to a third feature of analysis, namely, deduction. If a theory is correct, it should lead to a conclusion that can be tested as either right or wrong. Put in language you learned earlier, a theory should lead to a hypothesis that can be tested. Deduction is simply saying, "All right, if my hunch is correct, what should happen next?" If what should happen, according to your theory, does not, then you are wrong. Said Holmes, "It is impossible as I state it and therefore I must in some respect have stated it wrong." Theorize, hypothesize, test. And finally, declared Holmes, "It is an old maxim of mine that when you have eliminated the impossible, whatever remains, however improbable, must be the truth." Consider the politics of taking exams. Your professors have power over you in their evaluation of your work, your grade. Where there is power, there is politics. Assume that you have decided to dabble in politics in this way: you have carefully listened to class lectures, taken notes and read the texts. You formulate a theory of "what she wants" or "what he will ask on the exam." Your theory leads you to study certain things and to ignore others (to separate the essential from the immaterial). Exam day arrives, and you test whether you have "stated it wrong" or right.

Knowledge, observation, and analysis are essential to Holmesian logic and are also the requirements for understanding political logic. Use them, and you will be practicing not only political thinking but politics as well.

DEMYSTIFYING POLITICS THROUGH POLITICAL THINKING

"Men in general judge more by the sense of sight than the sense of touch," wrote Machiavelli in *The Prince*. One thing he meant by that was that people usually let vague impressions (sense of sight) take priority over a concrete understanding that can be derived from direct experience (sense of touch). This is especially true in regard to politics. One of the most common impressions of politics is that it is complicated, confusing, and beyond understanding. If you struck up a conversation with someone about politics, how many times do you think the response would be, "Well, I don't keep up on that because politics just doesn't make any sense to me"? Politicians, of course, take advantage of the idea that their craft is beyond understanding. Many officials know that when people believe that politics is confusing and corrupt, they will not bother to participate. The fewer citizens who take part, the more freely the politicians can act without public accountability.

But as Sherlock Holmes remarked in *A Study in Scarlet,* "It is a mistake to confound strangeness with mystery." Politics is strange to most people, there is little question of that. Yet politics need not be mysterious. In fact, thought Machiavelli, politics is no mystery at all. Rather, it is a very understandable human enterprise. It occurs where there are people, and so by understanding politics we will learn about people. Indeed, Machiavelli wrote *The Prince* and the *Discourses* to remove the mystery of politics, and Walter Lippmann, in *A Preface to Politics,* said: "We must put man at the center of politics, even though we are densely ignorant both of man and of politics. This has always been the method of the great political thinkers. . . . But one difference we in this age must note: they made their political man a dogma—we must leave him a hypothesis. That is to say, that our task is to temper speculation with scientific humility."

Why demystify politics? That which is no longer a mystery to you, you can control. Indeed, as we shall argue in the chapters to come, politics is a means by which you can control your own destiny.

How can we demystify politics? Don't "confound strangeness with mystery." Something mysterious cannot be understood, but something merely strange can. By learning about politics and by developing skills of political thinking, you can remove the strangeness. You will then have demystified politics and be in a better position to control your political fortunes.

The purpose of this textbook is to assist you in learning about politics, to remove its strangeness, and to help you demystify it. To that end we have thus far introduced you to the teaching of Niccolo Machiavelli, the logic of politics, and a few principles of political thinking. Our message to this point has been simple: politics involves everyone—you, us, your acquaintances, strangers. The very act of reading this book is political. For by learning about politics, you are engaging in politics and political thinking.

"It is a mistake to confound strangeness with mystery."

—*Holmes*

"The custom of praising the old and condemning the new does exist, but it is not always wrong. Sometimes such a judgment has to be correct since human affairs are always in motion, either rising or declining."

—Machiavelli

"The changing world that confronts us is both new and old. it is never wholly what it used to be, and therefore the old rules are never wholly reliable. It is never entirely new, and therefore we are fools if we do not look for guidance in the book of experience."

—Lippmann

"Data! Data! Data! I can't make bricks without clay!"

—Holmes

"Demand for the solution of a perplexity is the steadying and guiding factor in the entire process of reflection."

—Dewey

"Men in general judge more by the sense of sight than the sense of touch."

—Machiavelli

Part

II

Power, or the Clout of Politics

The Value and Vice of Power

It contained more than 800,000 square miles. It stretched west of the Mississippi River to the Rocky Mountains and through much of the Southwest. To acquire it would double the size of the United States. And best of all, the ruler of France, Napoleon, with his eye on a nice profit, was willing to part with this Louisiana Territory for only $15 million. But there were two problems. If a treaty of purchase were arranged, Napoleon's action would require approval of the French legislature, and President Thomas Jefferson's purchase of the territory would require the approval of the American Congress. Napoleon, an autocrat with virtually unlimited power, solved his problem simply: he ignored the French legislature. Jefferson, however, was a republican, a leader who believed in government by the consent of the governed. "I know of no safe depository of the ultimate powers of society but the people themselves," he asserted. His power, he thus thought, was strictly limited, not absolute like Napoleon's.

In defining the powers of government and his as president, Jefferson believed that the Constitution of the United States should be interpreted narrowly. He wrote to a friend, "the Constitution of the United States is the result of the collected wisdom of our country." But the Constitution said nothing about the power of government or of the president to acquire territory. If the Constitution was to be interpreted strictly, then the national government was limited to those powers specified in the Constitution; it was a government of power granted by the Constitution, not implied by that document.

How was Jefferson to solve his dilemma? His first thought was to amend the Constitution to allow the national government to acquire territory. His advisers, however, argued that his proposals for amendment would take too long for approval. Napoleon might change his mind, and the coveted bargain might be lost. They recommended, instead, that because the good of the nation was at stake, the president could fairly assume that the Constitution implied sufficient power to make the purchase. Jefferson agreed with the political logic of the times and circumstances and forwarded the treaty to the Senate for approval. Accepting the view that the power to acquire territory was implied by the power of the government to make wars and treaties, the Senate ratified the Louisiana Purchase in October 1803.

THOMAS JEFFERSON: PARADOX OF POWER

He was a tall man, but he slouched. He was an excellent writer, yet was a poor speaker who never gave an exciting speech. He was a forceful leader but a shy person. He was a man of great compassion and also violent animosities. He believed that all men were created equal; yet he was a slave owner.

These were only a few of the many paradoxes of the complex, princely politician and political thinker who became a legendary figure in the history of the United States. Perhaps the greatest paradox in the career of Thomas Jefferson (1743–1826), however, involved political power. Jefferson had no personal thirst for power. He liked neither the publicity nor the judgments made of the powerful. He wrote, "I find the pain of a little censure, even when it is unfounded, is more acute than the pleasure of much praise."

Like it or not, Thomas Jefferson understood political power and rarely failed to exercise it when he had the opportunity. And he had many opportunities, opportunities that embroiled him in numerous political conflicts. Sometimes he won; sometimes he lost. While in his early thirties and in the Virginia legislature, he wrote and achieved passage of a controversial statute establishing religious freedom. He was also part of a successful movement of social reform. But his term as the governor of Virginia left him so unhappy that he decided to retire from politics at age thirty-eight. Thus would have ended the political career of the man who had but a few years earlier been one of the authors of the Declaration of Independence.

But Jefferson's retirement was short-lived, and soon he found himself a member of Congress and again involved in the power struggles of national politics. From 1785 to 1789 he was active in international politics, serving as the U.S. minister to France. He came away from his European experience convinced that the reigning kings, nobles, and priests of the continent were scarcely princes, but instead "fools" and "idiots." With the founding of a new government under the Constitution, Jefferson returned home to serve as secretary of state in the administration of President George Washington. He again entered quickly into a conflict of power, this time as leader of the opposition to the policies of Alexander Hamilton. That leadership saw him help found a group called the Republicans, the forerunner of today's Democratic party, and he was elected Vice-President (1797–1801) and then president of the United States (1801–1809).

As president, Jefferson's exercise of power was astute, deft, and subtle. He began in a conciliatory way. In his inaugural address—the first ever delivered in Washington, D.C.—he stressed that "every difference of opinion is not a difference of principle. . . . We are all Republicans; we are all Federalists." He did not assault Hamilton's Federalist economic policies which he previously had opposed. Rather, he reduced expenditures, nibbling away at the Federalist program and thus weakening both the Federalist program and the party. But with the Louisiana Purchase, he rewarded his agrarian supporters, thus strengthening the Republicans' rural interests in their conflicts with the commercial and mercantile Federalists. "What is practicable must often control what is pure theory," wrote Jefferson.

Not all his power ploys, however, were so well conceived or successful. He sought to bring the Federalist judiciary into line by threats of impeachment and unsuccessful efforts to remove Federalist judges from office. Equally heavy-handed was Jefferson's 1807 Embargo Act. The act forbade U.S. trade with England and France, two nations locked in the bitter Napoleonic wars and each preying on American commerce. Jefferson thought that he could bring both nations to heel by withholding food, goods, and needed supplies. It was an act of coercion from a man who had once written: "What has been the effect of coercion? To make one-half the world fools, and the other half hypocrites." The embargo did not force England and France to terms; instead, it seriously disrupted U.S. trade and brought an economic crisis to both Federalist commerce centers and Republican farms and plantations.

To the untrained observer, Jefferson's thinking and his actions appear inconsistent, and they were. But Jefferson as a political thinker and prince knew politics well. He understood political logic, and it was the logic of politics that created the paradoxes of power that Jefferson so ably illustrates.

It is hard to say what might have happened had Jefferson stood firm in his view that he had no power to purchase the Lousiana Territory. It might well have been lost, and the United States would be considerably different today. But as a princely politician, Jefferson knew that power must be restrained in order to control its vices and must also be exercised in order to exploit its values. In this chapter, we shall expand on that idea and show you the two faces of political power, its value in social affairs and the vice it sometimes becomes.

WHAT DO PEOPLE WANT OUT OF LIFE?

If you are like most people, there are some things you want out of life and others you do not. The specific things that people want differ widely, be they as concrete as a particular model of stylish automobile or as vague as something called happiness. So diverse are the things people desire and seek that it defies one's talents to think of all of them. People who study politics do not even try. Instead, they try to classify the kinds of things people value. Two such scholars, Harold Lasswell and Abraham Kaplan, wrote a book in 1950 entitled *Power and Society* in which they offered two general categories of things people value.

First are those things that people such as yourself need and/or want to maintain and improve your physical being. They are things you want because your welfare depends on them. Hence, such values are welfare values. There are four classes of these values:

- People want well-being. Most of us want to be healthy, to be safe in our homes and away from them, and to have food, clothing, shelter, and the like.
- Wealth also contributes to welfare. Not everyone wants to be wealthy, but a certain amount of wealth (income, necessities, material goods, and services) is desirable to all of us.
- Some people value skill. Defined broadly, skill is proficiency in an activity. It may be playing baseball or bridge, operating video games, building skyscrapers, flying aircraft, cooking a meal, or anything else. Skill can promote welfare.

- Enlightenment is valued. Just to survive from day to day, you require some information, knowledge, facts, and insight. Just to drive an automobile you must pass a test of driving rules (enlightenment) and proficiency (skill).

You have probably noticed that these welfare values overlap; that is, because you value one type of thing, you value another. For example, if you want to earn a high income, it helps to know what you are doing and to be skilled at doing it. Thus one value can be used to get another (skill and enlightenment to get wealth, wealth to get well-being). Something has instrumental value when it can be used to get something else; it has intrinsic value when it is wanted for itself. Some college students cram (enlightenment) to pass exams (well-being); others do so just to learn more about a subject (enlightenment). For the former, their information is a means to an end; for the latter, it is an end in itself.

These observations about welfare values hold as well for the second category of things that people want. In dealing with one another, people want to be treated in certain ways. What you value in your relation with other persons constitutes *deference* values:

- People want respect and thus seek status, honor, recognition, reputation, and prestige.
- One thing that many persons desire in dealing with others is "to feel good about themselves." This sense of goodness—even of virtue, morality, and righteousness—is rectitude, knowing you have "done the right thing."
- Most people seek affection, from friends and confidants, to love and be loved.
- Finally, many people want power; they want to participate in making decisions that affect themselves and those with whom they deal, sometimes intimately, sometimes casually.

Respect, rectitude, affection, and power—if you have these, people will take you into account, they will defer to you. Like welfare values, they can be sought for themselves or as means to another, and as you have doubtless guessed, welfare values can be used to obtain deference, and deference, welfare. Thus did Thomas Jefferson use enlightenment (for him and his advisers) to secure the well-being and wealth of the United States, by exercising his power as president to acquire the Louisiana Territory.

THE VALUE OF POWER

Power then, is a value. Like any other value, power can be exploited to secure other values, or it can be valued in its own right. In either case, it has a close, unbroken tie to politics.

Power is the capacity to direct or influence people to do what they otherwise would not. Consider each item in this definition. Capacity means action. We know that a weightlifter has the capacity to press a certain load when he does so. You have the capacity to stay awake in class when you do it. When you are powerful, in other words, people know it by what you do. You may do it openly or secretly, directly or indirectly, in public or in private, but you do it. Jefferson had the power to acquire the Louisiana Purchase because he actually did so.

But acting is not enough. A capacity for power means acting either to direct or influence others. Through direction or influence people take part in making decisions that affect themselves and others. Direction implies coercion, and influence implies persuasion. In a little book entitled *Power, Influence, and Authority,* political scientist David V. J. Bell hinted at the difference between coercion and persuasion. If someone says to you. "If you do *X,* I will do *Y,*" that is a typical case of coercion. You are being told that if you do such-and-such, the coercer will either give or deny you something. "If you prove to me that you have studied," says the instructor, "I will give you an *A.*" The power (capacity) to reward or punish lies with the instructor. But suppose that instead you are told, "If you do *X,* you will do *Y.*" No longer does what you value depend on the will of another; you will get what you want from what *you* do.

To direct another is to promise or threaten; to influence is to get another to do something by making him or her believe that it is what that person wants. Both direction (coercion) and influence (persuasion) can take two forms. One way to direct people is to use force. As long as politics has existed, there has been violence in some form or another—wars, murders, torture, intimidation, starvation, forced labor, and so on. As you will see in later chapters, such tactics have sometimes been very effective in getting people to do what they might not have otherwise. But as Machiavelli knew, violence has its limits. A rule based solely or too much on violence is self-destructive. It saps the will, energies, lives, and spirits of the ruled, and the ruler will find that there is little left to rule. Force and violence should be used sparingly, believed Machiavelli: "For it is the man who uses violence to spoil things, not the man who uses it to mend them, who is blameworthy."

Violence should thus be economized. One way to practice an economy of violence yet continue to direct people, is to achieve their consent through nonviolent means. Machiavelli found at least three sources of such nonviolent coercion. One was through a people's traditions, especially their religious yearning. If a ruler could closely identify with the people's religious customs and beliefs, then as spokesperson for that religion, the ruler's demands would carry religious authority. For example, monarchs who possessed a divine right to rule (were chosen by God to rule on earth) had only to command, not threaten. Second, Machiavelli believed that a ruler could build a reputation for being so good that the people, believing the ruler to be actually that good, would pledge their unflagging loyalties: "It is good to appear merciful, truthful, humane, sincere, and religious." This will work because "the masses are always impressed by the superficial appearance of things." Finally, Machiavelli argued that a prince should establish laws and institutions (such as legislative bodies and courts) that would also achieve a reputation for goodness. If so received by the people, the prince's subjects could be directed through such institutions to which they had submitted their loyalty.

If direction (coercion) has its violent and nonviolent aspects, so does influence (persuasion). The violent side of influence is manipulation. Manipulation is influence through deception, making people believe something that you do not believe. An obvious form is lying. As you saw in Chapter 2 in the tale of how Prime Minister Churchill had to deal with the case of Coventry in World War II, manipulation is part of the logic of politics. What is manipulated is the value of enlightenment, that is, information, facts, truth. Unlike coercive violence, which frequently strikes at persons' physical well-being through torture, murder, and the like, persuasive violence as manipulation abuses the human mind by making it believe what is not so. Unless economized, that form of violence can be as destructive as coercion is.

Finally, influence can involve people in an exchange of agreed and opposing points of view, the trading of benefits. In short, influence can be achieved through negotiation. You do it all the time. Say that you want to buy a used car. You look around, find what you want, and make an offer. "Too low," says the sales representative. "What will you take?" you ask. You get a figure. "Too high," you respond. From then on it is a matter of negotiating a fair price, guarantees of repairs, what you will "pay down," and other aspects of the deal. Negotiation, in short, is mutual influence, each side trying to influence the other to do what otherwise would not be done.

Power is the effort to get people to do what they otherwise would not do. If you try to get a friend to go out and buy a pizza and bring it back to you, and the friend says, "Sure, I was going out to get one anyway," your power might be minimal. If you see a sign that says "Swimming Prohibited" or "Smoking Prohibited," and you don't swim or smoke anyway, then the warnings have little power over your behavior.

In sum, power amounts to the carrot and the stick, the direction and influence exercised in violent and nonviolent ways through force and consent. We have sketched out these aspects of power in Table 4.1.

TABLE 4–1. Aspects of Power

	Ways of Acting	
Acts of Power	*Violence (Force)*	*Nonviolence (Consent)*
Direction (Coercion)	Physical threat, abuse, and annihilation	Appeals to tradition, reputation, and institutions
Influence (Persuasion)	Manipulation	Negotiation

Remember, these are varied aspects of power. Although we described coercion and persuasion, force and consent, violence and nonviolence separately, keep in mind that they shade into one another in several ways. Rare is the single political act that can be conveniently and neatly labeled as solely coercive force or coercive consent, persuasive force or persuasive consent. The aspects of power blend into one another imperceptibly, and all are intimately linked to politics.

POLITICS AS POWER

In early nineteenth-century Europe, the plight of the working class was dismal. Wages were low, working conditions were bad, and labor was bought and sold like any other commodity. Members of the working class wanted, but did not have, the things to bring them either welfare or deference. Conditions were poor throughout Europe, and in Great Britain they were particularly bad. Unemployment and poverty demoralized millions. In 1838 a working-class group formed an organization directed at improving their lot, called the Chartists. In a short time the Chartists became not just a group seeking better conditions but a mass movement demanding political and social reform.

The Chartists took their name from the People's Charter, a document they drew up that listed their demands: the annual election of the legislature, universal suffrage for all adult males, a secret ballot, equal electoral districts, abolition of property qualifications for membership in the legislature, and the payment of salaries to legislators. In 1839 one million people signed a petition supporting the Charter, but the British government did not meet their demands. In 1842 three million signatures appeared on petitions. Again the government did nothing. After a few years the Chartists faded away, their dream of "political power our means; social happiness our end" unfulfilled until well after the death of the movement.

Like groups throughout history hoping to achieve well-being, the Chartists looked to politics as a means of doing so. Put differently, they recognized that the principal means of obtaining the things they valued was achieving the value of power. Politics is what it is because it helps give power to the people. Bernard Crick, a British political scientist, expressed it thus: "Politics, then, can be simply defined as the activity by which differing interests within a given unit of rule are conciliated by giving them a share in power in proportion to their importance to the welfare and the survival of the whole community."

Governments have been based on how power was distributed among interests "in proportion to their importance to the welfare and the survival of the whole community." In his *Discourses,* for example, Machiavelli classified governments going back to the time of the Greek philosopher Aristotle. In Machiavelli's scheme there were three kinds of governments. First was monarchy, with power concentrated in the hands of a single ruler. Second was aristocracy, with power concentrated in a small, select group. Third was democracy, with power distributed more broadly among large numbers of citizens.

Under these three types of rule, who exercises power generally depends on what people possess and other key welfare and/or deference values. Consider, for instance, well-being as a source of political power. In some ancient communities, political power resided in the strongest member of the tribe, the man who proved again and again his strength on the field of combat. Or consider wealth. Daniel Webster thought wealth vital to politics: "Power naturally and necessarily follows property." But so too could power be distributed on the basis of skill, for instance, turning government over to military experts skilled in the techniques of war, or on the basis of enlightenment, fulfilling the wish of many that people be ruled by "philosopher-kings." The deference values of respect, rectitude, and affection might also be sources of political power. For generations, the powerful positions in British government were reserved for members of the English aristocracy. In the Puritan towns and colonies of America, rectitude was the key to having power: religious leaders were political rulers. And how often does the president of a school's student body or senior class turn out to be the most popular classmate, in other words, selection on the basis of affection?

Whatever the form of government, it may be ruled by the strong, wealthy, skilled, informed, respected, religious, or loved. But what Crick's definition of politics says, and he is close to Machiavelli in this, is that politics is distinctive because it distributes power not on the basis of any *one* of these other welfare and/or deference values. Politics allows people of all differing and competing interests (values) to share in power "in proportion to their importance to the welfare and the survival of the whole community."

As long as power in a monarchy, aristocracy, or democracy is distributed in accordance with political logic (that is, along the lines of Crick's definition), the governmental form might be labeled as good. But as Machiavelli noted long ago, this has not always been the case. What seems at first to be three forms of government are actually six, "three of which are very bad, and three good in themselves, but so liable to be corrupted that they become absolutely bad." Thus, as Machiavelli continued in his *Discourses,* "monarchy becomes tyranny; aristocracy degenerates into oligarchy; and the popular government lapses readily into licentiousness."

Power, then, is the essence of politics. So crucial to the nature of politics is the capacity to direct and influence people that governments can be classified according to how they place that power in the hands of one, a few, or many rulers. When power conciliates differing community interests, its exercise is broadly shared, or at least all social interests are taken seriously by the monarch, aristocrats, or populace. But the exercise of power, as Machiavelli pointed out, is "liable to be corrupted," producing governments that do not serve the demands of varied interests. Power, then, is not just a value but also can be a vice.

VICES OF POWER

The Chartist's slogan "political power our means; social happiness our end" has two points, that political power is an instrument for winning valued goals and that it is therefore good. Not all political thinkers have agreed. Some make an even stronger case for power, arguing that it is so valuable in its own right that power *is* happiness. Thus, if you were to read the works of the nineteenth-century German philosopher Friedrich Nietzsche, he would tell you that humans have a "will to power." If they carry out that will, they become virtually superbeings, superior to all creatures, including those humans who do not express their will to power. Wrote Nietzsche, "What is good? All that enhances the feeling of power, the Will to Power, and Power itself in man. What is bad—all that proceeds from weakness. What is happiness?—the feeling that power is increasing—that resistance has been overcome."

For Nietzsche, power is good, indeed, power is happiness itself. But if you were to accept the verdict of most writers, you would probably concur with William Godwin, an English political thinker, who wrote almost a century before Nietzsche that "power is not happiness." Godwin's view reflects a judgment of power popular among many philosophers, that power is not good but bad, indeed, even evil.

Why does power have such a poor reputation? How can it be a value, yet be judged as bad by many thinkers? In itself, political power is neither good nor bad. It may, however, serve good or bad ends. As much may be said for other values. For instance, strength—an aspect of well-being as a value—may benefit people or destroy them. Wealth may be coveted for good or ill. An assassin's skill at weaponry may lead to the murder of a political leader; the skill of a surgeon may save the leader's life. Enlightenment contributes to discovery of a cure for cancer and also to germ warfare. Similarly, the deference values of respect, rectitude, and affection have positive or negative uses. (Think of how one person may love another so much as to assume total direction for the other's "own good.")

In effect, then, power, along with any value, is neutral in itself. Used to purchase the Louisiana Territory, political power was judged by most historians as good. Jefferson, when he reluctantly exercised a power that he deemed he did not have directly but that was implied by the treaty-making power, said that in the future "the good sense of our country will correct the evil" of such power "when it shall produce ill effects."

The bad reputation of political power is that it has been abused. So many and varied have been the abuses that you could never learn all of the particular vices of power, though certain types reappear through history. At the top of the list is a common abuse of power, violence. Frequently ignoring Machiavelli's admonition for an economy of violence, rulers have used assassination, terror, martial law, and genocide to secure their ends.

But there are other, more subtle and not so obvious vices often served by power, some exploiting violence over the mind as well as the body. Deception, for example, has a potential for abuse. Just as power may be used for good or ill, any of its techniques may be so used also. War, a clear form of violence, people generally abhor. But if a nation's people feel that their very survival is at stake (as did Great Britain or the Soviet Union in World War II), war will become a means of salvation, a technique serving positive ends. So too with deception. Machiavelli argued that a prince must have the strength and courage of a lion and the cunning and deceit of a fox. "Thus a prudent prince cannot and should not keep his word when to do so would go against his interest, or when the reasons that made him pledge it no longer apply," he wrote. "A deceitful man will always find plenty who are ready to be deceived." Was Machiavelli advocating deception? As a general rule, no. As a tactic required in certain times and circumstances, yes. Following the dictates of political logic (recall Chapter 2), the consequences of hypocrisy at a given time and place determine whether it was virtue or vice. Deception, like violence, must be economized.

The following two examples of political deception demonstrate that "a deceitful man will always find plenty who are ready to be deceived." Judge for yourself if either or both made power a vice.

Case 1. Remember from Chapter 3 that during World War I President Woodrow Wilson established the Inquiry to help draft peace proposals. He did so in part to seize the initiative from the Allies, especially France and Great Britain, who contemplated a peace serving selfish ends. But he had another reason. Before the United States entered the war, the Allies—Britain, France, Italy, Russia, and Japan—signed secret treaties dividing up the lands of Germany, Austria-Hungary, and the Ottoman Empire. The Allies intended to enjoy the spoils of war. Wilson knew of the treaties, opposed them, tried to have them repudiated when the United States entered the war. But to the chagrin of the Allies and Wilson, before any action could be taken, the secret treaties were published for all the world to see. What did Wilson do? He used two deceptive techniques. One, he denied "official" knowledge of the treaties, although he certainly did know of them. Two, he put the Inquiry to work, not simply to move toward a stable peace, but also to come up with a proposal that would set Wilson apart from the intrigues of his allies and thus would save his world reputation. Were these the actions of a prudent prince?

Case 2. In 1964, Senator Clair Engle of California sought reelection. Brain surgery had left him virtually unable to walk or talk. To cover this up, his advisers prepared a forty-two-second televised spot announcement featuring Engle. Careful retakes and editing resulted in a tape with a fit and healthy man saying only, "The medical men have given me the green light and I am running." Engle died before the primary election, but his name remained on the ballot, and he received more than 100,000 votes! Was there prudence in this deception?

Perhaps you will draw lines easily in these two cases, perhaps not. Arguments could be mounted to justify or condemn the actions in each instance. Whether power is value or vice cannot be a clean judgment. Another potential vice of power, vindictiveness, suggests this as well. In 1798, the U.S. Congress passed the Alien and Sedition acts. The public rationale for the acts was a threatened war with France. The Alien Act made it possible for presidents, in time of war, to arrest, imprison, or banish aliens. The Sedition Act made it illegal to publish "false or malicious writing" against the nation, president, or Congress. Although seemingly directed at French aliens and sympathizers, the acts had bigger fish to kill. They were directed at the Republican party of Thomas Jefferson, in the hopes of keeping the Federalist party in power. Because French aliens supported the Republicans, and vice versa, the Federalist cause would be aided by frightening the French out of the country. The Sedition Act could also be used against Republican editors who criticized the Federalist president. The Republicans protested, and Jefferson drafted resolutions for the Kentucky legislature against the acts. Ten persons, all Republicans, were fined and imprisoned for alleged violations. Eventually heavy-minded Federalist enforcement of the acts and partisan interpretation by Federalist judges won sympathy to the Republican side. The Federalists backed off, but the Republicans won the election of 1800.

The Republicans obviously thought that the passage of the Alien and Sedition acts by the Federalist Congress and their enforcement by a Federalist judiciary were abuses of power. Citizens might assume from Jefferson's conciliatory "We are all Republicans; we are all Federalists" that there would be no vindictive reprisals against the Federalists by the Jefferson administration. You be the judge of what happened next. In 1803, Jefferson sent to the House of Representatives the case of Judge John Pickering, a Federalist. Jefferson wanted Pickering impeached, that is, accused of "high crimes and misdemeanors," according to the U.S. Constitution, and tried, convicted, and removed from office. Jefferson's message identified the crime—intoxication and profanity on the bench. The Republican House impeached Pickering for malfeasance, declaring him unfit for office because of loose morals and intemperance. The Republican Senate tried Pickering, convicted him, and removed him from office.

With this success the Jefferson administration then went after Justice Samuel Chase of the Supreme Court. At Jefferson's urging, the House of Representatives investigated Chase's conduct. As a result, although no illegality was alleged by the articles of impeachment, the House voted to impeach. A lengthy and bitter trial in the Senate, involving considerable behind-the-scenes intrigue, produced a majority vote for conviction. But because conviction requires, according to the Constitution, a two-thirds vote, the Republican effort failed.

You can decide whether the Federalist acts and/or the Republican impeachments were abuses of power. Certainly the Alien and Sedition acts took vast liberties with the Bill of Rights, and Thomas Jefferson, who seriously questioned whether the national government had the power to purchase the Louisiana Territory, was not so reluctant to use his impeachment power as a tool for partisan purposes. Both were efforts at political vindictiveness, actions argued to be in the entire community's interests when in fact they served one group at the expense of the opposition. In each instance, what one party praised as the virtuous use of political power, the other condemned as a vice. Just as opposing viewpoints make it hazardous to judge the value of power outside the times and circumstances of its specific exercise.

FORMS OF GOVERNMENT

In an oft-quoted line the poet Alexander Pope said, "For forms of government let fools contest; whate'er is best administer'd is best." The clever couplet is too simple. How power is organized and exercised go hand in hand; that is, forms of government and their administration are so closely bound that they jointly determine what is "best." Accordingly, they shape the degree that political power is value or vice.

Up to this point we have invited you to think about the general nature of power: its relation to other values, characteristic political quality, organization, exercise, and possible abuses. Now we shall turn to three ways that politicians throughout history have formed and shaped power to their designs. Think of these as three forms of government. You will see that each "is administer'd" in a fashion befitting the way that power in organized by that governing form. In the remaining three chapters of Part II we shall describe each of these forms as autocratic, republican, and totalitarian.

Any form of government, any way of organizing power, must address common problems. Each must coordinate the diversity of a society's members and establish social order out of social conflict. Each must specify what role the general populace will play in governing and what role the rulers will play. Each must establish a philosophic rationale, a doctrine, that justifies how it "is administer'd." Each must adapt to its social, economic, and cultural roots. Each must make laws and inform people what those laws mean. And each must find a role for politics, for how the people sharing in power will advance their interests, cooperate with others, and thwart still others. In the chapters that follow we shall compare autocracies, republics, and totalitarian regimes with respect to how they address these problems. After that, you can decide whether the form of a government is something over which you want to have only "fools contest."

"I know of no safe depository of the ultimate powers of society but the people themselves."

—Jefferson

"The masses are always impressed by the superficial appearance of things."
—Machiavelli

"Political power our means; social happiness our end."

—*Chartists*

"What is good? All that enhances the feeling of power, the Will to Power, and Power itself in man. What is bad?—all that proceeds from weakness. What is happiness?—the feeling that power is increasing—that resistance has been overcome."

—*Nietzsche*

"Power is not happiness."

—*Godwin*

"Politics, then, can be simply defined as the activity by which differing interests within a given unit of rule are conciliated by giving them a share in power in proportion to their importance to the welfare and the survival of the whole community."

—*Crick*

Chapter

5

Autocratic Power

The common people called her "Little Mother" or "Little Mother Catherine." The philosophers called her an "enlightened despot." The labels indicate approval, even affection. She was Catherine the Great, Czarina of All the Russians. Catherine ruled from 1762 to 1796, a turbulent period in Russia and one of wars and revolutions in Europe, Eurasia, and the American colonies.

The enlightened despot of Catherine's era differed from the autocratic rulers of the past. For example, such earlier monarchs as Louis XIV of France or Peter the Great of Russia not only held absolute power but they also exercised that power with little claim that they were doing so on behalf of their nation or its people. Many such rulers believed that they could do what they wanted to do simply because it was God's will. After all, they were on the throne because God had placed them there; hence, they ruled with "divine right." The typical enlightened despots of Catherine's era, however, made little mention of divine rights of kings to justify their rule. Instead, they stressed heredity or dynastic family ties as the source of their power and usefulness to society as the justification for exercising it. "Despot" meant power centralized in the ruler, and "enlightened" meant that that power was exercised on behalf of the nation and its people.

Before Catherine the Great, the Russians were ruled through a complicated, tyrannous code of laws called the *Ulozhenie*. One of Catherine's enlightened aims was to revise that code, modernize it, and temporize. She thus drew up her own code and presented it to her senate in 1766. Its contents reflected her own philosophy of rule and typified that of the enlightened despot. On the side of enlightenment the code preached charity, equity, patriotism, tolerance, reason, and wisdom. Hence, the rich should not oppress the poor; torture should be abandoned; the death penalty should apply only in political crimes; and sovereigns should serve the people, not people the sovereigns. But there was a despotic side to all of this. There was slavery in Russia; that is, the serfs were the property of their owners. Catherine did not abolish serfdom but merely urged that peasants not be reduced to serfdom without good reason and that they be treated humanely. Her code, which she called her "legislomania," granted that she would rule with tender, loving care but also with firmness, a respect for privilege, and a demand for order.

Few instances so typify the differences in autocratic character between Catherine's rule and that of earlier despots, such as Don Cossack Emelian Pugachev. In 1773, Pugachev began what was to become the most violent peasant uprising in the history of Russia. He claimed that he was the true czar, that is, Peter III, the husband of Catherine from whom she had usurped power after leading a revolt against Peter's rule. Pugachev announced that Peter had not died but had merely gone on a long journey and that he, Pugachev, was Peter returned. Pugachev, after declaring himself czar, issued a manifesto abolishing serfdom, taxes, and military service. He quickly won a mass following of serfs, workers, fishermen, farmers, and others. His forces marched down the Volga River, capturing towns, pillaging and looting, burning, and killing priests and landlords. It seemed that nothing could prevent Pugachev from seizing all power. But fortune intervened. At that time, Russia was at war with Turkey, and victories in two key battles brought a quick end to what had been six years of fighting. The armies of Russia turned to fight Pugachev. The rebel and his force lost their advantage and with it the support of the serfs. In the fall of 1774, Pugachev suffered a major defeat and while trying to flee was taken prisoner by his own lieutenants and delivered to the Russian army in exchange for their own freedom. In anything but humane and enlightened fashion, Pugachev was chained inside an iron cage mounted on a cart and moved from province to province in public disgrace. After a year of this, he reached Moscow for trial. Naturally, he was found guilty.

The penalty? Here Catherine demonstrated that she was no absolute tyrant, as in the days of old, but an enlightened despot. Pugachev's sentence was to be quartered, to be pulled apart piece by piece, limb by limb. But Catherine was compassionate. Unlike Louis XV of France,

CATHERINE THE GREAT: AUTOCRAT

She was German but became the empress of Russia. She remained on the throne for thirty-four years, no small feat considering the times. It was, to be sure, an era of autocratic reign: Frederick the Great in Prussia, Maria Theresa in Austria, Joseph II in the Holy Roman Empire. But it was also an era of autocratic loss: George III of Great Britain lost the American colonies in the Revolutionary War and Louis XVI lost his head after the French Revolution.

In 1729, Sophie Fredericka Augusta of Anhalt-Zerbst, a minor German principality, was born. Her nickname was "Figchen," but she would someday become Catherine the Great. When only ten years old, she met a young man, Peter Ulrich, grandson of Peter the Great, the former czar of Russia. Five years later, summoned by Elizabeth, empress of Russia, Sophie set out from Anhalt-Zerbst, never to return again. Her destination was Russia where she was to be considered as a bride for Grand Duke Peter, the same young man she had met years earlier. She passed the stern examination of the Russian empress, who sought a suitable wife for her heir, Peter, and in 1745, Figchen became Catherine, grand duchess of Russia.

But Catherine was not content to sit idly by and wait to become the wife of a czar. She believed that she was destined to become the ruler of Russia in her own right, and that belief led her to study Russian culture, read widely on government and political philosophy, cultivate members of the empress's court, and convert from her German Lutheran religion to the Russian Orthodox church. Her success contributed to her good fortune. In 1762, Empress Elizabeth died and Catherine's husband Peter III ascended the throne. But his reign was short. Less than six months later, a military revolt overthrew Peter, a revolt that Catherine helped instigate. One June 28, 1762, Catherine was proclaimed empress, a crown that she wore until her death in 1796. Scarcely a week after assuming power, her husband was assassinated under mysterious circumstances.

It was now up to Catherine to fulfill her destiny. Upon coming to power, she first announced her intention to enact domestic reforms. She did but stopped short of reforms that might threaten her authority. A legal code was revised, the use of torture restricted, and religious toleration advocated. Lowlands were drained, roads were built, construction flourished, and cities rose on the plains. She relieved government of financial debts by simply coining more money. People did not worry that this would devalue the existing money, for they trusted "Little Mother." But such domestic activity did nothing to end slavery, to lessen the prerogatives of the nobility, or to promote genuine religious freedom. In foreign affairs, Catherine added to the territory of Russia by nibbling away at Poland until it disappeared, by annexing the Crimea, and by conquering portions of Turkey. The price for much of this was war, but it was a foreign policy of expansion that Catherine thought worth the cost.

Catherine the Great ruled by force, intrigue, payoffs, and seduction. Force she brought to bear on foreign nations, internal revolts, and usurpers to her throne. Physical punishment, the confiscation of properties, and assassination were ruling tools to be used when necessary. Intrigue and plot helped bring her to power, and she did not hesitate to use them to maintain that power. She frequently rewarded members of the nobility for their loyalty and service with payments of vast sums of money and huge numbers of slaves (serfs). Catherine was also no stranger to seduction. During her time as grand duchess and empress, Catherine the Great had a dozen lovers, each serving not only sexual but also political purposes. By her first, she conceived an heir to her throne, the illegitimate Paul I. Her second lover she eventually placed on the throne of Poland, the better to bring that nation into line. Her third helped lead the revolt that brought her to power: she had realized she would need friends in the military. Another led her victorious armies against the Turks. Others were confidants and ministers of state. And each was rewarded with status, wealth, and the illusion of sharing the czarina's power. Status she did give— titles and privileges—and wealth she did give—the equivalent of more than $1.5 billion paid out to all her lovers. But in the true tradition of the autocrat, her power she always kept to herself. Even on her deathbed a secret decree was announced that deprived Paul from succeeding her.

---

who had once had a man tortured and then pulled to pieces by horses in a four-hour public ceremony, Catherine ordered that Pugachev's head be cut off before the quartering so that he would suffer no pain. Pugachev's key aides suffered similar fates: his minor accomplices had their nostrils torn out, and those that betrayed him were pardoned.

AUTOCRATIC RULE: PAST AND PRESENT

As you can see from the tale of Don Cossack Pugachev, the line between absolutist tyranny and enlightened despotism was finely drawn. Yet, these various types of autocratic rule are worthy of your consideration.

As seen in Chapter 4, Machiavelli designated six kinds of governments. Three were good—monarchy, aristocracy, and democracy—but in corrupt form gave rise to three bad kinds of government—tyranny, oligarchy, and licentiousness. These six governmental forms Machiavelli mentioned in his *Discourses* but grouped them under two headings in *The Prince*: "All the states and governments that ever had, or now have, power over men were and are of two sorts: either republics or princely states." "Princely states also are of two sorts: either hereditary, where the family of the ruler has been in control a long time, or else new." We can think along with Machiavelli and say that an autocracy is one variety of "princely state." As such, power is concentrated in either a single ruler or a small coterie of rulers. As Machiavelli noted, either the ruler or rulers obtain power by birth or by seizure.

The modern tradition of autocratic power dates back to the earliest days of the European monarchies. Usually by force of arms but often by claiming their right to rule was divinely inspired, kings organized monarchies that would outlast each one's reign. Because wars were costly and destructive and elections usually disputed, the means for passing power from one ruler to another was through inheritance. In this respect, then, early autocrats moved from claims of divine right to those of heredity as justification for their right to govern. But these monarchs did not rule alone. In England, for instance, kings sent sheriffs into local shires; kings in France governed through local officials called bailiffs. Royal courts were created to settle disputes. Military force was the monarch's way of enforcing laws over rivals, challengers, and recalcitrant subjects.

As you can guess, governing through local officials, courts, and the army required money. Slowly the tradition grew that the king could levy demands on vassals for money rather than require their military service, and as new towns formed in a kingdom, monarchs demanded money in exchange for royal charters for the communities. In spite of the king's power, however, should he abuse it and demand too much, resistance was likely. In 1215, for instance English nobles and local and church officials forced King John to recognize their rights through the signing of the Magna Carta. Such pacts were increasingly common in kingdoms throughout Europe. As a result, autocratic power gradually devolved from its concentration in the king's hands to the king and a council of nobles, or his "court."

In the thirteenth century, autocratic rule acquired another element. As the towns grew, a new class of people emerged, the *burghers*. Like the lords and bishops with whom the kings had to deal, the burghers had money; hence they too had to be taken into account. So the kings routinely began to call assemblies of town representatives to announce policies, demand money, and listen to complaints. These assemblies represented *estates,* important social classes including the clergy, nobility, and burghers. For that reason the assemblies themselves were called estates in most kingdoms, except on the British Isles where they were called *parliaments*. These were not, however, legislative bodies. Rather, the estates could state their grievances, but it was up to the ruler whether to respond.

This brief history of the development of autocracy suggests three types: [the single ruler acting alone, ruling with a court, and ruling through an assembly] The justification for autocratic rule took varied forms, namely, divine right or heredity, but ultimately the power rested more on coercion than persuasion, the threat of violence rather than nonviolent means. Then in the eighteenth century came another kind of autocrat, the enlightened despot such as Catherine the Great in Russia, Maria Theresa in Austria, and Frederick the Great in Prussia. Enlightened despotism added two more justifications for concentrating power in the person of an autocrat. One was that eighteenth-century rulers were truly enlightened in that they had ideals that they sought to achieve, such as building roads, towns, monuments, and museums. Second, the eighteenth-century rulers were truly enlightened in that they were wiser, better informed, and more skilled than the earlier autocrats were. Enlightened despotism, then, could be justified because the rulers did not seek power for power's sake but because they cherished idealism and wisdom.

But as the English philosopher Bertrand Russell said of power, "Much that passes for idealism is disguised hatred or disguised love of power." Autocracy as practiced by Catherine the Great exemplifies the merit of such an observation. For example, in order to seize the throne of

Russia in 1741, Elizabeth, the daughter of Peter the Great, unseated the reigning czar, Ivan VI. That was no great problem, for Ivan was only an infant (his mother ruled in his stead). Elizabeth had Ivan imprisoned in solitary confinement, and his only contacts with humans for the next twenty-three years were with two guards permanently assigned to him. Though Ivan was in prison, Empress Elizabeth still considered him a threat, as there was always the possibility that rivals to her throne might free Ivan and use him as a basis for revolution against her. Therefore she kept the location of Ivan's imprisonment secret. To his jailers he was known only as "Prisoner No. 1." Elizabeth left instructions that if there was any attempt to free Prisoner No. 1, the guards should kill him immediately.

When Catherine became czarina in 1762, did her enlightenment and her idealism produce a more humane policy for Ivan? After all, by that time No. 1 had spent more than two decades in a dark cell, surviving on meager rations, going about half-naked, without ever seeing the sun. Once Catherine reached the throne, her idealism would surely mean that a more merciful fate awaited the child born to the purple. But no, Catherine still feared Ivan. All she did was have No. 1 moved to another prison, making sure that his head was covered with a bag so that, again, he never saw the light of day. Catherine then repeated the earlier instructions to Ivan's guards; that is, No. 1 was to be killed immediately if there was any attempt to free him.

In 1764, a young army lieutenant was assigned to the detachment in charge of the prison where No. 1 was being held. Basil Mirovich was a bitter man who blamed his lack of success in life on members of Catherine's court, and he often thought of leading a revolt against her regime. Upon hearing of Prisoner No. 1, he grew curious. After several inquiries he deduced that No. 1 must be Ivan, the displaced czar of all the Russians. By releasing No. 1, Mirovich could instigate a revolt, march on the capital, and see Ivan restored to power. On July 4, 1764, Mirovich led an attack on the prison. With the aid of cannons and guns, he forced his way to the cell of Prisoner No. 1. Seeing only one guard, he demanded that the cell be opened. Inside he found the body of the prisoner that had been stabbed repeatedly. True to his vow, the second guard had acted as ordered and did not let Prisoner No. 1 be taken alive.

When news of Ivan's death reached Catherine, she declared, "The ways of God are wonderful and unpredictable. Providence has clearly shown me its favor by bringing this affair to a successful conclusion." Mirovich was tried, sentenced to death, beheaded, and his body burned. The soldiers aiding Mirovich were sentenced to run the gauntlet between rows of a thousand men armed with sticks. But strangely enough, Mirovich's coconspirator, Apollo Uzhakov, mysteriously drowned on the day of the assault on the prison. Was he Catherine's agent, paid to provoke Mirovich?

Some of Catherine's enlightened reforms were wisely conceived; others were not. Among the better ones were the introduction of vaccination for smallpox (she allowed herself to be immunized to prove to her subjects that it was safe), abolition of state intervention in commerce, recoinage of Russian currency, establishment of business guilds, and army reform. Not so wise was her policy to bring German colonists to the Ukraine and Volga areas. They were exempted from military service, given interest-free loans, and freed from all taxes. Her thought was that the Russian peasants would profit from the example of the industrious, hardworking Germans, but it did not work out that way. The Russians were jealous of the colonists' privileges and hated them for their preferred treatment.

Autocracy did not close with the era of enlightened despotism. But the contemporary world has fewer of what Machiavelli called hereditary princely states and more of what he called the new princely states. You need not look beyond the headlines of your daily newspaper or watch more than a few nightly television news shows to find examples. When in 1981 the Polish military established martial law and an army general was installed as ruler, autocracy won the day. When in 1979 the shah of Iran was deposed and the government of Ayatollah Khomeini took over, one autocracy replaced another. Military governments in Africa (for instance, Libya) or Latin America (Argentina) have all the characteristics of autocratic power. What are those characteristics?

THE LOGIC OF AUTOCRACY

At the close of Chapter 4 you learned that autocratic, republican, and totalitarian governments differ from one another in several ways. Let us now consider the characteristics of autocratic regimes and then in Chapters 6 and 7 you can compare them with the characteristics of republican and totalitarian governments.

How Is Society Possible?

Any group of people, no matter how large or small, is made up of persons who are unlike one another in at least some ways. Think of yourself and the members of your family. There are age differences, experience differences, and many others between you and your parents. They may have different ideas about how well you should be doing in school, how much money you should be spending, what career you should be planning, and so forth. And if you have brothers and/or sisters, you undoubtedly differ from them in several respects as well. All these physical and social differences in your family are differences in your values, namely, the welfare and deference values you learned of in Chapter 4.

Sometimes the differences among people are so small that they scarcely are aware of them. You and your spouse or intimate friend may have so much in common that people say, "Aren't they just right for each other!" But rare is the couple or the members of any group who do not have some differences of values. The larger the group is the greater are their differences, to the point that they may produce arguments, and in the face of a great deal of diversity—and the conflicts it can provoke—the group may break apart. It no longer can exist as a group. In a group the size of an entire community, nation, or country, the fact of great diversity raises the question, How is society possible?

A prime objective of any government is to answer that question, to bring social order out of social diversity, to make society possible. The way that an autocratic regime does this is by assembling a single social interest, or a very small set of common interests, and enforcing that interest at the expense of all those that differ from it. Think of the early autocracies. First a king imposed his interests over those of the nobility and Church. Then, as he needed revenue, the king found enough in common with these classes to take their interests into account in governing the realm. Later, the burghers joined the select estates represented in the social order.

Imposing one's will on others is never easy. If your parents demand strict obedience from you, no questions asked (that is, if they are autocrats), you might rebel. But if you try to intimidate them so that you can always have your way, they may resent it. Autocratic regimes must accept that the "have nots" are always threats to the "haves" and must be dealt with accordingly. Once again Catherine the Great serves as an example. Her predecessor, Peter III, was Lutheran. He had no love for the Russian Orthodox church, the dominant religion of the empire and sought to place his interest over the Church's by taxing and confiscating Church property. When Catherine seized power, she knew that she could rule only with the Church's backing, and so she revoked Peter's policies. She soon found, however, this was not the course of pragmatic sagacity, for part of the property confiscated from the clergy had been the Church's serfs, and the serfs threatened revolt if returned to the Church. Catherine did not need that kind of insurrection on her hands so early in her reign; hence, she practiced the Machiavellian precept: "A prudent prince cannot and should not keep his word when to do so would go against his interest. . . ." She withdrew her promise to the clergy and permanently placed the various properties of the Church under the government's power. For the most part, the Church acquiesced, except for Archbishop Arsenius Matsievich, a man of considerable influence, who attacked Catherine in sermons and public speeches. He even spoke of leading a revolt to place Ivan VI on the throne. That was too much for the czarina, so Catherine had the archbishop arrested. The Church protested, but Catherine was firm: she, not the archbishop, was the temporal head of the Orthodox church. Matsievich was tried, his office was stripped from him, and he was confined to a cloister to carry water and cut wood. Four years later, he was imprisoned. He died of cold and hunger ten years after uttering his protest. That is how autocrats make society possible.

Who Tells Whom What to Do?

In most groups some people who stand out, and they are often the ones who propose ideas, inspire other people, and help the group get things done. The others may talk about those ideas, do what they are told, and contribute to the group in other ways, but they are followers, not leaders. Think of any group to which you belong, and you will see that some are leaders and others are led, that some are princes and others are subjects. Who are the princes and subjects in autocracies?

As with any government, the doers, the leaders, the rulers constitute a political elite in autocratic regimes. That political elite is rarely large. Catherine's Russia was typical. The political elite consisted of the czarina, her close advisers, her "favorite" (her lover), and members of her court. Generally represented in this select group were the army, high governing officials, commercial interests, the nobility, and the clergy. Check your own university or college. You will probably find something similar, although, we hope, less autocratic. Usually you will find a president and a board of directors or a board of curators that represesnt the influential social and economic elements that support the school and high-level academic deans and vice-presidents. The instructors or professors you see daily in the classroom, or your fellow classmates, are less likely to be among the select princes, more often they are subjects.

What makes the political elite distinctive in an autocracy is that it is not only exclusive but also self-perpetuating. That is, the elite's interests are always present, and outsiders are rarely invited to join. The identities of the individuals in the autocratic elite change, but the same types of people (the autocratic interests that impose social order) reemerge generation after generation, ruler after ruler. To be sure, with the death of a ruling autocrat, such as Catherine the Great, the fortunes of some people fall and those of others rise. But by and large, the ruling few—army, nobility, clergy, burghers—do not vanish from the race, they merely jockey for new positions.

One way that the political elite perpetuates itself is by claiming the right to rule. The claim may be a direct descent from the gods, such as was, for centuries, the claim of Japan's emperors. Or it may be a claim that the members of the ruling elite are justified in their position because they are the true heirs of great people. Catherine was German, not Russian, and was in no way related to Peter the Great, but she spoke as the "true" heir to his earlier deeds.

Now what of the powerless, the prince's subjects? They are not invited into circles of power: "The man who makes another powerful ruins himself," wrote Machiavelli in *The Prince*. The lot of the principalities' inhabitants is to obey their ruler and to defer to superior morals, skill, enlightenment, and power. Folk sayings capture the essence of the distinction: "the rich men at his castle, the poor man at his gate" or subjects "suffer the powers that be."

What Is the Community?

Autocracies do not survive everywhere. Certain social and economic conditions keep them going. Princes understand this and act to promote those conditions. Catherine the Great spoke precisely to this point: "The Russian Empire is so large that any other form of government than that of absolute Emperor would be harmful to it" (note her concern for good and ill, typical of the enlightened autocrat); "any other government is slower in execution, and leaves the field open to passions which disperse the power and strength of the state" (note here that ruler and state are taken by Catherine to have the same interests). And she noted, "the internal institutions of a country should always develop in accord with the character of that country."

Catherine thought of Russia's size as vital to its character. But size is not the key in determining whether autocracy survives. François Duvalier ("Papa Doc," as his subjects called him) ruled over tiny Haiti as president for life (he died in 1971), with every bit the severity of any Catherine of Russia. What is more important is a nation's social and economic arrangements. Autocracies survive when social classes are rigidly defined and sharply divided from one another. The deference value of respect that we discussed in Chapter 4 is distributed among a very small segment of the population. Similarly, such welfare values as well-being and wealth are limited, through the nation's economic organization, to a small, select group of landowners. Autocracies historically have existed in agrarian societies that have not yet developed industrial underpinnings. The conditions favor the nobility and clergy (both likely to be large landowners), not the farmers, peasants, or laborers in towns and villages.

What Is Politics Like?

If you have followed what we have been saying to this point, you already have a good answer to this question. Autocratic politics and the use of coercion and violence go hand in hand. Some autocrats practice the economy of violence more effectively than others do; yet the overall character of politics feels the effects of force and brutality.

There are other political considerations that differentiate autocracy from republics or totalitarian regimes. First, underlying any form of government is a doctrine that defines the relationship of politics to society as a whole, that specifies what the government should do and how it should do it. In autocracies, religion and custom are vital to such doctrines. When Catherine (then Sophie) set out for Russia to marry the heir to the throne, she belonged to the Lutheran church, and her father insisted that she promise never to surrender that faith. She did so. But she probably crossed her fingers, for she realized even then that if she were ever to rule she would need to belong to the Russian Orthodox church. She was in Russia only a short time before she began the long and difficult process of converting her faith. But it was worth it, for she knew that so important was the Orthodox religion to Russian doctrine that no ruler could long occupy the throne who was not of that faith. Indeed, her husband, Peter III, who was not of that faith and would not make any effort to become so—indeed joked about its strange and mystical ways—paid the price: his reign lasted less than six months.

Traditions, accepted beliefs and ways of doing things, folklore, myths—they too are essential parts of political doctrine. People have died for their beliefs and so cherish them that they may accept coercive measures to ensure that their beliefs will survive. "As long as you keep their old way of life and do not change their customs, men will live quietly enough," Machiavelli advised a prince taking power in a foreign land. Catherine did so in Russia, but George III of Great Britain was less astute with respect to the American colonies.

What rulers think of the law also distinguishes the politics of autocracy. In autocratic regimes, laws are not considered to be rules that people make to facilitate living together. Instead, law is law because "things have always been that way" (custom), because it is "god given" (decreed by rulers with the divine right to do so), or because it is the "enlightened" decision of the ruler. No matter what its source, however, autocratic princes apply the same laws to different people in different ways. Or more precisely, a person's place in the community decides his or her fate. It is a little like your parents or other relatives, who may drink alcohol and smoke cigarettes, telling you that "nobody should ever do so, and that includes you." Why not them? Peter the Great (and later Catherine) decreed that any man wearing a beard had to pay a tax to enter the capital. The application of the law was arbitrary. Members of the court did not need to be clean shaven, but peasants had to be or pay the tax. Furthermore, the Church condemned men without beards as "heretics." So, in autocracies the rule of law is that the lower one's status is, the more arbitrary the outcome of the law will be regarding that person.

A third important feature of political life is how princes communicate with their subjects. In autocracies, communication is by proclamation with the masses, rumor and gossip with members of the court. Russian rulers such as Catherine ruled through *ukases*, proclamations of laws. (You might ask yourself if the course syllabus handed to you by your professor on the first day of class is a *ukase*!) Catherine was particularly adept at planting rumors in order to mask her actual intentions. As a player of power politics in Europe, she would balance off the threats and promises of foreign nations—France, England, Prussia, Austria, Turkey, Sweden, Poland—by means of skillful hints conveyed to ambassadors sent to Catherine from those countries. No nation was ever quite sure of Catherine's aims. Gossip can be used both by and against a prince. Throughout her reign, for instance, Catherine was forced to deny that she had ordered her husband to be assassinated. She did not help matters, however, by resorting to the fiction that Peter had died of "hemorrhoidal attacks and colic," when many knew otherwise.

Finally, the ruler's attitude toward politics is distinctive. Autocratic princes either regard themselves as above politics, hence not involved in the dirty business of power plays, or they try to limit politics to what takes place among members of their court. But political conflicts and any political opposition to the prince must be kept secret. Such conflicts may be tolerated in the prince's court, but they must not be made public. Most importantly, opponents must not be permitted to appeal for support outside the ruling class. Such would be revolt, thus treason.

Under these political conditions of a state religion, arbitrary law, rule by decree, and the politics of secrecy, autocratic princedom swings back and forth. Sometimes autocratic government is benevolent, violence economized, controls relaxed. The carrot replaces the stick. At other times, autocracy is malevolent, violence rampant, controls rigid. The stick reigns. If you grew up in an autocratic family, or know friends who did, you will recognize this pendulum that swings from nice to nasty and back again. In autocratic princedoms, whether rule is nice or nasty depends in large measure on time and circumstance. These, thought Machiavelli, contain "the seeds of all things, good as well as bad, bad as well as good." In times of prosperity, the autocratic prince can afford to be benevolent. Then, wrote Machiavelli, "a wise prince will think of ways to keep his citizens of every sort and under every circumstance, dependent on the state and on him; and then they will always be trustworthy." But when times are bad, many a princely inclination is toward the corruption of power. Then, as English writer Lord Acton said, "Power tends to corrupt and absolute power corrupts absolutely."

AUTOCRATIC PERFECTION

Whether exercised as nice or nasty, autocratic power has an overriding goal and tendency. Any form of government—autocratic, republican, totalitarian—has a logic unto itself. That logic is the perfection of some means of achieving social harmony. Autocracy's logic is the perfection of obedience: "Don't do as I do. Do as I say." This is a message many a parent gives a child (perhaps you?). Or you may have caught your instructor in an error. One would hope the instructor would admit it. But some do not. The same logic is at work. Obedience is the aim, perfect obedience. That is what Catherine sought, and in many ways she was very good at it. But the perfection of obedience is not the only goal of organizing power. Republics have their logic too.

"Much that passes for idealism is disguised hatred or disguised love of power."

—Bertrand Russell

"The attempt to combine wisdom and power has only rarely been successful and then only for a short while."

—Albert Einstein

"The man who makes another powerful ruins himself."

—*Machiavelli*

"The Russian Empire is so large that any other form of government than that of absolute Emperor would be harmful to it; any other government is slower in execution, and leaves the field open to passions which disperse the power and strength of the state ... the internal institutions of a country should always develop in accord with the character of that country."

—*Catherine the Great*

"As long as you keep their old way of life and do not change their customs, men will live quietly enough."

"A wise prince will think of ways to keep his citizens of every sort and under every circumstance dependent on the state and on him; and then they will always be trustworthy."

—*Machiavelli*

"Power tends to corrupt and absolute power corrupts absolutely."

—*Lord Acton*

Chapter

Republican Power

The people of France have seen it all: they witnessed the autocracies of monarchs and of the Napoleonic era; they survived a totalitarian regime in parts of their nation during the Nazi occupation of World War II; and they have, by current count, experienced five republics. The last of these five, the current Fifth French Republic, is a useful starting point for learning about republican power in general and the role of the republican prince in particular.

The Fifth Republic arose out of crisis, which began not in France but in Algeria. In 1830, France seized Algeria from Turkey. Conveniently located directly across the Mediterranean Sea from the southern coast of France, Algeria proved to be popular for French colonization. Despite European migration to Algeria and the establishment of a virtually separate European community, an Arab nationalist movement developed and sought independence for Algeria from France. The movement intensified after World War II, and by the 1950s Algeria was beset by guerrilla warfare. The nationalists demanded independence, but the more than a million Europeans in Algeria insisted on retaining French ties. The warfare between the two was bloody and protracted. The French army, in order to restore order and keep Algeria French, used severe measures—including torture—against the rebels. By 1958 it appeared that the resolve in mainland France to keep Algeria French was waning. Officials in the Fourth Republic were sharply divided over Algerian policy, divisions that brought the Fourth republic to seeming paralysis.

On May 13, 1958, officers of the French army stationed in Algeria decided to take matters into their own hands. They seized power in Algeria, formed the Committee of Public Safety to rule, and demanded that mainland France create a wholly new French government that would keep Algeria part of France. The French president responded by ordering the army to obey but took no measures to force the officers to comply. Unrest, even panic, grew in Paris. At that point, there was a crucial development. Key members of the Committee of Public Safety in Algeria, officials of the Fourth Republic in France, and influential newspapers began to speak openly of the "only solution" to the crisis: General Charles de Gaulle.

De Gaulle, a hero to the French in World War II, had been in retirement for a dozen years. He was approaching his sixty-eighth birthday. Would he be willing to return to public life, and if he were, what could he possibly do? De Gaulle responded swiftly and decisively to both questions. On the fifteenth of May he issued a statement to the press which was critical of the governmental regime under the Fourth Republic, asserting that it had followed a disastrous road, noted that in the past France had turned to him for salvation, and closed by stating that he, de Gaulle, was "ready to assume the powers of the Republic." Four days later in a press conference, he announced that he would return to head "the French Republic, if the people wished it." On May 27, de Gaulle issued another statement: he had started "the regular process for establishing a republican government," implying that this process must be legal. He would not seize power by unconstitutional means. Instead, he wanted the Fourth Republic to bestow power on him by exceptional means. Two days later René Côty, president of the republic, sent a message to the French parliament. Côty was turning to de Gaulle, "the most illustrious Frenchman," to establish a government "within the framework of republican legality" to "bring about a fundamental reform of our institutions."

De Gaulle accepted the offer. On June 1, 1958, he spoke before the National Assembly, the legislative body and center of power in the Fourth Republic. He asked, first, that the assembly grant him full powers to act for France for a period of six months. Second, he wanted the authority to draft a new constitution for the nation and submit it to a public vote for approval. The assembly granted de Gaulle's requests and thus ended the Fourth French Republic. By August, the constitution of the Fifth Republic was drafted, a document that placed far more power

CHARLES DE GAULLE: CIVIL PRINCEDOM

"The Cross of Lorraine was the heaviest cross I ever had to bear," said Winston Churchill after World War II. The Cross of Lorraine was the symbol of the Free French forces which, after the defeat of France in 1940 by Nazi Germany, fled to England. There the Free French continued the war against Germany, fighting with the Allied armies in Syria, Madagascar, North Africa, and even in the Soviet Union. The leader of the Free French was Charles de Gaulle (1890–1970), and Churchill's remark about the Cross of Lorraine was a reference to de Gaulle, a princely leader that Churchill respected but found exasperating. Yet, after World War II this heavy cross was to leave a significant imprint on republican politics.

By the time World War II broke out, de Gaulle had already devoted three decades to an army career and had attained the rank of colonel. He had fought in the First World War, been wounded and left for dead, for which he received the Legion of Honor "posthumously." But he was not dead, and when the Germans found him, they tended his wounds and made him prisoner. He made five attempts to escape, never with success. After the war he continued his army career, taught at the French military academy, and was appointed to the secretariat of France's Supreme War Council. From there he served in the Army of Occupation, then in the Middle East. In 1932 he returned to France to serve as secretary to a government body charged with organizing the nation's defense. For five years he was familiar with political affairs and all aspects of military policy.

But throughout this long career, de Gaulle was more than a military officer. He was also a lecturer and writer, and in 1927 he presented an important series of lectures on leadership. This experience did three things for de Gaulle: it helped him sharpen his already superior oratorical skills, build a reputation as a student of military affairs, and write a book that expressed his concern for France's military preparedness. In these lectures and two books (*The Edge of the Sword* and *The Army of the Future*), de Gaulle argued that the French had become dangerously complacent about the possibilities of war. The army had been weakened, its strength and readiness gone. And the French defense policy—which consisted of little more than a line of fortification along the frontier with Germany—was a fatal mistake. The next war, de Gaulle believed, would be fought with weapons such as tanks and airplanes which would make such fortifications useless. Few politicians heeded his warning, and when Germany attacked in 1940, its *blitzkrieg* (lighting war) quickly breached French defenses. The French government gave up, but de Gaulle, who opposed the armistice with Germany, flew to England to continue the fight.

From England, de Gaulle managed to rally the French people, urging them in radio broadcasts to resist the Nazi occupation. He was able to arrange for French armed forces to be stationed in various colonies of the French empire to support "Free France." He acted as a thorn in the side of Allied war leaders such as Winston Churchill and Franklin Roosevelt, who frequently ignored the Free French forces in planning major engagements. Roosevelt even tried to work through a rival of de Gaulle's, General Henri Giraud, but in the end de Gaulle triumphed. After the liberation of France, de Gaulle made a triumphal return in 1944. He was intrumental in setting up a provisional government to rule the nation until a new constitution could be drafted. But tension developed between de Gaulle, who believed in government by a strong president, and the National Assembly, which wished to be the seat of power. Concluding that there was no way to resolve the impasse to his satisfaction, de Gaulle resigned in January 1946 as head of the government. He was fifty-six, and his public life was apparently at an end.

But end it did not. In a carefully planned rally in June 1946, he spoke out against the proposed constitution of the Fourth Republic. Still the constitution was approved in a public election by a close majority. De Gaulle continued his opposition by organizing a political movement directed at carrying out a national revolution, the "Rally of the French People." The movement held mass rallies, with rabid de Gaulle supporters waving Cross of Lorraine banners. De Gaulle's speeches urged a new "association" under a new constitution, with a powerful leader for a powerful French state. His opponents thought that he sounded more like a dictator than a republican. After a few electoral successes, the rally seemed destined to be a major force in French politics. But as conditions changed, the rally waned, and de Gaulle grew frustrated. In 1955, he announced his retirement from public life: "Everything suggests it will be a long time before we meet again. It is my intention not to intervene any longer in what is called 'public affairs.'" Only a "rather unusual shock" would make him do so.

The 1958 Algerian crisis provided the unusual shock that recalled the symbol of the Cross of Lorraine to public life. De Gaulle returned to power, founded the Fifth French Republic, and served as president until 1969. His return to power in 1958 and the widespread popular acceptance of his regime at the time exemplify a form of republic that Machiavelli called a *civil princedom.* By this Machiavelli meant a princedom "by choice of his fellow citizens." In such a princedom, wrote Machiavelli, "success depends neither on skill nor completely on fortune, but rather on a kind of lucky shrewdness." De Gaulle displayed such shrewdness in ending the Algerian crisis, seeking constitutional reform, providing France with a nuclear weapons capability, and making the nation an independent force on the European continent and in the world.

But what if the prince in a civil princedom loses public favor? Wrote Machiavelli: "The prince must have people well disposed toward him; otherwise in terms of adversity there's no hope." So de Gaulle found his final fall from power. In 1962, he provoked a political crisis by ignoring constitutional amendment procedures to obtain a direct popular vote on an amendment that would provide for popular election of the president (until then the president had been chosen by an electoral college). Unless he had "the people's confidence," said de Gaulle, he would resign. The amendment passed with 62 percent of the popular vote, and de Gaulle later won a second term as president. But in 1969, de Gaulle proposed another constitutional amendment, and the people voted no. Perhaps thinking Machiavelli correct, that without the people being well disposed toward him there was no hope, de Gaulle resigned. This time his retirement from civil princedom was permanent; his luck had run out.

---

in the president than in the National Assembly (see Chapter 8). In a public vote in September, 80 percent approved the new constitution. Two months later de Gaulle was elected president of the republic. Although the crisis that wrecked the Fourth Republic was over, it took de Gaullle until 1962 to solve the Algerian problem. As we shall see later, he did so by following republican logic. That is, he came to power with the support of those who favored keeping Algeria a part of France, yet solved the Algerian problem by negotiating the independence of Algeria.

REPUBLICAN LOGIC

A prince knows that labels are often confusing. In fact, a prudent prince frequently calls things by names that they are not. How many times have you heard, for example, a political leader claim to have "whipped inflation," even though prices continue to rise? Perhaps costs are not increasing as rapidly as they did earlier, but they still are going up, not down. Inflation has been slowed, not stalled, not whipped.

You should keep in mind that governments too, may have misleading labels. Not all governments called republics are such. For example, after World War II Germany was divided into two nations, known best as West Germany and East Germany. In West Germany, people elect their political leaders from among competing candidates to hold office for specified periods. A constitution limits what those leaders can do, and periodically those officeholders must go back to the people and seek reelection so that if they win, they will stay in office, and if they lose, they will yield their power. In East Germany totalitarian logic prevails (see Chapter 7): power is concentrated in the elite of the Communist party, representing a relatively small percentage of the population. Popular elections have little to do with who governs, since there is only one candidate, a Communist, to vote for in any instance. West Germany calls itself the Federal Republic of Germany, and East Germany calls itself the German Democratic Republic. Consider also that the autocratic regime of Argentina is labeled the Argentine Republic; the totalitarian regime of Russia is the Union of Soviet Socialistic Republics; the autocratic regime of South Africa is the Republic of South Africa; and Mao Tse-tung exerted total power over the People's Republic of China.

Add to your confusion the fact that some republics do not even use a label—Australia, Canada, Great Britain are examples. Although historians note that the word *republic* was so odious at the time of the founding of the United States as to provoke opposition, ask yourself what word appears when you say the "Pledge of Allegiance."

Finally, confusion becomes exasperation when you add yet another term, *democracy*. For example, isn't the United States a democracy rather than a republic, or is it a republic rather than a democracy? That debate can, and has, raged seemingly forever. We think it not worth your time to argue the point, for in contrasting republican power with autocratic power and totalitarian power, the ideas of republic and democracy are very close. For our purposes, a republic may be considered to be a *representative democracy,* a government that lodges power in the people and wherein those people elect from among them representatives who hold office and make decisions for everybody. Candidates compete for votes in open elections, and if they win, they will hold office for limited periods of time and will govern under conditions that restrict what they can do.

Before exploring the details of republican logic, beware of one other point. Representative democracy differs from what political scientists call *direct* democracy In a representative democracy, the officeholders elected to represent people make governing decisions; in a direct democracy, the people gather to make those decisions. If you are a member of the group that meets and votes on what you will and will not do, you are taking part in direct democracy. When you vote for others to represent you, you are practicing representative democracy. Because the democracies of nations are of the representative variety, we shall speak therefore of the logic of republican power, not of direct democracy.

How Is Society Possible?

The American philosopher John Dewey wrote, "The key-note of democracy as a way of life may be expressed, it seems to me, as the necessity for the participation of every mature human being in the formation of the values that regulate the living of men together."Think back to our discussion of power in Chapter 4. You have power when you can take part in decisions that involve your life, the values you achieve and those you do not. If Dewey was correct, another way to think of democracy (or for our purposes, a republic that is a representative democracy) would be to say that it is a form of government that disperses power among the people. It does so by giving them the opportunity to participate in making decisions affecting their lives. You can think of opportunity in the same way that you did about capacity in Chapter 4; you have capacity or opportunity when you can persuade others to do what they otherwise might not. A republic encourages such action by letting people take part in their government.

Thus the republic allows diverse and perhaps conflicting interests to share in government. As indicated earlier, this does not mean that it is necessary to have every member of society take part directly in every decision that might have some bearing on that person's life. Instead, republican logic dictates popular control over how decisions are made. Elections make popular control work, but they must be special kinds of elections. As will be seen in Chapter 18, elections in autocratic and totalitarian regimes frequently have nothing to do with choosing rulers. Instead, voters are rounded up and given no choice but to vote for the regime. Republican elections, however, have distinctive characteristics.

- *They are free and open.* People qualified to vote cannot be kept from doing so, nor can they be forced, bribed, or otherwise intimidated to vote in a particular way. This is not to say that people cannot be required to vote. Some republics make voting compulsory, for instance, Austrialia, the Netherlands, Belgium, and Italy.

- *They are competitive.* There must be choices. When Charles de Gaulle returned to power in France in 1958, he gave the voters a choice; namely, they could vote *oui* or *non* on the proposed constitution of the Fifth Republic; if *non,* he would resign. More frequently, choice means among competing candidates, perhaps representing different political parties, points of view, or other interests.
- *They must be regular.* Officeholders are not chosen for life. But in autocratic regimes the tendency is to do precisely that. In 1964 François Duvalier was chosen president of Haiti for life. But in republics, elected officials hold their jobs for limited terms, and they may or may not be eligible for reelection.
- *They must be final.* This means that the election results must be peaceably accepted by winners and losers alike. The winners assume office, and the losers become a loyal opposition, criticizing but not rebelling against the freely elected government. Autocratic logic differs. In 1962 the Dominican Republic held its first free election after three decades of dictatorship by General Rafael Trujillo, assassinated a year earlier. The elected president was the founder of a political party opposed to the Trujillo regime. No sooner had he taken office than he was removed by Trujillo's former army generals and colonels. The "republic" in the Dominican Republic did not yet mean republican logic.

Elections in republics display these characteristics in varied degrees. Republican logic is not always perfect. For instance, in the United States sometimes only one candidate competes for a particular office in an election, and there have been instances in American history when votes were bought and sold. Indeed, in his first election for office, George Washington purchased votes by providing free liquor to those who would support him. Such instances do not destroy the entire fabric of a republic, but they do illustrate that republican logic—which calls for the perfection of participation through popular control—can be contradictory.

Who Tells Whom What to Do?

Republics derive from the ideal that power should be broadly distributed among a society's population. They follow Machiavelli's precept that "the governments of the people are better than those of princes." This is not to suggest, however, that there is no role for princes. Princes are necessary for republican survival, but they are subject to popular control. That assumption is strikingly different from the one that Catherine the Great made as czarina of all the Russians. Catherine had control of the populace; yet there was little popular control over her. The prince bound by popular control cannot command but must lead. Hence, political leadership is a vital principle of republican logic joined with popular control.

As an example of this principle in action, return to the case of Charles de Gaulle. Machiavelli taught that in politics "the causes of the success or failures of men depend upon their manner of suiting their conduct to the times." One defect of republics, he noted, is that "such changes are more difficult and tardy in republics" than in other governments; therefore, "necessarily circumstances will occur that will unsettle the whole state." The task of the princely political leader in a republic is to recognize that times and circumstances have changed and to adjust to them or, more accurately, persuade the people to adjust to them. This adjustment has distinct phases.

First, when changes "unsettle the whole state," the result may be difficult times—social unrest, economic problems, an unstable political period. A crisis may erupt, or at least what people consider a crisis. When the Algerian question came to a head on May 13, 1958, France faced a crisis. From 1786 to 1787 there was an economic depression following the American Revolution, and debtors in Massachusetts rebelled against the local taxing authorities ("Shay's Rebellion"). Many politicians viewed this as proof of a serious crisis demanding drastic action, the eventual remedy being the new Constitution of the United States. Into such crises strides the prince whose task is to reestablish order by a combination of direction and influence, force and cunning. Thus did Charles de Gaulle emerge in France. Thus also did the Founding Fathers reach the Constitutional Convention in Philadelphia in 1787 (see Chapter 8).

Second, having been brought to politics by crisis, the prince strives to set up a legitimate regime and then to wield personal power through it to resolve the crisis. Thus de Gaulle announced that he was ready to return to power, "if the people wished it" and if the Fourth Republic would offer him that power legally. That was accomplished when President Côty asked de Gaulle to form a government; de Gaulle accepted and then received from the National Assembly full powers for six months and the authority to reform existing institutions, thus founding the Fifth French Republic. (Similarly, the Founding Fathers met in Philadelphia in 1787 to amend the Articles of Confederation but, like de Gaulle, later created a whole new constitutional regime.)

Having established a legitimate regime in which the president of the Republic dominated the National Assembly, de Gaulle was prepared to exercise presidential power to end the Algerian crisis. That was not easy. He had come to power as a result of an insurrection by a military and political faction in Algiers committed to keeping the colony French. Although never explicitly stating support for such a view, by going to Algeria, de Gaulle implied that he sympathized with it. There he opened a speech with the phrase *Je vous ai compris* ("I have understood you"). What he did not do in the speech, however, was mention a "French Algeria" or the integration of Algeria into the French republic. Nor in the early days of his rule did he give the military faction much hope for a French Algeria. Many of the officers who had led the insurrection he transferred from Algeria to other assignments. Then in September 1959, he proposed "self-determination" for Algeria. He thus offered to negotiate with Algerian leaders seeking independence, while permitting the army to continue to restore order in Algeria, and ultimately to let all Algerians (native and Europeans) choose to be French or independent. This produced a second insurrection by the forces seeking a French Algeria, but it failed. De Gaulle then went further and proposed an Algerian republic and, more importantly, an election throughout France and Algeria: people could vote *oui* or *non* on de Gaulle's Algerian policy. In the 1961 election de Gaulle received a three-to-one margin of approval in France, over two-to-one in Algeria (although the Europeans in Algeria voted no). This produced the third and final revolt, the "Revolt of the Generals." De Gaulle countered this with a radio broadcast, carried throughout France and Algeria, ordering all soldiers to disobey the orders of the four generals leading the revolt. De Gaulle won the day. Three of the generals fled, and the fourth was imprisoned. Thereafter de Gaulle removed all dissident officers and officials who had aided the rebellion. The French army, de Gaulle made it clear, would be removed from Algeria and totally reorganized; a major inducement to the officer corps was de Gaulle's guarantee to make the French army an "atomic force" on a par with other nuclear powers.

Under conditions of considerable chaos and bloodshed brought about by terrorists intent on keeping Algeria French, de Gaulle negotiated a settlement with those seeking independence. In 1962, de Gaulle's policy was put to a nationwide vote. It was approved by over 90 percent, and in 1962 Algeria achieved independence. Using guile, rhetoric, force, and compromise, de Gaulle had ended France's ties to Algeria over the protests of almost a million French, most of whom eventually returned to the mainland.

There is a third and final phase in princely adjustment to changing times and circumstances, the establishment of institutions that guarantee that future rulers will govern under more stable conditions than did the founding prince. As you will see in Chapter 8, America's Founding Fathers did this through the Constitution. De Gaulle attempted to do so with the Fifth Republic. He was highly critical of the constitutions of both the Third and Fourth republics. Too much power was exercised by the National Assembly which was torn asunder by factions and parties unable to adjust to change. That, de Gaulle thought, was why the Third Republic was unable to prepare for war with Germany and the Fourth Republic was unable to deal with changing conditions in the French empire. Hence, the political leadership that can make popular control effective must be lodged in the president: "The cornerstone of our regime is the President . . . he is, indeed, the guardian of the independence and integrity of the country. . . . He answers for France. On the other hand, it is for him to assure the continuity of the State. In short, he answers for the Republic." As you watch and ponder politics in the future, it will be for you to judge the adequacy of de Gaulle's preparations. Thus far the

Fifth Republic has continued: de Gaulle resigned as president in 1969; his elected successor Georges Pompidou died in 1974; Valéry Giscard d'Estaing was elected to follow but lost in his reelection bid in 1981 to François Mitterand. What *fortuna* holds for the future remains to be seen. Once when still president, de Gaulle was asked at a press conference about who would follow him. With good-natured haughtiness he replied, "After de Gaulle, de Gaulle!"

What Is the Community?

Machiavelli taught, "Let republics, then, be established where equality exists, and, on the contrary, principalities where great inequality prevails. . . ." In practice, republics do not rest on a foundation of perfect equality. Look around you, and you will see that other people do not share the same quantity or quality of valued things that you do. Some have more of the welfare values of well-being, wealth, skill, and enlightenment; others have fewer. Nor are deference values of respect, rectitude, and affection evenly divided up among you and the rest of the populace. Equality refers to roughly even distributions, not perfect ones. Autocracies and totalitarian regimes rest on marked inequalities, republics on approximate equalities.

Indeed, it is precisely because most people are only approximately equal in social and economic matters that republican logic emphasizes another principle, *political equality*. Republican logic assumes that if people are viewed as politically equal and treated as such, this will maximize their opportunities for taking part in politics. Political equality, in other words, exists to maximize the opportunity for equal shares in political power, the view being that if people have political power they can use it as an instrument to obtain a greater share of welfare and deference values.

When Thomas Jefferson wrote in the 1776 Declaration of Independence that "all men are created equal," he voiced a commonly held view of his times. Being created equal did not guarantee equality in other respects. Governments, however, if properly conceived, could guarantee at least one form of equality, namely, political equality. And because in nature all people are created equal, any government that rested on political equality would be a natural protector of its people. Wrote Jefferson in 1790, "The republican is the only form of government which is not eternally at open or secret war with the rights of mankind." The rights, of course, were the natural rights derived from being created equal.

The principal device to ensure political equality in a republic is the vote. Republican logic, seeking the perfection of participation in government, demands that citizens be treated equally in voting. This implies, first, that every mature person should be allowed to vote: the principle of universal adult suffrage. Mature adulthood is a matter of age in republican logic, for example, in the United States, to vote, you must be eighteen or over. Second, each person should have only one vote; that is, the wealthy should not be allowed more votes than the poor are, or you, after graduating from college, should not be allowed to cast more votes than your friend can who has not graduated. Third, each vote should count equally in making decisions. The vote you cast for governor of your state should have no greater weight than your neighbor's does. Finally, derived from this political adjustment to the facts of social and economic equality is a rule, adopted not because it is necessarily right or wrong but because it is convenient. If each person has a vote and each vote counts equally, whose votes will decide what is to be done? The principle of majority rule thus applies—when people are divided, be they members of the electorate, legislature, judicial bodies, or whatever, the majority will prevail. This does not mean that the majority is right or the minority wrong, only that the majority has won a particular contest. Today's minority may become tomorrow's majority.

You have probably guessed that just as with the characteristics of elections dictated by republican logic, there are compromises with respect to political equality. Most republics place at least some restrictions on who can vote, perhaps requiring that they be citizens, not be in jail, have their names listed in official books in advance of the election, have resided in their neighborhoods or political subdivisions for a minimum period, or some other restrictions. Votes, furthermore, do not always count equally. As a result of de Gaulle's successful effort in 1962 to amend the constitution of the Fifth Republic, the French president is now elected by a direct vote of the people, each vote counting equally. In the United States, you do not vote directly for the president, but for persons called *electors* who are pledged to the candidate of your choice. If you live in California, a state with a large number of electors, your vote will count more than if you reside in North Dakota. For the president is chosen by the total number of electoral votes received, not by popular votes, as in France. And majority rule does not always prevail. Many towns in the United States require a two-thirds majority for approval in elections to decide whether they will increase taxes. Do all these compromises make such republics autocratic or totalitarian? Not so long as the basic principles that we have discussed—popular control, political leadership, and political equality—operate in the main.

Such principles have operated in nations that have a large middle class and much mobility from the lower clases into the middle class. Moreover, the economic base of republican regimes has typically been one of free enterprise, capitalistic markets, or a mixed economy in which many businesses and industries are under private control but are regulated by the government or in which some businesses are privately owned and others are under government control. Whatever the social and economic arrangement, however, the key community characteristic demanded by republican logic is equality in opportunities to exercise political power.

What Is Politics Like?

As seen in Chapter 5, autocracies thrive on the notion that there is only one true doctrine, usually religious, and condone no dissent from it. Totalitarian regimes rest on a similar doctrinal basis (see Chapter 7). In this respect, republican politics is largely nondoctrinal. This is not to say that there are no doctrines, ideas, creeds, or religious beliefs to which people are loyal. The point is that none stands as an official doctrine above popular debate. None is official truth from which there can be no dissent.

Republican logic takes a different tack. Politics rests on the principle that society is open to all kinds of views and that none is immune to criticism. Why? People are fallible; that is, they make mistakes. As long as people's actions, especially the actions of political officials, are open to public scrutiny, errors can be detected and corrections made. The same holds for political ideas. Because people err, the likelihood that any one idea is correct is slim, at least slim enough to warrant giving it close examination. As long as the principle of popular debate holds, competing points of view are encouraged and indeed are inevitable. Doctrinal politics is discouraged but is not inevitable.

But public debate requires support. If people are afraid to speak out, to criticize the status quo and to advocate other approaches, there will be no airing of diverse viewpoints. Few princes, no matter what their commitment to the republic, enjoy criticism, at least public criticism. Charles de Gaulle avoided it by controlling his public appearances. When he did appear in public, he sometimes encountered trouble. When he kicked off his campaign in 1958 to win public approval for the constitution of the Fifth Republic, he journeyed to an area of Paris where opposition was rampant—hostile demonstrations, violent protests, anti-Gaullist marches, and the like. Sizing up the situation, de Gaulle decided to make only a few public remarks, lead the crowd in singing the national anthem, and hasten away. He vowed that never again during the campaign would he appear where such public displays of opposition were likely. Instead, he used carefully orchestrated press conferences and media appearances to make his pitch.

James Madison, a princely figure about whom we shall say more in Chapter 8, wrote in the *Federalist Papers* that "in framing a government which is to be administered by men over men, the great difficulty lies in this: you must first enable the government to control the governed; and in the next place oblige it to control itself." One method of persuading the government to control itself, and also to enhance popular control, is to protect the liberties of people to speak out in opposition to their governors. For public debate to occur, another principle must operate, that of political liberty. A chief purpose of law in a republic is to protect the freedom of the people—regardless of their viewpoint, class distinctions, racial or religious or ethnic background—and to permit them to express their beliefs. This means freedom of conscience, speech, and association.

With these protections the attitude toward how people should become informed about politics differs markedly from that of autocratic or totalitarian regimes. Recall that in autocratic regimes proclamations and gossip are the sources that people must rely on to find out what is going on; in totalitarian governments a government-controlled mass communication system operates (see Chapter 7). In a republic, newspapers, periodicals, television, and the like are not appendages of the regime. To the degree that de Gaulle's France, for example, limited the amount of time that opposing points of view had access to television, as was the case when de Gaulle sought popular support for his policies via elections, the Fifth Republic was not as republican as logic would require.

Finally, then, what is the attitude of rulers and ruled toward politics in a republic? Simply put, politics should not only be tolerated but also encouraged. Politics in a republic is the means by which diverse interests express their demands; those demands can be conciliated; and decisions reflecting the widespread sharing of power can be made. Autocracies decry politics as irrelevant and unnecessary. Totalitarian regimes denounce politics as subversive. Republics accept politics for what it is, the logical result of the interplay of popular control, political leadership, political equality, popular debate, and political liberty.

BUT WILL IT WORK?

James McHenry was a delegate to the convention in 1787 that produced the Constitution of the United States. Many years later he wrote a book entitled *Anecdotes,* about what took place. He related a story about the American folk hero Benjamin Franklin, also a delegate: "A lady asked Dr. Franklin, 'Well Doctor, what have we got, a republic or a monarchy?' 'A republic,' replied Doctor, 'if you can keep it.'"

Franklin's point should be well taken for two reasons. One is that republican governments are fragile. They depend for endurance on a delicate balance of forces and tensions, between princes and subjects, changing times and circumstances, and a host of other imponderables. But equally important in Franklin's view was the phrase "if you can keep it." Whether republican logic will work, particularly the logic of the republic in which you live, depends on "if *you* can keep it." If you learn, understand, and practice nothing, then autocratic logic may seem reasonable to you. But if you want to take part in your government, mastery of republican logic is essential. There is another alternative, however, the totalitarian way. Consider it as carefully before you make up your mind as to whether the possibilities of people successfully governing themselves are so slim that as the American journalist and critic H. L. Mencken noted with humor and despair, "Democracy is the art and science of running the circus from the monkey cage."

"The key-note of democracy as a way of life may be expressed, it seems to me, as the necessity for the participation of every mature human being in the formation of the values that regulate the living of men together."

—John Dewey

"The governments of the people are better than those of princes."

—Machiavelli

"The cornerstone of our regime is the President . . . he is, indeed, the guardian of the independence and integrity of the country. . . . He answers for France. On the other hand, it is for him to assure the continuity of the State. In short, he answers for the Republic."

—de Gaulle

"The republican is the only form of government which is not eternally at open or secret war with the rights of mankind."

—Jefferson

"In framing a government which is to be administered by men over men, the great difficulty lies in this: you first enable the government to control the governed; and in the next place oblige it to control itself."

—James Madison

"Democracy is the art and science of running the circus from the monkey cage."

—H. L. Mencken

Chapter

7

Totalitarian Power

On November 7, 1938, in Paris, France, a young man by the name of Herschel Grynszpan approached the German embassy. He carried with him a gun, and his intent was murder. His intended victim was the German ambassador to France. Grynszpan's motive was that his parents had just been deported from Germany to Poland. The reason? The Grynszpans were Jewish. That was reason enough for deportations in Nazi Germany. Grynszpan arrived at the embassy and asked to see the ambassador. But an embassy councilor, Ernst von Rath, intervened. There was trouble, and in the struggle Grynszpan shot Rath, and two days later Rath died. His death was to serve as the excuse for one of the

ADOLF HITLER: DICTATOR

On first sight he was not a striking figure. He was short; his complexion was rough; he had a small, almost comic, toothbrushlike moustache; and his hair fell in an unruly way over his left eye. In conversation he spoke in a quiet, offhand, diffident way that made him seem ill at ease. Few would take this man to be the absolute ruler of conquered lands that stretched from North Africa to Norway and from France almost to Moscow. But first looks were often deceiving to his contemporaries. The eyes that seemed so pale as to go unnoticed from a distance were piercing—some said even hypnotic—when encountered up close. And the seeming lack of ease in personal conversation yielded to a dynamism, indeed arrogance, as he spoke to the people gathered to hear him.

Adolf Hitler (1889–1945), the *Fuehrer* (leader) of Germany from 1933 to 1945, was born in Austria, the son of a customs official. In school his record was adequate but hardly distinguished. He did display some interest in art and music, and so as a young man he went to Vienna in 1907 to study them. But fortune did not smile. The art academy refused admission, and for the next six years he survived the best he could, including wearing threadbare clothes, begging for food, and living in a house for the destitute. But Hitler also read, argued politics, and learned to paint. In 1913 he decided to try his luck elsewhere. Moving to Munich, Germany, he hoped to make a living as a painter. But when World War I began in 1914, Hitler enlisted in the German army. He became a runner carrying messages to the front lines. Before the war ended he had attained the rank of corporal, been gassed, and won the Iron Cross for bravery. Returning to Munich without work, his future was not bright. But here his army contacts helped, and he found work as a political agent of an army bureau. The bureau investigated suspected subversive activities and infiltrated various groups. As an agent, Hitler was also assigned to do some public speaking, a task he fulfilled with great relish.

He had not been on the job long when he received orders to check out a group called the German Workers' party. It was not much of a group—only six members. Hitler thought the investigation not worth much effort but attended a group meeting. He became mildly interested in the group's efforts, at least to the point of speaking before the meeting. He departed, thinking little more of the group and so was surprised to receive notification that he had been accepted for membership. So he joined, becoming the seventh member of a group that was to grow into the National Socialist German Workers' party, that is, the Nazi party.

By 1923 the party had grown sufficiently to test its strength. It plotted to overthrow the government of Bavaria, a political subdivision of Germany, in the hope of seizing power throughout the nation. But the plot failed, and Hitler received a five-year prison sentence, of which he served only thirteen months. In prison he wrote what was to become the bible of the Nazi movement, *Mein Kampf* ("my struggle," or "battle"). In spite of its 1923 failure, by 1933 the Nazi party had grown to be the largest in the German legislature. Much of that growth depended on Hitler's skills as a campaigner. In 1932 he ran for president and moved throughout Germany by automobile and airplane, from village to village, city to city. Although he lost the election, in 1933 the victorious candidate, President Paul von Hindenburg, invited Hitler to become chancellor, the effective head of the German government. Hitler accepted in

January, and by March 1933 the German legislature had voted to give Hitler dictatorial powers.

Hitler's "Thousand-Year Reich" lasted a mere dozen years. But in that span it perfected the totalitarian organization of power, the logic of total control. Within the Nazi party Hitler did not hesitate to use violence to keep hold of the reins of power: assassinations, murder, imprisonment, and purges were common. In the German nation he restored confidence in the government by building industry, superhighways, and a mighty military machine; he mobilized support for his policies (more than 88 percent of Germans voted to make him both chancellor and president) by means of propaganda, censorship, and intimidation; and he mounted an attack on the Jewish population of Germany that ended with deportations, concentration camps, and the mass murder of six million Jews. And in his dealings with other nations, by means of bluff and threat, guile, and war, he managed to become the most influential adventurer since Napoleon.

Time, circumstance, and unprincely judgment ultimately caught up with Hitler's total dictatorial control. The failure at economizing violence brought violence against Hitler himself. On April 30, 1945, scarcely a week before Germany was to become the conquered loser of World War II, the Fuehrer took the final step in maximizing violence: he committed suicide. Totalitarian power had played out its unique logic in Germany.

---

most brutal events ever to occur in a seemingly civilized nation, yet one all too typical of the terroristic use of power in totalitarian regimes.

News of Rath's death reached Adolf Hitler, the dictator of Nazi Germany while the Fuehrer was in Munich, Germany, with the leaders of his Nazi (National Socialist) party to celebrate the fifteenth anniversary of an unsuccessful attempt that he and others had made in 1923 to seize power in Germany. What Hitler had not been able to do by violent means in 1923, however, he had managed by more peaceful ways a decade later. Now his word was law throughout the Third Reich, Hitler's name for Germany's third empire.

Hearing of Rath's death, Hitler left the party celebration. He spoke briefly with Joseph Goebbels (see Chapter 27), an important minister in the Reich. Goebbels returned to the meeting of party leaders and announced that Rath's assassination had provoked anti-Jewish demonstrations in several parts of Germany. According to Goebbels, Hitler felt that as long as such demonstrations were spontaneous, no action should be taken against them. Several party leaders took this to mean that they were to organize "spontaneous" riots against the Jews. This they did, and with a vengeance.

The night of November 9, 1938, came to be known as the *Kristalnacht*, the "crystal night." The name has beauty and poetry, but the events commemorated were neither beautiful nor poetic. Nazis attacked Jews on the streets or broke into their shops and beat them. Jewish businesses were bombed, burned, looted, and destroyed. Jewish synagogues were burned, and Jewish homes were entered and destroyed. More than twenty thousand Jews were arrested, three dozen seriously injured, and an equal number killed. During all of this the police stood by and did nothing.

It is appropriate to begin any consideration of how power is organized in totalitarian regimes by brief mention of *Kristalnacht.* As you will see in this chapter, what went on in that single evening illustrates the logic of totalitarian power. In that logic, the use of force and terror, the whims of the dictator, and the perfection of total control are essential. You will find they differ in marked ways from the essentials of republican logic and autocratic logic.

TOTAL POWER: FICTION AND FACT

In 1949 the English writer George Orwell published a fictional account of life in a totalitarian regime. He called his novel *Nineteen Eighty-four.* The time of which Orwell wrote is now here, and his description of totalitarian logic has become a classic. The plot of the novel involves a brief period in the life of Winston Smith. Smith resides in Oceania, one of three great superpowers that comprise the world in 1984. Oceania is constantly at war with one or the other superpower, Eurasia or Eastasia. At least, people think that there is always war, for that is what their government keeps saying. There is no way of discovering otherwise, because the government has total control over all communications.

Oceania is a totalitarian state. All power resides in the members of the Inner party, a tightly knit and small elite within the single political party that governs Oceania. At the head of government is a dictator known only as Big Brother. Posters and pictures of Big Brother are everywhere. Whether or not such a person actually exists, no one can say. Even to wonder is dangerous because the Thought police is always on the lookout for such crimethink. Ruling in the name of Big Brother and the Inner party are four government ministries. The Ministry of Truth (Minitrue) supposedly deals with news, entertainment, education, and the arts; it actually engages in propaganda and rewrites history to serve the needs and wishes of the party. The Ministry of Peace (Minipax) deals with war; the Ministry of Love (Miniluv) maintains law and order; and the Ministry of Plenty (Miniplenty) handles economic policy, especially food shortages and rationing.

Smith works for Minitrue, and each day he rewrites stories that have appeared in past issues of the *Times,* the party-controlled Oceania newspaper. He rewrites the stories to bring them into line with current party policies. "Who controls the past," goes the party slogan, "controls the future: who controls the present controls the past." Smith takes pride in his work: it takes a special talent to invent history precisely as the party dictates. Yet, in the back of his mind Smith seems to remember another time when there was no party, no Big Brother. But since there is no record of it, such a time must not have existed. Yet, again, could it be . . . ?

As the novel unfolds, Smith's puzzlement leads him to do some foolish things. He purchases a diary and begins recording his innermost thoughts, and against all party rules he begins a clandestine affair with Julia, who also works in Minitrue. In a section of town near where the proles live (the common working people who are not members of the party), Smith rents a small room above a curio shop where he and Julia can meet away from the prying eyes of the Thought police. "Folly, folly, his heart kept saying: conscious, gratuitous, suicidal folly!"

And folly it turns out to be. The proprietor of the curio shop is an agent of the Thought police. Smith and Julia are arrested and hauled off to separate prisons in the Ministry of Love. There Smith is the victim of beatings, torture, and degradation, all at the hands of Inner party member O'Brien. O'Brien tries to convince Smith that all this terror is in Winston's best interests. All the party wants Smith to do is willingly to think as the party dictates, with no reservations, and to "love Big Brother." Smith insists that he does love Big Brother, but O'Brien keeps up the physical and mental torture. Winston finally breaks and admits that he hates Big Brother. O'Brien is pleased. At last Smith is being honest. Now real progress can be made. Smith is taken to Room 101, a torture chamber where each prisoner must confront whatever is his own private hell, that which the prisoner most fears. Smith fears rats. Rather than face the prospect of having rats scratch his eyes out, Smith disavows his love for Julia. Instead, finally, he wins "victory over himself." He loves Big Brother.

What Orwell tells you and all others familiar with his *Nineteen Eighty-four* is what life is like in a totalitarian regime.

Winston Smith was the victim of total power. According to Chapter 5, autocratic logic strives for the perfection of obedience, tries to persuade subjects to obey the prince's commands. In Chapter 6 you learned that republican logic aims for a different kind of perfection, that of popular participation in governing. The perfection that lies at the heart of totalitarian logic actually derives from a combination of, or a perversion of, the logics of autocratic and republican power. Totalitarian princes want people to obey. But as O'Brien said to Winston Smith, "It is not enough to obey him," speaking of Big Brother, "You must love him." "Love" here means actively and willingly participating in a prince's dictates. A totalitarian regime achieves obedience by giving people the illusion that they are taking part in the governing of their own lives through their loyalty (love) for a dictatorial prince. The essence of totalitarian logic, thus, is not the perfection of obedience, not the perfection of participation, but the perfection of mobilization. The masses are mobilized on behalf of a princely dictator.

In order to see how totalitarian logic works in practice, let us return again to the questions we asked about autocratic and republican regimes. With those questions answered, you will be able to compare autocratic, republican, and totalitarian politics.

How Is Society Possible?

Franklin Roosevelt, president of the United States during World War II (and whom we will discuss further in Chapter 9), remarked that "history proves that dictatorships do not grow out of strong and successful governments, but out of weak and helpless ones." The history to which Roosevelt was referring was the history of his times. The rise of totalitarian regimes, at least during his lifetime, proved his point: the inability of the autocratic government of Czar Nicholas II to deal with Russia's domestic problems and the crises produced by World War I led to the Communist dictatorship after 1917 of Vladimir Lenin and his successors; strikes and general unrest in Italy led Benito Mussolini to march on Rome in 1922, thus establishing a Fascist dictatorship; and the chaotic political and economic situation, and the inability of the leading political parties to cope with it, helped bring Adolf Hitler's Nazi regime to power in 1933. This is not to say that totalitarian dictatorships always emerge when governments appear weak and helpless. As seen in Chapter 6, the inability of the French National Assembly to deal with the Algerian crisis in 1958 did result in the downfall of the Fourth Republic. But another republic, not a totalitarian regime, replaced it.

More often than not, totalitarian power begins in social and economic crises so severe that opponents of the existing political order can use the turmoil to replace the autocratic or republican government with an entirely new political form, the totalitarian government. In the process, political leaders appeal to the masses to support them in seeking a revolutionary new order. By creating a completely new society, order is to be brought out of the diversity and the chaos that diversity allegedly produces. That new society will be built on principles contained in a revolutionary ideology. That ideology, be it Communist, Fascist, Nazi, or whatever, usually claims to be scientific. That is, the ideology stands as a factual explanation of the way things are and a prediction of how they will be. One prediction appears in all such doctrines, that if the masses follow the dictates of the totalitarian regime (dictates that supposedly derive from ideological principles rather than the capricious power-seeking whims and ambitions of the dictator), conflict will vanish, order will be restored, and happiness will be inevitable. If for some reason the ideological principles fail to predict political realities, it will not be the ideology that is in error, not the vision of the new society that is wrong. Rather, the enemies of the state, either foreign or domestic, have blocked the march of history and, therefore, must be rooted out. Thus we find Joseph Stalin (see Chapter 27), princely dictator of the Soviet Union, explaining why twenty years after the Russian Revolution the ideological promise had not yet been fulfilled: "The victory of socialism in Russia is not complete because the danger of intervention from capitalist countries continues."

Imposing a social order by trying to convince people to accept and believe a revolutionary ideology has its problems. Suppose that you were miserable and unhappy, believing that no one loves you and that

Power, or the Clout of Politics

you will never graduate and never get a job if you do. Your roommate tells you not to worry: simply turn your future over to astrology, that is, read your horoscope every day and act accordingly. You do but nothing changes. You reason fairly quickly that believing in astrology is not much help, and so you turn elsewhere. Totalitarian rulers, however, cannot have people turning elsewhere. No, everybody must love Big Brother.

To mobilize that love, dictators turn to coercion. Reason must bow to total power. Hitler put it thus: "The one means that wins the easiest victory over reason: terror and force." Totalitarian dictators do not follow Machiavelli's precept: they do not economize violence; they maximize it. And they do so not only against alleged enemies of the revolutionary ideology, for example, the Jews in Nazi Germany or the capitalists in postrevolutionary Russia. Totalitarian dictators maximize violence against members of their own ruling group in order to keep them in line.

O'Brien's torture of Winston Smith was a fictional case of an Inner party member maximizing violence to keep an Outer party member mobilized. Now consider two real-life cases. Shortly after he became leader of the Nazi party in 1921, Adolf Hitler established a paramilitary party unit. Its purpose was to discipline party members, dress in military outfits (members wore brown military shirts), march, and impress the German middle class with the party's respect for order. The unit began with the name of "Gymnastics and Sports Division" and then took the title of *Sturmabteilung* (abbreviated SA), for "storm detachment." But many people simply spoke of the SA as the "Brownshirts," and when Hitler came to power in 1933, it was the victory of the "Brown Revolution."

The commander of the SA was Captain Ernst Roehm. He had more grandiose plans for the Brownshirts than did Hitler. He wanted his private army to have a military role comparable to that of the Reichswehr, the German army. Moreover, he argued that the aims of the Brown Revolution had not yet been fully met, and so in 1934 he began calling for a "second revolution" to complete the task. Hitler disagreed on both points. He did not want to lose the support of Reichswehr generals by creating a rival military force, and he thought that a second, more radical, revolution would be premature.

The conflict between Hitler and Roehm intensified when the Fuehrer decreed that the SA must confine itself to political affairs, that any military role would be strictly limited. This rankled Roehm, and within a few weeks, rumors reached Hitler that he and the SA were plotting a revolt. Hitler did not bother to check out the rumors but instead decided to make an example of the "nest of traitors." In short order he set in motion a plan to have key party leaders that he *assumed* to be Roehm's accomplices arrested and executed. Then he personally went to a hotel in southern Germany where Roehm was staying. Revolver in hand, he entered Roehm's room, awakened him, and placed him under arrest. Hitler then sent a code word ("hummingbird") to his henchmen in

Berlin. That signaled that arrests and executions of other party leaders were to begin. Throughout the day and night of June 30, 1934, a brutal purge was carried out. Some party members were shot. Another was disemboweled by a shotgun blast in his own living room. Yet another was brought back from his honeymoon and executed. As for Roehm, he was placed in a prison cell, given a revolver with one shell, and told to draw the "right" conclusions. When he did not, his executioners wasted no time in placing two bullets in him. By the time the bloodshed was over, an estimated two hundred party leaders had been executed without trial. The Fuehrer had exercised the logic of total control.

So also did the dictator in our second example of maximizing violence, Joseph Stalin in the Soviet Union. Following the death of the Communist party leader Vladimir Lenin in 1924, Stalin assumed leadership jointly with two other party figures, Grigori Zinoviev and Lev Kamenev. Within a short time Stalin was able to expel from the party both of these potential rivals, along with a key figure in the Russian Revolution, Leon Trotsky. But expulsion was not enough. There would always be the possibility that any of these leaers, or others, might mount a revolt. So in 1934 when one of Stalin's closest aides, Sergei Kirov, was assassinated, Stalin blamed a "Trotskyist conspiracy." There followed a series of trials for treason in order to purge the party of conspirators. In these trials the accused—not only members of opposing factions but also Stalin's closest allies that for the slightest reasons had earned his distrust—were forced to confess to all kinds of crimes. Both Kamenev and Zinoviev were tried and executed. Trotsky, who had fled Russia, was axed to death in 1940 under mysterious circumstances. Before it ended, the party purge of the 1930s had touched all levels of Soviet society, instituted terror as the principal instrument of social control, made the secret police a feared arm of the party, and made spying, denunciation, concentration camps, and executions commonplace practices of governing. Stalin, like Hitler, paid little heed to Machiavelli's advice to princes: "Yet it certainly cannot be called *virtu* to murder his fellow citizens, betray his friends, to be devoid of truth, pity, or religion; a man may get power by means like these, but not glory."

Who Tells Whom What to Do?

The totalitarian mind would like to believe that the governing elite consists of people of high merit. The rule because they supposedly deserve to. In Nazi rhetoric this meant that rulers came from superior racial stock, the "Aryan" elite (tall, strong, white of skin, blue of eye, blond of hair) that had been sifted and tested through struggle. In Communist rhetoric, rulers emerge from a state of such perfect social mobility that rewards follow efforts, as contained in Karl Marx's phrase "to each according to his needs, from each according to his abilities."

In practice, however, the totalitarian elite consists of a relatively small inner party, governing in conjunction with a much larger outer party. Totalitarian regimes are one-party states; opposition political parties are not permittted. Only the party of the revolution—Nazi, Fascist, Communist, or whatever—is entitled to rule. All power is concentrated within the inner circle of that party. Ultimately, the most important concentration lies with the party leader.

The peculiar role of the political party and its leader constitutes one of the unique features of how power is organized in totalitarian princedoms. Typically, the political party in a totalitarian nation consists of a fairly small percentage of the total population. Of the overall number of party followers, there is a hard core of devoted members who are unquestioningly dedicated to the party's revolutionary aims and its leader. The party is organized as a hierarchy: units at one party level take orders from the next higher level which, in turn, takes orders from higher levels. As Hitler's "Night of the Long Knives" illustrates, insubordination can be dealt with harshly. The ruling party oligarchy and its dictator call the shots (literally). So important is the revolutionary party to totalitarian logic that the party is more powerful than are ordinary government organizations such as the legislature, courts, or bureaucracy. Just as Catherine the Great ruled through her royal court, Hitler and Stalin ruled through their revolutionary parties.

Typically, the dictatorial party is led by one person. This is what Hitler called the *Fuehrer Principle*. Even before Hitler, Lenin recognized the advantages of concentrating the party's power in a single leader, especially if Lenin were the leader. All dictators have taken the view, quite to the contrary of Machiavelli's, that "the governments of the people are better than those of princes," that republics suffer from indecisiveness and the inability to hold anyone responsible for decisions. Said Hitler: "We have to learn our lesson: one will must dominate us, we must form a single unity; one discipline must weld us together; one obedience, one subordination must fill us all, for above us stands the nation." Thus he defined his leadership principle; namely, the will of the dictator is the will of the people. The people rule because Big Brother rules.

And what of the people? What is their role? It is not to obey in passive ways, as in an autocracy. Nor is it to take part in making the decisions that affect them, as in a republic. The role of the people is to support, with great enthusiasm, the dictates of the leader. Either passive obedience or meddling in public affairs is suspect. It is a violation of the freedom provided by the party. Asserted Lenin, "It is true that liberty is precious—so precious that it must be rationed."

What Is the Community Like?

Socially, the totalitarian regime preaches equality. But it is a strange form of equality, one in which some are more equal than others. Put differently, only selected classes of people deserve to be treated as equals. In Hitler's Germany this meant those that he considered to be of the Aryan race. Jews he considered to be inferior, hence, unequal. To qualify for equal treatment in Stalinist Russia, you could not have been a businessman, a landowner, or private entrepreneur. Those were vestiges of the capitalist enemy that had to be destroyed. Only the workers, the proletariat, could expect equality. In short, only if your political function justified it—if your support for the regime was important—could you have a preferred place in the social scheme. If not, you could expect harsh and painful treatment.

Economic arrangements in totalitarian regimes differ according to the dictates of party ideology and the leader. Communist ideology and leadership calls for centrally directed, mobilized, and planned economic affairs. Private ownership of the means by which goods are produced and distributed is considered a capitalistic anachronism to be removed. Hitler's dictatorship took a different tack. Winning power as he did in 1933 during the midst of worldwide economic depression, Hitler faced the need to put people to work, stabilize the value of German money, and, most important, prepare to expand the empire, even if by war. Rapid industrialization was the order of the day. But that called for the support of private business, and German business leaders were suspicious of Hitler. So Hitler set out to court them. In confidential meetings with business tycoons, Hitler outlined an economic program much to their liking: he favored the elimination of labor unions, a program of public works and rearmament to be managed by businessmen, a private property, and the prevention of Communism at all costs. With a dictator at the helm of government, all these things could be accomplished. Business leaders came to believe Hitler could do such things, and after all, they told themselves, if he does have radical tendencies, we can still control him. In the end, however, in keeping with totalitarian logic, Hitler demanded and received total control of the economy, not business's control of himself. In his wooing of economic leaders, Hitler merely practiced a maxim that he believed true in all dealings: "An intelligent victor will, whenever possible, present his demands to the vanquished in installments."

What Is Politics Like?

Totalitarian politics is nasty, not nice. Whether the doctrine outlined in *The Communist Manifesto* by Karl Marx and Friedrich Engels, or the Nazi doctrine outlined in Hitler's *Mein Kampf,* totalitarian logic sorts the good guys from the bad and preaches that the bad must be destroyed. Both are like religions in their content and fervor. A totalitarian doctrine offers a theory of the world and how evil came into it, how that evil can be conquered and eliminated, a vision of paradise, and an accounting of historical forces beyond human control. There is no room in totalitarian doctrine for *virtu* or *necessita,* only *fortuna,* which sweeps all before it.

You need not know the intricacies of either the Communist or the Nazi doctrine. The essentials will show you the general picture (see Table 7.1). In the Communist vision, economic structures—the organization of such forces of production as land, labor, and capital—

Power, or the Clout of Politics

determine a multitude of things, including the kind of government, the society's class structure, religious beliefs, enjoyment and leisure pastimes, and the current thinking. In primitive times the ownership of labor (slavery) was the basis of the economic structure. Gradually however, slavery was challenged by feudalism, an arrangement based on peasants working the land, serving, and making payments to feudal lords. The emergence of the two economic structures, slavery and feudalism, led to a clash, out of which grew capitalism, a new economic structure based on ownership of capital (manufacturing, factories, and so on). But if capitalist businesspersons are to make profits, they must exploit their workers, pay them virtually nothing, make them work long hours, force them to buy high-priced goods, conscript them into armies to fight wars to expand capitalist markets, or whatever. The workers will become increasingly miserable. But for a while they do not realize how badly off they are: they are pacified and seduced by their religion, by the illusion that they have a role to play in their governments, because they vote in elections, and by popular entertainment. But soon their misery becomes so widespread and intense that capitalism sows the seeds of its own destruction. The workers rise up, for they have nothing to lose but their chains. Revolution breaks out, and a dictatorship of the proletariat is established. The wealth is redistributed, and the capitalists are weeded out. Communism becomes the economic structure. Ultimately, because everyone is happy, there is no more conflict. Government and politics, which had been used by the capitalists (the bourgeoisie) to keep workers in their places, is no longer necessary, and the state withers away. These are the essentials. Lenin added an important element by insisting that although the historical forces leading to Communism were beyond control, they could be pushed a bit. A tightly knit, highly devoted and disciplined political party must be the vanguard of the proletariat in advancing the revolution. This, he thought, had been done in Russia.

Nazi doctrine is less systematic but no less visionary. Hitler boiled it down to this: "Man has become great through struggle. Whatever goal man has reached is due to his originality plus his brutality. All life is bound up in three theses: Struggle is the father of all things, virtue lies in the blood, leadership is primary and decisive." Start with struggle. For Hitler the historical force beyond human control was force. "Only force rules," he said. "Force is the first law. Always before God and the world, the stronger has the right to carry through what he wills." And who is the stronger? Virtue lies in the blood. The basis of any strong society, Hitler argued, was the *Volk*, ("people") a blood-defined, racially defined, willed-by-God entity. Individual human beings come and go, but the *Volk* goes on forever. Only through membership in the *Volk* do individuals reach full flower. Only through the *Volk* do cultures prosper. "Everything we admire on this earth today," Hitler stressed, "is only the creative product of a few peoples and originally perhaps of one race." The key race is the Aryan, the superior German race: "If they perish, the beauty of this earth will sink into the grave with them." However, they

TABLE 7–1. Types of Government and Their Characteristics

	Autocratic	Republican	Totalitarian
Government seeks to bring order out of diversity by:	Authoritative enforcement of one of the diverse interests.	Letting diverse interests share in the government or the competitive choosing of the government.	Creating a completely new society such that conflict would no longer arise; by means of the guidance and enforcement of a revolutionary ideology that claims to be scientific, thus comprehensive and necessary, for both knowledge and allegiance.
Role of the inhabitants (i.e., the masses):	Passive obedience and social deference ("suffer the powers that be" and "the rich man at his castle, the poor man at his gate ....")	Voluntary and individual participation, hence partial and discriminating, never total, loyalty.	Mass participation and compulsory explicit enthusiasm (passive obedience is rejected as inadequate or suspect: "Who are those who are not the friends of the people but that they are the enemies of the people?")
The official doctrine:	Allegiance as a religious duty and government as part of the divine order.	Allegiance demanded and given on utilitarian and secular grounds.	Allegiance ideological and based on an all-encompassing conception of people as a product of impersonal forces, whether racial or economic. Inner reservations exposed and punished just as surely as open dissent.
Typical social structure:	A highly stratified castle or class structure.	A large middle class or bourgeoisie.	Egalitarian in aspiration; but in fact a social structure mainly determined by political function.
Position of the political elite:	Self-perpetuating and exclusive (almost always fortified by myths of descent from the gods or great people.)	A stable political class enjoying social prestige, though not exclusive. Subject to penetration by candidates from political and educational institutions designed to encourage mobility.	In theory a meritocracy based on perfect social mobility ("to each according to his needs, from each according to his abilities"). In practice a relatively small inner party with a relatively large outer party.

Typical economic organization:	Agrarian, preindustrial, usually aiming at self-sufficiency.	Market economy, capitalistic or mixed capitalist/government control.	Centrally directed and mobilized war economy or planned, centrally administered economy emphasizing rapid industrialization.
Attitude toward the law:	Law as customary and/or god given and sacred. Law as related to status: the lower the status the more arbitrary the outcome.	Law is produced from both custom and legislative statutes and applied generally; i.e., outcome not based on class, race, or status.	Laws of history or race—greater than people and interpreted and applied by party ideologists.
Attitudes toward diffusion of information:	Proclamations but no regular news: rumor and gossip as institutions exploited by both rulers and ruled, mainly oral communication.	Not all newspapers, periodicals under control of state. Effective operation of regime dependent on popular access to information and official access to accurate measures of opinion.	Mass communications controlled by state. Official encyclopedia preferred to books and novels. All art forms to be propaganda.
Attitudes toward politics:	Leaders either above politics or politics limited to secrecy of palace and court. Conflict and opposition tolerated as long as not public and as long as no appeals for support outside of the ruling class.	Politics always tolerated; politics equal to conciliation: opposition sometimes public and institutionalized.	Politics and opposition seen as subversive and not just personal intrigue or conspiracy, but a symptom of social contradictions yet to be eradicated. Politics a bourgeois sham.

Adapted with the author's permission from the larger scheme in Bernard Crick, *Basic Forms of Government: A Sketch and A Model*, New York: Macmillan, 1973.

will not perish if they use force in the struggle with inferior enemies, namely, the Jews. Once the Jews, who devised instruments "to subdue Aryan peoples to his rule" are vanquished, there will be paradise (just as in the Communist vision, paradise will arrive once the bourgeoisie are abolished). Finally, leadership is primary and decisive. This is the Fuehrer Principle. Through the Fuehrer's force, the *Volk* can rule for "a thousand years."

Reviewing these two doctrines gives you a clue to the totalitarian attitude toward law. Laws are not human products. They are laws of history, economic laws in the case of Communist doctrine and racial laws in the case of Nazi ideology. The dictator and the ruling elite discover those laws, interpret them, and enforce them. Laws are applied through a monopoly of force, every manner and means of armed combat, violence, and terror available, and against all enemies inside and outside the nation.

Totalitarian logic also dictates the attitude toward communication. All means of effective mass communication are under the control of, and thereby at the disposal of, the ruling elite. Newspapers, newsmagazines, radio, television, rallies, mass demonstrations, textbooks, art, music, film serve the regime's propaganda purposes. Thus a monopoly over all means of persuasion joins the monopoly over all means of coercion. This combination creates precisely the conditions for terror so well depicted in *Nineteen Eighty-four*.

Finally, what does the totalitarian mind think of politics? Politics is subversive, the tool of the bourgeoisie to subdue the worker or the tool of the Jew to subdue the Aryan. Political activity is, by definition, subversive; hence it must be removed with antisubversive measures. That translates into the use of a secret police to spy on everybody, friend and foe alike, to apprehend and execute those guilty of thoughtcrime. British political scientist Bernard Crick has written that "the person who wishes not to be troubled by politics and to be left alone finds himself the unwitting ally of those to whom politics is a troublesome obstacle to their well meant intentions to leave nothing alone." The totalitarian view of politics is that political activity is an obstacle that must be removed so that total power will not be disturbed in its desire to leave nothing alone.

COMPARING POLITICS

You cannot escape the exercise of power. Either you exercise it on others, share in its exercise, or it is exercised on you. Like governing regimes, you can organize power in different ways. Table 7.1 reviews the essentials of organizing power. In your daily relationships with other people, which do you choose? It is not an idle question, for you can be autocratic, republican, or totalitarian. As an autocrat you can try to impose your will on your associates with threat and guile, rumor and gossip, appeals to their loyalties ("If you really loved me, you would . . ."), and other tactics. As a republican, you might work closely with others in a free and open exchange of ideas, willingly settling for half rather than a whole loaf. Or you can be totalitarian. Kick people out of your group if they don't accept your dictates, betray your friends, force everybody to do your bidding, and like it! Any of the three approaches to power, whether exercised by governments or in everyday life, has its risks and rewards. What is your choice, Catherine the Great, Charles de Gaulle, or Adolf Hitler? "Dictators ride to and fro upon tigers which they dare not dismount," wrote Winston Churchill in 1936 in a prophetic book entitled *While England Slept,* "And the tigers are getting hungry." You might want to ponder that thought as you make your choice.

"You must love Big Brother. It is not enough to obey him; you must love him."
—*O'Brien in Orwell's Nineteen Eighty-four*

"History proves that dictatorships do not grow out of strong and successful governments, but out of weak and helpless ones."
—*Franklin D. Roosevelt*

"The one means that wins the easiest victory over reason: terror and force."
—*Hitler*

"Yet it certainly cannot be called *virtu* to murder his fellow citizens, betray his enemies, to be devoid of truth, pity, or religion; a man may get power by means like these, but not glory."
—*Machiavelli*

"It is true that liberty is precious—so precious that it must be rationed."
—*Lenin*

"Dictators ride to and fro upon tigers which they dare not dismount. And the tigers are getting hungry."
—*Churchill*

Totalitarian Power   **99**

Part

III

Princely Palaces Where Power Resides

Chapter

Palaces of Power: What Are They? What's There?

The summer of 1787 in Philadelphia was long, hot, and humid. The amenities of today did not exist. No air-conditioned meeting halls. No swimming pools. Not even running water, electric lights, or indoor toilets. But no one knew about those things then and so Philadelphia, being centrally located, was about as good a place as any in this outhouse society to gather to reform the Articles of Confederation. Still, by the second Monday in May when the convention was scheduled to begin, only a handful of delegates had arrived. They met day after day, waiting for a sufficient number to begin. Finally, by May 25 enough delegates were on hand to commence, but it was not until late June that delegates from as many as eleven states reached Philadelphia. Others wandered in for another two months. Actually, only fifty-five delegates met regularly, and only a dozen of those did the work. The Constitutional Convention was scarcely a popular assembly.

One delegate, James Madison, arrived with a plan. Some called it the "Virginia Plan," as it reflected the thinking of that state's delegation, and others named it the "Randolph Plan" after Edmund Randolph, its assumed author. Whatever its lineage, it envisioned the form of government that Madison favored. It called for a forceful national government with powers far greater than those contained in the Articles of Confederation. This government could act in areas in which the separate states were thought incompetent or in areas in which individual state action would disrupt national harmony; it could negate laws contrary to national intent, and it could take action, force if necessary, against recalcitrant states. And where was all this national power to be lodged? Primarily, it would reside in a legislative body consisting of two chambers, one to be elected by the people of the various states in proportion to each state's population and the second to be chosen by the first from nominations submitted by state legislatures. There would also be an executive elected by the legislature, a judiciary chosen by the legislature, and a "Council of Revision" consisting of the executive and members of the judiciary that could review and veto acts of the national or state legislatures.

The Virginia Plan first called for the concentration of powers in a central, national government. Second, those powers would eventually be centered even more in the popularly elected chamber of the legislature. There had never been anything so grandiose in scope proposed before, nor would there be again until France concentrated so much power in the National Assembly following the revolution still years in the future. Although the noted English legislator Edmund Burke, who had supported the American cause before the revolution and would oppose the French Revolution, had written in 1771 that "the greater the powers, the more dangerous the abuse," the advocates of the Virginia Plan proceeded undaunted. Nothing less than a national legislative body with power to define the extent of its own authority and that of the states would be satisfactory.

The delegates debated the plan for three weeks. Its opponents then offered an alternative. This scheme, the New Jersey Plan, also contained a legislative body. It, however, would have only one chamber and would represent each state equally. There would be an executive elected by the legislative body, and members of the executive could be removed from office by the legislative body or by a majority of the states. There would be a tribunal, with specified duties, appointed by the executive. But the two key provisions of the plan were (1) that the national government would have only the powers specified, which meant adding the power to tax and to regulate commerce to the powers specified by the Articles of Confederation; and (2) that all laws or treaties made by the national government would be binding on each state.

The delegates came to the nub of the matter: where would power lie in this new government? There were two more weeks of acrimonious debate. Finally, the delegates passed on the issue to an eleven-member committee to reach a compromise. It did: there would be a legislative body of two chambers, the lower chamber with one member for every forty thousand inhabitants and the upper with equal membership from each state (but votes in the upper chamber would be by individuals, not state delegations), and all bills to raise and spend money could originate only in the lower chamber. With that obstacle out of the way, the delegates bargained their way through other disputes, including slavery, the nature of the national executive, the national judiciary, and other thorny and not-so-thorny issues.

But what about the key question, that is, where was power to reside, at the national or state level and, if national, then where? In fact, the delegates did not reach a final decision, only a tentative one. They specified powers clearly intended as national, powers enumerated as those of the national legislature, namely, Congress. By implication it left powers not so named to the states. But it has taken almost two centuries of interpreting the provisions of the Constitution to work out a rough answer to the question of where power lies, and there is yet no definitive answer even today.

James Madison, who had foreseen a strong national government whose powers would supersede the states' authority, in short, compro-

JAMES MADISON: PALACE FOUNDER

"Between those tremendous mountain peaks of power, Hamilton and Jefferson, standing over against each other, Madison was the valley." This not very flattering assessment of the man that many civics textbooks call the "Father of the Constitution" was written by a U.S. senator, Albert J. Beveridge. The senator meant to suggest that Madison's role in the founding of the American republic was secondary and that Madison did little more than obey the dictates of his ally Thomas Jefferson in Jefferson's struggles with the leader of the Federalist party, Alexander Hamilton. But Beveridge's analogy is misleading. Madison was more of a Mount Rainier in his own right than a gap between the Grand Tetons.

James Madison (1751–1836) was of the Virginia gentry but received a "northern" education at Princeton University. He became involved in politcs early and by 1776 was a member of the Virginia House of Delegates. There he became acquainted with Thomas Jefferson, with whom he worked closely for the next half-century. After the American Revolution, Madison served in the Continental Congress and was a key figure in the movement to call a convention to revise the Articles of Confederation. The revision produced the Constitution of the United States, a document whose character was in large measure influenced by the thinking, oratory, bargaining, and persuasion of Madison. As joint author of the *Federalist Papers* (with Alexander Hamilton and John Jay), Madison mounted a forceful defense of the Constitution that was influential in its ratification.

With ratification of the Constitution, Madison became a member of the first U.S. Congress. There he pressed for passage of the first ten amendments to the Constitution, the Bill of Rights. With Jefferson he founded the Democratic-Republican party (later called the "Republicans," but actually the forerunner of today's Democratic party). Madison prepared the Virginia resolutions attacking the Federalists' Alien and Sedition acts (see Chapter 4). When Jefferson was elected president in 1800, Madison served as secretary of state (1801–1809) and then was Jefferson's successor as president, 1809–1817.

Such a career certainly suggests that Madison was more than a "valley." But was he indeed a valley compared with the two "peaks of power," Hamilton and Jefferson? Consider their records. Before the ratification of the Constitution, Madison and Hamilton shared the limelight as the two principal advocates of the document. They were not valley and peak, but equal protagonists on behalf of ratification. The other alleged power peak, Jefferson, was not even part of the debate; instead he was in France as America's ambassador. After ratification, however, Madison and Hamilton split. In 1790, four weeks before Jefferson returned to the United States, Madison launched an attack in Congress on Hamilton's financial plan for the new nation. Federalists began calling their opposition the "Madisonians," a name that was to stick until well after the Republican party appeared. Madison, not Jefferson, instigated the struggle that has become in American political folklore the Hamiltonians versus the Jeffersonians.

Madison also instigated the proposal to move the national capital to the South (to what is now Washington, D.C.) in exchange for support for Hamilton's desire to have the federal government take over all state debts. It was Madison who proposed, before the Constitution was even dreamed of, that the Continental Congress stabilize the economic situation by assuming the debts that the states had run up during the revolution. That idea, proposed in

1783, was to become a major plank in the Hamiltonian program in 1790. It was also Madison who proposed, again in 1783, that the national capital be moved to the Potomac River. That idea was to become a major goal of Jefferson in 1790. The two "peaks of power" made a bargain so that each got what he wanted, but both basic policies originated with the "valley," not the "peaks.".

A year later, 1791, it was Madison who sparked yet another great Hamilton-Jefferson controversy, over Hamilton's proposal for the federal government to create a national bank. Two weeks before Jefferson, as a member of Washington's cabinet, opposed the bank plan, Madison spoke against the plan in Congress. Again it is hard to sort the peaks and the valleys of power.

After Jefferson's election as president, Madison remained the forceful initiator of policy. As secretary of state, Madison recognized that Napoleon's army in Santo Domingo was having trouble putting down a rebellion there. He urged that the United States continue trading with the rebels rather than side with the French. Jefferson accepted Madison's analysis, and the rebels were victorious. Shortly thereafter, Napoleon decided to renounce his territorial claims in the area, including the Louisiana territory. Madison's decision regarding Santo Domingo paved the way toward the Louisiana Purchase.

Finally, as president, Madison recognized that times and circumstances had changed. As a princely practitioner of political logic, he understood that Republican policies, designed for an earlier generation, had to be adapted to meet changed times and circumstances. Almost as if following a Machiavellian precept ("You should never let things get out of hand to avoid war. You don't avoid such a war, you merely postpone it, to your own disadvantage."), Madison ignored the Republican policy of peace to lead the nation to war in 1812. Then the Republicans who had earlier reduced the national debt saw it increase to the largest in the nation's history. Moreover, Madison—who had led the fight against the first national bank on grounds that the bank was unconstitutional—signed the bill for a second bank passed by a Republican Congress. Madison and the Republicans had opposed tariffs but approved a protective tariff in 1816. Finally, Madison had previously argued that public monies could be spent only on matters specified by the Constitution, but he proposed federal funds for building roads and canals. In these efforts Madison had the support of Jefferson.

In the end, Madison was the equal ally of Jefferson for the opening sixteen years of America's nineteenth century, just as he had been Hamilton's equal in the fight for a new constitution. He made compromises throughout his political career in order to govern and, more importantly, to guarantee what he deemed a proper division of powers between state and nation, between nation and world, and among the various political institutions of the republic: presidency, Congress, courts, administration, and parties. Thus did he found and strive to balance the palaces of power.

---

mised his original plan. Not only did he do so with respect to the division of powers between national and state governments, he also did so with respect to limits imposed on the national legislature. If these compromises troubled him, he did not say so in public during the struggle for the ratification of the new constitution. In fact, he drafted a ringing defense of the Constitution and, in the *Federalist Papers*, implied that a government of limited, specified powers shared by the separate legal palaces of Congress, president, and courts was precisely what the delegates traveling to Philadelphia had sought in the first place. In a sense, he was correct. Although not achieving the whole loaf (the Virginia Plan), Madison had worked out an acceptable solution to a problem that he, as princely politician and political thinker, defined in ways similar to Niccolo Machiavelli's. In the remainder of this chapter, you can sharpen your princely skills by considering that problem, how Machiavelli and Madison, respectively, proposed to solve it, and thereby learn where the palaces of power are in politics.

WHAT'S THE PROBLEM?

You have learned enough about Machiavelli's political thinking to understand that for him nothing could be taken for granted. Indeed, the things that you take for granted in your daily life—daily routines, fairly predictable relationships with the people you know, expectations that you will get through another day even with some difficulty—are not givens at all. You must work to obtain comfortable routines, stability, and predictability in your life. Why? Because everything changes and if you fail to adjust to those changes, they will disrupt and even destroy your daily routine.

Politics, too, is constantly changing. It occurs in a world of flux, in which chance (*fortuna*) often renders even the best efforts meaningless. As Walter Lippmann (recall Chapter 3) wrote in his book *Preface to Morals,* "Whirl is King, having driven out Zeus." In short, chaos, not order, reigns. Said Machiavelli: "But as all human beings are kept in a perpetual movement, and can never remain stable, states naturally either rise or decline, and necessity compels them to many acts to which reason will not influence them. . . ."

James Madison also worried about change and how to cope with it. For Machiavelli the element of chance made change a threat to stability. For Madison is was human self-interest. He did not say that people were worthless; instead, he believed that they were motivated by selfish ambition, that they put their self-interests above those of other people and of society as a whole, and that they formed "factions" (people "united and actuated by some common impulse or passion"). These factions claw and tear at one another, creating chaos, confusion, and instability.

Machiavelli and Madison thus defined the same problem: in a world of constant change and continuing flux in which chance and selfishness breed fickleness, how is stable politics possible? You will quickly recognize that this problem is closely related to a question that any form of government must answer, namely, the question posed in Part II, How is society possible? If politics makes society possible in a universe of disorder, how then does one establish a stable and enduring political regime that will preserve social order?

WHAT'S THE ANSWER?

For both Machiavelli and Madison the solution to the problem of how to have a stable and enduring politics lay in large measure in deciding who was to have power and who was not. This is always an important question in politics, whether it be the politics of a nation or the politics of everyday life. Certainly, if you want to be princely in your conduct, you must have power; you must be able to direct and influence the decisions that will affect you. You create a stable politics in your everyday life when you know your power and its limits and adjust to changing times and circumstances. You can go only so far in demanding things of other people, though sometimes that may be quite far. But going too far, not knowing who has power and who does not, can prove costly.

From your reading of Part II you know tht different forms of government have different general answers to the question of where power should lie. Take first the autocrat. In Chapter 13 we shall outline the power struggle between two princely figures of sixteenth-century England: Queen Elizabeth I of Great Britain and Mary Queen of Scots. For now it is sufficient to know that when the air had cleared and both Elizabeth and Mary had died, James I became king of England in 1603. James's autocratic rule was turbulent, and his inconsistent religious policies antagonized protestants and Catholics alike. He spent funds lavishly and wastefully, and he surrounded himself with incompetent advisers. His opponents attacked him in the House of Commons, the lower chamber of the English Parliament. James would tolerate no such insubordination and simply dismissed Parliament and ruled without it from 1611 to 1621. When Parliament convened again, King James announced, "I will govern according to the common weal, but not according to the common will."

James's comment typifies the autocratic answer to the question that Machiavelli and Madison faced. For the autocrat, a stable politics is a personal politics. The autocrat's duty is to know the "common weal," what is good for the whole community. But this responsibility does not include worrying about the "common will," what subjects themselves think is good for them. You can readily see the problem here. Even if the autocrat is enlightened and truly does rule according to the common weal and successfully adjusts to changing fortune, ambitions, times, and circumstances, what will happen after he or she is dead? What guarantee is there that the successor will be princely enough to do the same?

Totalitarian regimes are not necessarily superior in this respect. Consider Benito Mussolini, dictator of Italy, who came to power in 1922 and ruled for two decades. Although he founded a political party, the Fascist party, to stabilize his position and his regime, his rule was as personal as that of any autocrat. "My program is simple," he said, "I want to govern." When he fell from power in 1943, so did his regime. Adolf Hitler's Thousand-Year Reich experienced the same fate. Admittedly, both Mussolini and Hitler were conquered in war. What about victorious totalitarian regimes? On the surface, such totalitarian politics is more stable. At least, for example, neither the regime of the Soviet Union or that of the People's Republic of China has collapsed with changes in leadership. Yet, in each case after the death of a stabilizing dictator (for example, Lenin or Stalin in the Soviet Union or Mao Tsetung in China), the ensuing purges and leadership struggles are evidence of Machiavelli's assertion that "necessity compels them to acts to which reason will not influence them. . . ."

Your grasp of republican logic will suggest a general answer to where power should reside in those regimes. Thomas Jefferson put it in sweeping terms: "I know of no safe depository of the ultimate powers of the society but the people themselves." The key here is "ultimate." Jefferson did not argue that power should be concentrated *in* the people but, rather, distributed *among* them, for "it is not the consolidation, or concentration of powers, but by their distribution that good government is effected." It is in precisely this idea of the distribution of powers that Machiavelli, three centuries before Jefferson and Madison, found similar answers to this basic problem of governing.

From everything you have discovered thus far about Machiavelli's thinking, you know that he believed in strong political leadership, princely leadership. When there was chaos, Machiavelli would turn first to a prince whose *virtu* would guide princely behavior in doing the *necessita* in the face of *fortuna*. A prince would find order under conditions of change and chaos. But like the personal politics of the autocrat or dictator, the personal *virtu* of the prince was only a short-term solution to the problem of making politics stable. Once the prince was dead, the conditions of disorder that called him or her into being would return. Successors would fight for power and divide the nation, and whirl would be king once more.

Therefore, a prince must establish the political regime in such a way that it will outlive him or her. In sum, there must be permanent arrangements that will permit later generations to adapt to changing times and circumstances, that will improve people's odds in their constant encounters with chance. What would be these arrangements, these political institutions?

As always, Machiavelli turned to history for the answer. He noted that there had been some regimes in which only the prince had power but which had not outlasted the prince. There was others in which the prince held power in collaboration with the aristocracy, or the nobility, of which the prince was a part. These too did not endure. A third possibility was a princedom in which the prince acquired power by popular approval and ruled in accordance with the common will (as James denied he would do). These also were short-lived. Obviously, these three alternative approximate the autocratic, totalitarian, and republican forms.

There is, however, a fourth possibility, which Machiavelli approved. He described it thus: "When there is combined under the same constitution a prince, a nobility, and the power of the people, then these three powers will watch and keep each other reciprocally in check." What he envisioned were three residencies, three palaces, of power. Each would be separate from the others. Each would share political power and would exercise that power, at least in part, so as to check the abuse of power by either or both of the other two. For Machiavelli was certainly realistic enough to grasp, as Madison later did, that if left alone and to their own devices, princes, nobility, or masses would surely abuse power. He would have accepted Madison's observation that "the truth is that all men having power ought to be distrusted." Thus people with power must be restrained in a mixed regime whose power is distributed among all classes of people.

Compare now the solution of James Madison. He too understood the principle that power must check power. In a passage from the *Federalist Papers,* Madison wrote: "Ambition must be made to counteract ambition. The interest of the man must be connected with the constitutional rights of the place. It may be a reflection on human nature, that such devices should be necessary to control the abuses of government. But what is government itself, but the greatest of all reflections on human nature? If men were angels no government would be necessary." It could be Machiavelli writing. How then would Madison represent all social classes in governing, thus distributing power among them so that they could check one another? He urged two means, and both, he thought, had been written into the Constitution of the United States.

First, Madison argued, there must be an "extended republic." One of the reasons that republics have failed is that they have been too small. Being small, it has been relatively simple for a faction to recruit support among people of similar self-interests, become a majority, gain control through popular elections, and then abuse that power by governing at the expense of other, minority factions. If a republic were larger, there would be more territorial space and more people. The greater the territory and the population are, the greater the differences will be among the people—in their opinions, values, religion, loyalties to politicians seeking power, and in the most "common and durable source of factions," that is, "the various and unequal distribution of property." So much diversity would reduce the likelihood of any single faction sharing sufficient interests with others so as to form a majority and gain power. Ambition would check ambition in an extended republic.

The second means for distributing power consists of political institutions, the palaces in which the power rests. Machiavelli thought of these as being the prince, the nobility, and the popular assemblies. Madison looked to the new Constitution and found these palaces to be the two-chambered Congress, the national executive, and the courts. Each was separate from the other. Take, for example, the selection of Congress, president, and judges: one house of Congress was to be popularly elected, the other chosen by the states; the president was to be elected by electors representing the states; and judges were to be appointed by the president with the advice and consent of the second legislative body. Each institution had constitutional powers allotted to it. These powers would overlap sufficiently so that the separate institutions could check and balance one another's actions. For a single faction to control all power, it would require capturing each palace, an unlikely event. And if that were not check enough, in the federal arrangement there were always the states with their separate domains. They too would exercise restraining powers over the national government, just as the latter would exercise restraints on the states.

The Madisonian scheme is obviously more detailed and formalized than the Machiavellian one. Yet the solution to stabilizing politics is the same: distribute power broadly and then check power with power. Pit power against power, palace against palace. Try to check the unfavorable odds of *fortuna* by reshuffling the deck.

But defensive backs on football teams do not always keep pass receivers from scoring touchdowns. Pitchers do not always keep batters off base. Hockey players do not always check their opponents. And soccer defenders do not always mark the offense. In short, establishing a plan is not the same as executing it well. Power balancing is not automatic. Mechanisms are devised and set in motion, but making them work is a matter of skill, and here the prince returns. But it is no longer the prince who had to bring order out of chaos, create appropriate governing forms, and then die knowing that there would no longer be a need for princely conduct. Rather, once stable institutions exist, there must be succeeding generations of princes to make them work.

No sooner had the new government authorized by the Constitution of the United States met than James Madison realized that its institutions must change with the times. As leader of a faction in Congress opposed to the financial plans of the Washington administration, Madison knew that he could not carry the day by simply letting the checks and balances work their will. He looked around and found that *fortuna* had already intervened. What he had thought was unlikely when he had contributed to the *Federalist Papers* had not only become likely, it had happened. A single faction, the Federalist party, had taken control of the palaces of power—Congress, the Washington presidency, the federal courts. Madison's response was to seek to do the same, to organize a majority faction to win the palaces of power. He began by forging an anti-Federalist coalition in Congress. He and Thomas Jefferson undertook a "botanical expedition" to study the flora and fauna of the midwestern and New England states; actually the trip was a political foray to attract local and state leaders to the opposition. In 1796 the two allies corresponded with state leaders in an effort to win the presidential election. (Federalist John Adams won, and Jefferson became vice-president). By 1800, the state legislatures and governors, the presidency, and Congress had become Republican. Only the federal judiciary eluded them, and as you may recall from Chapter 4, the Republican attack on the courts failed.

In mounting the Republican opposition to Federalist control, Madison did not turn his back on the principles or arguments he had used to

Princely Palaces Where Power Resides

advocate ratification of the Constitution. Rather, he recognized the consequences of the new government once it started operating. He understood that those consequences could be changed without violating the constitutional forms arrived at through the bargaining in the long summer of 1787. In that respect he played by the rules he had advocated in pursuit of the values he believed in; what he reassessed, in a Machiavellian way, was political *necessita* in the face of shifting *fortuna*.

THE MOST STATELY OF PALACES

If your aspiration is to be a prince, maybe even *the* prince, you now know what you're after: power. You know what it is and what it can do for you. You know how power is organized in autocracies, republics, and totalitarian dictatorships (whether those be within nations or in everyday politics). And you know how two princely political thinkers, Machiavelli and Madison, proposed to stabilize power. Now you need to know where to go to find power, what we have called the palaces of power. It is a good idea to study these institutions so that you will know what they are and what they contain. If you strip away the mystery of these august residencies of power, you will see that, more often than not, very ordinary people find their way to them. Like the Wizard of Oz, many are good (or bad) natured charlatans rather than princes. But remember that if you want to travel to such realms, you must take the initiative; nobody is going to invite you to the top. There is too little room in the most stately of power mansions, and so you must study them, demystify them, and learn their nooks and crannies. Then you will not only find your way there, but you may also excel.

There are many palaces of power in virtually any political regime. For the present, however, it is a good idea to confine your study to four: *Executives.* The executive establishments are known by the various titles given to the officials who occupy their palaces: kings and queens, presidents, prime ministers, premiers, fuehrers, chancellors, and the like. Such people are, first, the ceremonial heads of their government, and as such they embody the ideals and rituals of the nation. They do this in many ways, for example, by holding lavish dinners for other visiting heads of state or ambassadors, making tours of other nations and ceremonial public appearances, parading through the nation, and even throwing out the first ball at the World Series or presenting a trophy to the winners of international competitions. Second, these officials are the heads of government (although in some regimes the person who is the head of state, for example, the queen of England, is not the head of government as well—the prime minister in British politics). Heads of government are responsible for political leadership, proposing what to do, directing and influencing others to do it, drumming up support, fighting off the opposition, and carrying the day. In short, heads of government exercise considerable political power.

Legislatures. Legislative palaces too have several names: Parliament in Great Britain, Congress in the United States, the National Assembly in France, the Supreme Soviet in the Soviet Union, the Diet in Japan, the Knesset in Israel, and many others. They consist of assemblies of officials convened on a regular basis to make political decisions. What kinds of decisions they make and how they decide vary from one government to another. In some nations, for instance, the United States or Great Britain, the legislature has considerable discretion to propose, deliberate, debate, change, and pass laws. In others they merely do as told by the head of government, a condition more common in the Soviet Union. Some legislatures are popularly chosen to represent diverse, competing interests, and others are handpicked by the reigning autocrat or dictator. One other point of not: legislative palaces generally have two houses; that is, they are bicameral. Thus Congress consists of the House of Representatives and the Senate, the parliament of the Federal Republic of Germany has the Bundestag and Bundesrat, the Diet in Japan contains the House of Representatives and the House of Councilors. The reasons for this are to represent different interests in each house, to divide powers and duties, or simply to conform to historical tradition. But not all legislatures are bicameral. Nebraska's state legislature, for example, is unicameral, having but one house.

Bureaucracies. A bureaucracy consists of many governmental offices dealing with various specialized areas. These palaces exists to get things done, to apply the policies made by executives, legislatures, and courts to both general and specific situations. A vast portion of your everyday life feels the impact of bureaucracy: the quality of the food you eat, the water you drink, and the air you breathe must meet bureaucratic standards. How policies are applied is, of course, a matter of discretion. No two cases are exactly alike, and so in wielding bureaucratic power the official makes choices and, in so doing, makes policies. Your friend zooms through a radar trap at sixty-five miles per hour, and the police pay little attention; you drive fifty-seven and get pulled over.

Courts. Judges, the residents of judicial palaces, interpret and apply the rules and laws of a political regime to specific cases. This too involves discretion, and hence, the courts, no less than the executives, legislatures, and bureaucracies, make policies. For example, a major city in the southeastern part of the United States has a public drunkenness ordinance; namely, any person appearing in public in an inebriated state can be arrested, tried, and punished by fine and imprisonment if found guilty. The city also contains a major university, and so there is no lack of such arrests. But judges in the city's courts regard the law as so vague that they regularly dismiss the cases brought before them. Thus, what is the law, the ordinance passed by the city's legislative body or the actions of the judges? The same question can be posed with respect to national courts and laws. In fact, presidential acts, bureaucratic decisions, and congressional legislation cannot become law if the U.S. Supreme Court decides that they violate the Constitution. The same holds for legislation in France; that is, the Constitutional Council can question the legality of laws.

These are the palaces of power, the establishments of power, and they are powerful institutions. They can be used by princes to direct and influence people to do what they would not otherwise, and they are the ends of power, for they can exploit their power to preserve their own existence and survival. Before you enter and start roaming the halls of each of these palaces in the four chapters to follow, there are still a couple of general points you need to consider regarding how these palaces connect with one another in various political regimes.

First, some nations divide themselves into subunits, for example, provinces as in Canada, *lander* as in the Federal Republic of Germany, or states as in the United States. Each of the four political institutions— executive, legislative, bureaucratic, and judicial—exists in the national government and each of the subunits. *Federated* nations divide their power among the national government and the various subunits. In short, national palaces of power are supreme in designated areas of national politics, and each subunit's palaces govern matters in its jurisdiction. In *confederal* nations the palaces of power of the subunits are so powerful, as compared with national political institutions, that the subunits are almost independent of national direction and influence, or at lest must approve national decisions before they can take effect. Finally, in *unitary* nations, the governing subunits (cities, towns, counties, shires, and so forth) are extensions of the national government and derive their power from the central government. Examples of these distinctions are not hard to find: you will recognize the United States as having a federal government, Switzerland as having a confederal arrangement, and France as being a unitary nation.

Second, how executives and legislatures relate to one another is important. A key distinction applies to republican regimes. When the national executive, as head of the government, is independent from the legislature, thus conforming to Madison's principle of separation of political institutions, political scientists speak of presidential government. Thus the president of the United States or of the Fifth French Republic has independent constitutional authority and is elected separately from the members of Congress or the National Assembly. But when the head of government is a member of the legislature, is selected by the legislature, and must have the confidence of the legislature to remain in office, this is parliamentary government. Canada, Great Britain, Japan and the Federal Republic of Germany are examples.

POWER, POWER, WHO HAS THE POWER?

The powers distributed by constitutions, laws, and decrees to executive, legislative, bureaucratic, and judicial palaces are not necessarily the same as those that the institutions actually wield. Their effective power (how powerful governing officials actually are) may be greater or less than their formal power (how powerful they are supposed to be). As a student of princedom, be aware of that fact. Don't go looking for power where it does not exist, finding it where it isn't, or overlooking it where it is. Such mistakes have led to the failure of many an aspiring prince. The next four chapters will help you keep alert to that point.

Finally, it is worth remembering that there is nothing permanent about the distribution of power. It may reside in one place today but shift elsewhere tomorrow. Just when you think you are able to make people do your bidding, you will find that you cannot. Even the most autocratic or dictatorial of rulers is as much a victim of changing power alignments as is the dedicated republican. Reflect on what John Knox said to Mary Queen of Scots. Knox founded Scottish Presbyterianism in the sixteenth century, in the face of fierce opposition from his queen. In a book he wrote about the struggle, he recalled this brief conversation:

Queen Mary: Think ye that subjects, having the power, may resist their princes?
John Knox: If their princes exceed their bounds, Madam, no doubt they may be resisted, even by power.

A thought worth remembering as you prowl the palaces of power: no matter how powerful the prince, there is yet power to resist power. Uneasy indeed lies the head that wears the crown.

"The greater the powers, the more dangerous the abuse."
—*Edmund Burke*

"I will govern according to the common weal, but not according to the common will."
—*James I*

"My program is simple: I want to govern."
—*Mussolini*

"It is not the consolidation, or concentration of powers, but by their distribution that good government is effected."
—*Jefferson*

"When there is combined under the same constitution a prince, a nobility, and the power of the people, then these three powers will watch and keep each other reciprocally in check."
—*Machiavelli*

"The truth is that all men having power ought to be distrusted."

"But what is government itself, but the greatest of all reflections on human nature? If men were angels no government would be necessary."
—*Madison*

Chapter

What Happens in Kingly Castles and Presidential Mansions?

L'Etat, c'est moi. "I am the state," said Louis XIV, the king who brought France to an absolute monarchy for more than seven decades, from 1643 to 1715. It was a time of lavish regal living, pomp and ceremony, and concentrated political power in the hands of a stylish autocrat. It was court politics at its zenith. But regal attitudes are not the possession solely of kings. Within a century France had not a king but a dictator, Napoleon Bonaparte. And, said Napoleon, "I am the state—I alone am here representative of the people." Then, little more than another century passed, and France had a new hero, this time a republican ruler, Charles de Gaulle. He was no less regal in his claims. *Je suis la France,* he liked to say when in power, "I am France." And even leaving power the courtly claim remains, *J'étais la France,* that is, "I was France."

Perhaps, you say, this tendency to talk about executive power as royal power—whether autocratic monarchs, totalitarian dictators, or republican chiefs of state—is a French trait. For example, you surely would not expect to find such regal views of executive power voiced by political leaders in the United States. After all, the Founding Fathers passionately distrusted royal power. Thomas Paine wrote in *The Rights of Man,* "Monarchy would not have continued so many ages in the world had it not been for the abuses it protects. It is the master fraud which shelters all others." The framers of the Constitution took great pains to avoid any taint of kingly government. In the only public release that came from the Constitutional Convention, they said, "Tho' we cannot, affirmatively, tell you what we are doing; we can, negatively, tell you what we are not doing—we never once thought of a king." In fact, there had been some thought of a king, by Alexander Hamilton who was alone in favoring the idea and by Benjamin Franklin who thought that presidents should serve without compensation to guarantee that they would not entertain any monarchial ideas. There was also a brief debate over what to call the president. The designation of "His Excellency" won out but was never incorporated into the Constitution.

So the framers of the Constitution gave little consideration to a king. But consider this kingly tale related by Joseph Califano, a close adviser to President Lyndon Johnson, in his book entitled *A Presidential Nation*. Califano reported that Johnson was returning from a long trip, preparing to board a helicopter that would take him from the air base to the White House. A U.S. Marine staff sergeant saw the president heading toward the wrong aircraft. "Your helicopter is the next one, Mr. President," said the young noncom, trying to be helpful. Said Johnson with regal pique, "They're all mine, son."

Regardless of whether they are hereditary monarchs, military dictators, high chieftains of a political party, elected presidents, or prime ministers of governing parliamentary bodies, contemporary executives—very much in style and often in substance—are similar to the reigning rulers of earlier centuries. Executive power *is* courtly power, and executive politics is the politics of the court. So that you can address the royal workings of executive life and perhaps learn a few lessons on how you might live it, let us turn to the relation of princes to their courts.

THE POLITICS OF THE COURT

You will recall from Chapter 5 that as kingly power developed, the interests of the monarch did not always coincide with those of the local nobles, church officials, and commercial class of burghers, whose support the king required, and so the autocrats convened assemblies of these groups to explain policies and issue decrees. Gradually such assemblies, or parliaments, evolved into separate palatial institutions of power, separate from the monarch and his or her ruling clique and from the royal jurists who tried infractions of laws and made decrees. This evolution was the source of the separation of governing powers into executive, legislative, bureaucratic, and judicial authority.

By the eighteenth century, three types of relationships had developed, or were developing, between executive princes and other institutions. You are already familiar with these three, from earlier discussions, as well as with a fourth (the dictatorial) that reached its zenith in this century. First, there was the hereditary monarch who as head of state and government ruled with the advice of his personal councilors and parliament. Second, there was the hereditary monarch who served as head of state but who shared powers as head of government with a minister (prime minister or premier) able to command majority support among the members of parliament. Finally, there emerged in some nations (notably the United States) an elected head of state and of government, that is, presidential government.

There are, of course, important differences among the monarchial, parliamentary, presidential, and dictatorial exercise of executive power. But there are at least two similarities that distinguish executive power *as* power from the varied ways that power is exercised. One is court politics, and the other is what executives try to do.

The Trappings of Court Life

The politics of the court consists of what goes on between and among an executive prince (monarch, prime minister, president, or dictator) and the prince's personal ministers, advisers, friends, and entourage. Court politics came into vogue in early monarchies, and by the time of Louis XIV of France, it was the rage. By the reign of his successor, his grandson Louis XV, court politics typified what went on in kingly castles. Hence, the court of Louis XV is a convenient place to learn about the general character of court politics.

Louis XV, who reached the throne at the ripe age of five in 1715, never acquired the zest for governing that his grandfather had. This is not to say he took no interest in public affairs, for he did. But much of the daily grind of governing (reading and writing dispatches, receiving petitions and demands, making decisions, appearing in public, and so forth) Louis found tedious, in fact, boring. He had other interests: he liked hunting, women, and intimate dinners. And having come to the crown so young, advisers governed in his stead for several years. So Louis acquired a tendency that Machiavelli had remarked upon three centuries earlier: "Men almost always prefer to walk in paths marked out by others, and pattern their actions through imitation." Louis trod the executive path cut by the members of his court.

Who were Louis's courtiers? To begin with, there were members of the royal household—his wife the queen, his heir the dauphin, other children, grandchildren, and relatives. In some royal courts the monarch's spouse plays an influential role in governing. Not so with Louis's queen. She had charge of the court's social calendar and little else. The dauphin also had no major political role, heir apparent or not. In addition to the royal family there were Louis's councilors, the members of his council (or cabinet), including his secretaries for foreign affairs, finance, army, navy, and the like. Of course, these councilors had their assistants, assistants had deputy assistants, and so on, down the line. Then add to the court the large staff of personnel responsible for running Louis's various palaces and estates, people with such lofty titles as Keeper of the Bedchamber. Additionally, the court contained a large number of nobles and ladies of the court. Nobles served the king in some capacity (even if as nothing more than hunting partners), and the queen had her ladies in waiting. There also were various "hangers on," persons who at one time had performed some service and were kept on at court to curry the king's pleasure. Other full-time courtiers included the royal physicians, tailors, barbers, dress designers, and so on. Ambassadors from foreign nations, artists, musicians, philosophers, members of the clergy, and others wandered in and out of court life. And not to be ignored, especially in the court of Louis XV, were the monarch's "favorites." A favorite was simply Louis's official mistress of the moment. One of these, Madame de Pompadour, was for two decades a mover and shaker in the politics of Louis's court.

As you might expect, to be a member of the royal court was a high

MADAME DE POMPADOUR: PRINCESS AT COURT

In 1730, when she was nine years old, Reinette Poisson went with her mother to a fortune-teller. (The early eighteenth century was an era of renewed interest in matters of the intellect, so much so that we now know it as the Age of Enlightenment. Enlightened it may have been, but seers, soothsayers, and fortune-tellers were still very popular, even among the people of the upper middle class.) The fortune-teller looked carefully at the bright, obviously attractive young girl. "One day this child will become the king's mistress," predicted the seer. The prediction was correct: when Reinette was twenty-four, Louis XV of France took her as his favorite (mistress), bestowed upon her the title of Marquise de Pompadour, and presented her at court.

All that was not so unusual. In those days, reigning monarchs frequently had mistresses or lovers in addition to legal spouses. Catherine the Great certainly did (Chapter 5). But what made Madame de Pompadour unusual was that for twenty years she was not just Louis's mistress; she also reigned over court politics and became an influential figure in the governing of France and in international diplomacy. She typified the splendor and pettiness, conflict and intrigue, force and influence that has come to be a major part of court politics.

Jeanne-Antoinette Poisson (later Madame de Pompadour) (1721–1764) was born of middle-class parents. Her father was of humble origin but had made a modest success as a food supplier. Indeed, during the plague of 1720, he kept people in the Provence region of France from starving. For that he received a title from the duke of Orléans. Unfortunately, his luck turned bad, and he was implicated in a food-buying scandal. He fled to Germany and several years later was able to exonerate himself, but by then his little Reinette had grown. In the meantime, his wife had developed a reputation as something of a loose woman, the mistress to a former French ambassador to Sweden. These three things—Madame de Pompadour's bourgeoise background, her father's scandal, and her mother's reputation—dogged her the rest of her life. Those at the royal court (including the queen) were used to Louis's womanizing; yet never, but never, had he taken a mistress from the bourgeoisie, and they never let her forget it.

When she became the king's mistress in 1745, Jeanne-Antoinette was married. No matter, those things could always be arranged, and were. But insiders at the court assumed, given her bourgeoise family and marital status, that Madame de Pompadour would stay in the background of court politics and would soon be only a passing fancy of the king. They were partly right on the first point, partly right on the second, and totally wrong in the long run. During her years as Louis's lover, Madame de Pompadour took little active part in politics, though she did influence the dismissal of the comptroller general of finances as a favor to her uncle and family friends who found the comptroller difficult. Courtiers were outraged. The incident proved the power of the king's mistress, or so they thought. But aside from that incident and from playing a minor part in arranging the second marriage of the king's heir, she had little direct concern with politics. She confined herself to pleasing the king, organizing a court theater, and being hostess at informal gatherings in her chambers.

All that changed in 1751. She and Louis ended any intimate relationship as lovers; yet she did not fall from favor. In fact she grew closer to Louis XV, becoming his friend, confidante, agent, and adviser. Madame de Pompadour realized that if she learned politics and practiced it skillfully, she could make herself indispensable to a monarch easily bored by the pomp, ceremony, and tedium of political affairs. Politics served her as a tool for survival, as a way of fending off rivals, combating intrigues, and remaining the king's favorite, even though no longer so in the bedroom.

As a politician, Madame de Pompadour did many things. She received ambassadors and ministers, and sometimes with the king and sometimes for him, she received petitions and requests from those seeking royal assistance; "We shall see," was her reply. She was instrumental in appointing members of Louis's council (cabinet), ambassadors to foreign nations, and generals of the French army. She worked to persuade the pope to intervene in a conflict between the French clergy and the parliament. She played a key role in recasting alliances among European nations, working out an alliance that brought France close to its archrival Austria in the face of a threat from France's former ally, Frederick the Great of Prussia. For this she won the praise of Austria's monarch, Maria Theresa. This new alliance helped fuel the Seven Years War, the outcome of which changed the maps of Europe, North America, and Asia. Madame de Pompadour was also a major force in French theater, art, and architecture, purchasing and remodeling (among other buildings) the Hotel d'Evreux in Paris. It is now the Elysee Palace, in effect the White House of France, where the president of the republic resides.

Madame de Pompadour died of tuberculosis at the age of forty-three. During her lifetime her political enemies had conducted whispering campaigns against her, circulated damaging doggerels (a political weapon common to court politics), orchestrated demonstrations opposing her influence, and attempted to implicate her in the nearly successful assassination of Louis XV in 1757. But because of her political skill she nonetheless retained the confidence of the king. Upon her death, Louis XV had no way to recompense the memory of his former mistress and political adviser. All he could do was observe her funeral procession, from a balcony overlooking the distant avenue. He is reputed to have watched it pass out of sight and, with tears running down his cheeks, say, "Well, that is all the honour I can pay her."

---

honor. It carried status and respect, opportunities for making important contacts, and the prospect of wealth. In sum, court life concentrated the kinds of welfare and deference values (see Chapter 4) that people coveted. But to remain in court, one had to maintain the favor of the king. With so many people at the court, opportunities actually to see and talk with Louis were rare. Courtiers competed with one another to win the king's pleasure, and this bred intrigue, rivalries, plots, malicious rumors and gossip, self-serving flattery, and all manner of deceit. Because only one person, Madame de Pompadour, seemed always to have the king's favor, much of the court's politics revolved around her, as courtiers either tried to influence Louis through her or tried to provoke her fall from favor.

If Louis's palace typified court life for autocratic princes, how would it compare with the backstage politics in republics or totalitarian regimes? Consider first the totalitarian comparison. Two dictators had their versions of royal courts. Adolf Hitler surrounded himself with an entourage of loyal courtiers. Unlike Louis XV, Hitler was not married, and so there was no *füehrer* family. But there was his inner clique of ministers for war, armaments, air, propaganda, security, and so on, who had been with him since the early days of the Nazi movement. Hitler had personal confidants, first Rudolph Hess and later Martin Bormann, who controlled access to the leader. He, too, had personal staffs to cater to his whims, in the Reichschancellery in Berlin, his mountain retreat at Berchtesgaden, and his various military command posts. And there were wives, ladies of the court, hangers-on, personal pilot, personal chauffeur, and the like. Hitler too, had a favorite, his mistress Eva Braun whom he married at the end and who committed suicide with him right before the downfall of Nazi Germany. In similar fashion, Joseph Stalin had a full complement of courtiers to serve his Kremlin during his reign. And, as you know from Chapter 7, life at the dictator's court was as full of machinations as lurid as anything dreamed up in the time of Louis XV, for example, Hitler's plot against Ernst Roehm or Stalin's purge trials.

Are republican princes susceptible to the life of the court as well? The intentions of the Founding Fathers to the contrary notwithstanding, the president of the United States is deeply involved in court politics. First, the president's wife and children receive courtly treatment. Eleanor Roosevelt, the wife of Franklin Roosevelt, engaged in the politics of court and nation. Jacqueline Kennedy, President John F. Kennedy's wife, set a courtly living style for the White House. Rosalynn Carter advised President Jimmy Carter, and their daughter received the publicity of a princess. There are other royal trappings: cabinet members; a private set of baronial advisers on foreign, domestic, and economic matters; a publicity and public information staff; a White House staff that has multiplied in size by fifty times in only twenty years; an entourage of news reporters hanging on each presidential utterance; and private limousines, jetliners, helicopters, retreats, and prerogatives never imagined during the summer of 1787. But the American republic does not stand alone in developing a regal executive. P. Viansson-Ponte in a book entitled *The King and His Court* described the royal splendor and style of the presidency of Charles de Gaulle of the Fifth French Republic. Again there were all of the features of court life: banquets for one hundred guests, gala receptions, and formal parties at the Elysee Palace; Madame de Gaulle presiding over the "court" in splendor; and a trusted entourage.

What to Avoid at Court

The royal life sounds appealing. So much splendor, so many privileges, prerogatives, and perquisites! It could easily turn a prince's head. Indeed, one of the major threats to the princely conduct and exercise of executive power is the court. Executive decisions made at court frequently fall on one or the other of two extremes: they are either overly cautious or overly risky. The court of Louis XV provides an example of the first. During his reign, France was threatened by England, a nation seeking to expand, at the expense of France, its territorial holdings in North America and India. Louis XV took comfort in an alliance with Frederick II of Prussia, thinking that it would protect France against its traditional enemies, England and Austria-Hungary. But unknown to Louis, the Prussian emperor negotiated a secret alliance with England, hoping thus to profit from any French-English war and to gobble up a little bit of Austria. Certainly France would never come to the aid of Austria, thought Frederick.

But Empress Maria Theresa of Austria thought otherwise. Learning of Frederick's secret plans, she proposed to her court an alliance with France. But how to get Louis XV to entertain such a proposal from a former enemy? Knowing of the influence of Madame de Pompadour at the French court, one of Maria Theresa's ministers opened negotiations through Louis's favorite. Madame de Pompadour was deeply involved in the diplomacy, arranged secret meetings between Louis and the Austrian representatives, and helped work out the details. An agreement was reached, but Louis vacillated. He knew it would mean war with Prussia, a prospect that court rivals to Pompadour did not favor. Louis's indecisiveness scarcely matched Machiavelli's maxim: "You should never let things get out of hand in order to avoid war. You don't avoid such a war, you merely postpone it, to your own disadvantage." After much delay, Louis approved the treaty of friendship with Austria. By then, however, Frederick II had reached his understanding with England. And he did not wait but attacked first. In the end, after the Seven Years War was over, France had lost much of its empire, perhaps because of the earlier tactical error of not isolating Prussia sooner.

Now reflect on a second case, not of caution, but of risk. In April 1961, after only three months in office, the administration of John F. Kennedy supported an invasion of the Cuban coast by exiles opposed to the regime of Fidel Castro. U.S. navy, air force, and Central Intelligence Agency forces were involved in a landing on the Bay of Pigs. It was a disaster. Out of an invasion force of fourteen hundred, two hundred were killed, and twelve hundred were taken prisoner. It was a product of court politics. The Kennedy administration had inherited the idea of such an invasion from the previous administration of President Dwight D. Eisenhower. But Eisenhower had never approved of the plan because of major flaws in it. The Kennedy court, however, convinced itself that the plan was flawless. First, Kennedy's courtiers simply ignored the legitimate doubts expressed by a small minority. Indeed, it was seldom that such doubts were expressed, because the courtiers labored under the illusion that everyone agreed that the plan was perfect. Indeed, given the success of the Kennedy team in winning the presidency in 1960 for their prince, how could any plan that the courtiers approved have defects? In such an environment in which court members consider themselves invulnerable to failure and agree on a plan, dissent vanishes. Everyone wants to please the prince or those close to the prince. So what the prince and his court wanted, they got; it turned out to be perfect only in its failure.

These two cases illustrate what you must avoid at court. First, don't agree just to please the prince; and if you are a prince, don't trust those who go out of their way to be deferential and servile toward you. Too often princes think that their course of action (Louis's reluctance to offend Prussia, Kennedy's reluctance to ignore doubts) is the right one, simply because they are princes. Being treated as gods produces delusions of grandeur that contribute to failures to accept uncomfortable truths, consider alternative arguments, and adapt to changing times and circumstances.

Second, beware of court intrigues. Much of what courtiers do stems from a close reading of their leader's whims and utterances. The hope is to discover who is in favor and who is out and to identify with the ins. Louis's courtiers were ever watchful for signs of coolness between Louis and Madame de Pompadour, and they even recruited and offered replacements for the king's favorite. Pompadour was equally watchful and almost seemed to take a page from Machiavelli, who wrote: "Since transition from private citizen to prince presupposes either skill (*virtu*) or luck, it would seem that either one or the other of these two qualities might ease some of the difficulties, at least partly. Still, the less one trusts to chance, the better one's hopes of holding on."

Third, if you serve a prince, beware of identifying the leader of your cause with the cause itself; if you are the prince, beware of thinking that you are the cause you seek. Claims by Louis XIV and by Napoleon that "I am the state" and by de Gaulle that "I am France" are symptomatic of what to avoid. As a physician's receptionist, you may come to believe you are the medical clinic you serve, but if you resigned, you would discover that the clinic could continue without you, just as the Fifth French Republic survived the resignation of de Gaulle.

Finally, remember that the politics of the court take place wherever courtiers vie with one another for the favor of a prince—among rising executives in large-scale business corporations, in the showrooms of automobile dealers where salespersons strive to please the sales manager, among waiters and waitresses seeking the favor of the restaurant manager, and even among students competing for high grades from their professors. Remember that no matter what your career is, you may find yourself in court (that is, office) politics and should act prudently to achieve your aims.

WHAT DO EXECUTIVES DO?

The framers of the Constitution of the United States, aside from listing a few things that the president would do, simply provided the vague phrase that "the executive Power shall be vested in a President of the United States of America." They did not spell out what "executive

Power" was. Nor would you find it defined precisely in the written constitutions and unwritten practices of other governments, be they autocratic, republican, or totalitarian. In the end, executive powers consist of what executive princes do and what they are allowed to do by legislators, bureaucrats, judges, and competing power wielders.

This may be put another way, that the princely exercise of executive power is a continuous effort to define the expanse and limits of that power, a never-ending experiment in force and influence, coercion, and persuasion. You can test that experiment by considering how different executives have approached it.

Often princely executives act first and obtain authority later. Thus did President George Washington act in 1793. At the time, France and England were again at war. France, by treaty, was an ally of the United States, but given the dominant strength of the English navy, much would be lost and nothing gained by entering the war on the French side. Nor was there any desire to oppose a close ally. Washington took the matter up with his cabinet. There was a happy compromise, that the United States would stay out of the war completely. The United States would not then risk fighting England, yet would provide some aid to France by transporting supplies to France in U.S. ships. The Washington administration issued a proclamation of neutrality in keeping with the decision; that is, American citizens would be friendly and impartial to both sides. The proclamation, however, provoked a constitutional debate. Where was the power for the president to proclaim that the United States would remain neutral? No matter, the president had acted, regardless of opposition. More than a year later, Congress passed the Neutrality Act of 1794, recognizing and accepting the executive power that Washington had already assumed. This from a president who had said, "Government is not reason, it is not eloquence—it is force! Like fire, it is a dangerous servant and a fearful master; never for a moment should it be left to irresponsible action."

At other times, executives act after being authorized. In 1792, Congress gave President Washington the authority to call out the militia to quell insurrections against federal law or, if the states requested, against state laws. When farmers in Pennsylvania protested a direct excise tax on whiskey (because it would hurt their sales of grain), Washington sent a force of thirteen thousand to put down the threatened insurrection. This "Whiskey Rebellion," which was more threat than act, ended, and two rebels were convicted of treason but pardoned by the president. The incident proved to be a good opportunity to prove that the president had sufficient power to execute federal laws.

A third way that heads of government test the bounds of their executive power is to propose action requiring the assent of the legislative and/or judicial bodies or of the people. If they win assent, the power has been granted; if not, they may yet get their way. You may remember that President Charles de Gaulle proposed an amendment to the constitution of the Fifth French Republic, permitting the president to be chosen through direct popular election. Instead of doing as the Constitution required and first submitting the amendment to the National Assembly, de Gaulle asked French voters to approve or disapprove of his proposal in a popular election. The assembly censured him for this. But since his amendment received overwhelming approval, he had won his point. Presidents are not always so fortunate, as President Franklin Roosevelt discovered in 1937 when he was having trouble with the Supreme Court. The Court declared that certain legislative acts in his New Deal recovery program were unconstitutional. Congress was sympathetic to Roosevelt's plight, and members introduced several possible amendments to the Constitution to correct the problem by limiting Court power, yet never got around to acting on any of them. So Roosevelt took matters into his own hands and sent a bill to Congress to reorganize the federal judiciary, something Congress could do without amending the Constitution. His proposal was that whenever any federal judge who had been on the bench ten years or more did not retire within six months of his or her seventieth birthday, the president would have the power to appoint an additional judge to the court on which the unretired judge sat. No more than fifty judges could be so appointed, and moreover, Roosevelt's plan limited the size of the Supreme Court to fifteen justices. Although not an explicit attack on the Supreme Court, the intent seemed clear, namely, to change the Court's decisions by adding judges favorable to the president's program (the Court then had justices of retirement age). Roosevelt's opponents called the plan a "court-packing scheme." Even his Democratic supporters were divided over the merits of the proposal. Ultimately, the U.S. Senate rejected the proposal. Yet Roosevelt won the day. Partly in response to the proposal for judicial reorganization and partly in response to Roosevelt's landslide victory in the 1936 election, two justices that had been opposing New Deal legislation no longer deemed such statutes unconstitutional. This came to be known as the "switch in time that saved nine" (the nine Court justices). Moreover, one of the justices retired, thus giving Roosevelt the opportunity to appoint a more sympathetic member to the Court, after all.

Kingly castles and executive mansions do not stand in isolated wilderness. Executives must work their will in a setting of a variety of people, some working in harmony with the prince and others opposing princely actions. Under these circumstances, there is a fourth way to test the limits of executive power, by building support and appealing for help among interests outside the executive palace. This is what Madame de Pompadour did, acting in an executive capacity in support of King Louis XV during his reign. One of the most bitter political conflicts of Louis's reign divided both his court and the nation. It involved religion, at issue a requirement that a person near death must meet before receiving anointment and prayer from a priest. An official order of the Church required that any person in such a state must produce a certificate proving a prior confession to a priest. One religious faction thought that this requirement was reasonable, but another did not. The opposing faction asked that Parliament seek a change in the order. So when a church official refused to give last rites to an old priest who opposed the requirement, Parliament condemned the official. The King's Council then annulled the parliamentary condemnation. In the meantime, the old priest died, and a large crowd attended his funeral.

The conflict between the King's Council and Parliament, which stemmed originally from the religious infighting, grew intense. The King would issue a decree, and Parliament would refuse to register it, that is, give it official approval before it could become law. The council would then annul the parliamentary refusal, thus making the decree law without being registered. The disputes continued until Louis XV decided to stand firm. He issued another decree: in the future all matters concerning the requirement pertaining to last rites would be handled by the King's Council, not by Parliament. Parliament refused to register the decree, and so Louis had members of Parliament arrested and exiled to the countryside. But the public and local governments sided with Parliament, and so Louis recanted and called Parliament back. This merely started the confrontation all over again. Louis's government was an autocracy, but the words written by Machiavelli in regard to a "weak republic" could apply to it: the worst thing it "can do is to be indecisive, so that all the decisions it makes are made out of necessity, and if any benefit results from them, it is necessity, not . . . prudence, that brought it about."

It was into this crisis that Madame de Pompadour stepped. First, she had a trusted confidant appointed ambassador to the pope in Rome. By corresponding with the ambassador and using him as an intermediary, she entreated the pope to announce an encyclical (papal decree) that would modify the requirement concerning last rites. After painstaking negotiations, the pope agreed and modified the requirement concerning certificates of confession but did not negate the original order demanding them. The French clergy accepted the papal decree, and although parliamentary magistrates refused to be bound by a settlement devised in Rome via Madame de Pompadour's efforts, the intensity of the dispute waned. Madame de Pompadour later clarified what she thought the relationship of executive to legislative power should be. Speaking to a member of Parliament, she asked: "Who are you, you gentlemen of Parliament, to resist the will of your master? Do you not believe that Louis XV is as great a prince as Louis XIV? Do you believe that the present Parliament is made of better, more cultured, able magistrates than those in Parliament then? I wish it were! If only they were like that!"

There is another important tactic for defining the executive prerogative. It is to rally the support of a political party behind the actions and programs of the head of government. You will remember that this is precisely what James Madison did, first in combating the programs of the Federalists and then in securing the passage of Republican proposals. The political party has been one of the key factors in the growth of presidential power in the United States. In Great Britain the prime minister, by definition, requires party support. In inviting someone to form a government, the reigning monarch in Great Britain chooses the person who can command a majority of the members of the House of Commons. This normally means the designated leader of the political party with the largest number of seats in the House. (The prime minister must be a member of the House of Commons.) As long as the House does not vote against any measure requested by the prime minister and cabinet, executive power remains lodged in the chosen head of government. Given the strength of political parties in the British regime in this century, only three prime ministers have been forced to resign because they have not been able to command a majority of the House.

But the party that grants executive power can also take it away. This is especially the case in a totalitarian regime built on a closed, single party led by a dictator. During the late 1950s and early 1960s the prime minister of the Soviet Union was Nikita Khrushchev, once a member of Joseph Stalin's court. After Stalin's death in 1953, a lengthy struggle for power ensued, and Khrushchev eventually emerged the winner. But in 1956 and again in 1961, he did something that eventually brought him down: in a major address in 1956, he denounced the reign of Stalin. He went into detail regarding the Stalinist terror, concentration camps, purges, and the cult of personality that had grown around Stalin. The denunciation itself raised no immediate problem. For one thing, it was secret and kept within the Communist party. For another, inner-party members knew it to be true and, hence, no direct threat to them. But word leaked out of Khrushchev's attack, of the removal of Stalin's body from its honored burial plot, and of the general downgrading of Stalin as a party leader and figure. This did raise a problem. How, people began to ask, could the Communist party, which was the vanguard of the revolution and thus could not err, have been so wrong? How could it follow the lead of Stalin and have condoned his brutal exercise of executive power? The myth of the party's infallibility had been dealt a severe blow, and someone had to be the scapegoat. The party's chief theoretician, a powerful figure in party circles, formed a coalition in 1964 that overthrew Khrushchev. Thus the dictator who had used the political party to support his executive power saw that power vanish when the party turned against him.

ARE GREAT PEOPLE CHOSEN?

More than a century ago, an English scholar, James Bryce, came to the United States and wrote a treatise on the nation and its government, entitled *The American Commonwealth*. In one of the book's chapters, "Why Great Men Are Not Chosen Presidents," Bryce discussed what he saw as the problem. By "great," Bryce meant two things. First, a great man was an individual who would be remembered for his deeds, even if he had not been president. Second, he would have been great, even if he had not displayed rare qualities while president. Few presidents measured up to Bryce's standards, George Washington being one who did. Why was this, Bryce asked. The answer, he thought, was that "the ordinary American voter does not object to mediocrity. . . . He likes his candidates to be sensible, vigorous, and above all, what he calls 'magnetic,' and does not value, because he sees no need for, originality or profundity, a fine culture or a wide knowledge." President Calvin Coolidge later put it in more down-to-earth terms: "I think the American public wants a solemn ass as President. And I think I'll go along with them."

By now, you have probably learned a different lesson. The princely exercise of executive power does require originality. You cannot be like Louis XV and walk the path that others have walked. To improve your chances, you must adapt to changing times and circumstances and be original, profound, knowledgeable, and not so solemn that you cannot roll with the punches. Unlike Louis, you must be decisive. Have friends in court, but unlike the Kennedy administration, avoid courtthink. Like Washington, test and know the limits of executive power and use violence with economy. Practicing these guidelines may even make you one of the greats that *are* chosen to wear the purple, even though not born to it. After all, Madame de Pompadour wore the purple and certainly was not of regal birth. But she learned a crucial rule: the skillful practice of politics can afford opportunities closed to those who pay no heed to the craft.

"Tho' we cannot, affirmatively, tell you what we are doing; we can, negatively, tell you what we are not doing—we never once thought of a king."
—The framers of the U.S. Constitution

"Men almost always prefer to walk in paths marked out by others and pattern their actions through imitation."
—Machiavelli

"Still, the less one trusts to chance, the better one's hope of holding on."
—Machiavelli

"Government is not reason, it is not eloquence—it is force! Like fire it is a dangerous servant and a fearful master; never for a moment should it be left to irresponsible action."
—Washington

"Who are you, you gentlemen of Parliament, to resist the will of your master? Do you not believe that Louis XV is as great a prince as Louis XIV? Do you believe that the present Parliament is made of better, more cultured, able magistrates than those in Parliament then? I wish it were! If only they were like that!"
—Madame de Pompadour

"I think the American public wants a solemn ass as President. And I think I'll go along with them."
—Calvin Coolidge

What Happens in Kingly Castles and Presidential Mansions?

10

What Happens in Legislative Chambers?

One day in 1833, the lord chancellor of England invited two young and ambitious politicians to dine. It was the first time the two had met, but it would not be the last. One had recently lost an election to Parliament, and the other had won. The loser was Benjamin Disraeli, and the winner was William Gladstone. Disraeli was the prime minister from 1867 to 1868, was succeeded by Gladstone until 1874, who yielded to Disraeli until 1880, who once again gave way to Gladstone. During their careers they contested each other on measure after measure, law after law. Their rivalry over the years prompted each of them to recall the lord chancellor's advice to them during that first dinner meeting: "Never defend yourself before a popular assembly, except by retorting the attack; the hearers, in the pleasure which the assault gives them, will forget the previous charge."

To learn about legislative politics, there is no better place to begin than by studying the parliamentary duel between Benjamin Disraeli and William Gladstone. Attack and counterattack, charge and counter-charge—their struggles brought the legislature to its zenith as a palace of political power in the nineteenth century. The style and tone of what happens in legislative chambers has changed in the one hundred years since Disraeli and Gladstone squared off against each other; yet the essence of what people do, namely, legislate, and the requirements for princely action remain unaltered.

"ALL LEGISLATIVE POWERS HEREIN GRANTED ..."

"All legislative powers herein granted. ...": thus begins Article I, Section 1, of the Constitution of the United States. It goes on to vest those "legislative powers" in a Congress consisting of two bodies, a House of Representatives and a Senate. At the time of its writing, such an explicit statement of formal legislative power was unique in the world's history. But as you will recall from Chapter 8, a separate legislative power in governments had been evolving on a less formal basis for centuries. Remember, for instance, that English kings had been convening parliaments of nobles, the clergy, and burghers well before there were even colonies in North America. And remember also that before the American revolution, England and France had full-fledged legislative bodies in operation, which vexed Madame du Pompadour no end, and she said of France: "Parliament is in a great commotion. The King will remain firm. Those little republicans must yield to authority based on justice."

She, of course, thought of the existence of a recalcitrant legislative power as evidence of a Republican plot to frustrate the king. There is a germ of truth in this. A *separate* legislative power that checks and balances executive action has become a characteristic of the republican form of government. But this is not to say that legislatures do not exist in autocratic and totalitarian regimes as well, and for this reason it will help to review some of the distinctions among them.

First, consider what it means to legislate. To legislate is to impose or to agree upon a general rule governing the conduct of people. Consider your family, especially if you are a member of a large family. Suppose that at some point your parents announced that each week each of your brothers and/or sisters, as well as you, would receive a specified allowance. To receive it, each of you would be required to carry out some task: mow the lawn, take out the garbage, make the beds, vacuum, whatever. Thus, your parents established a general rule that would apply to everybody. This is a characteristic of legislation, that is, its generality, as it is intended to apply to everyone the same way and to endure over time. Now, suppose that your father or mother (or both acting jointly) had not simply laid down the "rule of allowance" but had proposed that some rule be made, opened the matter for discussion, and even taken a vote on what the rule would be. In short, the rule was not imposed but was agreed upon through the give-and-take of family members. This too, is legislation, but clearly republican rather than autocratic in its origins. But the fact that a piece of legislation (a rule or a law) is intended to be general and to endure does not mean that it is beyond modification. Changing times and circumstances often dictate changes in laws. Machiavelli, writing of republics, noted that "no republic will ever be perfect unless its laws make provisions for everything, and set up a remedy for every possibility, and establish the means of using it." He knew this to be impossible. All that republicans could hope for was that the institutions they established and the people they chose to lead them could adjust to changing situations. Legislation could not therefore be a once-and-forever kind of thing. The mere act of making a law, for example, changes things and thus requires new laws to adjust to those changes. Return to the case of the rule of allowance. If you and other members of your family have agreed that you will receive equal allowances for tasks performed, does this make you equal in all matters? Does everyone have the same restrictions as to how much time will be allotted to watching TV, doing homework, staying out on dates, and the like? Probably not. So new rules are necessary. Woodrow Wilson, long

BENJAMIN DISRAELI: MEMBER OF PARLIAMENT

In 1834 a young man dressed in the clothes of a dandy, with long black hair in ringlets and wearing gold chains, attended a dinner party in a fashionable London neighborhood. There he made the acquaintance of the prime minister of England, Lord William Melbourne. Impressed by the young man's wit and eloquence, Melbourne offered to help him get a start in politics. "Well now, tell me, what do you want to be?" asked Melbourne. "I want to be prime minister," replied the young dandy. Melbourne chuckled and said, "No, no. No chance of that in our time. No, go into politics, you will be right. But you must put all these foolish ideas out of your head."

Benjamin Disraeli (1804–1881) took half of Lord Melbourne's advice. He went into politics, but he did not give up his "foolish ideas." From 1867 to 1868 and again from 1874 to 1880, Disraeli became prime minister, Britain's head of government and leader of the House of Commons. His rise was scarcely meteoric. His ancestry was Jewish. His grandfather, Benjamin D'Israeli, came to London in 1748 and became a success in business. D'Israeli's son, Isaac, had no taste for business and instead became a writer and author. To his son Benjamin (who changed his name from D'Israeli to Disraeli) he bequeathed his distaste for business and his taste for writing. After Benjamin was expelled from school at age fifteen, for fighting to correct an insult to his ancestry, he tried both business and literature. First, he consumed book after book in his father's library, and then he became secretary to a lawyer. After that, he tried unsuccessfully to found a newspaper, made some disastrous investments, and went heavily into debt. To recover, he turned to writing. At age twenty-one he wrote a novel, *Vivian Grey,* using a pseudonym. At first, it was well received, but when the secret got out that such a young dandy had written the work, the very people who had praised the novel condemned it. A failure at school, business, and writing—where now would he turn?

He decided to bide his time, and for the next few years he worked at becoming known by London's fashionable society. By exploiting a few valuable contacts he obtained invitations to dinner parties, balls, receptions, concerts, and other social affairs. He became a fixture at social gatherings, a guest prized for his charm, brilliance, looks, style, and cynicism. And he continued writing. With his newly won social contacts, his publishing career grew more successful, and at this point, he turned to politics. But failure again seemed his lot: he ran for a seat in Parliament and lost. He ran again, and lost. Not until 1837, with the help of good friends, did he win a seat in the House of Commons.

There too, success was slow in coming. The first challenge for a newly elected member of Parliament is the maiden speech, the first time the member speaks on the floor of the House. In Disraeli's era, oratorical skills were vital to success. Failure to speak or failure at speaking was always a blow to the aspiring politician's ambitions. When Disraeli ("Dizzy," as he was called by his colleagues) rose to speak for the first time, he was a sight that brought hoots from the assembled Commons: dark complexion, a green coat, white waistcoat, black cravat, and covered with gold chains. Laughter and catcalls were his reception. But he learned his lesson, and in the future he was less ostentatious, lowered his voice, was less strident, and spoke briefly. As the years went by, he gave up the attire of a dandy, dressed in black, and so polished his speaking skills that he became, along with his adversary William Gladstone, one of the greatest orators of Parliament. *Virtu* overcame *fortuna.*

Disraeli became the chief spokesman in the House for the Conservative party. But in 1841, when the Conservatives won control of the House, Disraeli was not invited to join the cabinet, though his fellow Conservative, Gladstone, was. Disraeli remained loyal to the party, but in 1846, when the prime minister proposed repeal of the Corn Laws (laws forbidding the importation of foreign wheat), Disraeli led a party revolt. The issue split the party, with Disraeli bolting the party and Gladstone siding with the prime minister. In the end, however, Disraeli's followers carried the day. By 1858 he became the Conservative leader of the Commons. In the ensuing years, Gladstone became increasingly isolated from the Conservatives, and by 1865 he had become leader of the Liberal party. For the remaining years of Disraeli's life, the duel between "Dizzy" and the "Grand Old Man" (Gladstone) was bitter and continuous.

Disraeli's two terms as prime minister were periods of reform, which included electoral reform, better low-cost housing, recognition of trade union activities, legislation to clean up polluted rivers, protection of merchant seamen, and steps to redeem public land for public use. These were also periods of aggressive foreign policy: annexation of the Fiji Islands, annexation of the Transvaal, wars against the Afghans and the Zulus, acquisition of Cyprus, and the purchase of controlling shares of the Suez Canal.

In all these matters Disraeli not only had to lead his party, the Commons, and Parliament, but he also had to lead his monarch, Queen Victoria. Before Disraeli became prime minister, the queen had a poor opinion of him. But once they started working together, they got along well. Indeed, in 1874 the queen was relieved to see Gladstone leave the office of prime minister and Disraeli return to it. Said Disraeli of his success with Queen Victoria: "I never refuse; I never contradict; I sometimes forget." When he retired from the House of Commons, Victoria made Disraeli a member of the House of Lords, conferring on him a peerage as the Earl of Beaconsfield. "Earl!" said Gladstone, "I cannot forgive him for not having himself made a Duke."

---

before he became president of the United States, was a professor of political science at Princeton University and wrote a book about how the U.S. Congress works, entitled *Congressional Government*. In it he made the same point that we are talking about here: "Legislation unquestionably generates legislation. . . . Once begin the dance of legislation, and you must struggle through its mazes as best you can to its breathless end,—if any end there be."

Legislation, then, is a process of making laws and as such is general and continuous, perhaps endless. A third, related point is that the legislative chambers in which this process occurs are of different types. We shall designate these types as parliamentary, presidential, and assembly. In a parliamentary arrangement, for example, the governments of Great Britain, Japan, West Germany, Italy, and Israel, the head of government and his or her chief executive officers are selected from and responsible to the legislature. This legislative form evolved primarily in Great Britain, which has come to be known as the "Mother of Parliaments." The United States exemplifies the presidential arrangement, that is, the president and the members of Congress are chosen separately, and the president and cabinet members are not also members of Congress. Because the executive and legislative share powers as separate institutions, they check and balance each other and so are responsible to each other (see Chapters 6 and 8). Finally, in assembly government the supreme power is formally concentrated in the legislature, including executive and judicial powers as well as legislative. The governments of the France's Third and Fourth republics had such characteristics, as do the formal constitutions of the Union of Soviet Socialistic Republics and the German Democratic Republic (East Germany).

In parliamentary governments, the executive (the head of government) has the power to dissolve the legislature and call for the election of a new one. But under presidential separation of powers there can be no dissolution of the legislature; the president cannot dissolve Congress. With assembly government, the legislature itself has the power to dissolve itself, an unlikely act. Whether a legislature continues to sit or is dissolved and a new legislature chosen is important. A legislature is a representative body, for one of its chief reasons for existing is for representation. In some fashion or other (it varies across legislative bodies), a legislator is supposed to represent the people. Those people may be those who have nominated, appointed, elected, or otherwise chosen the legislator. The legislator is responsible to those people and can be removed by them but, in turn, has the power to act on behalf of the people represented and to make laws that are binding on them.

The practice of representation is as old as government and is, of course, a characteristic of representative democracy (republics). The effort to represent different kinds of people in legislative bodies was one of the reasons that two-house legislative chambers emerged in most nations. Machiavelli hinted as much when he wrote that "in every republic there are two different inclinations; that of the people and that of the upper class, and all the laws which are made in favor of liberty are born of the conflict of the two."

An excellent example of this "conflict of the two" took place in England during the era of Benjamin Disraeli and William Gladstone. Before the seventeenth century, parliamentary power had been concentrated in the upper chamber of parliament, the House of Lords. But after constitutional struggles in the seventeenth and eighteenth centuries, the political center of gravity shifted to the lower chamber, the House of Commons. This is not to say that the two chambers represented strikingly different types of people and social interests. To be sure, the lords were the upper class of which Machiavelli wrote, a body of landed aristocrats. By the early nineteenth century, the Commons was at least more reflective of the commercial and business classes that arose during the period of industrialization. But these were scarcely the "people" of which Machiavelli spoke, and to the degree that the middle class was even represented in Commons, they did not match the numbers of the landed gentry.

The reason for all this was the practice of representing "rotten" boroughs. A borough consisted of an electoral district represented in the House of Commons by one or more members. The precise number of such representatives depended on gurantees made by earlier generations of English monarchs. As industrialization changed the times and circumstances, the inhabitants of many such boroughs moved away. The boroughs retained their allotted number of representatives, though the other, more populous boroughs into which people were moving did not increase the number of representatives they could send to Parliament. So imagine the following: one borough in Cornwall—a remote coastal area—of less than 350 square miles, 350 voters, and 15,000 residents, sent 18 members to Commons, more than all the populous districts that comprised London sent!

But rotten boroughs were only part of the problem. The right to vote was strictly limited. The 230 boroughs were of four types, about equal in number. In "scot and lot" boroughs, every householder who had resided in the borough for six months and was not a pauper could vote. In "burgage" boroughs, only house owners could vote. In "corporate" boroughs, only members of the local government could vote. And in "freeman" boroughs, voting was limited to members of special groups, usually the trade guilds. Add to this that many of the four types of these 230 boroughs were "rotten," and you can see how votes could easily be manipulated, bought and sold, traded, and so forth. In one such borough one man owned ninety-nine of the one hundred buildings (burgages), each carrying one vote; therefore he controlled ninety-nine votes but did not even reside there.

When Disraeli and Gladstone launched their political careers, Parliament represented very few people, hardly reflected the interests of large industrial cities and towns, restricted the franchise, and manipulated the vote. Agitation for reform was intense. But Parliament was slow to undertake reform, with good reason, for those in control feared that they had everything to lose and nothing to gain. But in the face of mass protests and demonstrations in London, Brimingham, and other cities, it became apparent that Parliament would need to legislate. In 1831, a bill was introduced to redistribute the seats in the House of Commons and to extend the right to vote. Its features would eliminate most of the rotten boroughs, create new Commons seats for industrial cities, extend the vote to all men (not women) who owned or rented a house for a specified amount, and retain the vote for men who resided on lands worth a specified amount (called "forty-shilling" freeholders).

After bitter debate and public demonstrations, the bill passed by a majority of one vote, but suddenly it was defeated by passage of another motion, that representation of England in the Commons not be reduced. Parliament was dissolved, and the ensuing election campaign was waged on the slogan of "the bill, the whole bill, and nothing but the bill." Opponents of reform were soundly trounced, and when Commons met, the bill passed. But the House of Lords, which then as now was a body whose members are appointed not elected, rejected the bill. Protest swept England: castles were burned, jails were opened and inmates freed, and town halls and a bishop's palace were set ablaze. So the bill was introduced in Commons for a third time, and again it passed, and again the House of Lords sought to kill it. The prime minister tried to overcome the Lords' opposition by having the king appoint enough new members to the Lords to pass the bill. But the king refused, and the prime minister resigned. Again there were mass demonstrations and protests. Finally, the leader of the opposition to reform, the duke of Wellington, accepted defeat. He had one hundred of his followers in the House of Lords stay home and abstain from voting on the bill, and so, on July 7, 1832, the reform bill passed. As Machiavelli had observed centuries earlier, the "laws which are made in favor of liberty are born of the conflict" of the "two different inclinations: that of the people and that of the upper class."

TO PARLEY: HOW LEGISLATIVE CHAMBERS WORK

You can now surmise that legislatures do two principal things: they make laws and they represent. As passage of the English Reform Bill of 1832 illustrates, these two activities can overlap. What laws legislators make depend on whom they represent; the interests represented influence what legislation is passed. Consider at this point, then, what a fledgling legislator must learn in order to act in a princely manner, lessons that can be found in part, but not wholly, in the experience of the "Mother of Parliaments."

The French *parler* is a verb meaning "to talk," and the word *parliament* is derived from *parler*. This is a clue to how legislatures perform their overlapping tasks of lawmaking and representing, that is, by talk. If you have ever watched on television newsfilm clips of a congressional committee in action, you know that talk is the order of the day. This is made even more apparent if you have ever watched televised sessions of the U.S. House of Representatives or listened to live radio broadcasts of the Canadian House of Commons. Talk, talk, talk. Legislation is the politics of talk. This being the case, the main things that a legislator must know pertain to how legislative chambers work through talk. Here are things the legislator must learn, things that you too must know if you want to legislate in your daily life—in school, church, among friends, with employers and fellow workers, etc.

Learning to Whom to Talk

Depending on their type, legislative chambers organize themselves in different ways for talk. That organization is a hint to where the power resides, who is influential, and who is not. But first impressions can be deceiving. In a typical session of the British or Canadian House of Commons, members of Parliament rise and address their remarks to the Speaker. Yet their audience is not the Speaker, but leaders of their own political party and of other parties in the chamber. Party leaders and others in Commons may take notice of a member's remarks by means of signs, even shouts of approval or disagreement As leader of the Conservative party in the British Commons from 1867 to 1880, Benjamin Disraeli's tactic was to ignore all remarks addressed to him. He would sit almost motionless, eyes half-closed, seemingly oblivious. But then he would rise, throw his shoulders back in a carefully rehearsed manner, and in a moderate tone of voice dissect each point made in the debate with appropriate invective, cynicism, and mannerism. His tongue was greatly admired and feared. When he could say with aplomb, as he did of Gladstone, "He made his conscience not his guide but his accomplice," members of Commons accepted him as a power worthy of being reckoned with.

A legislative chamber such as the U.S. House of Representatives is different. Debate on the floor has its place but is hardly as dramatic as in the House of Commons. As Woodrow Wilson pointed out in *Congressional Government* almost a century ago, there are reasons for this. One is simply physical. The British House of Commons is a crowded hall. Members of opposing political parties crowd together on cushioned benches across from one another; a long central aisle divides the benches, and at one end the Speaker sits in a raised chair. On the front benches to the right of the Speaker sit the leaders of the "government," the party in power—the prime minister and the Cabinet—and on the benches to the Speaker's left sit the leaders of the party out of power, the "opposition." Said Disraeli, "No government can long be secure without a formidable Opposition." Physically, then, the House of Commons makes the tilt between government and opposition talk of great importance. Not so in the U.S. House of Representativies. Opponents do not face one another but sit at desks that fan out in a semicircle before the Speaker. Members address their colleagues from a podium in front of the Speaker. Of course, the government (the president and cabinet) does not even sit in the House and never appears for debate.

Differences in political parties also contribute to differences in the importance of debate as a mode of talk in legislative chambers. In Great Britain legislative power belongs to the leaders of the principal political parties. It is their task to pursue legislation that will command the support of party loyalists. Parliamentary struggles are party clashes. As Woodrow Wilson noted in comparing British and American politics, in the former these clashes are widely known because of duels between each party's highly visible and powerful leaders, Disraeli for the Conservatives and Gladstone for the Liberals, for instance. In American legislative chambers, party clashes, although frequent, are not the rule. Democrats vote for Republican programs and vice versa. Moreover, very rarely are Americans treated to the spectacle of princely party leaders in the House or Senate squaring off against one another in debate. There are party leaders, at least in name. In the House, for instance, the Speaker is the leader of the majority party, that party also elects the majority leaders of the House, and the minority party elects a minority leader. In the Senate there are majority and minority leaders as well.

But in the United States Congress, as in the French National Assembly—where many parties vie for power—the talk that the legislature uses to do its work does not center on the utterances of the party leaders, as in Great Britain.

Woodrow Wilson alluded to another difference in the role of talk in different legislatures. Although the British House of Commons, like any legislative chamber, screens proposed legislation via its standing committees, the common's committees are few in number (nine), do not generally deal with specialized subjects (one committee for agricultural policy, another for military affairs, and so on), and do not change the substance of the policies proposed by the government. Commons politics is party politics, and committee members represent party views. Talk in the Commons's committees is secondary to the talk of the Commons's debate or the discussions between the prime minister and cabinet. But in the United States, the talk takes place not in floor debate but in congressional committees, both in the House and the Senate. In the United States (and in most European republics, Japan, and other representative democracies), legislative chambers are divided into numerous standing committees, each committee specializing in certain issues. In the United States, committee members are selected by party leaders, with the majority party in each chamber receiving more seats on any committee than the minority does. So influential is each committee and its chairperson in shaping the legislation under its jurisdiction that Wilson referred to the standing committees in the United States as "little legislatures," which result in government by committee. Lying between the power of the committees in the U.S. Congress and the lesser power of the standing committees in the British Parliament is the French National Assembly, which has commissions rather than committees. Each commission has a *rapporteur,* or reporter, appointed for each piece of proposed legislation. The *rapporteur* studies the legislation, prepares the commission's report, and debates that report before the assembly. But unlike the situation that prevailed in the Third and Fourth French republics, in shaping the constitution for the Fifth Republic, Charles de Gaulle substantially reduced the power of legislative commissions and their *rapporteurs.* The commissions can propose changes in what the president of the republic and the government in power seek, but the whole assembly debates and acts on the president's proposals, not on legislation as written by the commissions, as was the case before de Gaulle.

The fragmentation of legislative power among a host of "little legislatures" in the United States both derives from and exacerbates the reduced power of political parties in American legislative chambers. This complicates the task of learning to whom to talk and who will listen. Instead of the demands of literally thousands of special interests being focused on party leaders and legislators who support the leadership, special interest groups often go directly to the legislators who are key members of powerful committees. Although a legislator's party ties are important to congressional actions, few congresspersons would today adhere solely to Disraeli's injunction: "Damn your principles! Stick to your party." Instead, principles take priority, at least the principles that represent, or at least coincide with, those of special interests supporting the congressperson in the give and take of committee and electoral politics.

Learning When and How to Talk

Regardless of to whom the legislator addresses talk, be it party or special interest leaders, and the type of talk that is most important—oratory in Commons debate, dialogues in congressional committees, or *rapporteur's* recommendations on behalf of commissions, for instance—he or she must learn the ropes. This means learning the rules of talk, the skills, and what to talk about.

Any legislative chamber has rules, written and unwritten. Written rules cover a host of practices, which may vary widely from one legislative body to another. For example, in the British House of Commons there is a difference between legislative proposals that members can introduce ("private bills") and the "government bills." The latter take precedent and are far more likely to be passed. If a party member wants to get a private bill passed, it stands to reason that it is a good idea to support the government or the opposition, in order for it to have much chance. In the United States, any congressperson can introduce a bill. The key is whose support it has—the president's, party leaders', or powerful special interests'? Whatever the source of support, it is rarely automatic. Simon Cameron, President Abraham Lincoln's secretary of war, summed up the problem: "You scratch my back and I'll scratch yours." In short, the time to talk is when it will win support. The tone of talk is "logrolling," promises of mutual aid among politicians so that each can obtain at least something of what he or she desires.

Thus the formal rules for introducing bills in a legislative chamber imply informal ways of taking advantage of them. This also applies to rules pertaining to other matters: what items can be considered by what committee, rules that govern committee deliberations, rules of general debate, rules on voting on final passage of laws, and so on. The critical thing to keep in mind if you aspire to legislative princedom is that such formal rules do exist. They can be used by you to your advantage or against you to your detriment. In any legislative body, those who master the rules are prized as tacticians who know how to get things done or, often more importantly, prevent them from being done.

It is also necessary to learn the informal customs and conventions of the legislative chamber. You know that from your own experience. You have surely been in some groups in which people pay little attention to one another, talk at the same time, ignore niceties, and even shout to get a point across. But you also are a member of other groups (the classroom?) in which the dialogue is more restrained, people take turns talking, ask for recognition to speak, and are courteous in the extreme. To get your point across and be successful in the first type of setting certainly requires different tactics and skills than it does in the second. For instance, the customs and conventions of the U.S. Senate differ considerably from those of many other legislative chambers. The Senate prides itself on decorum, etiquette, and courtly behavior. It is a long and honored tradition, once summed up by one of its more illustrious members, Daniel Webster: "This is a Senate, a Senate of equals, of men of individual honor and personal character, and of absolute independence. We know no masters, we acknowledge no dictators. This is a hall of mutual consultation and discussion, not an arena for the exhibition of champions."

Rules, formal and informal, govern when to talk, that is, when to take part in legislating. It also is important to know what you should talk about Modern-day legislators live in a world of specializations; and the questions that reach government require expertise: when does life begin, when does it end; how does a nation meet its energy needs; what are the possibilities of nuclear fission, fusion; what are the subtle causes of inflation, recession, depression, and what are their consequences? The list is endless. Given the amazing number of bills introduced into a legislative body—twelve thousand per year in Congress alone—covering highly technical matters, it is no wonder that most chambers screen them through standing committees specializing in that subject. Developing expertise in a subject is one road to legislative success, though this does not imply that such expertise is always required or that if obtained it will guarantee princely action. But knowing what to say has its compensations. Following his disappointment at the reception to his maiden speech in Parliament, Disraeli received this advice, which he practiced from then on: "Astonish them by speaking on subjects of detail. Quote figures, dates, calculations. And in a short time the House will sigh for the wit and eloquence which they know are in you." In short, those who want technical expertise will find it in you; those who do not will be relieved from the tedium by charm. Either way, you must know what you will be talking about before you start talking.

Learning When to Change Your Position

The main charge made against politicians is that they refuse to stand their ground. To castigate a politician, use the word *trimmer,* one who trims a ship sails with the wind, blowing first this way, then that. Trimmers have no principles, no standards, no morals. Benjamin Disraeli denounced William Gladstone as a scoundrel who changed his principles at will. Gladstone retorted that Disraeli had no principles, only ambitions. In fact, both were astute students of political logic. Each assumed the Machiavellian precept that as time changes, so does *fortuna,* that "time contains the seeds of all things, good as well as bad, bad as well as good." Disraeli put it this way: "Change is inevitable in a progressive country. Change is constant." Gladstone told his followers, "Time is on our side."

The career-long political duel between Disraeli and Gladstone illustrates that in politics, princes must be willing to change positions to suit the times. When the Reform Bill of 1832 was being debated, Disraeli favored it, because he thought it might favor his candidacy as a member of the Radical party. (It did not, and he lost). Gladstone opposed the reform measures. As a member of the Tory (conservative) party, he thought that the measures might precipitate a constitutional crisis. Now leap forward more than three decades to 1866: Disraeli was no longer a Radical; he was a Conservative. Gladstone was no longer a Conservative; he was a Liberal. The Liberal party came out in favor of additional electoral reforms. Gladstone proposed, because the Reform Bill of 1832 had not gone far enough, to extend the vote to skilled workers, who were likely to vote Liberal, and to create new parliamentary seats for cities, also likely to be Liberal. Disraeli said nothing and showed little interest in parliamentary reform. Gladstone's bill received a majority of five votes and then lost an amendment. The Liberals fell from power. In came the Conservatives with Disraeli as leader of the House of Commons. He convinced the conservatives to adopt an electoral reform of their own, much more radical than Gladstone's. Property rights and income would no longer be a qualification for voting, and every male householder would have the vote. Certain citizens would have *two* votes: the clergy, university graduates, and those paying direct taxes of more than twenty shillings per year. What did Gladstone do? He opposed the bill and proposed amendments. On all amendments to remove the double vote for certain classes of people, Disraeli yielded. By conceding on these points, he won sufficient Liberal support (over Gladstone's opposition) for his Conservative bill to enact the Reform of 1867.

This was not the last time the two adversaries shifted their positions. Nor was it the last time that liberalizing reforms would be the result. Gladstone, who had, before 1867, opposed the use of the secret ballot in voting on the grounds that the few who could vote had a public responsibility to reveal their choices recognized that with every male adult voting, his argument no longer applied. So in 1872 he successfully obtained ballot reform, despite the opposition of the House of Lords. Disraeli, in his turn, led the opposition's attack on Gladstone's policies as prime minister from 1868 to 1874. But when Disraeli returned to power, he not only accepted those policies, he embraced and extended many. In sum, at least in flexibility of positions, both Disraeli and Gladstone assumed the virtue of a principle that Disraeli put well: "In politics nothing is contemptible."

The Price of Talk

There is an old saying that "talk is cheap." By now you should realize that is not always the case. Power talk, the talk of legislative chambers, does not come cheap. To do it well, to be effective, and to get things done require considerable wisdom, skill, and finesse. Learning to whom to talk and who will listen, the rules of legislative talk, the resources and skills of effective talk, and when to say what is not easy. But talk you must, whether in the legislative halls of government or in the groups in your everyday life. "Real politics," said Disraeli, "are the possession and distribution of power." Both require the astute use of talk.

"Legislation unquestionably generates legislation. . . . Once begin the dance of legislation, and you must struggle through its mazes as best you can to its breathless end,—if any end there be."

—Woodrow Wilson

"In every republic there are two different inclinations: that of the people and that of the upper class, and . . . all the laws which are made in favor of liberty are born of the conflict between the two."

—Machiavelli

"No government can long be secure without a formidable Opposition."

—Disraeli

"You scratch my back and I'll scratch yours."

—Simon Cameron

"This is a Senate, a Senate of equals, of men of individual honor and personal character, and of absolute independence. We know no masters, we acknowledge no dictators."

—Daniel Webster

"Change is inevitable in a progressive country. Change is constant."

—Disraeli

"Time is on our side."

—Gladstone

"In politics nothing is contemptible."

—Disraeli

Princely Palaces Where Power Resides

Chapter

11

What Happens in Bureaucratic Offices and Managerial Suites?

In 1955, few people had ever heard of the obscure history professor who taught at the University of Malaya and had the unlikely name of C. Northcote Parkinson. Indeed, when he sent an article to a leading journal and it was published, the editors did not even include his name. They simply published the piece as "Parkinson's Law." The gist of the essay was built around the commonsense recognition that "work expands so as to fill the time available for its completion." If, for example, you have an entire semester to write a term paper that you know will take only an "all nighter," you will play at working on the paper, browsing around to find the right note cards, checking and rechecking books from the library that you probably do not read, asking your professor over and over again, "Just what do you want on this assignment?" The night before the paper is due, you undertake a crash program to finish, although you have been working on the project "all semester." In the years following 1955, when Parkinson's Law was published, C. Northcote Parkinson added other laws and maxims. Some people regard them as tongue-in-cheek observations about the human condition, but others accept them as invariable truths. In either event, one of the laws is directly related to what happens in the bureaucratic palaces of political power. It is Parkinson's Law of 1,000, and it says that any enterprise that employs more than one thousand people becomes a self-perpetuating empire with so many internal operations that it no longer needs any contact with the outside world. You might accept this observance as frivolous or serious, but in either case, the fact that you are reading this book is evidence that you have some direct, firsthand knowledge of it. In all likelihood, your college or university employs more than one thousand people. (Actually, one thousand is not a magic number, and some would say that it takes far fewer for an organization to become self-perpetuating, that is, to become a bureaucracy.) Therefore, you are centered in a bureaucratic palace of power. You sense this

each time you register for classes, deal with administrators and professors about grades, or try to live with dormitory regulations. Let that
experience be your guide as you make your way through the bureaucratic mazes of power in this chapter.

A MODIFIED BRANCH'S LAW, OR WHY
BUREAUCRACIES EXIST

C. Northcote Parkinson was not the only person to coin alleged laws of
the human condition, many of which apply to the politics of bureaucratic
power. Taylor Branch was another such lawmaker: Branch's First Law
of Crisis teaches that the spirit of public service rises and that the
bureaucracy multiplies much faster in times of crisis. This certainly was
the case in the United States during at least two major crises, the Great
Depression which prompted a growth in bureaucracy during President
Franklin Roosevelt's New Deal in the 1930s (see Chapter 18) and the
great increase in bureaucratic size during and following World War II.
Other examples also demonstrate the insight of Branch's Law regarding
the times when bureaucracy is most likely to multiply itself: the critical
period in the Soviet Union as it fought for survival in the 1920s, the
People's Republic of China during a similar trial in the 1950s, and the
growth of bureaucracy in Great Britain during World War II.

But what of the other aspect of Branch's law; does a spirit of public
service coincide with bureaucratic growth during critical times? One
example suggests as much. In the spring of 1918, Germany still had
hopes of winning the war it was waging against France, England, the
United States, and their allies. Peace had been reached with Russia in
January, Italy had been humiliated in combat in 1917, Rumania had
been removed from the war, and U.S. troops had not yet come in force on
the European continent. There were a few pessimists, such as Walther
Rathenau who thought a negotiated peace would be the best course.
Then came Germany's great spring offensive in 1918. It failed, and by
November the Allies, and not Germany, were the victors.

The Allies practiced an old political adage: to the victors belong the
spoils. For the Allies, the spoils of World War I were harsh reparations,
and so they demanded that Germany pay $32 billion for damages caused
by the war. Germany's postwar economy was already in a shambles, and
inflation was rampant. And to add to the situation, the Allies forced
Germany to cede rich industrial regions to Poland. Germany's new
political regime, the Weimar Republic, which had been formed after the
revolution overthrowing the imperial monarch (see Chapter 21) was
under siege by the Communists who preferred a dictatorship of the
proletariat and by the ultranationalists who wanted either the old
autocracy or a military dictatorship. Violence was the order of the day.
During the first four years after the war there were 376 political
murders, most by ultranationalists, which went unpunished.

By any standard, then, Germany was in crisis. Given the political and personal danger that any governmental minister serving the republic was in, any person accepting political appointment was putting a life on the line. A spirit of public service would have to prevail among those so endangering themselves. In this environment of crisis and violence, in 1920 Joseph Wirth became the German chancellor, or prime minister. He appointed Walther Rathenau as his minister of reconstruction to deal with the pressing problem of reparations. It was courageous of Rathenau to accept the position. He already had three strikes against him: he was a Jew and a liberal, and he supported the republic with enthusiasm.

Together Rathenau and Wirth took yet another highly unpopular step. They formulated a policy of "fulfillment" that recognized and accepted the Allies' reparations claims. By so doing, in spite of bitter criticism in the press and in the Reichstag (Parliament), the two hoped to persuade the Allies of Germany's good intentions and, by trying to meet Allied demands, prove that those demands were impossible. Germany paid the first installment on reparation (1 billion deutsche marks) in the fall of 1921. Rathenau then convinced the British and French to postpone the next installment and to hold an economic conference in April 1922 to discuss the situation. At that conference, when the allies failed to respond to Rathenau's policy of fulfillment, he took another course. Unknown to the British and French delegates to the conference—being held in Genoa, Italy—he held secret talks with the Soviet delegates in Rapallo, a short distance away. Out of that secret discussion came the Treaty of Rapallo, a treaty of friendship between Germany and the Soviet Union. For both nations it achieved several things. One, Russia would demand no reparations from Germany. This was important because France had been pressuring the Soviet Union to eek reparations so that France could then collect debts from the Soviet Union. Germany relinquished all claim to German property that had been confiscated by the Soviet Union after the Russian Revolution. The two nations restored full diplomatic recognition with each other and agreed to strengthen their trade ties.

But because of the course of events in Germany—the assassination of Rathenau, the development of the Nazi movement, and the fall of the Weimar Republic—the treaty had little practical effect, though it did convince the Allies that Germany was capable of an independent policy in foreign affairs. But more importantly, Rathenau's efforts, which ultimately cost him his life, demonstrated that Branch's Law does say something about both the rise in the spirit for public service and the growth of bureaucratic politics during times of crisis. But bureaucracies need not thrive only in crises. To learn about that, consider what bureaucracies are, their origins, and their types.

As seen in Chapter 10, legislation involves making general rules governing the conduct of people. Rules, however, are not applied in the abstract but are relevant to individual, concrete cases. Administration

WALTHER RATHENAU: MANAGER OR MARTYR?

It is perhaps strange that a man who spent less than two years in government during an otherwise long and successful career should have become one of the pivotal political figures of the first quarter of this century. But Walther Rathenau (1867–1922) was a product and a victim of what Machiavelli considered the driving force of human destinies, changing times and circumstances. Another factor that influenced Rathenau's career was the commonly held belief that in an increasingly bureaucratic society anyone who had demonstrated outstanding managerial skills in private enterprise could be equally effective at dealing with a nation's political problems.

A few years after Rathenau's birth, his father, who owned a small iron factory in Germany, came across an invention being displayed at industrial exhibits and expositions. It was Thomas Edison's electric light. Rathenau's father recognized its possibilities and bought the European patents for the invention. With borrowed money, he founded a small business that grew into an industrial empire, *Allgemeine Elektrizitatsgesellschaft* (AEG), the European equivalent of America's General Electric. Rathenau had a cordial but not close relationship with his father. Very early he determined to make himself financially independent of the elder, and so he gave up plans for an artistic career, for which many thought him exceptionally suited, and studied electrical engineering in college. After graduation, he worked for ten years in two isolated outposts, first at an aluminum factory in Switzerland and then as manager of an electrochemical works in a remote part of Germany. Rathenau's decade of isolation was important to him in several ways. First, he became a highly competent technocrat and was rewarded accordingly: he achieved financial independence and even contemplated retirement. Second, he became a skilled manager of people, finances, and industry. Third, with ample time for reading and reflection, Rathenau nurtured his love of philosophy and pledged to write on philosophy someday. He eventually became one of Germany's leading political thinkers and statesmen. Finally, Rathenau thought long and hard about his ancestry. He was a Jew but thought of himself as a German Jew. He realized, however, that however loyal and patriotic to the German cause he might be, any path to a political career would probably be blocked because of his ancestry.

Just as he was about to retire at age thirty-two, the AEG urged him to join the firm as a member of the board of directors and to manage the construction of power plants. This he did and built power stations in Germany, Italy, England, the Netherlands, Argentina, Russia, and elsewhere. He became a financial power, associated with eighty-four of the world's largest industrial concerns. "Three hundred men, all acquainted with each other," he said, controlled the economic destiny of Europe. He was one of them. Such power naturally brought him into contact with governmental leaders, and he was the personal friend of the German kaiser and Germany's political and military leaders. Yet his political views did not always square with those expected of a man of so much wealth and influence. Indeed, for his time, he was a social reformer. He wished to abolish hereditary wealth and the class structure and aristocratic culture associated with it. Through highly mechanized and skillfully managed industry, production would be vastly increased and German workers liberated. All this required the expertise of an enlightened manager to plan and organize (administer), centralize the distribution of goods (through a tight bureaucracy), and curtail the production of frivolous goods.

In August 1914, World War I began. Rathenau was like most Germans, in that he thought the war was a noble cause that Germany would eventually win. But unless Germany's stock of raw materials, as well as those from captured Belgium and northern France was carefully managed, Germany could not survive a long conflict. He convinced the war minister of this and was appointed as the head of a department responsible for war matériel. His administrative experience served him well, and within six months he had ensured that Germany's stocks were properly conserved and had established private companies under public control to maintain the war effort. His task completed, he resigned. But there was some bitterness, for the military personnel of the Ministry of War and the civilian businessmen he had dealt with resented his methods. He noted, "Neither of the groups concerned can forgive me that I, a private citizen and a Jew, have done the state some service of my own accord, and I do not think this attitude will change in my lifetime."

It did not change. When Germany lost the war and the Imperial Government of Germany was overthrown and replaced with a parliamentary democracy (the Weimar democracy), one of Rathenau's admirers entered his name in nomination to be the first president. But many political circles, especially those opposed from the start to the Weimar regime, regarded Rathenau as a liberal and a Jew, thus not qualified for the presidency. They hooted and laughed when his name came before Parliament, and so he withdrew. It seemed that he would have no future in political affairs. But *fortuna* intervened. As Germany's postwar economic crisis worsened, the skills of a financial manager became increasingly attractive to troubled politicians. After all, before the war, the American dollar would buy 4.2 German marks, but by the fall of 1921 this figure had inflated to 200. In that same year the German chancellor (prime minister) asked Rathenau to become minister of reconstruction in his cabinet. Rathenau agreed and, within a year, became foreign minister. In both offices, his task was to deal with the huge debt that the victorious Allies demanded that Germany pay to recompense them for the war—$32 billion. Rathenau was moderately successful. He convinced the English that Germany wished to fulfill its obligations, obtained a brief postponement regarding when payments would be due, reached an agreement with the Soviet Union by which it and Germany renounced war claims against each other, and made a little progress in efforts to open talks on modifying the size of the war debts.

Rathenau's accomplishments bred opposition among anti-Weimar elements at home. For having signed a treaty with Soviet Russia, Rathenau was branded as a Communist. For being willing to fulfill war obligations he was labeled anti-German. And there was always his ancestry. A marching song for the anti-Weimar forces went: "Shoot down Walther Rathenau, he's a goddamned dirty Jew." And that is what happened. On July 24, 1922, Rathenau was assassinated in Berlin by members of a terrorist organization opposed to the Weimar Republic and its policies. Word of the murder brought hundreds of thousands of workers into the streets throughout Germany, protesting and mourning Rathenau's death. He became more popular dead than he ever was while living, a much more beloved martyr than appreciated manager.

takes specific actions in particular cases, actions that apply the more general and enduring rules implied in legislation. Such administration requires at least two overlapping activities, organization and management. Organization is simply the means of dividing up work among people; management includes directing and influencing workers in their tasks.

Consider an example. You are enrolled in a college or university, and to graduate you must pass certain requirements that have been set by your institution. Think of those requirements as one aspect of legislation governing the conduct of students. But you know that such rules, although intended to be general and to affect everyone in the same way, are often applied to different students in different ways. The requirements say, for example, that you must take a certain course in order to graduate. You find yourself in the last semester of your senior year and the course is not offered. What do you do? You probably seek an exception to the rule—ask to substitute another course, take independent studies in the subject, or whatever. At some point some administrative official must grant or deny your request, that is, apply a general rule in a specific case. In the pecking order (hierarchical organization) of the college or university that that officer works for, he or she is responsible to someone else and has other people who work for and are responsible to him or her. The official is managed and manages.

How people administer, organize, and manage political power in order to apply general rules in specific instances is what constitutes bureaucracy. The term literally means "rule by the office" or "rule by officials." Walther Rathenau's efforts thus were bureaucratic. As minister of reconstruction, he was responsible for accepting the general rules imposed by the Allies on Germany (those governing reparations payments), seeking ways to fulfill and change those rules (organization), and directing and influencing other officials to comply (manage). In this respect Rathenau was a bureaucrat.

Bureaucracies have existed since ancient times. The pharoahs of Egypt and the kings of Babylon were served by priests who did their bidding, applying general decrees in specific instances. Oriental despots had their subalterns, scribes, tax collectors, and other administrative officials. Machiavelli recognized the existence of bureaucrats, although he did not call them that, in *The Prince*: "All kingdoms of which we have any knowledge," he wrote, "are governed in one of two ways." He then described two types of bureaucratic rule: "either by a single prince with everyone else as servants, who by his appointment and permission assist him in the task of ruling; or by a prince with the aid of barons, who hold that rank, not by the prince's grace, but by the right of birth in an ancient family." Today we would say that either the princely manager has the power to hire and fire subordinate bureaucrats or they are selected by other means and cannot be removed by the prince. When a president appoints members of cabinet, staff, and other officials, he or she is governing in the first of Machiavelli's two ways. But many public officials obtain their jobs by "merit appointment," by taking competitive exams and demonstrating their qualifications. The president does not appoint these bureaucrats, nor can he or she fire them. In short, like barons with rank by "right of birth," they govern independently of princely grace.

With the rise in recent centuries of the modern nation state, there has been a proliferation of bureaucracy. Autocracies, republics, and totalitarian regimes all have vast bureaucratic supporting networks. Even Communist regimes, which profess the doctrine of seeking the downfall of the state (see Chapter 7), rely on bureaucratic power. Indeed, in many respects, Communist regimes have perfected bureaucratic logic, which has produced some misgivings. These are reflected in the words of the first premier of the Soviet Union, Vladimir Lenin, when he appealed for support: "Support this state that I represent, this beastly political bureaucracy; it is needed now to make wars civil and foreign." Leon Trotsky, who broke with the Soviet regime in a power struggle with Lenin's successor, Joseph Stalin, was more pointed: "Bureaucracy is impregnated through and through with the spirit of mediocrity." Let it be said, however, that Trotsky made these remarks after Stalin, by becoming a master of bureaucratic intrigue and power, had triumphed over his opponents.

Different political regimes, of course, have different bureaucratic organizations. Generally, however, whether autocratic, republican, or totalitarian, at the top of each bureaucratic hierarchy are executive departments or ministries. At their heads are cabinet members or ministers charged with policy responsibility in a particular area—foreign affairs, commerce, finances, agriculture, labor, health, education, defense, and the like. Each department or ministry is then divided into subagencies. These may be called offices, bureaus, divisions, or, as in France, *directions*. The degree that the department or ministry head endeavors to direct and influence these subagencies varies according to the size of the organization, how the workers are chosen, who talks to whom, who controls the monies available to the organization, and other imponderables. Walther Rathenau, for instance, because of his preoccupation with negotiations on the reparations problem and his short time in office, scarcely could get involved in the day-to-day operations of the Foreign Ministry once he was elevated to its head.

There are other types of bureaucratic organizations, but the internal structure of each is approximately the same as that outlined. In the United States, for instance, there are independent agencies administering all activities in a particular area. The Federal Civil Service Commission, for example, supervises, examines, hires, fires, promotes, and in other respects administers regulations calling for the merit selection of bureaucrats (called civil servants). Government corporations resemble privately owned businesses but conduct their businesses on a nonprofit, self-sustaining basis for government. To ensure that Germany would have sufficient supplies of scarce materials during World War I, Walther Rathenau, as the manager of war matériel, created the equivalent of a government corporation. In the United States today, the

Federal Deposit Insurance Corporation insures the deposits of banks and savings and loans associations and is the source of the phrase you often hear in advertisements: "your money is protected by the FDIC."

EVELYN'S FIFTH RULE, OR WHO ARE PUBLIC FUNCTIONARIES? WHAT DO THEY DO?

A bureaucrat is a public functionary, one who works (functions) on behalf of a specific set of people (a public). As you know from Chapter 1, Niccolo Machiavelli was a functionary before he wrote *The Prince* and *Discourses*. He served as secretary to the Florentine Council and as a diplomat; in short, he too was a bureaucrat. Other political figures also served as public functionaries at some point in their careers: Thomas Jefferson as U.S. secretary of state, Charles de Gaulle in the French army, James Madison as U.S. secretary of state, Walter Lippmann for the Inquiry, and Walther Rathenau.

There is a misconception that such bureaucrats do not participate in politics. This notion seems from the belief that because functionaries only carry out the will of their publics, applying general rules in specific instances, they lack the decision-making discretion of executives or legislators. Administrative functionaries, so goes the view, "take politics out of government." By now you will recognize the fallacy in such thinking. The college or university official who might act on your hypothetical request to be excused from taking a required course certainly has the discretion to "bend the rules." And the princely figures discussed in preceding chapters, from Machiavelli to Rathenau, surely made decisions, even when they were bureaucrats. In effect, they managed things, just as the fictional official manages your educational standing by allowing you to avoid a required course or by forcing you to take it. Remember that managing involves directing and influencing people, the essential elements of political power, as discussed in Chapter 4. Administration, then, is simply another variety of politics, not a substitute for politics.

Ponder this bureaucratic situation. Pontius Pilate was the Roman procurator (a functionary, a bureaucrat) responsible for administering the province of Judaea. He found himself embroiled in a local conflict, the trial of a man that some people thought was a troublemaker and others thought was the son of God—Jesus Christ. Pilate had a decision to make. Should he commute Jesus' sentence, prevent his execution? That might lead the troublemaker to stir up more discontent. Pilate's economy of violence took him in another direction. He would let Jesus be crucified, thus quieting the unruly mob opposed to Jesus, asserting local control, and giving local power holders what they wanted. Pilate the functionary made an administrative, that is, political, choice. Needless to say, the long-term results were not what he anticipated.

Pontius Pilate's administration involved decisions that did not directly affect his superiors and the Roman bureaucracy of which they were a part. Sometimes, however, indeed one can say usually, bureaucrats find themselves immersed in the politics of their own organizations. Indeed, they must play bureaucratic politics if they are to protect their own organizations, practice power, and advance their own careers. Through his letters and dispatches to the Florentine Council, Machiavelli influenced the council's assessment of political realities. By that means he wielded power over his superiors and over the policies they followed.

The politics inside an organization influence the tenor of politics outside the organization and vice versa. Consider a more recent example than that of Pontius Pilate. In 1974, Alexander Haig served as President Richard Nixon's chief of staff, an important functionary position in the White House. There were strong pressures from outside the White House staff for Nixon to resign because of mounting evidence that he was implicated in a 1972 break-in at the opposing Democratic headquarters in the Watergate apartment complex, in a cover-up to hide such White House involvement, and in possible illegal bribes, payoffs, and other scandalous conduct. Playing bureaucratic politics within the White House staff, Haig isolated Nixon's supporters and then sought to persuade other members of the staff, Nixon's family, and Republican leaders that Nixon should resign. From there it was a matter of convincing Nixon that resignation was the best way out, because he could never avoid impeachment by the House of Representatives and conviction by the Senate. Haig became a backstage facilitator, using his bureaucratic influence to get his boss to do something that otherwise he might not want to do or would not have done.

Douglas Evelyn is another not-so-tongue-in-cheek lawmaker. His Fifth Rule of Bureaucratic Behavior says that "incompetents often hire able assistants." This was precisely the course recommended by Machiavelli. "There are, in fact, three sorts of brains," he contended. "One understands on its own, another understands what others tell it, and the third understands neither itself or other people." The wise prince must learn that "the first sort is superb, the second sort very good, the third sort useless." Better that a prince secure the services as functionaries of the superb or the very good, even though those brains may disagree substantially with the ruler on vital matters, than rely on the administrative capacities of the agreeable but useless. To take the opposite course of action might derive the nation of a valuable public functionary just at the time it most needs him or her.

Thus Machiavelli might well have applauded German Chancellor Joseph Wirth's 1921 appointment of Walther Rathenau as minister of reconstruction. For here was the prime minister of a republic selecting as principal administrator a man who had no sympathies for republics: said Rathenau, "I am a supporter of the idea of monarchy, not just out of distaste for election jobbery and rivalry, for lawyers and publicists." He also held the innate sentiment and conviction that the head of state— and he really seemed to mean any ideal public functionary—"should be a deeply responsible man, removed and withdrawn from all the desires, ambitions, and temptations of ordinary life; a consecrated man, and not an *arriviste* [opportunist or social climber] who has made a successful career."

Assuming that such "superb" and "very good" (to use Machiavelli's ideal) or "deeply responsible" (to use Rathenau's) public functionaries exist, what do they do?

MILES'S LAW, OR MANAGING THE POLITICS OF BUREAUCRACY

By now, you may well be saying to yourself, "So what? Sure, I'm affected by what bureaucrats do, but I'm not one, so what can I do about it?" You need not seek far for an answer. Bureaucracies permeate all walks of life. They are massive organizations that employ millions of people. The U.S. federal bureaucracy alone employs almost three million people. Granted, that is only about 3 percent of all civilians working as employees, but add local and state bureaucrats, and the total rises to almost fifteen million, over 17 percent. Then consider Parkinson's Law of 1,000 and reflect how many persons work in organizations of that size— corporations, trade unions, churches, factories, colleges, and so on. What it means is that a vast portion of Americans work in bureaucratic organizations, and so the chances are very good that you will as well. The more you know about the workings of public bureaucracies and functionaries, the more you will know about your everyday life now and in the future.

A bureaucrat's opinion on an issue or problem depends on the job that functionary has. Rufus Miles, once a career federal bureaucrat in the U.S. Department of Health, Education and Welfare (now the Department of Health and Human Services) phrased it this way: "Where you stand depends on where you sit" (Miles's law). Return to the example of your efforts to get a required course waived so that you can graduate. Your viewpoint may be "what is one course, more or less?" The administrator who decides your case has a different vantage point. What is at stake is the institution, its standards, rules, regulations, academic reputation: "Why, if we bend the rules for you we must for everybody; then where will we be?"

Bureaucracies heed an imperative; that is, bureaucrats engage in struggles to maintain and expand their organizations and their organizations' interests. Parkinson's Law has more than a germ of truth to it because organizations must expand their power base to survive; they must become self-sustaining in conflicts with other organizations, for money, resources, programs, contracts, the prince's favor. By the same token, the individual bureaucrat has a career to protect and advance. The bureaucrat's interests become identified with the organization's, the organization's with the clientele it serves, the clientele's interests with the nation's.

During the administration of President Dwight D. Eisenhower in the

1950s, his appointee as secretary of defense, Charles E. Wilson, appeared before a committee of the U.S. Senate considering his confirmation. Wilson had had much experience running private bureaucracies, namely, the General Motors Corporation (GMC). A senator asked Wilson, who was also a major stockholder in GMC, about a possible conflict of interest. Could Wilson, if the situation arose, make a decision adverse to the interests of GMC if it were in the nation's interests to do so? Wilson replied that he could but thought it unlikely that such a situation would arise. "For years I thought what was good for our country was good for General Motors and vice versa. The difference did not exist. Our country is too big. It goes with the welfare of our country. Our contribution to the nation is considerable." Members of the press reported and interpreted Wilson's remarks to be "what is good for General Motors is good for the country," a phrase widely used to criticize the Eisenhower presidency as favoring big business. Be that as it may, Wilson's comment reflects what many a bureaucrat comes to believe, rightly or wrongly, that what is good for the organization is good for the country.

One task of the bureaucrat, then, is to serve the organization, something you will do if you are so employed. Whether in a governmental or nongovernmental bureaucracy, your task will be to exercise political power within it. If you do your task well, you will expand the organization's budget, personnel, functions, and reputation and fight off threats to the bureaucracy's power from other quarters. What are the tactics that bureaucrats use to do this? They begin with their clients. A bureaucratic organization comes into existence for a purpose, to perform a service, undertake a task, serve a need, or solve a problem. Fulfilling that purpose normally involves dealing with specific publics, or groups of people. The Department of Agriculture deals with farmers, the Department of Commerce with business, the Department of Labor with workers, and the Department of Justice with lawyers, judicial officials, and others. If the organization does its job right, it will win support from those it serves. The Consumer Protection Agency that does what its name implies will gradually win the support of interests it serves. Some agencies exist to regulate groups rather than to serve them. But if those agencies regulate in the groups' interests or balance the groups' and wider interests, they too will win group support. In fact, the regulated groups become dependent on the agency's efforts for their survival. In the 1970s the U.S. federal government, which had regulated the airline industry since its inception, moved toward deregulation as a means of stimulating competition for routes, airfares, and passengers. A few airlines were not happy at the prospect of deregulation, fearing that they might not survive competition. For those airlines the regulating agency, the Civil Aeronautics Board, was more friend than foe.

The first rule of bureaucratic survival, then, is to represent and serve powerful interests, powerful clienteles. Some bureaucratic organizations, however, have no recognizable clientele but are formed to solve a problem or meet a need rather than represent specific interests. Those agencies pursue two courses, the first being to develop a clientele. The Department of Defense—in the United States as well as in other nations—generates a powerful support from contractors and subcontractors who share in the huge governmental outlays for weapons systems, armaments, and defense systems.

The second course is continually to define and redefine the bureaucracy's mission. This can be done in several ways. Again, a nation's defense department is an example. Even if a nation's defense posture with respect to its enemy is superior, there will always seem to be a new enemy or world trouble spot to justify increases in defense spending. The maxim is that a nation never has enough defense. Or if an agency has performed the mission set out for it when it was created, its survival will require defining a new mission. In the early 1960s President John F. Kennedy stated his nation's goal of landing a man on the moon by the end of the decade. The National Aeronautics and Space Administration (NASA) enjoyed budgetary largess, and in 1969, the goal was achieved. Did NASA go out of business after its success? No, it redefined its mission: space exploration was the long-term task, the moon landings only a portion of it. Although no longer the beneficiary of vast budget outlays, NASA survives with unmanned space explorations, space shuttles, and other programs. Or consider the Federal Bureau of Investigation (FBI) under its former head, J. Edgar Hoover (see Chapter 23). The FBI's original job was to investigate crime, end racketeering, and reduce the rampant gangland murders coinciding with the era of American Prohibition. But such a mission had far less appeal once Prohibition ended and World War II loomed. So the FBI found new things to do, namely, ferret out foreign agents and spies. After the war, the FBI turned to investigating Communists, thus taking advantage of the fears generated by tensions between the Soviet Union and the United States during the Cold War. In short, the FBI is a bureaucracy that heeds Machiavelli's exhortations about adapting to new times and circumstances.

Indispensability is another tactic. The U.S. Central Intelligence Agency (CIA) and its Soviet equivalent the KGB make the claim of being indispensable. In a world of intelligence and counterintelligence, information and disinformation, covert operations, assassinations, terrorism and counterterror, both organizations use the rationale that they are indispensable to their respective nation's survival. The U.S. Internal Revenue Service combines claims of indispensability (after all, if there are to be taxes, there must be tax collectors) with public relations tactics to produce the impression that the IRS is doing a good job, processing refunds with dispatch, helping people fill out tax forms, responding to inquiries, and so on.

A healthy public relations program is vital to bureaucratic survival. The U.S. Department of Defense has a public affairs operation that in itself—applying Parkinson's Law of 1,000—is a bureaucracy. It employs thirteen hundred specialists and has a budget well beyond $20 million per year. It sponsors traveling exhibits, lectures, TV and radio programs, films, weapons demonstrations, new releases for local news-papers, and even helps make Hollywood movies extolling the virtues of a strong defensive posture. But not all public relations need be so public. A favorite gambit of Defense Department officials when Congress is considering the organization's budget is to leak to the press secret information about the state of United States' or its enemies' (usually the Soviet Union) defense. The implication of such leaks is that failure to vote budget increases would seriously jeopardize the competitive posi-tion of the United States.

Public relations and news management (see Chapter 27) combine with the lobbying of legislative palaces to form a useful trio of tactics to enhance bureaucratic survival and growth. Bureaucratic lobbying takes place in all regimes, autocratic, republican, and totalitarian. The head of Nazi Germany's air force (*Luftwaffe*), Hermann Goering, con-tinuously lobbied Adolf Hitler, seeking new types of aircraft, weapons, armaments, and the like. His favorite tactic was to assure Hitler that the Luftwaffe could perform miracles and then to feed him false infor-mation regarding its actual accomplishments. In a republic, bureau-cratic lobbying is directed not at a dictator but at the executive and legislative palaces, for example, at Congress in the United States and at the government in Great Britain. But their claims for the success of an agency's programs may be no less extravagant than Goering's.

These, then, are tactics to promote bureaucratic survival and growth. If you work in a bureaucracy, you may find yourself using many of them. And if you occupy a bureaucratic position, you may find other tech-niques useful in managing yourself, your superiors, and your subordinates.

James H. Boren, the founder of the International Association of Professional Bureaucrats, devised what he called the Three Laws of Bureaucracy: (1) "When in doubt, mumble"; (2) "When in trouble, delegate"; and (3) "When in charge, ponder." Are these merely humor-ous, facetious observations? Not at all. Many of the qualities associated in the popular mind with bureaucracy—delay, red tape, passing the buck, obfuscation—serve the bureaucrat in useful ways. There may be good reasons for delaying a decision: to gather more information, assess its consequences, drum up support, wear down the opposition, and even avoid the decision altogether, especially if the functionary does not want to risk taking the blame. Red tape, the multiplicity of complex rules and procedures that must be followed before anything can be done, also serves bureaucratic ends. For one, demanding a full record of what goes on not only provides the bureaucrat with information, but it also covers the official in case of future criticism. Red tape also puts obstacles in the way of reaching a bureaucrat, thus keeping "them off my back." Passing the buck is an ancient ploy (Pontius Pilate even used it) that allows a bureaucrat to avoid responsibility for an unpopular, or unsuccessful, program. And obfuscation, "When in doubt, mumble," so clouds issues and situations that seemingly no one need take responsibility.

Bureaucracies and bureaucrats that uses such tactics, like the little girl who had a little curl right in the middle of her forehead, can, when they are good, be very very good, but when they are bad, be horrid. In fact, when horrid, bureaucracies can even be insane, as testified to by the elaborate bureaucracy constructed in Nazi Germany to execute the "final solution." In large measure, whether bureaucracies are good or horrid depends on the princes who rule them and on their skills, motives, and practice of bureaucratic power. Walther Rathenau was one type of bureaucratic prince, Hermann Goering another. What type will you become?

"All kingdoms of which we have any knowledge are governed in one of two ways: either by a single prince with everyone else as servants, who by his appointment and permission assist him in the task of ruling; or by a prince with the aid of barons, who hold that rank, not by the prince's grace, but by the right of birth in an ancient family."

—Machiavelli

"Support this state I represent, this beastly political bureaucracy; it is needed now to make wars civil and foreign."

—Lenin

"Bureaucracy as bureaucracy is impregnated through and through with the spirit of mediocrity."

—Trotsky

"There are, in fact, three sorts of brains: one understands on its own, another understands what others tell it, and the third understands neither itself or other people. The first sort is superb, the second sort very good, the third sort useless."

—Machiavelli

"At the head of the power ... there should be a deeply responsible man, removed and withdrawn from all the desires, ambitions, and temptations of ordinary life; a consecrated man, and not an *arriviste* who has made a successful career."

—Rathenau

"When in doubt, mumble. When in trouble, delegate. When in charge, ponder."

—James H. Boren

Chapter

12

What Happens on Judicial Benches?

During the early 1830s, a young Frenchman traveled to the United States. He was a keen observer of social and political life, very much in the tradition of Niccolo Machiavelli. His name was Alexis de Tocqueville. Out of his travels came a volume describing the poltical life of the then young republic, a work entitled *Democracy in America*. In one passage Tocqueville wrote, "There is hardly a political question in the United States which sooner or later does not turn into a judicial one." In many respects what was true in 1835 is no less accurate today, and although in many other nations the judicial role is not as important as it is in the United States, there is a close link between the judiciary and politics. In fact, what happens on judicial benches is politics.

MAKING THE SUPREME COURT SUPREME

Secretary of State John Marshall made a mistake, and Chief Justice John Marshall corrected it. Recall from Chapters 4 and 8 that in the early years of the United States there was a power struggle between two contending forces. The conflict pitted the Federalists, led by George Washington, John Adams, and Alexander Hamilton, against the Republicans, led by Thomas Jefferson and James Madison. You will also remember that in the elections of 1800 the Republicans were triumphant, securing control of the presidency and of Congress. The Federalists had to take a stand somewhere and chose the federal judiciary. In fact, just before losing control of Congress, the Federalists passed a court-packing bill that would have delighted President Franklin D. Roosevelt, who tried a similar tactic over a century later (see Chapter 19). Arguing that federal judges were overworked, too remote from the people, and too few in number, the Federalist leaders proposed to create new district courts, justices of the peace, and circuit judges. Because President John Adams was still in office, he would appoint Federalists and not Republicans to these posts. Moreover, the Judiciary Bill proposed to reduce the size of the U.S. Supreme Court from six to five members, thus reducing the likelihood that the much feared and hated Republican President Thomas Jefferson would be able to appoint any members to that body.

Today the Supreme Court is an august and powerful body. It is an equal, independent branch of the federal government, along with the President and Congress. But at the end of the eighteenth century, the Supreme Court was equal in name only. After ratifying the Constitution, Congress created a court system with the Judiciary Act of 1789. It specified that the Supreme Court, mentioned only vaguely in the Constitution, would consist of a chief justice and five associate justices. The "inferior courts" spoken of in the Constitution would be circuit and district courts. None of the three circuit courts would have judges of its own; instead, two Supreme Court judges "riding circuit" (that is, going into hinterland cities to hold court) and a district judge would make up a circuit court. (Obviously this placed a considerable burden on the Surpeme Court judges, and indeed, many found their health taxed and their careers shortened by it. The thirteen district courts consisted simply of a judge. The president, with the advice and consent of the Senate, would appoint all federal judges.

During this period, the Supreme Court was of such little consequence that it was given only a tiny room in the Capitol building to meet in. The justices liked to think of themselves as independent of the other two branches of government, but in fact they were far from it. The justices were political partisans, loyal to the Federalist party, and heretofore followed the lead of Federalist presidents and congressional leaders. But now a Republican was about to become president, and the Congress was Republican. How would the Court, which had not become supreme, respond?

During the final days of his administration, John Adams appointed John Marshall, then secretary of state, as the chief justice of the Supreme Court. Until Thomas Jefferson's inaugural as president, Marshall would serve in a dual capacity, as secretary of state and as chief justice; after that, Jefferson's appointee, James Madison, would become secretary of state, and Marshall—as Court justices were appointed for life—would remain as chief justice. Marshall had already made up his mind on one thing, that he would keep the Supreme Court out of partisan politics and adopt a low profile. Silence on public affairs became the rule for Court justices. Marshall even refused to vote in national elections so as not to show any party preference, and when the Court announced decisions, Marshall intiated the practice of reading the Court's ruling opinion himself rather than letting associate justices read individual opinions. Justices could read dissenting opinions, which were rare, but Marshall spoke for the Supreme Court.

As the time approached for John Adams to leave the presidency and Thomas Jefferson to assume it, Adams hastened, with the help of Secretary of State John Marshall, to fill with his party's sympathizers the new courts created by the Federalist Judiciary Act of 1801. Marshall worked late into the night before Jefferson's inauguration, signing commissions for Adam's appointees. This, he thought, would make the appointees judges, thus placing in office good Federalists who could be removed only by impeachment. The judiciary would be the last bastion of Federalist power.

This, however, is where Adams made his mistake. In the last frantic hours in office, Secretary Marshall left on his desk the signed commissions for forty-two new justices of the peace. They were legally signed, but he had neglected to deliver them to the appointees. His successor, James Madison, found the commissions, and under President Jefferson's instructions, Madison simply discarded seventeen of the commissions. Adams's appointees (Republicans called them "midnight judges") protested, but because the office of justice of the peace was a minor one, did not fight for their commissions. But William Marbury did decide to fight and asked the Supreme Court to issue a writ of mandamus as authorized by the Judiciary Act of 1789. Such a document would order Secretary of State Madison to give him his commission. Chief Justice Marshall responded by issuing a routine order requesting Madison to show cause why such a writ of mandamus should not be issued.

Lines were quickly drawn. The Republicans charged that the Supreme Court was interfering with presidential authority, and they moved to repeal the Federalist Judiciary Act that had created all of the new courts and judges in the first place. In the first midnight session in its history, the House of Representatives agreed with the Senate vote to repeal the act. Thus the "midnight judges," like Cinderella, vanished at midnight. That, however, was not the end of the matter, for still pending was William Marbury's complaint. Even though the repeal of the Judiciary Act of 1801 had abolished the very office for which he sought a commission, his case before the Surpreme Court—*Marbury v. Madison*—still had to be decided.

Republicans rejoiced, as they thought they had the Supreme Court between a rock and a hard place, as the saying goes. On the one hand, if the Court did not rule in favor of Marbury, it would be a tacit admission that it was not an equal, independent body, one that could rule on the acts of the other two branches. That would be a major Republican political victory. But on the other hand, if the Court ordered Madison to issue Marbury his commission, Madison (and President Jefferson) would simply refuse on grounds that the Court could not interfere with presidential matters, that the commission had long ago been destroyed, and the office to which Marbury had been appointed no longer existed. The Court would not be able to enforce its order, once again demonstrating its powerlessness. That too would be a major Republican victory.

Thomas Hobson was a seventeenth-century English stableman who rented horses. But he gave his customers no real choice of horses. He would say, "Take this horse now or wait around for the next available one." Because that "next available one" would never show up, the apparent freedom of choice of Hobson's customers was illusory, what we

JOHN MARSHALL: THE POLITICIAN AS JUDGE

"I think nothing could be better," wrote Thomas Jefferson in 1793 to James Madison, "than to make him a judge." Jefferson was writing about John Marshall. But although Jefferson and Marshall were cousins, it was not because of family ties that he wanted Marshall to become a judge. Rather, it was to get Marshall out of the way, to see to it that Marshall would be buried in the obscure "third branch of government," the judiciary, and not run for Congress. First cousins they were, but political allies they were not. To be sure, when Marshall had first decided on the practice of law as a career and had applied for a license, Jefferson, then governor of Virginia, had granted it eagerly. Had he known what was to transpire between him and his cousin in the decades to come, he probably would not have been so willing.

John Marshall was born in 1755 in the wilderness of colonial Virginia, and he did not leave the backwoods until he was a teenager. There were no schools in the wilderness, and so Marshall learned to read and write with the guidance of his parents. He read the Bible, Shakespeare, the English poets, Livy's *History of Rome* (shades of Machiavelli!), and commentaries on law. He developed a lifelong love of poetry, but it was the law that became his lifework. Because of his ambition, his father sent him off for schooling to an academy in a distant county. He spent a year there learning Latin, history, literature, and philosophy, and his closest friend was James Monroe, later to become the fifth president of the United States. Marshall returned home and was tutored by a clergyman living in his parents' home, but aside from a later five-month period studying law at the College of William and Mary, the future chief justice of the United States Supreme Court had no more formal schooling.

When barely out of his teens Marshall took command of a company of Virginia militiamen formed to fight the British in what became the Revolutionary War. He saw considerable action and rose quickly in the ranks. Under the command of his father's best friend, George Washington, Marshall fought at Brandywine, Germantown, Stony Point, and in other battles. He survived the long and miserable winter encampment with Washington's army at Valley Forge, from 1777 to 1778. There he served as deputy judge advocate of the army. He presided over and judged cases involving disputes between officers and soldiers, violations of military regulations, and other conflicts. He developed the skills of and a reputation for precise, clear reasoning. As well, he cultivated close relations with Washington and his aide, Colonel Alexander Hamilton.

As the war continued, Marshall returned periodically to Virginia. There he studied law briefly, was admitted to the bar in 1780, was elected to the Virginia House of Delegates in 1782, and married in 1783. By the war's end, he was busily engaged in building a law practice, becoming influential in the Virginia legislature, and raising a family. But it was not long until he, like so many other of Virginia's political leaders in that era, grew worried about the seeming inability of the Continental Congress under the Articles of Confederation to solve the nation's postwar problems. Thus in 1787, when the Constitutional Convention, in which his fellow Virginians James Madison and Edmund Randolph played key roles, proposed a new governmental form, a federation, Marshall joined the Federalist cause. As a delegate to Virginia's ratifying convention, Marshall was given responsibility for defending the new constitution's provisions regarding the judiciary. This was not because Marshall had any particular repute as a jurist. Rather, most of the convention's delegates were rustic, backwoods men. "Good Ol' Boy" John Marshall could appeal to their common sense, thought Madison. And he did. But he also voiced a legal and philosophical position that he invoked again fifteen years later in his famous case of *Marbury v. Madison.* "Has the government of the United States power to make laws on every subject," he asked, "Can they go beyond the delegated powers?" He answered, "If they were to make a law not warranted by any of the powers enumerated, it would be considered by the judges as an infringement of the Constitution which they are to guard. They would not consider such a law coming under their jurisdiction. They would declare it void."

Marshall remained a staunch Federalist for the rest of his life, and indeed at the time of his death was the last member of the Federalist party that had sought ratification of the Constitution, supported the presidential administrations of George Washington and John Adams, and fought the Jeffersonian-Madisonian Republicans tooth and nail. He became a prosperous lawyer and served many a wealthy client. He was President Washington' strongest advocate in Virginia but turned down repeated offers to join the cabinet or accept some other post. Finally, he did become a public functionary, serving as special ambassador to France in 1797. American–French relations then were tense. President John Adams appointed a three-member mission to work things out, and Marshall was one of the members. French Foreign Minister Charles Talleyrand (see Chapter 24), through three secret agents, demanded that the United States pay an indemnity, give France a large loan, and give him personally $250,000 to negotiate. In dispatches to Adams, Marshall warned of the plot and intrigue and counseled against the terms. When news of the events became public in America, there was an outcry against France. This "XYZ Affair" (named after the three mysterious secret agents) forced a softening of French attitudes and finally a compromise. Upon his return, Marshall received a hero's welcome.

Marshall was elected to Congress in 1799 but shortly thereafter acquiesced to Adams's request that he accept appointment as secretary of state. He knew that the Republicans were about to oust the Federalists from office in the election of 1800, and so he looked forward to a short period of service and to returning to Virginia and his legal practice. But *fortuna* intervened. Oliver Ellsworth, the chief-justice of the Supreme Court, resigned. President Adams offered the position to a former chief justice, John Jay. But Jay declined, noting that he had resigned from the position years earlier because the Court was a "weak" and "defective" branch. So Adams summoned Marshall. "Who shall I nominate now?" he asked his secretary of state. Marshall suggested names. Adams rejected each and then declared, "I believe I must nominate you." Marshall accepted on the spot, and what happens on judicial benches has not been the same since.

---

know today as a Hobson's Choice. Think of how many of those you have had in your lifetime! Politics is full of such choices, and Chief Justice John Marshall was faced with one in *Marbury v. Madison.* He handled it by creating another alternative.

Marshall began the Court's opinion by rebuking those who had disregarded the Constitution, namely, Jefferson. Marbury, he said, had a legal right to his appointment as justice of the peace (remember, Marshall as secretary of state had signed the commission). To withhold the commission, Marshall went on, was not warranted by law (of course, had Secretary Marshall delivered it, the commission would never have been withheld). But even though Marbury had a right to his commission and that right had been violated, could the Court do anything about it? Here the skills of the politician were those of the judge, and Marshall escaped his Hobson's Choice. The only relief that the Court could possibly give Marbury would be to issue a writ of mandamus, as requested. The power of the Court to do that derived from the Judiciary Act of 1789. But in giving the Court such power, said Marshall, the Congress had overstepped its boundaries and violated the Constitution. Why? Because the Constitution is very specific with respect to the kinds of cases that the Court can decide without appeal from a lower court. The "original jurisdiction" of the Supreme Court is defined in the Constitution, and Congress cannot expand it. Because that portion of the Judiciary Act of 1789 that expanded the Court's original jurisdiction was unconstitutional, the Court had no authority to issue a writ of mandamus. Therefore, although Marbury was entitled to his commission, he would have to seek elsewhere for it. The Court could not help him. The Hobson's Choice was not John Marshall's, but William Marbury's.

For the first time the Supreme Court had presumed to declare an act of Congress unconstitutional. *Marbury v. Madison* is thus paradoxical. Marbury was told, in effect, by a Court so powerful that it could declare acts of Congress to be unconstitutional that because of that power, it was powerless to help Marbury. Quite simply, John Marshall practiced Machiavelli's economy of violence. By using the Court's power to deny the Court power, Marshall thus assumed for the Court more power than anyone had ever granted it before, and as a practical political decision, the ploy worked. The Jeffersonians raised criticism but could scarcely say much in light of the fact that they had "won" the case; that is, the writ of mandamus had not been issued. With *Marbury v. Madison* behind it, the Supreme Court went on to judge other acts unconstitutional, those of Congress, of the president, and of state legislatures and officials. The Court became supreme.

What, you may ask, happened to Marbury? He never got his commission, never became a justice of the peace, and by the time his case was decided, he no longer cared. But late at night as he was musing by the fire, how often did he ponder Marshall's opinion in his case and compare it with something Marshall had said before there was a republic of the United States, a statement he made during the Virginia convention debating ratification of the Constitution? Said Marshall then: "To what quarter will you look for protection from an infringement on the Constitution, if you will not give that power to the judiciary? There is no other body that can afford such a protection."

"THEY AIN'T NOTHIN' TILL I CALLS 'EM": JUDGES AND LAW

You need not be a baseball fan to catch the drift of a little anecdote that was told about three umpires. The umpires were discussing how, when standing behind home plate, they determine the difference between balls and strikes. One umpire said, "Some's balls and some's strikes and I calls 'em as they is." A second umpire did not fully agree: "Some's balls and some's strikes and I calls 'em as I sees 'em." The third umpire thought a moment and then responded, "Some's balls and some's strikes but they ain't nothin' till I calls 'em."

Substitute "law" for balls and strikes and "judges" for umpires, and you will have a simplified summary of what happens in palaces of judicial power. In its broadest sense, the term *judiciary* refers to judges, their appointment and how long they serve, the courts on which they sit, the kinds of cases they decide (their jurisdictions), and how they proceed. In sum, the judiciary consists of what judges do. As the fable of the three umpires implies, judges decide disputes between people and the law "calls 'em as they is"), interpret the law ("calls 'em as I sees 'em"), and make the law ("they ain't nothin' till I calls 'em").

Review what we said about law in Part III. Laws are general rules meant to cover the conduct of everyone in a nation, or at least a specific category of people, and they are intended to endure. They are made through legislation, through execution by the heads of governments and their ministers, and through the discretion exercised by bureaucrats in applying them. In short, laws are made by politicians through politics. But despite being intended to regulate conduct in general, not everybody obeys the law. (How fast do you drive on interstate highways?) Or people may do things that they think are legal, only to find that law enforcement officers say that they are not. (Have you ever turned *left* at an intersection against a red light, with no oncoming traffic, thinking that because you can turn right in such cases, you can also turn left?) Or people may do things simply because they are ignorant of the law. (How many times have you, or will you, fail to enroll in a required college course because you do not know that it is required?)

For many reasons, then, conflicts arise between what people do, or fail to do, and what the law requires. Into this situation steps another politician, the judge, responsible for settling the dispute. Thus, for example, James Madison did not give William Marbury his commission: the Supreme Court had the task of deciding whether Marbury had a right to the commission, Madison was required to supply it, and the Court could not do anything about it. But saying that a judge is a politician charged with a political task does not imply that a judge is necessarily biased or partisan in conduct, as were the Federalist judges during the early days of the American republic. Judges may or may not approach their duties in an impartial fashion, depending on the judicial arrangements of a particular political regime. In an autocracy, such as that of Catherine the Great or of Louis XV, judges serve the autocrat's will. If they do not, they will not remain judges. Consider the fate of Sir Thomas More. More was the lord chancellor of England, a post that combined judicial and ministerial duties, during the reign of Henry VIII. As a young man, More, a celebrated lawyer, won the admiration of Henry, and they became close friends. Eventually Henry made More his lord chancellor. But when Henry tried to divorce his wife, an action forbidden by the Catholic church, he decided to remove England from the Catholic church and pressured Parliament to pass laws that would do just that. More recognized that sooner or later, disputes would arise involving Henry, parliamentary laws, and the law as he, More, understood it. So he resigned the chancellorship to avoid having to take a stand on such issues. Henry, however, would not be put off so easily. He wanted More's approval of his actions, and failing to achieve it, he had More tried for treason on grounds that More had opposed the divorce. But at his trial the king's lawyers never proved that More had uttered a word against Henry or his actions. More's crime, it turned out, was one of judicial silence. "For this my silence, neither your law, nor any law in the world, is able justly and rightly to punish me," said More at his trial. And indeed, the law was on More's side, but Henry VIII held the power and had his reluctant judge beheaded.

Nor are judges independent and impartial in totalitarian regimes. Judges exist to serve the dictator and the totalitarian ruling party. The most obvious manifestation of such purposes is the "show trial," a public trial of the regime's opponents or dissidents. The verdict of guilty is foreordained. The purpose of the trial is to put the accused on public display, provide a forum on which they can confess their guilt, and proclaim the superior political and moral authority of the regime. Recall, for instance, that during the early days of Joseph Stalin's dictatorship of the Soviet Union, he was opposed by Leon Trotsky (see Chapter 28). Trotsky was joined by a former Stalin ally, Grigori Zinoviev. When Stalin sought to purge the Communist party of all opposition, Zinoviev was tried in 1936 in a spectacular show trial. Zinoviev confessed to being guilty of all the charges brought against him, including being implicated in the murder of one of Stalin's closest aides. Zinoviev's inevitable execution obeyed the logic of totalitarian justice.

Justice is not blind in autocratic and totalitarian regimes, but the assumption is that in republics the judges will be independent and impartial, at least seeking the ideal of blind justice. How independent the judiciary is, of course, varies from one republic to another. As a minimum requirement for independence, judges are not permitted to be prosecutors as well. In short, the agency that brings charges of a law's violation cannot be the same as that deciding the case. In U.S. federal courts, for example, prosecutors are public functionaries of the executive, namely, U.S. attorneys separate from the district, circuit, and supreme court judges who render the decisions. By contrast, in France judicial officers are members of a common civil service, *la magistrature,* within a single ministry. However, the three elements in the ministry (the judges, prosecutors, and administrators) are independent of one another, which does not violate the demands of an independent judiciary.

A second requirement of independence is that the judges be protected from political pressures. This generally means that once appointed, judges will serve for life ("during good behavior" is the U.S. Constitution's language). Removal from office requires extreme measures: impeachment by a majority of the House of Representatives and conviction by a two-thirds vote in the Senate in the United States; resolutions by a majority of both the House of Commons and of Lords in Great Britain; and special action by the *Conseil Superieur de la Magistrature* in France. Bear in mind, however, that such protection does not mean the total removal of judges from political pressures. As the conduct of the U.S. Supreme Court during Franklin Roosevelt's administration illustrated (see Chapter 19), judges do read newspapers, pay close attention to election results, heed public opinion polls, and keep abreast of the political climate. Being human, their decisions are not above being influenced by such awareness. As Lenin proclaimed, "There are no more reactionary people in the world than judges." But they do match Thomas Jefferson's verdict: "Our judges are as honest as most men, and not more so. They have, with others, the same passions for party, for power, and the privileges of their corps."

PALACES OF JUDICIAL POWER

Since John Marshall's exercise of judicial power as chief justice of the Supreme Court, a third requirement of an independent judiciary has evolved, one not solely limited to the United States but peculiar to it in several respects. To understand it you need first to consider the types of judicial courts that exist, which requires an initial distinction that roughly parallels the difference in judicial procedures. In some republics—the United States, Great Britain, Canada, Australia, Scandinavia, and Switzerland are leading examples—all legal disputes are tried in courts as one commonly understands them. These regular courts hear both criminal and civil cases (cases involving crimes against the whole community, such as murder, versus cases concerning wrongs against private individuals that do not affect community welfare). A few of these republics try both criminal and civil cases in the same regular courts, and others have separate sets of courts for each type of case. Many Western European nations add administrative courts to the regular courts. Administrative courts offer citizens opportunities to protest what they deem arbitrary and illegal administrative decisions, that is, bureaucratic laws. France, for instance, has a two-tiered system of administrative courts, the first consisting of courts that try citizens' claims and the second serving as courts that try appeals of lower courts' decisions.

Depending on whether the republic is unitary, federal, or confederal (see Chapter 8), it may have separate sets of local, state, and national courts. In any event, there is a hierarchy of courts. At the lowest level are the courts that try very minor cases and perform relatively minor tasks. Included here are justices of the peace. Above such courts are the trial courts, where judges hear and decide most criminal and civil cases. In the United States, if you were charged with violating a federal law, you would probably be tried in a federal district court; in Great Britain the county and crown courts, in France the "tribunals of the first instance," and in West Germany the *Landsgerichte*. If you lose your case and can afford to, you may be able to appeal to an intermediate higher court to reverse the trial court's ruling. In the United States, federal courts of appeal exist for this purpose, in Great Britain a national Court of Appeal, in France regional courts of appeal, and in West Germany the *Oberlandesgerichte*. Finally, each republic has a final court of appeal, a truly supreme court: The U.S. Supreme Court, the British House of Lords, the Court of Cessation in France and Italy, and the West German *Bundesgerichtshof*.

It was at the Supreme-Court level that John Marshall introduced the final requirement of judicial independence, the requirement of what has come to be known as "judicial review." Simply put, it is the power that Marshall asserted in *Marbury v. Madison* to declare unconstitutional the acts of other government branches and agencies. This is not a power that rests in the supreme judicial body of every republic, however. In Great Britain, for example, parliamentary and not judicial supremacy is the rule. In the Fifth French Republic, the Constitutional Council, not a supreme court, reviews bills to determine their compatability with the constitution. A similar arrangement prevails with Italy's *Corte Constituzionale,* a special tribunal. In sum, John Marshall's princely act was innovative, elevating the Supreme Court to a position of equality and independence, but it did not necessarily set a pattern of judicial independence for all other republics to follow.

AND JUSTICE FOR ALL?: HOW POLITICIANS USE JUDICIAL BENCHES

Chances are that you have pledged many times your allegiance to the U.S. flag, and so you have often recited the last four words, "and justice for all." In the *Federalist Papers,* James Madison wrote: "Justice is the end of government. It is the end of civil society. It ever has been and ever will be pursued until it is obtained, or until liberty be lost in the pursuit." Justice, however, does not come easily. It is a product of a political process, the politics of judicial benches, and as with any politics, some people benefit more from justice than others do. There may be justice for all, but what is just for some interests may seem less so for rival ones. Even in the United States which, as you may now infer, has one of the most independent of judiciaries, justice for all is selective.

We shall start with the question of who is chosen as a judge. More often than not, in the United States and other nations as well, the answer is a politician. Because experience with the law involves politics, any person with a legal background (a lawyer, officeholder, lower court judge, or whatever) elected or appointed to a judgeship is a politician. Moreover, if the judicial bench is in, for example, the U.S. federal judiciary, the person making the judicial appointment—the president—is a politician, who has a strong inclination to appoint judges that will interpret the law in desirable ways or to appoint judges who deserve political rewards. For instance, in 1952 one of Dwight Eisenhower's rivals for the Republican nomination for president was Earl Warren, the governor of California. At a crucial point in the nomination struggle Warren helped swing key votes to Eisenhower, and he became his party's standard bearer. After Eisenhower's election, the position of chief justice appeared on the Supreme Court. Earl Warren received the appointment and, in the ensuing years, provided leadership to a Court that made some of the most widesweeping and far-reaching decisions in U.S. history. Sometimes, however, partisan judicial appointments backfire. After his election as president in 1968, Richard Nixon owed a debt to certain interests favoring the slowdown of racial desegregation. Nixon sought to pay that debt by appointing a southern conservative, Clement F. Haynesworth, the chief judge of the Fourth Circuit Court of Appeals, to fill a vacancy on the Supreme Court. Labor and civil rights leaders mounted opposition to the nomination, and the U.S. Senate rejected Haynesworth, the first major congressional defeat for the president.

Politics, then, determines who will become a judge, and the political climate influences that decision. This is particularly true in wartime. After the Japanese attack on Pearl Harbor on December 7, 1941, which opened hostilities between the United States and Japan and brought the United States into World War II, there was widespread concern about the possibility of Japanese agents residing in the United States. Suspicion extended even to U.S. citizens of Japanese ancestry, of which there were many. As a result, more than 100,000—two thirds of them U.S. citizens—Japanese Americans were forced to leave their homes and properties and were placed in "relocation centers," a drastic invasion of their rights as citizens and scarcely "justice for all." A few of the Japanese Americans filed court cases appealing the laws that placed them in detention camps. Ultimately these cases reached the Supreme Court for final decision. The Court pronounced the detention measures valid, but as antiespionage and antisabotage actions. Any citizen's loyalty that could not be successfully challenged, said the Court, warranted unconditional release from the relocation centers. Court rulings did not come until two and three years after the measures were taken that segregated the Japanese Americans. Although no Japanese, U.S. citizen or not, was ever found guilty of any act of espionage or sabotage, wartime justice ran its course. In so doing, did it—and on this *you* be the judge—live up to the Machiavellian precept regarding justice? "Those who have prudently constituted a republic have considered, among the most necessary things to organize, the protection of liberty, and according to whether this is well done or not, that self-governing state will last for a longer or shorter time."

Another reason that justice is political is that politicians often use the judiciary for their own ends. This happens in several ways. The most obvious is the show trials in totalitarian regimes, mentioned earlier. Such trials serve not only to demonstrate how the regime deals with dissidents but also to legitimize a change in policy directions. After the death of Mao Tse-tung, the founding prince of the People's Republic of China (see Chapter 17), his successors opted for a different ruling style. But any change in a totalitarian regime implies that the previous path, though thought to be true when trod, was wrong. If not, the new path is wrong. The only recourse is to prove that the regime had been taken off the true path by traitors to the cause. The trial during the 1970s of the "Gang of Four" (of which Mao's widow was one), served such a purpose for the new power holders in China. Previous errors were not those of the regime but of the gang. The gang's conviction thus justified the new direction to be taken in the future.

Political trials are not limited to autocratic or totalitarian nations but occur in republics as well. In periods of internal strife, disruption, or turmoil or when there is fear of foreign invasion or infiltration, political trials are held. In the early 1920s the United States went through such a period, and a robbery and murder at a shoe factory in Massachusetts produced just such a political trial. Two men were charged with the crime, Nocola Sacco and Bartolomeo Vanzetti. Although no evidence appeared at the trial that any of the money had been traced to the defendants, that they had possession of the car in which the killers fled, or that they had actually committed the crime, they were found guilty. What was known was that they were draft dodgers and political anarchists, and their radical views were emphasized at the trial. Controversy surrounded the fairness of the proceedings, but in the end all appeals failed, and Sacco and Vanzetti were electrocuted in 1927, seven years after their alleged crime.

Perhaps Sacco and Vanzetti, like many persons who come before the bar of justice in political trials, were scapegoats, persons on whom politicians could heap the blame and responsibility for conditions that the executives, legislators, and bureaucrats could not themselves correct. We will never know for sure, but we do know that judges often too serve as scapegoats. For example, unable to deal with rising rates of crime and the conditions that encourage criminal acts, many an office seeker or officeholder takes a "law and order" stance. Without much sleight of hand, such a posture translates into blaming judges for being too soft on crime, too lenient in sentencing, too sensitive to the rights of the accused, too hesitant in using capital punishment. When moral waves sweep a nation to "do something" about a social problem like drug abuse, sexual promiscuity, the breakdown of family life, or crime, judges frequently serve as the scapegoats who have failed to punish sin. As pressures mount there is at least some temptation for judges to turn away from the princely practice of economizing violence to the more politically popular one of being a "hanging judge" dedicated to solving social ills, justice or not.

Finally, courts may get embroiled in political controversy, no matter how much judges would prefer to apply a "government of laws, not of men." Tocqueville's axiom that "there is hardly a political question in the United States which sooner or later does not turn into a judicial one" is verified over and over. The Watergate scandal that ultimately brought down the presidential administration of Richard Nixon was only one of many instances in which the judiciary had a distinctly political role. One of the final acts in the Watergate drama was the Supreme Court's decision in *U.S. v. Nixon*. The Nixon White House had taped conversations in the Oval Office, many of which involved the Watergate affair. Investigators probing the president's connection with Watergate sought copies of those tapes. Nixon refused to provide the tapes on grounds that the president was immune to any such order. In a unanimous decision the Supreme Court ruled against Nixon. Fearing impeachment on the basis of the evidence that the recorded conversations would provide, Nixon resigned. "No more useful and necessary authority can be granted to those who are appointed to preserve a city's liberty," wrote Machiavelli, "than the capacity to bring before the people or before some magistrate or council charges against citizens who sin in any manner against the freedom of the government."

In the end, what can you expect if you ever have your "day in court"? Expect politics. It will not be the politics of the executive, legislative, or bureaucratic palaces of power, but politics it will be, all the same. And according to whether you understand it and play it well and to the lawyers who represent you and the judges who judge you, to paraphrase Machiavelli, your self-governing person "will last for a longer or shorter time."

"There is hardly a political question in the United States which sooner or later does not turn into a judicial one."
— *Tocqueville*

"To what quarter will you look for protection from an infringement on the Constitution, if you will not give that power to the judiciary? There is no other body that can afford such a protection."
— *Marshall*

"They ain't nothin' till I calls 'em."
— *Anonymous umpire*

"Our judges are as honest as most men, and not more so."
— *Jefferson*

"There are no more reactionary people in the world than judges."

—Lenin

"Those who have prudently constituted a republic have considered, among the most necessary things to organize, the protection of liberty, and according to whether this is well done or not, that self-governing state will last for a longer or shorter time."

—Machiavelli

Part

The Rulers and
the Ruled

13

Wielders and Victims of Political Power: Princes, Nobles, Rivals, Subjects

"Who says organization says oligarchy." Those words appeared in 1911 in a book entitled *Political Parties,* written by a young German scholar, Robert Michels. The statement closes a slightly more lengthy discourse that holds a lesson for all those who aspire to a princely political life: "It is organization which gives birth to the domination of the elected over the electors, of the mandataries over the mandators, of the delegates over the delegators. Who says organization says oligarchy."

Michels's words neatly summarize what has come to be called his Iron Law of Oligarchy. The law is simply that in any organization—a small group of people, club, school class, trade union, church, political party, or even an entire nation—power eventually falls into the hands of a relatively small group of people which rules over and on behalf of other members. This "law" holds for any governing form, and it is "iron" because it is unbroken in social experience.

The lesson in the Iron Law of Oligarchy is threefold. First, in any social setting some people lead, and others follow. Charles de Gaulle (see Chapter 6) understood this well when he wrote that "men can no more get along without direction than they can without eating, drinking, or sleeping." Perhaps your intuition tells you that this is true, or if not your intuition simply your observation of what goes on in the groups to which you belong. Some students are active in class politics, but others are not. Some lead, some follow.

What, you might ask, is such a big deal about that? The answer lies in what you do with what you know. Most people simply resign themselves to the Iron Law of Oligarchy (although they do not call it that) and spend the rest of their lives being told by others what to do. They do not play politics, they say. But you have already learned in Part I of this book that you cannot *not* play politics. In both your everyday life or in more formal settings, you are a political being. Resigning yourself to being told by others what to do is not avoiding politics, it is simply forgoing the opportunity to participate in the decisions that control your life. Opportunity is the key. When the Iron Law of Oligarchy says that power resides in a small group of people within any organization, it means that one has the opportunity to seek membership in that small group. You have the opportunity to be a wielder of power, for, in fact, most of your fellows will, by default, step aside.

There is a second lesson here. Another observer of politics, R. M. MacIver, wrote in 1947 in a little book called *The Web of Government* that "in the strict sense we cannot classify states by asking whether one man rules or a few or the many. The many, or, the people, never rule—the actual business of ruling is always in the hands of the few." But, wrote MacIver, the principal problem is less who rules than one of "the relation of the one to the few" and, even more importantly, "of the relation of the few who rule to the many who are ruled." As you know from Part II, that critical relationship means one thing in an autocracy, another in a republic, and yet another in a totalitarian regime. Even if you decide not to seek to be a power wielder, there is still reason to take an active part in politics. That reason is to make sure that your relation to those who rule you is such that they cannot do just anything they wish. An active political life keeps the power wielders accountable to you.

Finally, there is a third message that we need to keep in mind regarding the Iron Law. An oligarchy is a small group of power wielders, the few who govern the many. But the few consist of different kinds of people. Some are princes, those who make the essential decisions in the practice of power. Others are advisers, we shall call them nobles, who have a stake in how power is exercised (see Chapter 20). Finally, among the few there are rivals to the prince, opponents who would be princes in their own right. Such rivals, friendly and unfriendly, have their own cadres of nobles and supporters independent of those of the prince.

Just as the few, the oligarchy, includes people who sometimes share values, sometimes fight over them; so too do the many, the ruled. Some people follow the lead of the ruling prince. Others oppose the prince and follow the direction of rivals. And still others do not follow at all. These nonfollowers ignore what is going on, confine their politics to their everyday lives, and passively accept what is going on. Sometimes these nonfollowers benefit from what princes do, and sometimes they are the victims of power wielded by the few.

These distinctions among princes, rivals, and nobles and among supporting and opposing followers, as well as nonfollowers, mean little in the abstract, but they take on significance in concrete situations. Consider the Babington Plot.

HOW DO PRINCES DEAL WITH RIVALS?

Machiavelli wrote that "nothing is harder to manage, more risky in the undertaking, or more doubtful of success than to set up as the introducer of a new order." Why? Because "such an innovator has as enemies all the people who were doing well under the old order, and only halfhearted defenders in those who hope to profit from the new." What Machiavelli meant was illustrated in the times and circumstances prevailing when Elizabeth I became queen of England in 1558. At the time, there was a bitter religious dispute between the Protestants and the Catholics. Under Elizabeth's predecessor, Mary Tudor, the Catholics had dominated. Queen Mary was a stern ruler on behalf of the Catholic church, and to serve those interests she undertook a campaign of religious persecution. Parliament reinstated laws of heresy, and three hundred Protestant men and women were burned at the stake at Smithfield. It was not a happy time.

So when Elizabeth came to the throne she won ready acceptance among the Protestants who wanted no more of Mary's persecution. But Elizabeth as "innovator" did not have the good will of Catholics, "all the people who were doing well under the old order." In addition, given the serious financial, religious, and foreign problems facing England, many of the nobility who welcomed Elizabeth to the throne did not really think she would last and thus were "only halfhearted defenders."

Under the circumstances it is not surprising that Elizabeth had rivals for the throne. The most notable was a cousin, Mary Stuart, the queen of Scotland. For years, both as queen of Scots and after she was forced to abdicate that throne and seek refuge in England, Mary plotted to seize the English crown. After being forced to surrender power in Scotland because she had alienated both the Scottish nobility and her rank-and-file followers, Mary knew that the only way to recapture Scotland would be as queen of England. To that end she recruited a cadre of nobles who for one reason or another wanted Elizabeth deposed and sought popular support among English Catholics, who yearned for a return to the times when they were the dominant religious force in the land.

In this setting emerged the Babington Plot. For years Mary had been involved in schemes to unseat Elizabeth. Elizabeth knew this but, beyond keeping Mary imprisoned in relatively comfortable surroundings, took no action. It was difficult to prove Mary's intrigue, for the deposed queen of Scots was always guarded in her correspondence, the only means by which she could communicate with her noble following. But in 1585, all this changed with the Babington Plot.

One of Elizabeth's talents was to recruit loyal and able members of the nobility to serve her in administrative capacities. One such was Francis Walsingham. Walsingham organized a highly loyal, imaginative, and efficient secret service, a necessary tool of governing in any era, but particularly so in a time of intrigue and plots (see Chapter 16). Walsingham received word that a certain Gilbert Gifford was being sent to England from France, where he had been training for the priesthood, to try to make secret contact with Mary. When Gifford set foot on English soil, Walsingham had him arrested. Gifford was of noble birth, but not of admirable courage. He had his price and Walsingham quickly found it. Gifford consented to become a spy for Walsingham's secret

ELIZABETH AND MARY: RIVALS FOR POLITICAL POWER

By virtue of their blood relationship to Henry VII, the king of England from 1485 to 1509, Elizabeth and Mary were first cousins once removed. This gave Elizabeth, who was the queen of England from 1558 to 1603, a claim to that crown. Not only was she the granddaughter of Henry VII, she was also Henry VIII's daughter. But Mary, who was the queen of Scotland from 1542 to 1567, also had a claim. She was the great granddaughter of Henry VII and the grandniece of Henry VIII. Under normal circumstances Elizabeth's claim would have taken precedence, and there would have been no rivalry for political power. But circumstances were far from normal.

Elizabeth was the daughter of Henry VIII's second wife, Anne Boleyn. The problem was that the pope of the Catholic church (of which Henry was the "Defender of the Faith") refused to accept Henry's divorce from his first wife and excommunicated Henry for marrying Anne. As a result England completely broke with the Catholic church, and the Church of England was established, with Henry at its head. Henry subsequently tired of Anne, who had not produced a male heir, and schemed to have his wife charged with adultery. Anne was convicted and beheaded. Parliament then declared Anne's daughter, Elizabeth, illegitimate. Elizabeth (1533–1603) was only three years old at the time.

Henry VIII went on to marry, divorce (or execute), and remarry. His reign ended in 1547. There followed the short, unhappy reign of his son Edward (by Henry's third wife) and the harsh reign of his daughter Mary (who was labeled "Bloody Mary"). Mary died in 1558, a death celebrated in London with bonfires and cheering. Elizabeth, whose right to succeed to the throne had been reestablished in 1544, now became the queen of England at age twenty-five. Given the conditions of English politics at the time—the country was torn by religious strife, burdened with a massive financial debt, barely recovering from a major defeat to France, and threatened with annexation by Spain—few gave Elizabeth much chance for a long reign.

But Elizabeth had the princely qualities that matched the times and circumstances. She had prepared long and well to exercise political power. She was at home in French, Italian, and Latin and was a quick and able thinker, easily matching wits with those who opposed her. Her administrative skills were considerable, for she selected able, trustworthy advisers. As one who had come of age in the tumultuous English politics of the early sixteenth century, she was realistic about what could and could not be done with power. Having been imprisoned and threatened with execution, she knew the risks and *virtu* of an economy of violence. Through colorful pageantry and succesful projects she knew how to capture the support of her subjects, who called her "Good Queen Bess." And more important than any of these qualities, Elizabeth wanted not only to reign but also to rule: "I know I have the body of a weak and feeble woman, but I have the heart and stomach of a king, and of a king of England too!"

In spite of the sorry legacy left to her by her predecessors, Elizabeth moved quickly against each problem besetting England. She began with the financial difficulties. In the first six months of her rule, Elizabeth wielded a budgetary axe, spending only 40 percent of what Bloody Mary had spent in her last half-year. The savings went to pay off the huge national debt incurred by heavy borrowing, and by 1560 England's credit was better than that of any other nation in Europe.

Elizabeth and her ministers approached foreign policy with a consistent general strategy that produced shifting tactics but an unswerving course. The goal was to keep England out of open war until such time as the nation was strong enough to win. This called for shrewd bargaining, the occasional abandonment of commitments and allies as suited English interests, manipulation, and deceit. For example, while professing peace with Spain, Elizabeth did not hesitate to approve raids by her seaman on Spanish ships in the Western Hemisphere. Elizabeth even used her own virginity as a weapon of foreign policy. Rulers of foreign nations, eager to make alliance with England, proposed marriage. (She received fifteen proposals during the first two years of her reign.) Through cunning, flirtation, and guile Elizabeth forged a foreign policy that enriched the nation, built up English military power, and ultimately broke the might of Spain.

A prudent compromise moderated England's religious conflicts. Under that compromise the Church of England was regarded as Protestant in doctrinal beliefs, thus pleasing the vast majority of English people who wanted no link to Rome. But in ceremony and ritual the Church of England remained largely Catholic, thus pleasing those of that religious persuasion. But not all. For the better part of three decades Elizabeth had to contend with forces rallying around her chief rival to the throne of England, the Catholic Mary, queen of Scots.

Mary (1542–1587), the daughter of King James V of Scotland, became queen when but one week old. Her mother ruled in Mary's stead as regent and sent Mary to France. Because Mary's mother was French by birth, the French had considerable influence in Scottish affairs during the regency. And because Mary grew up in France and married the French king, Francis II, it is no wonder that Catholic France continued to influence the Scots after Mary returned in 1561 (after Francis's death) to Scotland as the reigning queen. Mary was a devoted Catholic and came under severe criticism from the Scottish Protestants, yet held firmly to her faith. Mary also had a devoted ambition, that is, to become queen of England as well as Scotland. To that end she married Lord Darnley, a cousin also descended from Henry VII. Should Elizabeth not keep the throne, Mary was ready to claim legitimacy as the next in line.

The queen of Scotland was stunningly attractive: tall with beautiful skin, dark brown eyes, auburn hair, and an irresistible charm. French was as much her native language as any other. Since she had been born to the purple and prepared since birth to assume political power, she was trained in its exercise. But in politics, Mary was a novice compared with Elizabeth. Ever receptive to plots and intrigue, Mary's grasp of the economy of violence was certainly not as subtle as Elizabeth's. The motto of each queen hinted at the differences in both ambition and tactics. Elizabeth's motto was "I see, but say nothing." Mary's was "My end is my beginning."

Mary, much like her granduncle and Elizabeth's father, Henry VIII, quickly tired of her marital mates and fell in love with her Italian secretary, David Rizzo. Mary's husband, Lord Darnley, took part in a successful plot to murder Rizzo. Shortly thereafter Darnley's house was blown up, and he was strangled to death. Three months later when Mary married the Earl of Bothwell, a man implicated in Darnley's murder, both nobles and subjects revolted, and Mary was forced to abdicate in 1567. Mary was thrown into prison, escaped the next year, but again her forces were defeated and she failed to regain the throne.

At this juncture Mary fled to England. Elizabeth outwardly welcomed Mary and gave her refuge. Privately, however, Elizabeth recognized that if Mary could no longer be queen of Scots, she might well try to become queen of England. So she made Mary a prisoner. Mary's response was to profess loyalty to Elizabeth, yet declare that she would not leave her prison except as queen of England. For the next two decades, until she was beheaded in 1587, Mary did not leave prison. Over that period of time, through correspondence that she thought was secret, Mary was involved in several ill-fated plots to secure her release and seize the throne of England. She plotted with English Catholics, the French, the Spanish, and sympathetic Scots.

In the end it was to no avail. Implicated in a plot to murder Elizabeth, Mary was tried and convicted. Even then she did not lose her flair for the dramatic. Thinking that events elsewhere might save her, she said, "Remember that the theater of the world is wider than the realm of England." Elizabeth, however, provided that "theater of the world" with a lesson. Elizabeth had two choices after Mary was convicted, that is, to put Mary to death by either judicial execution or assassination. The latter was favored by her advisers and even by other heads of state. It had the advantage of being private and simple. But Elizabeth chose a public execution. By so doing she once and for all served notice to her rivals what their fate would be, while leaving no doubts in the minds of Mary's sympathizers that Henry VII's granddaughter, not his great-granddaughter, would rule.

---

service. He was instructed to undertake a covert correspondence with Mary, secure her confidence, and report what was going on.

Walsingham and Gifford set a clever trap, one that Mary could not escape. Gifford arranged for Mary's letters from the castle where she was imprisoned to be placed in a waterproof case, then hidden in the false bottom of a beer keg, one of many transported regularly into and out of the castle. Mary's letters would be "secretly" sent when the empty kegs were picked up, and his letters to her would arrive in full kegs. Mary rested happily in the belief that she had a foolproof means of carrying on her secret negotiations. Actually, however, there was no secrecy. For when letters to Mary reached England from abroad, Gifford picked them up and gave them to Walsingham. Walsingham then had them decoded and copied and returned them to Gifford. Gifford then took the letters to the brewer, who placed them in the beer keg to be delivered to the castle. Mary's letters, in turn, would go through a reverse process: into the false bottom of the keg, to the brewer, to Gifford, to Walsingham, back to Gifford, then on the boat sailing abroad. (The brewer was the truly enterprising one in all this, for Mary paid him handsomely to help her with the plot, Walsingham paid him handsomely to aid the secret service, and in addition he demanded a higher price for his beer!)

At the same time this clandestine bit of spying and counterspying was going on, a group of nobles sympathetic to Mary's cause concocted a scheme to assassinate Elizabeth. One member of the band, Anthony Babington, knew Mary. When Mary wrote to him a letter not having anything to do with the assassination plot, Babington wrote to her what was planned: Elizabeth would be murdered, Mary would be freed, and a foreign force would march on England and place Mary on the throne. Mary responded to Babington with, first, a noncommittal letter. But then a second letter from Mary to Babington appeared in the beer keg. Mary not only agreed to the plot but welcomed it, even recommending how the deed be accomplished.

Of course, when the letter was decoded, it proved precisely what Walsingham and Elizabeth had hoped. With little further ado, the plotters were rounded up. When news of the foiled scheme was known, the citizens of London celebrated. Bells rang, and there were bonfires in the streets, merrymaking, marches, and the singing of psalms. Six of the principal conspirators were dragged through London, drawn and quartered, and hanged. Elizabeth was more temperate with seven other plotters: they were allowed to hang until dead before being mutilated. Perhaps this verified what Elizabeth once said, "I am your Queen. I will never be by violence constrained to do anything."

The Babington Plot provided Elizabeth with a solution to a problem that had vexed her since the beginning of her reign, that is, what to do with a rival to the throne. Now Elizabeth had the proof that she needed of Mary's rivalry. Mary was tried, found guilty, and sentenced to execution. She went to her beheading as she had lived, seeing no guilt in her actions: "As a sinner I am truly conscious of having often offended my Creator and I beg him to forgive me, but as a Queen and Sovereign, I am aware of no fault or offense for which I have to render account to anyone here below." From what you learned in Chapter 5 you know that the last part of Mary's utterance reflects the mind of a true autocrat.

THE FEW AND THE MANY

Machiavelli wrote, "Keep the aristocracy from desperation and satisfy the populace by making them happy; this is one of the prince's most important duties." This is what Elizabeth did in princely fashion and what her rival Mary failed to do. The care and feeding of the few, the nobles or the aristocracy, and of the many, a prince's or a rival's subjects, is a crucial task. How well a princely ruler performs it depends in large measure on the character of the nobility or of the subjects in question. Let us consider each.

What Is the Ruling Class Like?

Gaetano Mosca was a student of political leadership who lived in the nineteenth century. In 1896 he published a book entitled *The Ruling Class.* Mosca took a dim view of the capabilities of people to govern themselves, at least the masses of people. In fact, he believed that most people had no desire for self-government and were instead willing and eager to pass on the burden of making decisions to those willing to do so. He called this group the "political class," those people willing or able to compete for power. From this political class emerges a ruling class, a political elite, of people who actually reside in the executive, legislative, bureaucratic, and judicial palaces of power and control them.

Although the ruling class comes from the larger political class, those who achieve power and exercise it are unable to do so without the cooperation of the political class. Wrote Mosca, "The man who is at the head of the state would certainly not be able to govern without the support of a more numerous class to enforce respect for his orders and have them carried out." Moreover, in addition to the support of the "more numerous class," the ruler must take care to court the support of the ruling class, for "granting that he can make one individual, or indeed many individuals, in the ruling class feel the weight of his power, he certainly cannot be at odds with the class as a whole or do away with it."

The support of fellow members of the ruling class and of a sufficient body of the larger political class is, of course, not easy to secure. The rivalry between Elizabeth and Mary for the support of the English nobility demonstrates that. In fact, although Mary may not have thought so at the time, her days as a wielder of political power ended two decades before the Babington Plot, when she abdicated the Scottish throne, because she had alienated her sympathizers in the Scottish ruling class by marrying a man suspected of having murdered her own husband. The nobility immediately revolted under the leadership of Mary's bastard half-brother, a pro-English Protestant. In short, Mary committed the fatal error of ignoring Machiavelli's precept to "keep the aristocracy from desperation."

Elizabeth made no such mistake. Her domestic and foreign policies were aimed at wooing, not alienating, aristocratic support. By a prudent compromise that ended the worst of the religious strife, she courted both the Protestant and the Catholic nobility. By pursuing an aggressive naval policy, one that permitted her "sea dogs" to prey on Spanish shipping and bring home rich treasures, she pleased the military segment of the nobility, and by restoring financial stability, Elizabeth won the approval of commercial and mercantile interests.

Nobles, after all, are human, and they also—as de Gaulle stated— respond to leadership. Elizabeth capitalized on this by demonstrating the decisiveness and strength of her character. After Mary had been given refuge in England, she soon was involved in fomenting rebellion against the queen. Led by disaffected nobles, sincere peasants in northern England decorated with the red cross of the crusaders, took up arms, and undertook to hold Catholic services in defiance of the religious compromise that had been reached. The rebels also moved to free Mary. But Elizabeth acted quickly and with vigor. She had Mary removed to a more secure place of confinement, and her forces dispersed the rebels. Elizabeth then turned to an economy of violence, and thus the plot resulted in no executions for either religious or political purposes.

A prince will be in a better position to mobilize the support of the political and ruling classes if the members of those classes feel that the prince is serving their values and interests, that is, is promoting their welfare and deferring to their most important demands. This is frequently easy to do because the prince and the nobles come from the same segment of society, have common values, and want the same things. Mosca noted that the political class, from which the ruling class originates, consists of people with similar backgrounds who normally share the same ideas, ideas that grow out of similar educations, regular contact with members of the same social and economic class, comparable opportunities, and a privileged standing in society.

There is substantial evidence for Mosca's argument. In autocratic regimes—such as in Russia in the era of Catherine the Great, in France at the time of Madame de Pompadour, or in the Elizabethan Age in England—the political class consisted of people related through birth and marriage. As members of the same or related courts, their similar backgrounds certainly contributed to shared values and interests. Their conflicts and rivalries arose over who was to rule, for example, Peter or Catherine, Elizabeth or Mary.

But Mosca's point is also well taken in regard to the social backgrounds of members of the political class in republics. Political scientist Thomas R. Dye studied the economic and social characteristics of leaders of institutions in the United States and tried to answer that question in his *Who's Running America?*. Dye's procedure was to identify the top echelon of industrial corporations; the news media; legal firms; philanthropic foundations; civic associations; cultural organizations; colleges and universities; the military; and executive, legislative, bureaucratic, and judicial institutions. Examining the social and economic characteristics of these leaders, he tried to determine whether there was a pattern.

As you might guess, Dye did find such a pattern. For example, from an economic standpoint, most of a nation's wealth is concentrated in a relatively small number of large institutions. One hundred manufacturing corporations control half of this nation's industrial assets. Half of all banking assets reside in fifty of the largest banks. Fifty corporations control half of all the nation's assets in transportation, communications, and utilities. Two thirds of insurance assets are concentrated in fifty companies; 40 percent of all foundation assets are in fifty foundations; and half of all private endowment funds for higher education can be found in twenty-five universities. Ninety percent of television news is controlled by ABC, NBC, and CBS, and ten newspaper chains have one third of the nation's daily newspaper circulation. The list could be extended, but you should be able to see the picture: the few are the haves, and the many are more likely the have-nots.

How few? Dye found that approximately six thousand individuals in seven thousand positions have formal power over institutions that control roughly one half of the nation's resources in the areas he studied. This amounts to less than three thousandths of 1 percent of the nation's total population. Add to that the distribution of personal wealth: 40 percent of all income goes to the top one fifth of those receiving income, and the bottom one fifth receives only 5 percent of total income.

The relatively small segment of the total population is, of course, not the whole of what Mosca intended in defining the larger political class from which the ruling class derives. Obviously the number of people who compete for political power in the United States is far larger than six thousand. Yet it is noteworthy that over one fourth of the ruling class, those holding the top governing positions, have held high corporate jobs and that nearly 40 percent of those in top leadership positions in America's corporations have held government positions.

Granted that a large number of the members of the ruling class , but certainly not all, have ties to areas of concentrated wealth. Does this, as Mosca argued, contribute to a sharing of ideas regarding the exercise of political power? The question is not easily or readily answered. On one side you should recognize that there is no clear evidence of what Dye called an "interlocking" elite. That is, the people who hold the top positions in one segment of America's institutions—say, government, industry, or the mass media—do not often hold positions in one of the other segments. Eighty-five percent of the seven thousand top positions alluded to are occupied by a person who holds one position and no other. Being powerful in one institution does not necessarily mean exercising power in another.

You should realize also that all is not peace and harmony "at the top." There are factions that have differing points of view about what the government should do, and conflicts arise over federal versus state and local control of various programs, tax reform, energy programs, measures for dealing with inflation and recession, and other policy questions. But as Dye pointed out, and Mosca prophesied, these disputes take place against a backdrop of considerable consensus on general goals. Such matters as the fundamental worth of private enterprise, limited government, due process of law, and certain social programs are parts of that consensus. Means, not ends, provoke disagreements.

Dye suggested one other point that you should bear in mind in deciding whether Mosca was correct in asserting that the political class tends to have similar thoughts on how to exercise power. Dye noted that the initial costs for studying, planning, organizing, and implementing national policies are paid by corporate and personal fortunes. Resources from these fortunes are funneled into foundations which subsidize studies, planning groups, and other efforts aimed at finding solutions to pressing problems. Through those efforts a consensus develops regarding national priorities and goals. Members of the ruling class—the president, congresspersons, bureaucrats, judicial officials—take that consensus into account in making policy decisions. Indeed, they are so much a part of the consensus that they can scarcely think outside it.

This may come as no surprise to you, not if you consider the politics of your everyday life. You have a circle of friends of whom most have roughly the same social backgrounds, education, interests, and perhaps even aspirations. Through your daily contacts with such people you form an understanding of "how things are" that is the equivalent of the consensus formed among members of the political and ruling classes. If a problem comes up involving your circle of friends, there is a strong likelihood that you will think alike. To be sure, you may disagree over what precisely to do—to send out for a pizza or for a hamburger—but you all agree that you are hungry, must cram for final exams and thus cannot go out and that some kind of fast food is the answer. Deciding whether to allocate money for a superbomber or a missile system is perhaps a more critical decision; yet the policymakers involved make it with a common understanding that there is a common desire to build American defenses.

Communist regimes hold out the ideal of the classless society, the ultimate result of a dictatorship of the proletariat. In fact, however, totalitarian regimes do have their political and ruling classes, just as do autocratic and republican regimes. The Thousand-Year Reich, for example, had a strict hierarchy of classes and ranks, privileges and prerogatives, social climbers, jealousies, and backbiting. At the top was the Fuehrer, the target of all manner of sycophantic behavior aimed at currying his favor.

Or consider the privileged class of the Soviet Union. Its members have opportunities not even dreamed of by the mass of Soviet citizens. For example, the privileged shop in unmarked stores accessible only with special passes, obtained from the euphemistic "Bureau of Passes." In those stores are foods so short in supply that they are not available to ordinary shoppers. Other shops offer such otherwise unobtainable luxuries as stereos, tape recorders, perfumes, liquors, and imported chocolates. Members of the privileged rank drive expensive limousines, live in compounds restricted to the well-to-do, have vacation cottages, and receive all of the other benefits that go with being power wielders rather than ordinary riffraff.

Who are the members of the Soviet ruling class? Start with the Communist party. The party's Central Committee is an elite body, and membership in it is obviously highly coveted. Its Politburo, or policy bureau, is the apex of the Soviet class structure. It normally consists of 14 members and is a self-perpetuating body, meaning that its members choose their own successors. They also select the general secretary of the party, the ruler of the party and of the Soviet Union, today's equivalent of the "Czar of All the Russians." Going down the hierarchy from the Central Committee are the cabinet members, leaders and members of the Supreme Soviet (the legislative body), executive officials, and so on. Approximately 200,000 officials under the supervision of the Party Secretariat, under command of the general secretary, make up the party bureaucracy. The Communist party at large, with something on the order of 1 million members, constitutes the political class from which, returning to Mosca's theory, the ruling class is selected.

But in the Soviet Union the privileged class extends beyond those who struggle for power and those who exercise it. There are also other elites who enjoy the benefits of special status, including military officials, scientists, technocrats, artists, cosmonauts, writers, actors, editors, and many others. All in all, estimates of the total size of the privileged class—those in sufficiently prestigious positions to reap the rewards of high status, including relatives who also prosper—is several million. Yet considering the sizable population of the Soviet Union, the answer to the question of who is running Russia, like that to who is running America, is the few, and certainly not the many.

What About the Rest of Us?

In sum, what Mosca wrote almost a century ago appears true, regardless of the form of government; that is, there is "a class that rules and a class that is ruled." "The first class, always the less numerous, performs all the political functions, monopolizes power, and enjoys the advantages that power brings, whereas the second, the more numerous class, is directed and controlled by the first, in a manner that is now more or less legal, now more or less arbitrary and violent."

Certainly, most people do not have the characteristics, the power, and the glory that go with membership in the ruling class. Depending on the society that they live in, they may not be deprived of welfare and deference values, but their share of them is likely to be far smaller than that of the political nobility. Yet even though they lack the powers and privileges of princes, nobles, and rivals, they cannot be ignored. "It is essential for a prince to be on a friendly footing with his people," stated Machiavelli, "since, otherwise, he will have no resource in adversity."

Princes cannot rule with only the support of nobles. Rivals will always challenge and in that challenge mobilize an opposing cadre of aristocrats, as did Mary Stuart. That members of the ruling class may, as Mosca believed, share backgrounds and ideas does not mean that they will agree on which prince should actually do the ruling. By learning the lessons of politics you position yourself to take sides in such controversies, to exploit your share of the "resource" that Machiavelli insisted that princes need in "adversity." This is, in fact, how princes become princes. They learn things about politics that nobles, rivals, followers, and nonfollowers do not. Moreover, they do things in politics that others do not.

"Who says organization says oligarchy."

—*Robert Michels*

"Men fundamentally can no more get along without direction than they can without eating, drinking, or sleeping."

—*de Gaulle*

"Nothing is harder to manage, more risky in the undertaking, or more doubtful of success than to set up as the introducer of the new order. Such an innovator has as enemies all the people who were doing well under the old order, and only halfhearted defenders in those who hope to profit from the new."

—*Machiavelli*

"I know I have the body of a weak and feeble woman, but I have the heart and stomach of a king, and of a king of England too!"

—*Elizabeth I*

"As a Queen and Sovereign I am aware of no fault or offense for which I have to render account to anyone here below."

—*Mary Queen of Scots*

"Keep the aristocracy from desperation and satisfy the populace by making them happy; this is one of the prince's most important duties."

—*Machiavelli*

"It is essential for a prince to be on a friendly footing with his people, since, otherwise, he will have no resource in adversity."

—*Machiavelli*

"In all societies two classes of people appear—a class that rules and a class that is ruled."

—*Gaetano Mosca*

Chapter
14

What Do Princes Learn That Others Do Not?

It is always good sport to make fun of politicians. In America, poking fun at politicians, not baseball, is the national pastime. For example, the noted American journalist and critic, H. L. Mencken, liked to twit that "the smarter the politician, the more things he believes and the less he believes any of them." Will Rogers, one of America's greatest humorists, also had some things to say about the knowledge required to be a politician. He coined the slogan "be a politician; no training necessary."

One of his most pointed lines was "common sense is not an issue in politics, it's an affliction."

Such comments may well apply to the average politician. But we assume that if you are taking politics seriously (the evidence being that you have continued to read this book), you will want to be more than merely average. You aspire to princely politics. The princely politician learns more about politics than what people like to call common sense. The problem with common sense is that it is common, what everybody knows. Princedom demands something more, knowing what others do not. In this chapter we shall look at, first, what it is that most people learn about politics: what common sense is; and second, we shall explore what princes learn that others do not: the uncommon sense of princedom. With that in mind you will be better prepared to walk your path to princely behavior.

WHAT DO MOST PEOPLE LEARN ABOUT POLITICS?

If you were to remain an average American, what could you be expected to know about politics? Not a great deal. In spite of all the time and attention devoted to informing people about politics, through civics courses in public schools, the news media, and books and magazines, most Americans are not very interested in and are only moderately familiar with politics. Pollsters regularly take the public political pulse, and sometimes it is hard to find it beating. For example, in general, polls show that when asked, Americans do not really consider themselves up to date on what is going on in their nation's capital. Studies have indicated that fewer than four in ten Americans know what bodies comprise Congress, the House of Representatives and the Senate. One in five have expressed the belief that the Supreme Court is a part of Congress (think how that might send John Marshall whirling in his grave!).

Or move from textbook knowledge to current events. There, too, common sense is more common than informed. Research indicates that fewer than two thirds of Americans can name even one U.S. senator from their state, fewer than 40 percent can name both, fewer than half can name their congressperson in the House, and fewer than half can give the name of even one member of the nine-member Supreme Court. Finally, consider items in the news. On any given topic, no matter how saturated the news coverage of it, almost one fifth of Americans surveyed by pollsters show up as chronic "know-nothings": they have not even heard of the event, problem, issue, or crisis making the news.

Is such poorly informed common sense peculiar only to America? Evidence gathered in opinion surveys in other nations indicates that it is not. Whether asked to name political leaders, institutions, or simply current events, the result is the same in nation after nation—the level of popular information, common sense, about politics is remarkably low.

If detailed information about public affairs is what people do not learn, then what do they learn? What is the common sense of politics? To begin with, people learn what political scientists call a political culture. This means that people acquire a very general sense of what their government does and how it goes about doing it. To the degree that this general sense has any detailed meaning, it comes from how people think that government and politics affect their everyday lives. H. L. Mencken, of whom we spoke before, did not spend all of his time "damning politicians up hill and down dale," as he once put it. He also had some thoughtful things to say about how people react to government. His words capture the sense of political culture that people do learn. "The average man," he wrote more than sixty years ago, "at least sees clearly that government is something lying outside him and outside the generality of his fellow men—that it is a separate, independent and often hostile power, only partly under his control and capable of doing him great harm." What type of harm? Take taxes, certainly something that brings you in contact with government on a daily basis—income taxes, sales taxes, use taxes, property taxes, and on and on. Mencken expressed it strongly: "The intelligent man, when he pays taxes, certainly does not believe that he is making a prudent and productive investment of his money; on the contrary, he feels that he is being mulcted in an excessive amount for services that, in the main, are useless to him, and that, in substantial part, are downright inimical to him."

You need not agree with Mencken on taxes. That is not the point. What is important in his commentary is what it says about political culture. People do learn a highly general sense of what government is and does, what it should do and how it should do it. To repeat, that general feeling becomes important only insofar as politics touches our daily lives. Within this general sense of government, which we call political culture, people learn a few specifics. They are not textbook specifics or even detailed items of information; instead they are identities.

First, people learn to identify with a nation. They become "Americans," "Irish," "French," "Russians," "Japanese," or whatever. Princes recognize this and even encourage it as a means of rallying support among their subjects. When Mary Queen of Scots was growing up in France, she was largely isolated from the traditions, folkways, and customs of her native Scotland. After her return to Scotland, she had to learn many of those things that her subjects had learned as a matter of common sense, namely, what it meant to be Scottish.

Second, people learn something about what their national government is. This is not necessarily what institutions comprise it. Instead they learn to trust it or distrust it, take pride or shame in it, love it or fear it. One research finding that alarmed many political observers in the United States during the 1970s was that often children no longer seemed to learn positive feelings about their government. Whereas a decade earlier it was commonplace that most American children agreed with statements like "what goes on in government is all for the best and the government "almost rarely" or "never" makes mistakes, fewer than one third expressed those sentiments in the 1970s. Princely rulers, of course, must keep abreast of such shifts in common sense and either counter or take advantage of them.

Third, in addition to a sense of nationality and government purpose, people learn to think of politics as involving highly celebrated leaders. They think of politics not as what goes on within the palaces of power but as what certain political figures seem to do, their actions, personalities, styles, and flairs. Few rulers have tried so hard to capitalize on that element of common political sense as did Eva Peron, the First Lady of Argentina and wife of dictator Juan Peron. Eva Peron was a strikingly attractive woman who cultivated the style of a Hollywood movie actress, was a power in Argentine politics, accumulated great wealth, and lived a regal life-style worthy of any Catherine the Great, Madame de Pompadour, Queen Elizabeth, or Mary Queen of Scots. But she knew well that she could not court public favor with just that, and so she went to great pains to take advantage of her impoverished roots. She cultivated the speaking style and language of the working classes, created a program to make a public display of personally handing out money to the poor, and attacked in her speeches all wealth and privilege. "Anyone who knew me from the time I was a simple Argentine girl," she asserted, "knows that I could never have never enacted the cold comedy of oligarchical drawing rooms. I was not born for that." By careful manipulation of her public image, Eva Peron took advantage of the commonsense tendency to glamorize and romanticize, thus adhering closely to Machiavelli's admonition that a prince should be praised, not blamed; be known for liberality, not stinginess; and be loved, not feared.

Finally, people learn a general sense of civic obligation. Put differently, they learn to be citizens. This does not mean that they learn to be continuously active in the politics of their locality, state, and nation. (You will see in Chapter 15 that one of the things that separates princes from others is that princes are always active in politics but that most other people are not.) Rather, it means that they learn to think of themselves as citizens rather than subjects. In a world in which governments have become huge, complex, bureaucratic organizations at all levels, noted Mencken, "There are no longer any citizens in the world, only subjects." Be that as it may, most people still think of themselves as citizens. But it is a markedly idealized notion of citizenship, largely separate from everyday life. It is, in fact, the role of textbook citizen that people learn, not a citizenship of the supermarket, work place, or even the voting booth. The citizen role has about the same status, in the United States, say, as the Christian does. You have probably heard preachers denounce the "Sunday Morning Christian" who goes to church on the sabbath but does not practice the Christian spirit in daily living. The apathetic citizen decried by the political journalist or political scientist is of a similar ilk, one who espouses the virtues of the active political life but rarely incorporates those virtues into everyday living.

The common sense of politics, then, consists of what people learn of national identities, government in the abstract, the positions of their political leaders, and an idealized sense of civic obligation. Where do people learn such political cultures? A sense of nationhood, authority, and government certainly begins in the family. In many nations children acquire a sense of identity with a political party. This is not so common as it once was, yet still is an important political force. Studies in the United States, Great Britain, France, and other republics conducted before the 1960s found that most people learned to think of themselves as loyal to a particular political party—Democrat or Republican in the United States, Labor or Conservative in Britain. In more recent decades

EVA OR EVITA?

Eva Peron was not born to the purple; that is, she was not of royal ancestry destined to inherit political power. Yet in a seven-year period, from 1945 to 1952, she became a political power in her own right, and after her death at the age of thirty-three, she became a symbol of power, one that political factions in Argentina fought over in order to extend their direction and influence over that troubled nation. Even today, more than three decades since her reign as the First Lady of Argentina, the memory of Eva Peron lingers in the background of Argentina's politics, a potential weapon in the hands of power seekers perhaps willing to exploit it yet again.

She was born Maria Eva Ibarguren in a shack located in Los Toldos, a village that was little more than a stop on a railway line stretching across the Argentine pampas. She was the illegitimate child of Juana Ibarguren and Juan Duarte, who lived with his legal family on a nearby farm. The circumstances of her birth were not unusual, for in that year of 1919 more than one fourth of all children born in Argentina were illegitimate. When Eva was three, her mother moved with her and her sisters and brother to the more populous city of Junin. There Eva Duarte (her mother simply took Juan's last name) attended school for six years, the extent of her formal education. Informally she learned about the immediate world from the male residents of her mother's boardinghouse and about the more remote social universe from reading popular magazines and going to the Crystal Palace, Junin's movie theater.

Eva wanted to be an actress. At age fourteen she set out for Buenos Aires, the capital and leading metropolis of Argentina, indeed the largest city south of the equator. As an actress Eva had no native talent, but she had excellent substitutes, ambition and a desire for power and the lessons she had learned so well at her mother's boardinghouse, that in exchange for certain favors men would be only too eager to help her career. For the next decade Eva undertook a succession of male conquests, each of which brought her another step closer to her goal. She moved from taking minor parts in stage plays to roles in radio soap operas. Soon she became a popular celebrity on radio, a step that advanced her budding career as a movie actress. By 1943 she was the hostess of a prestigious radio interview show. Through that connection she made the acquaintance of the man who would soon become absolute dictator of Argentina, Juan Peron.

What began as a temporary liaison grew to much more. Eva became Peron's mistress, later his wife, and—most importantly—the key to much of his political dominance. On Peron's behalf Eva was a tireless public speaker, endlessly appearing before working-class crowds and appealing for support. The workers, who like Eva had flocked to Buenos Aires from the countryside, responded to her harsh, almost peasant manner and her simple, emotional language. She called them her *descamisados,* the "shirtless ones," that she would rally against the oligarchs and aristocrats. With Peron she forged an alliance of the working class and military which came to power in 1945.

The reign of Eva and Juan Peron was totalitarian. Like the regimes of Nazi Germany, Fascist Italy, or Communist states in Russia, China, and elsewhere, the Perons created the aura of a mass movement. Argentina became Peronist Argentina. Propaganda in the form of controlled news, orchestrated torchlight parades, rallies, speeches, hymns, and chants was the order of the day. Terror—intimidation, imprisonment, torture, and murder—was official policy. Elections were rigged, and friends and lackeys of the Perons held high office. Anyone critical of President Peron or his First Lady was charged, under the law, with "disrespect," a crime punishable by up to three years in prison. Eva perfected another ruling technique, the "campaign of humiliation," holding up to public scorn anyone who opposed her.

Yet during this reign of propaganda, terror, and humiliation, Eva was a popular figure. Indeed, many regarded her as a saint. But in this public role, the name of Eva gave way to "Evita": Evita, the little beloved one, the great benefactor, the beautiful humanitarian. Under her auspices the Foundation Eva Peron was created. Millions of dollars were funneled into this alleged charitable organization whose stated purose was to serve the poor. In fact vast sums earmarked for the foundation were placed in secret accounts in Swiss banks. Still, sufficient sums were doled out to the poor personally by Eva so as to leave the impression that she was indeed a saint. Each day thousands would line up in front of her office building waiting to get in and tell their tale of woe to Evita. She would listen with great sympathy, then reach under the blotter on her desk and hand each petitioner the amount of money necessary to make things better. Although the true nature of the totalitarian regime was well known, few *descamisados* could believe that the strikingly attractive Evita was a party to the thuglike rule.

In 1952 Eva Peron died of cancer. The announcement came over the radio at 8:25 P.M. on July 26. The exact moment is important. Before that time it had been the custom for radio stations to begin their newscasts at 8:30 each evening, but during the remainder of Peron's shaky reign, newscasts began at 8:25, always with the message, "This was the moment Eva Peron entered immortality." For now she was no longer a political power, but the highly prized symbol of power. Juan Peron, in a struggle to retain control, frequently appealed to the memory of Eva as means of sustaining the support of the working class. But in the end, in 1955, Peron fell from power. The anti-Peronists who replaced him moved quickly to expunge the name and memory of Eva from the public mind. But there was one problem: the embalmed corpse of Eva Peron. For more than two decades that corpse was a coveted symbol of Argentine political power, sought by anti-Peronists to keep its resting place from becoming a shrine and by Peronists as a tool to rally mass support. Eva's corpse, because of its symbolic importance, secretly rested for more than two years in a hidden laboratory in Buenos Aires and later was stolen and placed in a military warehouse. From there it traveled to a storeroom in West Germany, was buried in a grave in Italy under a false name, was dug up and carted to an attic in Juan Peron's home in exile in Spain, returned in 1974 to Argentina during Peron's second short reign before his death, and finally buried in a family tomb.

Almost sixty years after the birth of Maria Ibarguren, a musical, *Evita,* appeared on Broadway, which was loosely based on her life. In it the leading character sings, "Don't cry for me, Argentina, for the truth is I shall not leave you. . . ." It remains to be seen whether she actually has.

---

such studies reveal that fewer people learn such partisan identities, a point to which we shall return in Chapter 18 when we discuss how princes win power through elections.

Schools are also important places where most people learn about politics. Machiavelli thought that a nation's educational arrangements were so vital to politics that its civic nature depended on them: "It is true that men are more or less virtuous in one country or another, according to the nature of the education by which their manners and habits of life have been formed." Dictators are well aware of the importance of schools in teaching about politics. Adolf Hitler opposed letting education be free and open to everyone, for he regarded it as a possible threat. Any regime that allowed it would fall, even a republic: "Universal education is the most corroding and disintegrating poison that liberalism has ever invented for its own destruction." Joseph Stalin thought that a nation's education depended on what a ruler wished to accomplish: "Education is a weapon whose effect depends upon who holds it in his hands and at whom it is aimed." Regardless of the political aims, autocratic, republican, and totalitarian princes recognize that schools are vital to what people learn about politics and must be dealt with accordingly.

Churches are another forum for political learning, Machiavelli argued that any wise prince will instill and support a strong religious sentiment in subjects. Civic virtue can be advanced through religious practices. The sagacious prince, explained Machiavelli, identifies with the "miracles that are celebrated in religions, however false they may be." By doing so the prince takes on increased "credence with the people." Eva Peron understood this and made a great show of religious sentiment. Traveling in Europe in 1947 she sought an audience with Pope Pius XII, knowing that in predominately Catholic Argentina this would put her in good standing with her people. She hoped that the pope might even honor her with a high tribute. In fact, he did just that, awarding her the Grand Cross of the Order of Pius IX, the second highest papal decoration. Thereafter, Eva Peron made it a point always to draw public attention to the honor.

"Where the press is free, and every man able to read, all is safe." Thus did Thomas Jefferson highlight the combined influence of education and the final source of political learning for most people, the news media. Totalitarian regimes know the crucial role played by such media and, as you saw in Chapter 7, keep a tight control over the press. Republics provide a looser rein, but their political leaders sometimes take steps to manage news to the advantage of the regime, a process we shall discuss in more detail in Chapter 27. Certainly princes learn their common sense of politics as well, but they do not always treat what they learn in the same way as do others. Moreover, princes learn more and from other sources.

WHAT PRINCES LEARN ABOUT POLITICS

Most people give little thought to politics, as it rarely enters their minds that politics takes up a good portion of their everyday lives. To them politics is foreign, something that "politicians" involved in remote "governments" do. If the average person learns little of politics, it is largely because he or she regards politics as peripheral to daily hopes and aspirations. Not so for princes. Politics is no mere avocation for the prince, but an all-consuming vocation, an activity that absorbs all of his or her waking moments. Should you seek princedom, this is one of the first things that will set you off from others, that politics not only will be in your daily existence, but it also will be your life's work. It was for such people that Machiavelli wrote *The Prince,* explaining to them what they needed to learn in order to rule in a princely fashion.

As you discovered in Part I of this text, Machiavelli was a great believer in history as a prince's best teacher: "It is an easy matter for him who carefully examines past events to foresee future events in a republic and to apply the remedies employed by the ancients, or, if old remedies cannot be found, to devise new ones based upon the similarities of events." Rulers fail, explained Machiavelli, when they do not study the lessons of history: "But since these matters are neglected or not understood by those who read, or if understood, remain unknown to those who govern, the result is that the same problems always exist in every era."

As we now turn to the question of what princes learn about politics that other people do not, it will be useful for you to think back on the princely figures you have already met. Along the way we will have need to mention them again. What is the "common sense" of such princes as contrasted to the common sense of politics that most people learn?

Princes can be distinguished from nobles, rivals, and subjects because they know more than anybody else does. They know more because they take the trouble to find out, and they take that trouble because they recognize, along with Machiavelli, that chance (*fortuna*) is a large part of the affairs of people. No prince can fully dominate *fortuna,* but prudence indicates that every effort should be made to do so. "Fortune is a woman and the man who wants to hold her down must beat and bully her," wrote Machiavelli. He was, of course, writing in the vernacular of his time, and so you should not take his analogy literally. He was simply saying that the art of governing requires serious work. Eva Peron put it this way: "Nothing in my destiny is extraordinary; still less is due to chance."

Learning Political Lore

As an aspiring prince, where do you begin to fortify yourself against *fortuna?* Start with the study of history, the history of the nation, state or province, locality, group, or organization that you seek to direct and influence. Customs, traditions, folkways, and myths abound among any set of people and have great emotional appeal. If a prince could understand the political lore of his subjects, thought Machiavelli, he could appeal to it in order to win power and to exercise it. That is one reason that Machiavelli considered religion so important to successful rule, because religion contains much of a people's culture. "Everything that tends to favor religion [even if it is believed to be false] should be received and availed of to strengthen in." Catherine the Great took that axiom to heart. Soon after her arrival in Russia, you will recall from

Chapter 5, she converted to the Russian Orthodox faith, something that her husband, whom she later unseated, refused to do. When the time came to seize power, "Little Mother" was received warmly as Russian and not viewed as German.

Machiavelli believed that the best way for a nation to defend itself against external enemies was to build citizen armies. If citizens are to be willing to sacrifice themselves for their homeland, however, they must have a strong sense of patriotism and such a sense must be cultivated. One way to do that is by understanding and appealing to a people's national heritage. In World War II, Winston Churchill appealed to the British heritage; Adolf Hitler pointed to Germany's interrupted national destiny; and Charles de Gaulle portrayed himself as the embodiment of French culture. In regard to learning the culture of other nations, remember that the Inquiry, under Walter Lippmann's direction, tried to take into account religion, languages, ethnic, and historical patterns in drawing up a proposed peace treaty for World War I. When the Treaty of Versailles ignored much of that effort, it opened the door to the disastrous reign of *fortuna.*

Learning Political Models

The study of history offers you clues to your own and others' political culture. But history also teaches other things. By reading the biographies of princes who have faced a variety of problems and situations, you can learn two things, how they prepared themselves to deal with fortune and misfortune and how they actually handled both. During the era of autocracies dominated by monarchs such as Catherine the Great, Louis XV, Mary Queen of Scots, and Elizabeth I, great pains were taken to tutor future kings and queens in the policies and practices of great predecessors. For example, Catherine the Great, while still in her early teens, read and reread the lives of Cicero and Plutarch and poured through a classic of its time, Montesquieu's *Considerations on the Causes of the Greatness of the Romans and Their Decline.* Later, when she had become czarina of all the Russians, Catherine hired a tutor to instruct her own children: "The knowledge which they are to acquire should serve only to give them a thorough understanding of their role as Princes."

Republican princes can also profit from a close reading of political histories and biographies. Harry Truman was an avid student of history and insisted that many of the problems he faced as president of the United States were problems that other rulers had faced in earlier timses. Dwight Eisenhower, who became the Allied military commander in Europe and later president of the United States, not only studied history but also wrote it. One of his tasks as a young army officer was to go to Europe after World War I and prepare an official army history of the principal battles and battlefields of that conflict. What he learned about terrains, the disposition of forces, and possible supply lines was to be of immense value to him decades later when he commanded an invasion of precisely the same territory.

Totalitarian rulers have also been students of history. Adolf Hitler studied closely the campaigns of the Napoleonic wars but nonetheless repeated many of Napoleon's mistakes. In defending against Hitler's invasion of Russia during World War II, Joseph Stalin adopted the tactics of withdrawal, attrition, and patience that had worked so well when "Mother Russia" had successfully repelled Napoleon's armies in the early nineteenth century. Eva Peron provides an interesting contrast. She too read a great deal, but not historical tomes. Instead, as a young girl, she studied popular celebrity magazines, from which she learned something of how to prepare for a life in Argentine society. More importantly, she discovered who the powers of the entertainment industry were, and when she went to Buenos Aires to make her fortune as an actress, she carefully cultivated those powers. Even her acting career provided historical lessons, as she was regularly featured as the lead actress in radio dramas about historical figures, for instance, Elizabeth I of England.

History and biography provide a rich treasure of background material for any aspiring prince seeking appropriate ways to model one's behavior. Of course, as Machiavelli warned, times and circumstances change. Old remedies "cannot be found." But the prince who knows history stands a better chance of devising "new ones based upon the similarities of events" than does the historical know-nothing.

Learning the Rules

You learned from Part III that power resides in different palaces in different ways. to direct and influence events requires that a prince know the rules, institutions, and organizations that count most in exercising power and the appropriate procedures. The autocrat's princely court plays by different rules than does that of the republican or of the totalitarian, and it behooves a prince to find out what is fitting and what is not, what works and what does not. This means learning not only what the rules are but also how they can be interpreted to one's advantage.

Thomas Jefferson argued that the rules of the U.S. Constitution were clear, that they did not permit the federal government to establish a national bank in accordance with Alexander Hamilton's financial schemes. Jefferson lost that round. Later, when he became president, Jefferson had the opportunity to purchase the Louisiana territory. He had some misgivings about whether the Constitution authorized such action but in the end found an interpretation of the rules that suited his desires. The entire career of Chief Justice John Marshall illustrates that princes must learn the rules and how to interpret them. If they do so, they will have an advantage over nobles, rivals, and subjects who do not.

It is just as important to master the unwritten rules. When Benjamin Disraeli first became a member of the House of Commons, he dressed and acted like a dandy, a fop. That had contributed to his success in the drawing rooms of English high society but clearly was not within the rules of the august Parliament. Moreover, in his maiden speech in the Commons, Disraeli violated another rule, speaking too long and too shrilly. He quickly learned his lesson, assumed a lower profile, and built a reputation as one of the Commons's most able orators. Eva Peron mastered unwritten rules as well, carefully training herself to be graceful and charming in social gatherings with important political figures but to be coarse and almost peasantlike in appealing to her *descamisados.*

Learning to Present Yourself

Princes become celebrated persons by drawing attention to themselves, the kind of attention that results in being either "praised or blamed," according to Machiavelli. In Chapter 21 of *The Prince,* Machiavelli offered specific suggestions for acquiring a princely reputation, including planning and carrying out great designs, proving oneself competent in governing internal affairs of the state, being decisive, taking a stand, and demonstrating moderation and justice. He also made it clear that a prince must preserve his or her dignity "at all costs." Put in modern language, a prince must learn to portray a positive image before nobles, rivals, and subjects and to hide blemishes.

Acquiring a positive reputation requires developing skills that are appropriate to presenting yourself before other peopole, in formal and informal settings, with individuals, in small groups, and before large audiences: in other words, to communicate effectively. All of the princely figures so far described were polished communicators. Not all had precisely the same skills; rather they developed skills appropriate to their talents and personalities.

For example, the secretary to the Ten, Niccolo Machiavelli, became skillful at writing dispatches to his superiors in Florence. By controlling what he did and did not tell them, Machiavelli was able to monitor the flow of information between Florence and the various principalities to which he was sent as a diplomat. Writing skills were also the forte of Walter Lippmann. Madame de Pompadour and Catherine the Great were untiring in their devotion to letter writing. Catherine conducted matters of state through letters: Pompadour's uncanny talent at remaining a power behind the throne of Louis XV long after she had ceased to be his mistress can be attributed to her ability to write well: it was through her lengthy correspondence with ambassadors that she was able to cement the alliance between France and Austria before the Seven Years War.

Other princes develop rhetorical and oratorical skills. Adolf Hitler was a poor and disorganized writer but a mesmeric orator. The Nazi party rallies at which Hitler would speak at length was the main vehicle through which he gained the support of the people. Charles de Gaulle also was a masterful speaker. Before each TV address, de Gaulle would write out his speech and memorize it. This done, he would rehearse the speech before a mirror, using a tape recorder. Recognizing that such performances require the talents of a dramatic actor, de Gaulle—like Eva Peron—took diction lessons to establish an appropriate style and cadence. Princes who rely on the spoken word for communication know that the nonverbal gestures and mannerisms that go with the oral presentation are very important. Benjamin Disraeli had a trick of pulling his handkerchief from his sleeve and coughing softly into it in order to make a point. Adolf Hitler purposely began his speeches in an awkward, shy manner and then built up to a frenzy of waving arms and gestures that had profound dramatic effects.

Because they are good at communicating in some ways and not in others, some princes prefer to emphasize their strength. Thomas Jefferson was a poor speaker and preferred the written to the spoken word in communicating with allies and rivals. James Madison was a short, uninspiring person in appearance. Yet in one-to-one conversations the clarity of his argument would leave people with the impression that his reason, not his style, was important. Walter Rathenau developed skills of written communication, but they often resulted in seemingly obtuse messages. He was much better in small group discussions than in appearances before large audiences or in correspondence.

In sum, princes must learn how to present themselves effectively, to inspire audiences to make great sacrifices (as did Winston Churchill) or even great errors (as did Adolf Hitler), to change an entire regime (as did Charles de Gaulle), or to acquiesce to a corrupt one (as did Catherine the Great).

Learning by Doing

As noted earlier, princes are likely to be avid students of history, studying the past and learning from historical figures. But "book learning" is not the whole of it. Without exception the princely leaders we have discussed learned through practical political experience as well as academic study. Even Walter Lippmann, who is remembered today more as a political journalist and thinker than as a practical politician, was deeply involved in the political events of his nation and the world for more than half a century. More than abstract study forms the bases of princely conduct.

Princes also often lean by taking risks. Sometimes those risks pay off, and the prince discovers what worked. But ofher times the risks prove costly, and the prince learns from errors and mistakes. Benjamin Disraeli is an example, as he met with several disasters during his early political experience. Although he aspired to be prime minister at an early point in his political career, the many setbacks he suffered made it appear that this would never happen. Still he persevered, learned something from each failure, and continued to try to grasp *fortuna* by

MEASURING MACHIAVELLIANISM*

The MACH IV scale consists of several statements. No statement is necessarily correct or incorrect. You will probably agree with some of the statements and disagree with others. Read each statement carefully, and on a separate sheet of paper write a column of numbers from 1 through 20. For each statement indicate by number the amount of your agreement or disagreement.

If you agree strongly, write +3.
If you agree somewhat, write +2.
If you agree slightly, write +1.
If you disagree slightly, write −1.
If you disagree somewhat, write −2.
If you disagree strongly, write −3.

When you have indicated your opinion of each statement, calculate your score. Note that some of the items have an asterisk beside the number of the item and that others do not. First, consider all of the items without asterisks. Then convert your value for each item to a score, as follows:

$$+3 = 7, \ +2 = 6, \ +1 = 5, \ -1 = 3, \ -2 = 2, \ -3 = 1$$

Now do the same for all items with an asterisk, as follows:

$$+3 = 1, \ +2 = 2, \ +1 = 3, \ -1 = 5, \ -2 = 6, \ -3 = 7$$

Finally, add the numbers of your twenty scores.

A total score of 100 on this scale is neutral, neither Machiavellian nor non-Machiavellian. You can measure where you fit, above or below that neutral point. Don't make too much of what you find one way or the other, as this is only an exercise to give you a feel for what some researchers try to do in studying politics.

1. Never tell anyone the real reason you did something unless it is useful to do so.
2. The best way to handle people is to tell them what they want to hear.
*3. One should take action only when sure it is morally right.
*4. Most people are basically good and kind.
5. It is safest to assume that all people have a vicious streak, as it will come out when given a chance.
*6. Honesty is the best policy in all cases.
*7. There is no excuse for lying to someone else.
8. Generally speaking, people won't work hard unless they're forced to do so.
*9. All in all, it is better to be humble and honest than to be important and dishonest.
*10. When you ask someone to do something for you, it is best to give the real reasons for wanting it rather than giving reasons that carry more weight.
*11. Most people who get ahead in the world lead clean, moral lives.

*Reprinted with permission from Florence L. Geis and Richard Christie, *Studies in Machiavellianism* (New York: Academic Press, 1971).

12. Anyone who completely trusts anyone else is asking for trouble.
13. The biggest difference between most criminals and other people is that the criminals are stupid enough to get caught.
*14. Most people are brave.
15. It is wise to flatter important people.
*16. It is possible to be good in all respects.
*17. P. T. Barnum was wrong when he said that there's a sucker born every minute.
18. It is hard to get ahead without cutting corners here and there.
19. People suffering from incurable diseases should have the option of being put painlessly to death.
20. Most people forget more easily the death of a parent than the loss of their property.

---

the forelock. In the end he achieved his goal of miniserial political power. Winston Churchill, Charles de Gaulle, Walter Rathenau all achieved their major political successes long after most people have gone into the solitude of retirement to lick their wounds.

Two features of risk taking are common to most princes. First, think of how many of the princes/princesses you have read about thus far have decided very early in life that they were destined to have political power. For instance, Catherine the Great had visions of being an empress when only a little girl, long before she ever had the opportunity to go to Russia. Her dreams were not the idle fantasies of a schoolgirl; she knew that she would be a ruler! And so she cultivated the skills and contacts that would put her on that road. Or remember Benjamin Disraeli's early aspirations to reach greatness in British politics, the prophecy that the future Madame de Pompadour would someday be the king's mistress, and even Thomas Jefferson's thought that it would be a good idea to make his cousin John Marshall a judge in order to get him out of the way. Finally, there was surely little doubt in Eva Duarte's mind that she was setting out to find not just fame but power when she put herself and her cardboard suitcase on a train from Junin to Buenos Aires.

Second, there is an old saying in politics, "Start high to finish high." Princes aspire to high office early, and in order to achieve it they rarely devote much time to securing lesser positions. The seat of political power in Great Britain is the House of Commons, which is where men like Winston Churchill and Benjamin Disraeli set their sights. Adolf Hitler wanted to rule Germany, and Joseph Stalin wanted to rule Russia, and both toiled in the hinterlands to win support for their higher ambitions. But when they jockeyed for position, they jockeyed for high position. Although today we might consider a seat in the Virginia House of Delegates to be a minor political office, compared with the presidency of the United States, remember that when such princes as James Madison, John Marshall, and Thomas Jefferson began their political careers, starting at the state-legislative level meant starting at the top, as there was no government of the United States as we know it.

THE *VIRTU* OF TAKING POLITICS SERIOUSLY

Of all the things we have discussed in this chapter that separate the prince from others, the most distinctive is that unlike most people, princes take politics seriously. But despite being so seriously about their craft, princely politicians rarely win accolades. In fact, as we saw at the beginning of this chapter, there is a widespread tendency to heap scorn on all politicians, princely or not. So commonplace is the assumption that politics and politicians are bad, even evil, that one of the stocks in trade of the contemporary politically ambitious person is to deny such ambition, condemn politicians, decry the evils of politics, and seek power as a citizen or amateur who will "rise above politics." This power-seeking device is known to princes as well as amateurs. Indeed many of the princely rulers we have discussed thus far—for example, Catherine the Great, Charles de Gaulle, Adolf Hitler, Eva Peron, as well as others—were quick to jump on the antipolitics bandwagon.

Politicians who take their vocation seriously are open to another form of criticism. There is a strong likelihood that princely conduct, because it does follow the logic of politics rather than the more pleasing and attractive moral standards of a community, will be attacked as being immoral or, if not immoral, then certainly out of the ordinary, something darkly "Machiavellian." Social scientists have even devised tests to determine to what degree people display Machiavellian tendencies. As we close this chapter we refer you to Figure 14.1, a simple test to measure the Machiavellian trait. Take it and see how you do. You will then be prepared to consider a topic as important as what princes know that others do not, namely, the subject of our next chapter, what do princes do that others do not?

"Common sense is not an issue in politics, it's an affliction.
—*Will Rogers*

"It is true that men are more or less virtuous in one country or another, according to the nature of the education by which their manners and habits of life have been formed."
—*Machiavelli*

"Education is a weapon whose effect depends upon who holds it in his hands and at whom it is aimed."
—*Stalin*

"Fortune is a woman and the man who wants to hold her down must beat and bully her."
—*Machiavelli*

"Nothing in my destiny is extraordinary; still less is it due to chance."
—*Eva Peron*

"The knowledge they are to acquire should serve only to give them a thorough understanding of their role as Princess."
—*Catherine the Great*

Chapter

15

What Do Princes Do That Others Do Not?

It was a motley, ragtag band that set out on a mid-March day in 1930 from a tiny village in India. There were eighty of them, and their goal was to march 240 miles on dusty roads to the sea. When there they would simply collect salt from the seashore. But by doing so they would violate the Salt Act and, they hoped, bring the wrath of the British-controlled government of India down on their heads. Why, you might wonder, would they want to do that?

Since 1600, with the founding of the East India Tea Company, the British had designs on the Indian subcontinent, and as a result of incursions and wars, the area became part of the British Empire. One result of the Seven Years War so much favored by Madame de Pompadour was that the French surrendered to the British their claims on India. Benjamin Disraeli took pride in proclaiming Queen Victoria as the empress of India. But it was only a short time thereafter that the Indians began to get restive, and by the close of the nineteenth century, there was an active movement for Indian independence. Into this struggle during the First World War walked the man who dominated it until after the Second World War, Mohandas K. Gandhi, and it was Gandhi who led the 1930 March to the Sea to protest the Salt Act.

During the late 1920s the movement for Indian independence intensified, and on January 1, 1930, a group of Indian nationalists declared the nation independent of British rule. Gandhi proposed that January 21 then be celebrated nationwide as Independence Day. The British, of course, ignored both the declaration and the celebration, and so Gandhi decided to test the British resolve through a campaign of civil disobedience. He would find a law that the British had imposed on the Indians, a law symbolizing the nation's grievances, and then lead a movement in the peaceful disobedience of that law, hoping that passive resistance to other forms of British rule in turn would become so widespread as to force the British to negotiate independence.

Gandhi selected the Salt Act as the target of his protest. The manufacture and sale of salt were a government monopoly, and the possession of salt not secured from the government was prohibited. There also was a small tax on the purchase of salt. Gandhi recognized that a small band protesting the salt tax would scarcely bring the British to heel, but that was not his direct aim. What he wanted to do was to publicize to an uninformed world how the British, through such things as a tax on a necessity of life such as salt, exploited the impoverished Indians. For the most part the British ignored Gandhi's protest march. They let the sixty-year-old man, dressed in a loin cloth and with staff in hand, go on his way, reach the sea, and gather his salt. They made no effort to arrest him. But the provincial government ruling the seaside territory grew anxious, fearing that Gandhi was about to lead a raid on the government's salt depots. If he did, the government thought that it would be impossible to halt the spread of lawlessness. So the government played into Gandhi's hands by arresting him.

Gandhi's march to the sea and his arrest became symbols of the Indian protest. In themselves such acts had few tangible results. What they did do, however, was to arouse the Indians and intensify their struggle for independence. And when Gandhi called for a boycott of British goods sold in India, he got results. Before World War I, half of all British exports of cotton cloth had gone to India; by 1932 this had fallen to one fourth. In subsequent years the British began to respond, and by 1947 India had won its independence.

Gandhi's acts illustrate that princes do what most people do not: they lead. They lead by doing what is necessary in specific times and circumstances. As seen in Chapter 14, princes learn things that other people do not. That is their political *virtu*. We shall turn now to the things that princes do that others do not, their political *necessita*.

WHAT MOST PEOPLE DO (DON'T DO) IN POLITICS

Although everyone participates in the politics of his or her everyday life, relatively few are active in the governing of their local community, state or province, or nation. In gauging how active most people are in politics, the first distinction to make is between those who hold public office and those who do not. In any nation, most people do not occupy governing positions, and they do not reside in executive, legislative, bureaucratic, or judicial palaces of power. They are, in short, the governed, not the governors.

This does not mean, however, that they have no share in political power. They do. The size of that share depends, in part, on the type of regime that governs them. In a republic, for example, people have an indirect role in government, in that they elect their public officials and hold them accountable to their will. They have at least an opportunity for the active exercise of power. As you will see, only a few often take advantage of that power. Nonetheless, the opportunity is there, Autocracies, by contrast, do not permit the sharing of political power. Passive obedience, not active exercise, is the principle.

The genius of Mohandas Gandhi's princely leadership, in both South

Africa and India, was to turn this characteristic of autocracy against itself. He fought passive obedience with passive disobedience. Whether such a tactic would work against totalitarian rule is questionable, in a totalitarian regime, coercion and terror prevail. The choice is not between an active or passive share of political power but between support for the regime or possible torture and execution. However, Gandhi, rightly or wrongly, believed civil disobedience to be so powerful that it would work anywhere. "The willing sacrifice of the innocent," he said, "is the most powerful answer to insolent tyranny that has yet been conceived by God or man." For disobedience to be "civil," it must be "sincere, respectful, restrained, never defiant, and it must have no ill will or hatred behind it."

You should note one other thing about the distinction between those who hold public office and those who do not. Being a public official is no guarantee that you will be a prince. That depends on your *virtu* and *necessita* in the face of *fortuna*. Many public officials in many nations fall short of Machiavelli's princely requirements. At the same time, however, you need not be an officeholder to be princely. Gandhi is only one of many examples of princely figures that influenced the politics of their time, yet never held governmental positions. Martin Luther King, Jr., who borrowed much from Gandhi's teachings, is another example.

Let us now look at those republican regimes in which people do have an opportunity to exercise indirect political power. How active are they? That depends on the type of activity available and the nation. In measuring how active people are in politics, political scientists have devised a classification of types of political participation. The fourfold scheme is made up of voting, campaigning in elections, working in community politics, and working for oneself.

As you might expect, one factor that determines whether or not people vote is whether they are required to do so by law. Some nations make voting compulsory: Australia, the Netherlands, Venezuela, Belgium, Italy, and Greece are examples of nations that have some form of compulsory voting. In those nations the average percentage of the people eligible and registered to vote who actually do so ranges from 80 to 95 percent. Eligible and registered voters actually voting in republics without compulsory voting average from 60 to 90 percent. Overall, since the end of World War II, of twenty-eight nations regularly holding elections, the rate of voting in elections has been slightly below 80 percent.

Making such estimates is difficult. For example, in the United States in order to vote you must first be eligible, be a U.S. citizen eighteen years of age or older. You must also register, that is, go to a government office and prove that you are eligible. In estimating what percentage of Americans do vote, you will get a different figure according to which of these two electorates—the eligible or registered—you use as a basis for measurement. Thus, in presidential elections since 1945 an average of slightly more than 55 percent of Americans eligible to vote have done so. That does not compare well with the 80 percent in nations worldwide.

MOHANDAS K. GANDHI: SAINTLY POLITICIAN

It is a "nauseating and humiliating spectacle," thundered Winston Churchill in 1931, "of this one-time Inner Temple lawyer, now seditious fakir, striding half-naked up the steps of the Viceroy's palace there to parley on equal terms with the representative of the King-Emperor." Churchill was talking about Mohandas K. Gandhi, a man that millions of Indians called *Mahatma,* (a religious term meaning "Great Soul" or "Holy One") and the dominant figure in the struggle for Indian independence from British rule. By 1931 the British had opened talks with Indian leaders about the possibilities of greater self-rule in that portion of the empire, a possibility that Churchill did not relish. Now, he felt, one of the most troublesome characters in the history of the British Empire, Gandhi, was being elevated to equal status with the viceroy, the agent of British rule in India. No matter to Churchill that many people thought Gandhi was a saint; Churchill deemed it more accurate to label him with a play on words, a "fakir" (religious recluse and ascetic) pronounced much like "faker."

Gandhi was born in 1869. Although his family was not of high social standing—not of an elevated caste, to use the Hindu social classification—his family was better off than most. Gandhi was a descendant of a family of grocers, and his grandfather, father, and uncle had been prime ministers of local territories not under British rule. His mother was deeply religious, taking and living up to strict vows. These were the origins of the unique combination that marked Gandhi's life and career: a saintly presence and a political sagacity.

Gandhi finished high school and one year of college in India. A family friend argued that Gandhi should go to England and study law. Everyone agreed except his mother, who worried that her son might fall into bad ways in far-off England, eating meat and drinking alcohol. She was unaware that young Gandhi was already guilty of those sins, as well as having visited a brothel. Only if Gandhi would take vows not to touch wine, women, or meat, could he go to England. He so vowed and set off in 1888 for London. Let it be said that the friends he made while studying law urged him to break his word. But Gandhi was resolved: "A vow is a vow and cannot be broken."

In three years Gandhi became a member of the bar and returned to India. Although he managed to make an adequate living from his legal practice, he was not satisfied, and so when there was an opportunity to take on clients in South Africa—which had a sizable population of Indian nationals—Gandhi again left his native land. At age twenty-four he set out on what was to be a brief stay, but he was forty-six before returning to India permanently.

Gandhi's experiences in South Africa taught him many things that he would remember and practice for the remainder of his life. He encountered discrimination against Indians in South Africa and resolved to do something about it. But what could a minority community living under autocratic rule (many Indians were indentured workers living in conditions of virtual slavery) do? Gandhi thought that a program of nonviolent, passive resistance was the answer. He called it *satyagraha:* "Truth [*satya*] implies love, and firmness [*agraha*] engenders and therefore serves as a synonym for force. I thus began to call the Indian movement "Satygraha," that is to say, the Force which is born of Truth and Love or non-violence."

The program was derived from a Hindu religious principle, *ahimsa,* the vow not to do injury to any other being. It entails peaceful agitation and resistance to law, which often brings about arrest and punishment. But mass arrests and punishments raise and publicize doubts about the moral force of the law itself. When the program works, it forces rulers to negotiate changes in the offending regulations. For example, the Indians in South Africa were required to go through elaborate procedures to register their legal presence and to pay a fee for doing so. Gandhi wanted the practice abolished. In accordance with his doctrine of nonviolent resistance he first selected a specific grievance, not attacking the general issue directly. In this instance the specific grievance produced an even greater tightening of registration requirements, and so Gandhi organized a campaign of peaceful picketing outside registration offices to discourage Indians from complying with the new laws. It worked: large numbers of Indians did not register, resistance leaders were arrested (including Gandhi), and the Indian community was galvanized to greater resistance. The government finally decided to negotiate a settlement, and Gandhi and his followers were released from prison.

The settlement did not, however, include abolishing the tax on registration. Gandhi had not even included it as a demand. "The minimum is the maximum," he said. That can be taken to mean that in *satyagraha,* the minimum demand—easing regulations on registration—is the only specific request. Or it can mean that the specific minimum demand is only the prelude to a larger attack on the whole issue, in this case including fees for registration as well. As it turned out, Gandhi sought the latter. He organized Indian women to persuade the miners to go on strike, protesting the registration tax. They did and were arrested. Gandhi then called for a march (one of many he led in his lifetime) to protest the arrests. That also worked, and Gandhi was again put in prison, and so the miners again went on strike, paralyzing the territorial economy. The government relented and through the Indian Relief Act repealed the tax. Gandhi, again out of jail, proclaimed his work in South Africa finished and returned to India. General Jan Smuts, the minister primarily responsible for dealing with Gandhi's agitation, declared, "The saint has left our shores, I sincerely hope forever."

It was indeed forever, and Gandhi devoted the remainder of his life, from 1915 to 1948, to leading India's struggle, first for greater self-rule and then for independence. The political tactics learned in South Africa caused the British no end of grief. Nonviolent agitation, civil disobedience, strikes, marches, fasts, and hard bargaining were Gandhi's practical weapons. With them he not only dealt with the British but also reorganized and reoriented the Indian National Congress party (an important arm in the fight for independence), tried to instill a sense of pride in his fellow Hindus, and unsuccessfully tried to promote unity between Hindus and Muslims. In all these tasks he relied on both political and religious means. In his manner, Gandhi symbolized devout, dedicated religious belief in his manner (prayers and purifying fasts), his dress (giving up the Western garb worn by educated Indians and dressing instead in a homespun loin cloth), and his words (preaching always of Truth and Love).

But just because Gandhi practiced a saintly politics does not mean that he failed to practice a power politics as well. Gandhi simply and sincerely believed that his "truth force" was far stronger and politically effective than brute, physical force. Whereas a dictator such as Italy's Benito Mussolini could say, "There is a violence that liberates and a violence that enslaves; there is a violence that is moral and a violence that is immoral," Gandhi thought that all violence enslaved, was immoral, and thus was ineffective. "Non-violence," said Gandhi, "is the first article of my faith. It is also the last article of my creed." Ironically, violence ended Gandhi's life. On January 30, 1948, as he walked through a crowd on his way to a prayer meeting, a Hindu man who mistakenly believed Gandhi to be responsible for dividing India into Hindu and Muslim territories, approached Gandhi as though to touch his feet and fired three shots into his stomach. Gandhi fell, uttering his last words, "Rama, Rama" (God, God). Thus died the saintly politician.

But of registered voters the turnout rate is much higher, about two thirds in the most recent presidential elections. Compare that with India's, which is less than 60 percent, or Switzerland's, which is about the same as the United States'. Another way to calculate how often people vote is to measure the percentage of regular voters in a nation, those who vote frequently in both state and local elections. In nations in which it is possible to base guesses on reliable evidence, the percentage ranges from 56 for Nigeria to 93 for Japan (the United States has a percentage of 63 on this basis).

So if "most people" means a majority, then in republics at least we can say that most people vote. But, for example, when campaigning in support of candidates in elections, the proportions of people taking part are much lower. In the United States approximately one in four adults work in some fashion or another (often remote) for a political party, about the same as in Japan. But in Japan, half of the adults attend political rallies; only a fifth of Americans do so. As for actual membership in a political party, fewer than one in ten Americans or Japanese take part; in Austria, which by comparison involves people in party activity much more, still only about one fourth of adults are party members.

Similarly, in regard to people working in local community politics, the proportions are low, including being active members in community organizations, working with or helping local groups, and contacting officials within or outside the community to get assistance. About 10 to 30 percent of American adults do these kinds of things, compared with only 5 to 15 percent in Japan and India and less than 10 percent in Austria.

Finally, not many people contact either local officials or officials outside their own communities in order to promote their own self-interests. Less than 10 percent do so in the United States or Japan, and only slightly higher percentages in Austria, India, or the Netherlands.

What all this adds up to is that most people do little in politics other than vote. And if you recall from Chapter 14 what most people know about politics, few voters do so in any informed way. There are many reasons that most people are not more active in politics. In some nations legal restrictions discourage an active political life, and often it is a matter of not having the resources—welfare and deferential values— that encourage political activity. Finally, many people just do not care.

Whatever the legal, social, economic, or personal reasons, the fact is that politics is an activity of the few, not the many, and princes know

The Rulers and the Ruled

this. Indeed, because most people do not take part in politics, it makes it easier for princes to do so, and to do so in more ways. By the same token, because so few people play politics and thus use their shares of political power, it makes it easier for you to play, to get ahead, to use their share of power, and to prosper. In short, the political apathy of most people can contribute to your princely success. What, then, could you do that most people would not?

WHAT PRINCES DO THAT OTHERS DO NOT

You know that princes learn things that set them apart from ordinary people. Mohandas K. Gandhi is a good example of that princely learning. Unlike most Indians he was able to travel to England and receive legal training. But he did not stop there. While studying law he also studied Latin. He read widely, particularly in areas of religious study, and studied vegetarianism. Later in South Africa he devoted himself to a systematic study of the Hindu, Muslim, and Christian religions. By doing so, he was following the precept of Sherlock Holmes, to observe and ponder everything, for one never knows when it may have a useful application. Gandhi's knowledge turned out to be vital to his quest for political success. That, of course, is the point worth reemphasizing: because princes learn what others do not, they can do more.

Estimating the Social Bases of Power

Princes must be sensitive to what values that people adopt in given situations, values for which people will strive and perhaps kill and die. This means sizing up the distribution of welfare values—well-being, wealth, skill, and enlightenment—and the deference values—respect, rectitude, love, and power. Knowing who has these and to what degree helps princes decide on tactics that will permit changing the situation more to princely liking. Gandhi recognized that in India, as his experience in South Africa had taught him, it would be pointless to confront the British *raj* (rule) directly. For one thing, the British held all the important welfare resources: military and bureacratic skills, administrative enlightenment, wealth, and well-being. To be sure, there was a class of fairly well-to-do Indians, but they were deferential to the British *raj*, acquiescing to it. Most Indians were poor and would suffer in any direct confrontation with the British.

In his quest for *swaraj* (self-rule, self-government) for India, Gandhi devised techniques more in keeping with the values of the Indian masses. First, he relied on their religious devotion, thus capitalizing on the value of rectitude among both Hindus and Muslims. Second, he thought Indians capable of great love, for one another, for their enemies, and for him. Out of this combination of strengths, the Indian capacity for rectitude and affection, Gandhi forged his program of action, *satygraha*, or civil disobedience.

Satygraha became a practical strategy whose ultimate goal was political control, *swaraj.* Gandhi believed that if Indians could call attention to their specific grievances and win concessions, they gradually would become less servile to the British. They would win their self-respect, a deferential value that most Indians had lost centuries earlier with the coming of the British *raj.* By uniting their value resources—morality, love, and self-respect—Gandhi would have the weapons to seek political power.

Gandhi did not rely solely on *satygraha* to accomplish all of this. He joined civil disobedience to what he called his "constructive program," a program represented in the *khadi,* handspun cloth. Gandhi understood that India was not an industrialized nation, not even ready for such industry, but he preached that India must become self-sufficient. One way was for Indians to make their own goods, such as simple foods and housing. In this vein Gandhi taught that Indians should use spinning wheels to spin their own clothing. This may appear to you as a bizarre way of gaining a nation's independence and scarcely very practical. But there was more to the *khadi* program than alleged self-sufficiency: *khadi* became a tool for political organization. Gandhi organized programs of compulsory spinning for Indians of the upper classes, the relatively small intelligentsia, to remind them of the hardships of the poor and the tedium of manual labor. It would also remind them that although they might be profiting from the British *raj,* the rest of the nation was not. Moreover, by recruiting people into the *khadi* program, Gandhi also mobilized a well-trained and disciplined cadre for his program of *satygraha.* Thus his constructive program provided the army for successful civil disobedience.

Thus, to the degree that politics is like a game, princes must gauge the strengths and weaknesses of all the players. Then, in the spirit of the contest, princes must do something else.

Agitating Against and Exploiting the Rules

Machiavelli observed, "Nothing is harder to manage, more risky in the undertaking, or more doubtful of success than to set up as the introducer of the new order." Princes must accept these risks. Kwame Nkrumah, who experienced both successes and failures as president and dictator of the African nation of Ghana before his overthrow in 1966, recognized such risks: "We prefer self-government with danger to servitude with tranquility" But princes try to reduce risks by taking advantage of the rules of the conflict. It is against the rules in baseball, for example, for the pitcher to throw the ball at the batter. But an astute pitcher can exploit the rules, nonetheless, by throwing a few balls so close to the hitter that the batter begins to think that the ball is aimed at him, and thus the pitcher will achieve a psychological advantage.

Gandhi exploited the rules through agitation, stirring up public interest and controversy over an issue. Frequently people simply accept things as they are and do not bother to protest what they do not like.

"Let's not make an issue of this" is a saying with wide currency. An agitator, however, wants to bring issues to light or, if there are no issues, make them. Public officials seldom like agitators. Governors prefer that the governed not be stirred to action. When conflicts arise, it is a standard ploy to condemn the controversy as a "tempest in a teapot" and the work of "agitators." But Frederick Douglass, a slave who escaped to freedom and agitated for the abolition of slavery in the United States, put things in a different light: "Those who profess to favor freedom, and yet depreciate agitation are men who want rain without thunder and lightning. They want the ocean without the roar of its many waters."

Princes prefer to choose the issues and controversies on which they will take risks, hence agitate. Knowing just how far to go—that is, what the rules allow and how they will be applied—is vital to successful agitation. Gandhi was well aware, both in South Africa and India, that he could only go so far in protesting grievances before the rulers would take notice and respond. So he tried to control the tenor of the rulers' response by choosing the grievance, the issue, to battle. The Salt Tax was scarcely much of an issue to most Indians, but Gandhi's march to the sea made it one. He was sorely disappointed when he was not immediately arrested, for he viewed arrest as a key to publicizing the conflict, expanding its scope, recruiting new supporters, and forcing the British to make concessions. But with princely patience he waited (something that most people do not do), was arrested, and thereby forced the issue.

Adapting Necessita *to* Fortuna

Going far enough yet not too far is a princely art acquired by political experience. It requires knowledge of the social bases of power and of the rules permitting agitation. Yet, even with long experience and full knowledge, a prince may go too far, suffer the consequences, and not err the same way again. Again, Gandhi provides a case in point.

During World War I the demands for *swaraj* became strident among a radical segment of Indians. Gandhi approved of neither the extremity of their goals at the time (they demanded immediate and complete independence, but Gandhi still thought that some connection to the British would be useful and, in any event, a minimum condition that might later lead to independence) nor their terrorist methods. Alarmed by an increase in terrorism and general unrest the British decided to take stern measures and proposed the arbitrary arrest and internment of agitators. Gandhi opposed such measures and decided on *satygraha* as a response. But what form should it take?

Gandhi had a flash of inspiration, explained in a letter to a colleague: "The idea came to me last night in a dream that we should call upon the country to observe a general *hartal*." He was referring to an ancient Hindu method of protesting a ruler's arbitrary actions, by devoting a day to no work and no business, only fasting and prayer. The response to Gandhi's dream (unfortunately it ended in a nightmare) was enthusiastic. On the day of the *hartal* Gandhi spoke in a mosque in Bombay. All was peaceful. But in Delhi, demonstrators fought with the police and there were casualties. There were worse incidents in other regions. Gandhi's assumption that all would be nonviolent, for he believed that people were naturally peace loving, was a "Himalayan miscalculation," as he later said. The bitterness from these events left hostility and distrust against the British *raj* that remained until independence and drove many moderates into a more radical pursuit of *swaraj*. The lesson that Gandhi learned was not to act on impulse, as many others do. Moreover, if *satygraha* was to work, his followers must receive disciplined training, and he set himself to that task.

Princes must be wary. Sometimes, believing that a certain political tactic is the minimum thing to do at the time, princes often find that their followers are more interested in maximum results. Events can get out of hand, for political necessity has not been balanced against political fortune. Too err in this way is bad enough, but not to learn from it can mean disaster.

Practicing the Art of the Possible

In the musical production of *Evita,* a romanticized stage production based on the life of Eva Peron, a group of army officers sings the following song:

> *One has no rules,*
> *Is not precise.*
> *One rarely acts the same way twice.*
> *One spurns no device.*
> *Practicing the art of the possible.*
>
> *One always picks*
> *The easy fight.*
> *One praises fools,*
> *One smothers light.*
> *One shifts from left to right.*
> *It's part of the art of the possible.*
>
> *One always claims*
> *Mistakes were planned.*
> *When risk is slight*
> *One takes a stand.*
> *With such sleight of hand,*
> *Politics—the art of the possible.*
>
> *One has no rules,*
> *Is not precise.*
> *One rarely acts the same way twice.*
> *One spurns no device.*
> *Politics—the art of the possible.*

Of course, the song is intended to poke fun at politics and politicians and should be enjoyed as such. But if by now you're willing to accept that for good or ill political logic indeed dictates the types of behavior captured in this song, you can extract from it a few other things that princes must do that most people need not. Politics frequently requires that rules be vague, meanings imprecise, conduct flexible; that issues be used for practical gain; and that credit be grabbed and blame be strategically placed.

A principled, moral, saintly prince such as Mohandas Gandhi was no more immune to such political necessities than any other prince would be. He too recognized the imperatives of the art of the possible, and he practiced them. After his confession of "Himalayan miscalculation" in 1919, he toured India. Everywhere he basked in the glory of what his mass following believed to be the great success of his *hartal*. Did he fail to take credit for it? He was delighted by the turn of events: "Rightly or wrongly, I seem to command, at the present moment, in an excessive degree, the respect and the affection of the people all over India." Then with the self-confidence so important to the princely calling, Gandhi stated, "I am the one man who can today preserve the peace in India as no other man can."

So even if the *hartal* had been a miscalculation, it quickly fell into the category of "planned mistakes." Gandhi was also flexible in his stands, frequently changing them for no apparent reason. But he did have reasons. Within a year after proclaiming that the way to *swaraj* included a continued connection to the British, he took the opposite stand. All links with Britain had to end, even at the risk of violence. For such preaching he was jailed in 1920 and stayed there for the next three years. Why had he changed? He was adapting to changing times and circumstances. In art he hoped to promote Hindu-Muslim unity, and he sought to galvanize his followers by using the British *raj* as a scapegoat, blaming the British for the deterioration of a once great people. It was not the last time that he did not "act the same way twice." For example, early in World War II he preached that Indians should cooperate with the British; later in the war he helped promote a "quit India" rebellion against the British. After the war he opposed British plans for independence and then supported them. *Necessita* was a princely guide.

Taking the Job Seriously

Politics is a full-time job. For the dilettante it may be something to dabble in, and for the average politician a way to make a living. But for the prince, politics is not a diversion, not simply an occupation, but a way of life. Taking politics seriously is a requirement. Serious work, serious study, serious imagination all are part of the princely craft, not only for politics, but also for any endeavor in which one chooses to be princely—a profession such as law, medicine, or teaching; athletics; religious endeavors; artistic enterprises; and even making love.

One thing that occupies the princely politician is self-advice. Certainly a prince needs to have help and advice. But often the prince must seek his or her own counsel, which is where serious imagination comes in. Being able to place yourself in a prince's shoes is one way to learn about princedom; but being able to imagine what to do at a given time and place and to anticipate action and consequences before acting is the way to practice princedom. When he committed his great miscalculation in 1919, Gandhi failed to take into account what he might have done if he were a radical, violent nationalist seeking immediate independence. Thus he failed to anticipate the possible consequences of his *hartal*. In 1930 he did use his imagination in the selection of the Salt Tax as a specific grievance, deciding on the march to the sea and appraising the likely government response and mass response.

Self-counsel is an effort to calculate probabilities. The development of such foresight demands a dispassionate and hard-headed estimation of the way things are, in the tradition of Sherlock Holmes, "Data! Data! Data! I can't make bricks without clay!" (Chapter 3) Princes cannot permit emotions to overrule their judgment. Gandhi certainly did not. One of the great strengths he derived from his religious commitment was that despite believing that people should love one another, he did not let anger, fear, frustration, or any other sentiment guide his princely judgments of his adversaries. Thus he could deal with friend and foe alike on the basis of the facts of the situation at hand.

Such calculations helped Gandhi accomplish one of his last political successes. When India achieved independence in 1947, two nations emerged, the separate republics of India (mostly Hindu) and Pakistan (Muslim). Throughout his career Gandhi had opposed the partition of India into two nations. But characteristically, with independence at hand, Gandhi accepted the inevitable, shifted his stand, and did not protest the partition. But many Muslims still lived in certain regions of the Republic of India, such as Calcutta. The Hindus' and Muslims' fear of each other there resulted in riots, bloodshed, and atrocities. The Hindus blamed the chief minister of the region, H. A. Suhrawardy, for their plight, considering him to be an archvillain. Gandhi, now seventy-seven years old, sought to end the strife. Although no ally of Suhrawardy, he offered his help. Gandhi proposed that he and Suhrawardy live together without police or military protection in an abandoned Muslim house in a filthy, impoverished, mixed Hindu-Muslim neighborhood. At first Hindus felt betrayed and threw rocks at their house and broke the windows. But Gandhi and Suhrawardy appeared together not as enemies but as friends. Soon both Hindus and Muslims came from all over Calcutta to the house. They left shaking hands, marching arm in arm, and shouting "We are one." It came to be known as the "Miracle of Calcutta." Gandhi had correctly calculated the probabilities.

Persistence and dispassionate evaluation are requirements of princely performance. Gandhi would scarcely have approved of the implications but would have understood the logic behind Dirksen's

Three Laws of Politics that summarize these requisites. Everett Dirksen served as a member of the U.S. Senate, rising to the position of minority leader. His laws were simple: "Get elected. Get reelected. Don't get mad, get even."

Making Prudent Payoffs

In the end, princely success demands that princes be able to persuade nobles, rivals, and subjects—all those people who do not do what princes do—to do what they otherwise would not, to accede to the prince's rule. The principal political mechanism for this is the judicious distribution of rewards and punishments. These are all of the welfare and deferential values discussed previously. Their distribution is what politicians call "patronage," awarding such payoffs as jobs, money, and status.

Such payoffs are a problem for any prince. In a world of power what is one group worth compared with another? What should one person receive, contrasted with another? We have already said that to practice power a prince must accurately estimate the social bases of power. In accordance with that estimate, the prince should solidify his or her rule by distributing political rewards. Failure to do so can contribute to the erosion of princely power, even to open revolt.

Sam Rayburn, Speaker of the U.S. House of Representatives longer than any other person to hold that office and a political power in his own right, coined the dictum for distributing political payoffs: "If you want to get along, go along." Princes reward on the basis of service, "going along," to be sure. But they cannot equally reward everyone who goes along: there simply are not enough goodies to go around. Yet at the same time, the prince does not have the luxury to play favorites, and the prince would be foolish to do so, even if he or she could. To reward the few at the expense of the many may, of course, provoke discontent among subjects.

But there is a greater risk. If one or more groups consistently skim off the cream, there is danger in concentrating the payoffs in one or more such groups. Concentrated power in any form—power in the welfare values of well-being, wealth, skill, or enlightenment or the deferential values of respect, rectitude, love, or political position—can pose a threat. A broad distribution of payoffs disperses them among a multitude of power centers, decreasing the likelihood of any single power enclave's developing sufficiently to challenge the power of the prince.

This is the problem that the British *raj* faced in contending with the forces of independence in India. On one side were the British, with their control of military, economic, and political resources. But as Gandhi understood and preached, these were not the only sources of power. Respect, morality, and love also were significant. These, he taught, resided not in the British but in the Indian people, Hindu and Muslim. So he used those forms of power, which the British *raj* had permitted by default to become monopolized by their Indian subjects, against the seemingly more formidable concentration of military, economic, and political power of the British. It was that struggle that dominated the subcontinent for three decades of Gandhi's princedom.

POLITICAL GROWTH AND MATURITY

By this point you have probably realized that what princes do is to perform a highly intricate balancing act. They are close students of power, its distribution, and its social bases. They also are close students of rules, customs, and practices and constantly exploit them to princely advantage. They select which battles to fight and which to avoid, are light on their feet, and work with the devices that they deem appropriate to the changing times and circumstances and, above all, to shifting *fortuna*. On the surface the princely way of life may seem almost impossible to master. And as we shall argue in Part VIII, some believe that it is now beyond mastery. But if there is one trait that sets apart what princes do, it is that princes continue to grow and mature. Because princes take political work seriously, they never cease to learn to do or do to learn. Any prince who stops the lifelong process of political growth and maturing and the relentless effort to master the fickle finger of *fortuna,* stops being a prince.

To learn the intricacies of power one must exercise power—whether the power is physical, economic, technical, scholarly, social, spiritual, amorous, or political. To accomplish that, you must have it, you must get it. It is time to see how princes go about that task.

"The willing sacrifice of the innocent is the most powerful answer to insolent tyranny that has yet been conceived by God or man."

—Gandhi

"There is a violence that liberates and a violence that enslaves; there is a violence that is moral and a violence that is immoral."

—Mussolini

"Non-violence is the first article of my faith. It is also the last article of my creed."

—Gandhi

"Nothing is harder to manage, more risky in the undertaking, or more doubtful of success than to set up as the introducer of the new order."

—Machiavelli

"We prefer self-government with danger to servitude with tranquillity."

—Kwame Nkrumah

"Those who profess to favor freedom, and yet depreciate agitation, are men who want rain without thunder and lightning. They want the ocean without the roar of its many waters."

—Frederick Douglass

"Get elected. Get reelected. Don't get mad, get even."

—Everett Dirksen

"If you want to get along, go along."

—Sam Rayburn

Part

Taking Political Power

16

Taking Political Power Through Intrigue

William Marcy Tweed, better known to his cronies as "Boss Tweed," was a man of considerable political power. For decades during the nineteenth century, his organization, the Tweed Ring, controlled Democratic nominations, municipal elections, and appointments to public office in New York City. Unfortunately for Boss Tweed, the times and circumstances caught up with his misdeeds. After he and his allies defrauded the city of over $30 million through padded accounts and tax favors, the wholesale graft could no longer be concealed. Local newspapers published evidence of the corruption, and Tweed faced trial and conviction. The once powerful boss died in prison in 1878. During his reign, however, he offered many an insight into political realities, one being particularly relevant to us. Said Boss Tweed, "The way to have power is to take it."

This chapter and the two that follow it are about how princes take political power. "This transition, from private citizen to prince, presupposes either skill [*virtu*] or luck," observed Machiavelli. "The less one trusts to chance, the better one's hopes of holding on," he continued. Those "who become princes through their own strength of character may have trouble gaining power, but they find it easy to hold onto." In short, if you seek princedom, whether in your daily life or in the larger political realm, you will not find power presented on a silver platter. You must work for it. Princes do so in a variety of ways, three being especially noteworthy. In this chapter you will encounter the first, intrigue. The following two chapters will tell you about force and elections as other ways of taking power.

WHY INTRIGUE IS SO INTRIGUING

The dictionary defines intrigue as a secret maneuver, hidden scheme, covert plot, or conspiracy designed to achieve a denied, unavowed, or unstated purpose. Perhaps you need a passing grade in a course that you find dull, boring, and time-consuming. You could take a direct approach, study, try to get interested, and learn something. But intrigue is another—and you think less painful—possibility. So you drop by your professor's office and lavishly praise him or her for the teaching, text, and assignments. You ask a pertinent question now and then about something you "are having trouble with" (no matter that the question is irrelevant to the course so long as it displays your sly purposes). In class you appear to pay attention (what you will recognize as "sleeping with one's eyes open") or seem to take extensive notes—while actually writing a letter to a friend.

This is intrigue, seeking something that you say you are not seeking or do not even mention at all, that is, a passing grade. You keep hidden your real actions, daydreaming and correspondence, and your motives. Intrigue is common in the politics of everyday life: in families, among friends and enemies, in school, on the job, or trying to get repairs on a car, stereo, or anything else. It is thus not surprising to find it a venerable technique for taking political power. Although Adolf Hitler (see Chapter 7) captured one of the essentials of intrigue when he said, "The victor will never be asked if he told the truth," intrigue is not limited to totalitarian regimes. Intrigue helped Charles de Gaulle in the French Republic (Chapter 6) and was vital to Catherine the Great's seizure of autocratic power (Chapter 5).

Intrigue as a political technique is, of course, as old as the human race. Certainly the story of Adam, Eve, and the serpent in the Garden of Eden provides at least fabled evidence of that. Intrigue was a staple of power grabbing in ancient Rome where, as so often happens, intrigue begat intrigue. Consider the case of Aelius Sejanus, who was an ambitious Roman politician living during the reign of Emperor Tiberius (A.D. 14–37). Upon the death of his father, Sejanus succeeded to his father's position as prefect of the praetorian guard. The guard was an elite body of five thousand soldiers serving the Roman emperors. The guard's allegiance, however, was notoriously fickle but necessary for the emperor's survival. Sejanus courted the confidence of Tiberius and won it and then convinced Tiberius that there were plots against his life. To counter these, argued Sejanus, Tiberius should concentrate the guard in Rome—at the time it was scattered in small bands throughout Italy—and also should take refuge on the isle of Capri. Tiberius agreed to both suggestions. This, of course, left Sejanus alone in Rome to seize power at the first opportunity. But he had carried his intrigue too far. Tiberius was old but no fool. He became suspicious of Sejanus and of the praetorians, and so he sent Macro, a messenger, to Sejanus. Macro told Sejanus that Tiberius wanted to bestow honors on him, but Tiberius had given Macro a commission transferring command of the guard to Macro. The Roman senate convened to honor Sejanus, and at the close of the ceremonies, Macro read the commission. Sejanus was stripped of all offices and arrested for treason. Members of the guard took him into custody. Sejanus and all members of family, including his eight-year-old daughter, were executed. According to Machiavelli, "Experience teaches that, of many conspiracies attempted, few turn out successfully, because a man who conspires can hardly do so alone. . . ." The lesson came too late for Sejanus, though Tiberius did not escape either but was murdered later by Macro with the support of the venal guard.

Intrigue is not simply an ancient practice. many a secret scheme has surrounded the Oval Office of the White House. Indeed the cover-up of the break-in of Democratic campaign headquarters in 1972, the notorious "Watergate scandal," was intrigue that involved not only members of the president's court but President Richard Nixon as well.

Intrigue, then, can be a technique for seizing, distributing, and exercising power. When it works it has its rewards. For instance, intrigue has been at the heart of every power shift in the Soviet Union. Stalin conspired against Trotsky, Kamenev, and Zinoviev to seize power after the death of Lenin (Chapter 7). When Stalin died in 1953, another power struggle ensued. Five years of jockeying ended with Nikita Khrushchev's rise to the premiership in 1958, only to be ousted in 1964 by means of court intrigue. Plots and conspiracies also are a part of seeking lesser offices. The payoffs are apparently worth the risk. Special privileges are given to the Soviet ruling class—access to country homes and estates, exclusive shopping complexes, expensive automobiles, lavish entertainment budgets—indeed, all of the perquisites and privileges of the ruling elites in capitalist nations.

THE FINE ART OF POLITICAL HOMICIDE

Intrigue takes many forms, but it is convenient to divide them into two categories. The first is political murder, that is, assassination. The second, character assassination, is also violent. We shall turn first to murder.

The Unsolved Case of the Two Little Princes

The historical details are sketchy and often contradictory, but there is no question that in 1483 King Richard III came to the throne of England under conditions of intrigue. The identity of the victims of all the plotting is also clear. But who were the real plotters? That is the mystery.

After the death of King Edward IV, the rightful heir to the throne seemed to be Edward's son, the Prince of Wales, then only a young boy. Until the prince came of age, power would be in the hands of a regent or protector. Here the confusion and intrigue begin. There is evidence that before his death Edward had named his brother, Richard, the duke of Gloucester, as protector. Not so, said the prince's mother and members of a rival faction. Without informing Richard, who was in the countryside at the time of Edward's death, the maternal faction hatched a plot to have her named regent. But Richard got word of the scheme, marched on London, defeated the small force, and became protector of the prince, who was crowned shortly thereafter.

RICHARD III: MURDEROUS MACHIAVEL OR MACHIAVELLIAN PRINCE?

History has not been kind to the memory of Richard Plantagenet (1452–1485), who briefly reigned as king of England from 1483 to 1485. He has been charged with all sorts of crimes: conspiracy to murder, murder, renunciation of his own mother, forcing himself upon a woman who hated him, a plot to poison his wife and marry his niece, and usurpation. William Shakespeare captured the character of this evil genius in *King Richard III*. Relying on the historical accounts of his period, Shakespeare portrayed Richard as deceitful, deceptive, and a master of duplicity. Accepting Machivelli's equally negative appraisal prevailing in England at the time, Shakespeare put these words in Richard's mouth:

> Why I can smile and murder whiles I smile,
> And cry "Content" to that which grieves my heart
> And wet my cheeks with artificial tears,
> And frame my face to all occasions. . . .
> And set the murderous Machiavel to school.

Richard, in short, was such a skilled practitioner of intrigue that he could have taught Machiavelli—the alleged master of intrigue—a few things. How accurate is this historical and dramatic judgment?

To address such questions, one must first consider the times and circumstances of Richard's life. When Richard was three years old, the War of the Roses erupted and continued until his death. This war was between two rival families, each claiming to be the rightful heir to the English throne. The House of York wore the white rose as its badge, the House of Lancaster the red rose. Each had the support of contending nobles and subjects, and within each house were members seeking to advance their own selfish interests. An especially strong noble, one capable of hiring the services of soldiers from France and adding those forces to his own loyal tenants, could have a great deal to say about who would be king. By joining his army to one of the houses or to one of many rival members in the two houses, such a noble could make and destroy kings.

Such was the role of Richard Neville, Earl of Warwick. Warwick won the title of "kingmaker" for his intrigues and machinations. In 1460 Warwick took King Henry VI (of the House of Lancaster) captive after a battle. Parliament, however, refused to dethrone Henry, and so Warwick convened an irregular assembly, went over the heads of Parliament, and crowned a member of York as King Edward IV. The two houses immediately challenged each other in a seven-hour battle in a snowstorm at Towton, the bloodiest engagement on English soil. Edward triumphed. By able fiscal management and the avoidance of costly foreign wars, Edward freed himself from dependence on Parliament for funds, thus securing his reign. But Warwick, the kingmaker, grew restive. When Edward continued to defy him on foreign policy, Warwick revolted in 1470, forced Edward into exile, and restored Henry VI of the House of Lancaster to the throne.

At this point Richard Plantagenet, Edward's nineteen-year-old brother, entered the picture. In 1471 Richard led Edward's armies in a battle near London that defeated the House of Lancaster, killed Warwick, captured Henry VI, and restored Edward to the throne. Within a month the demented Henry died in the Tower of London, perhaps murdered by Yorkists. (It was common in this era for the faction winning power to remove all likely rivals, for fear that changing fortunes might resume the enemy challenge. The failure to deal with Henry VI the first time around had already caused Edward enough problems.) Rumors were, however, that Richard, unbeknownst to Edward but acting as his brother's "hit man," had killed Henry. In fact, Richard was leading the king's forces in another battle at the time of Henry's death and was far away from London.

There were other rumors. George of Clarence, the brother of Edward and Richard, had been executed, supposedly drowned in a vat of wine. Word had it that Richard, knowing that Clarence was ahead of him in the line of succession to the throne, had plotted the execution. According to this story, he had planted false accusations of treason regarding Clarence, and Edward had acted on such gossip. The facts say otherwise. Clarence had indeed been treacherous and had joined with Warwick and the Lancasters' cause. Edward accused Clarence of treason, and although Richard agreed with Edward's charges against Clarence and resisted the execution, Clarence still was killed.

The Shakespearian and historical version of Richard's marriage is that he forced Anne Neville to marry him for political and economic gain, though the real story is far more complex, too much so to permit a detailed account. Suffice it to say that Anne had been a pawn in Warwick's scheme in 1470 to restore Henry VI and the Lancasters to power. Warwick arranged Anne's marriage to a member of the House of York. But Anne's betrothed died in battle, and George of Clarence—not Richard—then asked for her hand. Anne was Clarence's sister-in-law, and because his wife had died, he could acquire a sizable financial fortune by adding his former wife's holdings to Anne's. But Anne did not see it that way. She fled from Clarence, was protected by her childhood friend, Richard, and married him. The marriage was not forced, but a match that pleased both.

Dramatists and early historians found the source of Richard's alleged calumnies in his physical appearance. Unlike his handsome brothers, Richard was thought to be deformed. History provides a nickname, "Crook-back." Yet again the facts are otherwise. One of Richard's shoulders was slightly higher than the other, not all that abnormal in human beings. But he had no hunchback, no withered arm, no clubfoot. Had he been so deformed, he would have had difficulty fighting in the heavy armor of the day, on horseback, and holding a spear and shield. Nor did he poison Anne, once she had served her political purposes, in order to marry his niece (a Lancaster) for additional advantage. Anne died of natural causes, much to Richrd's grief. The niece, it turns out, married Henry VII, the first of the Tudor kings and whose forces defeated Richard's at the Battle of Bosworth in 1485, ending the War of the Roses.

Edward IV died in 1483 at the age of forty, the victim of too much wine, women, and song. His heir was prince Edward, aged twelve. Custom and law called for a regent to rule in the prince's stead until he came of age. Myth has it that Richard, using guile and the force of arms, had himself first named regent, then king. In the deadly soap opera of winning power by means of intrigue, it is difficult to know who is scheming and who is schemed against. The "murderous Machiavel" version is that Richard marched on London with his army, accused the prince's mother of witchcraft so that she would not be named regent, forced Parliament to name Richard as regent for his nephew the prince, placed the prince in the Tower of London for "protection," charged that his

Taking Political Power

brother Edward's marriage had not been legal, thus pressed Parliament to declare illegitimate all of Edward IV's children, seized the crown, and murdered his nephews Edward V and Richard, duke of York, to prevent future rivalry.

There is another version, more in keeping with the princely demeanor that Machiavelli urged. It recognizes that Edward IV before his death had requested Richard to be regent. It takes note both of a plot instigated by Edward's mother and relatives to seize the regency and of Richard's decisiveness in quelling the intrigue. It accepts that charges were debated in Parliament regarding the illegitimacy of Edward IV's children. But these charges were not brought by Richard. In the constitutional crisis that seemed likely, Richard assumed the crown so as to prevent the accession of a boy king at that time. In short, Richard acted to preserve order. Finally, the princely version raises serious doubts that Richard murdered his nephews.

By all accounts, the reign of Richard III was successful, regardless of the intrigues and plots surrounding it. Richard was reputed to be a skilled administrator, introducing innovations in financial management. He also practiced Machiavelli's axiom that "a prince, therefore, should have no other object, no other subject of study, than war, its rules and disciplines." Even his detractors agree that in his brother's service and as king, Richard was a shrewd military tactician and a courageous battlefield commander.

"A horse! A horse! My kingdom for a horse!" shouted Shakespeare's King Richard III just before he died in battle at Bosworth. Perhaps the real Richard would have been better off with a good publicity agent.

That is one version of what happened. Another does far less credit to Richard. It says that Richard, upon hearing that his brother had died and had named no protector, moved with his military band and forced Parliament to name him protector. There was, according to this version, no rival plot. Richard had the young Edward V imprisoned in the Tower of London, declared an illegitimate heir, and taken the crown for himself. He also had another nephew, Richard, duke of York, imprisoned with Edward. Rumor had it—and rumor is always an important feature of intrigue—that Richard, fearing that he might be dethroned by sympathizers of the two princes, had them murdered and their bodies buried under a staircase in the Tower of London. This, combined with King Richard's long history of machinations and usurpations, spurred on the opposition. The result was an invasion by rival forces based in France. Richard was killed in battle, and a new king, Henry VII, came to the throne and ended the reign of terror.

Almost two centuries later, in 1674, workmen in the Tower of London were making renovations. They uncovered two skeletons, obviously the bones of two young children. Could these have been the bodies of the two princes allegedly assassinated on orders of the odious King Richard III? After all, no bodies, nor any other evidence of their death, had been found back in 1485. There were only suspicions. The assumption upon the discovery of the remains was that they were the two princes. By order of the king at that time, the bones were sealed in an urn and placed in a tomb at Westminster Abbey, the burial place of English monarchs. The urn bore the inscription, "Here lie the relics of Edward Fifth, King of England, and Richard, Duke of York, who, confined in the Tower, and then stifled with pillows, were privately and meanly buried, by order of their perfidious uncle, Richard, the usurper."

There is also the version that says Richard may not have usurped political power. After being named protector, Richard certainly knew that he could not trust the rival faction, made up of the prince's mother and her intimates: he could not let the devious mother rule, nor could he take the chance that Edward V would be used as a pawn in her game. Richard thus decided to set aside Edward V and the duke of York, reluctantly agreed that they be named illegitimate, and placed them in the royal apartments of the Tower of London for protection. At that point he assumed the throne.

Here the story takes on a mysterious twist. There were rumors that the princes had been murdered. But these rumors, without any supporting evidence, were apparently planted by Richard's rivals as a means of stirring up opposition. Moreover, such gossip was invaluable in mobilizing an invasion force in France. At the time of the invasion and the Battle of Bosworth at which Richard III died, the two princes were still alive in the Tower. Their death came after the battle, not at the hand of Richard but possibly on orders from Henry VII to guard against possible claims to his throne. Henry, not Richard, usurped power through homicide.

No evidence will unravel this mystery, not even if submitted to Sherlock Holmes. In 1933 the urn containing the bones of the two princes was unsealed. A five-day investigation by experts concluded that the bones were those of the two princes and that they had likely died before 1485—evidence of Richard's culpability. But not everyone is so sure. Using the methods for such investigation that existed in the 1930s it is generally agreed that the death date could be in error two years either way; that is, the princes might have perished after 1485, during Henry's reign. Moreover, the skeletons were unusually large for boys of the ages of the two princes when they allegedly died. Instead of being murdered at age twelve or thirteen—by Richard—they may have been as old as fifteen, thus living into the first years of Henry's reign.

Who murdered the two little princes? We will never know, but for your purposes it is not necessary. What the mystery suggests is that intrigue breeds intrigue. The princes were certainly victims of someone's grab for power, but whose? Perhaps Richard, long thought to be the assassin, was also a victim. Machiavelli asserted, "As for one's own subjects, even when no outside disturbance occurs, there is danger they may form a secret conspiracy; from such a plot the prince's best protection lies in not being hated or despised, and keeping himself in popular favor." Perhaps Richard was not a political murderer but the victim of character assassination, of unfounded rumors that made him hated so that he fell from popular favor as well as on the battlefield.

Tyrannicide or Expediency?

"Resistance to tyrants is obedience to God," stated Thomas Jefferson. Mohandas Gandhi would have agreed. But even though Jefferson also said that "the tree of liberty must be refreshed from time to time, with the blood of patriots and tyrants," for it "is its natural manure," he probably did not mean such blood should be taken by the assassin. As a victim of assassination Gandhi would probably not have approved of political homicide as a means of resisting tyrants. Yet tyrannicide, the slaying of tyrants, has always been a widely practiced means of taking power.

There are two schools of thought regarding whether it is morally justifiable to strike at tyrannical kings (or any other kind of rulers). One says that because tyrants derive subjects of their natural rights, it is not only lawful but honorable and morally necessary to suppress tyranny through assassination. The problem is that one can never be certain when such a justification will turn to license for expedience. It is a variation of the old argument of when the ends justify the means, and vice versa. "A great politician has to bother himself less with means than with the goal," said Adolf Hitler. But can the means be so immoral as to deny the goal? Students of the second school of thought regarding tyrannicide think so. Tyranny itself, they believe, may be moral. The tyrant may be God's agent sent to teach a lesson or accomplish works beyond the understanding of mere mortals. To strike the tyrant is to interfere with God's will.

St. Thomas Aquinas was a great moral and religious philosopher of the thirteenth century. So divine were his teachings considered that he had the nickname of "Angelic Doctor" (others called him "Dumb Ox" because he was so slow and cumbersome in his movements). St. Thomas tried in his teachings to reconcile Christian thought with everyday life, and so what he had to say about tyrannicide and political homicide in general derives from practical as well as moral considerations. He advised that three consequences of tyrannicide be weighed. First, if one is going to strike at the tyrant, the attempt must be successful. If not, the tyrant will become even more fearsome. Second, even if the assassination effort is successful, the plotters are likely to fight among themselves. Successful assassins may become victims. (Did this happen to Richard III?) Third, the successor to a tyrant, or any murdered ruler, may turn out to be worse than the victim; conditions may worsen through success.

Whether for moral or practical reasons, assassination is an action to be undertaken cautiously. Yet many political homicides result not from calculation but from rash action. Consider examples of various kinds of assassination attempts, successful and not so successful. There are lessons here on violence that may be avoided, *fortuna* that is not.

Some assassins act in the name of ideals. They may be patriotic: John Wilkes Booth, who killed President Abraham Lincoln, was sympathetic to the Confederate cause in the Civil War. The ideals may be religious or moral: Dietrich Bonhoffer was a Protestant minister who believed that Adolf Hitler was the "Antichrist" and plotted Hitler's murder (he was not successful). Or the ideals may be doctrinal: U.S. President William McKinley was murdered by a dedicated anarchist, Leon Czolgosz. Regardless of what they consider their high motives, patriots, moralists, or ideologues seldom take into account the practical consequences of their actions. Emotion, not calculation, informs their schemes. And if they are deranged, as seems to have been the case with Booth and Guiteau, they may serve as instruments of *fortuna* that no prince can anticipate, no matter what the princely *virtu* or *necessita*.

Then there are the calculators who kill for limited, practical, and workable reasons. In some instances the power wielders take matters into their own hands, either to win power or to thwart an attempt at a power takeover. The circumstances surrounding the murder of Peter, husband of Catherine the Great (Chapter 5) illustrate calculated murder in order to take power. The effective conspiracy of Adolf Hitler and his henchmen to murder S. A. leader Ernst Roehm in 1934 (Chapter 7) exemplifies the use of homicide to ward off perceived intrigue. In other cases rulers or aspiring rulers may obtain the services of professional assassins. During the administration of President Ronald Reagan, government spokespersons charged tht Libya's ruler, Muammar Gaddafi, had hired assassins to kill high-ranking U.S. officials, including the president. How much of this turned out to be genuine intrigue on Gaddafi's part and how much was a trumped-up charge serving the purposes of White Houe intrigue was unclear.

Sometimes assassination attempts are undertaken for specific goals, and yet are designed to serve higher ideals. Such was the case of the attempt made on July 20, 1944, on the life of Adolf Hitler. This was during the height of World War II, shortly after the invasion of the European continent by the United States and the Allies. The war was going badly for the Nazi regime. High-ranking officers in the German army, concluding that Hitler would lead the nation to disaster which would result in a peace treaty that would effectively end the military might of Germany, plotted to strike at the Fuehrer. The plan was carefully worked out. A young army officer, Klaus von Stauffenberg, was to travel from Berlin to Hitler's military outpost in East Prussia. He would carry into a briefing with the Fuehrer a briefcase containing a bomb, place it under the conference table, and then leave. The bomb would explode, killing Hitler and his top personnel. But *fortuna* intervened. The bomb exploded, but its full force was shielded by the large, heavy leg of the conference table. Hitler was badly shaken and one arm injured. But he was up and about quickly. Within hours, leaders in the plot and numerous officers not even involved were executed. Their bodies, strangled with piano wire, were photographed. German military officers forced to view the films were reminded of what St. Thomas Aquinas meant, that even the most carefully calculated plot may fail and that the tyrant would then take revenge.

THE FINER ART OF CHARACTER ASSASSINATION

Unless you rise high in politics, it is unlikely that you will ever be a target for physical assassination, that is, political homicide. But if you are at all politically active, as you are in the politics of everyday life, if not in a more formal government post, you will always be open to attacks on your honesty, reliability, and reputation. You are, in short, a target for character assassination. Machiavelli lived and wrote in times when political murder was commonplace. Execution, poisoning, regicide all were useful, if not acceptable, practices for taking power. Machiavelli warned princes about the dangers, but he was far less troubled about such physical threats to princes than he was about the dangers of character assassination. "The prince should try to avoid anything which makes him hateful or contemptible," wrote Machiavelli. "When princes cannot help being hated by someone, they ought first of all to try to avoid universal hatred, and when they cannot do this, they should try as hard as they can to avoid the hatred of the most powerful group around."

Given the times and circumstances under which Richard III took power, it was virtually impossible for any ruler to avoid some degree of hatred. Rival houses, or rival factions within a single royal family, had been contending for decades for the English crown. No ruler could long keep his or her reputation unsullied. Richard understood this, and he tried during his brief reign to avoid "universal hatred." To the degree that the general population of subjects cared about such things, Richard had a reputation as a brave and shrewd military commander, a wise and innovative fiscal administrator, and a clever political tactician in dealing with Parliament. But he could not "avoid the hatred of the most powerful group around," namely, the members by marriage of Edward IV's royal family. Believing, rightly or wrongly, that Richard had usurped the crown, his rivals wanted it returned to the rightful heirs in the name of Henry VII. To this end they used various forms of character assassination as a means of creating a "universal hatred."

One such tactic was rumor. Compared with today's sprawling metropolis, fifteenth-century London was little more than a village. News traveled by word of mouth, and so one of the most valued aides of any politician was, for want of a better term, the "plant" (social scientists today refer to "opinion leaders"). Such a member of court was a trusted friend of both powerful figures and ordinary townspeople. By dropping a hint or asking an intriguing question or by some other ploy the aide would plant rumors and gossip for political purposes. The rumor that Richard had murdered the two princes is one example. To be effective a rumor must, of course, be believable, and rumors about kings usurping the throne and murdering their rivals were certainly believable in England. Henry I had seized the crown from his older brother; King John displaced the rightful heir, Arthur, and saw to his murder; Edward II was dethroned and killed; and Richard II met his demise when Henry

IV seized power. Why then would it be so hard to believe that Richard III engaged in such practices?

In modern times rumor and gossip still play a major role in political intrigue. Joseph Goebbels (see Chapter 27), minister of propaganda in the Nazi regime of Adolf Hitler, developed what was called the "whispering campaign." In the tradition of the plant, influential people under Goebbel's orders started rumors to serve Nazi ends. These took many forms, for example, that Jews were plotting an attempt on Hitler's life, that a secret weapon had been found that would win World War II, or that a military thrust was on the verge of great success.

Politicians in republics are just as likely to exploit rumors and gossip as are autocrats or dictators. The "leak" (revealing confidential information to members of the press without disclosing the source) is a widely used technique in republics for winning and practicing power. Experts at political intrigue often use leaks to try to force people to leave office. For example, during the administration of President John Kennedy, his secretary of state was Dean Rusk, who had enemies within the Kennedy court. Hoping to remove him from office by arousing speculation in the press regarding Kennedy's confidence in his secretary, those enemies leaked a story to newspaper columnists that the president was searching for a new secretary of state. The reporter who published the story was one of Kennedy's closest friends. Rusk, however, held his ground, commenting only that "Washington is a very wicked city." Another series of leaks was instrumental in forcing President Richard Nixon from office in the Watergate scandal. One reason that the break-in (and its cover-up) at the headquarters of the Democratic party in 1972 became the focus of public attention was the reports published in the *Washington Post* telling of White House involvement. Many of those facts came from leaks by a confidential source identified only as "Deep Throat."

It frequently is possible to strike at a power holder by worming one's way into that person's confidence or the confidence of the power holder's superior, friend, or even spouse. Gregori Rasputin was a Russian monk who gained the confidence of the wife of Czar Nicholas II. Rasputin convinced her that he could cure their son, who suffered from hemophilia. By playing on her fears for the health of her son, Rasputin was able to influence the czarina and, through her, the weak-willed Nicholas. In the intrigue that surrounded that autocrat's court, rumors abounded that Rasputin was a secret German sympathizer (against whom Russia was fighting in World War I). Those who live by intrigue, as the case of Richard III amply proves, often die by it. In 1916, Rasputin was assassinated by a group of nobles.

Playing on human emotions is a time-honored tactic of intrigue. The variety of possibilities is almost endless among people prone to jealousy, envy, vanity, greed, fear, hatred, and ambition. The clever schemer can just as easily capitalize on generosity, love, patriotism, and naiveté. There is an old saying that "flattery will get you everywhere." It is certainly true that some rulers will shift their opinions in the face of appeals to their egos. Mohandas Gandhi, Catherine the Great, Thomas Jefferson, Adolf Hitler, Walter Lippman, Walter Rathenau all at one time or another were courted successfully through flattery. Machiavelli recognized this temptation and cautioned against it: "Courts are always full of flatterers; men take such pleasure in their own concerns, and are so easily deceived about them, that this plague of flattery is hard to escape." Being easily flattered leads to being contemptible, an almost certain source of a prince's downfall.

Rumors, gossip, leaks, intimacy and flattery are tools of political intrigue that seek to assassinate reputations behind the scenes. Another tactic is simply to make open denunciations of rivals, enemies, or even allies if the occasion calls for it. These denunciations may be true, false, or half-true. What so often makes them effective is that simply by responding to a charge the person denounced gives it some credence, thus playing into the hands of the assassin.

A prime practitioner of the smear tactic was Joseph McCarthy, U.S. senator from Wisconsin. During 1954 McCarthy made a series of speeches in which he charged that Democratic presidential administrations had been guilty of "twenty years of treason." In his ensuing campaign against those he thought were "soft on Communism," the senator denounced specific members of presidential administrations. His basic tactic was to call a press conference late in the afternoon, thus making his charge just in time to be published in the evening papers (television news as you know it today was virtually nonexistent), but not in time for reporters to get a denial of such charges from the officials denounced by McCarthy. Denials would appear in the next day's newspaper, but often on a back page, for by publication time McCarthy had already captured the front page with fresh denunciations. The tactic worked for a while, but ultimately McCarthy was censured by his Senate colleagues.

UNEASY LIES THE HEAD THAT WEARS THE CROWN

Thus the fine art of political homicide and even the finer art of character assassination combine to form the bulwark of political intrigue. As you strive for princedom, both in your personal life and in grander palaces of power, recognize that such tactics are not the province of any particular time, place, or political regime.

In 1895 Finley Peter Dunne was a cartoonist for a major newspaper in Chicago. He created a character, "Mr. Dooley," a saloon keeper given to offering bits of princely wisdom. In a memorable cartoon Mr. Dooley stated, "Politics 'ain't beanbag. 'Tis a man's game, an' women, childer, an' pro-hybitionists'd do well to keep out iv it." By now you should recognize a fallacy in Mr. Dooley's sagacity: politics, at least the politics of everyday life, is unavoidable. It is the province of everyone, and in these times and circumstances, so is the politics of more palatial power estates. But Mr. Dooley was right about one thing: "Politics ain't beanbag." Because you cannot "keep out iv it," you would do better to practice it in a princely manner, meaning that because it "ain't beanbag," staying on your toes helps. As Machiavelli warned, "the less one trusts to chance, the better one's hope of holding on."

"The way to have power is to take it.."
—*Boss Tweed*

"Why I can smile and murder whiles I smile."
—*Shakespeare's Richard III*

"The victor will never be asked if he told the truth."
—*Hitler*

"Experience teaches that, of many conspiracies attempted, few turn out successfully, because a man who conspires can hardly do so alone."
—*Machiavelli*

"As for one's own subjects, even when no outside disturbance occurs, there is danger they may form a secret conspiracy; from such a plot the prince's best protection lies in not being hated or despised, and keeping himself in proper favor."
—*Machiavelli*

"Resistance to tyrants is obedience to God."
—*Jefferson*

"A great politician has to bother himself less with means than with the goal."
—*Hitler*

"Washington is a very wicked city."
—*Dean Rusk*

"Politics ain't beanbag."
—*Mr. Dooley*

"The less one trusts to chance, the better one's hopes of holding on."
—*Machiavelli*

Taking Political Power

Chapter

17

Seizing Political Power Through Force of Arms

In October of 1922 a stocky, blustery man stood before the National Congress of the Fascist party in Naples, Italy. In a bellicose, threatening speech he proclaimed that force was a justifiable method for taking control of the government of Italy. His speech finished, he boarded a train for Rome. His militant followers from various regions of the country marched toward Rome as well. Four centuries earlier Niccolo Machiavelli had written in this same land that "it seldom happens that men rise from low conditions to high rank without employing either force or fraud. . . ." Benito Mussolini's "March on Rome" was to prove Machiavelli right. King Victor Emmanuel, instead of using his army to put down the march, requested the premier of Italy to resign and asked Mussolini to replace him. On October 30 Mussolini took office. By threat of force and the use of fraud Mussolini had seized power.

Mussolini was not the first ruler to use force of arms as a means of seizing power. The method is as old as politics itself. Nor was he the last. In this decade of the 1980s one can find numerous nations ruled by cliques that have seized power by military force. In Latin America more than half a dozen nations are ruled by the military, in Africa two dozen, in Asia and the Middle East another half-dozen; and in 1981 the military took control of a European government, Poland. Estimates vary, but from 1960 through 1978 thirteen Latin American nations experienced at least one military takeover of power; between the end of World War II and 1972 there were eighty-three attempted military takeovers in Africa, most successful, and forty-two more in Asia. Trotsky, who lost out in a power struggle in the Soviet Union to Stalin (see Chapter 7) observed that "not believing in force is the same as not believing in gravitation." Apparently many aspiring rulers agree.

This chapter examines force as a means of gaining political power. There are several techniques, including riots, uprisings, demonstrations, coups d'états, and terror. We shall begin with revolutionary conquest.

WARFARE—CIVIL AND NOT SO CIVIL

Chapter 16 showed that when successful, intrigue can be an effective way of taking power and even holding it. But when intrigue fails, it can bring disaster and thereby create the conditions for seizing power by force of arms. According to the Marquise de Sévigné, who chronicled the political and social conditions during the reign of France's Louis XIV, "Fortune is always on the side of the larger battalions." If not the larger, perhaps the more persistent.

The struggle for political power in China during the first half of this century is a case in point. For centuries China had been ruled by a long line of autocrats. All seemed peaceful and serene. But in the eighteenth and nineteenth centuries the autocratic order began to disintegrate. Western nations posed an increasing external threat, poaching, invading, and establishing commercial colonies. Within China warlords with their private armies fought in civil conflicts; bandits roamed the land; and secret societies plotted the overthrow of the imperial regime. In October 1911, open rebellion broke out, and there were general uprisings throughout the south of China. The armies of the Manchu ruling dynasty began to crumble before the forces calling for an end to the autocracy and the founding of a republic.

In northern China things looked better for the emperor. His chief of staff, Yüan Shih-k'ai, held his ground. So well did he repel the rebels that it appeared that the military forces of the emperor and the provisional republic would be locked for years in a protracted civil war. Then intrigue entered the picture. Wishing to avoid further bloodshed and because he sensed that fortune was turning against the poorly financed republican forces, the provisional president of the republic, Sun Yat-sen, decided on an economy of violence. He astonished friend and foe alike by offering the presidency of the republic to Yüan Shih-k'ai if Yüan would guarantee the abdication of the Manchu emperor. Taking a cue from the ancient Chinese scholar Sun Tzu who had written that "all warfare is based on deception," Yüan accepted the offer, unseated the emperor, and became president.

This duplicity ended the civil war and produced a republic born of intrigue and force of arms. But peace was not restored for long, thanks to Yüan's unsuccessful efforts at more intrigue. In 1915 the Japanese government presented China with "Twenty-one Demands," which would have turned control of China over to its stronger and hostile neighbor. Such a humiliating arrangement was, of course, unthinkable to most Chinese, but it was not unthinkable to Yüan Shih-k'ai, for it was he who had secretly negotiated the terms of the demands with the Japanese. His purpose was to end the republic, resurrect the empire, and name himself as emperor. When this became known, rebellion erupted. Yüan, his intrigue a failure, died shortly thereafter. Military commanders set themselves up as independent warlord rulers in the provinces of China, and things were much as they had been before the Republic had been formed.

In the years that followed, the republic gradually reasserted itself. First, it built a political party and army, the Kuomintang, under General Chiang Kai-shek. Second, the Kuomintang, at the insistence of the Soviet government that was supplying it with arms and training, joined the new Chinese Communist party. The alliance gradually beat back the forces of the rebellious warlords. But prosperous landowning factions in the Kuomintang had the ear of Chiang Kai-shek. They worried over Communist demands for land reform, and so in 1927 when it appeared that peace and harmony might be restored to China under the republic, Chiang turned on his Communist allies. Tens of thousands of Communists—peasants, workers, students—were killed by Chiang's forces. Out of the 25,000 members of the Communist party, 15,000 died.

But Chiang's swift and lethal stroke backfired. Many Kuomintang military commanders, outraged by Chiang's tactics, defected to the Communist cause, taking their armies with them, and members of the Communist party that had urged collaboration with the Kuomintang rebelled against the forces of the republic. One such member was a thirty-four-year-old military commander, Mao Tse-tung, who led his army against Kuomintang forces in the provincial stronghold of Changsha. But the Kuomintang's machine guns demolished Mao's forces, demoralized his troops, and forced retreat. In the weeks following, the ill-armed and outnumbered army shrunk to little more than a small band. In December 1927, they sought refuge in a mountain hideout in Kiangsi province in southeastern China. There, much like George Washington and John Marshall galvanizing their armies at Valley Forge, Mao devoted a long, miserable winter to rebuilding his revolutionary force.

For more than two decades Mao was virtually to write the book on how to seize power through revolutionary conquest. Mao understood through his direct experience what the Prussian military strategist Karl von Clausewitz had meant in his classic text on warfare, *On War*: "We see, therefore, that war is not merely a political act but a real political instrument, a continuation of political intercourse, a carrying out of the same by other means." Through violence, discipline, education, guerrilla warfare, imagination and unswerving persistence, Mao became what Machiavelli had called the founder of a "new princedom acquired with one's own arms and energy."

After reaching his mountain hideaway Mao had only eighteen hundred men left in his army. Not all of them had been with him in battle. Several Mao had recruited when his force met up with two bandit chiefs, whom Mao immediately made regimental commanders. All had to be fed, clothed, and protected against the harsh elements, requiring the cooperation of the region's natives. They were not enthusiastic about aiding the forces of a rebel and two bandits, and so Mao formed an independent government district composed of five villages. Laws were passed redistributing land from the landlords to the peasants. Any landlords opposing the district government were executed, to show that those who carry guns will use them if necessary.

MAO TSE-TUNG: THE PRINCE AS REVOLUTIONARY

"A prince should have no other object, no other thought, no other subject of study, than war, its rules and disciplines. . . . The quickest way to lose a state is to neglect this art; the quickest way to get one is to study it." Niccolo Machiavelli could have been writing about Mao Tse-tung (1893–1976), the founder of the People's Republic of China, had not the words come more than four centuries before Mao's birth:

During his life Mao was a librarian, laundryman, teacher, philosopher, poet, and politician. But what brought Mao and his Communist followers to power in 1949—a scant twenty-eight years after forming a political party of only a dozen members—was their mastery of the arts of conquest, persistence in the face of staggering losses, and unremitting warfare.

Mao was born in a small village in southwest China, the son of a peasant father and a devout Buddhist mother. By the standards of the times the family was fairly well off; Mao's father owned twenty acres of land when most families were lucky to have five. His father was a strong disciplinarian and a miser, and his mother was a gentle and generous woman. Like his father Mao practiced strong self-discipline, and like his mother he sympathized with the plight of the poor. Mao's early schooling, steeped as it was in the writings of Confucius, reinforced the values of discipline, order, and work. But on the side he read other works, including the romantic tales of bandits and heroes, many of whom stole from the rich to give to the poor.

At age sixteen Mao left his native village to attend an academy which offered a mixed course of study, a classic Chinese curriculum combined with modern subjects. The experience reinforced what became a lifelong belief in the strength of traditional Chinese values. But it also broadened Mao's horizons and taught him that his once mighty China had been torn asunder by internal strife and preyed upon by the imperialist nations of the West and by neighboring Japan. Reading about George Washinton and Napoleon and the emperors of a once great China, Mao was impressed again with what a princely hero might do to bring order out of chaos. He had not even seen a map of the world; yet he sensed there was more to it than he would ever find if he followed his father's wishes and became an apprentice to a rice merchant. So he decided not to return home but to seek more schooling, this time in Changsha, the capital of a province of more than twenty million people.

It was now 1911, a fateful year for China. Within a few months of Mao's arrival in Changsha, the imperial government of China was overthrown and replaced with a republic under the leadership of Sun Yat-sen. Sun was a Christian convert, educated in America, and actually was an American citizen. His Alliance party was formed to bring down the Manchu monarchy. Mao became sympathetic to Sun's cause, and as a result he committed his first political act. To defy the Manchu rulers, Mao and his fellow students vowed to cut off their queues, the braids that the monarchy forced the people to wear. Mao and a friend cut theirs off, but the other students got cold feet and refused to honor their vow. Mao did not hesitate and forceably removed the queues of the unwilling students. Here, as he did so often in his career, he demonstrated that he was decisive and ready to use force if necessary to realize his political aims.

During the successful republican revolt, Mao joined the regular army. But when civil war was averted, Mao found himself once more a civilian. What to do now, he pondered. He perused the advertisements that schools seeking students placed in newspapers and first considered attending a soap-making school. Like Mohandas Gandhi who thought that if India could become clean, it would be great, Mao thought that a clean China would be a great China. So Mao paid his entrance fee to the soap-making school. But he did not attend. A friend assured Mao that the newly formed republic would need lawyers. Why not help make China great by becoming a lawyer? Mao agreed, but not for long. For he then was attracted to learning economics, as China would need economists to restore greatness. He enrolled in a school, but the courses were taught in English (and Mao hardly knew the alphabet), and so he dropped out.

Like Benjamin Disraeli or Adolf Hitler, there was a period of drift in Mao's life; yet he did not waste it. Mao went to the public library, and for six months he studied the writings of Western philosophers. For the first time he saw a map of the world, learned the theories of socialism, and after this self-contemplation decided to become a teacher. So back to school he went, but this time without funds, as his father had cut off his allowance out of disgust for his seeming idleness. For the next six years, living on meager rations and wearing rough clothing, Mao pursued his studies. He read widely and learned to write. By the time he had earned his diploma, he presented himself as deliberate and thoughtful, well disciplined, persistent, decisive, and imaginative. Never quick to talk he would, like Benjamin Disraeli, listen carefully and then sum up the discussion lucidly and forcefully.

Mao's first job was as an assistant librarian. This again provided an opportunity to read and reflect. He also was responsible for giving lectures, a task that helped sharpen his oratorical skills. But most importantly he joined a society to study Marxism. He recognized that for Communism to take root in China and truly restore its greatness, some revision of Marxist thinking would be necessary. Karl Marx had written that Communism would triumph over the industrialized middle class, a middle class that had replaced the feudalistic privileged class that was exploiting the peasantry. Marxist teaching was that if a country were to become Communist, there must first be industrialization, then a middle-class victory, and finally the overthrow of the capitalist classes by the working classes. Mao, however, realized that Communism could work in China if based on the peasantry. There was no need to rely on an industrialized base. Communism could return China to greatness, yes, but a Communism built on rural peasants, not on the cities' working classes.

The end of World War I brought the circumstances that set the events in motion that eventually proved Mao correct. Japan had opposed Germany during the war, and now as spoils of that war, Japan demanded all the former German colonies located in China. The news that Japan was about to get its wish produced widespread protest in China. Student demonstrations erupted and spawned similar protests among other groups. Mao, like many an aspiring prince before and since, became an agitator, taking the lead in forming the United Students' Association and in publishing student magazines designed to spread the protest message. These efforts brought him recognition, a reputation, and an income. By 1921 Mao was no longer the peasant hick seemingly going nowhere. As one of the founders of the Communist party, his counsel was sought: should the party stay within the Kuomintang party, the heir of Sun's earlier success, or go its own way? Mao worked to maintain the alliance in a common effort against the Japanese. His counsel prevailed until 1927 when the Kuomintang army under Chiang Kai-shek attacked the Communist militia, killing more than five thousand.

For the next twenty-two years, with the exception of a truce during World

War II to mount a united campaign against the Japanese, the Red Army of Mao and the Communists and the Kuomintang army of Chiang waged a bloody, seemingly endless civil war. During that period, because he had been in charge of peasant training for the Communist party, Mao assumed command of the Red Army. By 1935 he had become supreme commander of both the party and the army. Combining guerrilla warfare, politicl indoctrination, and strict discipline Mao forged an army that in 1949 took power by conquest and force. The man who when scarcely twenty-five had been turned away from a local park by the sign "Dogs and Chinese not allowed" had gone on to preach that "political power grows from the barrel of a gun." Having used that gun, he stood where emperors had once reigned and proclaimed to the Chinese, "We have stood up. We will never be humiliated again. Let the earth tremble."

But Mao did not use violence against the common people, as to do so would alienate them: "The deepest source of the immense power of war," he later wrote, "lies in the masses of the people." "The army must be at one with the people and be regarded by the people as their own; then the army will be invincible throughout the world." Or as he was fond of saying, "The people are the sea and the army are the people in the sea." To preserve the support of the people, Mao treated the more well-to-do peasants with moderation. This raised the ire of some of Mao's lieutenants who believed his moderation was anti-Communist. When officers in the Twentieth Army revolted against Mao's leadership, Mao acted quickly. In a ferocious attack on his opponents, three thousand members of the Twentieth Army were executed. The man of moderation was also a man of steel.

Hidden in Kiangsi, Mao practiced another Machiavellian precept. Machiavelli had written (although whether Mao had ever read the words is uncertain) that "the prince should never turn his mind from the study of war; in times of peace he should think about it even more than in wartime. He can do this in two ways, by training the body and training the mind." To train his troops' bodies Mao drilled and disciplined them, teaching them how to survive under the worst of conditions and how to live off the land. To train their minds he stressed political instruction. Every man learned not only how to fight but what he was fighting for. The basic beliefs of Communism received repeated emphasis so that each soldier understood them well enough to go out and teach the peasants and recruit them for the "people's army." Mao was adamant that his soldiers learn correct behavior. They were not to rob, plunder, or steal when conquering a territory. Rather, they were to assist the population and win its approval and support. Unlike the forces of Nazi Germany foraging through the Russian Ukraine in World War II, with mass torture and slaughter that produced hatred among a people that at first had welcomed the Germans as liberators, Mao's forces combined conquest with conversion.

As his Red Army grew in numbers and strength during the isolation in Kiangsi, Mao came down from the mountains to battle the forces of the Kuomintang. But he avoided all-out confrontations unless necessary and instead perfected the art of guerrilla warfare. The simple essentials of his tactics are contained in a verse:

> *When the enemy advances, we retreat,*
> *When the enemy retreats, we advance,*
> *When the enemy rests, we harass him,*
> *When the enemy avoids the battle, we attack.*

For Mao, unlike the Marquise de Sévigné, fortune was not always to be found on the side of the larger battalions, but on the side of the crafty. The slyness of the fox, not the brute strength of the lion, would win the day.

Nobody would be excluded from Mao's people's army: "Everyone has his strong points," he said, and "he should be encouraged to develop and put to good use those strong points, however limited they may be." "Even the lame, the dumb, the deaf, and the blind could all help in the revolutionary struggle." In 1933, after years of trying, the Kuomintang army encircled the Red Army. There seemed to be no escape. Artillery fire bombarded the Red Army, and it was clear that either the army must escape the "wall of fire" or perish. After a year of bombardment the Red Army finally broke out of the encirclement. But once out, where would it go? Mao was by this time supreme commander of the Red Army and the Communist party, and he proposed a bold plan. Instead of remaining in the south of China and fighting the forces of the Kuomintang, which were superior in arms and numbers, he would take the Red Army across four thousand miles of terrain—through jungles, mountains, deserts, and swamps—to the remote Shensi province. There the army would fight not the Kuomintang but the Japanese. The Chinese people would then know that the Communists rather than the Kuomintang were the true liberators and protectors of their nation. In a battle with a hated external enemy Mao would win the war over his internal foes. The insight proved to be the turning point in the struggle for political power in China.

The "Long March" of 1935 took its toll: of ninety thousand who broke out of the Kiangsi, only twenty thousand reached Shensi. For every mile of the Long March, five soldiers perished. Others were left along the way to form guerrilla groups; many were too ill to keep the pace of three miles per hour for twelve-hour days; and a few deserted. But the Red Army persisted. Of course, Chiang Kai-shek was not pleased at Mao's success, and in late 1936 he flew to south Shensi province to direct an attack on the Communist base, only to be arrested by one of his own generals and turned over to the Communists for trial by a "people's court."

Mao again used his imagination and an economy of violence. Instead of taking the opportunity to rid himself of his hated foe, Mao had Chiang released. In exchange Chiang agreed to renew his collaboration with the Communists, a collaboration that had been broken off in 1927 when

Chiang turned on his allies. Together the Kuomintang and Red armies would fight the Japanese, and although the alliance was not easy, that is what happened. But in 1946, China's third civil war in forty-five years began as Kuomintang and Communist forces resumed their battle. However, this war did not last long. In battle after battle, the Communist armies prevailed, and by September 1949 it was all over. Chiang Kai-shek fled mainland China to form a republic in Taiwan. Mao founded the People's Republic of China.

Even for those who do not seek political power by force of arms, there are lessons in the story of Mao's quest. The successful prince, either a violent revolutionary like Mao or a nonviolent revolutionary like Gandhi (see Chapter 15) is imaginative. Mao's Long March and Gandhi's March to the Sea both were bold moves that captured the loyalty and dedication of their followers. Mao, again like Gandhi, insisted on strong self-discipline, for himself and for those whom he led. Each understood the value of patience and persistence. Each met defeat but survived to become even stronger. And each wanted to restore the dignity and greatness of their people, Mao in China by force of arms and Gandhi in India by passive resistance. Finally, both changed the map of the world.

COUP D'ETAT: THE QUICK AND THE DEAD

Revolutionary conquest requires extreme measures—protracted war; a change of political regimes as well as rulers; and dramatic social, economic, and cultural reforms. Seizing power by means of a coup d'etat is a more modest approach. The term is French, meaning literally "stroke of state." A coup is a sudden, forceful stroke against a regime's rulers and includes deliberate violation of constitutional forms and procedures. Instead of a broad transformation of government, as in revolution, a coup replaces one set of governing elites with another. Once in office the new elite may well move toward fundamental political, social, economic, and cultural reform, but this is not generally the case. A notable exception came in France in November 1799, when Napoleon Bonaparte (see Chapter 29) led the "coup d'etat of Brumaire." That coup created a governmental form that placed the legislature in the nominal control of the executive, consisting of a first consul and two assistants. Before long, however, the first consul—Napoleon—gained total control, was made emperor, and instituted sweeping political and social reforms.

More common are coups d'etat that involve infighting among those who control key government resources, usually factions within the military. With loyal (for the moment) fellow officers the pattern is for a general, admiral, colonel or other commander to order the military forces to seize control of governmental office, arrest the ruling officials, (perhaps killing them in the process), and take charge. The police, local officials, radio, television, and newspapers generally fall in line. Properly executed, such coups use minimal violence and bloodshed, at least in their initial phases. Seeking no fundamental changes in the way things are but instead seeking power for its own sake, one elite replaces another, the rich get richer, and the poor get poorer.

Military coups are common in Latin America and Africa. For example, in 1973 there was a military overthrow of the government of President Salvador Allende: his socialist rule was ended and Allende was murdered. Brazil, one of the largest and richest nations south of the equator, has been under military rule since 1964. In Africa Libyan Colonel Muammar Gaddafi has been in charge since toppling King Idris in 1969; and Burundi, the Central African Republic, Comoro, Congo, Equatorial Guinea, Ghana, Guinea-Bissau, Liberia, and Somalia—to name a few such nations—have regimes that have come to power as a result of coups. Asia is not immune either, as evidenced by the military takeover in Bangladesh in 1982. Even the Soviet-backed regime in Poland, threatened with unrest and labor strikes, resorted to a military coup in December 1981, to replace one set of rulers with another.

Once in power as a result of a coup, a new elite strives to consolidate and solidify its holdings, frequently resulting in harsh measures. Argentina is a case in point. After Juan Peron's second term in power ended with his death by heart attack in 1974 (see Chapter 14), his wife Isabel assumed the presidency. She had taken on far more than she could handle, and the inevitable coup came in 1976. Isabel was imprisoned, and General Jorge Videla became president. To preserve its authority, the new elite engaged in widespread assassination, secret arrests, and torture, ruling techniques that have been the staple of Argentine politics for a long time. Videlia was, of course, replaced by another military president in another coup, but nothing changed in Argentine politics. The game of musical chairs continued unabated, and in June 1982, General Leopold Galtieri, the man who had led Argentina to defeat in a war with Great Britain over the Falkland Islands, paid the price: he too fell from power.

Vilfredo Pareto was a sociological theorist who studied elites. He remarked on the tendency in modern nations for each ruling elite to be replaced by another elite, either by being overthrown or compromised. Pareto observed that there were two major types of elites. One consists of innovators who plot, scheme, and manipulate to achieve dominance, and the other is made up of persistent, forceful, and conservative persons. Pareto theorized that these two types of elites, the changers and the preservers, alternated in power, and he called this the "circulation of the elite." But the military coup d'etat defies this pattern in at least one respect. The changers do plot and scheme, but when the new elites come to power, they do not change things but conserve the old order for their own selfish advantage.

There have been exceptions in recent decades. In 1952 there was a military coup that overthrew the Egyptian monarchy. Shortly thereafter Colonel Gamal Abdel Nasser removed President Mohammed Naguib (an army general) and took control. Under his rule far-reaching changes began, changes that were carried even further by Nasser's successor, Anwar el Sadat, before his death by assassination in 1981. Similarly, in 1967 democracy in Greece came to an end for a seven-year period because of a military coup. Repressive measures produced demands for a return to constitutional democracy, and so the elite that had produced the 1967 change became itself a victim of change.

The history of seizing power by coup d'etat suggests that certain conditions aid and abet such measures. If the military is not under civilian control, for example, the rulers will be looking for trouble. Moreover, if a nation's armed forces are concentrated in a limited geographic area, rather than dispersed over a large expanse, there will be a potential for trouble. This potential is heightened in nations in which a single city or metropolitan area dominates the nation's politics: Buenos Aires in Argentina, Rangoon in Burma, Istanbul in Turkey, or Warsaw in Poland. The conditions for successful coups also depend on a central, state-controlled communications system, especially radio and television. Finally, much depends on the nature of a nation's military might. If there are three powerful, independent military services—army, navy, and air force—rival generals and admirals will jockey for position, each plotting against the others.

Combine these possibilities and you will have the situation that Mao Tse-tung warned against. Although a skilled military leader himself, Mao recognized the danger of a military force beyond control. In his case he meant control by the Communist party. The party controls the gun, he taught, and the gun thereby serves the party.

DRAWING A CROWD

You undoubtedly have been in a crowd at least once in your life, probably many times. At sporting events, celebrations, parades, and rallies, you become part of a crowd. Politicians may take note of such gatherings, especially if they think that by appearing before them they can enhance their own popularity in some way. But these crowds are scarcely the kind that have anything to do with seizing power by force. Yet there are crowds that do; indeed in certain political arenas, crowds and force go hand in hand. When they do, a prince's ability to stir up a crowd is vital. A crowd at fever pitch can be employed as a weapon of violence more effectively than can bombs, tanks, planes, or guns.

One politician who understood this well was Joseph Goebbels, the minister of propaganda in Nazi Germany (see Chapter 27). Goebbels studied the works of the nineteenth-century social theorist Gustave Le Bon. Le Bon was particularly interested in the behavior of masses of people and believed that when people acted as members of crowds it was possible to get them to do things they would never do acting alone: "It is crowds rather than isolated individuals that may be induced to run the risk of death to secure the triumph of a creed or an idea, that may be fired for enthusiasm for glory and honor." And so "the improbable does not exist for a crowd."

Goebbels learned this well and took particular note of Le Bon's view that one thing that would draw and stir up a crowd was to give them a hero, preferably a god, and a sacrifice, something to fight against, to hate, and to purge from the face of the earth as a mark of purification. Goebbels gave the Germans Hitler as a god, through several carefully orchestrated public appearances and techniques, and he gave them the Jews as an enemy to sacrifice.

The manipulation of crowds to seize power involves what you might think of as the "Four S's," sin, suffering, sacrifice, and salvation. The people are told that they have sinned or been sinned against. Hitler did this by railing before audiences against the perfidious leaders that had sold out Germany during World War I. They had given Germany a "stab in the back," an unpardonable sin. This, Hitler explained, was the source of their suffering: Germany's economic woes, lack of respect among the world of nations, internal chaos, and so on. To atone for this sin and to remove the suffering, there must be sacrifice. That sacrifice was twofold, sacrifice in the name of the German Reich, the fatherland, and its Fuehrer; and sacrifice of humanity by purging the evil within, the Jewish population. Such sacrifice, devotion, dedication, and service would bring salvation.

Hitler, like Mao, combined the weapon of the crowd with that of force of arms. Mao's bold stroke of moving the Red Army four thousand miles away incorporated the principles of crowd psychology. The imperial and Kuomintang leaders had sinned against the people by being selfish, hastening China's fall from greatness, permitting the intervention of foreign powers in China's affairs, and fomenting internal disorder. All of these enemies, foreign and domestic, Mao was able to symbolize in the Japanese. By turning the Red Army north to Shensi to fight the Japanese, Mao provided the opportunity for suffering (the Long March), sacrifice (both Chinese lives and the hated external enemy of Japan) and salvation: "We will never be humiliated again. Let the earth tremble."

In addition to the psychology of crowds, their physical properties are important as well. A crowd is a collection of people in physical proximity to one another (in the streets, an arena, or a similar locale) who are in direct and temporary contact. There is strong rapport among the members of the crowd, so much so that they can stimulate one another to do things.

Crowds develop either spontaneously or through manipulation. When Japan made its Twenty-One Demands in 1915, and the duplicity of President Yüan Shih-k'ai became known as well, there were spontaneous uprisings and demonstrations in various Chinese cities. In contrast, in 1927 when Chiang Kai-shek turned his Kuomintang forces against the Communists and all the members of the Communist party were expelled from the Kuomintang, the Communist leaders tried to fight back. They called for mass revolts that they hoped would produce a general insurrection against Chiang throughout the cities and country-side. This "Autumn Harvest Uprising" failed and led Chiang to inten-sify his campaign against the Communists, ultimately driving them and Mao to retreat into the mountains of Kiangsi. But popular uprisings, spontaneous or manipulated, do not always fail. Recall from your knowledge of history that the legendary Boston Tea Party provided a rallying symbol for the American Revolution, and similarly, when the people of Paris stormed the Bastille prison in 1789, the act symbolized the end of the autocratic regime.

Not all crowds produce riots, uprisings, and violent demonstrations. Mohandas Gandhi's *hartals* in India, you will recall, were work stoppages designed not to provoke violence (although sometimes they did) but to express passive resistance to the British *raj*. Similarly, the March on Washington in August 1963, led by Martin Luther King, Jr., was an expression of support for civil rights legislation, not a grab for power. It was more akin to Gandhi's March to the Sea than to Mussolini's March on Rome.

"CONFUSION, INDECISION, FEAR: THESE ARE MY WEAPONS"

"Confusion, indecision, fear: these are my weapons." The words are Adolf Hitler's. Hitler came to power by "peaceful means; that is, he was invited to form a government to rule Germany in accordance with constitutional procedures. But his peaceful assumption of power had behind it a long string of terrorist tactics. His Nazi party had won seats in the German legislature through intimidation, beatings, threats, and force of arms as much as by legitimate election techniques. His success was no less a seizure of power than was Benito Mussolini's. And just as Mussolini effectively used terror to put an end to the Italian republic, so too did Hitler in abolishing the Weimar democracy.

As a means of seizing and enhancing political power, terrorism shares several characteristics with the other forceful methods we have discussed. Like assassination it may involve deliberate homicide for political stakes. Like revolutionary conquest and civil war it frequently means protracted warfare to destroy a reigning regime, usually by using paramilitary forces. Even so, however, terrorist leaders may collaborate with disaffected elites within the ruling class when it is in their interests to do so, an action characteristic of the coup d'etat. Terrorism also uses crowd psychology: "Confusion, indecision, fear: these are my weapons."

But terrorism has its own distinctive character as well. For example, terrorists do not restrict assassination to a few highy placed government officials. The Red Brigade, a terrorist organization operating throughout Europe, especially in Italy in the 1970s and early 1980s, was just as likely to kill businessmen, educational leaders, and others as it was to kill public officials. Similar techniques of violence may be directed at people outside the government, even the general populace. Bombs placed in banks, shops, restaurants, subway stations, churches and synagogues, airplanes, theaters, and other public places do not distinguish the social and/or political class of their victims. The Red Brigade has kidnapped governing officials—former Italian Premier Aldo Moro, U.S. Brigadier General James Dozier—and also relatives of members of the business community. "Knee capping," the terrorist technique of spraying machine gun fire at knee level and rendering many victims cripples for life, is not always selective.

One reason that terrorism is not selective in its victims is that as a tactic of violence it sets modest short-term goals and patiently endeavors to wear down the resistance of its opponents. This means the will of not only officials of the incumbent regime but also private citizens and the general populace. Terrorists believe that victory in the long run will be theirs, that sooner or later, people will grow weary of the confusion, indecision, and fear that permeates their daily lives. When that point comes, as with Mussolini's March on Rome, the reins of power will be turned over to them. No price is too high to pay for such a prospect, even being hunted from continent to continent, arrests, trials, torture, and execution. Even if the terrorist organization is repeatedly put down, terrorists believe that in the end victory will be on their side.

In this respect terrorism shares an assumption made by Mao, not only in his revolutionary conquest but in his struggles against external enemies as well. Being a Marxist, Mao believed that the march of history would result in the inevitable triumph of Communism over capitalism. But he saw no reason not to nudge history along. A people well organized and disciplined, no matter what their number, could survive any protracted conflict. Whether a people's army, guerrilla band, or terrorist brigade, a dedicated group could overthrow the better financed and armed forces of capitalist imperialism. Had he not proved so in his native China? On the basis of this belief Mao developed his theory of "limited war." Highly trained and disciplined bands should fight a series of wars in country after country. One by one, the enemy nations' will to resist would erode in the face of "continuing revolution." The imperialist nations, he asserted, were "paper tigers," frightening to view but in fact powerless.

Terrorism is a worldwide phenomenon. Terrorist bombings are possible in the cities, towns, and villages of all nations, in Paris as well as Belfast, the countryside of El Salvador as much as the outskirts of Beirut, the jungles and plains of Latin America or Africa, and the subways of London or Washington, D.C. Many of the tactics employed owe much to a careful reading of Mao, though terrorism did not begin with Mao. the term itself, *terrorisme* in French, comes from the French Revolution's "Reign of Terror." In 1793 and 1794 the Jacobin faction, faced with both internal insurrection and external invasion, decided to take stern measures to maintain its power. Passage of the Law of Suspects enabled the arbitrary arrest of anyone of noble birth or who had held office before the revolution. A revolutionary tribunal had the authority to try and execute those accused of sabotaging the regime. As many as ten thousand may have suffered that fate, the most famous being Queen Marie Antoinette, who was guillotined.

Long before the Reign of Terror, however, terrorist techniques had been developed by dissident groups. The "zealots" in Palestine in A.D. 70 attacked crowds on holidays, a practice still favored by some terrorists. In India strangulation with silk ties was the preferred technique of "thugs." Since then, terrorist tactics have changed with the technology of death. "Bomb throwers," "guerrillas," "skyjckers," "knee cappers," "freedom fighters," and various other designations pass in and out of the lexicon of terrorist politics.

As demonstrated by the Reign of Terror in France, official terrorism is also widely practiced to keep dictatorial regimes in power, not merely as a means of securing power. Once in office, terrorists may continue to use the psychology that got them there, namely, specific applications of intimidation and violence against selected targets who oppose the regime. Again the purpose is to wear down the opposition and to exhaust their physical and mental capacities to resist. The intent is not to destroy such opposition groups but to convince them to accept the new regime. It is not enough to have enemies or dissidents admit under duress that "$2 + 2 = 5$"; they must believe it sincerely, totally, and unquestionably.

In this respect, then, terrorism (whether to seize or hold power) differs from the numerous cases in which marauders seeking power and tyrants wielding it have tried to wipe out entire classes or races of people. Terrorism is a political tactic aimed at converting ("brainwashing" is a frequently employed synonym) people to positive acquiescence of their lot. Genocide, the systematic, planned annihilation of a racial, cultural, or political group, seeks not to change minds but to expunge the alleged enemy from the face of the earth. The "Holocaust" against the Jews in Hitler's "final solution to the Jewish problem," is one example.

USING VIOLENCE TO ECONOMIZE VIOLENCE

In another distinction between terrorism and genocide there is something to learn about force of arms as a means of seizing and holding power. Revolutionary conquests, coups d'etat, crowd incitement, and terrorism all use violence. An aspiring prince who seeks power through such means (Napoleon Bonaparte, Juan Peron, Adolf Hitler, Anwar el Sadat are a few examples of those using these respective techniques) has a choice. A would-be prince can either maximize or minimize the violence inherent in each method. Make no mistake about it, violence is part of any of the means of forceful power discussed in this chapter. But each can be used with or without discretion to win and hold a people or to destroy and alienate them. In short, each method of violence, paradoxically perhaps, offers an opportunity for the economy of violence.

Consider again the case of Mao Tse-tung. A man who says that "political power grows from the barrel of a gun" does not probably strike you as a man of peace. But Mao was a man seeking power, and as with any such political figure his motives were complex, sometimes even contradictory. Be that as it may, he assessed his times and circumstances and set himself upon a course of achieving political power by revolutionary conquest, a most violent means. When he had to use the full force of arms, he certainly did so and did not hesitate to execute landowners or even members of his own Twentieth Army that rebelled against him. Remember also, however, that when he had the opportunity to execute the hated Chiang K'ai-shek, he found it more politically prudent to negotiate with and then release his captor. Mao also gave strict instructions to the Red Army to help the people of the lands conquered: no robbery, looting, burning, pillaging, or destruction. That too was politically wise. Even though using a violent technique to seize power, Mao found it appropriate to practice an economy of violence.

Contrast Mao's leadership with that of another group seeking power over China, the forces of its powerful neighbor, Japan. Japan did not economize violence to win the hearts and minds of the vanquished: far from it. In July 1941, with things going very much their way, the Japanese unleashed a campaign against Mao's forces, a campaign called the "Three Alls," standing for "burn all, loot all, and kill all." With vastly superior forces, the Japanese killed, burned, and looted their way across north and central China. Before it was over, eighty thousand soldiers of the Red Army were dead or wounded, and one third of the population of Shensi had been killed. This was not terror but genocide on a large scale. But the Three Alls failed. Even the Chinese who detested Mao and his Communists could not stomach the Japanese campaign. Instead of turning on the weakened Communist base in Shensi, the anti-Communist Chinese joined with Mao. Building tunnels underground from village to village (a guerrilla tactic later incorporated by Vietcong forces in their war against the U.S. forces in Vietnam and by the Palestinian Liberation Army in its efforts to terrorize Lebanon), the people provided safe passage ways for the Communist soldiers.

There is a folk saying and moral precept that "those who live by the sword die by the sword." Perhaps true, but swords can be wielded in different ways, and the prudent prince knows the difference.

"It seldom happens that men rise from low conditions to high rank without employing either force or fraud."
—*Machiavelli*

"Not believing in force is the same as not believing in gravitation."
—*Trotsky*

"Fortune is always on the side of the larger battalions."
—*Madame de Sévigné*

"All warfare is based on deception."
—*Sun Tzu*

"A prince should have no other object, no other thought, no other subject of study, than war, its rules and disciplines. . . . The quickest way to lose a state is neglect this art; the quickest way to get one is to study it."

—Machiavelli

"Political power grows from the barrel of a gun."

—Mao

"War is not merely a political act but a real political instrument, a continuation of political intercourse, a carrying out of the same by other means."

—Clausewitz

"The people are the sea and the army are the people in the sea."

—Mao

"Even the lame, the dumb, the deaf, and the blind could all help in the revolutionary struggle."

—Mao

Chapter

Winning Political Power Through Electoral Campaigning

"Behold a Republic!" cried Huey Long, "Whose every man is a king, but no one wears a crown." Huey Long was a southern politician who rose to power during America's Great Depression. Before his death by assassination he had won the governorship of his native Louisiana (1928–1931) and served in the U.S. Senate (1931–1935). Some people thought him a friend and savior of the "little man", others viewed him as a ruthless demagogue, America's version of Adolf Hitler. In either case, he was a product of time and circumstance and had the ability to capture political power through the art of electoral campaigning.

What were Long's skills? They were numerous, the skills that any politician must have who seeks power not by intrigue or force of arms but through elections. Principal among these was his ability to arouse a sense of communion among his followers, to convey a sense of excitement to a crowd, and to make himself its spokesman. He was, in sum, a dramatic actor who could play as many parts on the electoral stage as there were audiences to the performance. Before his "pea pickers," as he called the farmers and downtrodden, he played the role of knight errant promising to slay the "octopus" oil companies who controlled the state government and robbed the poor. Before slightly prosperous middle-class audiences he adopted the posture of a responsible reformist offering plans for free school textbooks. Appearing in front of college teachers he was suave, sophisticated, and cultured. But a rural audience he would entertain with jokes and stories, and he would court a French-speaking group in southern Louisiana by playing the flamboyant drinker and womanizer, an adopted son of the district.

Huey Long also knew the value of gimmicks to electoral warfare. His slogan, "Every man a king, but no one wears a crown," captured the essential ideal of republican rule, that everyone shares political power. Was Long also just another "every man?" To prove it he would ask members of his audience how many wore silk socks. None. He would ask how many wore cotton socks. All. Then he would remove one of his shoes, exposing (of course) a cotton sock, but with the big toe sticking through. Crude it was, but for its time and place an effective campaign device.

Machiavelli observed that a "private citizen becomes a prince" through "crimes" (intrigue) and "intolerable violence" (force of arms). But there is another path, one appropriate for a republic. It "depends neither completely on skill [virtu] nor completely on fortune, but rather on a kind of lucky shrewdness," said Machiavelli. It is to rise "by the favor of the people." Today this means winning political power through elections. In this chapter we shall examine how princes do that. First, we shall look at the purposes that elections are supposed to serve, and because not all elections are alike, we shall describe the different kinds. Finally, we shall examine how politicians campaign to get elected and reelected.

WHAT IS THE ELECTORAL ALTERNATIVE?

As seen in Chapter 6, the principal purpose for elections in a republic is to permit the governed to choose, freely, who will govern them. Republican elections may do other things as well. Recall from Chapter 6, for example, that Charles de Gaulle called for free elections in order to permit French voters to approve or disapprove of the constitution of the Fifth Republic. Subsequently, there were other elections to decide on the acceptability of constitutional amendments and other issues.

In such "referenda" elections the voters vote directly for governmental policy rather than choosing public officials to do so. Depending on the constitutional requirements of the republic involved, such referenda may be called by the ruling regime (as did de Gaulle), the constitution itself (many state constitutions in the United States require popular approval of amendments), popular demand (for instance, Switzerland permits citizens to petition for an election in order to challenge an act of the national legislature), or popular initiative, that is, forcing officials (by obtaining a required number of residents' signatures) to put an item on the ballot not previously passed by legislative action.

Such free elections, whether to choose public officials or policies, should be distinguished from the controlled elections frequently found in autocratic or totalitarian regimes. Joseph Stalin once proclaimed the constitution of the Union of Societ Socialistic Republics as "the most democratic in the world." On the surface he was correct, at least to the degree that all citizens except the certifiably insane are eligible to vote and 999 of every 1,000 do! But the choice given them in elections is literally "take it or leave it." Only one candidate for each office, from the Communist party, appears on the ballot. To vote for the candidate the citizen need only fold the ballot and drop it in the ballot box in full view of everyone. To vote against the candidate, however, the citizen must go to a booth and cross out the candidate's name on the ballot, a procedure with obvious risks. Similarly, totalitarian regimes hold referenda on policies, called *plebicites*. The Nazi regime in Hitler's Germany held a series of plebicites to approve or reject the Fuehrer's actions. Given the consequences of not doing so, the regime overwhelmingly won such plebicites.

The controlled elections typical of autocratic and totalitarian regimes thus are not a means of winning power but of imposing power already secured through intrigue or force of arms. Popular referenda in republics pertain to policies rather than candidates. What ends, therefore, do free elections of public officials serve in a republic? There are three theories.

One is that when voters go to the polls to choose their rulers from among competing sets of candidates, the electoral verdict will state the "popular will," that when competing candidates take conflicting stands on issues and proposed policies, the electorate's judgment not only will decide who will govern but also how they will govern. By selecting one set of candidates over another the voters have said, in effect, "We elected you to get done the things that you said you would do." Thus, in this view an election directly chooses policymakers and indirectly chooses policies. According to Part IV, on the relations between rulers and ruled, however, you will probably recognize the problems with this view. For one, many voters are not sufficiently informed about the candidates' stands to make wise decisions about policies when choosing among office seekers. For another, candidates are not always eager to take clear-cut stands on issues (for fear of alienating and losing votes rather than winning them). Hence, it is no wonder that voters see no differences. Finally, the times, circumstances, and voters' (not to mention nonvoters') welfare and deference values change. What they voted for or against yesterday might not be the same as today. Elected policymakers cannot simply look to the election results as reliable guides for what to do in the day-to-day business of governing.

A second view says that voters do not send their governors a message, let alone decide which policies they prefer. What they do is choose among candidates representing different political parties. The party that wins the most votes and/or seats of power has the responsibility to govern as it wishes, for a specified period of time. When that ends, the election again serves as a means for voters to assert "popular control" over the policymakers by reelecting them or throwing "the rascals out." This view, too, has problems. It assumes that the voters identify their interests with one or another political party, choose among those parties, in retrospect evaluating the conduct of the party in office, and choose between the "ins" and "outs" in subsequent elections. Again, Chapter 14 should help you ponder these assumptions. People are no longer as ready as they once were to identify their interests with political parties, nor do they make prospective or retrospective judgments on the basis of party loyalties. And keep in mind that in many republics there are several political parties seeking power, each representing radically different points of view regarding how the government should be run. Rarely does any single party win a majority of legislative seats or clear-cut control of the executive palaces. Consequently, the parties must compromise their stands and build coalitions. As Charles de Gaulle noted with respect to France, the likelihood of consensus, let alone the uniformity of opinion, is slim: "How can one conceive of a one-party system in a country that has over two hundred different varieties of cheese?"

A third view believes that electing public officials says little about the popular will or popular control. Elections are essentially devices for winning political power and symbolizing popular support for the government and acquiescence to its rule. In this view elections are dramatic, seasonal rituals. By taking part in the ritual, the voters demonstrate their loyalty and devotion to the political community (that is, to "America," "France," "the republic," or whatever), its regime, and procedures. For members of the electorate, the ritual reassures and soothes any doubts and frustrations they may have about the way things are going, quiets anxieties, reaffirms their beliefs in justice, creates hopes for a better future, and promises a new beginning. Prudent aspirants to political power recognize these emotional aspects of elections and adapt their campaigns accordingly.

Machiavelli recognized that it was important for a princely ruler of a republic to appeal to the emotional side of subjects. "The people are always deceived by false appearances of good unless they are persuaded otherwise by someone worthy of their confidence," he wrote. "When the people have no one to trust, ruin may sometimes ensue." It is by capitalizing on the fact that when free elections offer subjects the opportunity to discover someone to trust, someone to whom to give their popular support—more so than to express the popular will or exercise popular control—they serve as means for princes to win political power.

"The ballot is stronger than the bullet," said Abraham Lincoln. In short, when properly exploited, the election is more useful than intrigue or force is in achieving power.

IT'S NOT JUST HOOPLA: CAMPAIGNING TO WIN AND HOLD POWER

Marcus Tullius Cicero was a republican politician. His name is not a household word today, but it was in the Rome of the caesars, so much so that Caesar Augustus thought him a threat and had him executed. But during his life, in addition to being an officeholder, orator, and philosopher, Cicero was a campaign consultant. (A campaign consultant advises people running in elections on how to win them.) In a letter to his brother Quintus, Cicero offered his views on what Quintus should do to win a campaign for a Roman consulship, a high governmental office: "Consider what the state is: what it is you seek: who you are that seek it. Almost everyday as you go down to the forum you should say to yourself, 'I am a *novus homo*' ["new man"], 'I am a candidate for the consulship,' 'This is Rome.'" There is an abundance of prudent advice contained in that statement, advice just as relevant today to the aspiring prince seeking power through election as it was two thousand years ago.

"Consider What the State Is"

"This is Rome," wrote Cicero. What he meant by that, and what every campaign manager since his day has meant, is that a candidate must be familiar with the nation and electoral district in which he or she is running.To begin, this means knowing the demographic makeup of a candidate's constituents. What types of people live there? What are their racial and ethnic backgrounds? How do they make a living? How much money and other wealth do different groups have? How well educated are the constituents? How old are they? What portions are male and female? Where do people live, and in what kind of housing? Who lives in the city, the outskirts of cities, in rural areas? The "conciliation of people," wrote Cicero, is one of a candidate's tasks. To perform it well, the aspiring politician must know what the people are like. "Take care to have in your mind a chart," Cicero wrote of Quintus's district, "laid out according to the tribe of each town and learn it by heart."

Huey Long certainly did that. His ability to attract pea pickers, blacks, French-speaking Cajuns, city workers, college graduates, and other diverse groups was no accident. He learned his chart well. Long also knew "what the state is," something Cicero also emphasized. Candidates must also know their constituents' social habits, including folklore, traditions, prejudices, and values. A big toe sticking through a cotton sock was, of course, part of Long's campaign hoopla. But it was more than that; it was Long's way of courting and identifying with his constituents. Like all campaign hoopla it was artificial; that is, on a daily basis Long wore silk, not cotton, socks. But as Cicero advised, "in a business lasting only a few months [an electoral campaign], it seems probable that the artificial may be the more effective."

There is a third thing to know about the state, and that is the candidate's constituents. In addition to demographic characteristics and social habits, a candidate must understand his or her constituents' hopes and aspirations, anxieties and fears. Herein lies the source of campaign promises, sometimes implied and sometimes blatant. Cicero advised his brother to adjust his behavior to his constituents' emotions, "a concession to the necessities of the moment." Wrote Cicero, "when you cannot do a thing you should either promise or put your refusal pleasantly: the latter is the conduct of a good man, the former of a good candidate."

In considering "what the state is" in order to win power by means of election, few campaigners have surpassed Abraham Lincoln. Before 1858 Lincoln had been a moderately successful politician in Illinois, and then in that year he ran for the U.S. Senate. Although defeated, his performance in a series of debates with his opponent, Stephen A. Douglas, drew national attention. Lincoln was no longer a local politician, and Republican party leaders began to mention him as a presidential possibility. Lincoln openly denied such ambitions. Privately to a friend, however, he confided, "The taste is in my mouth a little."

If taste it was, Lincoln savored it in several ways. In 1859 he traveled over four thousand miles and made twenty-three speeches in Indiana, Ohio, Iowa, Kansas, Wisconsin, New York, New Hampshire, Massachusetts, and Connecticut. Commonplace though such speaking tours may be in today's jet age, they required untold dedication in mid-nineteenth-century America. At each stop he made the acquaintance of men who, not coincidentally, would be delegates to the 1860 Republican National Convention. Moreover, he tried to guide party policy by means of correspondence with political leaders across the nation.

But as one of several indications that Lincoln knew what the state was, consider this. In 1859 he secretly purchased a weekly newspaper in Springfield, Illinois. The paper was pro-Republican, publishing mostly in German with an occasional article in English. Why did he make such a purchase? One possibility is that the census figures indicated that there were 1.3 million immigrants in the United States, more than one half of them German and living in the northern states. The weekly newspaper served as a vehicle for reaching what Lincoln knew was to be a vital portion of his constituency. By taking a stand against a law that forbade any foreign-born naturalized citizen to vote or hold office until two years after being awarded citizenship, Lincoln endeared himself to the leaders of the German and other foreign-born communities. "Let your first care be to acquaint yourself with the knights"[opinion leaders], Cicero had written, "for they are comparatively few, then make advances to them." Lincoln may not have read Cicero's letter to Quintus, but he practiced the advice.

ABRAHAM LINCOLN: PRINCELY CAMPAIGNER

One hundred years after Lincoln's birth, schoolchildren in Springfield, Illinois, celebrated February 12 with the following ditty:

> A blend of mirth and sadness, smiles and tears;
> A quaint knight errant of the pioneers;
> A homely hero, born of star and sod;
> A Peasant Prince; a masterpiece of God.

They were referring to Abraham Lincoln (1809–1865). The Lincoln legend is so well known and enduring that only its barest outlines remind us of his life and career. But sometimes those outlines are hard to pin down. For instance, so appealing has become the mythical figure of Lincoln that at least fifteen locales have claimed to be his birthplace, in Kentucky, North Carolina, Tennessee, and Indiana. Authorities now agree on a plot of land in Larue County, Kentucky. In any event, the family moved around, and by 1837 Lincoln had reached Springfield, Illinois, where he practiced law and embarked upon a political career.

Lincoln's early years, although much romanticized in legend, bore similarities to those of other princely figures. He recognized the value of a broad education and to this end was a self-taught and avid reader. One anecdote—and about Lincoln there are countless such stories—relates his self-teaching techniques. He practiced reading aloud to himself (something John Marshall also did). Asked why he did so, he explained that it gave him the advantage of learning by sight and sound, thus enabling him to recall better what he was learning. But he did not confine himself to books. He also enjoyed mixing with his fellows, observing them closely and listening and telling stories. He developed a sense of how people would respond in differing situations, always able to find a parallel.

Lincoln's lifeblood was politics. From the time he began practicing law, he was first, last, and always a politician. In princely fashion he endured defeats, only to return to the political fray and later victory. Even before practicing law, Lincoln was first defeated for a state legislative seat (1832) and then was elected and reelected until 1846 when he went to Congress as a member of the House of Representatives. Twice as a member of the state legislature he ran for Speaker of the Illinois house, and twice he lost. From 1849 to 1854 he was out of elective office, but not out of politics. He campaigned both inside and outside Illinois for the presidential tickets of the Whig party and in 1856 made more than fifty speeches for the ticket of the new Republican party.

By 1858 Abraham Lincoln had been active in well over a dozen election campaigns, either on his own behalf or supporting some other candidate. The experience had taught him several things. For one, it had sharpened his oratorical skills. Appearing before audiences that ranged from small groups of people to large gatherings had taught him how to win and hold attention, how to present himself to people and make favorable impressions. He became his own best image maker. He became a keen analyst of issues, learning which issues might win him support, which ones he should exploit, and which ones he should avoid. He developed the ability to recognize popular concerns and to adjust to them, turning them to his advantage. Finally, he made influential contacts with political leaders, not only in Illinois but throughout the nation.

Yet for all of this, he was still largely a local politician. He had experienced his ups and downs, and so many downs that at one point he had almost decided to abandon politics and stick to the practice of law. However, his persistence paid off. In 1858 he received the Republican party nomination to run against the incumbent Democratic senator from Illinois, Stephen A. Douglas. It was not an enviable task. In those days U.S. senators were chosen not by the direct vote of the people, as they are today, but by the state legislatures. Thus the Lincoln-Douglas campaign was actually conducted on behalf of Republican and Democratic candidates for the Illinois legislature.

In the 1850s election campaigns were of intense interest. Campaign speeches were occasions of high drama and great entertainment and were avidly followed, as though the orators were engaged in a sporting contest. Lincoln knew that he needed an appropriate forum to challenge the better known and highly regarded Senator Douglas. He proposed in a letter, therefore, that he and Douglas would "divide time and share the same audiences." This would save both of them considerable time, wear, and tear as they traveled. Douglas accepted, and out of this came the now famous Lincoln-Douglas debates. Actually they were more joint appearances than debates; yet their dramatic impact was the same as that of a duel. Criss-crossing the state through seven towns the candidates followed a standard format: one would speak for an hour, the second for an hour and a half, and the first would then close with a one-half hour reply. At the next stop on the circuit the candidates would reverse the order of their speeches.

In the end Lincoln lost the election, but he won the campaign, a victory that meant a great deal for his political ambitions. The number of popular votes cast for Republican and Democratic candidates for the legislature was about the same. Had there not been a slate of third-party candidates, and had the state legislature been apportioned more favorably to the Republicans, Lincoln might well have been elected. But the Democrats retained control of the legislature, and Douglas was returned to the U.S. Senate. How then did Lincoln win the campaign?

When the campaign began, Douglas was a politician with a national reputation who was seeking reelection to enhance his presidential ambitions. By engaging in a series of debates with a lesser-known politician he helped his challenger build a national image. The debates received unprecedented news coverage, as it was the first time that national correspondents had traveled with the candidates, reporting both the substance of the exchanges and the colorful events of the campaign. The result was a gold mine in public relations for Lincoln. Moreover, Lincoln too had his eye on more than a Senate seat. Recognizing Douglas's ambitions—which might in the future run counter to Lincoln's—Lincoln manuevered Douglas into taking positions on the slavery issue that alienated the "Little Giant" (Douglas's nickname) from the southern Democrats. This too contributed to Lincoln's new national image. Finally, of course, the fact that Lincoln and the Republicans almost upset the favored Douglas helped enhance Lincoln's stature among politicians within the national Republican party.

In 1860 Abraham Lincoln received the Republican nomination for president. He had said earlier in a response to a question about his presidential ambitions that "only events can make a President." But in Machiavellian fashion he also understood that the prudent, princely campaigner seeks some control over events. Through extensive speaking tours in Kansas and Missouri, the Midwest, New York, and the East, Lincoln promoted his presidential chances while denying direct interest in the nomination. In the presidential election of 1860 the Republicans defeated a Democratic party badly divided on the issue of slavery.

Lincoln's victory triggered events that looked as though they might un-make, not make, a president—namely, the secession of the southern states from the Union and the ensuing Civil War. The Lincoln legend credits him with a princely resolution of that conflict and justly so. What it too often ignores, however, is that Lincoln, in spite of his preoccupation with the war, never ceased campaigning. He understood well that in order to exercise power in the interests of preserving the Union, he had to retain that power. Two stories offer a sense of his thinking.

"Lincoln is letting his whiskers grow," people noticed in January 1861, before Lincoln traveled to Washington for his inaugural. Why, after fifty-two years, had Lincoln decided to grow a beard? No answer is certain, but one explanation offered is that a beard would enhance a presidential image. A girl in New York had suggested as much in a letter to the president-elect, and another letter from "True Republicans" in New York urged Lincoln to "culti-vate whiskers and wear standing collars." Was reelection already on his mind?

The second story concerns the Emancipation Proclamation. On January 1, 1863, Lincoln signed a proclamation declaring that in all areas in which people were still in rebellion against the Union, slavery would be abolished im-mediately and completely. Long before this, however, the abolitionists had pressed Lincoln to take such action, arguing that emancipation would show that in the Civil War the North had fought a moral cause with "God on our side." But until he found it politically feasible to do so two years after taking office, Lincoln countered these earlier demands with and eye toward the 1864 presidential election. "It would be nice to have God on our side," he said, "but we must have Kentucky."

The Lincoln of legend is manysided: "Self-Made Man," "Rail-Splitter," "Honest Abe," "Great Emancipator," "Savior of the Union," and "the greatest character since Christ." Add to that constant and princely campaigner.

It was in appealing to another segment of his constituency that Lincoln demonstrated even greater sagacity. In appraising the overlap-ping and competing groups that comprise an electoral constituency, advised Cicero, "consider and weigh carefully the amount of influence each possesses." Lincoln recognized that the vote of the laborers, both in the cities and the rural areas, would be crucial in any presidential contest, and so he sought an issue that would appeal to the labor vote. He found it in slavery. But exploiting that issue was ticklish. Lincoln had never been an abolitionist one who sought an immediate end to slavery. in fact, he did not even speak out against slavery until 1845, when he was well into his political career. Then he spoke of it as a "monstrous injustice" but could see no way of eliminating it in "any satisfactory way." In fact, he strongly implied that he did not favor abolition, for if that were done, "what next? Free them and make them politically our equals." No, he said, his feelings would not permit that, and even if they would, "those of the great mass of whites would not."

Here was the nub of the problem. Lincoln understood that the hopes, aspirations, anxieties, and fears of the white laborers did not permit their full support of abolition. The abolition of slaves would mean competition with white labor in the marketplace. Thus a stand for abolition would sacrifice labor votes; yet a stand against it would also alienate the large bloc of abolitionists. How to appeal to both, seemingly contradictory, interests? Lincoln's solution was the containment, not the abolition of slavery. He argued against letting slavery spread to free states where it did not exist: "We want them [the free states] for homes of free white people." Where slavery did exist it would die a "natural death." In sum, slavery (1) was morally wrong, an appeal to abolitionists; (2) should be prevented from spreading, an appeal to white laborers; and (3) would die a natural death, a compromise appealing to abolitionists, laborers, and even some slave owners. Lincoln understood his constituents, adjusted accordingly, and won both his party's presidential nomination and the office itself.

"Consider What It Is You Seek"

The office that an aspiring politician seeks does much to shape the methods used in campaigning. Cicero's brother, Quintus, like Abraham Lincoln, was ambitious and sought the highest office that the republic had to offer. "Seeing that you are seeking the highest place in the state, and at the same time that there do exist sentiments opposed to you, you must positively employ every method, and all your vigilance, labour, and attention to business," recommended Cicero. It is still sound advice for you today, whatever the office you seek—in a club, school, professional organization, or local, state, or national government.

During Cicero's time, running for office was called *canvassing*, a term still in vogue in Lincoln's day. Today we say *campaign* instead of *canvass*, but what Cicero said about it remains the same: "The canvass for office resolves itself into an activity of two kinds, of which one is concerned with the loyalty of friends, the other with the feelings of the people." In short, win the support of one's followers and win the hearts of others. The three "P's" involved in that joint enterprise are planning, polling, and promoting.

If you aspire to princedom, the first thing you must think about is yourself; that is, do you really want to go to the time, trouble, expense, and pain of seeking office? Because the answer to that involves Cicero's third admonition, "Consider what you are that seek it," we shall set it aside for the moment. But assume that you have thought about running and decide that you will take the plunge. What next? The answer is plan, plan a campaign organization and a campaign strategy.

In ancient times the word *campaign* referred to the period that an army spent in the field. In an electoral campaign, just as in a military one, one needs an army to fight battles. Machiavelli explained: "The armies with which a prince defends his state are either his own or are mercenaries, auxiliaries, or mixed. . . . Mercenaries and auxiliaries are useless and dangerous." In modern election campaigns, a candidate has the same choices as did Machiavelli's prince. Should you seek office, for instance, you may choose to build your own campaign organization, borrow the workers of some influential groups (auxiliaries), or hire people to run your cmpaign (mercenaries). Whether your auxiliaries and mercenaries prove useless or even dangerous depends what you do with them.

Living as you do in the United States, you need no reminder of what election campaigns are like.There are so many of them that you could hardly have missed them. Every four years Americans elect a president, some members of Congress, some governors, some state legislators, and other officials as well. Midway through that four-year period Americans again elect other congressional and state and local officials. During the other years of that four-year period, many states and localities hold other elections to choose officials or policies.

Campaigns began to take on the character that emerged early in the history of the republic. Similarly, that character was emerging in other nations, England being the most notable, and then in the late nineteenth and early twentieth centuries in Western European nations, the English-speaking world, and elsewhere. In the earliest period candidates built their organizations around auxiliaries; that is, they obtained the support of groups already in existence, rather than trying to start from scratch. The most common of such groups was the political party. In a republic a political party is simply a coalition of people with both common and conflicting interests who join together to win support in elections for their candidates so that the party may capture office and control the government.

As the chief auxiliary for candidates in the early campaigns, political parties promised many resources. Parties supplied financial support, organized rallies of supporters before whom their candidates spoke, introduced candidates to influential power brokers, mapped out speaking tours, provided an army of workers who contacted individual voters on behalf of the candidates, and saw to it on election day that those voters reached the polls and supported the party's slate of nominees. In return for such resources, party leaders asked that loyal party members be appointed to offices and that preferred policies and programs be followed. As a result, policymaking (Chaper 24) was greatly influenced by partisan considerations.

Political parties have not been the only auxiliaries around which candidates organize their campaigns. Groups with more narrowly defined concerns—for instance, to improve the lot of the workers, to advance the interests of the railroads, or to promote various commercial ventures—offered their support in exchange for a sympathetic hearing in government circles. Sometimes such special interest groups operated through the political parties, supporting the candidates by contributing to the parties that nominated them. This was more frequently the case in nineteenth-century America and in such parliamentary republics as Great Britain than it has been in twentieth-century America or in many other nations. More frequently, special interests groups operated independently of political parties, directly making their contributions to and seeking favors from the candidates.

The character of campaigns as you recognize them today began with an emphasis on auxiliaries: political parties and special interst groups, with special interests working through the parties. Winning power through the electoral alternative, then, meant winning party support. Abraham Lincoln recognized this and through speaking tours and corresponence constantly courted prospective delegates to the 1860 Republican National Convention. Although Lincoln had serious competition for the nomination, his careful exploitation of party contacts paid off, and he received the nomination.

Although candidates still rely a great deal on the party auxiliary in organizing their campaign armies, party influence has decreased, especially in the United States. There are various reasons for this. One is that in the United States many local communities insist that candidates run in "nonpartisan" elections, elections in which political parties cannot legally participate. Another is that in many nations the political parties no longer command the loyalties of voters as they once did. Instead of thinking of themselves as steadfast Democrats or Republicans (as in the United States), Laborites or Conservatives (as in Great Britain), or Liberals and Conservatives (as in Canada), people regard themselves as independent of party wishes and switch their loyalties from election to election (recall the discussion in Chapter 14). As noted, the trend has been for special interest groups to work directly with the candidates. For example, in the United States laws regulating how candidates raise the finances necessary for their electoral bids enhance the opportunities of "Political Action committees" (PACs) to contribute large sums to candidates. As the number of PACs has increased they have replaced the political party in the vital task of financing election campaigns. Finally, candidates depend less on speaking tours and party rallies as forums in which to talk to the voters and more on the media of mass communication—newspaper, radio, television, and direct mail advertising.

Machiavelli taught that the prince either has his own forces or those of auxiliaries and mercenaries. Today's campaigning prince requires all three, and a serious candidate must gather an army of volunteers. In fact, there are two such volunteer armies. One consists of those who freely and willingly give their time and other resources to a candidate. They knock on doors, type letters, lick envelopes, make telephone calls, donate their homes for campaign functions, and perform an untold number of other tasks for the candidates of their choice. The larger, more efficient, and well organized a candidate's volunteers are, the less dependent the office seeker may be on party or special interest support.

Indeed, one way in American politics for candidates to capture their parties' nominations for office is to mobilize a winning volunteer effort in party primary elections. There have been recent notable examples of this tactic, some successful and others not. In 1972, for example, George McGovern was given little chance of winning the presidential nomination of the Democratic party when he set out to do so. Yet by organizing a grass-roots effort of volunteers in party primaries, he was able to win enough delegates for the nomination. Similarly, Jimmy Carter in 1976 relied heavily on volunteers in his successful quest for the Democratic nomination for president. Four years later, however, John Anderson, seeking the republican presidential nomination, fell short of victory, in spite of his volunteer forces.

There is a second type of volunteer force, one of paid volunteers. They are part of a candidate's "own" army in Machiavelli's sense, in that they are loyal workers, but are mercenaries in that they are paid and thus might just as easily have been hired elsewhere. As in anything, you get what you pay for, and, paid volunteers may—as Machiavelli noted—be "useless and dangerous." The 1964 struggle for the Republican presidential nomination is an example. It pitted U.S. Senator Barry Goldwater of Arizona against Governor Nelson Rockefeller of New York. In the crucial California primary election the Goldwater forces had a multitude of volunteer workers freely giving their services out of dedication to his cause. Rockefeller, largely because of his belated entry into the nomination fight, was forced to raise an army of paid volunteers. The matter-of-fact and routine approach of Rockefeller's volunteers proved to be no match for the intensity and enthusiasm of the victorious Goldwater forces.

There are other mercenaries in modern election campaigns besides paid volunteers. It is here that the remaining two of the "Three P's," polling and promotion, join organizational planning. In today's world, major campaigns appealing to large numbers of far-flung voters still adhere to Cicero's maxims of charting one's constituency and making promises. But when constituencies contain vast numbers of voters—in an entire nation, province, state, or district—it is not easy to do as Cicero urged, "review the entire city, all colleges, districts, neighborhoods." Nor is it possible to meet each voter, "having your house full of visitors before daybreak." Polling and promotion are substitutes.

Through public opinion polls, candidates survey the views of the electorate. A poll is simply a means of finding out the characteristics of constituents and what is on their minds, by interviewing a relatively small but representative cross-section of them. To be valid and reliable indicators of what people think, polls must be conducted in accordance with required techniques and standards. Here enters the *pollster,* a specialist in measuring public opinion. Rare is the candidate capable of conducting a public opinion poll that is not "useless and dangerous" (that gives no useful information or yields false information), without consulting a professional pollster. For this reason, pollsters, acting as campaign mercenaries, have become key actors in modern campaigns throughout the world. Working on behalf of a variety of candidates and in far more elections than any single candidate could possibly run in during a lifetime, pollsters are the modern-day answer to Cicero's demand to "consider what the state is."

On the basis of what the pollster advises and in conjunction with what a candidate's other advisers counsel, the campaign organization of volunteers, auxiliaries, and mercenaries plans the strategy and tactics of the contest. This is the third "P"—promotion, which includes defining the issues of the campaign, working out the candidate's stands on them, sizing up and working out attacks on opponents, and carrying out a campaign to communicate all of this to prospective voters in order to galvanize supporters, neutralize the opposition, and win at least the short-term allegiance of those who are undecided.

Promotional activities are the province of specialists who make their living by advising campaigners. A complete list of this cadre of mercenaries is impossible, but a few examples follow:

1. Professional campaign consultants who organize and coordinate the candidate's overall campaign.
2. Public relations personnel who write press releases presenting the candidate and campaign message in the best light.
3. Press secretaries who keep on friendly terms with journalists, responding to questions and keeping alert for potential problems.
4. Advertising specialists who devise, film, and edit the candidate's televised commercials.
5. Fund raisers who know the techniques of raising money to finance the campaign.
6. Budget specialists who allocate and keep track of vast amounts of campaign expenditures.
7. Lawyers who help keep the candidate within the law or see that loopholes are exploited and evasions are not detected.
8. "Advance" personnel to precede the candidate on speaking tours and to orchestrate the details of appearances, meetings with local influentials, and news coverage of the candidate.
9. Specialists in organizing telephone banks, those volunteers designated to call voters and give them the message.
10. Direct-mail specialists with computerized mailing lists that are the basis of appeals for financial support and votes.
11. Speech writers, even joke writers, that polish a candidate's words.
12. Hair stylists, grooming agents, makeup artists, voice and diction coaches, and specialists in weight control—anyone who might help the candidate seem more pleasing to the eye, ear, and psyche.

As this partial list suggests, promotional mercenaries are interested not only in communicating the candidate's electoral message but also in promoting what the candidate is or, sometimes more importantly, what the candidate seems to be. That brings us to the third of Cicero's recommendations concerning how to win power through elections.

"Consider Who You Are That Seek It"

When the Illinois Republican convention to choose delegates to the national convention took place in 1860, John Hanks, a friend of Abraham Lincoln, carried in two fence rails bearing the inscription "Abraham Lincoln, the Rail Candidate for President in 1860: Two rails made from a lot of 3,000 made in 1830 by Thos. Hanks and Abe Lincoln—whose father was the first pioneer of Macon County." Cries went up from delegates, "Lincoln! Lincoln! Speech!" Lincoln, still denying that he was interested in the presidency, rose to cheers of "Three times three for Honest Abe, our next President." "Identify your work." they shouted. Lincoln examined the rails. "It may be that I split these rails," he said. Looking further, he went on, "Well, boys, I can only say that I have split a great many better-looking ones."

So began the image of "Honest Abe Lincoln, the Rail Splitter." Cicero advised his brother, "So true it is that men are more taken by look and words than by actual services." Cicero was talking about what modern-day campaign advisers call *image*. A candidate's image consists of how he or she appears to the electorate, either because the candidate seeks to appear that way and contrives to do so or because people see—and want to see—in the candidate certain things that cannot be obscured, or both. Machiavelli called it *reputation*. Whatever the label, every aspiring prince must take it into account.

Cicero advised Quintus to take stock of himself before all else. Of what material did he consist? Did he have sufficient ambition to seek office? Could he stand the "deception, intrigue, and treachery everywhere?" If he could, then he should campaign. But what else must the candidate take into account about his or her qualities in order to win power through election? There are three principal questions: Do people know who you are? What do they know you to be? What do you want to be, and can you make them believe you to be this?

Cicero told his brother that every day he should say to himself, "I am *novus homo*." What Cicero meant was that his brother was seeking high office for the first time. There was a "newness" to his brother's name that made him unknown to voters. Contemporary political consultants would say that Quintus lacked "name recognition." People rarely vote for a candidate they have not heard of. So Cicero gave advice that contemporary campaign consultants would give you if you were to seek office: first, make yourself known.

It was to make himself known that Abraham Lincoln invited Stephen A. Douglas to meet him on the same platform during the Illinois senatorial campaign of 1858. Appearing with the nationally recognized Douglas helped Lincoln, still a relatively obscure politician, to catch the eye of journalists, political leaders, and party notables. To continue to build his name recognition, Lincoln went on speaking tours. By 1860 he was no longer an unknown. In more recent times there has been similar emphasis on making known the unknown.

When Jimmy Carter set out to capture the presidential nomination that he ultimately won in 1976, he was a relatively unknown former governor of Georgia. His only other "claim to fame" was that he had appeared on a national network television show, "What's My Line?" a show in which panelists tried to name which of three contestants was in a given line of work The panel did not identify Carter as a governor. So obscure was he that journalists dubbed him "Jimmy Who?" when he announced his candidacy for president. Yet by painstaking organization and tireless efforts in his early campaigning, Carter achieved victory in the first test among the candidates for his party's nomination, the party caucuses in Iowa. From then on he was no longer "Jimmy Who?" but "Jimmy What?"

The question of "what?" pertains to what people know about the candidate. This campaign consultants refer to as the candidate's *position,* meaning that a candidate—or product, idea, or simply any individual such as yourself—holds a position in people's minds relative to that of the other candidates, products, ideas, or individuals. Take as an example car rental firms. Hertz used to advertise that it was "Number One." The success of that advertising was not lost on Hertz's main competitor, Avis, and so Avis returned with "We Try Harder." Such messages positioned the two companies in the popular mind.

Abraham Lincoln positioned himself to run for the presidency in 1860 by exploiting the slavery issue. All other potential candidates favored either the abolition or the extension of slavery and based their positions on moral grounds. Lincoln, as you have seen, took his position on economic grounds. He distinguished himself from others who might seek the presidency by opposing slavery: opposing its extension but not supporting abolition, only its natural death. Jimmy Carter answered the "what?" question in 1976 by running not as a liberal or conservative (as were all his competitors for the Democratic presidential nomination), but as one who could be trusted to give America "a government as good as its people."

Finally, there is the question of which qualities a candidate possesses or does not possess that should be emphasized in a campaign. This is the problem of crafting a candidate's image. An image has two sides. One is what people may come to think of a candidate as a political leader. Specifically what do they believe about the candidate's background, experience, and preparation for the office sought, and what political interests (parties, special interests, groups, and the like) do they think the candidate serves? The second side is how people regard the candidate as a person, both from the standpoint of personal qualities (honesty, integrity, decisiveness, energy) and dramatic qualities (appearance, speaking abilities, capacities to stir up an audience, work with people, identify with popular hopes, aspirations, anxieties, and fears).

It is in building name recognition, positioning, and image management that the most influential mercenaries in modern-day campaign armies thrive. Drawing on findings from public opinion polls, promoters package candidates for appropriate electorates. Such packaging is itself not new to election campaigns. Even Cicero recommended it: "Above all in this election you must see that the Republic entertains a good hope and an honorable opinion of you."

Successful campaigners have always understood it. Abraham Lincoln's references to his humble origins, his absence of pleasing physical qualities, and his self-made success combined with his humility, home-spun humor, and candid assessments were carefully calculated to present what he thought was indeed the "real" Lincoln, "Honest Abe, the Rail Splitter." What has changed is that no longer is such promotion the province of simply the candidate and a few advisers but now is handled by a growing industry of mercenaries.

"WHAT DO WE DO NOW?"

"What do we do now?" is the qustion raised in the film *The Candidate,* in which Robert Redford played a young, idealistic candidate who had been successfully packaged to win high office. Having won he realized that he knew nothing about how to govern. Winning political power—whether by intrigue, force of arms, or free election—is not the same as practicing it. Yet as you move on to Part VI to consider the princely exercise of political power, remember that although obtaining and practicing power differ, how one achieves power influences what one can do with it. What one does with it determines whether one can hold onto it and, if it is lost, get it back again.

"Behold a Republic! Whose every man is a king, but no man wears a crown."
—*Huey Long*

"How can one conceive of a one-party system in a country that has over two hundred different varieties of cheese?"
—*de Gaulle*

"When the people have no one to trust, ruin may sometimes ensue."
—*Machiavelli*

"The ballot is stronger than the bullet."
—*Lincoln*

"Consider what the state is: what it is you seek: what you are that seek it."
—*Cicero*

"When you cannot do a thing you should either promise or put your refusal pleasantly: the latter is the conduct of a good man, the former of a good candidate."
—*Cicero*

"Only events can make a president."
—*Lincoln*

"The armies with which a prince defends his state are either his own or are mercenaries, auxiliaries, or mixed. ... Mercenaries and auxiliaries are useless and dangerous."
—*Machiavelli*

Part

VI

Practicing Power

Chapter

19

The Reality and the Dilemma of Power: The Problem of Ruling

Fortuna did not smile on the presidency of Herbert Hoover. By all accounts, an intelligent, hardworking, and humane man, only a few months after taking office he was saddled with circumstances that he could neither understand nor control. He came into office convinced that the economic boom of the 1920s was permanent, that endless economic growth would end poverty and hunger in the land, and that all Americans would soon have "two chickens in every pot, and two cars in every garage." Hoover's philosophy and experience would not admit otherwise. But in the fall of 1929 the unthinkable happened: the stock market crashed, plunging the nation and the world into a sustained period of economic scarcity that older Americans still remember as the Great Depression. During the next years, banks and businesses failed, wages fell, unemployment climbed, and desperation and fear pervaded the nation.

Herbert Hoover was a man of strong principles, committed to the traditional American values of rugged individualism and free enterprise. He believed so strongly in these principles that he thought that the economic downturn was temporary and could be cured by the business establishment and that American self-reliance and neighborly voluntary aid would see people through the crisis. So he resisted government action to help the many desperate people and kept predicting that the economy was "fundamentally sound" and would thus soon lead to a plane of prosperity higher than ever before. Every time he said that things got worse, and because people began to doubt his wisdom and compassion, his reputation suffered. He was soundly booed at a World Series game. He became highly unpopular, associated with the businessmen that people blamed for the Depression. In the minds of many of the needy and dispossessed, he ranked with Ebenezer Scrooge and Marie Antoinette in insensitivity, refusing to institute policies to help the desperate and often dispossessed farmers and the huge numbers of unemployed workers. Nevertheless, he remained true to his principles, arguing that public aid to feed the hungry "would have injured the spiritual responses of the American people. . . ." He ran for reelection in 1932 on these principles.

But principles do not win elections or successfully rule. Princes do. Hoover's opponent in 1932 was New York Governor Franklin D. Roosevelt. In many ways, Roosevelt seemed an unlikely candidate for president, especially from a party pledging to change things for the many. He might not have seemed to have the popular touch any more than the dour engineer Hoover did. Roosevelt was not a deep thinker or a serious man like Hoover. Indeed, early in 1932 before the election, Walter Lippmann wrote in his newspaper column that Roosevelt was "a highly impressionable person without a firm grasp of public affairs and without very strong convictions. . . . [He is] a pleasant man who, without any important qualifications for the office, would very much like to be President." Yet as it turned out, the very quality that Lippmann thought he lacked—"strong convictions"—which of course Hoover had, became Roosevelt's strong suit. The country wanted more than a change; it wanted somebody to *do* something, even if it were wrong.

When Roosevelt took office on March 4, 1933, economic conditions could not have been much worse. In retrospect some historians are still astounded that there was not a revolution. But all agree that if something had not been done *soon*, economic conditions would have led to an unprecedented upheaval. When Roosevelt took office, most of the banks in the country were closed. Cities were defaulting on their payrolls. Unemployment had now hit over one fourth of the labor force and more than one third of nonfarm workers. Large parts of the agricultural Midwest was in ruins, the land spent in the "Dust Bowl" and the farmers migrating elsewhere. There was real starvation and despair. The big institutions of the country—government, business and finance, newspapers—were in danger of collapse in a revolutionary tide, perhaps like the one that had just swept into power in Germany.

Roosevelt's now famous first inaugural address set the tone for what he sensed needed doing: "This nation asks for action, and action now." And Roosevelt offered that. Working his aides, cabinet, and bureaucracies at a murderous pace, Roosevelt dazzled the nation with the flurry of actions, orders, and legislation, now termed the *Hundred Days*. He declared a bank holiday, even though the banks were already closed; all he did was *keep* them closed. What he did was not so much an economic move but rather a political move: it had the effect of a call to action, a precedent of decisiveness, and a reaffirmation of belief that a political program boldly taken can solve economic problems.

The new Democratic-dominated Congress he called into special session. A hastily prepared legislative program was rammed through a Congress as much caught up in the dizzy atmosphere of crisis as everyone else was. Some bills were scarcely debated on before they were passed. FDR acquired the emergency powers of a virtual dictator. The flurry of legislation and regulations offered something to everyone: the

FRANKLIN ROOSEVELT: PATRICIAN REFORMER

The early life of Franklin Delano Roosevelt might seem to have been an unlikely spawning ground for a great reformer. Born into a wealthy and patrician Hudson River Dutch family, his upbringing resembled that of a Victorian English gentleman and might have bred in him an insensitivity to the plight of the common people, lazy contentment with the life of the leisure class, and an uncritical defense of the status quo. On the contrary, young Franklin was taught the duty of *noblesse oblige,* the idea that the privileged should use their position to lead and also to lead to do good. Roosevelt was trained, at home and at school, to become one of those remarkable creations of democratic societies: the aristocratic reformer who advocates the interests of the common person, even though he or she is not one of them. His wife Eleanor, the niece of President Theodore Roosevelt, shared his concern for social justice and supported his entry into public service.

Thus Franklin Roosevelt's march to princedom was underscored by his confidence that he had a right to lead and also that he had a duty to lead on behalf of the many. But more than that, Roosevelt had the "common touch," an unlikely trait in someone brought up in an environment of servants, governesses, and gardeners. Throughout his career in politics, he was able to present himself, easily and naturally, as a kind of aristocratic democrat, appealing to people as someone above them but able to communicate to them, articulate their feelings and wants, and be warm and friendly and able to learn from them.

Roosevelt was never a good student, but he was handsome, articulate, and energetic. He entered the New York State Senate in 1910 and quickly became a progressive leader, advocating reform legislation. He was influenced by the reform tradition pioneered by his Republican relative Theodore and went to Washington to become assistant secretary of the navy under the Democrat Woodrow Wilson. In 1920, although only thirty-eight, he so impressed the party leaders that they nominated him for vice-president on a ticket that lost. He clearly seemed to be a man with a future. But in the summer of 1921, that future seemed ended: Franklin contracted polio and nearly died. He lived but lost the use of his legs forever; he could never after that walk without help and had to be lifted out of cars. But he was indomitable, refusing to retire from politics and coming back to make a rousing speech at the 1924 Democratic convention.

In 1928, Roosevelt was persuaded to run for governor of New York to strengthen the national and state ticket. Even though Hoover won in a sweep, Roosevelt was narrowly elected. As governor during the early days of the Depression, Roosevelt began to develop those governing habits that were to serve him so well as president. Roosevelt had to strong political assumptions or ideological tenets to which he was tied. So from 1930 to 1931, when the Depression hit New York state hard, Roosevelt began to experiment with state relief and recovery measures. He began to gather a "brain trust" of academics with new ideas about how to meet the challenge of such a catastrophic economic downturn. From political mentors such as Al Smith and Louis Howe, he learned how to play politics well, dealing effectively with urban machines, labor leaders, legislatures, and the news media.

Roosevelt's political training, personality, and advisers stood him in good stead when he campaigned and won in 1932. Unlike the stolid and stubborn Hoover, Roosevelt seemed to advocate movement, dynamism, experimentation, and *doing something*. Despite his physical infirmity, he appeared to be the one on the move, ready to meet the challenge, upbeat and confident, symbolized by the cheery tune that was his campaign song, "Happy Days Are Here Again." During the campaign, he was vague about what he was going to do and indeed even reaffirmed some traditional political shibboleths that were later quickly abandoned, such as "balanced budgets" and "free enterprise." But people sensed that Hoover was static and Roosevelt kinetic. For example, Roosevelt broke with tradition, flew to the 1932 nominating convention, and addressed it personally instead of waiting for weeks to be ceremoniously asked. He seized the moment to address a large national radio audience, rally the convention, and signal that he was willing to break the old rules to meet the future.

In office, Roosevelt the president, much to the surprise of many, became the central American political figure of the twentieth century, perhaps the most powerful leader of the twentieth century, and maybe even one of the greatest American presidents ever. He was elected president four times, breaking another precedent; enjoyed widespread popularity even though the New Deal did not really cure the Depression, and became in death the symbol of reform that set the agenda of the Democratic party in subsequent decades. When he died, many millions reacted as if he had been a member of their own family. There were many people who could not remember anyone else as president or conceive that someone else could be president. And in truth, to many people the presidents since, from Truman on, were just not *the* President in the way that Roosevelt was.

Roosevelt was so breathtaking a speaker, adept a politician, and obvious an extrovert that even his political enemies admired him, as in the words of Republican William Allen White, "We who hate your gaudy guts salute you!" Historians and ideologists will debate forever the effectiveness and wisdom of what Roosevelt did with the New Deal and the Grand Alliance, but no one doubts what he was: a consummate politician who loved politics, was good at it, and ruled a nation without parallel, until his death at Warm Springs, Georgia, in 1945.

---

farmers got the Agricultural Adjustment Administration; business, the National Recovery Administration; labor, wage-and-hour and collective-bargaining guarantees; the unemployed, relief, home buyers, home loan help; and so on. Roosevelt went on the radio in "fireside chats" to explain to the people what he was doing.

The New Deal was a set of improvised moves designed to meet, or at least give the impression of meeting, the economic malaise. It is still not clear how successful it all was, but it did give people hope, a sense of economic security and the promise of restored economic prosperity. The country began to think that the government was on their side, willing to try new things to put the country back to work and not tied to the dogmas of the past. "At the end of February," wrote the now converted Walter Lippmann, "we were a congeries of disorderly, panic-striken mobs and factions. In the hundred days from March to June, we became again an organized nation, confident of our power to provide for our own security and to control our own destiny." That is a not inconsiderable political achievement for one hundred days. The pace and improvisation of those initial days established Roosevelt's reputation as a democratic reformer and forged the Roosevelt coalition that would endure long after Roosevelt himself had gone.

FIGURING OUT HOW TO RULE

Suppose for a moment that you are suddenly thrust into the job of ruler of a country. All else is prologue; now you are the prince. People defer to you; you are whisked around in a limousine with a security escort; you move into a mansion. You are escorted your first day in power into a palace and an ornate office. You sit down behind an elaborate desk. Your aides stand around ready to serve your every whim. So then what do you do?

If you had not prepared for that moment, you would no doubt be terrified. Now you may think it fanciful to imagine yourself in such a position, but actually the problem of the prince is not very different from the problem you have in using academic power in your college career or in whatever it is you wind up doing. At the beginning of your college career and at the beginning of every school year, do you sit down and take stock of what you will have to do to succeed? In other words, do you *plan* what it is that you are going to do, anticipate what might happen (especially what might go wrong), and then act accordingly? How much of your college career, or your life in general, do you stumble through mindlessly, without forethought or afterthought? On the other hand, if you do plan, do think about what you are doing, and do try to do a good job, you will be practicing power. You will be using what the political philosopher Hobbes called the "present means to secure some future apparent good." Perhaps you will not be faced with curing a Depression, as Franklin Roosevelt was, but your problem is similar: figuring out how to rule, how to use power in practice to obtain desired results.

To help you out a bit, let us look again at what Roosevelt did at the start in order to practice power successfully. In the interim between the November 1932 election and his inaugural in March 1933, Roosevelt planned what to do once in office. He spent most of the time conferring with his advisers about what to do first and gathered around him the people he wanted to appoint to the cabinet and bureaucracy. He conferred with the new Democratic leadership in the Congress. All of this was done in secret. Roosevelt waited and kept his mouth shut. He committed himself to nothing and built the suspense as to what he would do.

Perhaps most importantly, in the interim he avoided any cooperation with the defeated Hoover. Economic conditions worsened sharply after the election, and Hoover tried to talk Roosevelt into taking joint action on several matters. Aside from the formalities of exchanging public letters about the need for national unity, Roosevelt would not be drawn into any joint decisions. Hoover made several overtures, but to

Roosevelt it appeared that Hoover was trying to draw him into Hoover's policies and his excuse for why the Depression occurred, thus justifying Hoover's actions. Roosevelt was not about to associate himself with them, and so much to Hoover's dismay, he said nothing and did nothing until he took office.

GETTING OFF TO A GOOD START

One of the political types that fascinated Machiavelli was the founder of new states. For example, he wrote about the founding of Rome, when (the legend goes) Romulus murdered his brother Remus and established the republic. Machiavelli advised:

> And this should be taken as a general rule: it rarely or never happens that a republic or kingdom is well organized from the beginning, or completely reformed, with no respect for its ancient institutions, unless it is done by one man alone; moreover, it is necessary that one man provide the means and be the only one from whose mind any such organization originates; therefore, a prudent founder of a republic, one whose intention it is to govern for the common good and not in his own interest . . . should try to have the authority all to himself; nor will a wise mind ever reproach anyone for some extraordinary action performed in order to found a kingdom or to institute a republic.

Indeed, we should forgive Romulus for murdering his brother, because "while the action accuses him, the result excuses him; and when the result is good, as it was with Romulus, it will always excuse him; for one should reproach a man who is violent in order to destroy, not one who is violent in order to mend things."

Machiavelli, like many other political observers, was convinced that extraordinary times called for extraordinary princes and extraordinary politics. At such times, politics as usual will not suffice; getting things started or restarted requires something unusual, innovative, revitalizing. "Success attends those who conform to the times." What Hoover did not understand, and Roosevelt did, was that politics as usual had not worked, that the Depression was an extraordinary occurrence, and that people wanted someone to restart—to "reform"—the depressed economy. Hoover thought Roosevelt was without principle ("A chameleon on plaid," he called him), when actually he was simply a better politician who recognized the temper of the times. Roosevelt refused to cooperate with Hoover, not only to keep making Hoover look like the villain, but also because he sensed that the extraordinary new prince needed to act alone on a fresh start not tied to the usual politics of the past and the old and discredited prince. Roosevelt in power quickly gathered to himself virtual dictatorial powers, not because he wanted to be a dictator, but because he knew he had to have extraordinary powers in order to do what was necessary to overcome the Depression. Roosevelt in the flurry of the one hundred days did many things that were ill conceived, hastily applied, and contradictory, but people were willing to forgive the means because of the new hope the New Deal gave them. Machiavelli and Roosevelt both understood that the starting point of any enterprise was crucial. When you set out to do something, getting off to a good start is the most important. When you form a project, or reform what you are doing, you should think hard about the best way to proceed. For example the crucial point of a school year is the first days in which you form your habits of self-rule. You should plan what you are going to do, assert your independence of parents and friends to set your own schedule, study the school and your teachers in order to understand how they think and what they expect, cultivate people who can help you, anticipate what problems might befall you, discipline yourself to work habits, and constantly reevaluate how you are doing.

Suppose that it is midway through your sophomore year. Looking back on your grades, you realize that you are not doing too well. Why? "The teachers all hate me." "My boy/girl friend takes up too much time." "The dorm is too noisy." Nonsense. If you are not inordinately stupid and are willing to look at yourself honestly, you will know what the trouble is. The trouble is your habits of self-rule, or rather your lack of them. So it is time to reform, change your habits, and do better. Like Roosevelt, you have to take extraordinary measures, like studying more and dumping that clinging vine you've been dating, in order to bring about an extraordinary change. In Roosevelt's case, getting off to a good start meant going a long way to curing the Depression, by reforming the way in which things had been done; in your case, it means reforming those habits at the beginning of a school year that will aid your academic success or reforming later to stop those habits that are getting you D's and F's.

ESTABLISHING YOUR RULE

Between the election to the end of the one hundred days, Roosevelt established his rule; he built his reputation and his power by establishing his habits of ruling. First, he kept his own counsel. Nobody knew what he would do, and he was not saying. He built mystery and suspense in regard to his intentions, which as any movie buff knows, makes the climax all the more exciting. Notice also that Roosevelt had as little as possible to do with Hoover, and by doing so, he placed the blame on him. In the campaign, of course, he cast Hoover and the Republican "money changers" as the villains. During the interim and during his rule, he continued to use them as the cause of the current plight. Maybe that was unfair, but it was politic. Remember the play on the old dictum: "When the Great Scorer comes to mark against your name, he'll write not whether you won or lost, but where you placed the blame." Blaming the "people who created this mess" gives one considerable flexibility to end the mess. Hoover and the Crash were to be central to Democratic rhetoric for decades. So Roosevelt spurned Hoover so as to avoid any alliance with or taint of the old prince; Hoover was to be too useful as a symbol to be treated kindly.

Roosevelt also gathered his team around him. He was putting together an administration and therefore wanted people for a variety of political and administrative reasons. Allies and aides have to be more than good administrators; they also have to meet political criteria. Roosevelt's cabinet, for example, included both Democrats and Republicans, the first woman cabinet member, conservatives and liberals, and a geographic mix. All had some political use to him. Too, none of them had presidential ambitions, or were likely prima donnas, and so none of them would upstage or publicly embarrass him. The prince was going to speak with a single voice, and anybody who did not like what he said could go (some did).

But Roosevelt not only recruited political and administrative help. He also sought the help of intelligent people, a collection of advisers on difficult economic and policy matters who came to be called his "brain trust." Because the extraordinary times made new approaches critical, Roosevelt wanted new ideas, no matter how harebrained. So the intellectuals suggested ways of combating the Depression, which Roosevelt either used or did not use, as he saw fit.

As Roosevelt met with his team, they planned what to do first. If the country wanted action, as Roosevelt sensed, the question was not only planning what to do but also deciding what was most important and needed doing first. So they decided on a general agenda with priorities— the banking crisis first, a special session of Congress to consider a set of relief measures, and more far-reaching New Deal programs to follow. Roosevelt won in a landslide and brought with him huge Democratic majorities in the Congress. He had a "mandate" and a Congress willing to do his bidding. But he had been in politics long enough to know that that would not last. He realized that at the start he had to ask for as much as he could before the mystique of the mandate dissipated.

The ensuing whirlwind of action communicated decisive action, setting in motion a wide variety of programs designed to ensure economic security (unemployment compensation) and restore economic prosperity (the agriculture bill). Given the gravity of the situation, Roosevelt was content to institute measures that were contradictory, such as economizing on one part of government spending and going into debt on another. The proliferation of agencies and programs brought overlapping functions and waste. But for Roosevelt the point was to do something and to worry about the problems later.

Roosevelt also was careful to convey his image. He appeared in public as decisive, energetic, upbeat, and on top of things. He had the political initiative in those first days, and he was going to capitalize on it by establishing his rule. He did so through the vigorous and exhausting pace he kept, exhorting others to get to work, reaffirming his confidence in recovery, and assuring everyone that the government cared. His reputation as a leader was established in those days, and no subsequent amount of criticism and debunking could undo it.

President Roosevelt was willing to adjust. Even though a program or policy had been set in motion, to him that did not mean that it was carved in stone. Rather, he was willing to try things and, if they did not work, to try something else. He likened himself to a football quarterback who knows what the next play will be but beyond that, "future plays will depend on how the next one works." Unlike Hoover, who operated from immutable economic premises, FDR developed policy as a political strategy. He saw politics as supply and demand: give people what you think they want, and if they do not want that, give them something else. Adjust policy and change programs as necessary. If a new threat or discontent emerges, meet it with a new experience. Roosevelt's New Deal was guided less by ideology than by politics. When Senator George Norris asked him, "What are you going to say when they ask you the political philosophy behind the TVA [Tennessee Valley Authority]?" "I'll tell them it's neither fish nor fowl," said FDR, "but, whatever it is, it will taste awfully good to the people of the Tennessee Valley." Roosevelt knew that political benefits and political support were inextricably linked, and so he adopted programs and policies with politics in mind.

Roosevelt knew that he could not do everything. Despite the awesome power he wielded and the massive actions he set in motion, he realized that he would be able to accomplish just so much. "I have no expectation of making a hit every time I come to bat," he admitted. He fought for what he wanted but accepted defeats, compromises, and frustrations with grace and wit. He accepted half-victories easily, brokered many administrative and legislative deals, and turned opposition into opportunity. When he was attacked by big business and Republican newspaper magnates (such as William Randolph Hearst), he lashed back with rhetorical flourishes about "money changers" and "the resplendent economic autocracy," proving all the more to the mass of Americans that he was on their side, or as he said of himself: "They loved him for the enemies he had made."

Finally, Roosevelt enjoyed his job. He liked politics for its own sake, enjoying the give and take, the push and pull it involved. He loved being at the center of action, and indeed he liked being the center of attention, as he was a bit of an extroverted ham. He probably would not have liked the closed and conspiratorial politics of an autocracy or totalitarian state, but he did like the open exchange of republican politics. He was not afraid of using power, in both its nice and nasty forms. He could charm legislative leaders over drinks or threaten to fire underlings who resisted him. All in all, Roosevelt dealt with the most serious problems—the Depression and world war—with an aplomb and enthusiasm that kept him fresh and interested in whatever was happening.

This profile of Roosevelt should give you some idea of the characteristics and actions by which Roosevelt established his rule. It might be wise to consider cultivating similar habits in your own life, perhaps at the beginning of the school year. You do not have to imitate the prince in every way, but it might be wise for you—if you wish to be a good student and reap the rewards from doing so—to plan what to do, in what order, seek the aid of intelligent people (for example, take the toughest courses from the best and most challenging professors), adjust and reflect on what you are doing and how well, do what you can but do not fret over failures, and even enjoy and take pride in fulfilling the role of student well. Think of how many fellow students you know who are not successful.

POLITICAL CHARACTER

Franklin D. Roosevelt, then, is an example of someone whose princedom blossomed because he had the right combination of political qualities and political conduct. Practicing power requires the development of political character. Simply put, character is what one is and what one does. Roosevelt had a distinctive political character, whose qualities served him well in political ruling. Much has been written on the qualities that are desirable in a good Prince. There probably is no perfect set of qualities, as it may be desirable to have princes with different traits at different times for different purposes. But we can use Machiavelli and Roosevelt to point to some characteristics that have worked.

What character traits should a prince have? This is that aspect of Machiavellian *virtu* that the prince brings with him or her as part of his or her psychological makeup. "A man's character," wrote Sophocles, "is his fate." This is true in that qualities help or hurt a person in practicing power. What qualities did Roosevelt possess that helped or hurt him? Remember that Roosevelt came into office at a bleak and frightening period. What could be more politically helpful than a leader who was confident, cheerful, hopeful, composed, and energetic? Roosevelt was the antithesis of the cold and distant Hoover. Whereas Hoover appeared as a Scrooge who refused to help the cold and hungry, Roosevelt appeared as a generous town father who understood the people's plight and was eager to help. Perhaps in the long run, Hoover's strict capitalist approach might have worked. But the political occasion called for liberality, and Roosevelt had it. On another occasion, people might want a prince who is stingy but reduces taxes and deficits; but that was not the case in 1932. In two chapters of *The Prince* Machiavelli commented on "praise and blame" and "liberality and stinginess," that "something resembling virtue, if you follow it, may be your ruin, while something else resembling vice will lead, if you follow it, to your security and well-being." As for liberality, "the generosity that earns you that reputation can do you great harm." It is true that government projects in times of economic depression increases taxes and deficits, which may be harmful in the long run. But as economist Maynard Keynes told Roosevelt, "In the long run, we are all dead." What Machiavelli did not consider is that in the short run, liberality was the political quality appropriate for the time.

The same difficulty arises with decisiveness. Machiavelli noted the vice of being indecisive and that "it is well in all deliberations to come at once to the essential point, and not always to remain in a state of indecision and uncertainty." But elsewhere he urged caution rather than decisiveness. The point again is that one quality may be called for at one time, and another called for at another time. In 1932, Hoover seemed weak and indecisive, unsure of what to do and unwilling to do very much. Roosevelt had the quality of decisiveness, and indeed the hundred days "came at once to the essential point," which was to act. But in other circumstances Hoover may have seemed cautious and Roosevelt reckless. Political virtue and political vice depend on whether they are called for by the times.

But whatever the qualities called for, the prince must *seem* to have them. It may be that a prince is not decisive or generous, but if he or she appears so, then in an important political sense he or she will be. "It is good to appear merciful, truthful, humane, sincere, and religious. . . . Everyone sees what you seem to be, few know what you really are," Machiavelli observed, and "the prince should try to avoid anything which makes him hateful or contemptible. . . . What makes the prince contemptible is being considered changeable, trifling, effeminate, cowardly, or indecisive; he should avoid this as a pilot does a reef and make sure that his actions bespeak greatness, courage, seriousness of purpose, and strength. . . . [H]e should maintain such a reputation that nobody will even dream of trying to trick or manage him."

Whatever qualities you may have are important only if other people believe that you have them. Perhaps Hoover was in fact decisive and generous, but he could not or would not communicate that politically; Roosevelt could. Perhaps in fact Roosevelt was not what he seemed. But he quickly established his political reputation and what he actually was or was not became irrelevant. The reputation established his rule and had real political consequences in restoring people's faith in the government.

Many people have decried Machiavelli's apparent advocacy of hypocrisy. But that is not quite the important thing. In order to rule, princes must communicate those qualities demanded by the political situation. If they help them master the situation, it is irrelevant whether they actually are what they claim to be. Suppose that in private, unbeknownst to his public, Roosevelt was a hypocrite, who was not at all what he seemed in public. Nonetheless, the political effect of what he appeared to be was beneficial, whether or not he believed it. Suppose that Hoover actually was what he seemed and therefore was in good faith; Roosevelt actually may have not been what he seemed and therefore was in bad faith. Hoover then was sincere and ethical, but that led to bad political results. Roosevelt then was insincere and unethical, and that led to good political results.

Political reputation is established when princes play political roles. Role playing is how they convey their political qualities. Princes may have to play many roles. Machiavelli used his famous animal metaphor:

"Since a prince must know how to use the character of beasts, he should pick for imitation the fox and the lion." Princes may have to seem to be many things—chief executive, head of state, defender of the faith, commander in chief of the military, manager of the economy, war leader, and so on. It is politically important for them to convey their role as prince. Roosevelt was expert at playing public roles. He could be a fox. (When asked why he dealt with some of the more unsavory machine bosses in his party, he replied, "They may be SOBs, but they're *our* SOBs.") He also could be a lion, lashing out viciously at his Republican opponents. Roosevelt was a complex and accomplished political character, conveying those qualities through role playing that established his reputation and thus rule. He was what Machiavelli called a *virtuoso,* who like the musical virtuoso, could play politics with professional ability.

The other side of the coin of political character is political conduct. To establish your rule, you not only have to be, you have to do. It is not enough to bring the right political characteristics to the practice of power. Establishing rule means that you also have to act. It is not enough to be generous; you also must use power to effect political generosity. It is not enough to be decisive; you also must decide. You may have the appropriate political qualities called for by the times, but if you cannot use them to get things done, they will be useless. Hoover claimed to be generous and decisive, concerned about the massive unemployment and attempting to do something about it; but it was too little, too late. Roosevelt, by contrast, did a great deal very quickly and kept doing it. Hoover was certain of his principles but doubtful about what to do; Roosevelt was uncertain of principles but did not doubt that something had to be done.

Roosevelt's political conduct in the first months of his administration established his rule, and his decisiveness and generosity were demonstrated quickly by what he did. As Machiavelli declared, "Nothing gives a prince more prestige than undertaking great enterprises and setting a splendid example for his people." The New Deal was undertaken as a great enterprise, mobilizing institutions and creating new ones, in order to concentrate effort and enthusiasm for a program of recovery. To that end, Roosevelt developed an agenda: what was to be done, in what order, at what pace, with what scope, and to what end.

An agenda is a recognition that one cannot do everything but that one can do something. The hard part is deciding what needs to be done and how much. Roosevelt's brain trust and his cabinet developed the legislation and executive orders of the hundred days, determined their priority, decided that because the country wanted action that they would ask for a lot very quickly, gauged the scope of their agenda, and developed their short-term and long-range purposes. Like any prince, Roosevelt was dealing with three kinds of agendas: stated, hidden, and fortunate. The stated agenda of the New Deal was to use government action temporarily to relieve suffering and restore prosperity. The hidden agenda, if there was one, was to establish a permanent welfare state and governmental controls that would prevent a future economic collapse. Roosevelt eventually began to say that "government has the final responsibility for the well-being of its citizenship." The fortunate agenda includes the incidental and unsuccessful items and the proper response. In other words, *fortuna* forces items requiring action onto the agenda of politics. The rise of Huey Long, labor unrest, and the recession of 1938 forced Roosevelt to deal with them. But the agenda was completely changed on December 7, 1941, when the Japanese attacked Pearl Harbor. Winning the war took precedence over domestic concerns but, ironically perhaps, ended unemployment and depression!

Like most other princes, Roosevelt developed a style of decision making; that is, he developed ways and means by which decisions were reached on the agenda of the New Deal, and on how they could best be implemented. The trick, of course, is finding a successful style of decision making. Princes have tried many different methods of making decisions: some like conflicting advice, others prefer committee concurrence, and still others decide alone. In any case, the method is not important if the decision-making process uses good political logic, if the right political decision is made at the right political time and achieves the right political result. Roosevelt liked conflicting ideas, multiple sources of information, wide ranging options, all of which he could sort out in his "flypaper" mind. Like Machiavelli, he believed that decisions should be based on information, but he also was interested in more subtle kinds of information than staff reports and statistics. When his wife was to make a tour somewhere, he told her, "Watch the people's faces. Look at the condition of their clothes on the wash line. You can tell a lot from that. Notice their cars." Roosevelt knew that the political logic of decision making was not entirely rational; it had to be supplemented with hunches, guesses, and political instincts.

Decision making involves not only knowing what to decide but also what *not* to decide. Roosevelt knew that there were certain items that he could not include on his political agenda, no matter how he felt about them. So, for example, he never challenged the South's segregation laws. The country was not ready for it, and challenging would have shattered the New Deal coalition, which included the Democratic South. Practicing power includes facing harsh realities and insoluble dilemmas, the evils that you may not be able to undo and the choices that will be unpopular. Roosevelt apparently knew about black treatment in the South and that he was limited in what he could realistically do. Later on, he knew that the war would halt his program of reform but that the spread of Fascism had to be stopped.

Ruling is also choosing, meaning that princes must take risks. Political logic is oriented toward results, which includes taking risks. What are the potential costs and benefits of deciding to do X? Roosevelt knew that there were risks in the legislative assault of the hundred days but that there were greater risks in not doing anything. On the one hand, the New Deal would draw the enmity of the powerful few and might even worsen the class conflict between the few and the many. It might not work, it might backfire by making things worse, it might create resentment by increased taxation, and so on. On the other hand, by doing little or nothing Roosevelt risked being branded as another Hoover and inviting social upheaval. So taking the first risk seemed more politically logical than the latter did. As Machiavelli argued, "No leader should ever suppose he can invariably take the safe course, since all choices involve risks. In the nature of things, you can never try to escape one danger without encountering another; but prudence consists in knowing how to recognize the nature of the different dangers and in accepting the least bad as good." Roosevelt calculated the risks and chose the course that he thought had the best chance of bringing economic recovery and political benefit. This was not only the search for the "lesser evil"; politics is not only the art of the possible but also the art of the approximate. Roosevelt chose those policies that he thought would best approximate what could be done.

Roosevelt was also adept at making and implementing decisions with a clear eye on what effect they had, whether they worked, and what reactions they brought. Roosevelt did not assume that just because he believed that policy X would have effect Y that it would naturally work. That was the mistake that Hoover had made, trusting his preconceptions toward work as a law of nature. Roosevelt probably had that in mind when he remarked that "economic laws are not made by nature. They are made by human beings." Programs that seemed to work were expanded, and those that did not were abandoned or altered. Briefly in the early days of the New Deal, Roosevelt had broad support. But he knew that it could not last and was ready when business and financial figures attacked him and formed right-wing groups such as the Liberty League. Roosevelt anticipated that this hostile reaction would occur and used the groups as whipping boys. This solidified the positive reaction to the hundred days among the many, linking them all the more closely to FDR by raising the fear of a return to Hooverism and rule by the "economic royalists." Roosevelt understood one of the fundamentals of republican political logic: with the support of the many, the hatred of the few can be blunted, despite their power. During the Depression, it was the positive reaction of the many to Roosevelt and the New Deal that prevented revolution, and not the magnates of industry and finance. Roosevelt was adept at anticipating reactions, knowing which positive and hostile reactions to expect, and which to choose for political advantage.

On the whole, Roosevelt became one of the most remarkable political characters of the twentieth century. His reputation survives him, evoking admiration in subsequent presidents as diverse as Lyndon Johnson and Ronald Reagan, as well as among many ordinary people who see him as one of the principal figures of our time. No one could have predicted it in 1932, but the qualities and conduct of political character quickly unfolded in Roosevelt's initial use of power.

PRACTICING POWER: WHAT'S IN IT FOR YOU?

Roosevelt is a prime example of someone who was good at establishing rule and thereby practicing power. Even though what he did may seem remote and awesome, it differs little from what you will have to do in whatever walk of life you choose. The habit of ruling requires discipline, the disciplined application of qualities in action. Your character will come out in how you establish your rule. This may simply be the self-rule you establish at the start of a school year or how you rule others in a business, classroom, or military unit. Like Roosevelt, at first you would be wise to establish your agenda, your style of decision making, what can and cannot be decided, the risks you are willing to take, and what reactions you may expect from what you do. What you do, as student or in a career, involves the art of the approximate no less than in Roosevelt's. Roosevelt's political character was to serve him well. You should hope that you can develop habits of rule half as good.

"Reform if you would preserve."
—Roosevelt

"They loved him for the enemies he made."
—Roosevelt, quoting Andrew Jackson

"A man's character is his fate."
—Sophocles

"Since a prince must know how to use the character of beasts, he should pick for imitation the fox and the lion."
—Machiavelli

"They may be SOB's, but they're *our* SOB's."
—Roosevelt

"Government has the final responsibility for the well-being of its citizenship."
—Roosevelt

Chapter

②⓪

Finding and Using Political Help: Practicing Power with Advisers

In 1610, the Estates-General, the traditional representative body of the French nation, was called by the king for one of its infrequent meetings. A clergyman, the bishop of Luçon, had been selected by the clergy to deliver the traditional address to the throne. Such addresses were sometimes pietistic and laudatory, but not this one. The young bishop made a brilliant survey of current political problems, which was impressive enough for its political intelligence, not always found in clergymen. But the address is of interest to us today for one key passage, in which the bishop drew the king's attention to the singular qualifications of the clergy for helping the king in state matters.

The calling of the priesthood, argued the bishop, made priests peculiarly fit for positions requiring the king's trust. Priests were obliged to acquire knowledge, live by a strict moral code, and govern themselves prudently. But these were also the qualities that the king would desire in those that he wanted to serve state interests. Further, priests were freer than were laypeople from wordly concerns, since they did not marry, had no need to accumulate wealth, and were forbidden to seek earthly rewards and the pleasures of the flesh. Therefore priests could be trusted to serve king and country honorably and effectively.

The brilliant and self-assured bishop did not, of course, mention any names. But it did not escape the royal attention that he clearly had himself in mind. Indeed, the queen-mother began to use him in the byzantine intrigues of royal power that beset France at that time. The bishop acquitted himself well but for years was frustrated in gaining the power that he wanted, and for a while fortune turned against him and he was exiled. But he finally gained the trust and respect of the young King Louis XIII, who used the bishop to mediate in his eternal conflicts with his cunning and powerful mother. For his many services, the bishop was made a cardinal (1622) and finally, at the age of thirty-nine, prime minister, head of the Royal Council (1624). From then until his death in

RICHELIEU: THE KING'S MAN

Armand Jean du Plessis de Richelieu was from birth in delicate health, but sure what he wanted his life to be. His father was a functionary for Henri III, and when the sickly child survived, king and court were entertained at his christening. At the banquet, the child's crib had a streamer with the motto "Armand for the King," dedicating him to the service of the crown. Armand was originally destined for a military career, and his brilliance at his studies augured a future as a career soldier. Early on, his sense of his own superiority and ambition to succeed was evident to all. The motto he chose for a school essay was "who will be my equal?" Disciplined, graceful, with a capacity for hard work and a brittle intelligence, he appears from his teenage years onward to have impressed everyone with his bearing and brains. "He had the intention of all that he did," it was remarked of him; he was determined to exercise authority and power, knew he was good at it, and did it in the political role he carved out for himself, as adviser to the king.

When his elder brother became a monk, Armand was asked by his family to become a priest, because they had the title to the bishopric of Luçon. Armand dutifully did so, realizing that this might be another route to power and influence. He mastered theology and impressed the pope with his intelligence, to the extent that he granted dispensation for Richelieu to become the bishop of Luçon several years before he reached the required canonical age. Richelieu ruled Luçon with the administrative skill and attention to practical problems that were to become his trademark. It was during this period that those aspects of political character that we discussed in the last chapter came to the fore: finesse and ruthlessness, intellectual power, flexibility, thoroughness and seriousness; the development of an agenda (relieving the tax burden of his flock, drawing up a simple catechism), a ruling style of dignity and richness, and a reputation as being intelligent, fair, concerned, and able.

After a decade of intrigue and frustration, in 1624 repetitive Richelieu began to rule France with the intellect and subtle maneuvering that was to serve the monarchy so well. It was Richelieu's resolute and unswerving political goal to make Louis—and the monarchy after him—the master of his kingdom and France a leading power in Europe. When Richelieu took office, there was considerable doubt about both. The monarchy was threatened by various internal groups, unfair taxation, a quarreling royal family, and the ambitions of Spain and other states in the context of the religious split brought about by the Reformation. When Richelieu died, the monarchy was rich and powerful, the internal divisions had been quieted or crushed, and France was preeminent in Europe, a unified nation that was to culminate in the career of Louis XIV, "the Sun King." Louis XIV could say "I am the state" because of the achievements of Richelieu.

Richelieu was a tenant in office at the convenience of Louis XIII. Louis came of age in a turbulent and warring family and was himself unstable and somewhat irresponsible. But he was certainly smart enough to know that if he could not rule effectively, he had found someone, Richelieu, who could. Louis devoted himself more to horses and women than to affairs of state, but he gave Richelieu his wholehearted support, creating a powerful monarchy in spite of himself. Richelieu recognized the political necessity of the relationship, and his political conduct always carefully deferred to Louis and the crown. And he was always grateful to and even affectionate toward Louis, saying of him, "The capacity to permit his ministers to serve him is not the least of qualities in a great King."

Serve him Richelieu did. We associate forever with Richelieu the Machiavellian principle of *raison d'état* (reason of state). Richelieu's fixed purpose was to serve Louis and France, and so every act, every situation, every person, and every institution had to be subordinated to that. Reason of state was his guiding political principle. For example, even though an officer of the Catholic church, he was interested in the French Protestants, called the Huguenots (though only to the extent that they were loyal to Louis), and tolerated their religious differences and protected them from Catholic persecution. Similarly, he backed the German Protestants in their rebellion against the Catholic emperor. The political logic of reason of state carried political considerations above religious principle, in effect supporting religious toleration in exchange for political gains. Like Machiavelli, Richelieu thought that religion had its pragmatic uses for politics, to the extent that it aided purposes of *raison d'etat.*

Richelieu had the reputation of being merciless, but he was so only for political reasons. He believed that the factious state of French society was such that it had to be ruled with an iron hand, and there is no doubt that he did. He drove his old ally the queen mother into exile, executed intriguers and duelists without batting an eye, deposed or executed unruly provincial governors, and besieged a Huguenot stronghold so fiercely that two thousand people starved before it surrendered. "France under Richelieu," one observer has remarked, "had little internal history—the death-rate among the Cardinal's enemies was too high." But if Richelieu's rule was cruel, it was done with an eye to the economy of violence. He enforced the executions of young nobles who dueled, not because he enjoyed it, but because he saw it as a menace to peaceful society and civil government. "The question is," he wrote to Louis, "do you wish to make an end of dueling or of your own power?"

Finally, even though Richelieu was a master political intriguer, he was no hypocrite. He openly admired Machiavelli, wrote of *une vertue male* "Machiavellian *virtu*") in his *Political Testament* and, surprised that no French writer had written a defense of Machiavelli, induced a writer named Machon to do so. He supported autocracy because he thought it was in the national interest, and he played politics for the same reason. "Man is immortal," he told the king, "his salvation is hereafter; the state has no immortality, its salvation is now or never." His maxims of ruling revolve around helping the king to rule and how to use advice: "Secrecy is the first essential in affairs of state." "[I]t is most certain that those who have the greatest gifts are sometimes the least capable of taking advice." "In judging crimes against the state it is essential to banish pity." However, it is experience and not book learning from which good political advice can be gleaned, for "the capacity of counselors does not require a pedantic knowledge: none can be more dangerous in a state than those who will govern kingdoms by the maxims they find in books."

1642, Armand Jean du Plessis, known to us as Cardinal Richelieu, was the effective ruler of France, an adviser who helped his king and country by practicing power.

"Advice is worth exactly what it costs—nothing," goes the folk saying, but nothing could be more untrue. Advice, for one thing, is never free—you pay a price for seeking and accepting help. For another thing, advice is not always worthless. Could you have learned to read English, drive a car, or get through registration without help? Advice is simply some recommendation or information that someone gives you to help you make a decision or take some course of action. An adviser is someone whose knowledge you use to help you get what you want. If you do not know what to know or what to do, it makes sense to seek out someone who does know. It is the wise person and prince who is not afraid of asking for help. No one can rule alone. You have to know what good help is, where to find it, and how to use it. To that end, in this chapter we shall look at political help, in particular at the career of one of the great political advisers, Cardinal Richelieu.

Richelieu is an example of what Machiavelli called "a general and unfailing rule: that a prince who is not shrewd himself cannot get good counseling, unless he just happens to put himself in the hands of a single able man who makes all the decisions and is very knowing." Louis XIII was the classic case of someone smart enough to know that Richelieu had the superior political mind, and so he let him rule. There are many other cases of princes too stupid to listen to smart advisers or princes who think themselves so smart that they do not need advice. But if you are serious about practicing power, you will need help. The question for you then becomes how to recognize and use the Richelieus of your time, but not to let them dominate or mislead you. In other words, if you are going to establish and sustain your rule, you must learn how to use advice and advisers. Or conversely, if you have ambitions of becoming close to the throne, then you will have to learn how to become an adviser and give advice. This chapter will be divided into two points of view: first, that of the prince who wants to get good help and, second, that of the adviser who wants to give good help.

ALL THE KING'S MEN

Machiavelli stressed that "choosing his ministers is a matter of no small importance to a prince, since they will be good or bad, depending on his judgment . . . when they are able and loyal, you may be sure he is wise, because he knew enough to recognize their ability and command their loyalty." Further, "a prince should always take counsel . . . but when *he* wants advice, not when other people want to give it." The problem for the prince, then, is how to get good help and then how to use it. This is not easy, but it is crucial. There are not many Richelieus around, and finding them, recruiting them, and commanding their loyal help is a real political task. It is a sad fact of ruling that your help can hurt you if you do not get the right people and do not use them wisely. There are apparently only limited ways in which they can help you, but unlimited ways in which they can hurt you. So it is important that you organize your rule so that they will help more than hurt.

Suppose that you have just opened a small business, making some "high-tech" piece of electronic equipment. If you are smart, you will try to recruit good help. You will seek out veterans of the industry who can advise you on the basis of their experience. You will recruit the best electronic engineers and technicians you can afford. You want good accountants, administrative help, secretaries. If something is not working right, you will bring in consultants who can identify what is wrong. If someone is not working, you will fire him or her and get somebody else. You will learn whose advice and help is worthwhile and whose is not. You will learn on whom you can rely and on whom you cannot. You will cultivate the former and get rid of the latter. If you find and use good help well, your chances of business success will grow.

If you become a political prince, the problem will be even more difficult. The businessperson who follows bad advice and tolerates bad help may just lose money. But in politics, you can lose your job or even your life by following bad advice, and your state may suffer grievous political losses. If Louis XIII had not followed Richelieu's advice, factionalism may have worsened at home, and Spanish influence in Europe might have increased, both of which might have cost Louis his throne and life and France its independence and power. So how do you determine to whom you should listen?

There are no absolute guidelines, but first you can identify whom not to listen to. Human political experience is replete with examples of princes who came to grief for taking the advice and getting the "help" of fools and scoundrels. So what follows is a brief look at the kinds of people that show up to offer their services but that should be avoided at all costs.

From your point of view on the throne, look out over your court and the administrative apparatus you have set up. Who is working, getting things done, on top of the job, and knows what is going on—and who is not? Among your staff or in the bureaucracy, what do you see? (You had better see.) Do you observe a "happiness-for-lunch-bunch," a group that goes to lunch at 11:30 and returns at 2:00? Do you constantly get a "first thing Monday morning" reply to requests for answers? Do you get the impression that some of your help are time servers, opportunists, political hacks, and downright incompetents? Then it is in your ruling interest to get rid of them, because they are not going to serve you well. They are not interested in your success.

Too, if you have any sense, you will avoid help and advice that is not disinterested. By that we mean avoiding advice from someone who has an emotional stake in the outcome of something or even your success. For this reason, advice from your spouse, family, friends, or relatives is probably bad. They wish you well, and the advice they tender is probably what they think you want; they may then reinforce you in a decision that is disastrous. Seek the advice of someone who does not love you. Certainly don't trust the advice of the self-interested, those who may try to use you for their own interests, such as flatterers and yesmen. Princes have gotten themselves into trouble because they surrounded themselves with people who always agreed with them, stroked their egos, and thought their every idea a brilliant one. But they have gotten into equally as much trouble by heeding moralists and idealists who gave them moral or ideological but not political advice. It is also astonishing to find the extent to which princes have listened to crackpots. Astrologers, holy persons quack doctors, you name it, have been used by princes. One example will suffice. The last czar and czarina of Russia, Nicholas II and Alexandra, were much taken by an itinerant holy man named Rasputin, who said that he had the power to cure their son of hemophilia. His spell over them was such that by 1916 he was practically running the Russian government himself. His appointments were charlatans and crackpots like himself. What they did was so catastrophic that it hastened the 1917 revolution, the rise of the Bolsheviks, and of course the execution of Nicholas and Alexandra. Rasputin "helped" them into loss of throne and life. Political princes are beset by people with harebrained ideas, but with the proper precautions, they can be kept away.

So bad help and advice are always a danger. Your problem as a ruler is not only keeping the bad away but also recognizing and using well the able and loyal. The prince's advisers are to keep you from falling. But where do you find the able and loyal? In your past experience, you have come into contact with people that impressed you and that you trust, and so you recruit them. Or you ask people you trust to recommend people. Or maybe you seek out people with reputations as knowledgeable and experienced in certain matters. The prince's advisers come from a variety of places. Usually rulers develop a working relationship with their advisers through a trial-and-error period. In whatever case, remember Machiavelli's point that the quality of the prince's advisers reflect on the prince: "The first notion one gets of a prince's intelligence comes from the men around him." If they are not wise, this will mean that he is of weak or unformed political character, and you will come away having formed "a poor opinion of the prince, because he made an error in his very first choice." The basis for selecting help and seeking advisers is to find people who are going to give you political intelligence and not reinforce you in your irrational prejudices, feed your ego, appeal to your worst instincts, help you rationalize inaction or failure, while away the hours in idle chatter, or protect you from bad thoughts. They are supposed to help you rule and should be selected and used on that basis.

HOW TO USE THE PRINCE'S ADVISERS

When you come to power, you will have to organize your government. Because you cannot rule alone, you will have to use political and administrative help to aid you in a variety of jobs. Running a government of any size requires many different skills: administrative, military, diplomatic, scientific, and so on. Clearly, you will need several different kinds of talent. But whatever kind of job is to be done— administrative, advisory, liaison—the first principle must be that those who serve, serve on your terms and at your convenience. You are the prince and therefore the boss; it is your job to rule and theirs to help; you have to rule them in order to further your larger purpose of ruling. Think of how many modern princes have gotten themselves into political trouble because they could not put their own house in order. As Machiavelli understood, how much reputation can princes maintain if their underlings criticize them, break from policy, say stupid things, are caught in scandals, leak embarrassing things to the press, join the opposition, and on and on?

It is a common but often fatal mistake of princes to think that because they employ help, their relationship to them should be anything other than political. True, it is normal for you to take an interest in, and like, many of the people who work for you. But that does not mean that you have an obligation to them that overrides or interferes with your task of political rule. The political logic of the prince-and-help relationship is this: you expect them to be loyal to you, but if they become political liabilities, they cannot expect you to be loyal to them. As prince, you must always remember the principle of expendability: all help should be dispensed with when they are no longer useful. To remain loyal to help after they have become a political burden is to invite disaster.

This is not to say that you must treat your advisers like slaves and threaten them daily with the chopping block. Your relationship with aides and staff, cabinets and other kinds of deliberative groups, and political allies is often based on strong attachments, such as friendship and long association. But the fact is that the relationship is political and that because of that they are expendable. You expect them to work, to help you, to be loyal, and they can expect that you will reward them for this, but if they become political trouble, you should abandon them without losing any sleep.

Put yourself back at the helm of that struggling small business. Suppose that you have an old friend who works there and in the past has done good work for you and has drunk beer with you after work. But now he is more trouble than he's worth, drinking on the job, messing up equipment, lowering company morale. If, because he is your friend, you cannot face dealing with him quickly, either straightening him out fast or firing him, then your company and your economic princedom will suffer.

In your relationship with your help, to the extent that you will not exercise power over them—to the point of firing them—they will hold a kind of power over you. At your best, you want to stir feelings in them: affection, because their loyalty derives from that, but also respect and fear. They work for you for a variety of reasons, but if you can inspire them, you can maximize your power over them. If they love you, that is all to the good, but at the least you want to command their respect and fear. As Machiavelli observed, ". . . since men love at their own inclination but can be made to fear at the inclination of the prince, a shrewd prince will lay his foundations on what is under his own control, not on what is controlled by others. He should simply take pains to not be hated. . . ."

However you rule your advisers, your power over them permits you to use political help and advice for your princely purposes. There are many ways you can use such persons. For example, as president or prime minister, you may recruit a cabinet to represent parts of your political coalition. Thus, cabinet officials are selected in part because they represent religious, geographic, ideological, or some other political grouping. You may even have to select someone who is not the most qualified in an administrative sense but who meets certain political qualifications.

But there are many other, often more subtle, uses for your political help. A cabinet officer, for example, may serve as a useful lightning rod to displace political hatred away from you. If you are elected, for example, as an anti-labor union prince, one way to take the heat off yourself might be to appoint an aggressive and outspoken labor minister who thus becomes the object of the labor unions' hatred. President Nixon used Vice-President Spiro Agnew for this general purpose, sending him around the country to speak out against the antiwar demonstrators and to the party faithful, provoking reactions to Agnew by both faithful and demonstrators but freeing Nixon from becoming directly embroiled in the conflict. Nixon no doubt understood this, as Eisenhower, when president, had used him, and others, for the same purpose. During World War II, General Eisenhower asked Marshal Georgi Zhukov of the Soviet Union how the Red Army cleared mine fields. Without batting an eye, Zhukov replied, "We march through them." Eisenhower used Nixon, Dulles, and others to march through his mine fields.

In this regard, Eisenhower appears to have understood better than have most recent American presidents the dispensability of servants. Advisers are functional as long as they are helpful; when there is trouble, failure, or scandal, they may become useful only as fall guys. Taking the blame is the burden of the advisers, not of the prince. When Eisenhower's chief of staff Sherman Adams was implicated in a scandal (he had accepted gifts from a questionable figure), Eisenhower at first demurred, sounded out others' opinion, and then summarily dismissed him. By contrast, Nixon held onto Richard Haldeman and John Ehrlichman much too long; Carter defended Bert Lance too strongly; and Reagan had several people in his administration who hung on long after their political usefulness had gone. When there is trouble, princes should put political distance between themselves and the figure in trouble and should get rid of him or her at the first opportunity. There are plenty of ambitious people out there willing to replace them, and a prince's willingness to fire them serves as an example to others in his or her employ.

At times, you may even want to get rid of several employees at once. Such wholesale firings are called purges and are designed to achieve some political purpose, such as to "shake up" your administration, get rid of cabals and cliques, and prove that you are doing something to rectify a bad situation. We already mentioned how Hitler and other dictators used purges to get rid of potential rivals and possible conspiracies and to convince other powerful backers that they were willing to purge undesirable elements. President Carter purged his cabinet in 1979 after his "crisis of confidence" speech, but other than getting rid of people he thought disloyal or less than competent, the shake up did not have the desired political effect on the many that he had hoped for. On the other hand, a purge can backfire badly. Nixon's famous "Saturday Night Massacre" during the Watergate crisis was a mistake, for it made those fired into heroes. Nixon failed to calculate the political "firestorm" from the purge, and it hastened his fall from power.

There are many other uses of princely advisers—as troubleshooters, spies and shills, liaisons to particular groups or institutions, money raisers, and so on. You have to ride herd over a variety of people doing your bidding in a variety of ways. In some measure your political success will depend on how well they do your bidding and, as we have emphasized, how willing you are to rule those around you. With that in mind, let us point to some ways in which *not* to use the prince's advisers.

HOW NOT TO USE THE PRINCE'S ADVISERS

So far we have stressed that the relationship between you, the prince, and your helpers and allies is political. Since that is the case, your relationship with them is one of power. But remember that power relationships can work both ways. Your advisers may well try to exercise power over you. An aide may try to set your schedule so that you see people that he wants you to; an adviser may urge a course of action by means of a compelling argument; a political ally may argue for a policy that favors her group or industry. They all are using the form of power we termed *influence,* trying to affect how you think and act politically. But remember always that you are the prince and that you do not have to do what they want. You do not have to let them rule you. Let us point to some of the ways that you do not want to use—or be used by—the prince's advisers.

Do not let them lead you. In conference with aides, consultative bodies, or whatever, don't let them talk you into something. One of the striking things about the Watergate tapes detailing conversations between President Nixon and his staff was Nixon's willingness to be led by them, especially Halderman and Ehrlichman. They seemed to maneuver him into positions or courses of actions. Being led means that someone else is telling you what to do (often unbeknownst to you), and that can spell trouble. There are examples of princes who after deciding on something in one political body (say, in a conference with the heads of foreign powers), go home, and have their mind changed by aides, thus infuriating and confusing their allies by reneging on the agreement. If you do not master your help, it can have unfortunate political consequences.

Do not let your advisers lie to you. They are supposed to provide you with political intelligence, bringing rationality to your administration and information to help you decide. If you do not know what is really going on, then you are trying to rule in the dark. If they keep telling you that everything is all right, and it turns out that it is not, you will be the one who is blamed. But it is understandable that if they screw something up, get into trouble, and so on, they will want to keep it from you. It is wise, then, to have spies and informants to keep tabs on what your people are up to. It is also wise to keep reminding yourself that you may indeed want to be lied to and that your advisers are just catering to your own wishful thinking. So they may doctor economic statistics, the body counts of enemy dead, popularity polls, and so on to make you feel good. If you are willing to lie to yourself, you will find plenty of people who will help. But obviously that is insane for ruling. Rulers, like anyone else, hate to face uncomfortable truths. The Nazi air force chief Hermann Goering once reprimanded a Luftwaffe general for telling Hitler that American planes had penetrated German territory, denied "officially" that they were over there, and reported to Hitler that the first reports were wrong. At this point in the war, Hitler wanted to deny reality, and an ally (Goering) wishing to curry favor with the Fuehrer, lied to him.

In this respect, political scientist Irving Janis identified a decision-making malady, a sort of collective self-delusion by prince and advisers that he called *groupthink*. Janis studied various decision-making groups who made truly bad, even insane, decisions—the Bay of Pigs, the invasion of North Korea, the escalation of the Vietnam War, the Iranian hostage rescue mission, Reagan's attempt to reduce Social Security. Why were they so bad? Because, Janis argued, they were decided by cohesive groups who shared the fantasy of their own invulnerability, power, and morality and screened out thoughts of problems or failure. Princes can be seduced as easily by the amiable confidence of such coherent groups as anyone else can and can accept their advice with the assurance of success. So to avoid disasters that flow from groupthink, political princes should establish principles of decision making that encourage criticism, doubts, alternatives, reappraisals, conflicts, debates, and perhaps most of all, facts. If you discover that facts are being withheld or suppressed, it is time to shake up the decision-making apparatus.

Do not let your advisers get too close. Aides, advisers, and allies often will take advantage of your friendship or softheartedness. You will be asked to forgive mistakes, venality, corruption, public embarrassments, and so on, all of which will cost you politically. Even your own family, as Presidents Carter and Reagan can well attest, can become a political liability. After President Warren Harding began to discover the corruption that his pals (the "Ohio Gang") had perpetuated after he had put them in positions of trust, he remarked that it was not his enemies that were giving him trouble, but his friends. Remember Machiavelli's remark about how much one is judged by how one rules one's own house. For that reason, you had better be unforgiving and tough, even with your own family.

Do not let your advisers defy you. If you have aides or allies who disagree with you publicly, ridicule you, or undercut you, don't tolerate it. You can find plenty of talented people who will serve you anonymously and loyally. There are ways you can rein in the defiant. Abraham Lincoln had a cabinet officer who openly defied him. According to the story, Lincoln had him come in to his office, gave him pen and paper, and dictated as he wrote and signed his own letter of resignation. Lincoln then took the letter, put it in his desk drawer, and said "I'll fill in the date." End of problem.

There are many other difficulties that you can have with your help. Basically, your problem is to extract from them good help with a minimum of intolerable problems. Always keep in mind Machiavelli's warning: "When you notice that your minister is thinking more of himself than of you, and that everything he does serves his own interest, a man like this will never make a good minister; you cannot possibly trust him." Above all, see to it that your advisers are serving your political interest and are not doing things in which you, rather than they, are being used.

HOW TO BE A PRINCE'S ADVISER

Let us now take the other point of view, that of the prince's adviser. What do you have to do to become an influential adviser, aide, or ally to a prince? There have been many different ways of becoming a political influence at court, consider, for example, Woodrow Wilson and Colonel House, Madame de Pompadour and Louis XV, Hitler and Martin Bormann, Nixon and Henry Kissinger, James I and the duke of Buckingham. Whatever the relationship, the adviser is powerful because he or she does have influence over how the prince thinks and acts. Cardinal Richelieu was so influential as to be in many ways the prince himself. Let us return to Richelieu for further clues to how to be a princely adviser.

How did Richelieu do it? With care, patience, and persistence. Richelieu demonstrated that gaining power, even in an advisory capacity, takes much effort and much time. But by the time Louis XIII elevated him to power, Richelieu's reputation was established, even among his enemies. Richelieu had something that Louis recognized and needed: political intelligence. Unlike many other princes, Louis was aware of his own limitations, could see the political logic of letting Richelieu rule, and indeed became grateful for Richelieu's successes, as they consolidated his kingdom. Too, Louis was smart enough to follow Machiavelli's dictum that "the prince who wants to keep his minister obedient should think of his welfare, honor him, enrich him, load him with honors and offices." Louis gave Richelieu wealth, pomp, an entourage that traveled with him, offices and benefits he thought fitting for the first minister of France. There was even a measure of affection between prince and counselor, although Richelieu was careful never to let it interfere with his political judgment.

Thus Richelieu consolidated his political position because he did good political work. He seemed to be able to triumph over the political passions of his age—royal-family jealousies, petty palace quarrels, romantic disputes among the nobility, the religious fanaticism of both the Catholic clergy and the Huguenots—through his cold, calculating mind and single-minded sense of purpose. He had a cool head and a clear sense of priority. In one of the early memoranda he sent to Louis he stated, "Physicians hold it for an aphorism that an internal weakness, however small in itself, is more to be feared than an external injury, be it never so large and painful. From this we learn that we must abandon what is to be done abroad until we have done what must be done at home." Richelieu set out on a complicated course of action that eventually dispensed of internal problems and concentrated more and more on increasing French power in Europe. Neither Louis nor his enemies could score him for a lack of success. Indeed, nothing succeeds like success.

Too, unlike the many intriguers against the crown, Richelieu posed no threat to Louis's position. Louis was still king, if sometimes in name only. Richelieu was brilliant in his handling of Louis, always deferential and respectful, careful about titles, and couching every proposal (some already set into motion) as advice. The introductory epistle to his *Political Testament* concludes: "the advice I give to Your Majesty has no purposes beyond the welfare of the state and in particular of yourself, of whom, Sire, I am the ever humble faithful, obedient, devoted and thankful subject and servant." Richelieu was the master of the problem that faces all those who would exercise power in a subordinate political role: how do you use power without seeming to be a threat to that person for whom you exercise power? Richelieu was able to serve without being servile.

Richelieu's standing with Louis was such that the thought of replacing him was impossible. Richelieu's power was enhanced by the fact that for Louis he was indispensable. This does not mean that someone else was not constantly trying to undermine Richelieu's influence with Louis; but at key moments, and with Richelieu's help, Louis would realize that he needed him and back him. Once when the king was ill, he was nursed by the queen mother and the queen, both of whom used the occasion to criticize Richelieu to the bedridden Louis. Realizing this, Richelieu followed Louis to the queen mother's residence and sneaked in on them, saying, "I wager that you are speaking of me." The queen mother was irate, but Richelieu in dramatic gesture fell on his knees at the king's feet! The king retreated to Versailles to consider the matter; Richelieu was summoned, not knowing if he would be deposed in favor of the royal family; but when he knelt, Louis raised him in an emotional gesture. Eventually Richelieu, with Louis's acquiescence, drove the queen mother into exile. Louis had been reminded of Richelieu's indispensability.

Richelieu's power was enhanced because he was successful in becoming the single voice advising Louis. Eventually he undercut all rival or opposition voices and alone had Louis's ear. Most of the time. There were constant and strange threats to Richelieu's power over Louis. Once, for example, the king's conscience was troubled by a confessor who told him that his immortal soul was in trouble because, at Richelieu's direction, he had signed treaties with heretic (Protestant) princes. Richelieu became alarmed that the king's religious scruples might undermine his carefully crafted foreign policy, and so he had the confessor replaced by another who would follow Richelieu's simple instruction: "Do not, I ask you, meddle with matters of state." On another occasion, Louis became infatuated with a handsome and impetuous boy named Henri de Cinq Mars. Richelieu let things alone for a while but after some time became aware through his elaborate secret service that the boy was plotting with the Spanish to murder Louis and make himself monarch! The boy had loosened Richelieu's grip on Louis by means of the king's blind infatuation with him. But Richelieu quietly gathered the damning information on the conspiracy, to be presented to the king only when the cardinal thought that he had enough; anything less would result in his own fall. When Louis and his favorite set out for the battlefront, Richelieu went after them. Even though he was a sick and dying man who had to be carried in a litter, he was not about to let the king out of his grip. Finally, Richelieu acquired a copy of the secret treaty that Cinq Mars and his conspirators had negotiated with the Spanish. The moment had arrived: Richelieu's confidential secretary confronted Louis with the evidence. The conspiracy was broken, the boy executed, and Richelieu's hold on Louis and state policy restored.

Finally, Richelieu was a success as the king's adviser because he was devoted to his job and his master's political interests. He was always on top of things, seeking information, plotting and planning, using people like chess pieces, never resting or relenting in his purpose. When trailing the king in the Cinq Mars episode, he reproached a secretary who had not reported from the king's entourage for a day or two, for neglecting to inform "a person, who, like myself, has a passion for affairs of state." It may seem strange to think of the calculating cardinal as passionate, but his passion was for politics. On his deathbed, he was still urging the king to be firm against the conspirators. He had prepared his *Political Testament* to be used by Louis after his death; he was not going to leave the king and his kingdom to chance even after he was gone. Richelieu's devotion to political duty was complete: he had struggled against great opposition, often at the risk of his life, to make the French monarchy great. He was indifferent to criticism or hatred, once writing, "Those who work for the State should imitate the stars. The dogs bark, but they shine none the less and revolve in their courses."

HELP IS ON THE WAY

In this chapter, we have looked at ruling from two points of view. In either case, what does it mean for you? If you are going to rule, you will have to rule over those people who are supposed to help you. You will have to make sure that they really do help you. Not only must you develop skill at judging and recruiting the kind of talent you want, but you also must ensure that your advisers do what you want. Gathering the right combination of trustworthy ability around you to help you rule is absolutely crucial. You can probably tell that a prince is in great political trouble if his or her help is unruly.

On the other hand, perhaps you would prefer the role of adviser or helper, whose talent is in some more specific job. Many people prefer responsibilities delegated to them by a prince, but not the power that the prince exercises. Very few people are able to match the skill of a Cardinal Richelieu, who developed the role of the powerful adviser to the point of being almost unique. But then, very few of us have the political talent of a Richelieu. One thing is certain: if you run an enterprise and find yourself in trouble and in need of help, you had better hope for, and look for someone of Richelieu's caliber to help you.

"The capacity to permit his ministers to serve him is not the least of qualities in a great King."

—*Richelieu*

"Man is immortal, his salvation is hereafter; the state has no immortality, its salvation is now or never."

—*Richelieu*

"The capacity of counselors does not require a pedantic knowledge: none can be more dangerous in a state than those who will govern kingdoms by the maxims they find in books."

—*Richelieu*

"Choosing his ministers is a matter of no small importance to a prince, since they will be good or bad, depending on his judgment ... when they are able and loyal, you may be sure he is wise, because he knew enough to recognize their ability and command their loyalty."

—*Machiavelli*

"A prince who is not shrewd himself cannot get good counseling, unless he just happens to put himself in the hands of a single able man who makes all the decisions and is very knowing."

—*Machiavelli*

"Those who work for the state should imitate the stars. The dogs bark, but they shine none the less and revolve in their courses."

—*Richelieu*

"Do not behave like a wet hen."
—*Father Joseph, to Richelieu during the Spanish invasion, 1636*

Chapter

21

How Do You Rule Through the Few?

In the first book of the Greek philosopher Plato's *Republic,* there is a famous and still relevant debate. Socrates, who was the subject of Plato's dialogues, was discussing the question of justice, when he was interrupted by Thrasymachus, who insisted that Socrates was on the wrong track:

> "Listen, then," Thrasymachus began. "What I say is that 'just' or 'right' means nothing but what is to the interest of the stronger party ... in every case the laws are made by the ruling party in its own interest; a democracy makes democratic laws, a despot autocratic ones, and so on. By making these laws they define as 'right' for their subjects whatever is for their own interest, and they call anyone who breaks them a 'wrong-doer' and punish him accordingly. That is what I mean: in all states alike 'right' has the same meaning, namely what is for the interest of the party established in power, and that is the strongest. So the sound conclusion is that what is 'right' is the same everywhere: the interest of the stronger party."

Socrates spent the rest of the first book refuting Thrasymachus, but not to everyone's satisfaction. For many people since have thought that Thrasymachus and Socrates were arguing at cross-purposes. Thrasymachus was stating what in fact is the case, and Socrates was stating what should be the case. Socrates was interested in the value of political justice; Thrasymachus was looking at the empirical fact of how power defined and used justice. Socrates was in the normative tradition of trying to discover political values; Thrasymachus was in the Machiavellian tradition of trying to discover political facts. The two perspectives are related, although they often do not know it.

Suppose that you belong to an old, conservative family that is traditional and stubborn in its views. You and others of the younger generation would like to be given money to go to college or buy a house and so forth. But all the money is controlled by, say, a grandparent or a maiden aunt who is very stingy with it and will not give you any to help you go to school. When you ask why, you are told that it would not be "right" for them to do so. Some reason is given: they earned it, you would misuse it, it is bad for your character to be given help. Perhaps you do not think it just that they have all that money and will not use it to help a younger relative. But you are not the "stronger party" and cannot define what "right" is because you do not have the power to do so. Somebody else's definition of what is just prevails. More importantly, you do not get the money. That is what Thrasymachus meant: whatever true justice is, justice in fact is linked to powers. Grandma or Aunt Martha has the power to say what is just and thus to control who gets the money.

Thrasymachus and Grandma return us to that universal political tension of which Machiavelli spoke: the conflict between the few and the many, or what today we call the elite and the masses. This conflict has taken many forms in many different places and is not confined to the Marxist kind of conflict among economic classes. There are many kinds of "haves" and "have nots" and different outcomes to such conflicts. But conflict there is, and dealing with it is one of the toughest problems for politicians practicing power. Their solution may be just or unjust, depending on how they do it and what you think is just, but it is not an easy task. The conflict between the few and the many can, after all, result in anarchy and revolution, a diseconomy of violence, at least for a while.

The political question for practicing power is, as always: Who benefits? Who gets the welfare values? Who gets the deference values? The "justice" of it becomes political because power is instrumental in deciding who gets what. Suppose that you marry into a family like the one described above. You become the "leader" of it when its numbers turn to you for leadership. You know something of the structure of authority in the family, their values, finances, and desires. You know there are disruptive conflicts. So how do you deal with them?

If you are going to rule the family, you cannot escape the fact of the power of the few. But you also know that disruption and revolt are possible among the many. So essentially you have three political choices: you can side with the few, you can side with the many, or you can try to balance them off. There are advantages and disadvantages to all three. In your mythical family, siding with the few has the advantage of gaining the confidence of those who already have power; siding with the many has the advantage of the support of most of those in the family; and balancing has the advantage of trying to keep in the good graces of both sides. On the other hand, all these ruling strategies have political disadvantages: siding with one side is liable to gain the enmity of the other, and balancing can gain the enmity of both. Our point is simple: any human group, be it family or state, is likely to be divided along the lines of the few and the many. Your political problem then comes to be how you use the few and the many to rule.

The problem, in general terms, is one of political support. If you are going to rule, you are going to have to decide whose support is crucial, even indispensable. Perhaps you are genuinely committed to helping the many and achieving just benefits along the lines of "the greatest good for the greatest number." But the political fact may be that that admirable goal is affected by the power of the few. In any case, one ruling strategy common to autocracies, totalitarian states, and even republics is to rule through the few. How you gain their support, who they are, and how you can use them to rule are the subjects of this chapter.

POWER BASES OF THE FEW

Before we look specifically at the career of Bismarck and the German elite, let us acquaint you with the nature of elites by looking at the American elite. Recall our discussion (Chapter 4) of what people want out of life: welfare values and deference values. Everybody, we contend, wants these things more or less. This means that the few (elites) want them and that the many (masses) want them too. We can term these groupings as *welfare elites* and *deference elites* among the few, and *welfare masses* and *deference masses* among the many. Whatever strategy you think wise in ruling, you should understand both sets of political, economic, and social groups. In the next chapter we shall look at the many. Here let us look at the American few.

Typical welfare values include well-being, wealth, enlightenment, and skill. In the United States, this means that the rulers—presidents in particular—must take into account the power of various welfare institutions that control welfare values. The few—the political strata of American society with the most power—influence the practice of power because they control how those values are defined and put into practice. Well-being includes the desire for health and safety, but American medical, police, and military establishments control the political agenda as to how well-being is implemented. No matter what you may think about private medicine or nuclear weapons, these establishments have power over policy. The American masses may or may not share the elite definition of how well-being should be furthered, but if you are going to rule, you will have to take into account such establishments.

Or consider wealth. Whatever you may think about the distribution of income in America, it is a fact that the wealthy few have a great deal of power, and so you will have to contend with them as a fact of established power. Similarly, the intellectual establishment (the value of enlightenment)—the media institutions and their spokespersons, leading universities and intellectuals, newspaper columnists like the late Walter Lippmann—are the few who hold the power of ideas. However unreasonable their ideas may seem, they have great influence over what is done. Another welfare value is skill, which in America is established in the technocratic institutions, engineering, space, electronic, and so on. By having such power over technology as we deem necessary (such as nuclear power plants), political rulers need their help and depend on their technical advice in decisions.

The power bases of American deference elites resides in identifiable institutions and circles. A key deference value is respect, by which elites from old upper-class families are accorded status or honor and may be more likely to be recruited for leadership positions (for example, the Roosevelts). But respect may not be so powerful as affection, especially because someone famous drawn from the celebrity establishment has power over opinion (à la Reagan or Jane Fonda). Lastly, a deference value of import is rectitude, which in America resides in large degree in religious institutions and leaders, who have power because they are the guardians of morality.

If you were to practice power in America, the structure of established power among the few would be both a problem and an opportunity. The few are a problem because they may try to prevent you from doing what you want to do (for them or the many). On the other hand, they are an opportunity because they can give you support and help you do what you want to do, again either for them or the many. Elites can prevent you from doing what you think is politically wise, but they can help you by sponsoring or supporting what you want to do; or they can help you by acquiescing and adapting to what you are doing. But they must be won over before you can do anything. You may have to rule through the few in spite of themselves. It is a curious and recurrent fact that often the few do not see what is in their own interests and oppose political actions designed to keep them in power. Czar Nicholas II and the Russian aristocracy opposed reform measures that might have saved them, and as we discussed in Chapter 18, Roosevelt's New Deal may well have saved the American wealthy who were so adamantly opposed to it.

Elites mediate change. Because of their powerful position in any society, they have the most to say about what is to be done. Perhaps the problem in ruling through the few is to convince them to use that power to cope. Elites may be divided, complacent, arrogant, shortsighted, and not very bright. They are not necessarily on top because they are intelligent, unified, benevolent, or prescient. The American elite, for example, is an elite for a variety of reasons, including inherited wealth, nepotism, political connections, beauty, fame, and so forth, all of which do not necessarily make it politically astute. But because you have to deal with the Machiavellian universe of constant change, you will have to win over the political elites in order to do what needs to be done. Let us now look at the career of someone who successfully did rule through, and in spite of, a rather stupid and hidebound elite.

THE GERMAN ELITE AND BISMARCK

Prussia was a minor German state that began to emerge in European politics in the eighteenth century. It was ruled by the autocratic Hohenzolleren kings, who eventually gained control over the landed aristocracy, the *Junkers,* and developed an efficient civil service and army. But the outlook of the Prussian elite was feudal and despotic, and they resisted the Enlightenment tides of revolution and liberal democracy. Into the nineteenth century, there was no unified Germany, only a loose and warring confederation of petty states, constantly shifting their allegiance between Austria and Prussia. Despite the ever-growing Prussian military and industrial power, the caution and stupidity of the Hohenzolleren kings was such that despite the advent of German nationalism, there still was no German state as such.

Too, the Prussian elite did not understand the political tides of the nineteenth century. With the growth of the industrial elites (such as the Krupp family) came a new middle class with liberal ideas about parliaments and constitutions and an expanding working class with notions of a welfare state an even socialism (Karl Marx, remember, was a German). But the Prussian elite was incapable of dealing with these great changes, and their response to the revolutionary upheavals of 1848 was increasingly reactionary. Given their feudal and conservative outlook, they generally did not have the political perspicacity to mediate change by taking advantage of political opportunities, providing a political role for the key elements of both the few and the many by sweeping them up in a movement of German unification and nationalism. Such a far-reaching grab for power and German leadership was beyond the imagination of the Prussian elite.

But it was not beyond the imagination of one of their numbers, a member of the Junker-landed nobility, Otto von Bismarck. In his long career as the minister-president of Prussia, he helped bring Prussia, and eventually the German Empire, to power in Europe and as a society into the modern world, at least in terms of the society and culture of Germany. He helped adapt the welfare an deference values of the Prussian and then the German elite to the changes of the nineteenth century, for eventual good or ill. He strengthened the power of the German army, which was to emerge from the nineteenth century as the unparalleled defender of the national well-being of the fatherland. He increased the wealth and skill needed for national power and tried to create a German national identity. He accorded respect for the established institutions, the monarchy, the Junkers, and the army, and at least during the famous *Kulturkampf* ("cultural battle"), tried to give a Lutheran stamp of rectitude to the new German state. Although he never gained much affection for himself, through his political successes he did increase the degree of nationalist affection that people associated with the agents of Prussian success, the monarchy and the army.

How did Bismarck do it? How did he transform an obscure and feudalistic kingdom into a world power? He did it by ruling through the few. The Prussian many were not a viable political force, and of course the German many did not exist as part of a unified nation. Too, the hierarchical class structure and beliefs of Prussia would not permit republican participation by the many. So if Prussia were to become the unifying force that would create a powerful Germany, it would have to

OTTO VON BISMARCK: ELITE MEDIATOR

Most observers of Bismarck readily admit that he was one of the great politicians of all time, but they also agree that he was not a nice person. Although from a very different culture, time, and enterprise, Bismarck, if pressed, might have agreed with the statement of American baseball manager Leo Durocher when someone remarked to him that, at least, the losing manager was a nice guy: "Nice guys finish last," replied Durocher. Bismarck did not see himself or Prussia as a nice guy, and he was not about to finish last in what he called "the chess game of politics." Born into the ruling elite, he had a barely concealed contempt for the monarch and ruling class he served so well and a very high opinion, no doubt somewhat justified, of his own political talents, so sadly lacking in his peers. His conversation, memoirs, and letters reveal his arrogance and self-confidence. "Politics is less a science than an art. It is a subject that cannot be taught, one has to have the gift," he said, not adding that he thought that he himself indeed had the gift, with which many of his contemporaries might grudgingly agree. His attitude toward the Prussian few and his famous opportunism are revealed in his famous statement: "Because they have yet scarcely outgrown the political nursery, the Germans cannot accustom themselves to see politics as a study of the possible." The Junker mind was still in the feudal past, he thought, and even though he was a Junker, "... I would have to be blind or imbecile not to see things as they really are."

Bismarck's practice of power was guided by the political principle of *Realpolitick,* the idea of the pursuit of state power above all other considerations. Bismarck thought that a leader like himself had a responsibility to state interests that enjoined the practice of the "politics of reality." He once scolded his kaiser, Wilhelm I, for imprudent remarks to a foreigner, forbidden, he thought, "on account of *raison d'état.*" Although he had a mean streak, when it came to calculated policy, he had no peer. He was always cautious and moderate, realizing the limits of what he could do in both foreign and domestic policy and able to play off different interests until he could figure out his next move on behalf of the German Empire. After the defeat of Austria in 1866, he convinced the kaiser and army not to punish Austria severely, as he was already plotting his next move against France and needed a strong and agreeable Austria on his side. He was quite willing to use war as an instrument of policy, but only as a last resort and with the probability of economical results. Bismarck was the statesman who said that the great political questions are settled by "blood and iron," but he also condemned "romanticism," arguing that "it is unworthy of a great state to fight for something which does not affect its own interest ... woe to any statesman who ... fails to find a cause of war which will stand up to scrutiny once the fighting is over."

Bismarck came to be called the "Iron Chancellor" (who died, as some wag noted, of hardening of the arteries), but he was often less than that. The constant pressures of power often caused him fits of nerves and temper, orgies of eating and drinking, and periods in which he would leave Berlin to brood on the folly of all human effort. He was genuinely moved by the carnage he witnessed in the wake of the war with Austria and was quite sincere in his traditionalist social and religious convictions. He believed firmly that Germany could be unified and wield power only through the powerful and established few. Yet his quest for that goal shows his pragmatism. Despite his public contempt (done because it was politically useful) for parliamentarians, liberals, socialists, and Catholics, he made deals with all of them, sometimes gained their support, and even gave them what they wanted. In other words, the effect of what he did for the political necessities of a situation made him the ally of those elites who in principle he despised. He was not one to, as he said, "tie one hand behind our back on principle."

He was so devoted to his political task that his skill and achievements still dazzle. But it was not without its price. He gave new force to the Prussian habit of extraconstitutional and even illegal acts taken by authority, which weakened the legal and parliamentary forces in the German Reich after Bismarck, and of course was practiced by the Nazi totalitarian state. Bismarck would probably have thought the Nazis thugs; yet he too was capable of some rather repressive acts. He collected taxes illegally, suppressed hostile newspapers, indicted opponents, expelled the Jesuits from Germany, banned the Social Democratic party, and hectored his opponents. He had to deal with a hostile parliament that opposed him at every turn, and he once remarked, "A statesman wise in constitutional matters has said that all constitutional life is always a series of compromises. If compromise is made impossible . . . the series of compromises is broken and is replaced with conflicts. Since the life of a state cannot stand still, conflicts become questions of power; whoever has the power in his hands then proceeds according to his will." Many others, including Richard Nixon, have defended the right of rulers to use extraordinary power when it is deemed necessary, but with Bismarck it was a habit rather than an exception.

Despite his power and achievements, Bismarck never was popular and made many enemies during his long rule. But many, and certainly the kaiser, saw him as indispensable and even infallible. He knew better, once commenting, "This trade teaches us that one can be as clever as the cleverest in the world and still at any moment find oneself walking like a child in the dark." And his dispensability was clear enough when in 1890 Wilhelm II commanded him to resign. In retirement, the bitter Bismarck stated that in drawing up the Constitution of 1871, he gave too much power to the crown and not enough to Parliament! After he died, the new and unstable kaiser flaunted the power that Bismarck had built for the German Reich and helped the world blunder into World War I. Wilhelm II lacked the political skill of Bismarck and, like many other arrogant and stupid monarchs, knew nothing and learned nothing. He certainly had not studied history, as Bismarck had. "For me," said the Iron Chancellor, "history existed primarily to be learned from. Even if the events do not repeat themselves, at least circumstances and characters do."

---

be done through the few—the monarchy, the army, the civil service, the Junkers, and the few political activists, such as Catholics, liberals, and socialists. Bismarck was able to do it through brilliant political maneuvering that appealed to various welfare and deference values that benefited various elites (and the groups they represented) at different times. Whatever Bismarck believed in, he was willing to forget it at the time that he needed to achieve a political result.

Let us look at a few examples of Bismarck in action. The first major question facing Bismarck was how to dominate the German Confederation—the loose coalition of all the petty German states of central Europe—rather than Austria. Bismarck concealed his real intentions while doing everything to undercut Austrian influence in the confederation. He opposed all Austrian efforts to reform it to benefit them and talked Wilhelm I out of attending a congress of princes called by Austria, thus wrecking the idea. He prevented Austria from joining the German Customs Union and quarreled with them over a hundred different issues. Finally, he provoked them into war when he felt that the time was ripe to defeat them, which was after he signed a secret treaty with the Italians. The Austrians then had to commit a large portion of their troops to fight the Italians, and the expanded and efficient Prussian army decisively defeated them.

But Bismarck was not through. He refused to let the kaiser or the army punish the Austrians, since he had use for them in the future. What he wanted was control of the German confederation, to be run by Prussia. He concluded secret treaties with southern German states such as Bavaria to prevent Austrian control of them, thus breaking the peace treaty he had negotiated with the Austrians even before it was signed. This, along with the acquisition of Schleswig-Holstein, became the basis for the German Reich. The Prussian parliament, with whom Bismarck had feuded, was so impressed that they voted to legalize all of the Bismarck's formerly illegal taxations and expenditures and in addition gave him a large cash gift.

Then Bismarck turned his attention to France, who expected to be compensated for its neutrality and mediation during the Austrian war and peace. Bismarck had previously hinted that Prussia would not mind if France took Belgium and Luxembourg, but now he hesitated. Alarmed by the country's rise, the French press and public became ardently anti-German. During a complicated dispute over the Spanish succession, Wilhelm withdrew the Hohenzollern candidate, but the French overplayed their hand, demanding that the kaiser publicly declare that he would interfere no more and in effect submit to French will. The ambassador who delivered this message to the vacationing Wilhelm irritated him, and he cabled Bismarck that the facts of this last exchange should be made public. Bismarck, sensing the occasion, edited the telegram to make it seem that Wilhelm had snubbed the French ambassador and that the ambassador had provoked trouble. He then released it to the German press and to all European chanceries, where it quickly made its way into the French press. The alleged snub inflamed French public opinion, and the alleged provocation stirred German public opinion. Quickly Bismarck had what he wanted: a showdown with the French. Germany went on to win the Franco-Prussian war, gain Alsace-Lorraine, a billion-dollar indemnity, and become the leading power in Europe. All this in less than ten years!

In all this, note that Bismarck was using elite actors and institutions for his political purposes and that the German monarch was maneuvered into doing what Bismarck wanted, even though he was formally his superior. But Bismarck could not rule without the kaiser, and so he had to rule through him, by keeping his confidence, convincing him that Bismarck knew what he was doing, catering to his ego and status, and most of all by succeeding. With the support of the kaiser, Bismarck could cajole or bully other elite actors into doing what he wanted. It was difficult to attack Bismarck as long as the kaiser backed him and he was successful. When the old kaiser died, Bismarck could not get the full support of his son, Wilhelm II, and Bismarck was dismissed, much to the dismay, by that time, of the political elites of other countries, who saw Bismarck as a stabilizing and wise political force and the youthful kaiser as impulsive and overconfident.

This was so because after the buildup of German power, Bismarck pursued a policy of maintaining peace abroad and creating a German society at home. He was always aware of the limits of power and had no dreams of world empire, unlike Wilhelm II and Hitler after him. Bismarck saw clearly the limits of German power if the other European states—England, France, and Russia—united against Germany. So Bismarck worked successfully to make the most of Germany's gains and to prevent such a foreign coalition from forming against Germany. A policy of peace, then, was in Germany's interest, a political and not a moral calculation, to be achieved by Bismarck's favorite political method: divide and rule.

Similarly, Bismarck ruled at home by playing off elite actors and forces against one another, making alliances with one group at one time and then with another at another time. He had the support of the liberals in Parliament for his moves against Catholicism. But after he concluded an alliance with Catholic Austria, he abandoned the anti-Catholic measures, made a coalition with the Catholic party, and opposed the liberals. He opposed the Social Democrats and socialism but in the famous "revolution from the top" granted workers practically every measure that the socialists favored: accident and illness insurance, old-age pensions, medical and hospital services—the whole gamut of "welfare state" measures. He did this to buy off the growing Social Democratic vote, by undercutting their leadership.

Much of Bismarck's domestic program exemplifies the elite mediation of change. Bismarck recognized the growth of liberal and socialist ideas espoused by the new elites as a threat to Prussian, militaristic, and industrial notions of social organization. For good or ill, he sponsored measures that directed or undercut political change. He remolded the liberals into a probusiness party (they opposed his welfare state measures as interfering in free enterprise), made his peace with the Catholics, and fought the socialists through antisocialist laws and the welfare state. He appealed to a variety of welfare and deference values when they served his political goals and made and unmade coalitions with elites in like fashion.

THE POLITICAL STRATEGY OF ELITISM

Bismarck tells us much about the political strategy of elitism, ruling through the few. Elitism is most feasible in societies in which deference values include respect for authority and hierarchy. That is, some societies have established elites and institutions that are accorded high respect, rectitude, and affection. An autocratic monarch, for example, rules because he or she commands authority as the vested and established power at the top of the political and social hierarchy. An aristocracy claims to have a right to rule because of its superior status. An established church supports the authority of monach and aristocracy by teaching deference values such as obedience. In such societies, elites rule by virtue of their position. But this does not mean that they will rule well.

Established elites often make political mistakes that prevent them from ruling well. Often the elites become isolated and insensitive. Monarchs, prime ministers, or presidents can become so protected and separated from common life as to not know, or care, how bad off the people are. The many may resent rulers who do not seem to understand their plight. Perhaps Marie Antoinette did not actually say "Let them eat cake" in response to a crowd's call for bread, but the people believed she did, and that sort of insensitivity to suffering damages the reputation of an elite (in her case, it eventually did more than damage her reputation—she was guillotined during the French Revolution). Nothing does more to weaken the position of an established elite more than to be seen (by other elites or the many) as irresponsible and self-serving. For example, if tax laws written by an elite favor the rich few at the expense of the many, the elite is asking for trouble.

If you are going to rule through the few, like Bismarck, it is helpful to cultivate in the few some sense of their responsibility to rule well. Their claim that they have a right to rule must be supplemented with what is called *noblesse oblige,* an obligation for noble rulings, to be sensitive, caring, and responsible; to serve the public interest (the interests of both the few and the many); and, above all, to practice politics skillfully. The few can sustain their claim to the right to rule only by keeping their reputation, and that is maintained by means of political sensitivity and success. Take again the example of taxes. If an elite has the foresight to write tax laws that are "progressive"—that is, that tax the wealthier more than the common people—its reputation among the people, and thus their popular support, will help sustain it as an established elite.

The Prussian Hohenzollern kings, and indeed Bismarck himself, were unlikely candidates for a responsible and politically astute political elite in fast-changing nineteenth-century Europe. The Hohenzollerens, including Frederick the Great, were not in the forefront of enlightened despotism, and the Junkers had traditionally been a narrow-minded, reactionary, and stuffy class, jealous of their privileges and fearful of change. But remember that there is a difference between preventing change and mediating change. The monarchy and landed aristocracy of Prussia attempted to prevent change and even to undo change. But a ruling class, as Bismarck understood, cannot sustain itself forever if it does not adapt. So by his power over the few, he undertook to transform them into a responsible and effective political elite, taking them out of the parochial and feudalistic perspective of Prussia into ruling a modern and powerful state and empire.

Think what might have happened if there had been no Bismarck to serve monarch and state but, rather, a series of the more typical bloodless and unimaginative chancellors. There might have been no Germany, or perhaps a very different Germany; Austria might have become the dominant power in central Europe; and Prussia might have remained an obscure petty state. But Bismarck in a sense forced Prussia and Wilhelm I to be great, adapting to many of the social and economic changes of the times and sponsoring change (such as the welfare-state measures) instead of falling before a revolutionary elite (the socialists) who might have swept them from power. Bismarck understood the obligation for noble ruling, and the German elite was sustained in power, and German power and values were advanced beyond their wildest dreams.

Noblesse oblige, the obligation for noble ruling, is the political logic of elitism. An elite cannot justify its rule solely on the basis of its superior birth, status, wealth, or whatever. It certainly cannot demand obedience and privilege simply by existing. Bismarck understood and practiced elite ruling, making the elite give leadership and political success to state and society, providing a uniform direction to what became German society and offering power and wealth to the new German national state. The Bismarckian elite functioned by advancing the welfare and deference values of the German many, which, not incidentally, promoted the interests of the few of the ruling classes. The Hohenzollerns, Bismarck, the Junkers, the military, and industry all were er powered and enriched by the unification and modernization of Germany, but Bismarck's success had so impressed both the few and the many that no one begrudged them the welfare and deference values they accrued.

The career of Bismarck illustrates that for elite ruling in politics nothing succeeds like political success. After Wilhelm II dismissed Bismarck in 1890, the elite rule deteriorated. Wilhelm was not a good politician, being unstable, temperamental, and impulsive. The fear of German power that he flaunted so readily led to political coalitions against him, an arms race, and eventually the idiocy of World War I, which discredited and brought down forever the House of Hohenzollern, Junker rule, and many of the traditional features that had stabilized the changing society. Wilhelm II seemed to symbolize for the growing Social Democratic movement in Germany what Machiavelli warned against; "... the haughty manners and insolence of the nobles and the rich [which] excite in the breasts of those who have neither birth nor wealth, not only the desire to possess them, but also the wish to revenge themselves by depriving the former of those riches and honors which they see them employ so badly." Political elitism is as political elitism does, and if it does not—as Wilhelm II did not—then political populism, the rule of the many, will.

SO IS THRASYMACHUS RIGHT OR WRONG?

Thrasymachus, you will recall, observed that rule was selfish, that "right" was defined by might, and that power was exercised "for the interest of the party established in power." Bismarck's career shows that Thrasymachus was right in one sense and wrong in another. He was right that elites rule with their own interests in mind (remember the Iron Law of Oligarchy that we talked about in Chapter 13) and that they enjoy the benefits of political power and privilege. However, an elite that rules only in its own interest is inviting trouble and may contain, as did the French and Russian monarchies, the seeds of its own destruction. The few can justify their rule as right by virtue of their political success. But simply being the strongest party will not be enough if the elite cannot rule. Might ceases to be mighty, and claims to right collapse, as they did for Wilhelm II in 1918.

What Machiavelli and Bismarck recognized was that the rule of the few could not be separated from the many. Thrasymachus noted that the "strongest party" could include a democracy, the rule of the many. But for Machiavelli, the few and the many were a dialectic, in which power resides in both parties and from which much political tension arises over who gets what and who rules for whom. Machiavelli discussed this extensively in *The Prince,* Chapter 9, in which he argued that a prince, even though his orientation was toward elitism, must rule with the interests of more than his own few in mind. Bismarck did just that, giving form to the latent German nationalism among the many and benefits in the form of the welfare measures he enacted. The prince's political problem includes ruling both the few and the many. The prince is the one who has to be the "stronger party," as the success of Bismarck and the failure of Wilhelm II remind us. Remember the Machiavellian argument, that if you choose to rule through the few of the many, the interests of nobody will be preserved or advanced unless you practice power and practice it well.

"So the sound conclusion is that what is 'right' is the same everywhere: the interest of the stronger party."

—*Thrasymachus*

"Since the life of a state cannot stand still, conflicts become questions of power; whoever has the power in his hands then proceeds according to his will."

—*Bismarck*

"I listen for God's footfall, and seize the hem of his garment as it brushes by invisibly."

—*Bismarck*

"It is unworthy of a great state to fight for something which does not affect its own interest."

—*Bismarck*

"One conclusion only can be drawn: the prince must have people well disposed toward him; otherwise in times of adversity there's no hope."

—*Machiavelli*

"Nice guys finish last."

—*Leo Durocher*

Chapter

22

How Do You Rule Through the Many?

The inauguration in 1829 of Andrew Jackson as president of the United States remains one of the classic expressions of the bond between the many and their princely champion. The Washington aristocracy was aghast at the sight of the unseemly and unruly crowd that descended on the capital, pushing and shoving to get close to their hero. Many thousands of people—frontiersmen in buckskin, workingmen, ordinary folk clearly not part of the elite—pushed up the Capitol steps close to the portico where General Jackson was to take the oath of office. When Old Hickory appeared, the throng cheered madly. After he took the oath and gave a short speech, cannons were fired and the mob closed in on the new president. It was with the greatest difficulty that he pushed his way through the friendly crowd to a waiting carriage. At the White House, the doors were opened for the new president to meet the people informally, but an immense crowd appeared, according to one observer, of "all sorts of people, from the highest and most polished, down to the most vulgar and gross in the nation." The crush became so great again that Jackson finally had to retreat to his hotel. The crowd then turned its attention to the great quantities of food and drink provided, in the

ANDREW JACKSON: POPULAR PRINCE

In the movie *The Alamo,* one of the coonskin-hatted Tennessee volunteers defending the Alamo responds to an alleged demand for surrender from Mexican commander Santa Anna by indignantly asking, "Who do he think he am? Andy By God Jackson?" The affection and awe in which Americans held Andrew Jackson was noted by foreign observers of the time. By the time Jackson became president (at age sixty), he was already a national legend—the soldier boy of the Revolutionary War who had been wounded by a British officer, the self-made aristocrat of the Tennessee frontier, the fiery-tempered gambler, the duelist who had killed a man in a duel and carried a bullet in his body from another, but most of all the military hero of the Battle of New Orleans in the War of 1812 and the Indian campaigns. As president he seemed to be the personification of the new American democratic society and national aspirations.

He was also, by all accounts, an imposing figure who commanded fear and respect. Tall, straight, with deep-blue eyes and a piercing stare, he had a temper that he used for full effect. "No man," wrote a contemporary, "knew better than Andrew Jackson when to get into a passion and when not." Jackson's public character included great presence: when people saw him, they would cheer and applaud. He had the same effect on the few. When he reached New Orleans to defend it against the British, he was invited by the Creole elite to an elegant party in his honor. He appered in a uniform of blue cloth and yellow buckskin, as befit a man of authority and power. He charmed the Creole ladies with his manners and reassured the men that New Orleans would be safe now that Andrew Jackson was in command. As he left, the Creole ladies buzzed to the hostess, "Is this your backwoodsman? Why, madam, he is a prince!"

Although Jackson was always a popular leader, he was not liked by powerful figures and indeed was much vilified in his campaigns for office and by opponents of his policies. He was especially vulnerable because he had had to marry his wife Rachel twice. His opponents circulated "coffin handbills" to the effect that Jackson was an adulterer and a home wrecker, that his mother was a prostitute, that he was the son of a mulatto, and was guilty of various other crimes such as dueling, drunkenness, and cockfighting. Jackson had to develop a thick hide in politics and, given the life he had lived and the illnesses that constantly beset him, an iron will.

But his roots in the "democracy" was the true source of his strength and political agenda. The White House was open to common people as never before. One member of the Washington elite criticized a typical White House gathering as being "a motley crowd," including everyone from "the Vice President to an intoxicated canal labourer in a dirty red plaid cloak. . . . It is a striking picture of *democracy,* and truth to tell, it strikes me with disgust." But most Americans loved it: the government was theirs, and Jackson was the personification of their political and social values. Jackson was a master of political organization and propaganda and rewarded his political friends. He created the spoils system, by which political friends got federal jobs and contracts. (It was a Jacksonian senator, William Learned Marcy, who coined the phrase "To the victor belongs the spoils.") But Jackson's faith in the ability of the common person was unshakable, and he defended such "rotation in office" as a democratic process and justified his appointments on the grounds that "the duties of all public officers are . . . so plain and simple that men of intelligence may readily qualify themselves for their performance ... no one man has any more intrinsic right to office than another."

Jackson was a politician on the side of the democratic majority, at least in principle. The inhumane removal of the Indians to the West, which resulted in the death of many thousands, was done to benefit the white many who wanted to settle new regions, and it was a highly popular move. Jackson knew that his political fate depended on his popular support, and he always remembered that in whatever he did. "I do what I think just and right," he often said, but somehow what he thought just and right always turned out be the thing that his democratic many wanted done. In his famous bank veto message, he explicitly stated his political philosophy:

> It is to be regretted that the rich and powerful too often bend the acts of government to their selfish purposes. ... In the full enjoyment of the gifts of Heaven and the fruits of superior industry, economy, and virtue, every man is equally entitled to protection by law; but when the laws undertake to add to these natural and just advantages, artificial distinctions, to grant titles, gratuities, and exclusive privileges, to make the rich richer and the potent more powerful, the humbler members of society—the farmers, merchants, and laborers—who have neither the time nor the means of securing like favors to themselves, have a right to complain of the injustice of their Government. There are no necessary evils in government. Its evils exist only in its abuses. If it would confine itself to equal protection, and, as Heaven does its rains, shower its favors alike on the high and the low, the rich and the poor, it would seem an unqualified blessing. In the act before me there seems to be a wide and unnecessary departure from these just principles.

Jackson retired amidst popular veneration. At his successor Martin Van Buren's inaugural, it was he who was the object of homage. On his way back to the Hermitage, he was greeted by cheering crowds everywhere he appeared. He wrote of himself that he was "opposed throughout my administration by the talents, wealth and money power of the whole aristocracy of the United States, but nobly supported by the Democratic republicans—the people ... was filling the summit of my gratification, and I can truly say, my ambition."

---

process breaking the White House china and glasses, and generally wrecking the place. If you tour the White House, you still see the scars of the Jacksonian democrats that celebrated their hero's triumph with plebian gusto.

To many of the aristocracy that had ruled the country hitherto, the inaugural augured the "reign of King Mob" and the "triumph of Jacobinism" (the Jacobins were the extreme party in the French Revolution). The incumbent that Jackson defeated, John Quincy Adams, sniffed that "the only principles yet discernible in the conduct of the President were to feed the cormorant appetite for place, and to reward the prostitution of canvassing defamers." What Adams and the ruling elite did not understand was that the "appetite for place" was part of Jackson's appeal to the democratic mass. He represented what they wanted, and his electoral victory was for them not mob rule or Jacobinism but a triumph for themselves, the rule of the many.

Andrew Jackson, his stump speakers were fond of saying, was "a man of the people." He was one of them, the best of them, the leader of them. He was a self-made man born in a log cabin who had become a national hero and the champion of the common person. He was not part of the established few but rather was roughhewn and common, like the many that loved him. He instinctively identified with the common people, and they with him. When the great crowd cheered him at the inaugural, he was moved, bowing low to the "majesty of the people." "His strength lay with the masses," wrote one contemporary, "and he knew it."

He also knew how to translate that strength into politics. During his campaigns and presidency, Jackson knew that his political support lay with the newly enfranchised common men, especially those on the frontier. Jackson was the first American politician to understand and manipulate the changing nature of American society and republican politics. Before him, presidents had been elite leaders of the revolution, part of the Virginia dynasty, or, like Adams, the son of a founding father, John Adams. They were men of birth, reputation, and learning, but they cannot be said—Adams least of all—to have had the common touch. Jackson sensed that the new common men did not want to be ruled by their betters by position, but by their betters by achievement. Jackson personified someone who was their equal in a sense but also was one of them who had achieved, risen from the bottom to the top, as they all hoped that they or their children would too. Jackson championed the "politics of opportunity," representing the interests of the many. Jackson's ironclad support among the democratic many who voted him into office became a precedent for how to rule through the many.

POWER BASES OF THE MANY

"The rule of a prince," stated Machiavelli, "results either from the power of the people or that of the nobles, depending on which has a chance to prevail." We have already talked about Machiavelli's republican sentiments, as well as his understanding of the dialectic between the few and the many. In Chapter 9 of *The Prince,* Machiavelli argued that it was probably better to have the many on one's side than the few, as the many have the power of numbers, which is an almost irresistible form of support. If it is a choice of having the support of the few or the many, choose the many. Obviously, in republican politics in which one is elected and given power by the masses, the support of the many is preferable.

But Machiavelli also recognized that in other than republican politics, princes may rise and rule through the many. He observed, "Of course a man who becomes prince through the good will of the people ought to keep them well disposed toward him. . . . But even a man who becomes prince against the will of the people, with the aid of the nobles, should try above all things to win over the populace; he can do this quite easily by taking them under his protection." Elsewhere Machiavelli discussed how tyrants could rule through the many: "Whence it is that those tyrants who have the masses for friends and the nobles for enemies are more secure in the possession of their power, because their despotism is sustained by a greater force than that of those who have the people for their enemies and the nobles for their friends." How do you get the people on your side? Machiavelli advised: "Ascertain what the people really desire," which he thought was always "to revenge themselves on those who have been the cause of their enslavement" and to "recover their liberty." Thus for Machiavelli the many became the "greater force" that a prince in practically any political system could mobilize as the base of his support. The many are the strongest party, and those rulers who rule in their interest have the most powerful political base.

Actually there are many things that you can do to establish your power base among the many, as Machiavelli concluded: "The prince can earn the good will of his subjects in many ways, but as they vary according to circumstances, I can give no fixed rules and will say nothing on them ... a wise prince will think of ways to keep his citizens of every sort and under every circumstance dependent on the state and him; and then they will always be trustworthy."

What ways you can use does indeed depend on circumstances, but you must read those circumstances and benefit the many with those things they want. Recall our discussions of welfare values and deference values. If you are going to rule through the many, you must identify welfare masses and deference masses and use your power to realize the interests of the many. You must identify, articulate, and realize these groups' values. To the extent you can give them (or at least make them believe you are trying to) welfare values, such as wealth and security, and deference values, such as honoring their way of life, you will be rewarding them for their support. This popular support then will become your political base of practicing power.

You can see the political logic of ruling through the many by a moment's reflection. Let us use again the homely example of ruling a large family. Suppose that the aged grandmother has a large fortune but that the younger members of the family all are struggling to get through school, buy a house, or pay off loans. Through either persuasion or force, you gain control of the family fortune with the support of most members of the family, by promising that you will use the money to help them. And you deliver, spreading the money around to help the many of the family. At least for a period of time, you have the support and admiration of those you helped, but you can also see the conflict and problems that this family policy creates. For one thing, the powerful few—the matriarch and her backers—may resist giving up the money or claim that you are wasting it by giving it to college students who will, they claim, use it for drugs and sex. Too, you may use up the money and then incur the ingratitude of the many, who in effect ask, "What have you done for me lately?"

As we stressed in the last chapter, the relationship between the few and the many—in family politics or in national politics—is dialectical, because the division between the few and the many is universal, and in some way you have to mediate this difference. But you also have to choose in whose interest you will rule, and one of your choices is to rule through the power of the many. The advantage of seeking a power base among the many is that you will be taking a stand against privilege and for the maximum dispersion of welfare and deference benefits.

Let us take two common benefits that are central to the political logic of ruling through the many. First think of a common welfare benefit: economic security. The many desire their own well-being in terms of their own wealth, safety, and health. If you can spread benefits among the many and increase real income among them, make them feel safe at their work site or home, and make them healthier, then you will be appealing to a welfare mass that will become a base of political support. Santa Claus would get more votes than Ebenezer Scrooge. In a republic, then, when the leaders need the votes of the many, the government budget will increase when elections approach. The politician who promises and delivers the most benefits usually wins, right?

Not always. The benefits promised cost money, and in the politics of the many there is always a tension between costs and benefits. The government budget may always be too small in a democracy, but the government budget is also always too large. People want benefits, but they also do not want to pay taxes. If they cannot see how they would benefit from a new welfare proposal or think that someone other than themselves may benefit, then they may not vote for the benefit. On the other hand, if they elect someone who takes away benefits that affect them, they then may vote for someone who will restore them. It is true that the many want to have their cake and eat it too. Your problem in practicing power through the many is calculating benefits and costs and deciding which strategy is best for maintaining the support of the many. One strategy is to make the few pay most of the taxes and to spread the benefits among the many. Another strategy is to cut benefits and taxes, giving both the rich and the poor more wealth. The trick is to find the right political combination at the right political time. If you can create conditions of both economic prosperity and economic security, your rule is likely to be secure.

Similarly, ruling through the many requires that you pay homage to the deference values of the masses. If your many has family, religion, life-style, and morality values, you can make those values part of your ruling. For example, you can defer to the life-style of the many by appearing to live like them. Think of how many recent presidents you have seen photographed in Western dress or denims, at cookouts, going to church, expressing their support of religion, extolling the virtues of family life, and so forth. But leaders not only dramatize common values, they also enact them as policy, for example, making "moral" laws that support popular ideas about morality. However, there are difficulties and pitfalls here too. Masses are often divided into groups, identifiable along racial, ethnic, religious, regional, or some other lines. In that case, it becomes dangerous for you to become too closely identified with one set of deference values to the detriment of another. Ruling a country divided, for instance, along Catholic and Protestant lines (recall the problems of Elizabeth I and Mary Queen of Scots) makes things difficult. The best ruling strategy, although certainly not an easy one, is for the prince to pay homage to all important groups and their values, but not to become identified with any one to the resentment of the other. Machiavelli noted that "because every city is divided into professional guilds and family groupings, he should be inward with these people, and attend their gatherings from time to time, giving evidence of his humanity and munificence, yet avoiding any compromise to his dignity, for that must be preserved at all costs." Your dignity is preserved by being evenhanded in your relations with mass groupings but by keeping your distance from all of them. The last thing you need in ruling through the many is to become caught up in group conflicts over religion, race, or some other division.

Building a power base among the many is fraught with many other difficulties. People are fickle, and thus your support among the many may erode if political *fortuna* turns against you. The few will become emboldened to attack you, and political rivals may arise who try to woo the masses away from you. Discontent among the many often develops quietly, exploding into electoral or even violent revolts against your rule. For this reason, you must discover ways of finding out what the people are thinking and what you can do to quiet discontent, mobilize or rekindle support, and prevent your power base from slipping away from you.

To this end, it is politically wise to have methods of gauging public opinion. In modern societies, politicians use opinion polls to ascertain moods and trends among the public. But polling is expensive and time-consuming and should not be relied on solely. There are older, less precise, but nonetheless quicker ways of finding out what is going on out there, and this can be carried out by a second requirement of ruling through the many: political organization. Princes from time immemorial have used spies and agents to find out what people are thinking or doing. Often this was done to crush revolts and kill potential rivals. But if you are ruling through the many, you cannot always respond to discontent by crushing it. To a large degree, your support among the many depends on your popularity among them. Thus you will want to use public opinion and political organization as expedients to keep the many on your side. New discontent means for you plotting new expedients to sway public opinion your way. Political organization mobilizes opinion for your ruling purposes.

Throughout history there have been many different kinds of political organizations built among the masses. The most familiar is the political party, especially the mass parties with organizational structures that reach down into grass-roots levels. Other political orders also have parties. The Soviet Union, for instance, is dominated by the CPSU (Communist Party—Soviet Union), which is a political organization down to the cell level at its base but is crucial to Soviet rule because it organizes the masses and informs the rulers of what people think and want. The old-fashioned American urban political machine, such as the Democratic machine in Chicago, organizes people at the ward level and gives the machine bosses a way of knowing the masses' feelings. The ward heeler, cell leader, or whatever, is a quick if imperfect source of vital political information.

The political strategy of ruling through the many we shall term *populism*. The populist approach to practicing power is a contrast to elitism. Whereas elitism views power as exercised from the top down, populism views power as exercised from the bottom up. Populist leaders, at least in their rhetoric, believe in popular sovereignty and not in elite privilege. They espouse benefits for the masses and champion the cause of what one American politician called "the constituency of the hard up." The populists' power base depends on what they can deliver for the many, how well they fight the enemies of the people, and how closely leaders and followers identify with each other. We usually associate populist politicians with democratic politics, but not necessarily. The Perons in Arentina, Kemal Atatürk in Turkey, Mao Tse-tung in China, Mussolini in Italy, and even Hitler used populist methods in their approach to power. "Revolutionary despots" like Juan and Evita Peron may be autocrats, but autocrats who rule through popular support. In the democratic countries, one of the pioneers of populist rule was Andrew Jackson.

THE POLITICAL STRATEGY OF POPULISM

Andrew Jackson ruled through the many. He was the first presidential candidate who appealed to the rising tide of common men who had recently gained the vote. The election of 1828 brought out a million new voters, enfranchised by the easing of suffrage requirements and enrolled by a vigorous and exciting campaign run by the political parties. Jackson's "stump speakers" toured the country, organized rallies, torchlight parades, barbecues and dinners, distributed buttons and hickory-leaf hats, and most of all extolled "Old Hickory" as "the candidate of the people." Jackson was a common man, not unlike the emerging democratic and capitalist society full of common men, who had become a rich man, national hero, and spokesman for the aspirations of the new voters. Jackson was a democrat (many historians trace the Democratic party to the Jacksonians) by birth and conviction as well as politics.

In power, Jackson pursued the political strategy of populism. This meant that every policy, every political event, was evaluated in terms of populist political logic: what should you do for your political constituency, the many? We could point to many things Jackson did that endeared him to his followers, but none more striking than the "Bank War."

The Second Bank of the United States (BUS) had a charter from the federal government. The bank served many useful functions, such as providing sound currency and credit. But many ordinary people, especially on the frontier, hated the BUS. Many thought that they had been ruined financially by the bank and that it was a "monster," a concentration of economic power in the hands of a few easterners to the detriment of their interests. Jackson and his followers knew that the bank was powerful, outside the control of the president and that it bribed congressmen and rigged elections, propagandized through newspapers sympathetic to it, and could threaten the ruin of many people through monetary policy. The many saw the BUS as the ally of the few, and therefore their enemy. To Jackson's democracy, the bank's power and arrogance were symbolized in its leader, an arrogant, effete Philadelphia aristocrat named Nicholas Biddle. Biddle's contempt for Jackson and the populace was scarcely concealed, as, for example, when he addressed a group of Princeton University alumni after the Bank War: "It cannot be that our free nation can long endure the vulgar domination of ignorance and profligacy. You will live to see the laws reestablished— these banditti will be scourged back to their caverns—the penitentiary will reclaim its fugitives in office, and the only remembrance which history will preserve of them, is the energy with which you resisted and defeated them."

Many historians considered Biddle an economic wizard but a political idiot. Although Jackson's antibank sympathies were well known, in his first term he did little to fight the bank, and his new cabinet of 1831 included probank men. The congressional charter of the bank ran until 1836, when Jackson could be presumed to be leaving office. But Henry Clay, who had been nominated in 1832 to run against Jackson, advised Biddle to apply for a recharter. They had many allies in Congress and thought that Jackson would not risk vetoing the recharter during an election year. If he signed the new charter, this would preserve Biddle's power, but if he did not, it would give Clay an issue that might defeat Jackson.

Jackson immediately sensed that Biddle and Clay were trying to maneuver him into a political dilemma. Not one to back down from a fight, Jackson saw the political challenge: "The bank is trying to kill me, but I will kill it!" Jackson put his best writers to work on the famous veto message, which was to serve as a propaganda document during the campaign. As already noted, he appealed to the have-nots who deserved equal protection by government, especially from high-handed institutions such as the BUS. He appealed to nationalism, conjuring up foreign stockholders in the bank exercising undue influence over American affairs. The struggle against privilege and aristocracy put Jackson firmly on the side of the many. Biddle and the bank became the symbol of the power of the few, and Jackson as the defender of the many. By fighting the bank, Jackson represented those mass desires to "recover their liberty" (Machiavelli), which they feared the BUS was undermining, and to "revenge themselves" against the economic oppression they believed the bank had brought them.

Biddle and his allies scorned the veto. It was a "manifesto of anarchy," said Biddle, "such as Marat or Robespierre might have issued to the mobs" during the French Revolution. Biddle even had thirty thousand copies of Jackson's veto message printed and distributed, thinking that people would see the error in Jackson's argument. The tactic backfired, because the political logic that people saw in Jackson's message was a populist one: the bank was an agent of the few against the many and had to be destroyed before it destroyed them. Jacksonian orators during the campaign cast the president as the champion of the workingman, the merchant, the farmer against the aristocrats and the monied interests. Jackson's party was well organized at the grass roots, held rallies at which Jackson was praised and Biddle scorned, and turned out the vote. Jackson won reelection and set out to destroy the bank at all costs.

Jackson withdrew federal funds from the BUS and put them into "pet banks" controlled by his allies. Biddle called in loans and raised the interest rate, bringing about a recession in 1833–1834. This, he thought, would make Jackson look bad and prove again the need for the BUS. But Jackson turned this around to his political advantage, arguing that the bank had caused the economic distress to get back at him and by so doing had proved that such concentrated economic power in the few was dangerous and had to be destroyed. "I have it chained," he said of the BUS, "the monster must perish." In a brutal political struggle with the bank, his own cabinet and party, and Congress, Jackson persisted and slowly but surely did in the bank. The economic issues and consequences of the Bank War have been much debated since, and indeed Jackson's destruction of the bank may have been bad economics. But bad economics is often good politics. Politicians are not economists; they are politicians. Jackson understood the political logic of fighting and winning over the bank on behalf of his political constituency. From Jackson's point of view, the BUS was a powerful institution that threatened the power of the government, the presidency in particular, and of course his own power. If it could threaten the well-being of his political constituency, it could threaten his own political power. It was an economic war as much as a political war, and Jackson knew it. The bank was trying to kill him politically, and so he would use politics to kill it. It was classic populist politics.

PROBLEMS OF POPULIST RULE

Not everybody is as successful as Andrew Jackson was in ruling through the many. Think, for example, of how many American presidents have been defeated or driven from office. Many populist dictators have fallen into public disfavor and been swept from power. You can rule through the many only if they will let you, and there may be many problems with populist rule.

First, the few may simply be too powerful for you to rule through the many. Elites are, after all, entrenched and powerful, with advantages of institutional control, wealth, education, customs of deference, and the like. All these things may make it difficult to challenge their power successfully. You may be forbidden access to the masses. There may be strong traditions of nonparticipation. People may be content with elite rule. For any number of reasons, you may not be able to break the grip of elite rule.

But even if you can gain access to the many and they respond to your leadership, you may have to do things that will undermine your rule. Ruling through the many involves ironies that result from the political logic of populism. Andrew Jackson, for example, broke the power of the BUS, but at the price (at least one school of thought holds) of economically hurting the ordinary citizens that he thought he was protecting. Ruling through the many, just as ruling through the few, may force you into bad policies just because they are popular. Bad economics may for the moment be good politics, but it is still bad economics; in the long run, what is politically expedient for the moment may come back to haunt you.

Similarly, to rule through the many, you may have to overpromise. Overpromising involves the obvious political danger that you will not be able to deliver on your promises. The many will feel that you lied to them or are not a prince because you do not have the power to gain for them what you said you would. Too, by having promised to deliver welfare or deference values that the many want, you may be forced into bad policies. You may have to spend more money than your government has, getting you into debt (and thus increasing the banks' hold over you) and creating inflation. There may be popular religious figures with undue influence over your foreign policy, forcing you into unwise positions.

You also may have to succumb to the temptation of demagoguery. A demagogue is a leader who inflames popular passions to achieve some political end. Demagogues may appeal to racial, religious, and ethnic hatreds; class envy; national pride; indeed the whole gamut of base human emotions. But politicians who try to rule through the many often feel that they have to appeal to mass feelings that translate into political support. Hitler and Mussolini could harangue crowds into frenzy by such demagogic appeals, as could the Perons with their "shirtless ones." But like religious revivalism, the fervor produced does not last, and your base of support may evaporate quickly. But as the careers of Hitler and others demonstrate, you can go a long way on waves of political enthusiasm skillfully used. But the logic of demagoguery also includes its illogic: it makes sense to use it if all else fails, but it may have its price. For example, a common demagogic appeal to the many is the "bad man" argument. "There are bad men out there who are the cause of our plight, and so we need to oppose and fight them." Such appeals have proved useful for demagogic princes in stirring up war fever (the enemy is at the gate), reigns of terror (the enemy is within and must be liquidated), and material confiscations (the enemy's assets must be taken by us, as he acquired them wrongly and will use them against us). Scapegoats are always available and always guilty. But initiating such actions does not mean that you can control them.

In revolutionary times, when politics is not normal, demagogic appeals to and the control of crowds can be a potent form of power. But such crowds often demand revenge in the form of blood. Mass rumors and hysteria, mercurial changes in public opinion, and the mobilization of crowds by other leaders can make your control of the many very tenuous. In such situations demagoguery often produces a diseconomy of violence, resulting in military rule and perhaps your own political and even physical demise. The Jacobin "Reign of Terror" in the French Revolution was so extreme that it inspired counterrevolution and overthrow, bringing about the execution of the Jacobin leaders. Revolutions, especially in their demagogic phase, do indeed devour their own children.

Labeling a group or foreign power as a villain has many other pitfalls. Obviously it does not like being made the political scapegoat and may take political action of its own, trying to cast you as the villain. If it is a foreign power, dealing with it in realistic terms may be very difficult if for domestic consumption you have labeled it as evil. Why, your followers may ask, are you dealing with the devil? The revolutionary Iranian government found this problem in dealing with the Americans over the hostage issue. Those leaders that wanted the crisis resolved were constantly beset by the demagogic appeal of other figures equating America with Satan, which made the more practical leaders seem compromised and even traitorous. Similarly, American politicians who have tried to talk with the major Communist states (the Soviet Union and China) have been thwarted by recurrent efforts to label these states as evil.

Finally, there is the enduring question of how to produce among the many virtue rather than corruption. Machiavelli warned that a corrupt republic was difficult to rule because the people were corrupt and unruly and might require dictatorship. The deterioration of the virtuous Roman republic into the corrupt empire is the topical subject of Machiavelli's *Discourses* and is also the subject of Shakespeare's *Julius Caesar*. Maintaining civic and economic virtue among the many is not easy. If you choose to rule through the many, you may have to give them what they want (welfare and deference values) in order to satisfy them and keep yourself in power; but that may corrupt them by making life too easy. They may be more willing to live off the state, less willing to work, and, with more income, indulgent in habit. Increased levels of mass education may make the many more suspicious of, and even cynical about, their rulers. The spread of moral rectitude may make them less reluctant to prepare for or fight wars, which a widespread moral code may tell them is immoral. "Civic virtue," for Machiavelli and many others, includes the willingness of citizens to sacrifice and die for the interests of the state. But that may be hard to sustain if you rule through the many: telling people to sacrifice and die because "it's good for them" or "good for the state" may not be adequate. To sustain a growing and viable economy, for instance, may require people who are willing to work long hours for low wages; but when people have reached the level of shorter workdays for higher pay and the economy falters, how many will be willing to return to the virtues of hard work for low pay? When the many hear that political message, they may simply find another prince who will promise them more for less.

THE PROBLEM OF THE TYRANNY OF THE MAJORITY

There is another problem of ruling through the many that requires a separate word. This is the problem of the tyranny of the majority, common in large, modern mass societies. It was first recognized by the great French observer of Jacksonian America, Alexis de Tocqueville, who traveled around Jackson's new democratic society and then wrote, *Democracy in America*. In it, Tocqueville argued that there was a tendency, inherent in the political logic of a democracy, for such a society—and thus by extension its government—to deteriorate into a new kind of tyranny, a tyranny exercised over everyone by everyone. In a democracy, the majority is ascendant; therefore they create an egalitarian culture in which equality is the key value. Everybody believes that he or she has a right to achieve but also that everybody should be roughly like everybody else, and so the majority tyrannizes thought, custom, and of course politics. When the people rule, Tocqueville argued, corruption is inevitable, because the society produces a mass consisting of "an innumerable multitude of men, all equal and alike, incessantly endeavoring to procure the petty and paltry pleasures with which they glut their lives."

If Tocqueville was correct, this means that ruling the many in the modern world requires princes who understand the logic of majority tyranny. It may also be observed in "totalitarian democracies" such as the Soviet Union and populist dictatorships such as Peronist Argentina. Ruling through the many, remember, is not necessarily any more benevolent than any other kind of rule is. And consider this: if you are going to rule through the many, you may be as much a prisoner of the tyranny of the majority as anyone else. Why? Because to rule, you will be forced into the political necessities dictated by the power of public opinion and tastes. You may be forced into bad policies, idiotic gestures, evil deeds (such as persecutions), and so forth, simply because the source of your political power expects it. The people may exercise a partial tyranny over what is done politically, even though it may make no sense. In this case, political illogic rather than logic reigns, proving the point of Henrik Ibsen's: the enemy of the people is the people themselves.

WAS THRASYMACHUS RIGHT AGAIN?

Thrasymachus observed that justice and right were what was in the interest of the stronger party and that in a populist state the many will reign through the power of their numbers. Anyone who belongs to a group of more or less equals (such as a sorority or fraternity or club) knows how much power the others can exercise. Former Speaker of the House Sam Rayburn's rule for a successful career in the House of Representatives holds for many groups: "To get along, go along." In some measure, even princes who rule successfully through the many have to go along with popular opinion and wishes. Perhaps Andrew Jackson in his heart of hearts knew that his war against the Bank of the United States was not altogether economically wise or necessary, but he also knew the political logic of ruling through the many. Given what he represented to and knew about the many, like Martin Luther, he could do no other. He did what he thought was in the interest of the stronger party.

Yet the many are not fools. They are not necessarily swayed by demagoguery or are vindictive and revengeful, irrational and stupid. One of Machiavelli's chapters in his *Discourses* is entitled "The People Are Wise and More Constant Than Princes." If the many can be misled, he explained, so can princes; the many can support republican institutions and laws better than princes alone; alliances with republics are more stable; and because political wisdom is widespread in a virtuous republic, it will in the long run be more stable.

The debate about the proper role of the many in politics began with the Greek philosophers, and we cannot settle the issue here. Practicing power is one choice you have in ruling. The career of Andrew Jackson illustrates that ruling can be done well if one understands the political logic of ruling through the many. To a large degree, how benevolent and successful one's rule is depends on the virtue or corruption among the many. But also to some degree, ruling well through the many depends on the prince. "A multitude, without a chief," asserted Machiavelli, "is useless." The many can be led, but they can also be misled.

"It is to be regretted that the rich and powerful too often bend the acts of government to their selfish purposes."

—Jackson

"The people ... was filling the summit of my gratification, and I can truly say, my ambition."

—Jackson

"To the victor belongs the spoils."

—William Learned Marcy

"The rule of a prince results either from the power of the people or that of the nobles, depending on which has a chance to prevail."

—Machiavelli

Practicing Power

"Ascertain what the people really desire."

—Machiavelli

"The people are wiser and more constant than princes."

—Machiavelli

"A multitude without a chief is useless."

—Machiavelli

"Fetters and headsmen were the coarse instruments which tyranny formerly employed ... [but] in democratic republics ... the body is left free, and the soul is enslaved."

—de Tocqueville

Chapter

23

Using Political Culture: Governing Through Symbols

When you go to the capital city of any major political power, you will no doubt be struck by its buildings and monuments. The monuments tell you of the great events and princes of the past and the glories and heroes that established the power that prevails. The buildings are likely to be forbidding and forbidden, and you may be struck by the power that the buildings themselves communicate. The Kremlin, the walled headquarters of the Soviet Union's ruling elite, symbolizes the tradition of autocratic power dating back to the czars. The British Houses of Parliament symbolize the tradition of parliamentary self-government and the ancient heritage of constitutionalism and nationhood. The buildings of Brazil's new capital, Brasilia, symbolize the aspirations of a developing nation.

The buildings in Washington, D.C., also communicate something about politics. The monuments there celebrate the American past and heroes. The bureaucratic buildings are sober and efficient looking. The White House is guarded, and tours are controlled through the rooms in which well-known events took place. The Congress building (the Capital) communicates the nation's parliamentary heritage. Each building is a "signature of power," telling the visitor something of what goes on there and who has the power. You cannot just casually walk into the Oval Office and say hello to the president.

While in Washington, you might want to take the official tour of one of the most imposing and popular public attractions: the Federal Bureau of Investigation. The building is massive and functional, having cost altogether $126 million, the most expensive office building ever constructed by the federal government up to the time it opened. The guided tour is quite impressive. Many thousands of tourists yearly trek through the chamber of horrors of American crime. You can see the hat that John Dillinger wore on the night he was gunned down on a street in Chicago, as well as many other trophies of FBI lore. The tour guide will tell of the many ingenious traps the FBI set for kidnappers, murderers, bank robbers, and spies. You can see the massive collection of guns and armaments the FBI has collected. All in all, you will come away with the impression of a superefficient and legendary organization, still infused with the spirit of its creator, for whom the building is named, J. Edgar Hoover.

SYMBOLS AND POLITICS

Machiavelli commented that much of politics is appearance. He was aware that politicians acted in public, and thus what the public—the few and the many—thought of them was important. Princes must play roles such as those of the fox and the lion; they must "appear merciful" and the like; they will always "find plenty who are ready to be deceived" they should undertake "great enterprises" which have "enthralled and preoccupied the minds of his subjects"; they should "give the impression of being a great man"; they should "entertain his people with festivals and spectacles"; they should "reassure the public mind by such acts as will restore calmness and confidence"; they have to concern themselves with style; and they may have to use fraud and deception.

This does not mean that all princes are insincere dissemblers or that all politics is a con game. But it is true that ruling means using appearances, because through appearances people are convinced to obey. "Everyone sees what you seem to be, few know what you really are," Machiavelli pointed out. Think of your own relations with family and friends: how much of "what you really are" do they know about, and how much of what they know of you is "what you seem to be?" Are't there things about yourself that you don't tell other people? Don't you try to manipulate the impressions that other people have of you? Isn't it true that to the extent that you get them to do what you want depends on your ability to control what other people think? Aren't you concerned with appearances?

Think about your first date with someone you wanted to know better. Didn't you rehearse what you were going to say, plan the evening, take care about how you looked, and use gestures and talk to determine what the other party thought of you? In other words, you were trying to appear as what you thought the other person wanted you to be. In fact, you may or may not have been what you claimed to be, but by managing impressions of yourself, you appeared to your date in the way you wanted. You were acting, shaping your behavior in such a way as to affect the opinion of your audience.

Notice how much in a situation like this you require the language of theater. We are all actors on the great stage of life, whether we are performing in good or bad faith. Not everybody who goes out on a date is a con artist, nor is every relationship a con game. But we all more or less understand the drama of relationships, and could write a story of our lives. And we all sense the politics of life's little dramas. If you get out of the date what you want, you did so because you were a political actor.

All right, you say, but what does my dating have to do with public buildings and J. Edgar Hoover? Actually, more than you might think. Those who see drama in life base this on the idea that people use symbols.

When we communicate with one another, our behavior is symbolic, using language, gestures, props, and costumes in order to structure appearances. We use symbols to name things, to make sense of the world and ourselves, and to give meaning to relationships. We do not just think them up, of course; we live in a society that has a symbolic environment and teaches us symbols. A nation is a symbol that we are taught to believe in. The nation, as well, is collectively engaged in a large symbolic drama in order to realize its destiny. All of a nation's welfare and deference values are expressed and celebrated in political symbols, including monuments and buildings.

Politicians also sense that they are in a political drama that requires acting. We all are familiar with the dramas of American politics: the convention speech, the debate, the news conference, the campaign rally. How well politicians act in that drama depends on how we, the audience, react to the show and the actors. Political actors must understand the symbols of power and the power of symbols and must cultivate the dramatic arts, including that sense of an occasion's drama, about which Machiavelli wrote. As we have noted time and time again in this book, the ability to rise to the occasion and dramatize one's power is an important political skill.

Politicians also must understand that they are acting in a cultural drama. Politics always takes place in a culture and, indeed, is part of the symbolic environment of that culture. The politics of your date takes place in the context of culture, with its symbols and myths of courting and mating, institutions of marriage and the family, values such as chastity and modesty, and of course college traditions concerning sex. Your use of appearances on the date takes place with culture in mind. If you want to appear to the other as moral, you must communicate that; if you want to appear to the other as sexually available, you must communicate that. The politics of the date is part of the cultural drama, in this case the drama of romance.

Political scientists use the term *political culture* to refer to the cultural drama of politics as it is conducted in each culture. The way that the Japanese, Russians, or Nigerians conduct politics is affected by the distinctive features of their cultures. If you have ever been to a foreign country, you no doubt noticed its different customs. Politics is part of a country's own cultural drama, and accordingly, American politics is part of the American cultural drama.

This is why the old saw, "there is no morality in politics" is incorrect. Recall what Machiavelli said about religion, which is also part of a culture: politics must exist, but it exists in the cultural context of religion, which is one of the symbolic values of a culture. To rule a prince must at least appear religious, and pay homage to important deference values. Moral codes are important to politics, helping set the agenda of politics and limiting what is done. Princes who flaunt the moral code and cultural values of those they rule are playing with political fire.

Quite to the contrary, princes cloak themselves in the symbols of culture and become the political actors who enact the cultural drama. In politics, the political actors must become moral agents, representing on the political stage the people's desire to see their candidates win and their way of life secured. Princes appear to their people as the political representatives of all that they value and act for them to see that their values are defended and advanced. A king becoms a crusader, freeing the Holy Land from the infidels, fighting crime and alien doctrines and ideologies, legislating the will of God, persecuting unbelievers, and in general upholding those symbols in which we believe. The political drama as enacted by princes is indeed a morality play.

There is another old saw that is untrue: "You can't legislate morality." Morality is constantly being legislated or decreed by moral agents in politics. People may ignore the legislation or decree, but they will feel better because morality has been given political sanction and even the backing of the state. Moral forces once outlawed alcoholic beverages in the United States, when the government enacted Prohibition. Morality was legislated by constitutional amendment, therefore reinforcing the morality of abstinence; the fact that it did not stop drinking was not as important. In the future, if abortion is outlawed by the moral legislation of a constitutional amendment, a moral value will be backed by political power; but surely no one seriously believes that abortions will end, or even be much curtailed. Pragmatic politicians legislate morality for symbolic and not realistic reasons.

Legislating morality is a good example of *symbolic politics*. Many people are concerned about the fate of the cultural symbols they value and turn to politics in order to maintain those symbols. Several political conflicts are over symbols, for example, holy wars, in which people kill one another over whose god should be worshiped. Politicians are often caught in the middle in such conflicts, because a compromise over symbolic values is often difficult to work out. The political logic of symbolic politics militates against neutrality, fence straddling, or compromise, and often favors politicians who are willing to be swept up by a

J. EDGAR HOOVER: SYMBOLIC GOVERNOR

J. Edgar Hoover was to the federal bureaucracy born. He was born in Washington, D.C., the son of a superintendent of the U.S. Coast and Geodetic Survey. He went to public school in Washington and even considered becoming a Presbyterian minister. After high school, he worked his way through night law school and then went to work for the Justice Department. Significantly, he went to work there at a time when the government was being urged to respond to popular complaints about the "radicals" and "agitators" in the country. The then attorney general, A. Mitchell Palmer, responded by persecuting, arresting, and deporting many people connected with the so-called leftist ideologies. Much of this popular hatred was formed from the frustration and hard times in the wake of World War I and was directed at immigrant Catholics and socialists, who threatened jobs, religion, the chastity of our daughters, and the American way of life. The Palmer raids were a kind of symbolic politics, in which popular hatreds and fears were directed at a convenient and visible target. Hoover got an early glimpse of the cultural drama in which legal administrators are involved and how they can make symbolic responses that dramatize a government agency as the protector of popular morality.

Hoover was the director of the FBI from 1924 until his death in 1972. He was an adept bureaucratic politician, surviving various attempts to depose him and acquiring such a formidable reputation that no administration, Democratic or Republican, dared fire him or demand his retirement (he ruled the FBI well after retirement age). *Fortuna* even smiled on him at one point. When the Roosevelt administration came to power, the new attorney general-designate, Senator Walsh, was planning to fire Hoover but died before he took office. By the time Hoover died, his power was so great that his ever-increasing budget requests from Congress were always passed intact, and his support from powerful groups and a large segment of public opinion was solid. (After his death, revelations about illegal and dubious FBI activities ordered by Hoover tarnished his reputation, and Congress moved to limit the power of subsequent directors.)

Hoover is an example of an administrative genius who created a bureaucratic empire by means of clever politics and organizational esprit de corps. During his long directorship, he enlarged a marginal bureau in the Department of Justice into an enormous federal agency. He was quick to expand the activities of the bureau and was jealous of its turf. Hoover himself became an institution: he never married; the bureau was his life, and he devoted himself to its care and nurturing. If toward the end of his life he had become, for many, an anachronism, for others he still represented in his bulldog countenance and law-and-order stance, the embodiment of the Federal Bureau of Investigation.

---

moral tide. But if they join the wrong morality, they may suffer political loss. In symbolic politics, then, the question is whose morality will be honored.

Here again it may be choice of the morality of the few or the many. The powerful few, for example, control institutions (such as churches) and want to see their moral concerns enacted. But popular morality, especially in republics, has the power of public opinion behind it. If you as a political actor can become a symbolic moral agent of popular morality, you can also become a powerful political figure. To do so, you have to champion popular values and appear to represent popular symbols. To understand more fully how this process works, let us look at the career of one of the more successful practitioners of the political dramatic arts, J. Edgar Hoover.

THE POLITICS OF SYMBOLIC GOVERNANCE

Hoover was a bureaucratic politician who governed his FBI and the leadership of the forces of law and order by becoming a "symbolic governor." Many observers of bureaucratic politics have commented on Hoover's political acumen. Richard Gid Powers, in his book *The G-Man: Hoover's FBI in American Popular Culture,* discussed how Hoover used popular culture to build the image of the bureau and its director. When Hoover became the director of the FBI, he instituted many organizational reforms, demanding high qualifications and standards of conduct from agents, establishing a training school, and eliminating patronage hacks and political influence in the bureau. Even though some thought that his demands were somewhat puritanical, Hoover's internal discipline was legendary: he forbade agents to drink in public; insisted they be neat, clean, and courteous; and fired those who he thought were morally deficient. The reputation for professional efficiency came from the public discipline of the FBI agents.

But Hoover sensed that the FBI could be much more than just a federal agency respected for its efficiency. Rather, the FBI, and indeed himself, could become the symbol of the popular moral crusade against crime and subversion in the popular mind. Since in fact crime and subversion could not be eradicated, the reputation of the FBI would have to be established at the symbolic level in people's minds. But how to do that? Hoover finally decided to dramatize through the new mass media the symbolic role of the FBI in fighting crime. In that way, when each new threat, real or imagined, emerged, the FBI's actual ability to meet the threat would be unimportant. What would be important was that it appeared to be the moral agent defending popular morality and that no amount of statistics in critical reports by crime commissions and criminologists could undermine that appearance. As Powers pointed out, the public moral agent who defends popular morality in the wake of widespread fears will be defended by the populace because they will see that agent as popular morality in action. "When King Canute," added Powers, "began giving orders to the waves his popularity probably soared."

The first important wave to which Hoover began giving orders was the crime wave that began to stir public concern in the late 1920s and especially during the Depression of the 1930s. Hoover's response to this public concern demonstrated both his skill at symbolic politics and his genius for publicity. The growth of organized crime (like Al Capone and the Chicago Mob) and the rise of the Depression-era criminals (Bonnie and Clyde, Pretty Boy Floyd, and so on) increased the public's interest in crime. Dramatic logic called for a governmental response. The public's morality insisted that crime be stopped because it did not pay. Hoover no doubt knew that crime did pay, and paid well, but that a dramatic response, in the form of a moral crusade, was called for, and that something and someone had to be the symbolic personification of that crusade. So he began to involve himself in publicizing the bureau. But he also knew that what the FBI and Hoover could actually do was limited. Hoover did succeed in urging that the federal government, led by the FBI, assume the task of fighting the crime problem but leave the task of actually controlling crime with state and local governments. Hoover opposed the FBI's becoming a "national police force" because that would give it the direct responsibility for catching criminals. When, inevitably, it did not, its symbolic role would be threatened. A symbolic crusade requires a prince who personifies the holy mission, but it is the foot soldiers who do the actual combat.

Hoover cultivated the media of popular culture to dramatize the G-man (government man) and Hoover as the leaders of the symbolic crusade against crime. Though he had previously been unknown to the public, he became a celebrity, widely known from his speeches to civic and police groups, his articles in popular magazines, his name in gossip columns about his vacation or nightclub habits, his portrait in police chiefs' offices around the country; and spectacular publicity stunts such as filmed arrests of wanted criminals. In crime comic books, Hoover was a character who often appeared, often to end a story with a homily about crime's not paying. He was depicted as a hero to American youth, although he seemed more like a stern high school principal who lectured them on their duty to society and the penalty for crime. By the late 1930s, Hoover was "Mr. FBI."

The FBI was famous too. Hoover enlisted popular culture in an effort to make the bureau and the FBI agents into cultural heroes. Hoover enlisted ghost writers who turned out articles, radio scripts, and movie plots. The FBI cooperated in comic strips and comic books that glorified the G-men's triumphs over criminals. Toy companies marketed junior G-man badges, guns, and detection kits. Children played cops and robbers, the G-men against the hoodlums. The stories involved the Bonnie-and-Clyde hoodlums and gun molls being outwitted by the clean-living and science-armed agents. The agents were all Dick Tracys at the national level. But "adult" fare was not ignored either: Older Americans may remember radio shows such as "G-Men," "Gangbusters," "The F.B.I. in Peace and War," "This Is Your F.B.I." and, on TV, "The FBI" and "The FBI Today." In all these shows, the embodied moral force of the community was represented by the idealized FBI agent. The fictional agent was a clean-living version of the action detective; not the rough and cynical private eye, but rather a public detective who is honorable, intelligent, and scientific in his approach to crime. He defends not the private morality or sense of honor of the private eye (as in "The Maltese Falcon"); rather the FBI agent defends public morality and honor, and seeks not revenge but "law enforcement." In these stories he is a moral agent who acts responsibly and correctly in his defeat of the criminal, bringing a modern professional approach to a moral crusade. "G-Men" stands for "Government Men," which, according to legend, was shouted by "Machine Gun" Kelley as government agents charged him in service to the higher morality of the community.

Hoover responded to the later fears of crime waves by FBI activities, all faithfully dramatized in popular culture. By the 1940s, Hoover had established working relations with radio, movies, pulp writers, comics, and toy manufacturers. He controlled what they used and at times even the script. The FBI "suggested" certain themes to the exclusion of others. Obviously, they did not want stories about FBI failures or civil rights violations. The heroic image had to be preserved, as well as Hoover's role as moral agent for traditional cultural values. In Hoover's public speeches and comic book homilies, as well as in the stories on radio and TV, the crime was always the result of an individual violation of the traditional moral code. Hoover always disdained "maudlin sentimentality" in dealing with crime, condemning those who saw the criminal as a persecuted being, and remarked that "justice is incidental to law and order." His attitude might have been bad criminology, but it was good politics. By taking the hard line on crime, he appealed to the popular mind as the symbolic leader who dramatized their desire for revenge. With that kind of public reputation and support, Hoover could symbolically respond to each new threat and "reassure the public mind." Powers noted that in a 1939 speech Hoover defined democracy as "the dictatorship of the collective conscience of the people."

During World War II, for example, the G-Man of popular culture no longer spent much time fighting domestic desperados. Rather, he fought Nazi (and sometimes Japanese) spies who were trying to steal secrets and blow up defense plants. After the war, people became afraid of Communism with the rise of the Soviet Union. But more than that, they became afraid of domestic communism, and various witch-hunts began. Through popular culture, Hoover's FBI led the fight against "Communism" at home and Communist spies from abroad. Throughout it all, Hoover's rhetoric spoke of the "collective conscience" and represented it in the fight of good against evil. He warned again and again that the roots and the success of crime were in "moral decay" and called for more ardent crusades against the forces of evil. Whomever the enemy was at a particular time, they could win only by undermining our morals. The threat was then linked to what many parents worried about: the corruption of our children.

The drama of the FBI, then, became a heroic fight against alien threats. In popular culture, the threat was always from outside the community of good people. When the aliens were actually foreigners, or controlled by foreigners, that made the threat all the more dramatic. During the "Red Scare," radio programs such as "I Was a Communist for the FBI" and the TV program "I Led Three Lives" dramatized FBI infiltration and thwarting of Soviet espionage. Critics have argued that

FBI's success against Soviet activities was not all that great, but as far as the public was concerned, they were great because the dramas of popular culture depicted them as such. With the rise of the civil rights movement, the FBI was reluctant to become involved, missing a chance to dramatize themselves as a new kind of moral agent. Finally, they became involved in infiltrating and thwarting the Ku Klux Klan (later depicted in a made-for-TV special, "The FBI versus the Ku Klux Klan"). For the most part, however, the latter-day TV shows, "The FBI" and "The FBI Today" avoided scripts dealing with civil rights, antiwar protest, police brutality, antitrust violations, or anything else remotely connected with controversial political issues, sticking instead to the old tales of bank robbery, kidnapping, and espionage. Indeed, Hoover apparently had influence not only over scripts, but which actors were acceptable: "Inspector Erskine" of the FBI was played by Efram Zimbalist, Jr., Hoover's personal choice. (Some say that in Hoover's later days at the FBI, he demanded that agents conform to the "Zimmy image," making reality live up to art!)

With the rise of the antiwar and radical groups of the 1960s, Hoover had a new "alien" enemy which the FBI could fight. While many Americans cheered the FBI pursuing and harrassing such groups, there no longer existed the solid community which backed the FBI's crusade against America's enemies. Now many agreed with the protestors, or at least saw their point. They also were more difficult to catch. Perhaps more importantly, the FBI lost its appeal as the moral agent in the crime dramas of popular culture. Maverick cops (as in the movies "Dirty Harry," "The French Connection," and "Serpico") replaced the clean-cut professional FBI agent as hero. If mass audiences identified with cops, it was more likely to be an underground character such as "Baretta," the harrassed and varied police of "Hill Street Blues," or the handsome youngsters of "Chips."

Since Hoover's death, the reputation and the power of the FBI have declined. Congress moved quickly to limit the director's power; its image sank in the Watergate scandal; and other federal agencies gained jurisdiction over certain segments of law enforcement. But the FBI's decline was clearly augured by its loss of control over popular culture and therefore over itself as the one federal agent of the popular morality. When popular audiences no longer believed in the G-man as a moral force and not just another policeman, the FBI lost much of its symbolic status. But for at least three decades, the G-man and Mr. FBI were leading actors in a morality play of America versus the enemy.

POLITICS AS DRAMA

Hoover's career is an example of politics as drama. Whatever the director and the FBI were in reality, in appearance they were an important political symbol. Hoover's power was not in the statistics of crime detection but, rather, in the symbolic drama of crime fighting and "gangbusting" in the popular mind. This can be seen in Hoover's annual testimony to Congress requesting larger budgets: last year, he would always say, the FBI was never more successful in fighting crime; however, crime has never been more rampant and the threat to law and order never greater; therefore larger efforts and expenditures are required. In formal logic this argument is fallacious; but in political logic, given Hoover's reputation and goals, it was irresistible. Hoover's power was not power over crime or subversion; it was the power to dramatize crime and subversion. Hoover succeeded as a bureaucratic politician because he made himself and the FBI into a myth. Through the manipulation of the popular imagination, Hoover and the FBI became larger than life, the moral agents that act for us on the political stage, and therefore unassailable. It is remarkable that such impenetrable political armor could be made out of symbolic clothing. There is a fundamental political truth in the ancient children's tale about the Emperor's New Clothes. Princes rule in part by clothing themselves in mythic garb, the garments of political culture. Hoover was able to rule for so long because people believed in the myth that he created. If now people view FBI agents with a more critical eye, seeing them as mere employees in a large bureaucracy who are not to be trusted anymore than other police officers are, it is because they have lost their mythic political symbolic status that Hoover cultivated for them. They no longer are dramatic actors in a cultural drama of good and evil, but functionaries in the real world of police bureaucracy versus criminals. They have then lost their political *mystique*.

There are many different ways to govern through symbols. Politics, princes must understand, is an art, in part a dramatic art. Playing out the myths of a political culture is a pragmatic route to power. Responding to political anxieties by dramatizing oneself as a moral agent defending social values produces political support. Espousing important political symbols to be upheld and even enforced by the state rallies the collective conscience. Lastly, appearing as the heroic protector of lives, fortunes, and honor gains an important place in the popular mind.

Using drama in politics is a powerful way of securing power. But if in political dramas you dramatize yourself as the hero, this means there has to be a villain. The conflict becomes a simplistic one of the good guys versus the bad guys. There has to be an enemy. Now in reality, things are not that simple, but the popular mind will not admit of that. The easy characterizations of the many simply identifies Us versus Them. Politicians thus cast themselves as cultural heroes defending the faith.We are peaceloving, virtuous, and sinned against; they are warmongering, evil, and aggressive. By such dramatic casting, you may capture popular passions in a crusade against evil. But remember the price that you may have to pay: spending money on armaments to allay fears of invasion or annihilation; finding and punishing enemies in witch-hunts; injecting into politics hatreds that may be hard to control; and oversimplifying the realities of politics. If this seems immoral, remember what we said at the beginning: in politics, somebody always gets hurt. Even if it is the FBI symbolically solving the problem of crime on radio or TV shows, or capturing spies in the movies, the image created of the enemy has real world consequences.

"Everyone sees what you seem to be, few know what you really are."
—*Machiavelli*

"It is important . . . to reassure the public mind by such acts as will restore calmness and confidence."
—*Machiavelli*

"When King Canute began giving orders to the waves his popularity probably soared."
—*Richard Gid Powers*

"[He] who defends popular morality will come to be defended *by* popular morality. In fact he *becomes* popular morality in the minds of those who cannot distinguish between a thing and its representation."
—*Richard Gid Powers*

"Democracy is 'the dictatorship of the collective conscience of our people'."
—*J. Edgar Hoover*

"A prince should . . . entertain his people with festivals and spectacles."
—*Machiavelli*

Chapter

Making the Rules: Lawmaking and Policymaking

One of the recurrent fascinations for Machiavelli and for many other observers of political history is the founding of new states that through the sagacity of a ruler or a succession of rulers survive and prosper. Machiavelli today might point to the early United States, which through a succession of more or less competent rulers (Washington,

HENRY II: MAKER OF A FEUDAL KINGDOM

Henry Plantagenet, known to history as Henry II (1154–1189), may well have been England's greatest monarch, no small feat given the talent that has graced the throne of England. He was rawboned and fierce, given to fits of temper but nevertheless ambitious and shrewd, with a good memory and a desire to seek any knowledge that he could use to make his rule more effective. He was as consumed with the political problems of ruling as were the other powerful Norman kings who had preceded him, William I and Henry I. Henry II was well aware of the anarchic and hostile forces extant in England and France, as he had inherited a kingdom rent by nineteen years of civil war, a bitter succession fight, and innumerable intrigues, both inside and outside the royal family, bent on bringing down his throne. He was the compleat monarch, never forgetting the precept from falconry that his mother Matilda had preached to him: "Show your friends and allies their reward, keep it dangling before their eyes, but remove the bait before they can seize it; thus you will keep them devoted and eager to serve." For Henry, sometimes this political rule worked and sometimes it did not, even in his own family.

When Henry was eighteen, he married the thirty-year-old Eleanor of Aquitaine, the ex-wife of Louis VII of France. Eleanor was willful, beautiful, and the political match of any man. She and Henry were married for political reasons, giving Henry the dukedom of Aquitaine and thus the largest empire in Christendom but also setting the stage for centuries of strife between England and France. Together they formed the most powerful political force in Europe, but this did not stop them from quarreling and even warring. They spent twenty years trying to dominate each other but led separate lives. He was famous for his unbridled lust, and no household maid or daughter or wife of a vassal was safe from him. Eleanor tolerated his celebrated public romance with fair Rosamund but became his most dangerous political enemy, plotting with their sons civil war against him. (She also was no puritan, having a taste for young troubadors.)

At her court in Poitiers, Eleanor was far from the control of Henry in London. While the restless Henry, the ultimate man of action, conducted his throne from horseback—he liked to make decisions and do royal business while hunting—trying to make England into a respectable kingdom, Eleanor schemed against him at her court. All the baronial malcontents who disliked Henry's tough rule (he taxed the rich barons mercilessly) found their way to Eleanor's presence. She and their sons Richard and Geoffrey conspired against him, even convincing the heir to the throne, young Henry, to join them. But in 1173 King Henry crushed the rebellion, captured Eleanor and had her imprisoned in a castle for fifteen years. She refused his attempts to divorce her and in prison kept up her intrigues against him, maintaining her relations with French bishops and politicians and encouraging Henry's sons to rebel again.

Henry's major political achievement was in ruling a vast empire, ranging from the Scottish highlands to the Pyrennes. Like other medieval kings, he married his daughters to secure family alliances with the rulers of Saxony, Sicily, and Castile. His wealth, territorial holdings, alliance with Eleanor, and political reputation made him one of the most feared and respected of kings, and he raised England to its greatest prestige during his reign. But for all his political achievements, he could not rule his own family, all of whom envied and wanted his throne, though none of them had his ability. At Eleanor's urging, their sons finally rebelled against him by attacking his possessions in the continent. Henry, old and tired of fighting, set out once again to fight his own sons. In 1189, he died on the battlefield—some say of a broken heart—when he learned that even his beloved son John had turned against him. Henry turned his face to the wall, saying, "Shame, shame, on a conquered king!"

Henry was succeeded by the pompous and incompetent Richard the Lion-Hearted of undeserved legend, who spent little time in England, leaving the kingdom to the mercies first of Eleanor and then the disastrous John, of Robin Hood legend. John appears to have been as bad as the legend suggests, and his infringement on baronial rights led to the barons' forcing him to sign one of the landmark documents of constitutional history, the Magna Carta. John did not have what Machiavelli called "the knack of command" that was so impressive in his father Henry.

Adams, Jefferson, Madison, Monroe) associated with the Revolution and the founding of the nation, established a legitimate and effective government that endured. Machiavelli noted that "a new prince taking charge of a completely new kingdom will have more or less trouble in holding on to it, as he himself is more or less capable. . . . And it is worth nothing that nothing is harder to manage, more risky in the undertaking, or more doubtful of success than to set up as the introducer of a new order. Such an innovator has as enemies all the people who were doing well under the old order, and only halfhearted defenders in those who hope to profit from the new." But, he insisted, wise and powerful rulers determined to overcome adversity could through their "strength of character" rule new states, indeed bringing better rule than the country may have had before.

It is in such political crucibles that it is most instructive to look at domestic rule. What kinds of laws and policies lead to successful ruling? For it is at such times that domestic rule is most problematic, because a new regime and rulers are not secured by tradition, habit, or settled ways of ruling. There are many examples of such new states, but let us here discuss the domestic practice of power by looking at one of the most spectacular successes: the Norman kings who ruled England after the conquest of 1066, especially perhaps the best, Henry II.

RULING YOUR STATE

The Machiavellian view of politics stresses that ruling is always a precarious undertaking. Perhaps the most precarious rule is a new state, because as Machiavelli observed, "[S]tates which spring up suddenly, like everything else in nature which springs up in a day, cannot have a network of roots and branches; they are destroyed by the first storm that strikes." But it is precisely such new states and the princes that master them that are the most instructive. Machiavelli wrote about such mythical lawgivers and founders as Moses, Cyrus, Romulus,

Theseus, Solon, and Lycurgus "that fortune provided nothing for them but an opportunity; that gave them material, on which they could impose whatever form they chose." Such political state builders are remarkable because they create a new political form where one did not exist before, often against—or even because of—great odds.

In A.D. 1066, the Norman ruler William conquered England. Anglo-Saxon England was ethnically mixed and politically divided but nonetheless resented the invasion by the foreign, French-speaking Norman army. The Norman kings, beginning with William the Conquerer, were faced with the most difficult of political tasks: creating a new political "form" with the Anglo-Saxon "material" that was universally hostile to the new ruling class. The new Norman state was precarious, a small ruling group trying to rule over a million hostile and rebellious native English. The only way that the Normans could survive as rulers was to create a network of roots and branches that could resist the inevitable political storms that would strike.

Beginning with William, most of the Norman kings showed a genius for government. In Anglo-Saxon folklore and in Hollywood, the Normans made good proto-fascist villains, bleeding the virtuous Saxon peasants. Indeed, the myth of the Norman yoke even appeared in seventeenth-century revolutionary propaganda in England. But in fact, the Normans were rather good rulers and were so by necessity; they had to be because they were strangers in a strange land, and the only way they could survive was to be efficient. At the outset, William moved quickly to consolidate his new kingdom. He completed his conquest by 1071 and declared that all of England belonged to him. He then rewarded his military allies and granted fiefs to the Anglo-Saxon landholders in return for their loyalty. William thus established his own feudal system, with great fiefs near the frontiers for protection. Castles could be built only with his permission, and all of his vassals had to pledge their loyalty to him. Unlike other feudal systems, which had a weak central government subservient to the landed aristocracy, William established a strong central government with sovereign powers over every class and institution, and he retained such powers as coining money, building castles, conducting wars, and punishing major crimes. In short, William understood the necessity of creating a centralized state with sufficient powers to rule over both the powerful barons and the potentially powerful Anglo-Saxon masses.

Beginning with William, the Norman kings recognized the political logic of ruling a new and foreign state. They had to establish and control a centralized state in order to prevent the rise of hostile centers of power or rebellious forces, but they also had to respect local traditions and customs. For that reason, the Normans maintained or adapted Anglo-Saxon political institutions. William retained the Anglo-Saxon judicial system and shire courts to hear local cases. The shire court was presided over by a king's representative, the sheriff, giving him the power of the crown and making him the local symbol of the king's justice. William also retained the institution of the *fyrd,* the local Anglo-Saxon militia, and cultivated its loyalty: when some of the Norman barons revolted against him in 1086, William called out the Saxon militia against them. Indeed, William taxed the rich Normans mercilessly, lessening the burden on the poorer and less willing Saxons. William also conducted a survey of the resources of the land, written down in the famous Domesday Book. The survey was so thorough that it caused resentment, as it discovered resources as yet untaxed; yet it had the effect of not only increasing revenue but also making taxation more fair.

William was shrewd enough to understand the value of retaining in new form old Anglo-Saxon institutions and ruling practices. Two were especially helpful in consolidating Norman rule: inquiry and consultation. In inquiry, the Normans cultivated the practice of hearing cases and disputes in a wide variety of forums—inquest, commission, the courts. William also retained the Anglo-Saxon practice of investigating the cause of death of a discovered body and punishing those responsible (rather than just massacring the nearest village or whatever), including the right of the crown to summon the leading men of the community to give information. The Anglo-Saxons also had a regular consultative body called the *witenagemot,* an assembly of the great laymen and churchmen of the realm, who advised the king on matters of policy. William retained this in Norman form (the *curia regis*), giving the barons and others the perception that the king did not rule arbitrarily, but with the help of their advise and counsel. This institution finally became so entrenched that the feeling grew that the king had to consult them, to "parley" with them on important matters. After 1258, the barons had the power to insist that the great council meet three times every year with the king, and they called it *Parliament.*

It was then, through the necessities of political rule, that the English institutions of Parliament and common law emerged. The Normans could have ignored the traditions of inquiry and consultation, but at their own political risk. In domestic politics, especially in precarious situations, there is no substitute for good government. Or put another way: good government is good politics. This may seem like a truism, but it is one of the best ways to stay in power. The Normans had their share of bad rulers, but they had enough good rulers do enough good things that they survived, and eventually they were assimilated into English culture, as was their language, making English an amalgam of Anglo-Saxon, Norman French, and Latin.

WHAT ARE YOUR DOMESTIC POLITICAL GOALS?

Imagine yourself in the kind of political situation we have described. Suddenly you are the ruler of a group of people with whom you have little in common: you do not speak their same language; they resent you as an alien ruler; many of the things they do seem strange and puzzling to you; and they threaten your position. They outnumber you; their leaders scheme against you; anything that goes wrong is blamed on you; and nobody would mourn your death or fall from power. Not, you will agree, an enviable political position. But as the Norman kings remind us, also not an impossible one. Let us look at some of the things that you can do to master domestic politics.

In a general sense, your domestic political goals are simple: you have to maintain enough political control and curry enough political support to remain in power. You do this by ruling well. The Normans were able thus to maintain political control of the country. William established the new institutions and practices by which the government kept the peace. The king's law, the king's courts, and the king's highways extended his governmental power throughout the realm. William's barons and the local militia remained loyal during uprisings, thus providing him with enough military and police force to repel any trouble. William was so successful against lawlessness that for the first time in memory "a man of any substance could travel unmolested throughout the country with his bosom full of gold." Both the proud and powerful barons and the unruly and resentful Saxons were kept quiet by the government's power and ability to enforce the law. The attempt by the Norman government to be fair in the administration of justice was also a stabilizing political force. Many people felt that even though Norman justice was harsh, at least it was fair. The tradition of common law (based on Anglo-Saxon customary law) codified the laws, and Norman judges enforced them. By so doing, they avoided the cumulative grievances and resentments that spring from a sense of injustice, and emerge politically in hostile outbursts and support for rebellion.

William and subsequent Norman kings also understood the political uses of bringing prosperity. Norman policies were designed to aid trade and commerce. By building the king's highways and making them safe, merchants could feel safe traveling; indeed, the existence of good highways meant that they could travel. Norman feudalism and law regularized property relationships, making people feel that their property was secure. Courts and the royal bureaucracy gave people "title" to their holdings, which meant that they could not be taken away arbitrarily. The Norman kings understood that they had a stake in general prosperity: to the extent that the realm prospered economically, so did the royal treasury. It is hard to tax a poor people. Beginning with Henry I, the new English kings set out not only to increase the royal treasury but also to make government finances more efficient. When Henry and his officials discussed financial matters, they sat around a table covered with a checkered cloth to help their computations; consequently the English treasury came to be called the exchequer. With general prosperity and high compliance with taxation because it was fair, the monarchs had plenty of money to build English military power.

The line of kings after William also learned how to run the government. Henry I, for example, was as interested as his father was in mastering the machinery of government. Much of the business of government can be boring and tedious, but attention to detail gives the general impression that one is on top of things and that nothing escapes one's scrutiny. It was said of Henry II that he was "the king who never rested." Not only do you maintain control over policy by paying close attention to what your government is doing, you also gain a reputation for political omnipotence, of knowing everything of importance in your realm. (It also was said of the Byzantine emperor Justinian that "The emperor never sleeps.") Henry I selected a few trusted noblemen who divided up the labor of government, the rudimentary beginnings of cabinet administration: a justician who acted as the king's representative and as regent when he was gone; a chancellor who supervised documents, records, and correspondence and kept the great seal; and a treasurer who kept financial records and the king's treasure. From such beginnings the royal bureaucracy expanded over the centuries to include widely differentiated administrative roles.

But ruling a realm is not merely an administrative task. All public administration is political. Administrative decisions and policies should be determined according to their political consequences. The political control of the state and the political support needed to continue in power are inseparable. For that reason, domestic rule must be conducted with constant attention to maintaining the political coalition. The Norman kings were not totally independent of the powerful interests in their realm: the barons, the Church, and to some degree, the Anglo-Saxon masses. The *curia regis* was regularly convened as a political strategy, to give the barons the perception that they were being consulted and that their interests shaped royal policy. The local sheriff gave the king a representative among the people and an ear to local discontent. But as we have stressed again and again, ruling with your political coalition in mind may well present you with a dilemma. It may be that ruling fairly and giving your political supporters what they want is incompatible. In the matter of taxation, for example, if you exempt the barons, the people will become overburdened and resentful. The Norman kings are instructive in that they were able to make the rich barons and others pay more than the common folk did. Henry I devised new ways to get revenue from the rich, such as accepting *scutage* from his vassals rather than military service and giving privileges to towns if they paid higher taxes. Such ingenious administrative methods maintained the Norman political coalition while furthering its goal of ruling fairly and thereby remaining in power.

The greatest Norman kings are examples of how far one can go by ruling well, even under the most adverse circumstances. Out of political necessity, they created the mechanisms for the first modern state. By bringing good rule to England, they avoided the fate they might have suffered if they had been irresponsible tyrants. If the Saxon folk did not love them, they eventually came to respect them, and the Norman rulers gained widespread compliance with law and taxes and acquiescence in their rule. "How to deal with men he learned," it was said of William the Conquerer, "when to smite and when to spare."

HENRY II AND THE BUSINESS OF KINGSHIP

Henry II came to the English throne at the age of twenty-one, after a destructive period of civil war (1135–1154), which demonstrated to both Normans and Saxons the ruinous disadvantages of not having a strong ruler. Drawn from another hated French dynasty (the Angevin), Henry nevertheless brought England thirty-five years of benevolent rule, making many policy innovations and building an empire. Despite his intemperate fits of fury and depression, he left an indelible mark on English history through his attention to the business of kingship. His remarkable energies were directed throughout his reign to the absorbing passion of his life, the political mastery of his realm. He wanted to be a better king than even William and Henry I, a veritable "lion of justice."

Henry's domestic agenda aimed at first recreating political order and then extending the rule of law throughout the land. After his coronation, Henry acted: he sent home the foreign mercenaries that had accumulated during the long civil war; he had destroyed the more than eleven hundred unlicensed castles that had sprung up during the period of anarchy; and he revoked the royal grants of land and office made by his predecessor's cronies. He faced recurrent revolts, including those led by his own sons, but was always able to rally support from loyal barons, the Church, and the Saxon militia. Henry died on the battlefield fighting yet another revolt led by his sons, but for most of his reign, England enjoyed long periods of domestic peace.

Such periods gave Henry the opportunity to advance his twin goals of increasing the royal treasury and extending royal law. He knew that a king's power depended on his revenue and, like his grandfather Henry I, thought of ingenious ways to refill the royal treasury. Besides the revenue gained from his own estates (which was considerable, since Eleanor's holdings alone were greater than those of the king of France), he levied and enforced a wide variety of revenue-generating measures. Following the Norman tradition, he imposed the heaviest taxes on his barons, including stiff rates to permit marriages to landed widows. Henry sold charters to towns, successfully collected contributions from the English church, even from a new tax collected from knights who did not go on crusades. Henry was unceasing in his pursuit of revenue, and few, even among the most powerful barons, were willing to challenge openly the "lion of justice."

Henry's greatest domestic achievement was in extending the rule of law throughout the country. In the best Norman spirit, it was all done for sound political reasons beyond Henry's knowledge and appreciation of the law. Like William, he understood that an efficient and equitable administration of justice was crucial to the success of his rule. In terms of revenue, an extensive system of royal courts meant a constant flow of money into the royal treasury through the fines and fees collected. A just and universal enforcement of the law also served the political function of undermining revolts based on a widespread sense of injustice, by gaining the respect and compliance of the Saxon people. These dual political purposes meant, however, that Henry had to impinge upon the traditional responsibilities of two judicial institutions, the baronial and shire courts and the church courts. But Henry was determined to consolidate royal sovereignty, including sovereignty over the institutions of the feudal baronage and the Church.

Henry gradually gained control over the secular courts, by decreeing that certain crimes were restricted to royal justice and expanding the circuits and owners of itinerant justices. He made a large variety of writs available for a fee, which made the powers of the court available to a large part of the population. For example, if one man claimed that another had seized his land, he could buy a writ that gave power to agents of the crown to "repossess" the land and hear the case in a common court to which the seizer was "summoned." There twelve "lawful" local men were summoned to tell the truth about the land, and their testimony would be used to decide the case. Henry made a regular practice of summoning "juries" (from the French *juré,* a body of men under oath) to bear witness, evolving into the jury system familiar in Anglo-American law.

Henry also tried to bring the church courts and canon law under the royal administration. The English church, supported by the pope, had jealously guarded its right to try certain kinds of cases in church courts according to canon law, such as cases involving clerics accused of a secular crime. Henry hoped to break this power and to that end appointed his old friend and loyal chancellor, Thomas à Becket, as archbishop of Canterbury. But what Henry did not reckon for is captured in the old saw to the effect, "Where you stand depends upon where you sit." Someone appointed by a politician to a job—judge, bureaucrat, diplomat, or whatever—takes on the role once there, and does not necessarily do the bidding of whomever did the appointing. Becket, thusly, defended the Church's rights, much to Henry's chagrin. The battle between these two strong-willed men went on for years, with Becket refusing to bend on the Church's rights. One evening, celebrating Christmas, Henry's loyal and hard-drinking barons brought up the power and stubbornness of Becket, provoking one of the legendary royal rages. Henry rhetorically asked this gathering whether there were no men in his kingdom who would rid him of this meddlesome priest. This loss of temper turned out to be a political disaster for Henry, for four overzealous knights took him at his word, went to Canterbury, and murdered Becket in the cathedral. Henry was horror-stricken and swore to the pope that he had had no part in such a stupid act, but nevertheless he was forced to do abject penance. Worse, he had to yield on the issue, and the English throne for a long time had to acquiesce to the independence of church courts and laws, a severe defeat for Henry's goal of extending royal secular justice.

Despite this setback, Henry's legacy to England was considerable. He established a royal bureaucracy, extended the rule of law, and made the crown wealthy. The lion of justice, at least for long periods, met those classic domestic political goals that William had instituted. The word is deliberate: what the Norman kings "instituted" was *institutions,* the Latin root of which means "to set up." Institutions, once set up, become part of the political habits (the "roots and branches") of a regime and people, and become difficult to dismantle or ignore, as part of the political traditions of the country. Henry was succeeded by Richard the Lion-hearted, who overtaxed the country and spent all his time abroad at war; yet there was not a descent into anarchy again. Richard was succeeded by his brother John, whose overtaxation and violations of the legalities established by Henry led to a baronial revolt. Baronial rights were restored in the historic Magna Carta, which the barons forced John to sign and obey. Through misrule, John helped the development of Parliament, civil rights and criminal procedure, and most of all, the institution of the king's ruling by common consent and according to the principle of "what touches all should be approved by all." Perhaps the Norman kings, good and bad, hastened the demise in England of unlimited monarchical rule, on the one hand, by establishing the rule of institutions and, on the other, by enough misrule to bring the demand for more institutionalized rule.

ON IMITATING THE ACTION OF THE LION

"Even if he cannot follow other people's paths in every respect," stated Machiavelli, "or attain to the merit of his originals, a prudent man should always follow in the footsteps of the great and imitate those who have been supreme." The Norman kings, and Henry II in particular, provide us with examples of political talent creating a domestic state capable of rule under adverse circumstances. The domestic prince must be a lion of justice like Henry, in which case, he or she has a chance to maintain the political control and curry the political favor necessary in order to accomplish domestic political goals.

"Show your friends and allies their reward, keep it dangling before their eyes, but remove the bait before they can seize it; thus you will keep them devoted and eager to serve.

—*Matilda, mother of Henry II*

"[A] new prince taking charge of a completely new kingdom will have more or less trouble in holding on to it, as he himself is more or less capable."

—*Machiavelli*

"[S]tates that spring up suddenly, like everything else in nature which springs up in a day, cannot have a network of roots and branches; they are destroyed by the first storm that strikes."

—*Machiavelli*

"The emperor never sleeps."

—*said of Justinian*

"How to deal with men he learned, when to smite and when to spare."
—*The Anglo-Saxon Chronicle, on William the Conquerer*

"Where you stand depends upon where you sit."
—*American political maxim*

"Even if he cannot follow other people's paths in every respect, or attain to the merit of his originals, a prudent man should always follow in the footsteps of the great and imitate those who have been supreme."
—*Machiavelli*

Chapter

25

Reason of State: Warmaking and Peacemaking

In Chapter 14 of *The Prince*, Machiavelli wrote that "a prince . . . should have no other object, no other subject of study, than war, its rules and disciplines . . . the prince should never turn his mind from the study of war; in times of peace he should think about it even more than in wartime." These thoughts may seem a bit chilling when we contemplate the melancholy history of warfare. But we are also reminded that Machiavelli himself was a skilled diplomat, good at conducting negotiations for the purposes of reaching peaceful settlements. Thus Machiavelli represented in his career the two objectives of interstate relations: warmaking and peacemaking.

In Machiavelli's day a new political concept began to circulate: reason of state (*raison d'état, Staatsrason*). Although Machiavelli did not originate the term, his diplomatic communications presumed a realistic state interest. People began to express what everyone in politics had always known and what had always been practiced: that relations between states are governed by a struggle for power in which the states pursue their own political interests. The German historian Friedrick Meinecke, in his book *Machiavellism: The Doctrine of Raison d'État and Its Place in Modern History* traced this idea. "The State," Meinecke explained, "is in bond to the natural laws of the struggle for survival" and must recognize "the iron logic of power." He thus called for

TALLYRAND: MASTER DIPLOMAT

Charles Maurice de Talleyrand-Perigord, known to political history as Talleyrand, was a remarkable politician in many ways, not the least of which was that he was a political survivor. Indeed, his biographers speak of the political lives of Talleyrand, as he managed to participate in and survive the turbulent politics of France, beginning with the regime of Louis XVI and ending with the Revolution of 1830. Talleyrand lived from 1754 to 1838 and in that long life managed to become a bishop of the Catholic church, a servant of Louis's regime, a delegate to the Estates-General of 1789, a figure prominent in the French Revolution, Napoleon's foreign minister, a schemer against the emperor when fortune began to turn against him, the foreign minister to the restored Bourbon regime of Louis XVIII, the French representative at the Congress of Vienna, the grand chamberlain, and a participant in the Revolution of 1830.

Talleyrand's long and varied career suggests that he was an adaptable and adept politician, serving a succession of masters well, all of whom may have been a bit suspicious of him but recognized his political skill. There is something astonishing about such political survival, given the vicissitudes of politics and the tendency of new rulers to get rid of figures associated with previous princes. (In our century, political survivors such as China's Chou En-lai and the Soviet Union's Andrei Gromyko come to mind.) In his last undertaking in 1830, Talleyrand swore allegiance to Louis Philippe, whom he had just helped put on the throne, by exclaiming, "Sire, you are the thirteenth!" But the fact that he had served thirteen different rulers did not mean that he always had had respect for them. Of the Bourbons he said contemptuously, "They have learned nothing, and forgotten nothing." Indeed, of his peers at the Congress of Vienna, he impatiently sneered, "Too frightened to fight each other, too stupid to agree." Nor did political service mean that he would remain loyal to a ruler to the bitter end. One of Talleyrand's political talents was strategic treason, whereby he knew that the political game was over and offered his services to a new prince. He served Napoleon well but abandoned the emperor when the tide ran against him, actually greeting the allies when they entered Paris in 1814 and forcing the senate to depose Napoleon and form a new government. At Vienna, the Russian czar angrily accused Talleyrand of being a "traitor to the common cause." "That, Your Imperial Majesty," he replied, "is a question of dates."

Although Talleyrand's loyalties may be questioned, his political acumen and survivability may not. The English diplomat and historian Harold Nicholson wrote that "in Talleyrand the sense of proportion and the sense of occasion transcended opportunism; they amounted to genius." His legendary skepticism and pessimism ("The more things change, the more they remain the same" is probably his most famous aphorism) did not prevent him from believing that temporary political solutions were possible. He defended his political shifts: "I have never conspired in my life, except at those times when I had the majority of France for an accomplice, and when I sought with it the salvation of the country." Talleyrand was, Nicholson wrote, "both versatile and corrupt: but in his desire to give peace to France and Europe he was abundantly consistent and sincere." Talleyrand's closeness to the seat of power gave him an insight into the political arts denied to most of us, and his writings abound with Machiavellian observations on ruling: "In politics as elsewhere one must not love too much; it confuses; it lessens the clarity of one's view—and it is not always counted to one's credit." His response to events was almost never moral, but rather an assessment of their political consequences. When he learned that Napoleon had executed the duke of Enghien, Talleyrand bitterly exclaimed, "It is more than a crime, it is a mistake." His judgment was not on the moral rectitude of the event, but on the political wisdom of it. Talleyrand was always a moderate, a compromiser, a greaser of the political treads. At Vienna, he thought that the balance of power in Europe could be ensured only if the great powers were "animated by a spirit of moderation and justice which will preserve the equilibrium." Moderation seemed to him the best way to achieve political results: "Stability," he wrote, "frequently adds something to perfection, and perfection itself cannot add anything to stability."

"the discovery of the necessary character of political action ... the mighty kernel of truth in Machiavelli's *Prince*." Does this mean that foreign policy is immoral? Quite the contrary, argued Meinecke. Reason of state enjoins political rationality, the calculation of the political logic of state interest. To the extent that a prince lives up to the Machiavellian model, he or she will repress passions—hate, greed, revenge, and so on—and use political reason. Likewise in interstate relations, Meinecke stated, Machiavellism does not preach the end as justifying the end, but rather the idea that the end controls the means. The correct use of political logic makes warmaking and peacemaking highly rational games, definitely not a political sport for the fainthearted, dull minded, weak willed, and most of all, the political novice.

THE RECOURSE TO VIOLENCE

We all are familiar with the fact of violence in everyday life. Remember the schoolyard bully who, because he or she was bigger and meaner, could make life miserable for everybody else? Most of us have witnessed teenage fights, family quarrels, perhaps even more serious violence, such as robbery or murder. We know that violence is a part of life, and that often people can get what they want by recourse to violence. Criminals, for example, use illegal violence to get their way. "You can get more with a gun and a polite request," said Al Capone, "than just [with] a polite request." As the fictional Vito Coreleone of "The Godfather" said, you make people offers they can't refuse.

But the violence of the schoolyard or the street is nonpolitical. When we get into the realm of politics and government, we are talking about political violence. In Chapter 17 we talked about gaining power through force of arms, or revolutionary violence. This too is illegitimate violence, although of course if the violence of the movement leads it to gain power, the violence will be legitimated. Rather than criminals, the revolutionary terrorists and guerrillas become heroes, and the government officials and troops become the criminals. In politics, what you are labeled depends on whether or not you win.

All governments claim the right to use violence to accomplish political ends. The hard core of power is violence, including its threat or actual use in both domestic and foreign relations. Ruling means that one has to use political means adequate to accomplish political ends, and that includes recourse to political violence. This is a fact of power from which many of us shrink. Remember what we said about the economy of violence. In politics, like it or not, one must sometimes use violence in order to achieve political results. If politics is "a science of the controlled application of force," the political test is how well violence is used.

The fundamental imperative of ruling is keeping the peace. A prince cannot accomplish anything else unless there is civil order. This is called the *Hobbesian imperative*: according to the seventeenth-century political philosopher Thomas Hobbes, a prince has the duty to use the organized power at his disposal to produce at least a minimal peace. Without social peace, no other political purpose can be pursued. This means that one must use force and the threat of force. The great German political sociologist Max Weber perhaps said it best when in he defined an association as political "if and in so far as the enforcement of its order is carried out continually within a given territorial area by the application and threat of physical force on the part of the administrative staff."

Much of the domestic, official, "legitimate" political violence carried out by rulers and their police and armies is excessive and unjustified. Machiavelli warned that a prince should "make himself feared in such a way that, even if he gets no love, he gets no hate either . . ." and that "when princes cannot help being hated by someone, they ought first of all try to avoid universal hatred." Otherwise, excessive suppression can result in more violence and even the prince's downfall. But in any case, the use of official sanctioned violence in domestic polititics is a universal, if unpalatable political reality.

THE RECOURSE TO VIOLENCE IN
FOREIGN RELATIONS

During the French Revolution and the Napoleonic wars in Europe, a Prussian military officer named Karl von Clausewitz wrote a book based on his experience in and reflections on this period, entitled simply *On War.* In this book he made the now classic statement in regard to the political recourse to violence in foreign relations. "The war of a community . . . always arises from a political condition and is called forth by a political motive. It is therefore a political act. . . . War is therefore a continuation of policy by other means. It is not merely a political act but a real political instrument, a continuation of political intercourse, a conduct of political intercourse by other means. . . . All wars may be regarded as political acts." This thoroughly Machiavellian view has had great influence. When Lenin went into exile in Finland in 1917, one of the books he took with him was *On War,* and his notes made there emphasized that war was not only a political act but also the ultimate instrument of politics. Mao Tse-tung said in this connection, "politics is war without bloodshed, and war is politics with bloodshed."

Warmaking, the recourse to organized political violence, is an ancient and sanctioned form of politics. Interstate relations, from the ancient city-states and empires to the present superstates, have always included war or the threat of war. Virtually all states have claimed that under some circumstances the use of war is justified. Nearly all politicians have understood that in interstate politics one can often get more with guns and polite requests than just a polite request. With the recourse to war, you try to make political people offers they can't refuse. And they do the same to you.

Therefore princes must study war and accept that they may have to threaten to use or actually use war to get what they want. This does not mean you have to be a bully or a criminal; it means simply that the game of interstate relations includes as one possible means, recourse to organized violence, or war. Many such power games include war as an ultimate sanction. According to Machiavelli and Clausewitz, war should not be used for irrational or emotional reasons—revenge, for example—but for reasons of state. War is one of the rational political options open to princes to accomplish political purposes. For politically rational reasons, wars can solve problems. In disputes among nations, there may be no other way to solve a border dispute, conflict over regional hegemony, or other sorts of political conflicts. The American Civil War, for example, was the violent climax of the regional and moral conflict that had divided the United States almost from its beginning. It was a bloody, bitter war that has had repercussions down to the present. Yet the war did end slavery and in that sense did something good. Similarly, World War II in Europe defeated an aggressive power that threatened Western civilization. In both these cases, an argument can be made that war solved problems or secured worthwhile values and thus was justified. It may even be argued that both the American Civil War and World War II economized violence. The persistence of slavery in the South would have perpetuated misery, and the persistence of Fascism would have perpetuated the death camps.

A policy of war also may produce domestic benefits. Wars and the mobilization for war stimulate the national economy. One of the standard strategies for ending depressions and unemployment is mobilizing for war. The depressions in the United States and Germany in the 1930s were ended by rearmament. A foreign threat may also be the only way to unify a divided country, giving everyone a common fear and hatred. When irrational domestic divisions threaten to get out of control, a prince may be able to abate them by focusing attention on a foreign foe. By becoming the war leader defending the nation against foreign aggression, the prince may increase his or her popular support.

But a policy of war also has its political dangers. The threat of war makes people afraid and anxious, and they may heed the call of a political rival who will sue for peace. Actual war, if it drags on or leads to defeat, obviously may undermine the ruler's position. Indeed, the domestic costs of warmaking may often outweigh all the possible benefits.

Consider, in this regard, the Vietnam War. The United States committed itself to an ever-increasing involvement in Vietnam, by means of a series of short-term decisions rather than a long-term evaluation of the political or military wisdom of fighting the war. Not only did policymakers not think out the political rationality of the war, they also did not dream that it would produce the domestic reaction that it did. They were apparently guided by the law of political delay: let's keep putting off what we believe will be bad consequences if we lose. The Johnson administration, in particular, was guided by the political fear that if Vietnam fell to the Vietcong, it would suffer domestic political losses to the Republicans. Thus it would not withdraw, nor could it risk World War III by the nuclear destruction of North Vietnam. But the middle position left it with a stalemate. So the administration and the military kept raising expectations which were less and less convincing. The draft affected more and more families, and increasing numbers resisted it. Finally, Vietnam became a cause for the reform movements of the time, creating a powerful antiwar coalition. By 1968, the country was in such turmoil that Johnson decided not to run for reelection, but the domestic conflict over Vietnam persisted. In retrospect, the political losses suffered by Johnson, and in some measure, by Nixon, may well have been greater than those they might have suffered from a refusal to commit the country to the war and thus risk the domestic reaction to a Vietcong victory.

War, therefore, must be used with caution and discretion. A ruler does not want to get caught in the trap of fighting the wrong war with the wrong enemy at the wrong place in the wrong time. Usually getting involved in such a quagmire involves the political mistake of overextension. Military power of even the greatest magnitude—such as the Roman legions, the British navy, or the American nuclear arsenal—is nonetheless limited. Great powers may have great resources (sometimes called the *ingredients* of power—wealth, weapons, troops, industry, intelligence, good generals, and so on) but this does not mean that such power is unlimited. Rome, for example, was a powerful state that overextended its power by trying to dominate too many people in too many places. By expanding its "rim of power," it exhausted its resources and will. Vietnam was an example of trying to expand the rim of American power in a place that might not have been worth the price. The lesson of the past misapplication of military power is ultimately a political one: choose your fights carefully.

Perhaps the classic example of military overextension leading to political disaster was Napoleon I's invasion of Russia in 1812. By then the French Empire controlled a large part of Europe, but its conquests were tenuous because they had aroused nationalism and resentment against Napoleon's imperial rule. Despite that, Napoleon lusted for more and decided to invade Russia, completing his domination of

Europe. The outmanned and outgunned Russians retreated, burning their crops so that no food would be available to the French, and even let Napoleon enter and burn Moscow. General Mikhail Kutuzov avoided a showdown, arguing simply that one day it would snow and that the army would be destroyed by the Russian winter. He realized that Napoleon had overextended himself badly. Napoleon's retreat from Moscow in the winter became a nightmare, and less than a quarter of his army survived. This defeat encouraged others to strike against him, and in 1813, Napoleon was defeated and exiled. The policy of warmaking had led him to his downfall.

Yet it is often difficult to avoid using war and the threat of war as a political means. If you are reluctant to "rattle your sabers," other powers may take that as a sign of weakness and undertake foreign adventures. It is often argued that the European powers in the 1930s followed a policy of appeasement, by which they capitulated to each of Hitler's demands and by so doing emboldened him to seek even larger gains. A strong defense and communicating to potential aggressors that you are willing to use military force are deterrents. However, the existence of military power also makes other states afraid and encourages them to build up their own military power so as to be equal or superior to yours. This makes you afraid, and so you do the same, thus leading to an arms race, with competing powers trying to outdo one another in military power. Such races may heighten tensions and, rather than preventing war, make it more likely.

WHAT DID YOU DO IN WORLD WAR III?

"Compared to war," said General George S. Patton, "all other forms of human endeavor shrink into insignificance." That is debatable, but certainly everything else shrinks into insignificance in the age of nuclear warfare. The political logic of warmaking remains the same as before, but the advent of nuclear bombs with the means to deliver them to distant targets complicates things, to say the least.

Let us consider the potential for warfare between the two major nuclear powers, the United States and the Soviet Union. Since World War II, these two powers have been adversaries, competing for power in many ways. On one occasion, the Cuban missile crisis of 1962, they came very close to nuclear war. Since then, both sides have been expanding and complicating their military capabilities, especially in the area of nuclear weapons. Now both sides are capable of "overkill," that is, killing practically everybody several times over in either country.

Both sides are acutely aware of the danger of their power struggle, and both know that a nuclear war would be devastating to their own country. Yet the struggle and the accompanying arms race go on virtually unabated. Why? Because neither side feels that it can risk not staying in the struggle, not trusting the other side enough to disarm.

Two political scientists, Richard Neustadt and Graham Allison, pointed to the nuclear paradox: "In a world of mutual superiority, neither nation can win a nuclear war, but each must be willing to risk losing." Let us consider this. Both sides have such great nuclear power that if war comes, both will lose. If one side attacks the other, the latter will be able to destroy the former in retaliation. Thus nuclear war is irrational, the ultimate diseconomy of violence. A political act that results in the partial or even total decimation of one's own population, massive destruction of cities and industry, and radioactive pollution of the environment surely must be counted irrational. So both sides don't want nuclear war, and know that the other side doesn't want war either. But if one side is not willing to risk nuclear war, the other side can win political objectives by bringing the dispute to that level of risk. So in order to advance their political objectives, both nations must take the ultimate Machiavellian risk, even though they do not want to and even though they understand the dangers.

Could one side just leave the game unilaterally? It could, but in politics that is unlikely. The two have sought some ways to reduce the risk, such as the "hot line" between the Kremlin and the White House. But the nuclear game may well become more rather than less dangerous in the future. For one thing, the technology of nuclear war is so complicated that the risk of accident is increased. (World War III will not be a mistake—it is planned down to the last minute detail—but it might well be an accident.) For another, new players are entering the game and might begin it. As the number of players expands (as many as forty countries may have nuclear weapons by the end of the 1980s), the probability of their use increases, as well as the possibility of everyone's using them, escalating such a war into a worldwide nuclear holocaust. But perhaps the most likely scenario is one resulting from political *fortuna*. If the tides of world politics turn against one side and toward the other, the losing side may become desperate and irrational and initiate a war in a last-ditch gamble to win, or at least to destroy the other side.

What would happen in World War III? Suppose that you live in or near a major American city. In case of war, this is what would happen: The missile would emerge from an underground silo in the Soviet Union and approximately thirty minutes later would fall within a hundred yards of its target. In less than ten seconds, a fireball would spread out, vaporizing the downtown; a huge crater would be scooped out; and debris would be hurled everywhere. A wall of heat would move out as far as eight miles, starting fires in the suburbs, followed by a shock wave that would knock over buildings and throw people through the air. A mushroom-shaped cloud would form above the city, raining deadly radioactive particles in a forty-mile diameter. Hundreds of thousands of people would die immediately, and many more would die within days of injuries or radioactive poisoning. The survivors would live in a nightmarish world: no clean food or water, few or no doctors or medical facilities, the city reduced to rubble, and gangs fighting each other for food or loot.

In an all-out nuclear war, the long-term environmental and social consequences would be devastating. The nuclear clouds would affect agriculture for centuries, through both radiation poisoning and changes in the weather. The number of genetic mutations in animals and humans would increase. Despite Soviet and American government plans to return things to normal after such a war, most experts agree that that would be unlikely. The survivors may envy the dead as they forage through the rubble, huddle in shattered buildings, hide from roaming bands of scavengers (both human and animal), and abandon the legacy of civilization in a new dark age.

You might think that such a prospect would make nuclear war unthinkable, something that policymakers would reject out of hand. But not so. In both the Soviet Union and the United States, there are important policymakers and opinion leaders who maintain that a nuclear war is winnable. The "hawks" on both sides argue for more armaments, plans for civil defense and evacuation of cities, postwar recovery plans (such as issuing emergency change-of-address cards at post offices in cities hit by nuclear bombs), contemplation of first strikes against the enemy for a knockout blow before it can recover, and a willingness to tolerate large-scale casualties and the destruction of their own country in order to achieve their political objectives.

Such thinking might well seem insane to you, and many people would agree with you. After all, politicians are playing with your life, the lives of future generations, the fate of your country, and even the human race as a whole. The world has already been engulfed in two devastating world wars in this century, and many experts think that a third and even more devastating world war is nearly inevitable. Perhaps the Third World War began when both sides to the conflict accepted the idea that they had to defend themselves with weapons they could not possibly use without committing suicide. In any case, you will live to see whether the unthinkable does happen. And don't fool yourself: it can indeed happen, and the chances are very good that it will.

WHAT HAPPENS WHEN PEACE BREAKS OUT?

If the total warfare of nuclear holocaust seems impolitic, we will be faced with the ancient and vexing problem of bringing about peace. Is peace simply the breathing space before yet another war (peace has been defined as "the temporary absence of war"), or are there ways to bring about peace for long periods of time?

But there is historical precedent for peacemaking that actually works for long periods of time. The Machiavellian understands that even though war is possible as a political outcome, peace is possible too. If you enjoy a life lived in peace, it will be because of the success of politics. That depends, we reiterate, on the politicians exercising that highest of all Machiavellian political skills, diplomacy.

The success of peacemaking depends on several factors, all of which can be shaped and guided by diplomats. In politics, if parties to a conflict do not want to reach an agreement, it is unlikely that they will do so. In that schoolyard scrape we mentioned above, if the bully really wants to punch you in the nose, no amount of sweet reason will dissuade him. On the other hand, if he sees that everyone will gang up on him if he attacks someone, he may see the desirability of reaching an agreement: "If you don't punch us in the nose, we won't gang up on you." People may desire an agreement for a wide variety of reasons, not the least of which is that they are encouraged to do so for fear of reprisal. People may also just get tired of fighting, spending a lot of money on war, and constantly living in fear of death. So peace may become politically popular as well as wise. At the end of the Napoleonic wars, most countries were financially drained, tired of the killing, and desirous of peace. The desire was there; the political question was how it could be achieved.

This brings us to one of the most famous examples of peacemaking: the Congress of Vienna that settled the peace of post-Napoleonic Europe. But the fact that all parties concerned wanted peace is by itself no guarantee that peace will break out. After the downfall of Napoleon, there still remained political interests that had to be reconciled in order to bring about peace. In other words, besides agreeability, another condition of peace is reconcilability. If conflicting political interests cannot be reconciled, no amount of goodwill will be able to prevent the outbreak of hostilities again. They can be settled by negotiation, coming to a political agreement that satisfies the parties involved to the extent that peace is maintained. In that sense, the reverse of Clausewitz is also true: peace is a continuation of policy by other means, a political act, a continuation of political intercourse by peaceful means. Peace is a political strategy.

There is, however, another necessary condition for the creation of peace: the negotiating skill of the diplomats involved. If politicians sense that peace is an idea whose time has come, discover ways to reconcile issues, and use negotiation to bring agreement to fruition, then peace will have a chance. It takes hardnosed politics to give peace a chance. Think again of situations in which you may have been part of a task group, with the charge to come to an agreement on something. All sorts of things prevent reaching an agreement—personal feuds, inertia and delay, disagreements, even appeals to violence. In any event, it is likely that if your group reached an agreement, it did so because the necessary conditions of negotiation prevailed. In politics, peace is often an idea whose time has come, and the role of political negotiators is to find ways and means to seize the time and make peace.

The political logic of peace was much on the minds and agenda of the important politicians at the Congress of Vienna. In long and torturous negotiations, they finally found ways to forge a general European peace. The important figures there arranged parties, balls, and hunting for the lesser nobles and diplomats from the many small European states and principalities. "Congress dances," observed one weary diplomat, "but it

Practicing Power

does not march." But the social life served two crucial political functions: it kept the less important statesmen busy at romance and other forms of play, occupying them while the serious negotiators hammered out the details of the peace in small, private conferences; and the hunting, concerts, and the like also took up time. The serious negotiators knew that they could not be in any hurry to conclude the peace. If the peace were to last, it could not be made in haste, but only through long and considered negotiation.

There were three skillful negotiators who forged the peace at Vienna: Prince Klemens von Metternich, Viscount Robert Stewart Castlereagh, and Talleyrand. They brought with them the ingredients for peacemaking—the desire for an agreement (Castlereagh said that he came to Vienna "not to collect trophies but to bring the world back to peaceful habits"), the confidence that the issues involved were reconcilable, and considerable negotiating skill. But there was another question that hung over the conference: how was France to be treated?

It was here that Talleyrand played a crucial role. He exploited the differences among the great powers and sided with lesser countries who resented being ignored. He soon was accepted into the inner circle of decision making at Vienna and by January 1815, was in alliance with Austria and England, threatening Czar Alexander I of Russia with war unless he relented on Poland. But Talleyrand's major achievement was essential to the success of the congress: his diplomatic skill not only made him part of the inner circle of power, but it also made France an equal part again of the European community, and therefore not a country to be unduly humiliated in defeat, forced to pay debilitating reparations or give up many rights and territories. Remember that one of the key elements of successful negotiation is not to injure the prestige of one of the parties. By understanding this, the negotiators of the Congress of Vienna restored France to normalcy, making it a part of the relative balance of power that, with few exceptions, held until 1914.

By comparison, consider what happened at the Versailles Conference after World War I, when the defeated party, Germany, was not treated as an equal. Even though President Woodrow Wilson, one of the "Big Four" at that conference, warned that "only a peace between equals can last," he condoned the victorious powers' punishment of Germany, making it take the blame for the war, pay huge reparations, and disarm. Unlike the negotiators at Vienna, those at the Versailles Conference did not understand the political reasons for magnanimity. The restoration of Germany as an equal power in Europe, like France a hundred years before, might have restored a relative balance of power in Europe and might have created a stable Germany. Woodrow Wilson, the great political idealist, had several political cards that he could have played at Versailles that could have helped to bring about an amicable peace. But he would not use them and finally agreed that Germany deserved what it got. Such an attitude caused great resentment in Germany and created the conditions for great inflation and depression, unstable government, and the rise of the Nazis, who claimed the Versailles treaty was the cause of Germany's misfortune. Perhaps all that could have been avoided by a magnanimous treatment of Germany.

WILL PEACE BREAK OUT?

If it does, it will be the work of Machiavellian politicians using the full range of negotiating skills to bring it about. Peace will not come about just because we all desire it. (Indeed, not all of us, including powerful interests, do desire it.) Woodrow Wilson, many observers agree, desired a just and lasting peace as a political ideal. Yet the man of principle at Versailles was not also sufficiently a man of politics to bring it about. The political ideal of peace has to run the gauntlet of political reality, an often torturous and painful route that does not open up easily just because one's motives are good. At Vienna, Talleyrand (and the others) committed immoral acts, lying, double-crossing, dividing and then using the divisions, saying one thing and then doing another, and so forth. Yet out of that came a durable peace. At Versailles, Wilson was moral, but the peace did not last. His good motives assured that he meant no evil and indeed meant great good; yet his unwillingness to use evil for political reasons helped bring about great harm. Moral goodness does not guarantee political success.

In the years to come, the fate of humankind will be decided on what is done with nuclear weapons. This is foremost a moral question, but it is also a political question and in the final analysis can be decided only by politics. If we are to avoid nuclear holocaust, we will need moral Wilsons to define the ideal, but we will also need political Talleyrands to ensure its preservation.

"In politics as elsewhere one must not love too much; it confuses; it lessens the clarity of one's view—and it is not always counted to one's credit."
—*Talleyrand*

"A prince . . . should have no other object, no other subject of study, than war, its rules and a discipline. . . ."
—*Machiavelli*

"All wars may be regarded as political acts."
—*Clausewitz*

"Only a peace between equals can last."
—*Woodrow Wilson*

"Stability frequently adds something to perfection, and perfection itself cannot add anything to stability."
—*Talleyrand*

Chapter

26

The Arsenal of Political Means

By 1917, Europe had been engulfed in world war for two and a half years. Already millions had died in the struggle on two fronts, and the stalemate seemed endless and increasingly pointless. Germany, in particular, wanted something to happen to relieve it of the burden of fighting on two fronts, and something did: revolution broke out in Russia. The corrupt and antiquated czarist state, under the pressure of the war and domestic unrest, collapsed before the riots and mutinies that spread all over Russia. A provisional government replaced the deposed Czar Nicholas II. The Allies recognized the new government in the hope of keeping Russia in the war. The Germans immediately sensed that if they could persuade this new revolutionary government to sue for peace, it would free countless German troops to turn to the West for a final blow against the Allies. On April 2, 1917, the United States entered the war against Germany, which made the Germans even more desperate to make peace with the Russians. But it also meant having a government in Russia that wanted to abandon the war and was willing to deal.

German intelligence decided on a bold idea. It began to make secret contacts with the revolutionary party—mostly in exile—that was not part of the postczarist government but wanted to take Russia out of the war. This was the Bolsheviks, the Russian Communists. The Germans were, of course, in no way their ideological allies, but operated in the spirit of Bismarckian *Realpolitik*: given the gravity of the situation, we will deal with the devil himself if he can help us get what we want. If the Bolsheviks could seize power or simply create enough chaos, Russia could effectively be taken out of the war. Besides, the Germans reasoned, the Bolsheviks could not hold power for long anyway, and so they were only a temporary expedient that would not trouble them in the future.

The Germans conducted secret negotiations with the exiled Russian Communists, and in late March 1917 a German agent was sent to Switzerland to meet with the acknowledged leader of the Bolsheviks, Vladimir Ulyanov, known to the world by his political pseudonym,

LENIN: THE REVOLUTIONARY PRINCE

Valdimir Ilyich Ulyanov was born in a provincial town, the son of Russian-German middle-class parents. Vladimir and his older brother Alexander did well in school, and the brother went away to Petrograd to a university, where he became involved in a student's plot to assassinate the czar and, despite the pleas of his mother to the czar, was executed. Vladimir, who had just turned seventeen, became, after that, irrevocably committed to the revolutionary left and the overthrow of the czar. At the university of Kazan, he became involved in a student protest meeting and was arrested and expelled. The policeman who supervised the expulsion asked him, "Why do you revolt, young man? You are up against a stone wall." "A wall, yes," he is supposed to have replied, "but a crumbling one, and one which will soon collapse." The czarist wall eventually did collapse, with his help.

In his many years of political agitation, Lenin developed his very practical approach to the realization of Marxist revolutionary goals. He disagreed with those who thought revolution in Russia had to be economic before it could be political; that is, an industrial revolution would have to create a bourgeoisie and proletariat before a Marxist revolution could occur.

Lenin's legendary energy, zeal, asceticism, and combativeness led him into endless disputes with other revolutionary figures and groups in the decades before the revolution. He was involved in many plots and intrigues against the government and other revolutionary groups. He was arrested and spent time in Siberian exile. Eventually he was forced into exile and wandered from country to country, all the while maintaining his contacts and polemics with the other Russian revolutionaries. Like Marx himself, Lenin (with his ever-faithful and long-suffering wife Krupskaya) spent time in London and, like Marx again would go to the reading room of the British Museum and read and write. There is an apocryphal story that long after the revolution and Lenin's rise to power, a journalist retracing Lenin's steps inquired there, asking an elderly guard if he remembered an anonymous bald and bearded Russian man who used to come there regularly. The guard did remember, saying, "Yes, he used to come here regularly, read all day, and then leave. Then one day he didn't come back and was never heard from again."

Lenin was a great revolutionary but was also moody, cantankerous, intolerant, and even contemptuous of the Russian masses whose cause he espoused. His wife was scrupulously loyal to him during all the years in poverty and exile, even though he had an open love affair in Zurich with a glamorous Frenchwoman. He was also capable of cruelty and cynicism. The British philosopher Bertrand Russell talked to Lenin in 1920 and asked him about socialism in agriculture: "He explained with glee how he had incited the poorer peasants against the richer ones, and they soon hanged them from the nearest tree—ha! ha! ha! His guffaw at the thought of those massacred made my blood run cold."

Yet Lenin almost single-handedly kept the Bolsheviks in power. His prestige and political skill were such that the new Soviet Union persevered despite civil war, foreign intervention, and poverty and backwardness. But Lenin's health gave out, especially after an assassin's bullet nearly killed him, and he died in 1924 of a brain hemorrhage at the age of fifty-three. He died without naming a successor, though warning of the dangerous habits of Stalin (see Chapter 27). Churchill maintained that only Lenin could have prevented the Stalinist horrors that befell the Russians: "He alone could have found the way back to the causeway. . . . The Russian people were left floundering in the bog. Their worst misfortune was his birth . . . their next worst—his death."

In death, Lenin was promoted to immortality and still lies in state in his tomb in Red Square. Almost every morning a line of Russians waits in sun or snow to view the embalmed body of the bald man with the beard who was never heard from again. More than a hundred million people have filed through the granite mausoleum since 1924, and the Soviet leaders view parades from atop his tomb, the symbolic base of Soviet political authority. One sees Lenin's icon and name everywhere in the Soviet Union. The young Lenin provides a model of the new Soviet man in children's schoolbooks, and in Soviet oratory, books, and song, he is the "genius," the "great," the "immortal," worshipped in every form of popular culture. The frequently seen poster reminds the Soviets that "Lenin Lived. Lenin Lives. Lenin Will Live."

Lenin's legacy to Russia and the world is still controversial, but his influence, especially as a political tactician, has been great. He was influential not only in setting the Soviet ruling style but also on young nationalists in remote places. His ability to combine Marxist theory with the political logic of practice appealed to young intellectuals such as Mao Tse-tung and Vietnam's Ho Chi Minh. When Mao said "A revolution is not a dinner party," he was echoing Lenin's sentiment about such a political struggle: "To make an omelet, you have to break eggs." It is likely that one's attitude toward Lenin may be affected by whether one is part of the omelet or one of the discarded and broken eggshells.

Lenin. The negotiations were sensitive, and Lenin was cautious. He wanted assurances from the new Russian government that he and his cohorts would not be arrested on arrival. Too, he was concerned about how it would look for him to be transported by the Germans, and so he insisted that he and his colleagues be sealed in the railroad car they would take across Germany into Russia, in order to counter any later charges, by being able to say they had had no contact with their German carriers. There was an unscheduled stop in Berlin, where apparently Lenin and the German contacts did discuss financial arrangements for helping the Bolsheviks disrupt Russia; and indeed between April and the Bolshevik seizure of power in November 1917, between 6 and 10 million deutsch marks were invested in the Bolshevik party.

The Germans and Russian revolutionaries made a deal of truly Machiavellian proportions, for practical and political reasons. The Germans were aware of the magnitude of the gamble they were taking, and it is indeed a great irony that the reactionary regime of Kaiser Wilhelm II was instrumental in bringing the Soviet Union to power. The Germans were also aware of the human political weapon they were loosing on the world. "Nevertheless," wrote Winston Churchill, "it was with a sense of awe that they turned upon Russia the most grisly of all weapons. They transported Lenin in a sealed truck like a plague bacillus from Switzerland into Russia."

Churchill was in no sense an admirer of Lenin, but he did recognize that Lenin was a potent political force because of his grasp of political means. Lenin was not a political figure dedicated to reconstructing Marxist dialectics in obscure pamphlets and debating doctrines in cafes. He was a man of political action, willing to use whatever means was necessary to achieve his political ends. While waiting to return to Russia in 1917, he wrote, "It would be indeed a grave error if we tried now to fit the complex, urgent, rapidly unfolding practical tasks of the revolution into the Procrustean bed of a narrowly conceived 'theory' instead of regarding theory first of all and above all as a guide to action." Upon his return, Lenin plunged into action, organizing the Bolsheviks in their political struggle with the various other parties in the revolution. Against incredible odds, by November the Bolsheviks had seized power; by the next spring, they had made peace with the Germans; in the summer, the czar and his family were executed (although not at Lenin's order, and indeed the perpetrators were arrested and five executed for the murder); the civil war was eventually won; and despite international hostility and great hardships, Soviet rule was established. A major reason for this was Lenin's grasp of the variety of political means available.

ON MAKING POLITICAL OMELETS

Perhaps some of our readers think of Lenin as an evil man, who did evil things and created something evil. But clearly he did not think so, nor do the Soviets. It may be that he was simply more flexible and frank about the necessity of using whatever political means were necessary to achieve an end than most and thereby not evil but simply freer from humbug than most politicians. Being frank about what you think is not necessarily the same as being evil. Republican or autocratic politicians are not necessarily morally superior to totalitarian ones when push comes to shove: Truman used the atomic bomb, and the Shah of Iran ran a brutal secret police. Look at the political problem from Lenin's point of view: he and his party were faced with a reactionary and repressive regime with which there was no compromise. Because they were in a desperate struggle to realize their political goals in an hostile world, this meant that they had to consider any political means available if it contributed to that goal.

Now recall Machiavelli's famous statement: "In the actions of all men, and especially of princes who are not subject to a court of appeal, we must always look to the end." Lenin was no cynic or opportunist simply seeking power for its own sake. He sincerely believed in the Marxist promise of a glorious future and that that end made the means worth it. His orientation toward politics was in that sense always pragmatic. (One of his strategic books is entitled, *What Is to Be Done?*) He opposed those that thought the Marxist revolution would arise spontaneously among the masses after the full development of capitalism. "The inevitable," he argued, "takes a lot of hard work." That work includes doing things that are not strictly ethical. But in revolutionary activity, given the odds against you and the promise of what you will create, you cannot handicap yourself with ethical restraints, especially because the other party in the political struggle will not either. Lenin's approach to the political questions of means is as frank as Machiavelli's: when you commit yourself to political action in a situation with no rules and no holds barred, do what you have to do unhesitatingly, and do not fool yourself about what you're doing.

The tactics of a revolutionary party may seem remote from your life, but reflect a bit on this question. All of us have to use means to get what we want—a good grade, a date, a summer job, a good relationship with our parents. And all of us have more or less some kind of code of ethics. But situations vary, the intensity of our desires varies, and what we are up against and feel is necessary vary. We may feel as though we must use political means—power—to get what we want. Suppose you ask a girl (boy) you like for a date, and she (he) asks you if you're seeing anyone else. Even though you are, you tell her (him) no. You lied, but you didn't want to spoil your chances with this girl (boy) you want to date. You can tell her later, when she (he) likes you better, and you can safely bring it up. Ethical? No. Political? Yes. It is easy to condemn a political operative such as Lenin for using deceptive and brutal means to achieve his political purposes. But the cast-the-first-stone rebuff to that is that we all are political operatives. In the politics of everyday life, we choose political means that are not always within the bounds of ethical codes. Consider this universal ethical injunction: never lie. Could we really exist in daily life without every lying? Do you always say what you really feel, tell your parents what you actually do at school, turn down a gift of money from an aunt, even though you do not need it? Think of the secrets you keep. Is it ethical to keep these secrets? What would your life be like if everyone important to you knew them?

Let us take a related example, manipulation. "Manipulation," wrote Robert Goodin, "involves bending another's will." When you use the power of communication to deceive someone into doing what you want, that is manipulation. Such deceptive use of someone else is unethical; never manipulate. Yet could we get what we want in everyday life if we did not manipulate? Doesn't the dating game involve manipulation, indeed oftentimes mutual manipulation? Both parties on a date try to affect the impressions the other has of them. Have you ever feigned interest in some subject the other party obviously is enthused about, but of which you care nothing? Studies have shown that women on dates will often "play dumb," so as not to upset their male companion by appearing smarter than him! Men are equally capable of such subtle manipulation on dates. In order for the date to work, both parties have to be dishonest to some degree, to conduct the relationship in a state of "bad faith." The politics of the date necessitates a mutual exchange of accommodations, including secrets, flatteries, half-truths, deceptions, and lies. By doing so, the daters may get along well, and the date be a success.

If you reflect on the means you use in everyday life, you will realize that it is not easy to cope within the strict confines of a code of ethics. Machiavelli was one of the first thinkers to face the conflicts and dilemmas of what we should do, can do, have to do, and in fact do do. If ethical action is practical and useful, then we should do only those things that are ethical in terms of some code of conduct—religious, philosophical, institutional, or legal. But the fact is, Machiavelli argued, that life, including political life, is not that simple, and one has to do things that are ethically dubious and even unethical. Remember his argument that "the conditions of human life" simply do not allow you to be good all the time.

Let us consider some familiar problems. The absolute ethical position on lying is that you should never lie or, conversely, should always tell the truth. But in the politics of everyday life, could you in fact cope by always adhering to the truth? Psychologists have long pointed to the little self-deceptions, called *rationalizations*, that we use to convince ourselves that we are all right and that what we are doing is all right. The philosopher Jean-Paul Sartre pointed out the ways in which we use "bad faith," pretending that something is necessary when it is actually voluntary. The woman who says she has no choice but to put up with her lover's abuse of her is lying to herself about what she has to do. In the politics of self, we use lying as a means to cover up what we do not want to face about ourselves.

The hard Machiavellian question, then, is whether we could successfully play the politics of everyday life without using means that are less than ethical. In our own way, we are always calculating the costs and benefits of what we do and how we do it. Getting caught in a lie may be too much of a risk to be worth it. Offering excuses may eventually produce the "boy who cried wolf" effect: people refuse to believe you anymore. If you get the reputation of an "operator" whose word cannot be trusted, you may find it difficult to get what you want. On the other hand, if you do not tell small lies, offer excuses, and downright lie to people, would you get what you want?

Remember that from the Machiavellian viewpoint, ethics is a political strategy. For example, sometimes honesty is the best policy, and sometimes dishonesty is the best policy, depending on the costs and benefits involved. Telling the truth may sometimes be best, because it builds your reputation for credibility, increases people's willingness to trust you, disarms those suspicious of you, and makes you appear ethical. In terms of pragmatic rule, being honest may at times be the best political strategy to get what you want. In that sense, the ethical stance of telling the truth may be the best political strategy.

But in the pragmatics of life, dishonesty may also be a political strategy, the necessary if unethical means to a desired end. If you ask yourself whether the end is worth the means, you are assessing costs and benefits and political goals, not ethical considerations. Do you agree with comedian W. C. Fields that "anything worth having is worth cheating for"? What are you willing to risk in order to get what you think worth having? What are the costs and benefits of lying, intimidating, manipulating, bluffing, and so on? Can you exercise power in everyday life without using such means?

High-stakes politics may involve the hardnosed calculation of means. Indeed, politics is such that you may be faced with difficult choices, what we shall call the *paradox of means*. Suppose that you are involved in a political struggle with your opponents. Certain dubious means are available to both sides: duplicity, violence, lying, assassination, and other such things. If you are not willing to use such means, and your opponents are, they may win and you may lose. On the other hand, if you do use such means, this may mean that your opponents will have to respond in kind, making the conflict more intense and vicious and perhaps leading to your loss. In other words, you can lose by not being willing to use all means available, and you can lose by being willing to. Being ruthless does not guarantee your success and can backfire if you scare off people; but not being ruthless clearly does not guarantee success and may even ensure failure.

What Machiavelli argued for was a choice of means. The calculation of means is a difficult question of political logic: what political means should I use in these circumstances to achieve certain political ends? What are the risks, costs and benefits? If I do *X*, will they respond with *Y*? In politics, means are a political and not a moral judgment. Political means involve the use of power, and it cannot always be bound by ethics.

But politics and ethics may coincide. It may be good political strategy to be ethical. Political candor does have its uses, gaining you the reputation of being honest, and so forth. But it is still a political and not an ethical consideration. A political judgment may also have an ethical result, but that is coincidental too. Sparing your enemies after a military victory may be ethical, but it should be done for political reasons. The primacy of politics over ethics was best captured in Talleyrand's response to Napoleon's execution of the duke of Enghien: "It is more than a crime, it is a mistake!" The Machiavellian view is that politicians have to be more concerned with their mistakes in political judgment than with their crimes of ethical lapse.

THE SOVIET POLITICAL OMELET

In our discussion of political means, we focused on the career of Lenin for several reasons. First, in the Russian revolutionary movement of which Lenin eventually became the leader, the great diversity of means available is illustrated. Lenin and the Bolsheviks developed a political doctrine regarding the use of means, both for gaining power and then maintaining it. Finally, Lenin and the Soviet state he created exemplify both the power of means to accomplish large political goals and the inevitable question of whether it was worth it.

Lenin's orientation toward practical political means was first illustrated by his famous pamphlet published in 1903, *What Is to Be Done?* The Russian Marxists at this time were bogged down in organizational and philosophical differences. Lenin attacked the theoretical notion that the revolution would spontaneously emerge from the masses and that the Marxist organization should "follow in the tail" of a mass movement. The revolutionary theory of Marxism, he maintained, was not just an economic program, it was an injunction to revolutionary action. But who can take revolutionary action? What should be done, Lenin advised, is to create a cadre of professional revolutionaries who will act for the masses, educate them, lead them, and be the vanguard of the revolutionary movement. This party would be freed of the constraints of bourgeois politics and morality because its purpose would be revolutionary. Because of the magnitude of the political struggle and the power of the enemy, all means have to be considered and used if necessary in order to bring about the revolution. However, the means must be rational, decided as politically wise by the party, planned and executed by the party, and not done without party approval. Lenin opposed the terrorists who bombed and assassinated at random: killing should be planned and selective, done when it serves a specific and political and logical party purpose.

In principle, then, the Leninist view of political means is totally pragmatic: everything is a potential political instrument to be used to serve the party's and the movement's interests and goals. Communist parties seek what they believe to be a moral goal: the overthrow of capitalism and bourgeois society and the institution of a higher order that serves humanity. But bringing that about necessitates flexibility of strategy and openness of means. As Alfred Meyer pointed out, the political stance of Leninism is Machiavellian: "The practical morality of the communist movement is therefore a morality of expediency: whatever works is moral; whatever does not, is immoral."

Lenin stated what many other politicians had in fact practiced but not preached. (Indeed, something of the same doctrine was asserted by the Jesuits in the defense of the Catholic faith.) Likewise, Americans have been told for decades that their government has to do immoral things in order to achieve national political goals: be willing to fight an all-out nuclear war, bomb civilian populations, spy on and sabotage foreign powers, assassinate foreign leaders, spy on American citizens, lie to the public, give arms to repressive states, and so on. All this is justified as regrettable but necessary and sounds much like a morality of expediency.

Lenin thought that the Bolshevik professional revolutionary should be hard, disciplined, ruthless, adaptable, and able to calculate what means are appropriate to circumstances. He wrote that "there must be no doctrinaire attitude . . . against changes in strategy and tactics." "If I pursue an enemy," he argued, "who does not move in a straight line but zigzags, than I too must zigzag in order to reach him." Revolutionaries will succeed only with cunning and calculation: "Bolsheviks do not believe in miracles. . . . We must count on the worst." Politics is "a most coldblooded war." Concentrate on what can be achieved rather than dreams of total victory: "The most important task . . . is fighting the danger of being carried away by vast plans." The goal is power, power for the party to make the revolution and, once in power, to create the new Communist order and encourge revolutions around the world. In power, the new state has to use whatever means necessary to create the new Communist society: "A Communist who says that one should never dirty one's hands . . . that he is going to build Communist society with clean hands, is an empty phrasemonger."

The shaky new Soviet regime staggered along for years, fighting hostility from abroad and a civil war at home. When the civil war against the White Russians (czarists) was won, the regime was close to political collapse. The draconian measures of "war Communism" had brought economic ruin to the country and a considerable loss of political support. Lenin realized that drastic changes were called for to preserve the regime and thus instituted the New Economic Policy (NEP), in which he reintroduced private enterprise in agriculture, trades, and small industry, benefiting small businessmen and farmers. The terror was relaxed, and some degree of freedom was permitted in the arts and sciences. Lenin, of course, had no idea of reintroducing capitalism or bourgeois democracy, but he did see a temporary use of such measures as a necessary "zigzag" on the path to socialism.

Part of Lenin's legacy to the Soviet Union, world communism, and politics in general is his espousal of Machiavellian means to achieve political ends. It is likely that the Soviet political omelet could not have been created by someone less ruthless and daring. As we shall see, the legacy would have both pragmatic and demonic results (Chapter 27). In any case, the Soviet "operational code"—how Russia is ruled and how it conducts politics with other states—is much influenced by Leninist pragmatism and opportunism.

ON TEACHING POLITICAL EVIL

By saying the things that he did, Lenin, like Machiavelli, gainied the reputation of a "teacher of evil." Aside from what we may think of Communism as an economic and political system, or of the Soviet Union as a power, is what Lenin said about political means evil?

Suppose that all those statements about means were put into the mouth of someone you feel more favorable about—perhaps, George Washington. If he had said pithy things about political zigzags, dirty hands, and politics as a coldblooded war, we might think it just good political sense rather than evil. Politicians in republics and autocracies occasionally use most of the means that Lenin used and probably agree that politics is a cunning and calculating game. So if we translate the Leninist principles of revolutionary politics into more neutral language, maybe it will be more familiar.

Wolfgang Leonhard, a Marxist scholar, summarized Lenin's position on political tactics in general terms: First is to gain political allies and exploit all conflicts and failures among one's opponents. Second, make compromises and concessions in the here-and-now without losing sight of your long-term goal. Third, always strive to influence your potential mass political base and win them over for your political objectives. Fourth, master all political fighting methods in order to use them properly. Fifth, respect your enemy and never underestimate its strength. Finally, concentrate on the main political task and do not be misled, diverted, or discouraged from it. Lenin, like Machiavelli, did not teach political evil; he taught political expediency, that in the world of politics, good and evil means both are instruments of political action. Lenin was not interested in ethical goals, but rather in political ones: therefore political tactics could not be evaluated in terms of their ethical excellence but instead their political usefulness.

What Lenin understood and articulated was that political means—strategies and tactics—should not be left to chance. Means have to be studied, selected, and used. Means are a political instrument, something used to effect an end. Political struggles are not always pleasant, and so sometimes the means have to be unpleasant. You have to be up to the struggle and willing to play rough in order to be successful.

If you are thinking about getting into politics, you have to ask yourself what you would be willing to do. Is the political game worth the candle? Are you capable of doing the things necessary to gain and exercise power—deception, manipulation, half-truths, lying, breaking promises, dirty tricks, propagandizing and image-building, laying traps, betraying trust, intimidation, cover-ups, and on and on? If you are not, if you are squeamish and shrink from the battle, then maybe you should stay out of politics. But remember: in the politics of everyday life, the question of means also will come up, and the same agonizing choices and moral questions will assert themselves. At least you can be consoled by the knowledge that great politicians have gone through the same agony in power. Historian Richard Hofstadter wrote of Abraham Lincoln during the last months of his life: "Now he could see the truth of what he had long dimly known and perhaps hopefully suppressed—that for a man of sensitivity and compassion to exercise great powers in a time of crisis is a grim and agonizing thing. Instead of glory, he once said, he had found only 'ashes and blood'."

Lenin caused his share of ashes and blood, but we have no evidence that he agonized over the broken eggshells of the Russian revolution. What we do know is that he admired Machiavelli, and understood the arsenal of political means available for use. He knew that in politics you have to act, and you have to use political means to get what you want. Perhaps Lincoln, and most of the rest of us, could agree with Lenin when he would so often quote Napoleon: *On s'engage, et puis—on voit*—"You commit yourself, and then—you see."

"To make an omelet, you have to break eggs."

—*Lenin*

"A revolution is not a dinner party."

—*Mao Tse-tung*

"The inevitable takes a lot of hard work."

—*Lenin*

"In the actions of all men, and especially of princes who are not subject to a court of appeal, we must always look to the end."

—*Machiavelli*

"There is nothing so practical as a good theory."

—*Kurt Lewin*

"If I pursue an enemy who does not move in a straight line but zigzags, then I too must zigzag in order to reach him."

—*Lenin*

"You commit yourself, and then—you see."

—*Lenin (quoting Napoleon I)*

Chapter

27

Controlling Political Truth: Governing Through Propaganda

From Chapter 11, in regard to Walter Rathenau, you will remember the political turmoil of Germany's Weimar Republic. That turmoil continued until 1933, when the republic collapsed and was replaced by Hitler's totalitarian rule. Hitler and the Nazis triumphed for many reasons, not the least of which was their ability to sell themselves to the German people as the hope of a humiliated and scared country. They learned how to take advantage of certain events in order to communicate this to the public. The economic depression of the early 1930s was such an event.

But there were smaller, more personal events on which the Nazis also capitalized. In 1930, a young Nazi storm trooper named Horst Wessel was shot by another man in a fight over a woman. Wessel had been a

JOSEPH GOEBBELS: MASTER PROPAGANDIST

No name is more closely identified with political propaganda than Joseph Goebbels, "the man who created Hitler." But he was an unlikely candidate for the powerful Reichspropagandaminister in the Third Reich. He was not exactly the model of Aryan manhood: small, lame, dark, and something of a dandy. His small stature and limp made him look a bit absurd in the Nazi regalia of uniform and jackboots. But even his most ardent enemies admitted that he was intelligent. He was also cynical, ambitious, and calculating.

Unlike the other Nazi leaders, Goebbels was an educated man. He was born a Catholic, and his parents wanted him to become a priest. But he decided to become a scholar and was supported in this by a Catholic association. In 1921, he received his Ph.D. from Heidelberg University, studying under two Jewish professors. Like many another young unemployed German intellectual, he dabbled with political ideas, including Communism. He wrote poems, plays, and a novel. He wandered from job to job, woman to woman, and idea to idea until 1923 when the French occupied the Ruhr. He then offered his services to the leader of the saboteurs opposing the French, who refused him as a soldier but told him he could do important work as an "agitator and propagandist." By 1925, he had drifted into the National Socialist movement and by the next year had met Hitler and was touring with him on speaking tours. He had found his political cause and leader and eventually his job as a Nazi propagandist.

From Goebbels's diaries, we know that he was a strange combination of ardent belief and cold-blooded manipulation. He compared Hitler with Christ and indeed was much interested in Christ's life, but for political reasons: "I cannot think of a more fascinating personality in history than Christ . . . I know of no more powerful speech than the Sermon on the Mount. Every propagandist ought to study it." He and Hitler (who was also raised a Catholic) saw in Catholicism the organization and ritualism they could use in the secular religion of Nazism. Goebbels referred to the Mass as "the most tendentious rubbish ever to be inflicted on the intelligence of man, but mightily useful in proving man's capacity for absorbing nonsense." The Nazis' Nuremberg rallies and other elaborate rituals were spectacular quasi-religious pageantry designed for that purpose.

In the writings of Hitler and Goebbels, the philosophy of propaganda is stated about as baldly as it ever could be: "Propaganda," wrote Hitler, "is a truly frightful weapon in the hands of an expert." He was fortunate to find such an expert in Goebbels, who knew how to use such a frightful weapon. Goebbels fully shared Hitler's view that "the great masses of the people will more easily fall victims to a great lie than to a small one." Goebbels understood that political language is used for purposes of influence: "We do not talk," he explained, "to say something, but to obtain a certain effect." This meant that the political propagandist must abandon a commitment to telling the truth. He told a propaganda cadre: "The propagandist must construct his own truth. Whatever is right for the advancement of the Party is truth. If it should coincide with the factual truth, so much the better; if it doesn't, adjustments must be made. The great, the absolute truth, is that the Party and the Fuehrer are always right. They are always right." Elsewhere he wrote that "truth is what I make it."

Goebbels remained committed to the end to these political principles. Throughout his career as Hitler's chief spokesman, he responded to each new situation with new political "truths." He built a propaganda machine consisting of every medium of mass communication in Germany, turning every newspaper into an organ of Nazi information dissemination. He choreographed every major state event and decided how every political or military twist and turn was to be treated. He got into trouble with Hitler only once, when he had an open affair with a film actress, which infuriated Hitler, because Nazi policy and propaganda extolled the virtues of the family. Hitler broke it up, had the actress escorted by the Gestapo to her Prague home, and kept her under surveillance. But Goebbels got propaganda value even out of that, for soon afterwards Hitler was publicized in popular magazines as being a great marriage mender. After the scandal died down, Goebbels renewed his womanizing in a more discreet manner.

Despite his propaganda skill, Goebbels could not explain away the real truth of German defeats on the battlefield. Goebbels remained loyal to Hitler, joining him at the end in the Berlin Fueherbunker, which was fast being surrounded by the Russian army. He acted as best man in Hitler's wedding to Eva Braun and, after their suicide, announced to the remaining staff, "the heart of Germany has ceased to beat." He then had his six sleeping children killed by injection; his wife poisoned herself; and he shot himself. His body was to be burned to avoid discovery by the Russians, but it burned only partially, and so the charred remains were buried in an anonymous grave, the site of which remains unknown.

---

popular speaker at Nazi meetings and had written a poem published in the Berlin newspaper *Der Angriff*. Wessel was young and good-looking, the son of a Lutheran pastor, who had drifted into the Nazi movement. Wessel then took up with a prostitute and apparently acted as both her lover and her pimp. A former lover showed up one night in 1930 and shot him.

This squalid little tale in most cases would have stirred little interest, and Wessel would have died in the obscurity he deserved. However, Joseph Goebbels, the Nazi leader in Berlin and editor of *Der Angriff*, sensed an opportunity for publicity. He rushed to the hospital where Wessel lay mortally wounded and began to concoct the political uses of the story: he would turn Wessel into a Nazi martyr. Goebbels used the newspaper to turn Wessel into a heroic young man, the prototype of Aryan youth, who had been cruelly murdered by a Communist! Wessel lingered at the point of death for weeks, and in each new edition of *Der Angriff*, Goebbels editorialized about the heroic young patriot who had been wronged, and he called for revenge against the Communists (the Nazi's chief political rivals). Goebbels visited Wessel in the hospital daily and moved readers with emotional stories about the dying hero. A poem that Wessel had written was set to a folk tune and sung by ten thousand storm troopers in his honor. Finally, Wessel died, and Goebbels arranged for a massive funeral in his honor and gave the eulogy himself. The drama of the Nazi ceremony was heightened by the presence of Communist protestors who harassed the proceedings. His song was sung again, and the roll of the storm troopers was called, and at the end, Wessel's name was called, and all intoned in response, "Present!"

Horst Wessel in death was to become much more than he ever was in life. His image as a hero eventually was seen everywhere in Nazi Germany. In the Nazi years, the "Horst Wessel Lied" was sung at every official occasion, and at the Nuremberg party rallies it always closed the meeting. Every German child learned about Horst Wessel. Streets were renamed Horst Wesselplatz, and the now-banned Communist party headquarters was converted into the Horst Wessel Haus, a museum in his honor. Practically every German city of any size had a street or square named after Horst Wessel. Perhaps more importantly, Wessel became a symbolic role model, a hero whom young Nazis should emulate: he became Kamerad Horst, and according to Goebbels, "the mere sound of his name vibrates with something heroic, knightly, courageous. . . . A young man shows the movement how you can die if necessary, even must die."

Wessel's promotion to immortality was the work of one of the world's masters of propaganda, Joseph Goebbels. Goebbels understood the power of propaganda to persuade and how all the means of communication available can be mobilized for political purposes. Especially in the modern world, a large part of governing is through propaganda, controlled political truth communicated with the intent to persuade. The art and technique of propaganda are used in every kind of state, autocratic, republican, or totalitarian, whether or not the government has control over the mass media. Practicing power means having to use propaganda well, whatever the political order or situation.

POLITICAL APPEARANCE AND REALITY

Machiavelli spoke much of political appearance: "The mass of mankind are swayed by appearances . . . the deceiver will always find someone to deceive." Machiavelli believed that "it seldom happens that men rise from low condition to high rank without employing either force or fraud" and that the "prince who wishes to achieve great things must learn to deceive." Deceiving people by the manipulation of appearances is a widespread and ancient part of politics and, cynics might say, the central part. If there is any truth in the old charge that politics is a con game, then propaganda is one of the chief means of conning people.

Propaganda is a loaded word, connoting the use of lies to manipulate unsuspecting people into complying with some nefarious scheme. But actually propaganda is a much more inclusive practice. The word originated in religion, when in 1622 Pope Gregory XV convened a committee, the *Congregatio de Propaganda Fide,* to "propagate" the faith through foreign missions. But soon this term took on other meanings, including lying and twisting the facts. In its broadest sense, propaganda can include a minister giving a sermon, a peddler selling snake oil, a newspaper editorial making an argument, and even a professor giving a lecture. To propagate a message, you must communicate your message by ways and means that will have the desired effect on your audience. In that sense, propaganda is the intentional use of communication to influence others.

In this broad way we all are propagandists, because we all try to influence others. You may be quite sincere in what you believe but also quite willing to "shape" what you believe by trying to convince other people of its truth. Suppose in a conversation you argue for a certain belief. Don't you try to *propagate* that belief to the others in the group talking by putting the "best light" on your case? To paraphrase Huck Finn, we all tell the truth, mainly. If our intent is to influence, then we become propagandists. Basically, the logic of propaganda depends on the desire of people to influence others in their opinions and actions. When you talk to your girlfriend/boyfriend on a date about what you are going to do, you will use influence language.

By extension, the logic of propaganda is something we see everyday in advertising. The many ads you are bombarded with all day long are made by professional advertising agencies, armed with the latest in psychological research and aimed at getting you to consume, believe, give, act, or comply. Even though we all tell ourselves that we are immune from the influence of propaganda, a moment's reflection should disabuse us of that. You bought all those currently fashionable clothes without being influenced by propaganda, right? Indeed, when you applied to the school you now attend, they likely sent you a fancy brochure about the place, replete with pictures of pretty female and handsome male students, as well as claims about the quality of faculty and facilities. Was everything your school represented to you in that brochure true?

Unless you are a hermit, you are also besieged by political propaganda. Think, for example, of a presidential election year and the number of ads you are exposed to during the fall campaign. Just the television ads alone make up a goodly number, many of them slick "image" ads that convey very little hard information about the candidates. But you, like most other voters, see through the bamboozle and are not influenced by such ads, right?

Whether or not you are influenced by propaganda, a moment's reflection will let you see the political logic of propaganda. To practice successfully, you will have to gain influence over the opinions and actions of people. This means that you will have to communicate with masses of people in order to propagate your message. The message is presented so as to put the best light on the subject. The political intention is not to tell the truth but to exercise power through mass influence. It may be harmful to your political purposes to tell the truth. In any case, propaganda is used to communicate appearances to those far from the backstage of power. Propaganda is communication that shapes political appearances for mass audiences.

Clearly, your own experience with advertising should tell you that political propaganda is always not the truth. The advertisers are trying to persuade you, and thus their appeal may be directed toward your primal and social needs, unconscious desires, and irrational impulses.

But remember, the advertisers are not telling you the "truth" of the product, they are trying to sell it to you. Truth or lies are irrelevant to propagandists: if they can persuade you, without lying to consume, they will do so; but if they have to lie they will. Propaganda involves rhetoric, languages of communication used for effect. Language—words, gestures, symbols, images, and so on—is manipulated to convince you that you will really be sexy if you put on a certain perfume, successful and chic if you wear a certain brand of fashionable clothes, or healthy and young looking if you eat a certain brand of breakfast cereal. Advertising is the rhetoric of economic power, propaganda aimed at engineering the consumption habits of you, the consumer.

Political propaganda is the rhetoric of political power. In the many forms it appears, it always has the purpose of using the languages of political communication to persuade political audiences. Like advertising, you are probably wise to assume that it is done in bad faith. Whatever they are telling you, it is likely not to be the whole truth. The propagandists are trying to exercise power over you through political communication. They are communicating to you their own special kind of truth, what we shall call *political truth*. Political truth is a truth communicated for pragmatic political purposes, used for a while and then altered or discarded in favor of another more usable political truth. Political truth is "true" only if you can convince people that what you say is so and keep on convincing them. A political truth should be abandoned when it no longer has political use. Think of how much of politics is naming and renaming things for political reasons. Talleyrand pointed to this when he remarked, "An important art of politicians is to find new names for institutions which under old names have become odious to the public." Thus after a war "War Department" becomes "Defense Department," in which all weapons and war plans are "defensive." Political truth is concerned with political appearances. The propagandist's aim is to create a political reality by naming it and convincing people of the truth of the name. Because people do not know everything about what is going on, you can tell them through propaganda what the political story is. If you are adept enough, you can then rename the political story and create another political reality. As George Orwell pointed out in his famous essay on politics and language, the words used in political language convey ideas and images about what is happening, and if you have no other way to check the facts or do not trust the source of the story, you may well accept the tale told as true. Orwell noted the extent to which propagandists use "euphemism, question-begging, and sheer cloudy vagueness" to convey a political truth. Killing and displacing the peasants in the countryside becomes "pacification"; shooting your enemies becomes "liquidation"; preparation for war becomes "peace through strength"; a "blockade" becomes a "quarantine."

To a very large degree, then, the ability to control communications is power. If you can control communications, both the means and the message, you can control political truth. Political appearances as communicated become the political reality you have created for your audience. The propagandist mediates political reality for the many (and often for the few), creating the political truth for them by telling stories about what is happening. The political truth teller adjusts to new political circumstances by naming new political truths. The rhetoric of power is true to the extent that it works.

POLITICAL PROPAGANDA IN THE THIRD REICH

Joseph Goebbels was a genius in the use of mediated political truths to gain power. In retrospect, however sinister we may think the Third Reich, Goebbels's use of propaganda to create and then perpetuate Nazi rule is still a remarkable story. Germany, after all, had probably the best educated people in Europe, with its rigorous school system, great universities, and respect for knowledge and professors. You might think such widespread education would make Germans resistant to propaganda. But remember that Americans are prey to propaganda no less. In any case, Goebbels was well ahead of his time in the use of propaganda and employed methods of propaganda that now have become commonplace.

In the years before the fall of Weimar and Hitler's accession to power, Goebbels developed his range of propaganda techniques. He studied every aspect of communication, including past practitioners of the art. He studied Bismarck's (Chapter 21) methods, including the fabrication and editing of letters to be published in newspapers, "rumor squads" to spread lies and despair among opponents, the control of the press, and the creation of government press spokespersons. He read Le Bon's *Psychology of the Masses,* which included the idea that the many want godlike leaders and sacrificial victims. As he rose in power, Hitler and the other Nazi leaders began to recognize Goebbels's intelligence and skill at political communication, and eventually he became the head of propaganda for the Nazi state.

Goebbels once said of himself that he was "to the drama born." He brought to his job as Nazi *gauleiter* in Berlin, and later propaganda minister, the theatrical sense needed by every propagandist. To be successful at getting your political message across, you have to use all the techniques of theater. A theatrical performance works if the production uses all of the resources of dramatic presentation (such as good acting, lines, gesture, props, scenery and lighting, and costume) and the principles of drama (suspense, conflict, peripeteia, personification, climax, catharsis, and so forth). The key to Goebbels's propaganda genius was that he was a showman who understood that propaganda was effective to the extent that it was dramatic.

This attention to dramatic detail extended to the use of rhetoric. Goebbels realized that speaking before audiences was a dramatic art and thus was something to be studied and practiced. The Nazi message had to be dramatized through rhetorical devices. Goebbels wrote his own speeches with great care, using different colored inks to remind him of different emphases. Before he gave them, he rehearsed his speeches in front of triple mirrors, training himself to use voice and gesture for the best rhetorical effect. He coordinated the Nazi effort in the Reichstag elections of 1930 by selecting and training two hundred party members to form a cadre of public speakers. He put them through a crash course in speaking and then dispatched them to a wide variety of forums. The speakers were effective, helping the Nazis increase the number of seats they held, from 12 to 107.

Goebbels also insisted, both in seeking power and in power, on a constant stream of information. His goal was to get out the Nazi story to as many people in as many ways as possible, which meant a veritable deluge of information communicated through newspapers, loud speakers, posters, radio, movies, and so on. This included not only Nazi ideology and promises but also responses to specific events. Goebbels's Berlin newspaper, *Der Angriff,* was widely circulated and commented in colorful fashion on current events. When a leak of chlorine gas killed some people in Hamburg and, naturally, raised people's fears about chemical leaks elsewhere, Goebbels responded with an elaborate story that the German Communists, in league with the dreaded Soviet Union, were secretly importing such gas to use against the Nazis; not only that, they were also importing rats infested with bubonic plague in order to create social chaos and bring Germany under Communist rule! The Nazi party, of course, was dramatized as the only force standing against such a conspiracy. Goebbels's charges were often outrageous, but he believed with P. T. Barnum, that there was a sucker born every minute and thus that people would believe big lies or fall for big promotions. Goebbels even revived the ancient fable that the Jews engaged in ritual murder of Christian children.

But Goebbels also knew that propaganda was not just information. It had to be supported by imagery—pictures, movies, pageantry, slogans, symbols, myths. Goebbels wanted to communicate the idea that the National Socialist party was a movement, growing in power and support and marching forward toward the creation of a new Germany. Nazi posters were everywhere, picturing young Germans striding into the future and captioned by such memorable slogans as "Germany Awake!" or "Blood and Soil." The uniformed Nazi processions and parades, choreographed as political ritual, communicated the image of a unified movement with a historic mission. In power, Nazi pageantry, such as the annual Nuremberg party rally, became, under Goebbel's direction, spectacles with powerful imagery for both those present and those that saw movies such as *The Triumph of the Will.* An English diplomat stationed in Germany in the 1930s said that the Nuremberg rallies were the most beautiful thing he had ever seen.

In particular, Goebbels was concerned with creating and communicating the image of Hitler. Nazi newspapers portrayed Hitler as a paragon of virtue, as the hope of Germany, as the greatest political genius of the age, and eventually as an almost godlike figure of mythical proportions. In power Hitler was rarely seen in public, and Goebbels used this remoteness to create the *Fuehrerkult*. Goebbels introduced the term *Fuehrer,* making its use compulsory; made the official greeting "Heil Hitler"; and screened pictures and films of Hitler so that he was seen only with children and dogs at his mountain retreat or in full regalia as the chief of state greeting other foreign leaders.

Goebbels grasped the importance of mass communication to power and accordingly studied the media. The Nazi propaganda machine was formidable because Goebbels built it into an organization that utilized to the fullest every mass medium available. For example, he understood the potential of the new medium of radio. He ordered the expansion of the numbers and power of radio transmitters so as to reach larger audiences. He ordered the production of a cheap transmitter affordable to German families or at least a village. Collective listening was encouraged, with party "radio wardens" rounding up audiences and stopping work so that the workers could listen. In addition, Goebbels studied how radio could be used to produce certain sound effects, such as mingling and fading the sounds of marching boots, tanks, and planes to give the impression of a vast army on the march. He toned down Hitler's shouting and ranting—so effective in mass meetings but unsuitable for radio—so that Hitler's radio voice and style came across calmer and more reasonable sounding.

Like any good promoter, Goebbels knew the value of getting attention through a publicity stunt. In Berlin, he would arrange to have a party meeting in a hall in the heart of the Communist districts, fully aware this would be a provocation. He would advertise the meeting heavily and have the Nazi storm troopers march to the hall. Communists and others would crowd in to jeer. At that point, a fight would be started, and more storm troopers would appear. Goebbels would calmly direct the action from the stage, like a director giving stage directions. Once the fighting had subsided, he would launch into a speech while bleeding and wounded storm troopers were carried off the stage one by one at ten-minute intervals. Such stunts gained the party much publicity, dramatizing it, to at least some of the German people, as the defender of German nationalism. To others, of course, such stunts made the Nazis look like street thugs.

Nazi propaganda also personified the political conflicts in which Germany was involved. Goebbels's dramatic sense told him that the mass of people wanted politicians to have identifiable roles, such as heroes, villains, and fools. So Goebbels obliged, casting successful generals such as Erwin Rommel as heroes of the Reich. Jews were a standard source of villainy and were personified in stereotyped caricatures of Jewish bankers. Churchill was cast as the ultimate villain once it was clear that England was the enemy. Fools included those countries and politicians duped by the Jews and the British, such as, for a while, the Americans. Once the Americans entered the war, Roosevelt became a villain, with Nazi propaganda alleging that he was a mad plutocrat deranged because of his "Jewish" ancestry!

There is much else that was part of Goebbels's propaganda program. Despite the sinister aspects of the regime with which he was associated, Goebbels is still studied simply as one of the great practitioners of a crucial political art. His career illustrates many things, not the least of which how much power that a virtual monopoly of the means of communication can offer. Your control of political truth gives you a powerful weapon. Remember that your aim is to rule no matter what the type of government. Even in republics in which there are multiple sources of information, such as a free and critical press, as ruler you have powerful means of communication, which help you define the political truth you want and help keep secrets, thus preventing the press and the people from finding out things that you do not want them to know

But keep in mind what Goebbels understood: propaganda is aimed at the many. If they accept your definition of political truth, it will become difficult for the few—political opponents and the press—to dispute your word. Goebbels maintained that propaganda had two aspects: *stimmung,* current morale and ideas about politics; and *haltung,* conduct toward politics over time. *Haltung* requires a persuasive campaign to build support, trust, and deference that will last over time. Goebbels's long-term campaign to build the Fuehrer myth was designed to reinforce *haltung* among the many. But given the vagaries of politics, especially during World War II, he had to keep shoring up people's current feelings, especially their morale, or else their belief in the regime and the leader might be threatened. The difficulty was that maintaining *stimmung* became more difficult when Goebbels's political truth could be disproved by experience. The basic theme of "we are winning the war" became hard to believe in 1944 and 1945. Propagandists, then, are limited in their task by any competing source of political truth, be it enemy propaganda, a free press, political opponents, or falling bombs. But if they can convince the many, their control of political truth will give them great leverage against competing truths.

PROPAGANDIZING IN A REPUBLIC

Goebbels, of course, had the great advantage of controlling the means of communication in a totalitarian state that enjoyed for a long time considerable public support. Autocracies also exercise large control over the mass media, preventing competing sources of political truth from reaching the many. In republics, by contrast, there are constitutional and legal limits as to what one can do to control the press. The problem of a free press for the propagandist is a considerable one, but it is not insurmountable. If you are the public information officer, or head flack, for a politician—president, senator, governor, or whatever—your job will include using the free press for purposes of propaganda. There are several ways to do it.

Suppose that you are press secretary to the president. You are beset daily by the White House press corps. They want news and, more, they want the news behind the news. The president's reputation and policies, not to mention your job, is on the line. Press criticism and exposure can ruin the president's political fortunes. What you must do is control his political appearances as best you can to a press that may be independent and even hostile and over which you have imperfect control. Goebbels's example can give you guidelines as to what you can do.

Goebbels realized that propaganda ws theater. With that in mind, you can stage the president in a variety of forums on which the national press is obliged to report and which gives him direct access to the many. This has been called "presidential theater," those forums (such as a nationally televised address) in which the president can "go over the head" of the press and speak directly to the many. Similarly, when the president meets with heads of state, the press is kept at a respectful distance, photographing the great man with other great men and women.

Like Goebbels, you must cultivate the art of political rhetoric. This includes not only your own speaking ability and rhetorical devices but also those on your political team, most importantly your superiors. Just as Goebbels helped Hitler become an effective radio speaker, you will have to help your president utilize the mass media to best advantage. The electoral efforts of your party also should be coordinated in regard to rhetorical themes in keeping with the president's political programs and successes. Rhetoric should be controlled as much as possible to prevent gaffes, public disagreements about policy, and other needless blunders.

Goebbels insisted in a flow of information that got the story out. As press secretary, you can coordinate a wide variety of ways to disseminate information, getting the president's story out. Suppose that he comes up with a disarmament plan. Your job will be to sell it. You coordinate speakers from the administration (cabinet officers, undersecretaries, and so on.) and schedule them to speak to various important civic groups and conventions. You seek out and publicize the support of important political personages (for example, a former president). The press is given briefings on the plan, and the support of newspaper editors and other opinion makers is sought. The whole effort is designed to coordinate propaganda to tell the story of the president's bold and wise new proposal and thus garner support for it.

You can also utilize political imagery as propaganda. This can range from simply scheduling the president to appear with visiting dignitaries in the Rose Garden for a press "photo opportunity," to choreographing his appearance in an important political pageant or ritual, such as the commemoration at the Tomb of the Unknown Soldier on Memorial Day. The president's image in a more general sense, as learned from the polls, should concern you. How do people perceive him? What kind of image do you want to communicate? What can you do to overcome bad images, such as the perception that he consorts only with the rich and does not care about ordinary folk? Remember that the many know him only through his appearances, and therefore how they imagine him should not be left to chance.

Like Goebbels, then, you will have to spend much effort building the image of the president as a leader. For example, he will never take vacations but, rather, will take "working vacations." He will be pictured as decisive, hardworking, intelligent, and principled but practical, the man for the times. You will solicit testimonials from staff and cabinet officials, party officials, and congressional leaders as to his heroic qualities. He must be seen as both regal and a man of the people, with both kingly features and the common touch. The purpose of your political portrayal is to make him seem indispensable, a leader without whom the state would go to ruin.

You will have to study the media, most importantly their technology, organization, and customs. You will have to deal with a free press, and so you must understand how it works. If the president is to give a nationally televised address, for example, you will want to cooperate with the networks on the hookup, lighting, and set design in order to make him look good, as well as proper timing to gain the maximum audience without interfering too much with the regular television scheduling. You should study press organizations and people. Cultivating newspaper owners, television executives, and columnists and reporters takes an investment in time and money, but it may pay off politically in garnering editorial support, winning sympathy among reporters, and softening criticism all around. You may also have to find ways to intimidate or influence the press by means of harsher methods. If a reporter is consistently tough on the president, perhaps you can find ways to have her transferred to another beat. If a story is critical or embarrassing, a phone call to the managing editor may help soften additional such stories. All in all, you must stay on top of the press, remaining true to your task as chief propagandist and, using the press for your political purposes.

You will have to think up and stage publicity stunts. If your employer the president has a piece of legislation that has just been passed by Congress, have him sign it in some appropriate place to maximize its publicity value. For example, if it is an urban renewal bill, have him sign it in an urban slum; if a conservation measure, in a national park; if a bill to revitalize an industry, in the city most affected by the measure. Publicity stunts are one way to dramatize your boss in action through careful staging and media exposure.

Remember too, that propaganda must personify political conflicts. People want to hear a political story that tells them who the heroes, villains, and fools are, giving flesh to complex issues. Obviously your boss is the hero, the personification of what people hope for. But the selection of villains and fools must be carefully calculated. Sometimes it is wise to select for such a propaganda role an institution or group rather than an individual—"the special interests," "the big companies," "the idle rich," "the machine," "the politicians"—all of which connote in people's minds something sinister against which the president is fighting. All in all, your activities as a public information officer means that you will have to proceed in the spirit of Joseph Goebbels.

THE POLITICS OF PROPAGANDA

The political logic of propaganda requires that "mouthpieces" tell political truths. This makes many people uncomfortable and cynical, because it seems to indicate, according to journalist I. F. Stone, that "every government is run by liars." Recall what Machiavelli said about the necessity of fraud and the manipulation of appearances in order to rule. It may be bad ethics to use propaganda, but it is good politics. Remember also what we said about bad faith in politics: it may be impossible to rule in politics without propaganda, and therefore bad faith. Can you think of any government, now or in the past, that does not use propaganda? It is easy to say that governments and politicians should tell the truth, and not just the political truth. But it may not be so easy to conduct political rule without using propaganda.

In any case, the political propagandist should be aware of the political limits and dangers of propaganda. As the career of Goebbels illustrates, you can fake only so far. When reality intervenes, no amount of political propaganda will be able to convince the people any longer. If you are caught in lies—when the real truth contradicts the political truth—you may lose support and increase suspicion of you and your client. People may get into the habit of disbelieving, and so no matter what you say they will not believe you. To a large extent, successful politics depends on your ability to convince people to believe what you say; if they do not, you will be in political trouble. That is way the skillful use of political truth is so important, but also so tenuous. In politics, sometimes they believe, and sometimes they do not. To paraphrase the medicine man Sitting Bull (played by Chief Dan George) in the movie "Little Big Man," sometimes the political magic works, and sometimes it doesn't. After all, remember what eventually happened to Joseph Goebbels. You can go only so far in politics by faking it.

Like any other kind of political activity, propaganda has both a pragmatic and a demonic side. Propaganda is of great political use in "engineering consent," guiding people in their political beliefs and actions, making them feel part of a great political drama, and under-scoring the political truth of the state. But propaganda also has its misuses, bamboozling people into beliefs and actions that may harm them. Indeed, in its extreme form, one can imagine a world in which propaganda means total control of thought and action.

This is what George Orwell imagined the future would be like in *Nineteen Eighty-four*. In the Oceania of 1984, the political truth of propaganda is carried to its zenith. Winston Smith works for the Ministry of Truth, which administers propaganda on every subject. The past is constantly rewritten for present political purposes. People are constantly told that Oceania is winning the war, increasing plenty, and creating a new more perfect world. Indeed, during the middle of a speech, the enemy in the war is changed, the speaker adjusts, and the audience buys it! Oceania is in the process of creating a new language called "Newspeak," which as one of its creators tells Smith, is designed to "narrow the range of thought" and is built on the assumption that "orthodoxy is unconsciousness." O'Brien tells Winston later that "Whatever the Party holds to be truth *is* truth. It is impossible to see reality except by looking through the eyes of the Party."

Orwell's portrait of the future is a world in which propaganda controls reality. Clearly he thought that the future belonged to to-talitarianism and that the primary political means by which it would perpetuate itself by controlling what people know and do. In the world of *Nineteen Eighty-four* people are infinitely manipulatable and gullible, political slaves made so by the constant conditioning of propaganda. We may ask ourselves the uncomfortable question of how far along we are toward becoming that way ourselves and how much propaganda has destroyed republican freedom. After all, Goebbels helped transform a republic into a totalitarian state quickly. Perhaps advertising, political or otherwise, is helping condition us to accept an official reality and to narrow the range of our thoughts.

The reader may be wondering how he or she can resist the lure of propaganda messages and see through the sham. By studying propa-ganda, you can begin to see what they are trying to sell you. There is a lot of economic and political snake oil out there that you can resist if you try. Perhaps the best advice is to cultivate an attitude of skepticism. When you listen to a political speech or advertisement, remember the dictum proposed by the philosopher Bertrand Russell: "It is undesirable to believe a proposition when there is no ground whatsoever for suppos-ing it true."

"The great masses of the people will more easily fall victim to a great lie than to a small one."

—Hitler

"Truth is what I make it."

—Goebbels

"The mass of mankind are swayed by appearances ... the deceiver will always find someone to deceive."

—Machiavelli

"Every government is run by liars."

—I. F. Stone

"There is nothing that the masses hate more than two-sidedness, to be called upon to consider this as well as that. They think primitively. They love to generalize complicated situations and from their generalizations to draw clear and uncompromising solutions."

—Goebbels

"There's a sucker born every minute."

—P. T. Barnum

28

The Pragmatics
and Demonics of Power:
What Good and Evil
Can Governments Do?

Near the end of World War II, a Soviet artillery officer wrote a letter to a friend, in which he made a mildly deprecatory remark about Joseph Stalin, the dictator of the Soviet Union. The letter was intercepted and opened by military censors and routinely turned over to the Soviet state security authorities. The officer was arrested and sentenced to what in comparison with previous years under Stalin's rule was a lenient sentence: eight years at hard labor in a concentration camp. Stalin undoubtedly took no direct part in the incident but presided over a totalitarian system that doled out such punishments for seemingly trivial offenses. There were many thousands of such cases, but this one is memorable, for the young officer was Alexander Solzhenitsyn, later to become one of modern Russia's greatest writers, to win the Nobel Prize for literature, to write a vast exposé of the concentration camp system he termed the "Gulag Archipelago," and to be forcibly exiled from his native land.

In this last chapter on practicing power, we shall use Stalin's career to exemplify what we call the pragmatics and demonics of power. The questions we shall pose are not only political but also ethical: What price politics? Is political success worth the sacrifice? How do you judge? Stalin will help us answer.

HOW DO YOU GET ALONG WITH OTHER PEOPLE?

We have stressed throughout this book that you use power in everyday life. In a sense, every human relationship—father-son, mother-daughter, teacher-pupil, husband-wife—is a power relationship, in that they all involve rule. When people interact, they use power in order to

JOSEPH STALIN: SOVIET DESPOT

The political career of Joseph Djugashvili spanned the first half of the twentieth century. Born in Soviet Georgia, he became a seminary student and there, of all places, a revolutionary Marxist. (Like many of the other Bolsheviks, Joseph took a political pseudonym, Stalin, which means "steel.") He was short, scarred from smallpox, and had a thick Georgian accent. When he made his first radio address to the Russian people in 1941, they were startled by his accent. He was arrested several times during the revolutionary struggle and became one of the principal Bolshevik leaders during the revolution. But many of the other Bolsheviks, who were highly educated, brilliant conversationalists, and cosmopolitan, were contemptuous of the rustic and plodding Georgian. (Many of them, such as Lev Kamenev, Grigori Zinoviev and Leon Trotsky, might have been less rude if they had known that one day Stalin would have the power to have them executed—and did.)

The rise of Stalin to become a new despot, having powers that the most autocratic of czars could only envy, is a story in itself. How could the "colorless drone" who ran the Communist party's administrative offices become the absolute ruler who had only to pick up the phone to his secret police and order the internment or murder of any of his 200 million subjects? How could a man who was an outsider, from both Russia and the mainstream of the Communist movement, with no personal charm or oratorical ability become the virtually unchallenged ruler of all the Russians for almost a quarter of a century? How could any people give such a person that much power over them?

Part of the answer is, of course, that others did not really give Stalin almost unlimited power; rather, he took it. His extraordinary talent for political intrigue, for dividing and conquering, for playing people off from one another, for calculating the correct timing and measure called for by an occasion all served him well during the 1920s (after Lenin's death) in which, to everyone's surprise, he slowly but surely eliminated the other leading Bolsheviks. (Recall our brief discussion of this in Chapter 7.) The fall from power of rivals, the murder of Serjei Kirov (one of Stalin's closest aides), the purges and liquidation of real and imagined enemies all were engineered by Stalin's minions in the party and the secret police. In the purges from 1936 to 1938, by one estimate, he had killed 1,108 out of a total of 1,966 members of the Seventeenth Party Congress. George F. Kennan, then the American ambassador to the Soviet Union, wrote that Stalin once remarked that "there was nothing sweeter in life than to bide the proper moment for revenge, to insert the knife, to turn it around, and to go home for a good night's sleep." In eliminating his political enemies among the Soviet inner party, Stalin also satisfied a desire for revenge against those who had once scorned him. In the tradition of the Caucasus where he grew up, he adopted the tradition of calculated vengeance through political vendettas.

During his years of absolute power, Stalin exercised control, directly or indirectly, over virtually every aspect of Soviet life. He lived a strange, remote life, was rarely seen in public, and was thought of by many Russians as a kind of wrathful Old Testament God who would punish them if they thought or acted wrongly. He was obsessed with controlling what people wrote and read. Apparently he personally edited the manuscripts of famous Soviet writers and of course had many things banned (such as Dostoveski's works, which he admired but would not permit to be published). He believed that the ultimate weapon of political control was the dictionary. The Stalinist state machinery published the official truth in both the newspapers and the history books. History was constantly being rewritten for current political purposes. Everybody and everything in the realm of public expression were suspect. Even circus acts were criticized for "reactionary bourgeois tendencies." Soviet artists had to be very careful. The great music composer Dimitri Shostakovich, under suspicion, atoned by composing a piece entitled "Ode to Stalin's Afforestation Plan." There was good reason to be careful: Stalin often had artists arrested and even shot. The great Russian poet Mandelstam, himself later executed, once ironically remarked to his wife, "One should be happy to live in a country where literature was thought important; for where else do they kill people for writing poetry?"

Stalin's political operational code was very simple, according to Louis Fischer: any means are legitimate if they help achieve the desired end; people must be discarded when no longer useful; alliances are made to be broken; and ideas are worthless unless they help serve power. Stalin always strove to gain absolute power, never trusting his subordinates in the party or army. Some even doubt that he was committed to the goals of Soviet Communism but, rather, was a political cynic with a lust for personal power for purposes of domination, sadism, and revenge. Even with his inner circle and family (his daughter Svetlana defected to the West), he was brutish, suspicious, and domineering. Some psychologists have speculated that Stalin was an extreme case of megalomania, an insatiable desire for power. The megalomaniac seeks power as an end in itself and uses it to hurt others. At the height of his power, Stalin had himself extravagantly portrayed in the Soviet press as an almost godlike figure, the source of all wisdom and guide on the correct path to Communism. He imagined that associates, generals, doctors, and Jews all were plotting against him. Toward the end of his life, he wrote into Soviet ideology the doctrine of "transformism," the idea that his ideas governed nature and that he could transform physical and social reality at will.

Despite the "downgrading" of Stalin that occurred after his death, many Russians still admire him. With Khrushchev's speech condemning Stalin in 1956, there was an official period of "de-Stalinization." Stalin's body was removed from Lenin's tomb; the entry for him in the *Great Soviet Encyclopedia* was shortened; and he was rarely mentioned in the press. Yet the Soviet government and society still bear traces of his iron manner. Soviet citizens will still express their admiration for Stalin as a "strong boss" who would not put up with the "permissive society" of today. Despite the painful memories of the purges and terror and wartime sacrifices, both the reputation and ruling style of Joseph Stalin remain an integral part of the society he did so much to create.

---

accomplish the goals called for by the relationship. The relationship is ruled in some way.

Suppose (as in William Golding's novel *Lord of the Flies*) that you and a group of people are stranded on a desert island. Obviously the group must work out a system of relationships. Power will be used to define how the group is ruled and what rules will be in effect. But there are different ways in which the group might be ruled.

Indeed, the group could actually even disband, with the only rule being that "every man and woman for himself or herself." All on the island would seek food, shelter, and sex on their own. Whatever you get is yours, but you will have to defend it against the attacks of others. You, your possessions, and your companions all are in danger, as you sometimes have to sleep, and others can attack you then. Such a state of anarchy is uncomfortable but at least is logically possible. (Such a "state of nature" was described by the seventeenth-century political philosopher Thomas Hobbes in his book *Leviathan*, as one in which "the life of man [is] solitary, poor, nasty, brutish, and short.")

Most of us can see the logic of a group's staying together, the necessity of getting along with one another, stabilizing relationships, dividing up the labor, economizing effort, maintaining peace and order, and establishing rule. What we give up in freedom we gain in predictability.

The fact is that we want power exercised over us. On that desert island, we would quickly see the necessity of power being exercised and, at least in some ways, the wisdom of having someone with power tell us what to do. We may speed in our cars from time to time, but we can see the logic of having rules of the road enforced by the police. Most of us would grant the legitimacy of governments' using power to stop crime, enforce contracts, and regulate potentially dangerous behavior such as driving drunk and the like.

This argument we shall call the *pragmatic logic of power*. We expect politicians to do certain kinds of things, and we hope that they do them well. A government is supposed to function, and politicians are supposed to have the political and administrative skills necessary to make them work. Throughout this book we have extolled the virtue of political competence in great politicians who have used power to produce good results. We have also condemned political incompetence as something that reduces bad results. Even with the best of intentions, political amateurs and idiots have misused power, and many people have gotten hurt in the process.

"Power tends to corrupt," said Lord Acton, "absolute power corrupts absolutely." People who have power can be mean and vengeful, stupid and stubborn, and beset by deep psychological maladies, all of which they may visit on other people. They have what we shall call the *demonic illogic of power*. In the wrong hands, power can be a demonic force, a destructive rather than a creative power. We all want power exercised over us, but not too much so. We do not want to be overtaxed, overregimented, overly abused. Rather than simply the misuse of power by incompetent fools, here we have the abuse of power, often by quite competent maniacs, producing evil effects.

There are alternative ways to set up a society and government in order for everybody to get along. People can be forced to get along, they can consent to get along, or more likely, something of both. But the political logic of relationships does allow for different bases for rule. Let us look at three ways that relationships can be ruled.

Suppose that the group on the island agrees that it would be smart for them to get along because they have different things they can do and can thus help one another. They can exchange goods and services, trade, bargain, and deal, and have a government that acts as a honest broker. They all will benefit if they agree to help one another in whatever ways they can. That is the basis of an exchange society, ruled by a power that enforces the rules of help. This is often called the *politics of accommodation,* based on the logic of mutual help.

On the other hand, the group might agree that they all love one another and that they are committed to one another because of their mutual affection based on values they hold in common. This is the basis for an affective society, ruled by a power that enforces the rule of love. This is often called the *politics of redemption,* based on the logic of mutual love.

There is a third alternative. Suppose the group agrees that they do not love one another and that they do not even want to help one another. Indeed, they do not really like or trust one another very much. Peace is always precarious, and people are prone to be untrustworthy and violent, and so they must have a government with the power to subjugate all of them. Because they all fear one another, and thus are a threat to one another, they must have a government that rules over all of them by means of fear. They all will benefit if they agree to obey a power that rules by making them afraid of the consequences of disobedience. This is often called the *politics of subjection.*

We have discussed all three types of politics and politicians before. James Madison, for instance, was an advocate of the politics of accommodation, that society and politics could be rationally based on exchange, interest, and compromise. Gandhi espoused the politics of redemption, mobilizing the power of affection to achieve a political purpose. Catherine the Great was an autocrat who ruled by means of the politics of subjection, making her subjects and rivals afraid of her.

Each type of politics also has the potential for abuse, for the demonic illogic of power. The politics of accommodation becomes demonic, for instance, when trading and bargaining lead to highly unequal political and economic results, creating a large gap between the powerful and powerless and the rich and poor. The politics of redemption can become fanatical, forcing everybody to live up to the letter of the law and punishing those who are reluctant or do not believe. The politics of subjection can be excessively oppressive, with all the subjects living in constant fear and with large numbers of people being arbitrarily victimized.

There are, of course, many examples of such demonic politics, or at least politics with demonic results. Perhaps Herbert Hoover's rule is an example of the demonics of accommodation, because he refused to help the many who were suddenly needy. Certainly Hitler's depotism is an example of the demonics of political redemption, because of his fanatical pursuit of war and genocide. The worst despots, from Nero to Idi Amin, ruled according to the demonics of subjection.

So these are the ways the island could be ruled. Indeed, many other kinds of human relationships are in effect ruled this way. Think of families you know—are they based on help, love, or fear? Oftentimes they are a mixture. Boy–girl relations in high school or college often possess all three. The boy and girl help each other in studying, love each other, and maybe fear each other. Often either boys or girls will dominate the other, even keep the other in physical fear.

Governments can also be mixtures. Accommodation may give way to redemption in wartime or during periods of zealous reform. The West German government now practices a pragmatic politics of accommodation but once, during the Nazi period, used a quite fanatical and demonic politics of redemption. All states practice subjection of some sort, enforcing the law and punishing transgressors, but some, such as the czars of Russia, were more excessive than others were.

Like all of us, then, governments are capable of both pragmatic and demonic rule. How you treat other people is not very different from what governments and rulers do to people, differing in degree but not in kind. You use power in your relationships with other people, which involves the use and abuse of power. Thus you can and do treat people either pragmatically or demonically. How do you get along with other people? Do you "rule" them through help, love, or fear, or a combination of these? Do you use these powers to rule with pragmatic or demonic results? Does how you rule other people have good or evil consequences? Long ago Plato said that "the State is man writ large." Think about that: the same kinds of relationships that appear in politics are only what you do in your relations with other people writ large.

THE DISECONOMY OF VIOLENCE

Politics can produce some good results by economizing violence; that is, the controlled and rational application of political rule can produce pragmatic results by advocating peace and order. This may not be the most exalted ethic ever imagined, but it may be the best result that politics, as politics, can produce. In politics, we have asserted, somebody always gets hurt. But we have seen examples of rule and rulers who, in the context of their times and political order, can bring about pragmatic rule. We might term this a Machiavellian ethic: political peace has its price, but it may be the best that can be achieved under the circumstances and certainly is a prerequisite for all other human purposes, individual or social. What is loosely termed the *public interest* is served by the correct use of power.

The incorrect use of power is the diseconomy of violence. The demonic illogic of rule can produce uneconomical results from the excessive use of power beyond political necessity. The diseconomy of rule is politically illogical, producing bad results beyond political necessity. The political trick is knowing the difference between the pragmatics and demonics of politics, between the economical and the uneconomical use of power. Politicians often lose sight of why power is being used. A variation of the

Practicing Power

political pragmatic rule is, am I using power here for a sensible political purpose, or am I using power for vindictive, personal, and illogical reasons? In the latter case, it is likely that you are using power for an unethical, or at least a politically unwise, purpose.

Let us return to that desert island. Suppose that one person, supported by other, physically strong people, gain power. The new ruler has a demonic streak and begins to imprison, torture, and execute people. You are afraid for your own safety and life. You are afraid that the ruler and his or her supporters suspect you of hating them and wanting to overthrow them. Imagine yourself in a state of virtually total control, not only over your actions, but even over your thoughts. This is a state of demonic terror, in which you are reduced to being a potential or actual victim of unlimited power. Here power is sadistic, aimed not at the pragmatics of rule but at the demonics of victimization. It is not a comfortable state, as concentration camp survivors can attest.

The basic ruling option in politics is, again, either minimizing or maximizing the amount of pain in the world. This, of course, is a simple utilitarian ethic, but it fits the pragmatic rule that by their political fruits ye shall know them. In politics, this is always a ratio, a calculation, a trade-off: is what I am doing politically going to minimize, relatively speaking, the amount of pain in the world? Or will it increase the amount of pain in the world? How much pain is necessary in order to achieve a desired political result? Are the sacrifice and the suffering worth the effort?

Even though most of us would agree that it is better to minimize than to maximize pain, in actual practice, producing such results is not always easy. The turbulent whims of political *fortuna* may call for the *necessita* of tragic choices. But the *virtu* of practicing political pragmatics can produce an *ordini* with a relatively small amount of political pain, though the economy of violence in wartime or in corrupt societies may involve a great deal of violence. The pragmatic rule of the economy of political violence is simply that direct coercive power should be used only to produce political order. For Lincoln during the Civil War or Churchill during World War II, this was a very high level indeed. Even in the pursuit of pragmatic political goals, with no desire to commit acts of excessive violence, such acts may occur by miscalculation or the excessive zeal of subordinates. The tragic political choices that must be made in crises are messy, bloody, and unjust. But they must be made: remember Machiavelli's argument about the necessity of calculating whether cruelty is well or badly used. It may be necessary to use cruel methods to prevent even more violence.

But the demonic illogic of political violence goes beyond the utilitarian principle, for it aims not at pragmatic rule but, rather, at maximizing the amount of political pain beyond what is necessary to produce pragmatic political results. Political rule is both demonic and illogical— that is, it uses bad political logic—when it commits itself to a diseconomy of violence.

THE ILLOGIC OF POLITICAL CORRUPTION

The diseconomy of violence is the worst form of political corruption. There are many forms of political corruption, many of them relatively mild and some even endemic to certain regimes. Corruption is a malady of individuals and states, contracted when they abandon principles or depart from political sense. Republican regimes, as critics from Plato onward have warned, are prone to the corruptions of demagoguery and anarchy. Because republics are based on popular participation, they can be corrupted by a leader who appeals to mass emotions and prejudices. Republics also can deteriorate into anarchy, in which the masses follow no leader and divide up into ungovernable, warring factions. Autocracies can become stagnant and decadent. The political elite at the court of the autocrat can become inflexible and cruel, crushing all dissent, revolt, or reform. They can also become decadent, with the petty elite at the top enjoying wealth and opulence while the rest of society suffers. All such maladies can result in a diseconomy of violence, such as civil wars and revolutions.

But totalitarian regimes have the most potential for political corruption, if by that we mean a departure from or a perversion of the economy of violence. Totalitarian regimes, at least in theory, can maintain order, enforce unity, and achieve state goals through the coordination of effort, as probably no other kind of regime can. But if power corrupts, then the highly centralized and unlimited power of totalitarian regimes has the greatest potential for political corruption. Totalitarian corruption at its worst takes the form of demonic overcontrol of the individual, physically through the use of terror and psychologically through the use of mind control. By terror we mean the political use of arbitrary physical coercion and abuse as a demonic means to visit pain on a subject population. By mind control we mean the use of psychological manipulation as a means to expand the regime's control of the individual. This is not to say that these corruptions do not appear in republics or autocracies. Republics use advertising and other forms of propaganda to manipulate the people's minds, and autocracies often use terror to crush revolt. It is just that totalitarian regimes have fewer constraints on their use, and thus the likelihood of using the demonics of unlimited power is greater.

The positive political logic of political systems inspires them to perfect the system's political ideals or goals. Thus an autocratic system aims at establishing hierarchical order and obedience; a republican system seeks to introduce pluralistic balance and popular participation; and a totalitarian system works to produce revolutionary collectivism and mobilization. This we shall call the *perfected logic* of pragmatic political systems. But the opposite and perverted political outcome is also logically possible, and this we shall term the *negative political logic of political systems,* the perfected corruption of demonic power run amuck. At the absolute logical extreme, unlimited political power would exercise complete control over and maximize the amount of pain visited on its subjects.

Such a horrible system can be imagined but in reality has never been approached. But the logical potential is there. Many states are in fact limited in what they can do and thus are mixtures of the pragmatic and demonic. Let us look further at the rule of someone who was both a pragmatic and demonic prince, Joseph Stalin.

THE PRAGMATICS OF STALINIST RULE

By the late 1920s Stalin was virtually the complete political master of the Soviet Union. In policy debates with his opponents, Stalin advocated the position that he termed *socialism in one country*. Stalin argued that if the Soviet Union and the socialist ideal were to survive, they would have to do it by themselves, and do it quickly. The Bolsheviks understood that they were a new force in a hostile political world and that nobody was going to help them. Stalin understood the pragmatic political logic of rapid industrialization and modernization. The country would have to emerge from the Dark Ages into the modern age in half a generation, or otherwise the Soviet experiment would fail.

Stalin's pragmatic goal, despite all his mistakes, was one of the greatest and quickest industrial and social revolutions in history. A backward, illiterate country overnight became a great world power. Everything went into heavy industry, dams, and vast projects. The forced collectivization of agriculture freed labor for industrial projects. Peasant agriculture was medieval at the beginning of this period, to the point that the farmers were still using the same kind of wooden plows used by their ancestors a thousand years before. Cities grew rapidly. The whole nation was sent to school and taught both literacy and technical skills. With enormous effort and sacrifice, the Soviet Union had become a major industrial and military power by the time of World War II. Despite the destruction of cities and factories during the German invasion, the Soviet Union emerged from the war as the prominent power in Europe and the rival of the United States in military power.

Was the sacrifice worth it? Perhaps only an iron totalitarian dictatorship could have brought it off, coordinating long-range plans to achieve stated goals. Stalin envisioned pragmatic political goals, realized the urgency of bringing them about, and set the country on a course of economic growth that culminated in the defeat of the Nazis and the achievement of world power status. The ordinary Soviet citizen is better off today in practically every material way—per-capita income, health, job security, and so on. The pain caused one generation decreased the pain for subsequent ones. Thus a good case can be made that the rapid and exhausting economic programs of the Stalinist era were justified.

THE DEMONICS OF STALINIST RULE

But balanced against the pragmatic results of Stalin's rule are the human costs. However economically necessary the collectivization of agriculture may have been, it was handled in a brutal manner and resulted in the death and dislocation of millions of people. Stalin remarked to Churchill that it was worse than Hitler's war, but inevitable. Many peasants, including the wealthier ones called *kulaks,* resisted until death or deportation. They slaughtered their livestock, murdered collective farm heads, and even led armed resistance. But Stalin persisted, squeezing as much food as possible out of the countryside. The political strength and future of the Soviet regime lay in the support of the workers and the party in the industrial cities. If someone were going to starve, it would not be them. Stalin apparently took the ruthless and even cynical position that famines in the countryside were natural, cyclical phenomena and that this would just be one more cycle, but also the last one. In the long run, perhaps Stalin's policy fed more than it starved, but that sort of political logic was lost on the victims of the famine.

The terror unleashed in Stalin's Great Purge is often explained away by simply saying that Stalin was a madman, a paranoiac, a new and equally insane Ivan the Terrible. But the hard fact was that Stalin had, from his point of view, good political reasons for unleashing the terror. For one thing, dramatic movements such as purge and terror, capped by public "show trials," served the purpose of diverting attention from the failures of the regime and the discontent among the many. The portrayal of Trotsky and other "traitors" as sinister threats to Soviet society, and thus the new well-being of the people, helped solidify Stalin's support and, conversely, convey the message that opposition to Stalin was treason, because it aided the enemies of the people. Stalin was also aware that given his background in the conspiratorial history of Bolshevism, that conspiracies were possible. With the exile of Trotsky and his followers and the rise of Hitler, the possibility of domestic intrigue tied to a foreign foe was all too real. Thus Stalin could kill two political birds with one stone. He could eliminate, through purge, all possible conspiracies and rivals and commit the Soviet state to another movement, which would inspire new enthusiasm for and drive to the regime. The only way to shake things up and to rid the regime of enemies was through terror.

Stalin did not shrink from the task. The terror was vast, virtually complete, and in a sense unending. Everybody was a potential suspect, and no one could feel safe from the dreaded knock on the door at midnight. The secret police suspected everyone, including themselves (Stalin had two heads of the secret police shot). The purges, in effect, eliminated all potential opposition, by killing or imprisoning all the important Bolsheviks. Trotsky was killed in Mexico in 1940 by one of Stalin's agents. Stalin then replaced all of them with loyal people who owed their promotion to him. Stalin's eternal vigilance, through the "atomization" of Soviet society, ensured his rule.

For Stalin, there was no doubt a kind of inexorable political logic to the Great Purge and the policy of purge in general. If we accept his assumptions, the terror and other equally brutal policies did help the Soviet regime survive World War II and thereafter. But the question remains whether all the political pain that Stalin caused was necessary or whether it was excessive and unnecessary. Could Stalin have achieved Soviet objectives without such harsh measures? Could someone else have collectivized agriculture, industrialized Russia, defeated the Germans, and fought counterrevolution and civil disunity without terror, concentration camps, and great human costs? Is there a political logic to demonic politics?

For all those that suffered and died because of Stalin, there is not. But beyond that is the fact of Stalin's legacy on the Soviet ruling style. Stalin successfully created the first totalitarian government in the world and, to a large degree, the way Russia is still ruled. In many ways, he invented the principle and practice of totalitarian rule, with both the few and the many living in fear and anxiety and with the potential for people to be victimized for no apparent reason. The diseconomy of violence that Stalin created involved not only physical costs in those killed or imprisoned but also psychological costs in what political scientist Alex Inkeles called "the institutionalization of anxiety." The Stalinist terror, wrote Inkeles, affected those who were not arrested by creating in everyone a deep sense of insecurity by making them feel that they might have done something "wrong," although they were not sure exactly what: "The non-victim, looking at the actual victim, can never find out why the victim was victimized, because there are different and contradictory reasons for different victims, or there may have been no reason at all. . . . It is this compulsive conformity which the totalitarian regime wants. It gets as a derived benefit from the influence of the terror on the non-victim, who puzzles over the reasons for the treatment of the victim. Anxiety has been institutionalized." Or more succinctly, poet Bertolt Brecht wrote: "The victim is always guilty."

Stalin practiced the demonic politics of subjection by introducing into Soviet politics the idea of demons and witches, which fed political fears that the enemy was all around and could even be us. It is politically corrupting because it eliminates trust, shatters confidence, and makes everyone live in a state of perpetual anxiety. To fight the demons that threaten us, we must be just as demonic in our rule. The demons must by physically purged, whether they were witting or unwitting agents of the devil; the demons must also be purged from our minds by means of controls. The introduction of demonology enjoins a politics of "victimage." Because everyone is guilty, everyone is a potential threat. Thus everyone becomes a potential victim, someone to be sacrificed in order to ensure the survival of the regime and the position of the leader.

Since Stalin's death, the Soviet regime has departed from the perverted logic of victimization. Stalin has been condemned officially for his "theoretical and political mistakes," and many prominent victims of the purges have been rehabilitated as heroes. But, Stalin is still greatly admired by many ordinary Soviet citizens as a "strong leader," though the Soviet Communist elite so far has shrunk from the thought of another such leader and the diseconomy of violence he unleashed. The post-Stalinist regime has leaned toward a pragmatic politics of subjection, but Soviet leaders must ponder from time to time whether the regime could deteriorate again into another cycle of demonic politics.

ORWELLIAN LOGIC

We have mentioned George Orwell's chilling vision before. Here we only need mention that Orwell's portrait was in some measure based upon Stalin's rule, carrying the demonic illogic of that rule to its node. Orwell correctly saw in Stalinism the seeds of ultimate political corruption in a system dedicated to the maximization of control over its subjects. Orwell's futuristic Oceania expands the principle of victimage to everyone, and equates power with the ability to make subjected victims suffer. In the famous recognition scene, O'Brien states the principle to Winston Smith. Oceania is ruled for the sake of maximizing power, he tells Smith, not for any notion of a political good. Rather the Party rules Oceania by asserting its power over its subjects constantly. How? By making them suffer. Otherwise how could we be sure that they are obeying our will and not theirs? The goal of the Party is to maximize the amount of suffering it can cause them. "Progress in our world," gloats O'Brien, "will be progress towards more pain." Every value, humane feeling, or life instinct will be abolished. Every one will be a potential or actual victim controlled by omnipotent power. "If you want a picture of the future," he says, "imagine a boot stamping on a human face— forever."

So the demonics of power has an almost unlimited potential for causing pain. Orwell's vision simply states what totalitarian regimes have the politico-logical potential to become. Such a potential should make us all appreciate limits on political power, and the pragmatic use of power. In politics, we have said, somebody always gets hurt. But the question is, how much? Politics, it has been said, is a choice between evils, and thus ethically is a quest for the lesser evil. Certainly our discussion of the demonics of power should remind you of that. When we get frustrated with the compromises and deals of republican politics, perhaps we should remind ourselves of the argument made by Charles Frankel: "The greased palm is bad but it is preferable to the mailed fist."

"There was nothing sweeter in life than to bide the proper moment for revenge, to insert the knife, to turn it around, and to go home for a good night's sleep."

—attributed to Stalin

"Power tends to corrupt; absolute power corrupts absolutely."

—*Lord Acton*

"The State is man writ large."

—*Plato*

"A new prince, above all others, cannot possibly avoid a name for cruelty, since new states are always in danger."

—*Machiavelli*

"The victim is always guilty."

—*Bertolt Brecht*

"If you want a picture of the future, imagine a boot stamping on a human face—forever."

—*O'Brien, in Orwell's Nineteen Eighty-four*

"The greased palm is bad but it is preferable to the mailed fist."

—*Charles Frankel*

Part

VII

Losing Power

Chapter

29

Ruling Badly: Losing Power Through Incompetence

In the famous movie "The Wizard of Oz," Dorothy and her friends are awed by the great and wonderful and very mysterious wizard who rules Oz from his palace in the Emerald City. Like everyone else, they are cowed in his presence but later discover that he is a humbug, a con artist who uses special effects to scare his subjects. When Dorothy scolds him, "You're a very bad man!" the Wizard replies, "Oh, no, my child, I'm a very good man. I'm just a very bad wizard." It is no secret that the history of world politics offers example after example of politicians who were bad wizards, losing power because they were incompetent and ruled badly. Even so, the many precedents of bad rulers have not stopped later rulers from also doing the same incompetent things and being brought down. "There is nothing new except what is forgotten," said Mademoiselle Bertin, Marie Antoinette's milliner. The fate of her employers should have been warning to succeeding rulers (but sad to say, in cases too numerous to mention, it has not), and political upheaval (and much suffering for both rulers and ruled) has still been the rule.

WHAT IS POLITICAL COMPETENCE?

We all have some idea of what competence is. All of us try to cope with life, using whatever means we can to accomplish personal ends. Some of us learn to be competent at some things but not others. Our talents and aptitudes vary greatly, as does our ability to understand and use them. Take school: you are good at some subjects, not so good at others. Some are not good at school at all. They may be dumb, bored, confused, or lazy, but they don't display much academic competence, and really should not be in school at all. But most students gain some competence at something, and if they are smart, pursue and cultivate that at which they are good, translating that into something they can do in the adult world and even teach others—mathematics, law, fashion merchandising, even politics. If you fool around in school, you will not have learned any competencies, and wind up being a failure.

The Machiavellian perspective teaches that life is a risky business and that competence at the various roles you play is the only possible way that you can successfully cope. The principle of competence is your personal *virtu,* your ability to do well what you set out to do. For example, you may be a failure at marriage. To a large degree, this may be because you are incompetent at the marital virtues—fidelity, compatibility, sensuality, and so forth. True, you may be the victim of circumstances, of *fortuna.* You may marry someone who is incompetent at marriage, or events (war, depression, illness, an interfering family) may doom the relationship. But we all are victims of circumstance; the test of competence, at marriage, politics, or whatever is to master circumstance and rule.

This book has followed Machiavelli and praised those famous men and women who were politically competent. We have also stressed that you do not have to become a politician per se to learn the Machiavellian lesson that competent action is the way to accomplish goals. We shall now look at negative cases to learn from them. For examining what political princes have done to lose power can also reveal how to use power well.

ON SITTING ON POWDER KEGS

Louis XVI, Marie Antoinette's husband, was competent at his favorite pastimes, locksmithing and hunting, and he devoted much of his time to them. But he did not cultivate or exercise much competence at politics. By 1789, after fifteen years of rule, he was sitting on top of a political powder keg and did not know it. It is true that to some degree that Louis was a victim of circumstances. In other times, he might have reigned and died without incident.It is also true that he inherited many of the deeply rooted social and economic problems that came to a head in his time. But he did not appear to have tried to understand what was going on, nor did he take strong measures to try to solve those problems. He belonged to a dynasty that had had competent kings (Louis XIV) that he could emulate, and he was also educated enough to know that kings had been deposed because they were bad rulers (Charles I of England in the previous century). In 1776 the ousted minister A. R. J. Turgot warned Louis, "Remember, sire, that it was weakness which brought the head of Charles I to the block." What was to happen to Louis was not new, but it happened because he forgot that it could happen and did not try to stop it.

Too, it was not as though Louis did not have warnings. Many of his advisers and observers of developments in France warned that just beneath the surface was the potential for trouble. But Louis blithely ignored the warnings and continued his usual routine. Observers were also aware that the drift into political chaos called for political mastery from a leader who was not there. Gouverneur Morris, a visitor from America, wrote in early 1789, "Gods, what a theatre this is for a first-rate character!" And one of the Mirabeaus remarked: "We live in a time of great events but little men."

Louis was not a bad man. By all accounts, he was pious, earnest, and dignified. But he combined all the worst traits of a bad ruler, at the worst possible time to display them. He was well meaning in the worst sense of the word. He was slow-witted and lazy, willing to let the mounting crises develop without concerning himself with the possibility of disaster. He was stubborn when he needed to be flexible and irresolute when he needed to be firm. He would take an agonizingly long time to make a decision and then, when led by another adviser, change his mind, usually at precisely the wrong time. He was beset and confused by conflicting advice and dismissed under pressure his most talented ministers, who might have solved France's financial crisis.

Perhaps even worse, he took advice from and wilted under the pressure of his wife Marie Antoinette. She was politically ignorant, but she pushed him almost unfailingly in the wrong direction. She was not only a political liability in giving amateurish advice; she also was distrusted and hated by both the laity and the nobility. She was a foreigner, the "Austrian bitch," who, it was rumored, might be a traitor. It was also rumored that she was an adulteress and lived an extravagant life in the midst of great poverty. People believed the tale that when she was told the people had no bread, she replied, "Let them eat cake." Despite all these liabilities, she never tried to cultivate popularity among the people, which she could have, by sponsoring charities and the like. To many she came to symbolize the insensitivity and arrogance of the monarchy, even though she may not have deserved it.

In any event, Louis and Marie Antoinette were not prepared, by either education or experience, to govern even in quiet times, much less during the crisis of the late eighteenth century. Louis vacillated, compromised, stood adamant, gave in, attempted to flee, and all in all was baffled by the rapid turn of events. At best, he might have solved the problems that would have prevented the revolution and thus remained an absolute monarch; if not that, he might have transformed himself into a constitutional monarch and perhaps retained some political power and certainly his throne; but the worst happened: he lost his throne and his life (as did Marie Antoinette).

Perhaps it was politically unjust to blame and execute Louis (it certainly was politically unwise) for France's ills. But Louis might have avoided his fate if he had been politically competent. He even botched his attempt to flee, waiting too long and then unwisely letting himself be recognized in public, plainly not understanding Baltasar Gracián's thought: "It is a maxim of the wise to leave things before things leave them." In most great revolutions, at the onset of revolt, the country is usually being governed by someone who is inept at ruling, for example,

Charles I of England, Nicholas II of Russia, Shah Mohammed Reza Pahlavi of Iran, and so on. Even though impersonal historical forces and accidents of time and place contribute to the fall of kings, their own incompetence at politics is a reason as well.

What is worst of all about such political incompetents is that their failure to master crisis situations diseconomizes violence. We cannot blame Louis for the senseless violence of the September massacres or the Reign of Terror, but we cannot excuse him for helping create the political conditions that resulted in the breakdown of authority, law, and order and led to the violent competition for power among the warring groups that hoped to create a new state. Political incompetence has unintended but very real consequences in the havoc that misuse of power creates. By not facing and resolving the long-range and immediate problems of the old regime, Louis encouraged the incredible destruction of the revolution and Napoleon's empire.

Quantula sapientia mundus regitur, goes the Roman saying: "how ignorantly we are ruled." Not always and not necessarily. But there has been, sadly, more than enough political incompetence in human history to give that ancient lament universal meaning. Consider again the case of Louis. If he had understood his regime's fiscal mismanagement and indebtedness, he might have seen what disasters its continuation might lead to. Rather than hunt at Versailles, he could have tackled the difficult and thankless task of fiscal and tax reform. The nobles and clergy avoided taxation by means of their ancient privileges and thus left the tax burden to the new bourgeoisie and peasants and workers. Property and money were concentrated heavily in the few, and as the financial crisis worsened, so was the well-being of the many. But such reform was beyond the skill or interest of Louis, and France drifted into political revolution. "Politics," said Max Weber, "is a strong and slow boring of hard boards." Louis could work up no interest in the hard board of political reform.

Even if Louis had responded wisely to immediate events, he might have avoided having the political powder keg blow up in his face. As the financial crisis deepened between 1786 and 1788, a new minister Charles Alexandre de Calonne, clearly saw that there was only one way to end the spiral of debt and interest payments: make the privileged and wealthy pay a larger share of the tax burden, as there was more than enough wealth in the realm to make the regime fiscally sound again. The aristocracy and clergy resisted, and Louis gave in, dismissing Calonne; then when a new minister tried reform, he took away some of the political privileges of the aristocracy and the clergy but then caved in again when they resisted. His irresolution undermined his position with every major group in France and turned the financial crisis into a political crisis. In desperation, he called an Estates-General, which he could not control and which became the setting of the birth of the revolution. At every juncture, Louis vacillated and by so doing gave new impetus to the political defiance that finally resulted in full-scale revolution. By ruling ignorantly, both in the long and the short run, he let things get out of hand, and the powder keg exploded in his face.

But Louis was not the first or the last political incompetent to lose power. There are many other examples that we could point to, but let us here point to only two spectacular cases very much like Louis, those of Nicholas II of Russia and Shah Mohammed Reza Pahlavi of Iran.

THE FALL OF THE SHAH

In his book *The Anatomy of Revolution,* historian Crane Brinton compared the four "classical" revolutions, the English, French, American, and Russian revolutions. In each case he found some uniformities in the old regimes that had existed before the revolutions. First, all the societies in question were improving economically, and the revolutions originated not among the downtrodden but among those (the rising new rich, for example) who saw an intolerable gap between what they wanted and what they got. Second, in these prerevolutionary societies, there were bitter class antagonisms, with hatred directed at the ruling class and its privileges. Third, in each case the intellectuals—those who influenced ideas by writing and speaking—lost faith in the old regime and transferred their allegiance to the revolutionary cause. The governments also became ineffective, both in their normal operation and in their response to crisis. The institutions of the old regimes became cumbersome and inert, unable to cope with potential or immediate rebellion. The leaders of the old regimes lost confidence in their right to rule and adopted a deluge mentality. They become unable to handle financial crises and used force against revolt either stupidly or ineffectively, giving a new impetus to rebellion. When the revolutionaries won, they wanted to kill the leaders of the old regimes, and oftentimes they did. There was always a considerable struggle for power in the vacuum left by the collapse of the old regimes and usually a reign of terror in which many associated with the old regimes were executed. There was an attempt to create a new order that was more virtuous and harder to live up to than the old order was. But finally things settled down, usually with the emergence of a strong man who could rule. But the changes wrought by the revolution were not undone and to some extent revitalized the society. The revolution in time became central to the founding myth of the new regime.

The revolutionary process that Brinton described is one of political fragmentation, whereby a regime loses its ability to rule, and chaos ensues. In such times, the government loses its power over public opinion, among both the few and the many. People come to see the government, and the prince who heads it, as ineffective and illegitimate. As Machiavelli stressed, power ultimately is grounded in such opinion, the extent to which people believe one heads a government that does rule (is effective) and should rule (is legitimate). When such a ruler loses power over opinion, and people believe that he or she should not rule or cannot rule, then the ruler is in trouble. At that point, it may become wise to pack one's bags and find out where the fire exits are.

The most recent example of a ruler who fell from power because of political fragmentation was the Shah of Iran. The Iranian revolution had many of the classic features of revolution that Brinton identified. The shah's regime was thought by many to be stable and was praised by President Jimmy Carter as an "island of stability" in the unstable Middle East. The Shah was one of the most powerful rulers in the world, ruling an oil-rich country and building a massive military machine. Yet beneath the surfce, Iran was much more politically fragmented than many believed. It was a society that was improving economically but whose wealth was badly distributed. Class and ethnic antagonisms were bitter, and the traditional elites (such as the Muslim clergy) hated the new freedom and the "Western" traits of the urban middle class. The Shah's "White Revolution," aimed at industrializing and modernizing Iran, had the effect of infuriating and confusing the traditional elements while creating a "revolution of rising expectations" that frustrated the newly educated urban masses. Because both the traditional and modern elites were excluded from power, both directed antagonism toward the Shah. Intellectuals, both religious and secular, united in their condemnation of the Shah's regime. The Shah was not as grounded in political legitimacy as was thought. He was also not an effective ruler. Even though the regime was fabulously rich, much of it was drained off into the Shah's private fortune, fancy military hardware, extravagant and wasteful projects, and widespread corruption. As opposition mounted, the Shah's regime became more and more oppressive, antagonizing more and more people and being unable to stop riots and demonstrations. During the political crisis of the late 1970s, the Shah lost his resolve, and his allies in the government became more and more resigned to the political deluge to come. Like Louis and Nicholas, the Shah proposed becoming a constitutional monarch, but it was too late. He fled the country, and his regime collapsed. The Shah did not have an effective institution to protect him, in particular the military and police. He had no political legitimacy among any major group in the country, least of all among the Islamic many who resented his flaunting of traditional religious practices (for example, he allowed liquor in the country). The new revolutionary regime produced a struggle for power among the many factions that had supported the revolultion. They wanted to try and execute the exiled Shah and held American hostages in a futile attempt to force his return (he finally died in exile). The new regime conducted a reign of terror, executing many connected with the old regime (such as the top officials in SAVAK, the Shah's dreaded secret police). Ayatollah Khomeini, the new ruler and an Islamic *mullah,* and others dreamed of creating an Islamic republic ruled according to the principles of the Koran. The lessons of the Shah's fall are clear. Losing power is still possible for the mightiest of rulers, but the fall from power is not inevitable.

NICHOLAS II: THE LAST CZAR

Nicholas II was the last of the Romanovs, the Russian dynasty that produced little political talent (much less, say, than the Bourbons of France or Tudors of England). Nicholas displayed most of the worst traits of a political incompetent, probably more so than Louis XVI did. He really did not want the job of czar and called it "the awful job I have feared all my life." His father was a domineering man who helped make Nicholas timid and indecisive. As czar, Nicholas could never sustain any interest in a political program, events, or ministers who urged him to lead. His political convictions simply revolved around preserving "Holy Russia," the autocratic principle of czardom, and preventing anything that smacked of constitutional or administrative reform. But despite his ardent defense of autocratic privilege, he never had the will power to act like an autocrat; if he had, he might have prevented the revolution. He disliked competent administrators and consistently dismissed ministers (such as Count Sergei Witte) who tried to adapt to the rapidly changing Russian economic and political situation. Russia was riddled with discontent—in the decimated and defeated army, among the desperate peasantry, and among the growing industrial work force. But Nicholas was insulated from the realities and dangers of these changes. Yet in his own way, Nicholas may have sensed the winds of change with his fatalistic attitude: "Whatever I try," he said, "nothing succeeds. I am out of luck." "I have a secret conviction that I am destined for a terrible trial that I shall not receive my reward on this earth."

This kind of fatalism was widespread among the ruling class in early twentieth-century Russia and apparently, too, during the prerevolutionary period in France. As the French Revolution neared, people were reminded of the remark attributed to Louis XV. "After us the deluge." This sense of impending doom we shall term the *deluge mentality,* which paralyzes needed effort to control the processes at work and creates the feeling among those who rule that they are not equal to the task. Such political fatalism may become pervasive in a ruler like Nicholas, whose religious fatalism and political incompetence made him totally incapable of facing and dealing with the forces at work. Nicholas consistently discouraged the able ministers and elite reformers who saw the dangers caused by his stubbornness and stupidity, and they often gave up and became resigned to the collapse of the czarist system. Some even joined the revolutionary side, attempting to hasten the nearing political deluge.

Like Louis before him, Nicholas was married to a foreigner who was unpopular and who gave him bad but heeded advice. Alexandra urged him to resist all efforts for reform and to cling to the autocratic principle at all costs. When he took personal command of the army and was in the field, she—and through her, the "holy man" Rasputin—was by fiat the political power back in the capital of Petrograd. A Machiavellian interested in political competence and mastery could not imagine a more insane and self-defeating situation. Rasputin would make pronouncements to the completely gullible and believing empress, who would then communicate his "will" to the czar, who would then translate it into policy. This unbelievable situation finally ended when Rasputin was murdered, but it had made the czar seem so helpless and preposterous that afterwards practically everyone, from the Bolshevik exiles to the aristocrats in the capital, thought that very soon he would fall from power. By March 1917, the deluge mentality was so widespread that no one, except the hapless Nicholas, thought that he would last much longer. His own relatives warned him to sponsor reform or face revolution, to which he contemptuously replied, "I allow no one to give me advice." The British ambassador, representing the worried allies in the war, opined that the czar had lost the confidence of the Russian people, to which Nicholas replied, "Do you mean that *I* am to regain the confidence of my people, Ambassador, or that they are to regain my confidence?"

Needless to say, Nicholas was wrong again. It was the confidence of the people that was important, and there was none left. Despite repeated warnings, he chose to ignore the impending deluge and left Petrograd ignoring the outbreak of strikes and riots. "I shall take up dominos again in my spare time," he declared. Nine days after the beginning of the great revolution, when the desperate moderate politicians urged him to abdicate, he did so without a murmur. His fatalism prevailed again, and he had very little sense that his own incompetence had brought about the political chaos. But at least this attitude of fatalistic resignation was consistent. On this occasion, one of the politicians present said, "Your majesty, if you had done all this earlier, even as late as the last summoning of the Duma (the Russian parliament, which the czar had resisted since 1905), perhaps all that . . ." The czar broke in and innocently asked, "Do you think it might have been avoided?" Perhaps the same thought occurred to him in the moments before he and his family were shot by a local revolutionary group in June 1918.

THE PRAGMATICS OF JUSTICE

Ever since Aristotle, many observers of violent political change have agreed that the key to understanding such events is injustice. People revolt when they feel that the regime under which they live is unjust. what justice actually is has been debated ever since Plato's *Republic,* and we cannot settle it here. Our point is that people rebel when they feel that there is injustice and that a new prince will treat them more justly. People believe that they have a right to their just deserts and will probably respect and obey a prince if they believe that he or she is trying to give them what they think they deserve. This is the politicl pragmatics of justice: a leader and a regime are considered legitimate if people believe they are committed to them and are thought effective to the extent people believe that they deliver what they (the people) desire. If the gap between what they want and what they get is tolerable, the people will not be tempted by thoughts of revolt. Therefore there is a political logic to ruling justly.

This, of course, is easier said than done. The Machiavellian assertion is however, that people of power can anticipate and direct change in such a way as to avoid the fall. The rulers that we have discussed in this chapter did not have to fall. Louis could have faced and solved France's financial crisis. Nicholas did not have to be so stubborn and inflexible and could have made himself into a constitutional monarch and retained some powers. The Shah could have given the traditional religious figures at least some power in the government. In a family, a business, or a government, you can take steps to avoid falling from power. You have to use power in such a way that people believe that you deserve to rule because you are ruling justly. Making things not happen may well be the highest competence of the Machiavellian arts.

"There is nothing new except what is forgotten."

—*Mademoiselle Bertin*

"Remember, sire, that it was weakness which brought the head of Charles I to the block."

—*Turgot*

"Politics is a strong and slow boring of hard boards."

—*Max Weber*

"After us the deluge."

—*attributed to Louis XV*

"Do you think it might have been avoided?"

—*Nicholas II*

"Thus these princes ... who, after holding power for many years, finally lose it, should not blame fortune, but rather their own sloth; they never thought, during quiet times, that things could change (and this is a common failing of men: they never think of storms as long as the sky is blue). Then when the tempest breaks, their first thought is to run away, not to defend themselves ... The only good, safe, and dependable defenses are those that you can control yourself with your own energy."

—*Machiavelli*

Chapter

30

Losing Power Through Overdoing It

On state occasions—such as political holidays and memorials, rituals of succession, or times of trouble—it is customary and prudent for political leaders to engage in political oratory. During wartime when there are great casualties and domestic sacrifices, political rhetoric on such occasions tends to self-congratulatory. In such times of desperate political struggle, saying that "we are the good guys" is necessary to shore up morale. Such was the case in the fifth century B.C. in Athens, during the long struggle called the Peloponnesian War. To commemorate the deaths of Athenian soldiers on the battlefield, a great politician named Pericles gave a funeral oration. At such an emotional moment, Pericles managed to demean the Spartan enemy, pay tribute to the founding fathers of the Athenian city-state, and make a few self-serving political points; but mainly his speech contrasted the good guys with the bad guys, reaffirming for his audience an idealized version of Athenian democracy and wartime political intentions.

We have lived up to the faith of our fathers, Pericles said in effect. We are a free, independent, and prosperous people because of our virtuous political institutions. Our constitution is a "pattern to others"; our power rests with the many and not the few, and thus it is called a democracy. We are a free state, both in politics and daily life, tolerant of diversity but also respectful of laws and lawful authorities. We, the "best of all men," enjoy beauty and recreation, leaving "no room for dreariness"; and "because of the greatness of our city," trade flows in, and so we enjoy the products from distant lands as well as from our own. We also are "superior to our enemies" in how we approach war. Unlike the Spartans, we did not expel foreigners for fear of what they might learn; our trust is not in secrecy but in "native courage," relying not on compulsion but on bravery. We "have cause to admire our city," loving beauty and thought without becoming soft. We think not only about our own business but also about the government, because we run it; we are brave, not from ignorance, but rather from intelligence, realizing what we are fighting for. Athens is "an education to Greece," and our individual citizens "excel all men in brilliant quickness of wit and self-reliance in action"; this is not merely conceit: "let the power of our city bear witness—a power gained by the character that I have described." We alone, Pericles asserted, "prove greater than our reputation"; we alone give those we have beaten no cause to complain at being bested by "men like those." "Great are the memorials of our power," he proudly boasted, "there is no lack of evidence of it, to bear us witness both today and for the admiration of generations to come." We "have no need of Homer to praise us" because we have "laid open by our daring every sea and land, and everywhere left the lasting imprint of our services or our revenges." Those who fell in battle had "more at stake than men who have no such heritage," and like them, "may Athens be the passion of our lives" and be worthy of the example of the fallen soldiers.

Pericles was making a rhetorical statement about the political, economic, and social success of Athens, and so no doubt he was accentuating the positive. But he and the Athenians did have cause for self-confidence and pride. Athens was the envy of Greece, its most beautiful and influential city-state, with the most prosperous trade and the most imposing buildings. Athens' leadership in the war against the Persians had been decisive, and with good reason it still thought of itself as the preeminent city in all of Greece. Athens was the unquestioned cultural capital of Greece, producing (in the brief period of less than a hundred years) the most awesome array of human talent ever assembled in one place: playwrights Aeschylus, Sophocles, Euripides, and Aristophanes; sculptor Phidias; philosophers Socrates, Plato, and Aristotle; and the many other artists who built the Acropolis and the many other wonders of Athens. Athens also produced much political talent, men skilled at rhetoric, administration, and diplomacy, of which Pericles is the premier example. At that time, Athens was probably the most brilliant civilization ever to exist, or that ever may exist, and its influence on the world since is so vast as to be inestimable.

Yet within a few years, the glory of Athens was gone. It was defeated in a war, its political order caught between tyrannical and demagogic governments (the latter put to death the philosopher Socrates), and Athens never regained its political or intellectual preeminence. Within a few centuries, Greek civilization had changed, and the brief, shining moment of Athens was a thing of the past. The pinnacle from which Pericles spoke was the peak of Athenian civilization, to be lost in the war that he thought would be quick and relatively bloodless. That war and his speech were reconstructed by another of Athen's famous sons: the historian Thucydides, who wrote the story of the Peloponnesian War (431–404 B.C.), about how the Athenians lost political power and thus their great civilization. It is a story about overdoing it politically, about how grasping for more power can lead to ruin.

OVERDOING IT

We have stressed throughout this book the rough equation between what you do and what goes on in politics. In the last chapter, we noted that both you and politicians can lose power through incompetence. But incompetence is not the ony way that you can lose power. You can also lose power by overdoing it, by trying to do too much. You can be competent, even very competent, and still lose power by trying to extend your power over people, space, and time to the point that it dissipates by trying to control too much.

Suppose that when you first went to college, you took a normal course load and did well. Then you began to take extra courses and got in over your head. Your course load became too heavy, the work became burdensome, and your grades suffered. You tried to extend your power to too many subjects in too short a time, beyond your capacity to do well. You overextended yourself, and if you were smart, you either dropped some courses or next term went back to a more reasonable and normal load over which you could exercise your academic power more economically and constructively. Or you may take a job at which you become quite competent. Your power over what you do is adequate to do the job well. But you may reach for more power by taking on more tasks, to the point that you are not doing any of them well. By taking on too

PERICLES: DEMOCRATIC IMPERIALIST

The classical period of Athenian cultural glory and political ascendancy is often called the "Age of Pericles," with good reason. Pericles was one of a long line of notable Athenian politicians who formed the tradition of cultivating and practicing the "public arts"—oratory, debate, decision making, diplomacy, strategic thinking, and the presentation of the political self—in short, all those political skills that go into making princes. Pericles is an early example of a type of politician that was to appear again and again in history, the aristocrat as democrat, the person of aristocratic background and bearing who sponsors and leads popular democracy. (An American example is Franklin D. Roosevelt.) From 461 B.C. to his death in 429, Pericles was important in the tempestuous but creative civic life of Athens. He also is a good example of the importance of wise and continuous leadership to a democracy. This became evident after he died suddenly during the Peloponnesian War. Thucydides explained in his history that "it was democracy in theory, but the rule of the chief citizen in practice. But his successors, being more on a level with each other, and rivals for power, tried to please the people by giving way to them. And from that arose many mistakes. . . ." Plutarch pointed out in his *Lives* that Pericles already had pioneered the arts of demagoguery, thus giving his critics the spoils of empire, theaters and other public entertainments, paying them for public duties, and so forth, thereby encouraging "bad habits," which "changed [them] from a sober, thrifty people, that maintained themselves by their own labors, to lovers of expense, intemperance, and license."

Pericles was also, as this chapter will show, an ardent imperialist, who did not see, for all his political wisdom, the pitfalls of an extended imperial struggle with the Spartans. But his contribution to Athens and to civilization was still great. Pericles was a great builder, ordering the construction of the many public buildings of Athens. (They apparently were built by Athenians unemployed after the Persian War, as a kind of "full employment" policy to hire idle hands to construct public works.)

Pericles' olympian calm in public debate was legendary; his regal air and unflinching political realism often carried the day in the heated debates among Athenian politicians. Pericles was a political moderate, avoiding the extremes of any domestic or imperial policy. Perhaps this is what he had in mind on his deathbed when he said that the greatest thing he had done was "that no Athenian ever wore mourning because of me." Not literally true, but true enough so that in the idiotic devastation caused by the intemperate and adventurous leaders that followed, the Athenians finally appreciated the guidance of Pericles.

---

many jobs, your attention to each of them has become shortened to the point of neglect, sloppiness, and confusion. You may have built an empire at the office, but if you get sick or overextend, it all may collapse like a house of cards.

The Machiavellian strategy of living is to select what you can do well and to resist the temptation to try to do more. The Machiavellian view of life does not enjoin the endless expansion of power. The pursuit of power over other people and things can become—we cannot stress often enough—demonic, a megalomanic pursuit for more and more power. But Machiavelli discouraged the lust for power, of thinking that one could expand one's reach of power endlessly. He cautioned again and again that there were limits to what one could gain and control; and that the more power one had, the more of a burden that it would become, the more likely that it would corrupt, and the more danger that one's empire would collapse.

THE IMPERIAL IMPULSE

The "imperial impulse" refers to building and maintaining personal and political empires. *Empire* comes from the Latin *imperare,* "to command." So in a sense, any sovereign rule over territory or persons is an empire. But when we think of empire, we have in mind political dominion over peoples and territories through the expansion of the ruler's will over them. We may convince people to consent to our rule ("I should rule over you") or force them to consent to our rule ("I in fact do rule over you"). In our everyday lives, we have been part of, or built, empires in that sense. You may have grown up in a family that was the empire of your mother or father—they ruled the roost, it was their domain, you were one of their subjects. You may have even seen them try to extend their political empire to others, and perhaps try to sustain it over you even after you have gone away to school, work, or marriage. It is a common human impulse to want more, but the quest for more may lead us to build empires that extend beyond what we need or can control. Philosophers and historians have long talked of the common human quests for wealth, glory, and security. Politics is one of the ways in which we can seek these goods. As our political power expands, we seek still more wealth, glory, and security, establishing imperial rule in order to achieve them. But we can seek too much, and our greed can overextend our power and become counterproductive. We have then become the prisoners of power, unable to limit our lust for still more and afraid to give up what we have. At that point, the burden of our empire becomes an obsession, and we are in danger of being corrupted and even destroyed by the empire we have constructed around us. It is a heady thing to have power over wealth, to experience political glory, and to feel the security of dominating people and territory rather than their dominating you. But the higher you climb up the pinnacle of power, the thinner the air is the more precarious the climb is and the farther the drop is. Mighty are the empires that men and women construct, and mightier still is their fall.

But why do those who build empires go too far? Why don't they recognize and respect the limits of power? People who rule empires, be they a family or a state, often delude themselves into believing that what has worked in the past will work in the future, that the gods of luck are on their side and will continue to be, that they are infallible or destined to succeed, that nothing can go wrong, and/or that their political power and the glory are forever. But it is precisely that political attitude that brings trouble. People who have been successful in building imperial power are not humbled but, rather, are intoxicated by it and become arrogant, overweening, vain, and insolent. Power gives them too much pride, and pride bespeaks a fall.

The Greeks, who pioneered understanding politics as drama, had a word for it: *hubris,* a term we associate with Greek tragedy. In classical tragedy, man presumes against the gods by his godlike pride, thus trying to be like the gods. The mortal emotion of pride catches man in the excesses of his own making, by which means he is punished. The tragic hero exceeds the bounds of reason and restraint and by so doing creates the conditions of his own downfall. In Aeschylus' *Xerxes,* the great Persian king had an extensive empire, but his political fortune made him overly proud, and he began to think of himself as the "king of the world." He presumed against the gods by invading Greece without divine sanction. His passionate pride led him into presumptive folly and resulted in his destruction.

We are all capable of using more mundane forms of *hubris.* The reach for more and more power over people stems from our pride. We love ourselves so much that we extend that vanity to other people. We prove that our love for ourselves is justified by making other people love us or at least obey us. Our conceit is expressed in our power over other people. We have a right to rule them because of our superiority. We are mystified when others rebel against our rule, disobey us, follow someone else, and somehow do not see or admire the greatness. Such disobedience makes us all the prouder, and so we seek other ways to express our power. The successful pursuit of grades, money, and love partners proves that our pride in ourselves is justified, and our use of power good.

If the Greek tragedians were right, pride is the source of the imperial impulse. We want to build empires of which we can be proud and by building empires prove that our pride was justified. This is not restricted just to personal empires but also to political empires. As a city-state, tribe, or nation, we collectively come to take pride in ourselves and to believe that we have the right to rule others because we have the power to do so. We become afflicted with the imperial malady of seeking more and more power. The *hubris* of political power leads us to adopt an imperial attitude and lures us farther and farther into the imperial trap. We become the political victims of our own excesses. As the lawgiver Solon tried to warn, success—in acquiring wealth, allies, victories, all forms of power—breeds failure. Why? Success is power; power produces pride; pride leads to *hubris;* and *hubris* turns into excess and ruin. People indeed cannot stand political prosperity.

THE TRAGEDY OF ATHENS

The Athenians were drawn into the *hubris* of empire and became the first great political tragedy in Western history. By the time of Pericles' funeral oration, the Athenians had many reasons to be proud of themselves. But the confederation of Greek city-states of which Athens was the leader, that defeated the Persians was converted into empire. Athens refused to let its fellow city-states leave its domination and made them pay tribute in order to maintain the large Athenian navy. If a city-state tried to withdraw, Pericles would use the navy to force it to submit and punished it by increasing its taxes. The Athenians profited more and more from the empire and thus sought to enlarge it. In addition, they tried to install democratic governments in subject states, as Athens itself was a democracy; therefore its subjects had to be also. Pericles' self-confident attitude is typical of imperial power at its height, and he felt that Athens had the wealth, glory, and security that was its due because of its righteous empire.

The Athenian reach for more power produced two reactions, fear and envy. The other Greek city-states that were not under the Athenian thumb dreaded the prospect of being swallowed up in the expanding empire and envied Athens' domination of Greek commerce and wealth. The Spartans, in particular, having the greatest land power in Greece, were alarmed at the shift in the balance of power in Greece and gathered their own allies into a rival Spartan empire, rallied by fear and envy of the Athenians. Pericles was confident enough in Athenian power and "rightness" that he consistently provoked the Spartans, who were reluctant to challenge the Athenians. But when Pericles interfered with other city-states in the Peloponnesian League (Sparta's alliance), trying to lure them away from Spartan influence, the Spartans concluded that he was aiming for nothing less than the complete domination of the whole of Greece, including Sparta itself. "They could bear it no longer," wrote Thucydides, "they made up their mind that they must put out all their strength and overthrow the Athenian power by force of arms. And therefore they commenced the Peloponnesian War."

The Athenians' wealth, navy, reputation, and hegemony in much of Greece gave them the edge in such a conflict. Pericles entered it with confidence, believing that the war would be brief and Athens victorious. Yet Athenian confidence was untempered; overweening pride had led Pericles and the Athenians into the delusions of *hubris*. The Athenians did not account for the fact that most of Greece openly or secretly backed the Spartans. The Greeks thought that the Athenians would be the destroyer of Greek independence by means of its widening and avaricious empire. The Spartans thought that they were fighting a desperate struggle for survival. The Athenians did not consider that the Spartans had a warrior culture and were the toughest and most tenacious soldiers in Greece. From boyhood on, Spartan men were rigorously trained for war, and so the Spartan army would be difficult to defeat.

The Athenians also did not believe that things could go wrong, but they did. The Spartan army occupied Attica (the area of Greece where Athens was), forcing the rural population into the city. The plague broke out, killing large numbers of people, and it spread to the army, killing many valuable soldiers. The people blamed Pericles, and for a while he was repudiated. "After the second invasion of the Peloponne- sians [Spartans], wrote Thucydides, "a change came over the spirit of the Athenians. . . . Their despair was now complete and all vented itself upon Pericles." Pericles defended himself by reminding them of their pride in the empire: "You must support the city's reputation, "which depends on this empire of which you are all proud." You fight "to avert the loss of your empire." In any case, you cannot stop now, "for this empire of yours is now a despotism, which it may have been wrong to acquire, but which it is now dangerous to let go." Do not be led astray by those who would sue for peace; remember that Athens' name "stands highest among all mankind" because of its imperial power, "a power whose memory will remain forever" because "ours was the greatest and best-found city of the world." Pericles was shortly restored to power but soon died of the plague.

After Pericles' death, the tide began to turn against the Athenians. Their leadership became more erratic, desperate, and stupid. Dem- agogic leaders urged disastrous military expeditions like the Sicilian invasion. Athens, observed Thucydides, "lost her temper," and "kept grasping for more." The Athenians abandoned moral considerations and became more willing to commit atrocities. For example, a people called the Melians wanted to remain neutral in the war, but the Athenians sent troops there "in the interests of our empire." Thucydides reconstructed a dialogue between the Athenians and the Melians in which the Athenians argued that might made right, telling the Melians that "right, as the world goes is only in question between equals in power, while the strong do what they can and the weak suffer what they must." The Athenians then killed all the Melian men and sold the women and children into slavery.

The Athenian character and confidence then began to disintegrate. The arguments that won out in debates over policy and strategy became based purely on the question of what would profit the empire. In dealing with subject peoples, the Athenians' argument went, we cannot be swayed by the foes of empire—pity, democratic debate, or a sense of fairness. The burden of empire made the Athenians more and more irrational and reckless. "The cause of all these evils," wrote Thucydides, "was the desire for power which greed and ambition inspire." The Athenians were caught in the imperial trap: they felt compelled to sacrifice more blood, wealth, and honor in order to save their political possessions. To Thucydides, power had become their obsession and their destroyer. The lust for imperial power had drained their wealth, killed many of their people, and destroyed their character. Athenian democ- racy had become irrational demagogery, with endless plots, intrigues, and backbiting. Both rich and poor suffered the ever-rising costs of the war. People became cynical and self-serving, no longer believing in their gods, moral restraints, or the rightness of the Athenian imperial cause. "Fear of the gods or law of man there was not to restrain them." "Vices were esteemed as virtues . . . deceit was praised as shrewdness, recklessness as courage; loyalty, moderation, generosity were condemned as proofs of weakness." "That good will which is the chief element of a noble nature was laughed out of court and vanished. Every man distrusted every other man." Dissension in Athens increased, resulting in confused and irrational political decisions, feeble leadership, and even treason. With the help of the hated Persians, the Spartans finally wore down the Athenians' resources and will, and finally after an incredibly destructive war of twenty-seven years, the Athenians were defeated and their empire ended. The Spartans put in power oligarchs who conducted a reign of terror, ruling with the help of the Spartan army. But the Spartans were exhausted too, and soon the democracy was restored. But they too sought scapegoats, maintaining that Athens lost because of their abandonment of the gods, and so they tried Socrates for atheism and condemned him to death. Athens never regained its former power, nor Greece its moment of glory. The Athenian experiment in democracy and civilized self-rule was not attempted again for many centuries.

The political sin of *hubris* destroyed Athenian greatness in the primal political tragedy. A democratic empire is fragile, creating a political dilemma: to run an empire, you risk destroying democracy at home, indeed you may have to in order to do the things necessary to gain imperial rule; but if you want to preserve democracy at home, you may have to give up your empire. That the Athenians were unwilling to do. Their lust for more power led them to the excesses that eventually destroyed them. For all their greatness, they were not immune from what the historian Edward Gibbon explained in his *Decline and Fall of the Roman Empire* (1776–1783) as the "vicissitudes of fortune, which spares neither man nor the proudest of his works, which buries empires and cities within a common grave."

COMING APART

Many people think that individual life is tragic because we ultimately do not control it, all of us losing power by losing control over again and dying. Gibbon wrote of the Roman Empire: "All that is required for a civilization to disappear is time." It is also true that all that is required for you and me to disappear is time. Everything and everybody are eventually swept away in the shifting winds of time.

But that is not quite the lesson of Thucydides and the tragedy of Athens. The Athenians failed because of their *hubris*. They committed themselves to doing too much politically and entangled themselves in a mess that destroyed them. The political lesson for our lives and for political orders is to recognize what you can do, what you cannot do, and how to tell the difference. One of the time-honored ways, then, for coming apart is trying to exercise too much power in too many places over too many people. Again and again in history, both individuals and political orders have become embroiled in the wrong political struggle with the wrong adversary in the wrong place at the wrong time, with

Losing Power

terrible results. The trick is to be cautious without being timid, to use power without squandering it, to choose your fights and avoid quagmires, to take actions that conserve rather than spend your power, to fight the temptation to expand the rim of your power, and to resist the corrupting urge to acquire more dominion. Political fools rush in where wise princes fear to tread.

But perhaps Thucydides and the Greek tragedians were right: maybe there is a political logic, an imperial logic, that compels states to transform alliances into empires, rival empires to rise in response, and the fatal and mutually destructive conflict between them to be fought. Greek tragedy always has had a strong sense of the inevitable, of how the protagonists cannot resist tempting fate and seeking godlike power. The Athenians and Spartans seemed compelled to struggle: they could do nothing else but play out the drama to the end. The logic of empire impelled them to continue, even though the political quest had become demonic and self-destructive.

The question is not simply an academic one, for the historical analogy with the present is irresistible: could it be that the Americans are the Athenians and the Russians the Spartans? After all, didn't the United States and the Soviet Union join in fighting World War II? After that war, the coalition broke up, and both sides surrounded themselves with allies. The United States spent great amounts of money and effort building alliances, which, many have argued, has turned into an empire that we dominate politically and economically. We have become embroiled in "containing" what we believed are extensions of Soviet power into remote places—North Korea, Iran, El Salvador. We believe that we are the pinnacle of power and culture, that God is on our side, that this is the "American century." For a while some of the world lived under the umbrella of a Pax Americana, with the protection of our military garrisons, navy, and air force, financial assistance to client states, technical aid, and espionage. Perhaps we can compare in tone Pericles' funeral oration and President John F. Kennedy's inaugural address in 1961. Kennedy, like Pericles, hailed the democratic character that his country had produced, the civic virtue of its citizens, its great heritage, its patriotism, and its leadership of humankind. We are the good guys, the Russians the bad guys, but we are smarter and tougher; we shall win.

Our long struggle with the Russians is now longer than the Peloponnesian War and of course more global. But we may wonder if it will have the same outcome. Vietnam was part of our crusade to contain the spread of Communist power but became an example of a committed Spartan army (the Vietcong) that would not wear down despite the great amount of power applied. Vietnam also exposed weaknesses at home—doubts about the American mission, rancor over the money and people spent on the war, rebellion among the young and poor and black, and violent conflicts in the streets. Events such as the My Lai massacre were justified in much the same manner as the Melian massacre was. We began to speak of "the imperial presidency," which concentrated great power in a few, setting the stage for Watergate and exposing a "cancer" on our democratic institutions. Presidents came and went, all increasing our military hardware and reinforcing our commitment to empire, but the Soviets' power and influence increased. Perhaps we, following Kennedy, have become prisoners of our empire, the *hubris* of the overconfident and careless application of power that dissipates as we expand our rim of power to places remote from the center. When countries (such as China, Cuba, Vietnam, and Iran) turn against us, we feel that we have "lost" them. Our stubborn pride has made us drain our national wealth, overtaxing our citizenry and ignoring domestic problems; made us do dishonorable things (such as assassinate foreign leaders, bomb civilian populations, and "burn villages in order to save them"); and force our allies into becoming lackeys, abandoning democratic values for "national security." Convinced of our good intentions, we have reached for more and more power and felt all the more insecure after each episode of intervention, and so we turn to building a new weapons system or concluding a new alliance. The Russians, more cautious and circumspect, have tended to avoid direct confrontations but slowly but surely have built a spartan alliance and have let us destroy ourselves from within by squandering money and power, blindly rushing into military disasters, alienating our allies, breeding cynicism and doubt at home, and losing our belief in ourselves.

We shall see. If the United States does not go the way of the Athenians, it may well be the result of the rule of cautious, Machiavellian politicians who understand that power has to be handled properly, like nitroglycerin: don't throw it around or squander it, use it to create bridges and not passes, apply it in small doses gingerly and then only when needed, and if at all possible, don't use it at all. American democracy can come apart if politicians delude themselves with the intoxication of imperial power and pride. The check on recklessness is caution, on intoxication is sobriety, and on pride is humility; but to cultivate these virtues in leaders will take some doing. The pride of empire makes leaders shortsighted. As Machiavelli wrote, "But the ambition of men is such that, to gratify a present desire, they think not of the evils which will in a short time result from it." The true Machiavellian politician, to avoid the pitfalls of overreaching for power, has to take a larger view than most are capable of. But that is the only way to avoid repeating the Athenian tragedy.

"The Athenians kept grasping for more."

—Thucydides

"The cause of all these evils was the desire for power which greed and ambition inspire."

—Thucydides

The "vicissitudes of fortune, which spares neither man nor the proudest of his works, which buries empires and cities in a common grave."

—Gibbon

"But the ambition of men is such that, to gratify a present desire, they think not of the evils which will in a short time result from it."

—*Machiavelli*

"The attempt at total control does not merely corrupt, as Acton said; it debilitates. It undoes itself."

—*Gary Wills*

Chapter

31

Avoiding the Fall: Creating Political Stability

As the Roman Empire expanded in the first century B.C., the Roman republic was beset by revolution. The new wealth created by imperial rule brought with it problems. The Romans had prided themselves on their republican virtue, a nation of small landholders and soldiers, who, like Cincinnatus, lived simply and devoted themselves to their civic responsibilities. But Roman civic institutions and virtue had eroded with the advent of great wealth. A new class of rich men appeared who controlled large estates, armies, and government contracts (to build roads, for instance). They also acquired a taste for high living that shocked the traditionally restrained Roman patricians. The large estates had also dispossessed many plebian farmers, who were forced into Rome itself. The Gracchi brothers attempted reforms, trying to control the concentration of wealth and give land or welfare relief to the dispossessed. The Roman senate resisted such reforms, and the Gracchi were killed. In the next decades, the republic collapsed in the struggle among the reformers and their opponents and the opportunistic generals who vied for power. Julius Caesar was the most successful autocrat of this period, but he was assassinated by patricians intent on restoring republican institutions. For the next fourteen years, war continued in the Roman world. It seemed that not only the republic would perish but also Rome itself in an orgy of self-destruction.

In his attempt to rule a rapidly deteriorating empire, Julius Caesar was a failure. But so too were the patricians who killed him, as they had

AUGUSTUS: ROMAN REFORMER

The rule of Octavian (named Augustus by senatorial decree in 27 B.C.) was one of the epochal events in Roman and world history. The long period of civil strife that preceded the Augustan peace was so protracted and bloody that people were genuinely astonished and pleased that Octavian prevailed over the fractious parties. The praise of him may seem a bit overdone to us, but it is likely that Augustus was genuinely revered for the stability he provided. (Augustus means revered, from the grandiose title he was given: "Revered Emperor and Son of the Godlike Caesar.") Augustus was not interested in deification but, rather, in holding those offices in the Roman state that would give him effective control over the government. He never claimed in his lifetime to be a god, and when it was proposed that he be worshiped, he refused. (He was worshiped in the Hellenic world, but again, he permitted it for political reasons: it was customary in those states to have a divine monarch.) Augustus instead permitted the Romans to worship his genius! The old Roman belief was that every man had a guiding genius, and as head of a household, a man's genius guided its fortunes. In permitting a cult of his genius, Augustus was able to direct the patriotic worship of the state, of which he was at the moment the governing genius. (Later, of course, the Romans did deify living emperors, and the refusal to worship them as gods was considered treason, which was one of the reasons that the Christians were persecuted, as they refused to do so.)

Octavian was born into a relatively indistinguished provincial family and was brought up with republican discipline, in the country. His family had the good fortune to marry into the family of Julius Caesar when his star was on the rise. When only a teenager, it became clear that Octavian would probably become the male heir to the Julian line. When Caesar was murdered, Octavian discovered from his will that not only had Caesar adopted him as his son, but he had also left him three fourths of his huge fortune. But Octavian's claim to succeed Caesar was shaky—he was an obscure figure in the Roman capital, young and sickly and with little political or military experience. But Octavian soon proved to have consummate political ability, forging alliances with generals and legions, wooing the powerful senator Cicero, and maneuvering himself into the position of being the heir not only to Caesar's name but also to his power. His chief rival turned out to be Mark Antony, whose military skill and political following were well established. But Antony made a fatal political mistake: he became infatuated with Cleopatra, the queen of Egypt. Octavian, taking to Roman politics with gusto while Antony was in Egypt, convinced the Romans that Antony intended to conquer and displace Rome as the master of the world, ruling from Alexandria with Celopatra. When Antony divorced his wife, Octavia (Octavian's sister) married Cleopatra and proclaimed her son (presumably by Julius Caesar and thus Octavian's "brother" of sorts and of course a rival for power) the "King of Kings," which indeed made Antony look like a traitor. Octavian now had the support of both the elite and the masses, including those who still preferred Antony but jumped on the bandwagon to be on the winning side. At Actium (31 B.C.), Octavian easily defeated Antony with his legions (now believing Octavian's propaganda), and shortly thereafter both Antony and Cleopatra committed suicide.

Although his rise to power was bloody, Augustus became much respected by the Romans, not only for the success of his political rule, but also for the grace and decorum of his private life. He epitomized Roman restraint to the point of leading a rather dull life, devoid of all the extravagances often associated with the Roman aristocracy. (Perhaps this explains the rebellion of Octavian's only daughter, Julia, who was the scandal of Rome.) Despite being the automatic master of a vast empire and an adoring people, Augustus appears to have ruled without vanity, malice, or intolerance. He even allowed a certain amount of opposition and criticism, which his son-in-law Tiberius could not understand. Augustus explained: "My dear fellow, don't be childish and worry because people say hard things of me. It is enough if we can prevent them from *doing* us any harm." As an old man, he wrote a political testament, which summarized his accomplishments. It too had a political purpose other than vanity: its publication across the empire would stimulate the people's loyalty to the imperial order in the future. But Augustus was not totally unaware of and indifferent to what he had done. He busied himself in old age with the testament that everyone (wrote the historian Tacitus) "might read what he had done for Rome and the empire, for he knew well that when the lion was dead the dogs would bark again."

---

no program to return Rome to its republican past, or anything more than a hope that it could be restored to republicanism. They considered Caesar a tyrant who was robbing Rome of its liberties but did not recognize that Caesar had arisen in a chaotic situation in which the real problem was the restoration of order. Caesar was a strong ruler, but tactless, arrogant, and contemptuous of the political arts. But Octavian, his teenage grandnephew, adopted son, and heir, learned from Caesar's political mistakes.

THE PROBLEM OF ENDURING STABILITY

The political problem that faced Octavian was enormous. For decades Rome had been consumed by internecine strife and domestic instability. Roman society had changed, and there were new forces with which to contend. The republican system had clearly failed to bring domestic peace or to administer a vast empire well. For example, the governors of the imperial provinces had been political appointees, who often got their appointments through corruption and were interested only in "tax farming" their provinces for their own profit. But this was not a sound basis for imperial rule, as it encouraged revolt in the bilked provinces and did little to enrich the public treasury of Rome. There too were private armies, loyal to their generals who paid them rather than Rome, who looted the countryside and, worse, threatened the stable government. The cleavage between the rich and poor in Rome was large. The free poor had difficulty making a living and required public support. But this urban proletariat was capable of rising against the state. The legendary Roman family virtues had been dissipated by the wealthy in their quest for luxury and pleasure. (The Roman orgy was not entirely a myth.) The problems that Caesar Augustus (Octavian) perceived were great, but something had to be done. Could he restore the old institutions of the republic and the virtues that supported it?

Augustus did, and he did not. He understood that politically, like in everything else, you can't go home again. The republic had proved incapable of running the empire and was unstable in the wake of the social problems that had developed in Rome. Yet the Romans still respected the republican institutions and virtues "that had made Rome great." Augustus sensed that what was needed was to retain the form of the republican state and also to devise within that traditional framework a stronger, more centralized, autocratic state that would be a "re-form" of the old government. In that sense, Augustus was a political reformer, instituting new systemic reforms within the framework of the old system. He knew that attempting military or dictatorial rule, as Julius had done, would be only temporary and unstable. The political problem was not only to rule but also to ensure that stability would continue for a long time. Reform would retain the form of republican power, but the substance of power would be vested in an emperor, an absolute monarch who would not be called king (*rex,* a term that Caesar had unwisely used) but rather *princeps,* or "first citizen." Rome could not return to its original principles in full, but it could retain its form, through reform. "The genius of Augustus," wrote historian Herbert J. Muller, " . . . lay in his unconscious blend of conservatism and realism."

In a few years, Octavian had transformed himself from a well-placed military adventurer into a statesman and had reformed Rome into a stable government. He called himself "the restorer of the Roman Republic," but everyone close to the center of power knew that that was a legal fiction. Edward Gibbon, in his *Decline and Fall of the Roman Empire,* defined the imperial system as "an absolute monarchy disguised by the forms of a commonwealth." "Augustus was sensible," he went on to say, "that mankind is governed by names; nor was he deceived in his expectation that the senate and the people would submit to slavery, provided they were respectfully assured that they still enjoyed their ancient freedom." Even though the republic was a sham, nobody much cared because Augustine scrupulously honored the political tradition, and even more important, he restored peace (the Pax Romana) and imperial prosperity.

Gibbon accused Augustus of hypocrisy, and the Roman historian Lucian called him a chameleon. It is true that Augustus strove for absolute power by rough means and that he was not truly committed to the restoration of the republic. He was too much of a realist for that. But he was committed to Roman greatness and honestly tried to make the government effective and legitimate. In addition, he was a conservative in that he respected Roman traditions—dignity and decorum, family life, respect for authority—and so he played the part of a good republican "first citizen," living simply without ostentation. He took no special office or dress, lived in a modest house, ate moderately at banquets, and even had his daughters learn ancient and simple arts such as weaving and spinning. All this was designed to convey that the *princeps* was a model of republican simplicity.

Augustus ruled under this pretense for forty-four years and transformed Rome into a government that survived long after his death. When Augustus came to power, he used his immense wealth to pay the armies and the dole of bread, as the tax system had broken down. He made taxation a state function, ending the old practice of tax farming and standardizing the tax code. This stabilized revenues and made taxation fairer. Augustus personally paid for public works projects, providing employment and pride in the magnificent public buildings for which the capital became famous and which befit the seat of a great empire. Gradually, the Roman bureaucracy became famous for its efficiency.

Augustus garnered his power by eliminating potential sources of rivalry and by gaining allies in key groups. He insisted the senate continue to function and made it meet twice a month, even though it had no power; but he did purge it of potential threats (his greatuncle, remember, had been murdered by senators). Augustus also stopped the generals from raising their own armies. Even though he himself had come to power by means of his own loyal legions, he was not about to let another caesar do the same. He became the commander in chief of standing armies sworn loyal to the Roman state. This comand was firm because of the clever arrangement he instituted concerning frontier provinces. Augustus retained direct control over these provinces, where most of the legions were stationed, thus maintaining control over the army. Other "pacified" provinces he entrusted to the senate, but no troops. This gave the senate a sense of power and shored up its prestige. Augustus ruled by using institutions and people for his purposes, but keeping the real power to himself.

Even though he had stripped the patrician senate of any real power, Augustus secured its loyalty by enhancing its prestige and making it feel like a privileged elite. But Augustus also used the so-called equestrian class as part of the Roman civil service, for financial and military posts that he wanted in the hands of able men who would be grateful for the advancement. So the prefecture of Egypt (on which Rome depended for food), the praetorian guard stationed in Rome itself, and key provinces he entrusted to men of ability and not station. Augustus also reorganized the army with the same idea in mind, turning it into a legendary fighting force. He used it to consolidate the imperial rule in the provinces but recognized the limits of imperial outreach, ultimately abandoning imperial expansion and creating defensive frontiers behind which pacific Roman rule could be conducted. Augustus was popular among the plebians, who demonstrated at one point in favor of his being granted perpetual dictatorship. He increased the public dole fourfold and provided gladiator games and other sports, including a mock naval battle in which thirty ships and three thousand men took part! This policy of "bread and circuses" was used by subsequent rulers to keep the now powerless plebians quiescent.

There was much else that Augustus's reforms accomplished, but the total effect was one of enduring stability. Augustus created a political system that reformed Rome for a long time to come. Augustus's reign marked the beginning of the Pax Romana, the imperial rule that lasted for two centuries, maybe the longest period in Western history without a major war. He could not solve all of Rome's political and social problems, though he tried to. But he could not solve the political problem of succession. In theory, the senate elected the *princeps*. Augustus wanted to make the office hereditary but had no male heir. So he decided to adopt a son that he thought had talent, conferring on him powers and thus ensuring the succession of someone fit to rule. Sometimes this principle did not work: Augustus's chosen successor Tiberius was mediocre, and Caligula and Nero were catastrophes. But the Augustian system survived the terrible rulers, as the administrative machinery and army functioned well despite them. Eventually the emperor Nerva used the Augustan adoption method to select someone of ability, and this tradition produced some of Rome's ablest rulers, such as Marcus Aurelius. Augustus was also not able to restore the old state religion and piety for the old gods that he thought so essential to political stability. Nor was he able to return the Romans to the old morality and settled family life of yore. When Augustus was near death, the historian Tacitus wrote "the country had been transformed, and there was nothing left of the fine old Roman character." These two failures eventually led to the decline of Rome.

The achievement of Augustus offers many lessons, not the least of which is that political instability is not inevitable. Rather, political change is inevitable, but the deterioration of change into chaos is not. Augustus was one of those rare figures who successfully mediated change, combining the old and the new in an amalgamated system that had the ability to endure. But only for a while. The Augustan system brought political order and efficiency, but it was the end of Roman vitality. Safety was preferred to adventure, order to experiment, and dictatorship to self-rule. The Romans became contented and uncreative. The Augustan synthesis lasted in form, but the reform did not restore Roman vitality. During the long decline and fall of the Roman empire, the Romans demonstrated little power of political renewal.

THE POWER OF POLITICAL RENEWAL

Let us point to a personal example. When you enter college as a freshman, you may well come to school with a lot of enthusiasm, zest, and ambition. But as the semesters and years pass, it may become hard to sustain the energy and interest. You get used to school, and find a lot of it is boring. You may not be interested in a lot of required subjects, find that subjects you thought might be interesting are not, that some professors are dull and even incompetent, that the routine work of school is often tedious and pointless. So you find yourself losing your enthusiasm. Your attendance, studious habits, and grades suffer. You begin to wonder if it is worth it. At this point, you have reached a crisis in your self-rule. There are various things you can do. You can give up and quit school. You can continue doing badly, hating school and having fun. Or you can exercise discipline over yourself, changing your attitude and habits, restoring some interest and work to your life. You *systematize* your approach to school, and do better at it.

What you have done is not that different than what Augustus did. Your self-rule in school had become fragmented. To overcome that, you exercised the power of self-renewal, changing your ways, improving your efficiency, and succeeding at school. Now all through your life, you are likely to be beset by this problem. At work, marriage, or even leisure, you can become stagnant, bored, unable to sustain interest, with a feeling of hopelessness. If you succeed in these areas of life, it will be because of your ability of renewal. A successful marriage works in part by the ability of the parties to the relationship to renew the strength of the tie. By reforming, relationships are stabilized. But they are not necessarily revitalized. You may reform your approach to school and do better, but without enthusiasm. A marriage may be renewed by reform, but never regain the emotional vitality it had during the honeymoon. The peace of a reformed system may bring stability, continuity, and predictability, but lose a feeling of adventure and excitement.

In the long run, life can stagnate. People over time lose the power of self-renewal, and come to feel that they're in a dead end job, or that their marriage is a trap. People often put up with, plodding on despite the dread and boredom of it all. Too, life can deteriorate. People rebel by quitting jobs, breaking up their marriage, or such other forms of rebellion as drinking, fighting, and sabotage. In a wide variety of ways, after awhile people often lose the power of self-renewal.

Political systems often lose their power of self-renewal. They become stagnant and fossilize into a system that cannot change and adapt to new circumstances. The Romans of the Augustan Age stamped the motto *aeternitas* on their coins and clung to the myth of Eternal Rome even during its long fall, when it was eventually overrun by barbarians. The Romans also lost their ability to rule, became corrupt in their political and personal habits, and even became resigned to their decline. "What is the end of it all?" wrote Emperor Marcus Aurelius, "Smoke and ashes and a legend—or not even a legend." "Time," wrote Horace "depreciates the value of the world." The Roman political leaders after Augustus lost the power to cope, to learn, to keep alive their political ambitions. Without that power of renewal, their ultimate political fragmentation became inevitable.

Many have felt, Machiavelli and Gibbon among them, that one of the keys to the Roman decline and fall was political corruption. The origin of the word *corruption* comes from the Latin "to break," and that is the sense in which we use it here: how did the Romans break their state? What did they do, politically and otherwise, that eventually undermined their power to rule themselves wisely? When we think of an individual as "corrupt," we often think of him or her as tainted or diseased, as being not "virtuous." This notion of political health is an ancient one and is a useful metaphor. What excesses or defects were there in the Roman body politic that brought about the disease, decay, and death of the Roman state?

Machiavelli dealt with such questions in his *Discourses,* a commentary on the history of Rome by the Roman historian Livy. Using the metaphor of the body politic, Machiavelli noted that great states are thus subject to being "injured by time" and argued that it was "clearer than light that if these bodies are not renewed they do not last." What happens to such political bodies? They lose their power of self-government, either from being conquered from abroad or reduced to servility from within. For Machiavelli, the ultimate political *virtu* was republican liberty, by which a community of people governed themselves in the manner of early republican Rome. Rome's political *virtu* and the source of its imperial greatness lay in the commitment of its republican citizens to the common good. The primary commitment of the Romans was to the civil order and not to private or otherwordly concerns.

Let us put this argument another way. People can commit themselves to a variety of objects of affection, but three are basic and recurrent: self, state, and God. What Machiavelli seems to have meant is that a body politic is in a state of health if the commitment to oneself and to otherwordly religion is subordinated to, or at least coordinated with, patriotism. A state becomes corrupt when people do not care about it or love it anymore and replace patriotic passion for primary concern with oneself or one's god. When you care more about yourself than you do the glory of the state, you are more concerned about a private interest than a public interest and thus try to advance your own cause rather than the cause of the state. When you care more about the glory of God, you are not committed to the glory of the state. If the private individual and religion support the glory of the state, then they will legitimate patriotic fervor and sacrifice. If not, the state will suffer from neglect, disbelief, and hostility. The Christians, as Gibbon pointed out, helped hasten the demise of Rome with their otherworldly concerns, apolitical attitude, and refusal to pay obeisance to the state. But not so the early Romans, asserted Machiavelli: they were (at least in his imagination) full of "so much *virtu*" that patriotism was "more powerful than any other consideration," and so the Roman people were "for four hundred years an enemy to the name of king, and a lover of the glory and the common good of its native city."

In this view, political corruption stems from any other interest (or disinterest) that undermines the liberty and glory of the state. The Machiavellian ideal of self-government degenerates into corruption only when the people (often following the lead of a corrupt ruler or ruling class that sets a bad example) lose their civic *virtu*, their public spirit and love of the state. Machiavelli at one point called a corrupt political act as one "put forward by men interested in what they can get from the public, rather than in its good." The people are corrupt to the extent that they care more for their own selfish interests than for the state's interests, and the rulers are corrupt to the extent that they care more for power than for their own selfish interests. The collective power of the state thus dissipates into factious strife, and the liberty and power of the state soon disappear. Machiavelli believed that the true power of a state stemmed from its support by the people. When the people unconditionally support the legitimacy of the state, then its power is firmly grounded in the will of the people. When they do not, then it is on shaky ground and can be saved only by Augustan reform.

Machiavelli held out the hope that "blows" can restore a state to the *virtu* of its republican vigor. Both foreign threat and internal strife can be beneficial, he believed, because "those changes are beneficial that bring them back to their original principles. And those are the best-constituted bodies, and have the longest existence, which possess the intrinsic means of frequently renewing themselves." Great leaders may be able to stave off political corruption and death; indeed, if such a figure could appear in each generation and "would renovate its laws and would not merely stop it running to ruin but would pull it backwards, then you might see a body politic that was 'everlasting'." More importantly, if the *ordini* of a republic had the right arrangements, then the *virtu* might be perpetuated.

However, in the final analysis, Machiavelli reflected late Roman pessimism: in the long run, everything is corrupted and dies. If a republic, he stated, could be kept in "a perfect equilibrium," that would be "the best political existence." "But as all human things are kept in a perpetual movement, and can never remain stable, states naturally rise or decline." The power of political renewal is not perpetual, and the vicissitudes of time take their inevitable toll.

Machiavelli's concept of *fortuna* was based on the Roman goddess of fortune. In the centuries after Augustus, a strain of pessimism and fatalism regarding people's ability to control the future became more prevalent. The Romans thought much of fortune, chance, fate, destiny, necessity—believing those forces that determine our lives and fortunes as out of their control. Today we speak of *entropy,* the natural tendency of things to come apart in the long run. In politics, power in the long run also tends to come apart. Just as our individual power of self-renewal will dissipate, so it will with political power. Ultimately, we cannot control the corruption of aging and death. The same process may be inevitable with political orders, in that their power to rule themselves will eventually be undone by the temporal force of entropy. Neither our own selves nor the great states of history can, in the long run, avoid the fall.

This is a depressing conclusion and, as we shall see in the next chapter, a conclusion that Machiavelli did not wholly accept. But it is a legitimate conclusion if you live in a period of political disintegration. The late Romans sensed it and took up apolitical philosophies—

cynicism, skepticism, epicureanism. The Stoics taught the contemplation of the spiritual life. Popular cults and religions (of which Christianity was one) taught resignation and otherworldly concerns. People became concerned wholly with self or salvation, with having fun or being redeemed saved for another life. There was widespread disbelief in the Roman right to rule and an increasingly inability to control factions, armies, and provinces. Rome did not so much fall as just fade away, more and more unable to cope, disintegrating into political corruption and death.

ARE WE IMMUNE?

Is the American political order immune from the disease of political decay and death? Will we avoid, in the long run, the fall? It will depend in part on our political power of self-renewal, our commitment to the civil order, and whether or not all political systems die in the long run.

The historical analogy is oversimple but irresistible. Listen to some of the symptoms of Roman civic and social corruption and see if they do not sound familiar (drawn from a variety of historians): great inequalities of wealth, with great riches and luxury for a few amidst poverty and the public dole for many; the "bread and circuses" policy, which makes people used to living on public support and seeking entertainment in the huge sports colossi constructed for public diversion; a decadent obsession with sex and drugs; increasing adherence to cults and mystery religions; freakishness in the arts and music; crippling taxes to pay for military armaments and foreign imperial adventures; spasms of inflation followed by depression; conspiracy, intrigue, and murder among the political elite; mass revolts, draft dodging, and tax evasion; the inability to win border wars against the barbarians; a series of public works programs to deal with chronic widespread unemployment; trying to exercise military power in places remote from the center of power; and so on.

Since these and many more ills are part of the American political present, then perhaps we are witnessing a decline in republican institutions and patriotism. Perhaps our Augustus is yet to come. But we are aware of talk about political corruption, widespread public apathy and cynicism, the "imperial" presidency, and the decline of the "American century." Is our belief in the rightness of the American state more important to us than ourselves or our god? Do we still believe that "God blesses America?" Are we willing to die for the state? Will we become, like the Romans, so hopelessly immersed in factional and class strife, so disillusioned with the government, and so skeptical of solutions that the same creeping paralysis of rule that hobbled effective Roman government will affect us too? It has often been said that great civilizations become great because of their self-confidence, their pride in the state, and their commitment to a common political vision. When they lose those things, they wither and die. It takes considerable powers of political self-renewal to delay the decline and fall, but it remains to be seen whether we will have the political intelligence to renew ourselves and avoid the fate of the Romans. To a large extent, the ability of a state to govern itself successfully depends on the self-government—the political responsibility—of its citizens. We shall see whether the Americans of the future—will have the political *virtu* to sustain the health of the American body politic.

"Augustus was sensible that mankind is governed by names."

—*Gibbon*

"What is the end of it all? Smoke and ashes and a legend—or not even a legend."

—*Marcus Aurelius*

"Time depreciates the value of the world."

—*Horace*

[It is] "clearer than light that if these bodies are not renewed they do not last."

—*Machiavelli*

"But as all human things are kept in a peretual movement, and can never remain stable, states naturally rise or decline."

—*Machiavelli*

"My dear fellow, don't be childish and worry because people say hard things of me. It is enough if we can prevent them from *doing* us any harm."

—*Augustus*

"... he knew well that when the lion was dead the dogs would bark again."

—*Tacitus*

[Scipio] "burst into tears, and stood long reflecting on the inevitable change which awaits cities, nations, and dynasties, one and all, as it does every one of us men."

—*the Graeco-Roman historian Polybius, witnessing the fiery destruction of Carthage by the Roman general Scipio*

Part

Epilogue: Where Have All the Princes Gone?

Chapter

32

Where Have All the Princes Gone?

To produce a mighty book, wrote Herman Melville, you must choose a mighty theme. Readers can decide whether or not this is a mighty book, but it certainly has a mighty theme—the conduct of politics. We have ranged far and wide over time and space, areas of political life, and domains of princes, both good and evil, wise and stupid, successful and failing. We have seen both the pragmatics and demonics of power, the ability of politics to realize great good and commit great evil. We have seen the rise and fall of princes, regimes and empires, great rulers and poor ones. We have seen an array of human talent in history trying, and sometimes succeeding, to master, at least for a time, the politics of their time and place. You have just completed a grand tour of the realm of political princedom.

Well, you may ask, so what? What difference does this tour make to the conduct of my life? If you do take it seriously and use it, it might just make a difference. The value of any book and education in general is what you can do with it. Political science is no less an applied science than is engineering, English, or art: it has value to the extent that it guides and enriches our lives. In this epilogue, that is the question that we want to ask: now that we have come to the end of our story, what have you learned from it?

This is a question that you will have to answer yourself. Some of our readers will not learn anything; they will have wasted their time by reading (or not really reading) this book, as they have learned nothing from it. But others will learn many things, and some will learn a great deal. These students of politics are more likely to use in the long run what they have read, remembering what they have learned when they get out of school and put it to work. If they do that, then they will have grasped the essence of Machiavelli's advice, and this book will have succeeded.

WHAT HAVE YOU LEARNED?

If you have learned from this book, then you have learned something about politics. Machiavelli taught, and so do we, that we are not helpless in the world, that we do not have to be resigned to fate, that we can learn from the past, that we can use the lessons of the past to change our habits and goals, and that mastery of our lives and fortunes is possible. The Machiavellian is a realist, but not a pessimist. But learning about ourselves and the political world that we must master is not easy. *Politica est res dura,* the Latin proverb goes: "politics is a difficult thing."

In the introduction to his *Discourses,* Machiavelli outlined what he intended to do, to study the "wonderful examples of ancient kingdoms and republics" and their leading figures who are not "more admired than imitated." Machiavelli wanted to use history, to have "recourse to the examples of antiquity," to think about "imitating the noble actions" of ancient princes. The present can use the past for the future, "which should be the aim of all study of history." Other figures that you have read about in this book have urged the same approach. "The true use of philosophy," said Walter Lippmann, "is to help us live." In that spirit, we have used here the political experience of humankind to help our lives. If we have, as Machiavelli said of himself, "shown the way to others, who will carry out my views with greater ability, eloquence, and judgment," then the book will have succeeded.

But that depends on you. Political learning is difficult too, because you have to unlearn so much to learn about it. You have to overcome your prejudices, illusions, pet beliefs and theories, all the mental habits that prevent you from trying to deal with political reality. Knowing what is going on is enough without sugarcoating, ignoring, denying, or otherwise not facing the facts. The political world cannot be seen through rose-colored glasses. Neither can it be ignored or washed away. Reality, and political reality in particular, simply will not go away just by denying it.

The best princes we have studied in this book serve as examples— exemplars, even—of people who were capable of political learning. They learned that politics is hard; they were versed in political experience; they tried hard to learn what was going on and master the situation. Like yourself, they were successful to the extent they were willing to learn. They developed good political *habits*. They used a fund of learned insights to identify and act upon unfolding situations intelligently. They had trained themselves to apply their learned insights in new situations, responding flexibly as the opportunity developed.

So if you think about it, you have learned more than just some stuff about dead politicians. Rather more you have learned ways of thinking and acting that will help you live. You have learned that political learning itself is hard, and important, to learn. You have learned something of the uses of Machiavelli for your life. How you use what you have learned is up to you.

WHAT SHOULD YOU DO?

Now that you have learned all this, what should you do with it? Perhaps Machiavelli's principal message was to be smart, not dumb. The people that he admired ("prodigies of virtue and of wisdom"), and that we admire with him, were people of great political competence. In effect, if you are smart, you can be competent too. The world is filled with people who are incompetent or half-competent. The world always needs more competence, and in politics, where the lives and fortunes of many people are at stake, it needs it desperately. If you are smart, you can play the game of life well. You can figure out what you do well, cultivate the art and science of your talent, and elevate your work into a vocation. By "vocation" we mean the performance, with skill, affection, and care, of an occupation with professional responsibility. A person committed to a vocation doesn't just "do a job" or "fill a position"; rather he or she approaches a profession as an exercise in Machiavellian *virtu,* as something that needs doing, and can be done well.

In 1918, the great German sociologist Max Weber gave a famous lecture, entitled "Politics As a Vocation," in which he talked about one of our central themes here: that politics is—or at least can be—a noble vocation, something that can be approached with the responsibility that one expects of an important profession. The politician, Weber said, is subject to a "principle of responsibility" specific to the calling of politics in itself: "The honor of the political leader . . . lies precisely in an exclusive *personal* responsibility for what he does, a responsibility he cannot and must not reject or transfer. It is in the nature of officials of high moral standing to be poor politicians, and above all, in the political sense of the word, to be irresponsible politicians. In this sense, they are politicians of low moral standing. . . ." The politician, Weber went on to say, must have his passions, but they should be balanced by a "feeling of responsibility" and a "sense of proportion." The politician must avoid vanity: "The sin against the lofty spirit of his vocation . . . begins where this striving for power ceases to be *objective* and becomes purely personal self-intoxication. . . . For ultimately there are only two kinds of deadly sins in the field of politics: lack of objectivity and . . . irresponsibility." Weber addressed the Machiavellian dilemma: "Whoever wants to engage in politics at all, and especially in politics as a vocation, has to realize these ethical paradoxes. He must know that he is responsible for what may become of himself under the impact of these paradoxes. . . . The genius or demon of politics lives in an inner tension with the god of love. . . . Everything that is striven for through political action operating with violent means and following an ethic of responsibility endangers 'the salvation of the soul.'" But in the politician, no illusions are allowed: ". . . what is decisive is the trained relentlessness in viewing the realities of life, and the ability to face such realities and to measure up to them inwardly. . . ." The political "calling," Weber explained, requires those trained for it and mature enough to handle it: "Only he," he concluded, "has the calling for politics who is sure that he shall not crumble when the world from his point of view is too stupid or too base for what he wants to offer. Only he who in the face of all this can say 'In spite of it all' has the calling for politics."

You will have to decide for yourself whether you have the calling for politics. But Weber, and Machiavelli, and this book, gives you some idea of what is involved. Politics is not a vocation for everyone, just as not everyone has the "gift" to be a good lawyer, trucker, or outfielder. To be in politics, you are faced with a world that many find disagreeable, threatening, and even repulsive; and certainly not everyone has the talent or temperament to find a vocation in it. You may be scared by the responsibility of great power thrust into your hands like dynamite. You may be put off by the uncertain compromises, deals, half-victories, and frustrating defeats that are an almost daily part of your vocation. And of course you may be inhibited by the "ethical paradoxes." A character in Robert Penn Warren's novel *All the King's Men* put it succinctly, speaking of his Huey Long-like boss: "Maybe a man has to sell his soul to get the power to do good." Weber and Warren probably do not mean this literally. What they mean, and Machiavelli means, is that practicing politics as a vocation requires doing things that are equal to the tasks of the job. That includes domination, manipulation, dissimulation, violence; indeed the whole gamut of means by which you rule. The competent political professional must live with ethical ambiguity, with the paradox that if good comes out of politics, it has to be made by the bad.

Politics, then, is not for the faint of heart. But as we have seen again and again in this book, politics is a noble vocation, a profession with a tradition of excellence and accomplishment. In the United States, for a wide variety of historical and cultural reasons, the "professional politician" has a negative connotation. We prefer political amateurs to professionals, or at least politicians who bill themselves as amateurs practicing "antipolitics." One can only speculate as to why we feel this way. Perhaps we prefer political innocence to guilt or are afraid of politicians who are too competent. The problem is what we shall call the *demonics of innocence*: the amateur in politics is free from the guilt of playing politics well, but that ironically means that what needs to be done in politics, which only political pros can do well, will not be done. Thus innocence creates a demonic effect, by being unequal to the task of solving difficult political problems.

We here make a plea for Americans to value politics as a vocation. This is not to ask for a kind of Platonic elite of philosopher-kings, but rather for us to recognize—and thus encourage people to enter—politics as a worthwhile profession. It has often been argued that Americans do not make very good Machiavellians, and thus do not play the game of world politics very well. We do not like power, distrust politicians, and grow tired of politics, especially the responsibilities of empire. But the fact is that we are a world power, that we will not solve foreign or domestic political problems unless we play politics well, and that we are not going to live up to our political responsibilities unless we have— which means we elect—politicians who practice politics as a vocation.

We may feel more comfortable with apolitical amateurs, but they are still amateurs. Rather than preferring a nice (apolitical) man who means well, we should prefer a smart (political) man who does well. If we want to achieve political solutions, do we not need people with "trained relentlessness in viewing the realities of life, and the ability to face such realities and to measure up to them inwardly?" If we do not, then the argument is moot. But that ignores the Machiavellian reality: if we do not seek and find political mastery, then do not be surprised by what we do get. But then, that is true of any vocation: if you do not do it well, then the results may be bad. In politics, if it is not practiced as a vocation well, then the results may be disastrous.

The importance of this has recently been underscored by the eminent historian Barbara Tuchman, who gave a lecture entitled "An Inquiry into the Persistence of Unwisdom in Government" at the United States Military Academy in 1980. Why, she asks, does man make a poorer performance of government than of almost any other human activity? "In the late twentieth century, it begins to appear as if we may be aproaching ... suicidal incompetence." Woodenheadedness, zealotry, folly, stupidity—the list of crimes and idiocies is endless. But this is not to say that "men in office are incapable of governing wisely and well." But the mystery remains: for all his accomplishments in the arts, sciences, commerce, and even morality, "why is he so much less accomplished in government?" She thinks the root is "the lust for power": "Government remains the paramount field of unwisdom because it is there that men seek power over others—and lose it over themselves."

Politics, said Aristotle, is the master science. The reverse is also true: politics is the science of mastery, the correct use of power to gain beneficial political ends. This requires the exercise of power over others by people who have power over themselves. This includes both intellectual power (the power to think clearly about what to do in politics) and emotional power (the power to act on the basis of political reasons and not passion). The advantage of valuing politics as a vocation is that it professes competence and character in politicians, derived from their study of the master science, political science.

WHAT SHOULD YOU STUDY?

Suppose that you have chosen a vocation you wish to follow. What would you study? Why would you study at all? Well, you say, because to be a doctor, or carpenter, or homemaker, you have to study the field in order to know what to do. But what do you mean when you say that? What is involved in learning a vocation? Suppose you become a doctor. To practice medicine well, you acquire a body of knowledge, facts about the human body and how it works. You also acquire a set of values and ideals that go into the practice of medicine—the Hippocratic oath and norms of healing. But you acquire something else too, what we might call a philosophy of conduct. What you learn about the science and ethics of medicine is worthless unless you put it to use. So you learn what to do as a doctor, both in terms of how to practice medicine and also what is expected of a doctor as a social role. You learn how to *act* as a doctor. The vocation calls for rules for action.

This is also true for the study of politics. A political science includes a body of knowledge, a "science of facts." This is systematic, empirically based knowledge of the political experience of mankind. Political facts include, but are not restricted to, the knowledge gathered by survey or experimental method. This cumulative aspect of political science is gathered for use not only by political scientists but also by politicians. Too, political science includes the study of political values and ideals, a "science of values." Since politics involves the pursuit of goals, those that study politics should also investigate the wisdom and feasibility of political values. For example, we can study the actual operation of the "justice" system in the United States, but we should also study the ancient question "What is justice?" as a universal ideal and how it can be realized now. The science of facts is complemented by a science of ends.

But there is a third realm to political science, the "science of political conduct." This includes, but is not restricted to, a science of means. It also involves studying what can be. Between the realm of what is and what should be is what can be. Given the political facts and the political values we have, what then do we have to do in order to bring about certain results? Here political science truly becomes an applied science, a science of political action. By conceiving a philosophy of political conduct, the corpus of political knowledge that constitutes the entire discipline of political science is put to use. At least, a political science of action can tell politicians the limits and possibilities of what can be done. At most, it can actually make politics more intelligent and humane. Political science as a vocation would serve a clear political function rather than simply an academic one.

This is not to say, of course, that politicians will use political advice wisely, or even take it at all. But the Machiavellian tradition focuses study on the applied realm of political practice, and gives people in power knowledge they can use. It is oftentimes said that political science has very little bearing on politics. But if there is anything to the Machiavellian argument, this does not have to be the case, and indeed should not be the case. The tradition of advisor to power, of which Machiavelli himself was part, is one of the vital scientific functions of the discipline. The science of political mastery is something of great interest to wise rulers.

In a broad sense, this application of political science would teach the "lessons of the past." In the spirit of this book, it would garner knowledge of what princes have done to gain, hold, and lose power. It would stress the fragility of power, and the uncertainty and unpredictability of the consequences of political action. It would warn against applying the wrong historical lessons to present situations. It would urge not squandering power for light and transient causes, and to be cautious in the application of power. Above all, it would stress the vagaries of political *fortuna*: power has to be exercised with wisdom or the political sky may fall.

WHERE *HAVE* ALL THE PRINCES GONE?

There is a recurrent feeling in the late twentieth century that things are out of control. Many people feel that we are in an era like the late Roman Empire, in which the people in power are not equal to the challenge of the times. Presidents come and go, for example, but their ability to use power to solve large-scale domestic and foreign problems seems diminished. There seems to be no Roosevelt or Eisenhower in the offing. Many people think we are in a period of civic corruption, such as we described in Chapter 31. The "retreat" into privatism or religion by many suggests that we have given up on political solutions, and await the inevitable deluge. Some scholars who study the future contend we are headed for a new Dark Age, in which the great empires of the world break down— perhaps in a post-nuclear war age—into chaos, suffering, and the breakdown of civilization.

Others, no less pessimistic, see the exact opposite: a post-1984 world of iron controls, much like those envisioned by George Orwell. They see a world in which chaos is avoided only by the use of totalitarian rule, exercising an unprecedented amount of demonic power over the individual. Governments would master the scarcities and conflicts of the future by ending any exercise of human freedom. The price of existence would be absolute regimentation. Big Brother would be a kind of latter-day Grand Inquisitor, ruling through miracle, mystery, and authority over a sinister State armed with the technological means to control not only what you do but also what you think.

Yet neither scenario has to be, if Machiavelli and this book are to be believed. No political outcome in history is predetermined. It is true that oftentimes in history, no princes have emerged to master difficult times; indeed, sometimes the least amount of political competence is available precisely at the time it is needed most. There is no historical law that says that princes will emerge to meet the challenge of the times, or even that people want such a figure to emerge. It is even the case at times that politicians of *virtu* try to rule, but that things are too out of control for them to be successful. The future likely will not be a time in which it is any easier to rule, and it probably will be much harder. As Walter Lippmann said of that future, "The supreme question before mankind ... is how men will be able to make themselves willing and able to save themselves."

We will be able to "save ourselves" from the great political threats of the future by producing princes equal to the challenges. This is not a "great man" theory, nor does it absolve us of responsibility for the future. But with Machiavelli we do think that the future will be partly shaped by, and certainly reflected in, the kind of princes that emerge. If we are to avoid the demonic alternative from emerging, we shall have to be wise enough to prevent future Hitlers and Stalins from coming to power. If we are to conserve republican institutions and freedoms, we shall have to bring to power future Disraelis, and in moments of crisis, DeGaulles. If we are to weather economic or political crises, we will need future Roosevelts and Lincolns. If we are to survive, and even prevent, wars, we will need future Churchills. If we are to realize peaceful revolutions in the years ahead, we will need more Gandhis. If we need future constitutions, we will need more Madisons. If we need peacemakers, we will need new Talleyrands. In short, if the future is to solve its political problems, we will have to have princes who practice politics as a vocation, use power for benevolent rather than malevolent purposes, and somehow avoid the polar dangers of totalitarian overcontrol on the one hand and chaotic drift on the other. It will not be an easy task, but not impossible. If your life is made bearable in the future—or preserved at all—this will depend in part on the quality of princedom.

In the same lecture cited above, Professor Tuchman concluded: "Although professionalism can help, I tend to think that fitness of character is what government chiefly requires. How that can be discovered, encouraged, and brought into office is the problem that besets us." Character is the element of quality in the good princes we have dealt with in this book. They were distinctive and conspicuous political personages whose character was revealed by the responsibilities of power. For them, power did not corrupt, it elevated. They played the game of politics with the skill and fortitude one expects of champions. They led the political existence without being overwhelmed or consumed by it. They showed political character in the crucible of their times.

THE POLITICAL EXISTENCE

The princes we have talked about in this book led the political existence. The life of politics was the dominant part of their lives, their vocation. They tested their political *virtu* against the *fortuna* of their time. They were praised and condemned, supported and rejected, honored and satirized. They all struggled to succeed in politics, and sometimes some of them did. In all cases, sooner or later their political moment slipped away, and they passed and were forgotten like the rest. But not quite: we remember and celebrate them here. They could not conquer what Machiavelli called "the malice of time," yet what they did remains timeless, examples of what can be done with politics, for good or ill.

To live the political existence means that you have to act on a public stage in a play in which the script is largely made up as you go along. To act in the political play requires improvisation, doing the right thing at the right time to make the play go your way. There is a sense in which politics is all make-believe, the make-believe that comes true. The political play is about reality, with all the ambiguities, contradictions, enigmas, and paradoxes of the real world heightened and transformed in political dramas. Politics—to use the term of the existentialists—is absurd, a play without meaning but which is about creating meaning. Politicians use bad faith to create good faith, words to signify action, rationality to mobilize the irrational, logic to do the illogical. Politics always fails, but it is always necessary. Politics is insane, but is our only hope for sanity. We must cultivate our political gardens, but all gardens die.

To live the political existence means that you must understand this. There are limits to what politics can do. All political solutions are temporary, and create new problems. Politics is finite, occurring in a disturbed universe of changing times and circumstances. In such a Machiavellian universe moves the figure of the Prince: The person who governs with an understanding of these limitations and absurdities, yet exercises his or her mastery in the brief moment allotted them on the stage of political life. The political power and the glory is not forever, nor godly, but it has to be done, and can be done well. As students of princedom, we can admire political genius as one of mankind's more astonishing achievements. We can also now look with new insight on the smiling portrait of Niccolo Machiavelli.

FOR FURTHER READING

The following bibliography is not intended to be exhaustive, but only to give the interested reader some idea of the sources we have used in each chapter. This list provides further readings for students of politics who wish to pursue its study in more depth.

Chapter 1

Berlin, Isaiah. "The Originality of Machiavelli." *Against the Current: Essays in the History of Ideas.* New York: Penguin Books, 1982, pp. 25–79.

Buskirk, Richard H. *Modern Management and Machiavelli.* Boston: Cahners, 1974.

Fleisher, Martin (Ed.). *Machiavelli and the Nature of Political Thought.* New York: Atheneum, 1972.

Jay, Anthony. *Management and Machiavelli.* New York: Holt, Rinehart, and Winston, 1967.

Lyman, Stanford M. and Marvin B. Scott. *A Sociology of the Absurd.* New York: Meredith Corporation, 1970, pp. 12–27.

Machiavelli, Niccolo. *The Chief Works and Others* (3 vols.). Allen Gilbert (editor and translator). Durham: Duke University Press, 1965.

Machiavelli, Niccolo. *The Portable Machiavelli.* Peter Bonadanella and Mark Musa (editors and translators). New York: Penguin Books, 1979.

Machiavelli, Niccolo. *The Prince.* Robert M. Adams (editor and translator). New York: W. W. Norton, 1977. A Norton Critical Edition with readings.

Maughm, W. Somerset. *Then and Now: A Novel.* Garden City, NY: Doubleday, 1946.

Meinecke, Friedrich. *Machiavellism.* London: Routledge and Kegan Paul, 1957.

Merleau-Ponty, Maurice. "A Note on Machiavelli." *Signs* Evanston, IL: Northwestern University Press, 1964, pp. 211–223.

Parel, Anthony (Ed.). *The Political Calculus: Essays on Machiavelli's Philosophy.* Toronto: University of Toronto Press, 1972.

Pocock, J. G. A. *The Machiavellian Moment.* Princeton: Princeton University Press, 1975.

Skinner, Quentin. *Machiavelli.* New York: Hill and Wang, 1981.

Slack, Walter H. *The Grim Science: The Struggle for Power.* Port Washington, NY: Kennikat Press, 1981.

Villari, Pasquale. *The Life and Times of Niccolo Machiavelli.* New York: Greenwood Press, 1968. Originally published in 1892.

Wolin, Sheldon. "Machiavelli: Politics and the Economy of Violence." *Politics and Vision.* Boston: Little, Brown, 1960, pp. 195–238.

Chapter 2

Blumberg, Abraham S. "The Practice of Law as a Confidence Game." *Law and Society Review,* Vol. 1, No. 2 (1966), pp. 15–39.

Brams, Steven M. *Biblical Games.* Cambridge: The MIT Press, 1980.

Long, Norton E. "The Local Community as an Ecology of Games." *American Journal of Sociology,* Vol. 44 (Nov. 1958), pp. 251–261.

McDonald, John. *Strategy in Poker, Business, and War.* New York: Norton, 1963.

Orr, Robert. "Time Motif in Machiavelli." *Political Studies,* Vol. 17 (June 1969), pp. 145–159.

Stevenson, William. *A Man Called Intrepid.* New York: Ballantine Books, 1976.

Strauss, Anselm. *Negotiations.* San Francisco: Jossey-Bass, 1980.

Winterbotham, F. W. *The Ultra Secret.* New York: Dell, 1974.

Chapter 3

Dewey, John. *Logic: The Theory of Inquiry.* New York: Henry Holt, 1938.

Doyle, Arthur Conan. *The Complete Sherlock Holmes.* Garden City, NY: Doubleday, 1930.

Lippmann, Walter. *The Essential Lippmann.* Clinton Rossiter and James Lare (editors). New York: Vintage Books, 1965.

Lippmann, Walter. *A Preface to Morals.* New York: Macmillan, 1929.

Lippmann, Walter. *A Preface to Politics.* New York: Mitchell Kennerley, 1913.

Sebeok, Thomas A. *The Play of Musement.* Bloomington: University of Indiana Press, 1981.

Steel, Ronald. *Walter Lippmann and the American Century.* Boston: Little, Brown, 1980.

Chapter 4

Bell, David V. J. *Power, Influence, and Authority.* New York: Oxford University Press, 1975.

Crick, Bernard. *In Defence of Politics.* Baltimore: Penguin, 1964.

Lasswell, Harold. *Politics: Who Gets What, When, How.* Cleveland: Meridian, 1965.

Malone, Dumas. *Thomas Jefferson as Political Leader.* New York: Greenwood, 1979.

Merriam, Charles. *Political Power.* New York: Collier Books, 1964.

Russell, Bertrand. *Power.* New York: Norton Library, 1969.

Lasswell, Harold and Abraham Kaplan. *Power and Society.* New Haven: Yale University Press, 1950.

Chapter 5

Anthony, Katherine S. *Catherine the Great.* New York: Garden City Publishing, 1925.

Troyat, Henri. *Catherine the Great.* New York: E. P. Dutton, 1980.

Wittfogel, Karl. *Oriental Despotism.* New York: Random House, 1981.

Chapter 6

Maurois, Andre, *Disraeli*. New York: Time-Life Books, 1965.
Werth, Alexander. *De Gaulle*. Baltimore: Penguin, 1965.

Chapter 7

Bullock, Allan. *Hitler: A Study in Tyranny*. New York: Bantam, 1958.
Fest, Joachim. *Hitler*. New York: Harcourt, Brace, Jovanovich, 1974.
Hitler, Adolph. *Mein Kampf*. Boston: Houghton Mifflin, 1962.
Marx, Karl and Friedrich Engels. "The Manifesto of the Communist Party." *The Marx-Engels Reader*, Robert Tucker (editor). New York: W. W. Norton, 1972, pp. 335–362.
Orwell, George. *1984*. New York: Harcourt Brace Jovanovich, 1983.
Toland, John. *Hitler*. New York: Ballantine, 1981.

Chapter 8

Hofstadter, Richard. "The Founding Fathers: An Age of Realism." *The American Political Tradition*. New York: Vingate Books, 1974, pp. 3–21.
Roche, John P. "The Founding Fathers: A Reform Caucus in Action." *The American Political Science Review,* Vol. LV, No. 4 (December 1961), pp. 799–816.
Solberg, Winton U. (Ed). *The Federal Convention and the Formation of the Union of the American States*. Indianapolis: Bobbs-Merrill, 1958.

Chapter 9

Baker, Russell and Charles Peters. "The Prince and His Courtiers: At the White House, the Kremlin, and the Reichschancellery." *Inside the System,* Charles Peters and James Fallows (editors). New York: Praeger, 1976, pp. 3–16.
Bryce, James. *The American Commonwealth* (2 vols.). New York: Macmillan, 1912.
Califano, Joseph. *A Presidential Nation*. New York: Norton, 1975.
Levron, Jacque. *Pompadour* (New York: St. Martin's Press, 1963.

Chapter 10

Wilson, Woodrow. *Congressional Government*. Baltimore: Johns Hopkins University Press, 1981.

Chapter 11

Boren, James H. *When In Doubt, Mumble*. New York: Van Nostrand Reinhold, 1972.
Dickson, Paul. *The Official Rules*. New York: Delta, 1978.
Joll, James. *Three Intellectuals in Politics*. New York: Pantheon, 1960.
Kharasch, Robert N. *The Institutional Imperative*. New York: Charterhouse, 1973.
Parkinson, C. Northcote. *The Law of Delay*. New York: Ballantine, 1970.
Parkinson, C. Northcote. *Parkinson's Law*. New York: Ballantine, 1957.

Chapter 12

Corwin, Edward S. *John Marshall and the Constitution.* New Haven: Yale University Press, 1919.

De Tocqueville, Alexis. *Democracy in America* (2 vols.). New York: Vintage Books, 1954.

Jackson, Robert H. *The Struggle for Judicial Supremacy.* New York: Knopf, 1941.

Severin, Bill. *John Marshall: The Man Who Made the Court Supreme.* New York: David McKay, 1969.

Chapter 13

Dye, Thomas R. *Who's Running America* (3rd ed.). Englewood Cliffs, NJ: Prentice-Hall, 1983.

Fraser, Antonia. *Mary Queen of Scots.* New York: Delacorte, 1978.

Johnson, Paul. *Elizabeth I.* New York: Holt, Rinehart, Winston, 1974.

Luke, Mary R. *Gloriana: The Years of Elizabeth I.* New York: Coward, McCann and Geoghegan, 1973.

MacIver, Robert. *The Web of Government.* New York: The Free Press, 1965.

Michels, Robert. *Political Parties.* New York: Dover, 1959.

Mosca, G. *The Ruling Class.* New York: McGraw-Hill, 1979.

Neale, J. E. *Queen Elizabeth I.* Garden City, NY: Doubleday, 1957.

Chapter 14

Barnes, John. *Evita: First Lady.* New York: Grove, 1978.

Montgomery, Paul. *Eva, Evita.* New York: Pocket Books, 1979.

Taylor, J. M. *Eva Peron: The Myths of a Woman.* Chicago: University of Chicago Press, 1979.

Weber, Andrew Lloyd and Tim Rice. *Evita: The Legend of Eva Peron.* New York: Avon, 1978.

Chapter 15

Fischer, Louis. *Gandhi.* New York: New American Library, 1954.

Jack, Homer A. (Ed.). *The Gandhi Reader.* Bloomington: Indiana University Press, 1956.

Moon, Penderel. *Gandhi and Modern India.* New York: W. W. Norton, 1969.

Woodcock, G. *Mohandas Gandhi.* New York: Viking Press. 1971.

Chapter 16

Costain, Thomas B. *The Last Plantagenets.* Garden City, NY: Doubleday, 1982.

Shakespeare, William, "Richard III." New York: Penguin, 1959.

Chapter 17

Carter, Peter. *Mao.* New York: Mentor Books, 1979.

Tse-tung, Mao (Mao Zedung). *An Anthology of His Writings,* Anne Fremantle (editor). New York: Mentor Books, 1972.

Mao Tse-tung. *On Guerrilla Warfare.* New York: Frederick A. Praeger, 1962.
von Clausewitz, Karl. *War, Politics, and Power.* Chicago: H. Regnery, 1962.

Chapter 18

Sandburg, Carl. *Abraham Lincoln: The Prairie Years, 1809–1861: The War Years 1861–1865.* New York: Laurel, 1974.
Tufte, Edward R. *Political Control of the Economy.* Princeton: Princeton University Press, 1978.
Williams, T. Harry. *Huey Long.* New York: Alfred A. Knopf, 1969.

Chapter 19

Burns, James McGregor. *Roosevelt: The Lion and the Fox.* New York: Harcourt Brace, 1956.
Hofstadter, Richard. "Herbert Hoover and the Crisis of American Individualism." *The American Political Tradition.* New York: Vintage, 1973.
Schlesinger, Arthur M., Jr. *The Age of Roosevelt* (3 vols.). New York: Houghton Mifflin, 1959.

Chapter 20

Burckhardt, Carl J. *Richelieu and His Age.* New York: Harcourt, Brace, and World, 1965.
Janis, Irving. *Groupthink.* Boston: Houghton Mifflin, 1982.
Ogg, David. *Europe in the Seventeenth Century.* New York: Collier Books, 1962.
Richelieu. *The Political Testament of Cardinal Richelieu,* Henry B. Hill (translator). Madison: The University of Wisconsin Press, 1961.
Wedgwood, C. V. *Richelieu and the French Monarchy.* New York: Macmillan, 1950.

Chapter 21

Barker, Sir Ernest. *Greek Political Theory.* London: Methuen, 1947.
Crankshaw, Edward. *Bismarck.* New York: Viking Press, 1981.
Dahrendorf, Ralf. "In Praise of Thrasymachus." *Essays in the Theory of Society.* Stanford: Stanford University Press, 1968, pp. 129–150.
Pflanze, Otto. *Bismarck and the Development of Germany.* Princeton: Princeton University Press, 1963.
Plato, *The Republic.* New York: Basic Books, 1968.
Stern, Fritz. *Gold and Iron: Bismarck, Bluchroder, and the Building of the German Empire.* New York: Knopf, 1977.

Chapter 22

Pierson, George Wilson. *Tocqueville in America.* New York: Oxford University Press, 1938.
Remini, Robert V. *Andrew Jackson.* New York: Harper & Row, 1969.
De Tocqueville, Alexis. *Democracy in America* (2 vols.). New York: Vintage Books, 1955.

Chapter 23

Combs, James. *Dimensions of Political Drama*. Glenview, IL: Scott-Foresman, 1980.

Lewis, Eugene. *Public Entrepreneurship*. Bloomington: Indiana University Press, 1980, pp. 94–155.

Powers, Richard Gid. *G-Men: Hoover's FBI in American Popular Culture*. Carbondale: Southern Illinois University Press, 1983.

Powers, Richard Gid. "J. Edgar Hoover and the Detective Hero." *Journal of Popular Culture*, Vol. IX, No. 2 (Fall 1975), pp. 257–278.

Chapter 24

Anouilh, Jean, *Becket*. New York: Coward, 1960.

Eliot, Thomas Stearns. *Murder in the Cathedral*. New York: Harcourt, Brace, 1964.

Kelly, Amy. *Eleanor of Aquitaine and the Four Kings*. Cambridge: Harvard University Press, 1951.

Poole, Austin Lane. *From Domesday Book to Magna Carta, 1087–1216*. Oxford: Clarendon Press, 1951.

Walker, Curtis Howe. *Eleanor of Aquitaine*. Chapel Hill: University of North Carolina Press, 1950.

Winston, Richard. *Becket*. New York: Knopf, 1970.

Chapter 25

Brinton, Crane. *The Lives of Talleyrand*. New York: W. W. Norton, 1936.

Hobbes, Thomas. *Leviathan*. New York: Dutton, 1953.

Meinecke, *Machiavellism*. London: Routledge and Kegal Paul, 1957.

Neustadt, Richard E. and Graham T. Allison "Afterward." *Thirteen Days* by Robert F. Kennedy. New York: W. W. Norton, 1971, pp. 107–150.

Nicholson, Harold. *The Congress of Vienna*. New York: Viking Press, 1967.

Chapter 26

Goodin, Robert. *Manipulatory Politics*. New Haven: Yale University Press, 1980.

Leites, Nathan. *The Operational Code of the Politboro*. New York: McGraw-Hill, 1951.

Lenin, V. I. "What is to be Done?" *Selected Works*. New York: International Publishers, 1967.

Leonhard, Wolfgang. *Three Faces of Marxism*. New York: Holt, Rinehart, Winston, 1974.

Moorehead, Alan. *The Russian Revolution*. New York: Bantam, 1959.

Pearson, Michael. *The Sealed Train*. New York: Putnam, 1974.

Wolfe, Betram D. *Three Who Made a Revolution*. New York: Delta, 1964.

Chapter 27

Ellul, Jacque. *Propaganda*. New York: Vintage Books, 1973.

LeBon, Gustav. *The Crowd*. New York: Penguin, 1977.

Lochner, Louis (Ed.). *The Goebbels Diaries*. New York: Greenwood, 1948.

Qualter, Terence H. *Propaganda and Psychological Warfare*. New York: Random House, 1962.

Reimann, Victor. *Goebbels: The Man Who Created Hitler*. Garden City NY: Doubleday, 1976.

Wykes, Alan. *Goebbels*. New York: Ballantine, 1973.

Chapter 28

Medvedev, Roi Aleksandrovich. *On Stalin and Stalinism*. New York: Oxford University Press, 1979.

Deutscher, Isaac. *Stalin: A Political Biography*. New York: Oxford University Press, 1967.

Fischer, Louis. *The Life and Death of Stalin*. New York: Harper, 1952.

Kennan, George F. *Russia and the West under Lenin and Stalin*. New York: Mentor, 1962.

Tucker, Robert C. *The Soviet Political Mind*. New York: W. W. Norton, 1971.

Ulam, Adam B. *Stalin: The Man and His Era*. New York: Viking, 1973.

Chapter 29

Brinton, Crane. *The Anatomy of Revolution*. New York: Vintage Books, 1965.

Goodwin, Albert. *The French Revolution*. New York: Harper Torchbooks, 1962.

Moorehead, Alan. *The Russian Revolution*. New York: Bantam, 1959.

Chapter 30

Burn, A. R. *Pericles and Athens*. New York: Macmillan, 1949.

Cornford, Francis M. *Thucydides Mythistoricus*. Philadelphia: University of Pennsylvania Press, 1971.

Grene, David. *Greek Political Theory*. Chicago: Phoenix Books, 1965.

Jaeger, Werner. *Paideia*. New York: Oxford University Press, 1939.

Plutarch, *Lives of the Noble Greeks and Romans* (3 vols.). New York: Dutton, 1957.

Steel, Ronald. *Pax Americana*. New York: Penguin Books, 1977.

Thucydides, *History of the Peloponnesian Wars* (4 vols.). New York: Dutton, 1936.

Chapter 31

Blits, Jan. "Caesarism and the End of Republican Rome: Julius Caesar, Act I, Scene i." *Journal of Politics*, Vol. 43, No. 1 (Feb. 1981), pp. 40–55.

Buchan John. *Augustus*. Boston: Houghton Mifflin, 1937.

Gibbon, Edward. *The Decline and Fall of the Roman Empire* (6 vols.). New York: Dutton, 1954.

Grant, Michael. *The Fall of the Roman Empire: A Reappraisal for our Own Times*. New York: Clarkson N. Potter, 1976.

Rifkin, Jeremy. *Entropy*. New York: Bantam, 1981.

Wilkinson, L. P. *The Roman Experience*. New York: Knopf, 1974.

Chapter 32

Camus, Albert. *The Myth of Sisyphus and Other Essays.* New York: Vintage, 1955.

Jacobson, Norman. *Pride and Solace.* Berkeley: University of California Press, 1978.

Tuchman, Barbara W. "An Inquiry into the Persistence of Unwisdom in Government." *Esquire* (May 1980), pp. 25–31.

Warren, Robert Penn. *All the King's Men.* New York: Bantam, 1959.

Weber, Max. "Politics as a Vocation." *From Max Weber,* Hans Gerth and C. Wright Mills (editors). New York: Oxford University Press, 1958, pp. 77–128.

NAME INDEX